PREVENTION MAGAZINE'S
2,000
EVERYDAY
HEALTH TIPS
FOR BETTER HEALTH
AND HAPPINESS

PREVENTION MAGAZINE'S
2,000 EVERYDAY HEALTH TIPS
FOR BETTER HEALTH AND HAPPINESS

Previously titled *Everyday Health Tips*

WINGS BOOKS
New York • Avenel, New Jersey

Edited by Debora Tkac

Contributing Writers

Kim Anderson
Don Barone
Stefan Bechtel
Mary Blakinger
Richard Dominick
Sharon Faelten
Diane Fields

Denise Foley
Marcia Holman
Vicki Jarmulowski
Alexis Lieberman
William LeGro
Mike McGrath
Gale Maleskey

Jeff Meade
Ellen Michaud
Maria Mihalik
Eileen Nechas
Kerry Pechter
Cathy Perlmutter
Heidi Rodale

Michael Scofield
Tom Shealy
Debora Tkac
Lewis Vaughn
Russell Wild
Stephen Williams
Susan Zarrow

This 1993 edition is published by Wings Books,
distributed by Outlet Book Company, Inc.,
a Random House Company,
40 Engelhard Avenue, Avenel, New Jersey 07001,
by arrangement with Rodale Press, Inc.

Random House
New York · Toronto · London · Sydney · Auckland

Printed and bound in the United States of America

Book design by Anita G. Patterson

Library of Congress Cataloging-in-Publication Data

Everyday health tips.
    Prevention magazine's 2000 everyday health tips for
better health and happiness / [by the editors of Prevention
Magazine Health Books].
        p.   cm.
    Originally published : Everyday health tips. Emmaus,
Pa. : Rodale Press, 1988.
    Includes index.
    ISBN 0-517-08922-X
    1. Health.   I. Prevention (Emmaus, Pa.)   II.
Prevention Magazine Health Books.   III. Title.   IV. Title:
2000 everyday health tips for better health and happiness.
RA776.E92   1993
613—dc20   93-675
                                          CIP

8 7 6 5 4 3 2 1

Prevention® Magazine Health Book Staff
for Everyday Health Tips

William Gottlieb: *Editorial Director*
Carol Keough: *Senior Managing Editor*
Debora Tkac: *Managing Editor*
Sharon Faelten: *Senior Editor*
Kim Anderson: *Editor*
Don Barone: *Editor*
Marcia Holman: *Editor*
William LeGro: *Editor*
Ellen Michaud: *Editor*
Russell Wild: *Editor*
Jane Sherman: *Editorial/Production Coordinator*

Lisa D. Andruscavage: *Copy Editor*

Susan A. Nastasee: *Associate Research Chief*
Holly Clemson: *Assistant Research Chief*
Jan Eickmeier: *Senior Research Editor*
Christine Dreisbach: *Research Associate*
Karen Feridun: *Research Associate*
Ann Gossy: *Research Associate*
Staci Hadeed: *Research Associate*
Alice Harris: *Research Associate*
Karen Lombardi: *Research Associate*
Bernadette Sukley: *Research Associate*

Roberta Mulliner: *Office Manager*
Kelly Trumbauer: *Secretary*

Mark Bricklin: *Group Vice President, Health*

Book Design Staff
for Everyday Health Tips

Jerry O'Brien: *Art Director*
Anita Patterson: *Associate Art Director*
Peter Chiarelli: *Technical Artist*
Lisa Farkas: *Technical Artist*
Darlene Schneck: *Technical Artist*

Contents

chapter three: **YOUR HEALTHY HOME**

chapter four: **WORKING HAPPY**

chapter five: **SEASONAL WELLNESS**

chapter six: REST AND RECREATION

chapter seven: CAREFREE TRAVEL

chapter eight: BEAUTY AND GROOMING

chapter nine: STAYING IN SHAPE

chapter ten: LOVE AND ROMANCE

chapter eleven: CHILDREN'S HEALTH

chapter twelve: **YOUR HEALTHY PET**

How to Get in
Tip-Top Shape

Introduction

Psst, want a hot tip? Spicy foods can actually *burn* calories.

And here's a cold tip. The safest, most effective nasal spray for adults may be the kind intended for *children*.

And there are a lot more tips where these came from. Tips for coping with plummeting temperatures or a spouse's temper tantrum. Tips for dealing with a bad boss, bad food or a bad back. Tips for getting along with your kids, your co-workers, your cousins and your cat. Tips for every room in your house, every part of your body, every season of the year—everyday tips to get every aspect of your life in tip-top shape.

That's what *Everyday Health Tips* is all about: providing you with the biggest, best, most varied collection of health tips ever gathered in one place. It's as if we took a convention of health experts—nutritionists, dermatologists, psychologists, you name it—and signed them all up for this book. And at this super-convention, it's easy to "page" the doctor. He's always in—and always informative. You'll learn about:

- A simple 10-second technique that destroys cold germs.
- How painkillers like aspirin can actually *cause* headaches—and how to make sure they don't.
- The one controllable health factor behind 70 percent of all new cases of high blood pressure.
- A safe herbal tranquilizer.
- A special shoe that can reduce back pain.
- How heat can speed the healing of an infection.
- The five types of food that cause the most cases of heartburn. (Spicy foods are *not* on that list!)
- A diet that reduces arthritis pain.
- A common breakfast beverage that can stop an asthma attack.

And that's just a tiny sampling from the beginning of chapter 1!

Now here's a final tip, one you'll only get in this introduction: Don't read this book. That's right, *don't* read it. But *do* scan, skim and skip around. Because this book is made for browsing, for short and profitable visits, for finding the practical facts you need without having to plow through endless pages of scientific slush. Or think of it this way. This book is like a health-lover's fantasy of fast food: fun to consume, loaded with things that are good for you and ready right now. So go ahead, dig in—and tip the scales in favor of your good health.

William Gottlieb

Editorial Director
Prevention® Magazine Health Books

chapter one

MEDICAL CARE AND NATURAL HEALING

Fighting Infections and Colds

The forecast for this winter: Cold and windy with a 50 percent chance of scattered misery. Same as last winter. Isn't there *anything* we can do to prevent the annual onslaught of colds and flu?

Yes, say virus experts. We can stay away from people who sneeze and cough. Why? Cold viruses attack the upper respiratory tract. So when cold sufferers sneeze or cough, they spray fine droplets of virus-bearing mucus and saliva into the environment. Whether or not you're felled by a sneeze depends only on how big the droplets are, the distance between you and the sneezer and time.

Fortunately, sneezes become less potent when they finally hit the floor. And when they dry—which can take hours or even days—the virus dies.

HAND-TO-HAND COMBAT

You can also catch a cold from things like coffee cups, telephones or public drinking fountains, doctors say. But of all the things in your environment, the most likely object to give you a cold is the human hand.

"There's some evidence, with rhinovirus in particular, that you are apt to have the virus on your hands," says Jack Gwaltney, M.D., head of epidemiology and virology at the University of Virginia School of Medicine. And it's usually the people who are considerate enough to cough or sneeze into a tissue who spread the infection. The mucus seeps through the paper onto their hands, taking the virus along with it. And clinical tests have demonstrated that those with cold viruses on their hands can infect others.

How can you avoid the catch-and-transmit syndrome? Wash your hands frequently when you have a cold, Dr. Gwaltney recommends, or when you can't avoid being around someone else who has a cold.

THE ABC'S OF FLU

But what about the flu? Grandma called it grippe and most people call it the flu, but known by any other name it would hurt as much. That's because influenza is a viral infection that comes on suddenly, usually bringing fever, sore throat, runny nose, cough and a general weakness that can make it a chore just to move about. Your muscles and head may ache. You may get chills. You may end up flat on your back in bed. And you can expect to be miserable for two to seven days.

The common cold it's not. Flu viruses and cold viruses are completely different animals. And though cold and flu symptoms can vary dramatically from person to person, cold symptoms are generally milder and fewer—usually just sneezing or coughing, runny nose, slight malaise and inflammation of the air passages without fever or achiness.

Every year influenza viruses cause outbreaks, usually less widespread than the brutal pandemics that arise about once a decade. And the reason is their diversity and changeability. There are only three main types of flu virus: influenza A (the most prevalent), influenza B (a rarer breed) and influenza C (almost unheard of). But, at least in influenza A, there are many subtypes and many different new strains of these viruses that crop up. People often have no antibody protection against these mutations, and thus an outbreak begins.

Fortunately, most people recover from the flu. When they don't or when they have to be hospitalized, it's usually because the flu has led to medical complications such as pneumonia or has further weakened someone with an existing ailment.

The people most likely to be seriously threatened by the flu are those with heart or lung disease, pregnant women, the elderly, those confined to bed and the very young. In children, influenza brings a risk of the life-threatening neurological illness Reye's syndrome, which has also been associated with the use of aspirin-containing products.

The good news is that we aren't completely at the mercy of influenza. Here's what can be done to prevent it—or at least make it easier to endure.

Vaccination. Right now, the number one defense against influenza is flu shots. They can dramatically cut the number of influenza cases, and these days, reactions to vaccines are rare or minor.

In both Canada and the United States, flu shots are recommended for anyone over age 65, for adults and children with chronic disorders (like certain heart, lung, kidney, metabolic, immune or blood diseases), and possibly for those who take care of high-risk patients (medical personnel and family members, for example).

The anti-flu drug. Far too few people realize that there's an approved drug available that's being used to prevent and treat the flu. It's called amantadine hydrochloride, and it's 70 to 90 percent effective in preventing infections of influenza A (it's worthless against influenza B). If it's taken 24 to 48 hours after the influenza A bug bites, it can also cut the duration of the illness, perhaps by as much as two days.

Good nutrition. A healthful diet can't ward off the flu. It can't halt it once it starts, either. But clearly, your immune defenses function better when you're eating right.

"If you're properly nourished and in good general health," says Stanley Acres, M.D., chief of disease surveillance in the Department of National Health and Welfare in Ottawa, "your body will be in a much better position to endure the viral assault." And there's some evidence that good nutrition will also boost the power of flu shots.

TENDER LOVING CARE

Treating the flu—or a cold—is mostly a matter of relieving symptoms and consulting your doctor. The things that can really help are getting bed rest, drinking plenty of water and fruit juice, and taking aspirin (for adults only) or acetaminophen (the choice for children) to ease fever and achiness. Gargling with salt water or chewing on cloves—no more than four a day for adults, three a day for children—can relieve a sore throat. Using a humidifier, sitting up and slightly forward as though you were writing a letter and using your thumbs to massage the area under your eyebrows can ease the pain of a troubled sinus.

For a useless cough that doesn't produce any mucus, some doctors may recommend a codeine cough mixture or an over-the-counter preparation containing dextromethorphan.

A stuffy nose can be relieved by a decongestant, but inhaling steam also loosens mucus in the nasal passages, doctors report. That's why a cup of hot tea or—even better—a bowl of chicken soup (see the accompanying box) can also do the trick. And if you feel the need for a nose spray, some doctors suggest you can avoid the "rebound" effect—in which your nose is *twice* as stuffy after the spray wears off—by using one that's actually intended for children.

As to the age-old question, should you feed a cold and starve a fever, or starve a fever and feed a cold: It doesn't really matter. If you feel like eating, eat; if you don't, don't.

Lewis Vaughn

Foods That Soothe

Hot tea with a little honey is a tried-and-true remedy for a stuffy nose. "Inhaling steam loosens mucus in the nasal passages, helping to wash away infecting organisms," says Joseph Vitale, M.D., professor of nutrition at Boston University Dental School. "But chicken soup works even better. Nobody knows why, but no one will deny that steaming chicken soup is balm not only to the body but makes the spirits soar. And that can speed recovery.

"The warmth and affection with which food is offered has a very strong placebo effect. The message of caring that garnishes the soup, and other dishes you take pains with, may do more good than the food itself," he adds.

"For a more vigorous effect on your sinuses, try something spicy," suggests Irwin Ziment, M.D., professor of medicine at UCLA School of Medicine. "Mexicans living in Los Angeles who go for hot, spicy foods, even though they suffer exposure to smog, have fewer problems with bronchitis than non-Mexicans who have bland diets."

"Use lots of horseradish, mustard, cayenne, chili pepper and garlic on your food," he advises. "Enjoy oysters with horseradish and Tabasco, spiced shrimp cooked Creole-style in Tabasco or highly seasoned gumbo laced with garlic, which is an expectorant recognized worldwide. Such hot, spicy food—by loosening up your abnormal secretions—clears your sinuses, your nose and your lungs."

No More Headaches

I'm very brave generally, only today I happen to have a headache. — Tweedledum explaining to Tweedledee why he's unable to fight a duel with him, from *Through the Looking Glass* by Lewis Carroll.

You've got a headache and you don't know why. Oh, let's see now, what could it have been?

You hunched over your desk all day crunching numbers.

You cared for your screaming kids, your ailing patients, your sullen junior high school students.

You pounded the pavement on an all-day job safari in a market as dry as an African veld.

You drove 200 miles to stand in line in the hot sun at Six Flags over Georgia.

You fought with your spouse over who got butter in the jelly jar.

You watched three soaps, four game shows, a mini-series, and the colorized version of *The Maltese Falcon* on TV.

You went to a picnic, danced the polka, drank wine, ate cheese and hot dogs and were pulled into the mudhole in the tug-of-war.

You're Tweedledum stumbling upon the convenience of headaches as a catchall excuse.

Major or minor, headaches are a national pastime more prevalent than baseball, football and stock-car racing combined. Headache relief is a big business. There is a National Headache Foundation for headache researchers and headache sufferers. There's even the professional journal *Headache*.

Some researchers have named dozens of headache types, from migraine to ice cream to sex to vacation, but there are really only two major types of headache: tension, caused by contraction of scalp, neck and shoulder muscles, and vascular (the familiar migraine), caused by dilation of blood vessels in the brain. There's also a headache called a mixed headache that combines tension and migraine symptoms. What works to cure or prevent one type of headache may or may not work on another type, and the results also vary widely from person to person. Here's what the experts say about headache types and what to do about them.

TENSION HEADACHE

The pain in your brain is caused mainly by the strain. Tension headache, also known as muscular contraction headache, is estimated to account for 90 percent of all headaches. It's a constant, dull, viselike or bandlike ache, often with throbbing in the shoulders or neck. The culprit is mental, emotional or physical stress disguised as deadlines, discord, discomfort, depression. Scalp, neck and shoulder muscles tense up and ache, putting pressure on blood vessels and nerves in the brain. There are ways to treat and ways to prevent tension headache pain. Here are the methods most recommended by the experts.

Massage it away. You may not have to rely on drugs to get over your headache, says Seymour Diamond, M.D., director of the Diamond Headache Clinic in Chicago. Having someone massage your head, neck and shoulders helps relax taut muscles (see the box, "Relief Is Just a Massage Away," on page 5.

Warmth works wonders. Heat —a warm shower, a heating pad, a hot-water bottle, whatever—works the same way when applied directly to the head, neck and shoulders.

Hangover Helpers

The best way to prevent a hangover is . . . well, you know that. We won't insult your intelligence. But should you neglect prevention, here are some ways to ease the morning-after throb.

The hair of the dog that bit you is just as bad in the morning as it was last night, according to Seymour Diamond, M.D. Instead, he says, drink broth or bouillon to replace the electrolytes (essential nutrients) you may have lost in urinating the night before. The old standby, tomato juice, may work for the same reason. Liquids also replenish water lost to dehydration, a common side effect of alcohol. Eat honey on toast, says Dr. Diamond. The fructose (fruit sugar) in honey helps burn up alcohol.

Cold showers don't really work very well, says Dr. Diamond, but ice packs on the head can help. And forget trying to sweat the headache away. Saunas only dilate blood vessels more and cause more pain. Vitamin B shots don't work either, says Dr. Diamond.

Ice is nice. Ice packs placed on your head produce a numbing and cooling sensation.

Think it away. Biofeedback is another method that Dr. Diamond says has produced "excellent" results, but it requires training. Electrodes placed over your scalp and neck muscles are wired to a machine that produces one kind of audible tone that indicates when your muscles are being tensed and another tone when muscles are relaxed. Your goal is to learn to change the tone to the relaxed pitch by consciously relaxing your muscles and repeating relaxing phrases. After about four weeks of training, says Dr. Diamond, "the patient can often relax quickly at the first sign of a headache by sitting quietly and repeating the calming phrases."

Adjust yourself. It's tension prevention. Be aware of the way you hold your head while at work or driving or reading, says Dr. Diamond. Periodically change your position, stretch your neck and arms, bend your head from side to side and front to back a few times.

Find peace and relaxation. Along with biofeedback, says Dr. Diamond, meditation and progressive relaxation techniques can prevent tension headaches. Find yourself a quiet space for a few minutes or even half an hour. Sit in a comfortable chair, or lie on the floor, and begin to breathe deeply and regularly. Beginning with your feet, tense and then relax each muscle group in your body, working up your body until you end at your hands. Imagine the tenseness flowing out of your body through your fingertips while also imagining yourself in your favorite surroundings, whether on a tropical beach or a ski slope or before a glowing fireplace.

Take painkillers. Aspirin, acetaminophen (Tylenol), and ibuprofen (Nuprin) are all effective enemies of headache, says Dr. Diamond, and are by far the most popular. But be careful: It's well documented that both over-the-counter and prescription headache drugs can actually *cause* headaches—a rebound effect of taking them too often.

THE HEADACHE HEAVYWEIGHT

An inherited trait, the migraine is the Sherman tank of headaches. Most people who think they have sinus headaches actually have common

Relief Is Just a Massage Away

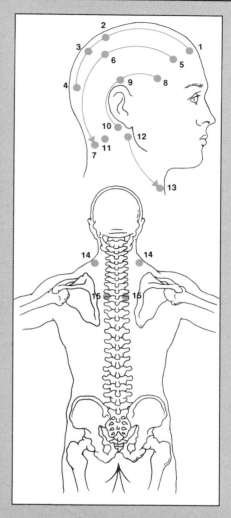

This is a massage-away-a-headache-by-the-numbers course, as adapted from *Massage: The Oriental Method,* by Katsusuke Serizawa, M.D., professor at the Tokyo University of Education. Massage loosens tense muscles. Have someone perform the massage so you can relax. Just follow the numbers on the illustration at the right, using a light touch and small circular motions, spending about 5 to 7 seconds on each point.

● Massage lightly with your fingertips at point 1, the center of the hairline at the boundary of the forehead.
● Continue back to the center top of the head at points 2, 3 and 4.
● Massage point 5 at the hairline on either side of point 1.
● Massage points 6 and 7 parallel to the course you took with points 2, 3 and 4.
● Now massaging in small circular motions with your palms, move back to the front hairline on either side of point 5 and massage points 8, 9 and 10.
● With the thumbs of both hands, massage points 7, 10 and 11 at the base of the skull.
● Using the index fingers and small, circular motions, massage points 12 and 13 on the neck.
● Now slowly turn the face upward and press either with your thumbs or with all 4 fingers on each hand on all the points from 1 to 13.
● Heighten the effect by massaging points 14 and 15 on the back.

migraines, says Dr. Diamond. Pain can be mild to severe, usually on one side of the head, and is often accompanied by nausea, vomiting, dizziness, tender skin and sensitivity to light.

A migraine is caused by dilation of brain blood vessels and thus is called a vascular headache. The expanded vessels press against nerve endings, which then release chemicals that cause pain. "Nearly everything under and including the sun" can trigger migraines, says Dr. Diamond. The main thrust of migraine therapy is to constrict blood vessels; usually simpler, nondrug methods are used first.

Control your diet. Dr. Diamond implicates food in about 25 percent of migraines and names certain foods and substances as proven migraine triggers: alcohol, avocado, bacon, bananas, broad beans, canned figs, cheese, chicken livers, chocolate, citrus fruits, coffee, herring, hot dogs, monosodium glutamate, nuts, onions, sausage, tea and yogurt. One or some or all of these could be your trigger, or it could be something not on the list. Discovering your trigger takes a little detective work: Eat or consume one of the suspects frequently for a month or two; if you don't get a migraine, move on down the line until you hit the right one, then eliminate it from your diet.

Reverse your blood flow. With biofeedback, you can learn to warm your hands by ordering your blood to flow into your hands and away from your head, thus constricting brain blood vessels. Doctors don't know why this happens, but it seems to work in about half the patients who go through a biofeedback training program, says William Speed, M.D., former president of the American Association for the Study of Headache. The American Medical Association also gives this technique its stamp of approval.

Put your vessels on ice. It numbs tender skin immediately and constricts blood vessels. A study by Dr. Diamond found that ice packs, especially the commercial gels, were effective in 80 percent of migraine sufferers; 53 percent of migraine and mixed-headache patients reported immediate relief.

The drug of choice. Ergotamine, a drug that constricts blood vessels, is the most effective drug in treating migraine and is the one most prescribed. But because it can have unpleasant side effects—diarrhea, nausea, dizziness, dry mouth—it is usually prescribed for those who have migraines only two or three times a month, says Dr. Diamond. Mild migraine can sometimes be helped by ordinary, over-the-counter drugs.

This drug can prevent migraine. A beta-blocker, propranolol, stops the action of adrenaline in your body. Adrenaline is the hormone that gets your heart racing when you're excited or afraid, making your blood vessels dilate. If taken for a year, propranolol may even "break your migraine cycle, once and for all," says Dr. Diamond. But this potent medication, often prescribed for high blood pressure and heart attacks, can have side effects.

THIS HEADACHE TAKES AN ENCORE

Cluster headaches are like guerrilla forces in a jungle war. They strike hard, fade, and return when you least expect them. Most cluster headaches last anywhere from 30 minutes to 3 hours and occur two or three times a day every day for a month or two, then disappear. The pain, say people who experience them, feels like someone is plunging a dagger or a poker through your eye.

Cluster headaches are a bit choosy about whom they victimize. They most frequently hit hard-driven, "macho" men between the ages of 30 and 50. These men, doctors say, usually smoke heavily, drink hard and push themselves to achieve impossible goals.

What can you do about them? Here are a few tips from headache experts.

Cool it. This advice applies to both your head and your fast-paced lifestyle. An ice pack on the head can help relieve the wracking pain of a headache.

Breathe deeply. Sucking in fresh lungfuls of 100 percent oxygen for 5 to 8 minutes will frequently relieve a cluster headache. The oxygen is available in tanks from a medical supply house or drugstore, but it should never be used for more than 12 minutes at a time. More than that can damage your lungs. You can use it for short periods, then turn it off and use it again later if your headache returns. But don't forget not to smoke around the oxygen. Otherwise you may not have a head to ache.

Go on the wagon. Anything that dilates your blood vessels can trigger a new headache when you're sitting out the lull in a cluster attack. So avoid alcohol. And if your doctor has you on some type of medication that dilates your blood vessels—nitroglycerine, for example—ask if there's an alternative.

Medicate. Since cluster headaches are not only painful but debil-

This Headache's No Picnic

There's nothing like a doctor with a sense of humor. Seattle neurologist R. Steven Singer, M.D., says there's such a thing as the picnic headache, "a product of the American summer scene."

Says Dr. Singer: "Picnics are designed to occur on bright, sunny days (trigger no. 1). The booze always arrives before the food, because the guy with the hot dog buns is a couple of hours late (trigger no. 2). When the food is served, it's hot dogs—and other forms of nitrites (trigger no. 3).

"The result is potentially a migraine before the ice cream course," which is why Dr. Singer and several of his patients wedge a few ergots (ergotamine, a migraine medication) in between the mustard and the 6-pack.

Relief Hitched to Marital Therapy

Can kind words soothe a headache? If they're from your spouse, they certainly might. At least that's what preliminary research conducted at the University of Manitoba School of Social Work, in Canada, uncovered.

Fifteen people who suffered from frequent headaches participated in the study with their spouses. The headaches ranged from tension headaches to intense migraines, and the couples were having marital problems that ran the gamut from disagreements about money and child rearing to infidelity. But the common thread running through all of the cases was the inability to communicate and solve problems.

Headache can become part of an unhealthy pattern that doesn't allow marriage partners to resolve differences, reported Ranjan Roy, Ph.D., who conducted the study. Many of the participants blamed their problems on their headaches or didn't want to address their problems until they felt better.

After an average of 7 marital counseling sessions, however, 11 of the headache sufferers experienced relief. And as an added benefit, 14 of the couples also felt that their marriage relationships were improved.

Dr. Roy cautions against overoptimism in this method of headache control, however, until more definitive studies are done.

itating, you may want to ask your doctor to prescribe a drug that can prevent them. Methysergide (Sansert), calcium channel blockers (Calan, Adalat), ergotamine (Cafergot), lithium and cortisone all seem to be effective in preventing cluster headaches. But not every drug works for every person, so you and your doctor may have to experiment before you find the right one.

TRY THE ESOTERIC

If your mind demands more imagination in its headache treatment, read on. Even self-described skeptic Dr. Diamond says he's learned not to discount what he might think are bizarre theories and treatments if they seem to work for some people. Here are a few offbeat techniques you might want to try.

Get juiced. In transcutaneous electrical stimulation (TENS), you get hooked up to 9-volt batteries and mild bolts of electricity buzz into your head. One study showed 55 percent of patients found some relief from their headaches. Dr. Diamond predicts positive results from current studies.

Gain from pain. Headache relief could be a side benefit of the brain's production of endorphins. These chemicals, the theory goes, kill the pain of exercise and cause "runner's high." Dr. Diamond believes endorphins could be the source of relief some migraine sufferers report after running. But exercise makes some people's headaches worse.

Hug a teddy bear. Teddy bears and security blankets may help stimulate the body's opioid system, a natural soother that's stimulated during childbirth. "They take you back to a time when you felt comforted," says Jane Roberts Gill, a clinical social worker at the Headache Research Foundation at Boston's Faulkner Hospital. "It's similar to the response created by petting a dog or cat."

Smell your headache away. Stop laughing. A Yale University research team is asking: If smell can immediately trigger emotions, can it *un*trigger emotions? Since most headaches are emotionally based (in our reactions to stress), so the smell theory goes, the smell of apple pie or the fragrance your first love was wearing can help you relax, and that relaxation may help cure your headache.

WHEN TO SEE A DOCTOR

Smells, teddy bears and low-voltage currents aside, there are times when a headache needs a doctor's attention. According to Dr. Diamond, the warning signs you should watch for, which may or may not indicate physical disease (implicated in only 2 percent of headaches), include:

● Daily or almost daily occurrence of headaches.
● A change in the nature of your headache.
● An increase in intensity of headaches.
● Neurological symptoms—such as weakness, numbness, dizziness—accompanying your headache.
● The need to take pain-relieving drugs every day or almost every day for a prolonged period.
● Lost workdays because of headaches.
● The occurrence of a headache whenever you physically exert yourself, whether during exercise or in the bathroom.

William LeGro

Better Blood Pressure

Do you have high blood pressure? Don't be too quick to say no—after reviewing all the evidence, top experts on high blood pressure have redefined what "high" really is. And it's lower than you think.

Members of the Joint National Committee on Detection, Evaluation and Treatment of High Blood Pressure now say that the old definition of high blood pressure (160/95 or higher) doesn't match the facts. After all, the health problems associated with elevated pressure (hypertension) can occur at pressures much lower than this. Reflecting the growing consensus among medical researchers, the committee members pointed out that high blood pressure actually starts at 140/90—below the levels that most physicians once considered normal.

The new standard means that the true number of people who have hypertension is far higher than once thought (over 57 million Americans!), and that almost half of them don't know they have it. Hypertension—which doesn't refer to a state of being "hyper" or tense—usually has no early warning symptoms. The only sure way to detect it is to have your blood pressure taken. And you should. Because high blood pressure is a threat to your life.

THE RISKS ARE HIGH

"Research shows that there's a progressive increase in cardiovascular risk as systolic pressure [the top and higher number] rises above 130 and diastolic pressure [the bottom and lower number] goes above 85," says Aram V. Chobanian, M.D., a member of the Joint National Committee on the Detection, Evaluation and Treatment of High Blood Pressure and director of the Cardiovascular Institute at Boston University Medical Center (BUMC).

"So even people with diastolic pressures as low as 85 to 89 (the 'high normal' category) should act to bring their pressures under control, especially since a significant percentage of high normals eventually become severe hypertensives," says Dr. Chobanian.

Such urgency is justified by the strong case that's still building against high blood pressure. Thanks to the Boston University/Framingham Heart Study and other research projects, it's now clearer than ever that hypertension is a major risk factor for stroke, coronary heart disease, congestive heart failure, kidney failure and lesser ills. Day by day, it speeds up atherosclerosis (hardening of the arteries), damages your nervous system and overworks your heart.

The ominous link between hypertension and death is now irrefutable: The higher your blood pressure (either systolic, diastolic or both), the more likely you are to die before your time.

A TREATABLE PROBLEM

Scientists are still uncertain why some people develop the problem and others don't, but they are sure about one thing: This puzzling disorder is the most treatable—and perhaps one of the most preventable—of all chronic ailments.

"Thirty years ago, relatively few people with hypertension could con-

How High Is High?

You have hypertension if your diastolic blood pressure is 90 or above or your systolic pressure is 140 or above. Isolated systolic hypertension (found mostly in the elderly) is a systolic pressure of 140 or more with a normal diastolic pressure.

Systolic Blood Pressure (the top and higher reading)	Classification
less than 140 ...	normal
140 to 159	borderline isolated systolic hypertension
160 or higher ...	isolated systolic hypertension

Diastolic Blood Pressure (the bottom and lower reading)	Classification
less than 85	normal
85 to 89	high normal
90 to 104	mild hypertension
105 to 114	moderate hypertension
115 or higher ...	severe hypertension

trol their blood pressures," says Dr. Chobanian. "But now practically everyone can achieve some degree of control, and most can bring their pressures down to the normal range."

For decades, hypertension researchers at BUMC and elsewhere have been debunking myths and advancing treatments. Here's what they're learning about what works—and what doesn't—in controlling America's most widespread cardiovascular health problem.

Lower your weight. Flab plays dangerous games with your blood pressure. Medical studies have shown that when body weight goes up, blood pressure goes up. When weight goes down, pressure goes down. On the average, a man's blood pressure jumps 6.5 points systolic for every 10 pounds of weight gain. A woman's pressure increases about half this amount.

"Our data suggest that overweight is one of the most powerful contributors to hypertension," says William B. Kannel, M.D., chief of preventive medicine and epidemiology at BUMC. "Our estimate is that as many as 70 percent of the new cases of hypertension in young adults could be directly attributed to weight gain."

Some contend that high blood pressure is somehow less dangerous in obese people (those more than 15 to 20 percent above ideal weight) than in lean ones, but the evidence refutes this. It's also not true that overweight people often have falsely high blood pressure readings because they have fat arms.

The most important news is that weight loss through diet alone can dramatically lower blood pressure *even if ideal weight isn't reached.* One estimate is that obese people can decrease their blood pressures an average of 8 to 10 points (systolic or diastolic) by losing 20 to 25 pounds. In some people, such a pressure drop is enough to take them right out of the hypertensive category.

Drink with one fist, not two. Drinking less than three alcoholic drinks a day should not raise your blood pressure. Drinking more than

Drugs against Hypertension

Do you need drugs to lower your blood pressure?

Generally, say doctors at Boston University Medical Center, you should first try nondrug therapies—salt restriction, weight loss, exercise and stress management—if you have a diastolic pressure of 90 to 95. After 3 or 4 weeks of such therapies, your doctor should be able to tell whether they're working. If they aren't, then drug treatment may be appropriate. Some people with a diastolic pressure of 96 to 99 can also go on nondrug therapy—if they're really willing to work hard.

Usually those at or above a diastolic pressure of 100 should be treated with medication right away. The higher blood pressure levels are just too risky to let them go unchecked.

that will. If a two-fisted drinker goes on the wagon, however, there's a good chance that his pressure will drop 10 to 25 points.

Leave the salt on the shelf. And that means at the supermarket as well as at home. There's an awful lot of salt hidden away in processed foods. Bologna, ham, cheese and bacon, for example, are loaded. So even if you're not adding a shake or two at the table, you're still getting far more than you need. How much more? Your body needs $1/10$ teaspoon a day, doctors say, yet you're probably eating 20 times that amount when all those hidden sources of salt are added in.

And too much salt can cause your blood pressure to soar—particularly if you're "salt sensitive." Researchers have recently devised tests that can tell you whether you are or not, but the tests aren't yet widely available. We do know, however, that if high blood pressure is in your family, there's a good chance you're one of the susceptible people.

Walk, run, cycle or swim. Working out for 30 to 60 minutes

three times a week can lower your pressure anywhere from 4 to 20 points (systolic or diastolic). But that's with the aerobic exercises mentioned. Isometric exercise—like weight training—should be avoided, since it can actually raise your pressure. But whatever exercise you choose, work into it slowly and with your doctor's blessing, especially if you're hypertensive or have other known cardiac risk factors.

Learn a relaxation technique. Studies have shown that techniques for stress-management—relaxation, biofeedback, yoga and meditation—can, in some people, produce a mild reduction in blood pressure for up to a full year. A few people may respond better than that, and others may not respond at all. For any of these techniques to work, however, you have to use them every day—especially in stressful situations.

Lewis Vaughn

Herbs
as Home Remedies

When you have a headache, you can either take two aspirins or munch on some willow bark. It's silly, of course. You wouldn't gnaw on a tree limb to get rid of a headache. But you wouldn't really be barking up the wrong tree if you did.

Concealed within the willow bark is an active pain reliever called salicin. For centuries, willow bark has been brewed by people of many cultures as a tea for headaches, rheumatism and fever. The aspirin we buy at the supermarket is a slightly modified, synthetic version of the age-old folk remedy.

Today, despite an abundance of commercial drugs, some people are turning to the old herbal cures. Why?

"A certain segment of the population has lost faith with the chemical era and they're afraid of the side effects of drugs," says R. F. Chandler, Ph.D., professor of pharmacy at Dalhousie University in Halifax, Nova Scotia, and a former member of Canada's Expert Advisory Committee on Herbs and Botanical Preparations.

But just because an herb is natural doesn't mean it's necessarily better or safer than a commercial drug. "God knows, nicotine is natural, but it's not safe," says Dr. Chandler.

Many herbs are safe, however, if used in moderate amounts in conjunction with an expert medical diagnosis. It's also best not to pick your own herbs but to buy them from a reputable producer. How is the herbal novice to separate the wheat from the chaff, the licorice root from the deadly nightshade? What's safe and effective? What isn't? And in those cases where an herb is good for you, how much is too much?

We asked several experts in herbal medicine for some practical answers.

Below is a list of some of the most effective herbal remedies, what they will do, and recommendations for safe "doses."

Feverfew for headaches. Despite its name, this natural remedy doesn't cool your fevered brow. But it might make what's under your brow feel better, especially if you suffer from migraine headaches.

Though it isn't known how feverfew blocks migraine attacks, one study showed that it can, at least for some. Researchers speculate that substances in the plant appear to make smooth muscle cells less responsive to certain body chemicals that trigger migraine muscle spasms.

How much feverfew should a person take, and in what form?

"If you take feverfew by eating the leaves, it should be in very small doses—from 50 to 60 milligrams, which is three or four of the little feverfew leaves each day," suggests Varro E. Tyler, Ph.D., dean of the Schools of Pharmacy, Nursing and Health Sciences at Purdue University. "Commercial preparations—capsules, for example—are hard to find, but some botanical wholesalers list them."

Some migraineurs who take feverfew mix it into foods to hide the herb's characteristic bitter taste.

Licorice for coughs. If you've taken commercial cough syrups, you might have benefited unknowingly from licorice, which has been used in cough remedies for generations. The use of licorice root as a medicinal herb dates back perhaps 4,000 years. Licorice was believed to help relieve stomach pain and mouth ulcers then, and there's some clinical evidence supporting that view today.

"The plant itself has very definite therapeutic effects," says Dr. Chandler. "It is a reasonably safe plant. But it does cause retention of water, which leads to retention of salt, which in turn leads to high blood pressure."

For this reason, you would be wise to moderate your intake of licorice if you have high blood pressure or heart disease. Too much licorice can lead to potentially dangerous heart rhythms. It is also not a good idea to eat much licorice if you are taking corticosteroid medications, since these drugs also cause water retention.

Garlic and Onion: Zesty Home Healers

Garlic and onion. We usually think of them more as toppings for pizza than as natural healers, but many believe that they're just as good in either role.

The claims made on behalf of garlic and onion are numerous, including reports that both these pungent plants reduce the tendency of blood platelets to clot. This may lessen the risk that a clot might block an already narrowed artery, causing heart attack or stroke.

If you use garlic, you should take about 1 small clove, and it should be raw, says Varro E. Tyler, Ph.D. "The more you cook it, the less potent it becomes," he adds. "All the active components of garlic are odoriferous. The deodorized varieties have more or less of the clot-reducing activity removed."

As for onions, Dr. Tyler says, eat as many as you like, preferably raw. Of course, you will soon notice that the one thing onions cannot do is help you make friends.

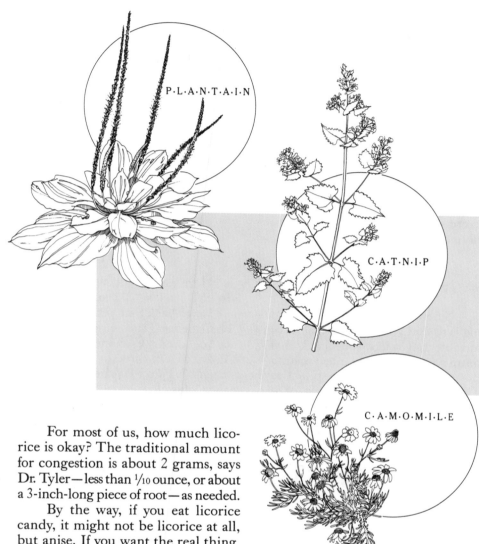

P·L·A·N·T·A·I·N

C·A·T·N·I·P

C·A·M·O·M·I·L·E

For most of us, how much licorice is okay? The traditional amount for congestion is about 2 grams, says Dr. Tyler—less than 1/10 ounce, or about a 3-inch-long piece of root—as needed.

By the way, if you eat licorice candy, it might not be licorice at all, but anise. If you want the real thing, check the ingredients.

Plantain for healing. Leaves of this spiky weed, commonly found on many lawns, have been widely used over the years to bandage and heal wounds. Its juice has also been used as a remedy for poison ivy. You're supposed to rub the crushed leaves on the affected area, says Dr. Tyler.

Valerian for the nerves. Looking for a natural tranquilizer that won't interact with alcohol, as some prescription drugs do? Try valerian. A small amount—about 1/4 teaspoon—in 1 cup boiling water is the recommended amount, says Dr. Tyler.

Soothing catnip. You'd never know it to see what this herb does to your cat, but catnip also appears to be a natural tranquilizer. "Most people who use it make it as a tea, using 1 to 2 tablespoons in a cup of boiling water," says Dr. Tyler.

Hops for relaxation. One of the most important ingredients in beer, hops is also the nutritional equivalent of easy-listening music. "Years ago, it was observed that the people who picked hops became tired and sleepy early in the day," says Dr. Tyler. "No one knew why until it was discovered that hops have mild sedative properties."

You can use hops in a couple of different ways. One way is to sleep on them. "I suggest putting hops in an old muslin pillow and trying it for a good night's rest," says Dr. Tyler.

Another way is to make hops tea, using a scant teaspoonful in 1 cup of boiling water.

Tummy-soothing capsicum. You probably know this hot-stuff herb best as chili pepper. Eat too much, and you might think your smouldering stomach will set off the smoke detector. But tummy torch it isn't. Capsicum has been used for years as a "stomachic" or "carminative"—a medicine that eases stomach pain and flatulence. Capsicum also has been used for diarrhea, cramps and toothaches, and you'll find it in some laxatives and muscle rubs.

If you'd like to try capsicum to relieve stomach upset, says Dr. Tyler, try it in small doses—no more than 60 milligrams, which is just a pinch or two.

"To use capsicum as a muscle rub, mix a little crushed red pepper with rubbing alcohol," he adds. "Keep it out of your eyes, whatever you do. And don't use too much. You could get blisters."

Camomile for digestion. "It's often thought of as an innocuous herb," says Dr. Tyler. "But camomile is an antispasmodic, used extensively throughout Europe for digestive upsets. It has no known toxicity. The only problem is an occasional allergy."

To settle your stomach with camomile, he suggests steeping 1/2 ounce in 1 1/2 cups of boiling water to make a strong tea. Let it steep 10 minutes. Drink it a few times daily, as needed.

Jeff Meade

Freedom from Back Pain

Can you get out of a car in one effortless motion? Work in your garden without wondering how you are going to straighten up at the end of the day? Make love with no fear that your body is going to kink up in some weird position that only an emergency medical team can undo?

You can if your spine is strong and flexible, able to bounce back from the stress of daily life. If it isn't that way with you, you can at least move in that direction by revitalizing the muscles, bone, cartilage and nerves that make up your spine. How? With a program of careful exercise, nutrition and lifestyle changes. Here's how to get started.

EXERCISE BUILDS STRENGTH

Even many surgeons who used to pooh-pooh its benefits now agree exercise can be your spine's salvation.

"Most back pains written off as disk problems are really muscle problems," says Willibald Nagler, M.D., physiatrist-in-chief at New York Hospital/Cornell University Medical Center, New York City. "Most people with back problems have back and hamstring muscles too tight for toe touching and abdominal muscles too weak for sit-ups."

The back and hamstring muscles support the entire structure of the back. They must be strong but flexible to allow you to bend over, sit or twist without straining your back.

The abdominal muscles, when strong, help to stabilize the lower back, the spine's most vulnerable point. Weak stomach muscles allow an exaggerated curve in the lower back, a posture that crimps disks and nerves.

To stretch the back and hamstring muscles, Dr. Nagler prescribes a series of exercises, including knee-to-chest pulls, cat curls and hip rolls. To tighten the stomach, he recommends half sit-ups with knees bent, alternate leg lifts, pelvic tilts and other exercises. See your doctor for instructions on these exercises.

ASSUME THE "S" STANCE

The trick to standing and walking is to find a posture that feels comfortable but offers your back maximum support. "We want to maintain the gentle 'S' curve of the spine," says Terry Nordstrom, director of the Department of Physical and Occupational Therapy and founder of the Back School of Stanford University. For some, in the case of swayback, it helps to pull in the stomach and tuck under the buttocks. This tilts the pelvis toward the back and provides cru-

cial support for the lower spine. Keep your knees slightly flexed, too.

When you're standing a long time, you can tilt the pelvis back and flatten the small of your back by placing one foot on a stool, chair railing or other object a few inches high.

SIT PRETTY

Here again, you want to maintain the back's "S" curve. "People with lower back pain tend to flop into a chair or sofa, throwing their backs into a drooping 'C' shape," says Edgar Wilson, M.D., director of the Comprehensive Pain Management Group at the Colorado Center for Behavioral Health. This posture overstretches the lower back ligaments while compressing the nerves passing out of the spinal column.

The easiest way to avoid slouching is to use a small pillow 2 or 3 inches thick behind your lower back when

The Best Doctor for Your Spine

Take 2 aspirins and call me in the morning—but whom do you call when your back is hurting?

One survey found that people got the most relief when they went to a physical therapist or a physiatrist.

No, we didn't spell the word physician wrong; we meant to spell it p-h-y-s-i-a-t-r-i-s-t. A physiatrist is a medical doctor who has been extensively

trained in all aspects of physical rehabilitation.

In the survey, 86 percent of the respondents reported being successfully treated for their back pain when they saw a physiatrist. It might be tricky finding one, though; many are not listed in the yellow pages. You can get their number by calling either your local medical society or a hospital near you.

you sit. And avoid prolonged sitting. Take a stand-up break every hour.

DON'T DRIVE YOURSELF CRAZY

If you're shopping for a new car, look for seats that offer good back support. Today many manufacturers are aware of the selling qualities of comfortable, supportive seating. Equip your older car with an orthopedic form. Keep the seat forward so your knees are raised to hip level; your right leg should not be fully extended.

NOURISH YOUR SPINE

Osteoporosis and arthritis add to the back problems of many older people, especially women. Back pain can be a sign of microscopic fractures in the vertebrae, as the spine slowly crumbles from age-related calcium losses. Many bone specialists today agree that, to prevent osteoporosis, most women should be getting at least 1,000 milligrams of calcium a day. That's about twice the current intake.

Vitamin D helps you absorb and use calcium. In one study, added vitamin D compound (calcitriol) reduced fractures in older women by 80 percent. If you're not drinking vitamin D-fortified milk or spending at least 15 minutes a day in the sun, consider taking 400 international units of supplemental vitamin D daily.

Trace minerals like zinc, copper and manganese are also vital to bone maintenance. Include shellfish, liver, nuts, seeds and whole grains in your diet to help meet these requirements.

Some researchers suggest that vitamin C could help maintain spinal disks because it helps form collagen, a tough connective tissue covering disks. Others have found that vitamin B com-plex also helps maintain bone and cartilage, as well as soothing nerves irritated by rubbing vertebrae. And some doctors use supplemental magnesium to help relieve the muscle spasms that can cause acute back pain.

CHECK YOUR FOOTGEAR

Any kind of pounding your feet take can show up as back pain, especially if your muscles are weak (strong muscles are good shock absorbers) or you're older (aging spinal disks become thin and hard, providing less cushioning for vertebrae).

Switching to flexible-soled shoes with soft, shock-absorbing cushions produced significant pain relief in many patients treated in the orthopedics department of an Israeli hospital. The cushioning shoe inserts reduced, by 42 percent, incoming "shock waves" from pounding feet.

Avoid heels higher than 1¾ inches, which shift body weight forward and exaggerate swayback.

DROP YOUR GUARD

Relaxed muscles are less likely to go into painful spasms. "People who have been in pain for a while tend to tighten their muscles to guard the area, which makes it almost like a block of concrete," says Dr. Wilson.

Gentle stretching exercises, like yoga, are a good way to relax muscles. Biofeedback and progressive relaxation training can help you relax deeply, even while you're active.

FIND YOUR PAINLESS POSITION

"The key for anyone in acute pain is to rest in a neutral, supportive position," says Nordstrom. "You can lie on your back with several pillows under your legs and your knees somewhat bent. That reduces the stress on your back quite a bit and is usually most comfortable.

"If you lie on your side, put a pillow or small roll under your waist and a pillow between your legs. If you like lying on your stomach, put pillows under your belly to support your lower back."

SLEEP LIKE A BABY

"Sleeping positions make a big difference," says Maggie Lettvin, former Massachusetts Institute of Technology fitness lecturer and author of *Maggie's Back Book*. Instead of lying on your back or stomach, she recommends sleeping in a fetal position—on your side with your knees bent at a right angle to your body—with small pillows under your waist and between your knees if needed.

LOSE THAT EXCESS BAGGAGE

Fat and back pain are an inseparable couple. "Especially when that weight is around their waists, people are likely to have back problems," Nordstrom says. The weight greatly stresses soft back tissues and compresses disks.

For maximum back protection and surest weight loss, combine diet with exercise.

Gale Maleskey

The Right Way to Bend

O-o-a-a-hhh! This is the distressing cry of a common species seen throughout the world: the bending-twisting-reaching person who is bending-twisting -reaching the wrong way. The baleful shriek usually signals the onset of pain, the start of disability and the realization that some stupid act has just been committed.

At one time or another, we've all hurt our muscles, bones and backs for the sake of the long reach or the big bend. Is such grief the inevitable fate of the body human? Probably. But there's hope.

Medical experts contend that it's possible to prevent many, if not most, of these injuries by teaching your body a thing or two about proper movement. Some authorities are quick to point out that there's a right way and a wrong way to drag a spare tire out of a car trunk, climb out of a lounge chair, stuff a briefcase into an airplane's overhead compartment or perform any other muscle-defying feat.

Here are some ideas for the right way to be a mover and shaker without destroying your back. But remember: These suggestions, though particularly useful for people with back and muscle problems, are no substitute for professional care.

The morning swing. In the A.M., don't sit bolt upright and try to

pop out of bed like a jack-in-the-box. That can be tough on your spine. Instead, roll over onto your side facing the edge of the bed, propping yourself up on your elbow. Swing your legs over the side of the bed and push yourself into a sitting position with your hands. Then use your hands to push against the bed as you get to your feet.

The backseat reach. You're in the driver's seat of your car and your briefcase is in the backseat. Problem: How do you get the briefcase to the front seat without getting out of the car or twisting your body into an excruciating half nelson? Answer: While sitting, rotate your whole body 90 degrees to the right (or turn and rest your knees on the seat, facing the briefcase), then grasp the briefcase and pull it toward you — don't try to lift it straight up.

The airport lift. You're in the baggage-claim area of the airport, and your suitcase is circling on the luggage carousel. How are you going to get your suitcase without straining your back or knocking a fellow traveler to the floor? Stand as close to the suitcase as possible, bend at the hips and the knees, tense up your lower

back muscles and slowly pull the bag toward you. Don't jerk it and don't lift it vertically.

The no-backache bow. To empty the dishwasher, thumb through a low filing cabinet, check a roast in the oven, look for something on a bottom shelf or do anything else that requires a low profile, don't stand and bend at the waist. Simply lower yourself on one knee or squat down.

The beach-chair shuffle. To extract yourself from a lounge chair (or any low chair), first scoot forward to the chair's edge, tuck your heels

back toward the front of the chair as far as they'll go and stand up, pushing off with your arms.

The car-trunk caper. To avoid ending up in traction, don't lift a heavy object out of your car trunk by bending forward from the lower back and holding the object at arm's length. Get as close as you can to the object, bend at the hips and the knees, tense up your lower back muscles and hoist the object toward you (not vertically), keeping it as close to your body as possible.

The overhead juggle. On an airplane, how do you heave your carry-on luggage into those overhead compartments without straining every muscle in your body? For one thing, don't try to heave anything—lift slowly and steadily instead. And, if possible,

avoid lifting heavy objects over your head. Otherwise, tense your back, stand just beneath the compartment, hold the load close to your body, and lift it in increments—first to your chest, then above your shoulders, then into the compartment. Reverse the procedure to get your luggage down.

The shoestring trick. If you have to tie your shoe, don't bend over while standing to reach your feet. You're asking for back trouble. Either get down on one knee or stand while resting your foot on a chair.

The tabletop prop. If you must bend over while standing to write on a desk or tabletop, do two things: Bend at your knees as well as at your hips and prop yourself on the writing surface with your hand or elbow.

The lowdown on scrubbing. If you don't do windows but occasionally scrub floors, try not to scrub them while sitting on your heels and bending forward. Instead, get down on all fours (with a towel under your knees to cushion them), keeping your head in line with your spine.

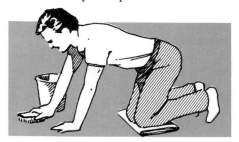

The bedspread crawl. When you make the bed, you bend at the hips and reach out over it to smooth the covers—this maneuver puts a lot of pressure on your spine. It's better to work kneeling on the bed with one knee, bracing yourself against the bed with one hand.

Lewis Vaughn

Healing With Heat

No matter what form it takes, heat affects your body the same basic ways: It relaxes you, or parts of you; loosens muscles and ligaments; dilates blood vessels; boosts blood circulation; increases metabolic processes; warms the skin and, of course, makes you sweat. Combined, these physical reactions may significantly enhance the healing process.

● Heat works to promote wound healing. When applied to a wound, heat raises the metabolic rate. The resulting increased blood flow carries away waste products and excess heat and provides a greater supply of nutrients and infection fighters to the affected area.
● Heat helps reduce the pain of arthritis and sore muscles.
● Heat relieves muscle spasms and helps reduce or control pain.
● Heat is even being used to treat cancerous tumors.

A FEW PRECAUTIONS

Different types of heat may work differently, and the form you use should depend on your doctor's recommendation. Moist heat is thought to penetrate deeper than dry heat and so may be better for sore muscles or injured ligaments; some skin ailments may benefit from less penetrating dry heat. Generally, locally applied heat, as in hot packs, can be better for some kinds of wounds and muscle and skeletal injuries; the overall heat of saunas and steam baths is what to go for if a feeling of whole-body relaxation is your goal.

Before trying any of these methods, however, be sure to consult your doctor. Heat is good therapy, but like any medicine, it can have adverse effects. If applied to a muscle or tendon injury, heat may be initially soothing, but there often is a rebound increase in pain after about 30 minutes, the experts say. (This is why you should

Heat Waves of the Future

Healing with heat has gone high tech with the coming of the laser beam. Here are some experimental treatments that quite possibly may become as routine as a tonsillectomy in the medicine of tomorrow.

● Yann C. Hwang, D.V.M., Ph.D., described a form of acupuncture used in China—though not approved in the United States—that employs a low-energy laser beam to relieve pain.
● A Swedish research team used laser heat to destroy psoriasis-ravaged skin on 3 patients, and they reported that new tissue grew and remained free of psoriasis during a 3½-year follow-up.
● Laser heat has also been used by a UCLA team to seal wounds in experimental animals, with less scarring.
● The heat of ultrasound is now being focused like lasers to fight glaucoma by destroying some of the cells that produce too much fluid in the eye.
● Cornell University researchers are working on another application that uses ultrasound to "tack weld" around the border of a retinal tear to prevent widening of the injury.

treat muscle or tendon injuries with cold for the first 24 hours before applying heat.)

For those with poor blood circulation, diabetes or heart disease, heat should be used only under a doctor's supervision—if at all. Heat is not advised for pregnant women, infants, young children or the elderly.

PACKING HEAT

Although hot packs have been used for centuries to treat wounds, John Rabkin, M.D., and Thomas Hunt, M.D., of the University of California at San Francisco, not only found out how a hot pack works to heal but how it may prevent infection. When the doctors applied hot-water bottles to closed wounds, they found that oxygenation increased with the higher temperatures, and blood flow in the area of the wounds rose threefold on the average.

More blood means more oxygen. Oxygen is vital to clearing bacteria from wounds, and so heat may play a role in preventing infection, the doctors say.

A hot pack can be a hot-water bottle, a heating pad, a Hydrocollator, or even hot towels. The most penetrating heat is given by a Hydrocollator. There are two types. One is a heating pad that can transmit moist heat. The other is a canvas-covered device consisting of several chambers filled with a mixture of sand and silicone. It's soaked in hot water, where the ingredients absorb the heat and retain it better than hot-water bottles, says physical therapist Alex Petruska, a specialist in sports conditioning and training and director of physical therapy for the Sports Medicine Brookline

Clinic in Massachusetts. The Hydro-collator can also conform to the shape of the body.

The advantage of a heating pad over a hot-water bottle is obvious: It stays hot. The disadvantage: It can burn you if you fall asleep on it. It's best to use one with a timer.

To avoid burns when using hot packs, place one or more towels between the hot pack and your skin. In general, apply the heat for 10 to 20 minutes two or three times a day.

SAUNAS AND STEAMBATHS

Researchers and physicians don't dispute the sauna's ability to soothe aching muscles. It can also warm up cold muscles, and can shorten—though not replace—the time you need for a regular warm-up before exercising, says Peter Raven, Ph.D., professor of physiology at Texas College of Osteopathic Medicine and president of the American College of Sports Medicine.

A major benefit you get from the wet heat of steam is the clearing of clogged breathing passages, says Ernest W. Johnson, M.D., professor and chairman of the Department of Physical Medicine at Ohio State University College of Medicine, in the journal *The Physician and Sportsmedicine.* A sauna's dry heat, Dr. Johnson says, irritates the trachea and bronchial tubes, while hot steam clears sinuses.

The primary disadvantage of steam heat is that your body can't dissipate heat as effectively as in a sauna because sweat evaporates more readily in dry air. In a steamroom, your own sweat lingering on your skin creates a stifling effect that increases your skin temperature, which in turn drives up your body's core temperature, even though a steamroom is kept from 50 to 70 degrees cooler than a sauna.

Some long-touted benefits of steambaths and saunas have now been disputed, however. Saunas, for ex-

An Ancient Practice against Ills

Moxibustion is an ancient Chinese medical treatment similar to acupuncture. Instead of inserting needles under the skin at specified "pressure points" on the body as is done in acupuncture, the practitioner of moxibustion holds a burning, cigar-shaped bunch of the herb moxa directly over the pressure point. The results are claimed to be the same as for acupuncture—namely, relief from just about whatever ails you.

Yann C. Hwang, D.V.M., Ph.D., of Tuskegee University, tested acupuncture, electroacupuncture (where the needles conduct an electric current) and moxibustion in baby pigs that were suffering from diarrhea caused by the bacteria *E. coli.* He believes moxibustion actually worked better than either form of acupuncture. Dr. Hwang says moxibustion may have relieved the diarrhea because of what may be the burning herb's effect on the immune system when applied to a pressure point.

The theory goes like this: Moxibustion, acupuncture and electroacupuncture each cause the body to release endorphins (natural painkillers) and the pituitary hormone ACTH. ACTH in turn steps up the body's production of the hormone cortisone. Dr. Hwang says a test-tube study showed that a very small amount of cortisone, as produced by moxibustion and acupuncture, enhances the immune system, which is why the piglets' diarrhea was relieved. A larger amount of cortisone, as produced by electroacupuncture, suppresses the immune system, which is why the diarrhea didn't respond as well to this treatment.

Dr. Hwang says moxibustion can be used for a variety of ailments, although it should never be used to treat an inflammation.

Two characteristics of moxa, though, may pose a problem to Western society, he says. One is that it sometimes leaves a scar from a mild burn on the skin that lasts for several days. The other? "It stinks. It smells like marijuana," says Dr. Hwang. "Sometimes the rural sheriffs can be very mean about it."

ample, will not raise your metabolic rate significantly and thus will not help you lose weight faster. Sweating in steambaths or saunas doesn't do much good in eliminating toxins from the body, nor does it cure colds or fever. In fact, steambaths and saunas may worsen some viral ailments.

INFRARED HEAT LAMPS

Heat lamps can be used for skin ailments that benefit from heat, says Dr. Hunt, like open wounds and psoriasis. Because the lamp doesn't touch your skin and emits dry heat, penetration is shallow. But a heat lamp can be dangerous: Misuse can cause burning, blistering and heatstroke.

William LeGro

Good Digestion Suggestions

Has this ever happened to you? There's a pause in conversation, not a sound to be heard in the room. Then, horrors, you feel it coming: A low, loud rumble begins under your ribcage. It's quickly followed by what sounds like a cascade of water over Niagara Falls. Finally, the thunder settles in your belly.

Now you're starting to sweat. Your eyes scan the rug, the ceiling, anywhere but the other faces. You start to wonder. Did the sound echo throughout the room? You shift in your seat, tightening your stomach muscles, hoping it won't happen again. Could they have possibly heard your stomach's serenade?

They did. Count on it. When your tummy talks . . . everybody listens.

Here's a rundown of the most common stomach ailments and what you can do about them.

FIGHTING FLATULENCE

You say you have more gas deposits than Mobil? One way to shut down the pipeline is to turn off the air.

The most common source of gas is swallowed air, says Harris Clearfield, M.D., professor of medicine at Hahnemann University Hospital in Philadelphia and an expert on gastroenterology. He says that some reasons for swallowing air could be "chewing gum, postnasal drip, rapid eating or poorly fitting dentures. In addition, drinking carbonated beverages such as soda and beer may increase the amount of gas in the stomach."

Certain foods are sources of gas, too. Such foods as cauliflower, brussels sprouts, dried beans, broccoli, cabbage and bran can cause trouble because they are not completely digested in the small intestine. When the undigested bits of food reach the colon, they are fermented by the bacteria that live in the colon. This fermentation often results in gas.

Another reason for gas trouble could be a lactase deficiency. Lactase is an enzyme that is normally found in the small intestine and is responsible for digesting lactose, the sugar found in milk and other dairy products.

"When lactose passes undigested into the colon, bacteria ferment the sugar, causing gas," says Dr. Clearfield. If you eliminate milk and milk products from your diet and the problem goes away, it could mean that you are lactose intolerant. You should check with your doctor, however, to make sure.

For routine gas, here are Dr. Clearfield's suggestions on how to alleviate the problem.

- Eat meals slowly and chew your food thoroughly.
- Check with a dentist to make sure dentures fit properly.
- Avoid chewing gum or sucking on hard candies.
- Eliminate carbonated beverages like beer and soda from your diet.
- Eat fewer gas-producing foods.
- Try exercises such as sit-ups to increase tone if abdominal distension is a problem.

If, after trying all these suggestions, you are still troubled by painful gas, see your doctor. Dr. Clearfield adds that studies show that antacids and other drugs do not really relieve gas pains.

HINDERING HEARTBURN

Plop, plop, fizz, fizz. Is this the sound of your after-dinner drink? If it is, you're not alone. The National Digestive Diseases Information Clearinghouse reports that approximately 10 percent of the U.S. population suffers daily from heartburn and that at least one-third of otherwise normal individuals have this symptom occasionally.

So why are we on fire?

Donald Castell, M.D., professor of medicine and chief of gastroenterology at the Bowman Gray School of Medicine, Wake Forest University, says it's the esophagus that's burning us. "At the point where the esophagus joins the stomach, the esophagus is kept closed by a specialized muscle called the lower esophageal sphincter (LES)," he explains. "The muscle of the LES relaxes after swallowing to allow passage of food into the stomach, but then it quickly closes once again. Backwash of stomach contents, called reflux, occurs when the LES muscle is very weak or, more commonly, when it inappropriately relaxes. Heartburn occurs when the reflux fluid irritates the esophageal lining."

Dr. Castell has some tips you can use to control heartburn.

- Avoid foods that affect LES pressure or irritate the esophagus lining—things like fried or fatty foods, tomato products, citrus fruits and juices, chocolate and coffee.
- Lose weight if you are obese.
- Elevate the head of your bed on 6-inch blocks.
- Avoid lying down after eating.
- Stop smoking. Studies show that cigarette smoking decreases LES pressure dramatically.

● Take an antacid to neutralize the stomach acid. Combined with a foaming agent such as alginic acid, it will form a foam barrier on top of the gastric pool.

Dr. Castell recommends that if the symptoms persist, or if you experience chest pains, you should consult your physician.

UNDERMINING ULCERS

Can you find the antacid section in the drugstore with your eyes closed? Has your two-Manhattan lunch been replaced by a two-Maalox lunch? When the stock market goes down, does your ulcer act up?

People who get stomach ulcers come in all shapes and sizes, just like the ulcers themselves. Ulcers most often appear in people over 40, but children have been known to have ulcers (most often caused by people over 40).

Peptic ulcers come in two varieties: stomach ulcers (also called gastric ulcers) and duodenal ulcers. Duodenal ulcers (found in the duodenum, the segment of the small intestine right after the stomach) are the most common type. They tend to be smaller than stomach ulcers and heal more quickly.

"Most people who develop duodenal ulcers produce more than the usual amount of stomach acid," says Juan R. Malagelada, M.D., professor of medicine at the Mayo Medical School, Gastroenterology Unit, Mayo Foundation, in Rochester, Minnesota. "Unlike duodenal ulcers, however, most stomach ulcers are not caused by the production of too much acid."

Scientists suspect that "the resistance of the stomach lining to acid and pepsin is lowered in those people who develop stomach ulcers and that even normal, or less than normal, amounts of these two substances can lead to the formation of an ulcer," says Dr. Malagelada. They believe that the lowered resistance of the stomach lining allows the acid and pepsin to break down the stomach lining in much the same way that these juices digest food. (Ouch!)

Dr. Malagelada says that scientists do not know what causes ulcers, but they suspect that it is a combination of environmental and genetic factors. He does, though, advise watching your intake of aspirin because aspirin, along with alcohol and caffeine, irritates the lining of your stomach.

If you do suspect that you have an ulcer, Dr. Malagelada suggests that

Six Tips for Avoiding Food Poisoning

It looked good. It smelled good. It tasted good. But somewhere in one of those dishes lurked tiny bacteria that left you with a big pain—nausea, diarrhea, vomiting and fever—and you realize (yikes!) you've been poisoned!

Food poisoning strikes millions of people every year—but it doesn't have to. Patricia Griffin, M.D., a medical epidemiologist at Atlanta's Centers for Disease Control, says that by following 6 simple rules, you can keep those bacteria from wreaking havoc.
● Keep food either hot or cold. Most bacteria die at temperatures above 165°F. They cannot multiply above 150°F or below 40°F, but in between they multiply rapidly, and that's the danger.

● Cook all meat, poultry and seafood thoroughly. Raw chicken, for example, is highly contaminated with salmonella and campylobacter. You can kill these bacteria by cooking foods to an internal temperature of 165°F. Leftovers should be reheated to 165°F, not just warmed up. Be cautious also about tasting your creations before they are thoroughly cooked. One bite can do it.
● Keep yourself clean. If you are cooking or handling food, wash your hands first.
● Always wash your hands between handling cooked and raw foods or raw meat and vegetables.
● Keep your kitchen equipment clean. After you handle raw meat or poultry, always scrub your utensils and cutting

board thoroughly with soap and hot water. Add a little chlorine bleach to the rinse.
● Wrap and discard foods in your refrigerator that are heavily covered with mold. Clean the refrigerator and examine nearby items.

If you have vomiting or diarrhea and you think you contracted food poisoning from eating out or from a commercially canned or processed food, call your local health department.

Food poisoning usually occurs within 1 to 6 hours after eating and should be over in a day or two. If your troubles persist and you become severely ill, call your doctor.

you see a doctor, who can prescribe one of several drugs available that will help neutralize your stomach acid or even reduce the amount of acid that your stomach produces.

CONQUERING CONSTIPATION

Thomas Jefferson had it. So did Mahatma Gandhi and Henry James. In fact, George Gershwin called it "composer's stomach." Constipation had all of these famous people singing the blues.

And now you've joined the chorus. The sound is deafening. Americans spend lots of money on laxatives, to the tune of $225 million annually.

Marvin Schuster, M.D., professor of medicine at Johns Hopkins University School of Medicine, defines constipation as the infrequent and difficult passage of stool. "As a rule, if more than three days pass without a bowel movement, the intestinal contents may harden and a person may have difficulty or even pain during elimination," he says.

Normal bowel movement frequency varies widely, from three movements a day to three a week. It's important that you know what is normal for you, so you can avoid developing a laxative habit. If a laxative habit does exist, substitute milder laxatives for stronger ones and then gradually withdraw the milder ones.

Dr. Schuster adds that "constipation is a symptom, not a disease" and that there are several ways to deal with it.

● Prevention is the best treatment. Eat a well-balanced, high-fiber diet that includes unprocessed bran, whole wheat bread, fruits, prunes and prune juice.
● Drink plenty of fluids and exercise regularly.
● Set aside sufficient time after breakfast or dinner, or after morning coffee, to allow for undisturbed visits to the toilet. Never ignore nature's call.
● Constipation is rarely serious, notes Dr. Schuster, although occasionally it may be a symptom of an underlying disorder. If your bout with constipation lasts longer than three weeks, check with your doctor.

PREVENTING PILES

. . . and they had emerods in their secret parts . . . and the cry . . . went up to heaven. — 1 Sam. 5:9-12.

And beyond. Hemorrhoids, also called piles (from the Latin word *pila*, meaning ball), afflict an estimated 50 percent to 90 percent of the civilized world.

You can get hemorrhoids any number of ways — from sitting or standing for prolonged periods of time, heavy physical labor, pregnancy, low intake of liquids and abuse of laxatives and enemas. But the most common cause is constipation caused by a shortage of fiber in the diet. This constipation makes us strain at something that Mother Nature never designed to be a workout, and we get stretched and blood-swollen veins in the anal area, which burn, itch and hurt.

Lester Rosen, M.D., a bowel specialist in Allentown, Pennsylvania, has

Expand Your Eating Awareness

"If we expand our awareness about eating, we can take care of 99 percent of digestive problems," says Deepak Chopra, M.D., an endocrinologist in Stoneham, Massachusetts, and author of *Creating Health*. Dr. Chopra recommends the following good eating policies.

● Whenever you're going to eat or drink — even if it's just half a peanut or a swig of juice — put the food on a plate or the drink in a glass, take it to the table and sit down. Eating should be a conscious act, not just something you do every time you walk past the fridge.
● While you eat, turn off all distractions, both internal (worries) and external (radio, TV, books, magazines). You should enjoy the *food*.
● Give your complete attention to the food. Enjoy the taste, be aware of the aroma and all the flavors — sweet, sour, salty, bitter, astringent and pungent.

● Be aware of the speed at which you're eating. If it's hurried, slow down.
● Before you eat, ask yourself if you are hungry, on a scale of 1 to 10. Many times, you eat just because you see the food there or because the clock says it's lunchtime — you're just following some automatic cue. You eat and afterward you feel ill.

some advice on how to stop the heavenly cries. "There's no question that more fiber in most people's diet could substantially reduce their hemorrhoid risk," he says. "Fiber is also important for people with existing cases of hemorrhoids, to help speed recovery." He also advises patients to change their reading habits. "I tell my patients not to make their bathrooms their libraries." It seems that just the act of sitting on a toilet can put undue pressure on blood vessels in the anal area. "People should try to restrict their toilet time to a maximum of about 5 minutes per sitting."

To treat hemorrhoids: See your doctor if you have blood in your stools. It may be just from hemorrhoids, but it could be something more serious. Dr. Rosen says over-the-counter products intended to shrink hemorrhoids are of limited value, but medications that keep the anal area clean (such as Tucks and Balneol pads) and those that help to control itching (such as witch hazel) may be worthwhile.

Probably the most soothing gift you can give your hemorrhoids is a sitz bath: warm, hip-deep water sprinkled with a few tablespoons of Epsom salts.

DEFEATING DIARRHEA

Spending more time in the bathroom lately, with your only reading material being the label of a Pepto-Bismol bottle?

Sidney Phillips, M.D., professor of medicine at the Mayo Medical School, says that most people suffer with frequent, watery bowel movements for one or two days each year. He says that most often the diarrhea is caused by viruses or bacteria that "infect the bowel and make it weep fluid. Contaminated food or water, public swimming pools and communal hot tubs are possible sources of these infections."

He adds that anyone with diarrhea should be "given fluids containing sugar and, preferably, salt. Regular nondiet soft drinks are a reasonable start. Commercial quick-energy drinks such as thirst quenchers may be even better." If diarrhea continues for longer than 24 to 72 hours, check with your doctor.

REDUCING RETCHING

It's bad enough that you're sick, but to be forced to kneel on the hard floor while you're sick is a little much to ask!

Those of you who've lived it know what we mean. Joel Wacker, M.D., assistant professor of medicine at the University of Wisconsin School of Medicine, knows how to put the brakes on vomiting. "To stop, the best thing you can do is to try and keep down plain, clear liquid. Eight ounces of water an hour would be a good place to start. To get some calories in, try flat soda pop or Kool-Aid with sugar in it. But make sure it doesn't have caffeine, which will irritate your stomach.

"Once the liquid stays down, work your way back to solids. Try Jell-O, then go on to solid foods like crackers or bread. Just work your way back slowly to a regular diet," Dr. Wacker advises.

Dr. Wacker also says that if you can't keep *anything* down and have been vomiting for 3 or 4 hours, you should contact a physician for treatment.

INTERRUPTING INDIGESTION

Yep, you ate the whole thing . . . and now it's eating you back. Indigestion is technically categorized as painful, difficult or disturbed digestion.

William Y. Chey, M.D., D.Sc., clinical professor of medicine at the University of Rochester School of Medicine, says a person is said to have indigestion if he suffers from several of a group of symptoms including "nausea, regurgitation of stomach contents into the esophagus, vomiting, heartburn, prolonged abdominal fullness or bloating after a meal, stomach pain or discomfort."

These symptoms can last for three or four days or longer. But if the symptoms interfere with your daily routine, you should see your doctor to rule out any serious problems.

But how do you spell relief? "Avoid greasy foods or solid foods containing meat," says Dr. Chey. "If you're lactose intolerant, eliminating all dairy products from your diet should provide relief." He adds that to ease the suffering, your doctor will probably advise you to follow a liquid diet and eat soft foods in small amounts until your symptoms subside.

Don Barone

Easing the Pain of Arthritis

If you're among the one million people who develop arthritis each year, you know that getting up and exercising while your joints ache can be trying. But think about your car after it sits idle for a few weeks. The engine may not want to crank right up and probably needs a little coaxing, but it runs great after it warms up.

In the words of Frederic C. McDuffie, M.D., vice president of medical affairs for the Arthritis Foundation, "People with arthritis must exercise their joints daily to ensure adequate joint mobility and muscle strength. An exercise program that's properly designed and implemented can keep joints flexible, help maintain muscle strength, build overall stamina, lead to a more positive self-image and create a sense of accomplishment."

Nowhere is the adage "Use it or lose it" more apropos than with arthritis. "The longer you sit around in pain doing nothing, the worse it gets," says Michele Boutaugh, Arthritis Foundation vice president for patient services. "You get stiffer and stiffer, and eventually you can lose the use of the affected joint."

If you need more convincing, just ask any of the 60 people who took part in a research project at the University of Missouri. They ranged in age from 21 to 83 and all had rheumatoid arthritis and osteoarthritis in their legs and feet. As part of the project, they did some water jogging—moving their legs in a jogging motion while in deep water. Since their bodies were lighter in the water, there was less strain on their leg and foot joints, and they were able to exercise and strengthen weak muscles. They also walked on dry land three days a week for about 30 minutes each day, says project researcher Marion Minor, a registered physical therapist with the University of Missouri School of Medicine.

After 12 weeks, their endurance and aerobic power improved and some had less stiffness and weakness, with more joint mobility. In other words, they were on the way to preventing or delaying the crippling deformities sometimes caused by arthritis, and they were leading fuller, more active lives, says Minor.

A WHOLE RANGE OF EXERCISES

Range-of-motion exercises help keep joints loose, improve muscle strength and restore movement that's been lost.

When doing any of these range-of-motion exercises, move the joint until you feel some pain, hold it there a moment, then move it a wee bit farther. If there's slight pain in the joint, be gentle as you move it through whatever motion is possible.

One of the more common range-of-motion exercises for aching hips calls for you to lie on your back with your legs straight and about 6 inches apart. Point your toes up. Slide one leg out to the side and then back. Try to keep your toes pointing up, and then repeat the exercise with your other leg.

A good range-of-motion exercise for arthritis in the shoulders is to stay on your back and raise one arm over your head, keeping your elbow straight. Keep your arm close to your ear. Return your arm slowly to your side and repeat the movement with your other arm.

Your physician or therapist will be able to give you more exercises specifically suited to the parts of your body affected by arthritis.

STRENGTHENING THE AFFECTED JOINT

A complete exercise program will also include strengthening exercises, because weak muscles add to joint

Start Your Day with a Stretch

You must get your body—specifically your aching joints—slowly prepared for exercise, so make stretching the first step before each workout. Here's one example of a safe, slow stretch: While lying in bed, stretch one arm up and then the other. Push your arms forward while opening your hands wide, then pull your arms back and close your hands. For your legs, pull your knees up toward your midsection, do a few, slow bicycle turns, then stretch your legs out straight.

Besides preparing you for your daily exercises, such activity also helps prevent morning stiffness. Also, to avoid injury and reduce stiffness or soreness the next day, it's a good idea to stretch as part of your cooling-down process each time you finish exercising.

Foods That Spell Relief

Researchers from the Albany Medical College and State University of New York at Albany compared the effects of different diets on patients with arthritis pain. One diet was typically American—high in saturated (animal) fats. The other was a diet higher in vegetable (polyunsaturated) fats, with almost no saturated fats. This diet plan was also supplemented with 1.8 grams daily of eicosapentaenoic acid (EPA), a factor found in fish oil.

EPA and other polyunsaturated fats are thought to reduce arthritis pain because they lead to the production of a type of prostaglandin that is less inflammatory, explain the researchers. And by the twelfth week of the study, the EPA group confirmed this. In that group, there was a drop in morning stiffness and there were fewer tender joints than in the group eating more saturated fats.

---

problems. These exercises can help maintain or increase muscle strength while putting as little stress on joints as possible.

Isometric exercises have the advantage of causing little joint stress. Basically, you're using your muscles to pull or push against a stationary object, which can be anything from a wall to a body part to an exercise belt.

Place your hands on a wall and push. You can feel your arm muscles working, but there's no joint movement. Another example is to sit in a chair and place your right hand on your right knee. Press your knee against your hand while allowing no movement of the arm or leg.

You need not do many isometric exercises to receive the benefits. Each routine held for a count of 6 seconds, three to four times a day, is enough.

Here are five keys to a successful exercise program.

Maintain a proper pace. Begin at a comfortable level and gradually increase the number of repetitions to avoid unnecessary pain. Use slow and steady rhythms, relax your muscles for about 10 to 15 seconds between repetitions, and breathe deeply and rhythmically as you exercise. Never hold your breath.

Mix exercise with rest and relaxation. The discomfort of arthritis will drain your energy and tire you quickly. Consequently, that means you'll need more rest than nonarthritic exercisers. Getting enough whole-body rest doesn't mean you have to go to bed and stay there, however. Strive for a balance of rest and activity. During a flare-up, you'll need more frequent and longer periods of rest than when your arthritis is quiet.

Most physicians recommend 10 to 12 hours of rest for each 24-hour period, divided between actual nighttime sleeping and short periods of lying down and napping during the day.

Exercise twice daily. This should be your routine for the rest of your life, unless the pain is too severe. In most cases, though, miss a day only if you must and not because you're too busy or in the wrong frame of mind. If you have to skip several days, start again at a slightly lower level.

Find a specific time and place. At first, you might try exercising at different times of the day until you decide what's best for you. Some people find that exercise first thing in the day reduces their morning stiffness.

Exercise when you're at your peak. This means when you have the least pain and stiffness and you're not tired. If you're taking a prescription pain medication, plan to do your workout when the drug is having the most effect. Even if there's slight pain, you need to do the range-of-motion exercises to keep your joints loose. If the joint is hot, inflamed, swollen, red or tender to the touch, move it gently through its range of motion. If in doubt, contact your doctor or therapist to find out how to adapt your exercises.

Tom Shealey

Allergy Relief

Gesundheit!

Whoever said life isn't fair must have been thinking about allergies.

Some of us can plow through thickets of poison ivy and emerge without an itch. Others so much as brush up against a few spindly sprigs of the stuff and they're digging holes through their socks for weeks.

For the majority of people, happiness is a warm puppy, yet dog fur brings thousands to heel. The reason is a difference in the sensitivity of the immune system.

Burdened with an overprotective immune system, a person with allergies is forever on guard against everyday things that don't bother the rest of us. It might be a slice of fresh garden tomato or a patch of clover, a glass of milk or an affectionate kitten.

In most instances, allergies are more annoying than debilitating. Coping often involves avoiding foods to which you might be sensitive or taking an antihistamine to dry up the occasional runny nose and soothe the itchy eyes of hay fever.

No matter what type of allergy you have, there's a good chance you can find relief. Here's some helpful advice based on the latest research and on interviews with allergy specialists.

Chew or sip more slowly. Sulfites are chemicals used to treat foods to make them look fresh. The U.S. Food and Drug Administration (FDA) has banned the use of the chemicals in supermarket produce or restaurant salad bars because they have induced fatal allergic reactions in people with asthma.

But we aren't rid of sulfites altogether. The FDA ban does not apply to prepared foods, such as potato products, frozen and canned vegetables, wine, beer, seafood, dried fruit, dry-mix salad dressings and soups.

Asthmatics and others who could be allergic to sulfites might be able to control an allergic reaction simply by eating or drinking more slowly. Up to 90 percent of all sulfite reactions result from the release of sulfur dioxide gas from food, caused by chewing and sipping, according to Ronald Simon, M.D., a member of the FDA's advisory group on food additives. The allergic reaction is the result of inhaling sulfur dioxide. Many asthmatics have learned to drink and eat more slowly and watch for the warning signs of a reaction — itching, warmth, flushing, chest congestion, abdominal discomfort, coughing and wheezing.

Tell your dentist about your allergies. Allergies also surface in the dentist's office. Fillings, dentures, caps, braces and crowns may contain the metal nickel, which causes allergic reactions in some people. Local anesthetics may also be preserved with a sulfite chemical. If you're allergic to either substance, tell the dentist before he goes to work in your mouth.

Avoid eyeglass rash. Spray a polyurethane coating on eyeglass frames occasionally to avoid the itchy facial rash that's caused by the interaction of sweat with eyeglass materials.

Keep kitty off the bed. Cat got your nose? Could be she's been sleeping in your bed. Kitty's attachment to your bed covers increases the amount of allergy-producing substances in your sleeping quarters a thousandfold. You don't have to hide your felines, just keep them out of your bedroom. The same rule applies to Rover. (For more information on pet allergies, see "Pets and Your Allergies" on page 356.)

Squelch that smoke. Cigarette smoke is bad enough, but for asthmatics, it could cause serious breathing difficulties. Secondhand cigarette smoke greatly increases the likelihood of an asthma attack for up to 4 hours, according to Australian researchers. Smoke evidently makes the asthmatic more sensitive to other allergens, like dust, cold air or exercise.

Just leaving the smoke-filled room might not be enough. By the time you make your exit, it could be too late. To avoid the complications caused by smoke, you have to bypass the smoke altogether.

Put the squeeze on your asthma inhaler. Asthmatics often use metered-dose inhalers to shoot a fine mist of medication into their bronchial tubes. But some people with arthritis or small hands have trouble squeezing the button atop the aerosol bottle. Others just have trouble coordinating the effort, pushing down on the top of the bottle and inhaling at the same time.

Glaxo, in North Carolina, has developed a plastic squeeze trigger, called VentEase, that slips over the inhaler to make it easier to use. To get one free, ask your doctor or pharmacist. Also check to see if your inhaler is compatible with this device.

Sniff for the hidden scent. Cosmetic and grooming-aid manufacturers sell a lot of products marked "unscented." But the fragrance may actually be masked with a chemical, ethylene brassalate. If you're allergic to fragrances, beware. Doctors believe you can react to this neutral scent just as easily as you might to any other fragrance. Read the label, and avoid ethylene brassalate.

Close your air conditioner vent. An air conditioner can do a lot of good for a person allergic to pollen or fungus spores. But if you keep the vent control in the open position, you're sucking outside air — and pollen — indoors. Pollen is extremely small, so your air conditioner filter probably can't screen it all out. Also, research shows that often there is a brief "burst" of mold contamination when the air conditioner is turned on because of mold inside the machine. So turn on the air conditioner and leave the room for ½ hour. This will give the molds in the room time to dissipate, resulting in cleaner, more breathable air.

Other people are very sensitive to cold air. So if you have your air conditioner temperature control set to "Arctic" and ice floes are forming in your living room, turn the temperature up to around 70°F.

Automobile air conditioners are subject to the same hazards, so keep the vent closed and run the air conditioner with the car windows open for a few minutes before you get in. And keep the temperature temperate.

Ragweed sufferers, beware of melons. Some people who are allergic to ragweed also develop itching or swelling of the lips, tongue or throat after eating watermelon, cantaloupe, honeydew, zucchini or cucumber. According to the Allergy Research Laboratory of Detroit's Henry Ford Hospital, these fruits and vegetables have allergy-producing proteins almost identical to those found in ragweed.

Avoid fur-bearin' varmints. If you're allergic to cats and dogs, it's likely you'll also react where the deer and the antelope play. If you're a hunter, that means getting someone else to handle animal carcasses. If you're a "hunter's widow," don't handle your husband's hunting clothes.

Go easy on shellfish. If you're allergic to shrimp, chances are pretty good you're also allergic to crayfish, lobster, clams, oysters and crab, according to physicians from the Clinical Immunology Section at Tulane University Medical Center. Common reactions include hives, nausea and shortness of breath.

Declare war on dust bunnies. Many people are allergic to substances found within their own homes, particularly dust. But you can keep dust down by doing any one of the following things.

● Have a contractor clean out your heating system. All it takes is a couple of carbon-dioxide fire extinguishers and just a little time.
● If you're redoing an allergy-sufferer's room, forget rugs. Instead, use linoleum in solid sheets, not blocks. Mold hangs out in the cracks between linoleum blocks.
● If you're wallpapering, purchase mold-free wallpaper paste. If you're painting, have mold preventive added to the paint. It'll cost about $1.50 extra per gallon.
● When you plaster, look for the one-coat variety that doesn't need sanding.

Stick to white glue. Many of the advanced "super" adhesives do dry more quickly and hold better, but some people who use them develop contact dermatitis. A few also develop other allergic reactions, such as asthma.

Consider using an air cleaner. Newer models are very effective at removing dust, pollen, cigarette smoke and mold from the household environment. Cheap models are considerably less effective, according to Harold S. Nelson, M.D., chairman of the American Academy of Allergy and Immunology's Committee on Environmental Controls.

Since an air cleaner can be expensive, Dr. Nelson recommends leasing one first to see if it does the job. Take time to decide whether it moves enough air, and try it out in your bedroom a couple of nights to find out how much noise it makes. When you use a filter, put it in the middle of the room, where it can do the most good.

Check out your contact lens solution. If you wear contacts and get itchy, teary or swollen eyes, it could be an allergic reaction to thimerosal, a mercury preservative used in contact lens solutions. Another common ingredient, the enzyme papain, can also cause allergic reactions. Switch to solutions that contain neither.

Wash poison away with rubbing alcohol. Here's what to do if you find yourself exposed to poison ivy or oak, according to William Epstein, M.D., professor of dermatology at the University of California at San Francisco. Wash the affected area immediately with rubbing alcohol, followed by water, and wash everything you might have touched with water. And don't use a washcloth, since this will also pick up and spread the poison.

Observe garden precautions. Yes, you can garden, if you observe a few precautions. Do your gardening in the evening. Most weeds unleash their pollen in the morning. Also, water the soil regularly to keep the dust and molds down and wear gardening gloves if you have sensitive skin.

Mike McGrath

A Piercing Problem

Some allergies have a familiar ring to them, namely earrings. You can be allergic to earrings for pierced ears.

There's been an upsurge in allergic reactions to the metal nickel, particularly among girls under 15 who have had their ears pierced. In fact, nickel allergy is the most common contact allergy among women.

The metal pins worn for the first 3 to 6 weeks after piercing contain minute quantities of nickel, which can make the body vulnerable to rashes when metal later comes into contact with the skin. Reactions are common with jewelry, metal buttons, wristwatches, brassieres and eyeglass frames.

Studies also show that girls with more than 1 hole in the earlobe—as in the current "pincushion" look—have twice as many allergies.

Researchers do not recommend ear piercing for children.

Eye Care

Most spiders have 8 eyes. Scorpions have up to 12. The marine flatworm holds the world record, with more than 100 eyes.

You have only two eyes and they must do it all: watch old "M*A*S*H" reruns, guide your car down dark and winding roads, read *War and Peace*, unsnarl Rubik's Cube and squeeze numbers into forms from the IRS. It can all get mighty taxing.

Amiel Francke, O.D., a Washington, D.C., optometrist and popular lecturer on eye care, says that during man's hunting, fishing and foraging days, the eyes were well adapted to the tasks required of them, and they were happy. But in these reading, writing and arithmetic days, where focusing up close for hours on end is part of everyday life, our eyes can sometimes feel glum. Indeed, quite stressed.

How do we know our eyes are stressed? They may appear tired, bloodshot and saggy. They may feel dry or itchy. You may have blurred vision. Or purple dots may stream across the sky. Stress-ridden eyes can also manifest themselves more indirectly, in general body fatigue, aches and pains. Perhaps worst of all, continual eye stress can lead to nearsightedness, says Dr. Francke.

GOOD PUPILS DON'T HAVE STRESS

What can you do about it? Well, you could take up full-time hunting and foraging. Or you could pick up a number of hints from the experts that will make life in this twentieth century a lot easier for you and your two little globular friends.

Tarzan no couch potato. Since eye stress is so much the product of how we live, Dr. Francke says our oh-so-civilized lifestyle is the first thing

When to Stop Using Drops

Nonprescription eyedrops come in 2 varieties: The "gets-the-red-out" kind contains medication to relieve the burning and irritation of eyes affected by allergies, colds and environmental irritants. The "artificial tear" kind is slightly salty distilled water (usually with preservatives) to moisturize eyes that feel dry.

Both can be helpful, but neither should be overused, says Eric Donnenfeld, M.D., an ophthalmologist and corneal specialist in Rockville Centre, New York. The medicated drops, he says, can cause more problems in the long run than they'll solve. And whereas the artificial tears can be used more freely, the *need* to use them for too long is an indication that you may have a medical problem.

How long is too long? No one should use eyedrops more frequently than once every 4 hours, and for no longer than 2 consecutive weeks before consulting an eye-care specialist, says Dr. Donnenfield.

Try this alternative. The eyelid contains oil glands that keep the eyeball lubricated. Sometimes these glands get clogged, and you get that dry-eyed feeling. Instead of eyedrops, Dr. Donnenfeld suggests trying a warm washcloth over the eyes for 5 to 10 minutes, 2 or 3 times a day. "It is a very simple home remedy that can remove the crust, open the pores in the lid glands and allow the eyes to be lubricated more effectively," he says.

we should address to de-stress our eyes. That's not to say you need to live like Tarzan in order to have happy eyes but that you incorporate "lots of outdoor activities and exercise" into your life. This will provide needed breaks for your eyes and relaxation for your whole body—of which the eyes are an integral part.

Tarzan no tied to desk. While at the office, a few Tarzan-like antics throughout the day can mean the difference between sad eyes and glad eyes. Dr. Francke recommends frequent breaks from any kind of close work. Walk around. Touch your toes. Swing your arms. Reach for the sky. Gaze at the horizon.

Tarzan no read in bed. Close work done at home—reading, writing,

watching TV—should not be done lying in bed, says Dr. Francke. "The muscles that help you see don't work well" in the prone position. Furthermore, if you're sick at home, steer clear of close work. "When you are sick, all of you is sick. This is one of the worst times to do paperwork or read. Listen to the radio or *listen* to TV instead," suggests Dr. Francke.

FUN WAYS TO RELIEVE THE EYES

Some might call them techniques for relieving eye stress. Robert Kaplan, O.D., M.Ed., of Portland, Oregon, prefers the word "games." Why? "So people will enjoy them, and relax as they're doing them," says the author of *Seeing beyond 20/20*.

So relax. And play Dr. Kaplan's games for de-stressing the eyes: Palming, Zooming, Shifting and Doing the Groucho Marx.

Palming. A treat for your eyes is "palming." Simply cover your closed eyes with the palms of your hands and luxuriate for several moments in the complete blackness. Be gentle! Don't push against your eyes.

Zooming. Stretch your eyes by zooming: Focus on your thumb at 4 inches from your eyes, then look out toward the horizon as far as you can see. Hold for several seconds. Repeat.

Shifting. "Jog" your eyes. Look left to right, up to down, then roll your eyes in circles. Don't strain.

Become a marxist. Do "The Groucho Marx": Raise and lower your eyebrows, looking as silly as you can. (Cigar optional.)

SPECIAL TIPS FOR SPECIAL STRESSES

Here are some suggestions for dealing with specific sitations that can strain your eyes.

At the wheel. William Johns, head of safety activities for the American Trucking Association, offers your eyes these tips for driving.

● Always keep your eyes moving — don't allow them to become fixed in a hypnotic stare at one point on the road in front of you.
● At night, with dazzling headlights coming at you, avoid looking into them by using the white line on the right side of the road as your guide.
● Take frequent breaks. Get out and walk around often. Nap if necessary.

Reading, writing, and arithmetic. To minimize eye stress while doing desk work, Dr. Francke suggests:

● Work when you are most fresh — in the morning, not at night.

● Arrange a comfortable space: Have good ventilation, loose clothing and an area free from noisy distractions.
● Make certain the room is well lit and your body is not casting shadows on your work.

TV and movies. TV and big-screen theaters can both be big eye stressors, says David A. Newsome, M.D., professor of ophthalmology at the Louisiana State University Eye Center. The reason, he says, is that people usually don't sit properly — with their eyes level with the screen.

For TV, he suggests a comfortable chair, not too close to the screen, with a light on somewhere in the room. For the cinema, he suggests sitting at least far enough to the rear so that your head isn't tilted back (forcing your eyes into an unnatural position). For either kind of viewing, Dr. Newsome advises you to monitor your blinking, as it has a tendency to slow down when the action picks up. "Blinking keeps the eye lubricated and washed," he says.

Computing. Working at a computer is about the most stressful of all things for your eyes. "Computers combine all the evils of a twentieth-century eye-stressing lifestyle," says Dr. Francke. If you use one regularly, do not pass chapter 4. Do not collect more eye stress. Turn to "Your Health and Your VDT" on page 154.

TWO EYES OR FOUR EYES?

Constant eye fatigue, headaches or blurred vision may mean that you need glasses or that the glasses you have are the wrong ones. As a preventive measure against eye stress and near-sightedness, Dr. Francke suggests that if you do regular close work, you do so with glasses that magnify and reduce strain.

The American Optometric Association recommends you have annual eye examinations.

Setting Your Sights on Shades

Whether it's the Clint Eastwood, Elton John or Jackie Onassis look you're after, the most important thing about sunglasses shouldn't be their appearance but their function: to block glare and reduce eye stress. Tom Loomis, past president of the Sunglass Association of America, has a few pointers on how to buy the best shades.

● Slip on the glasses in question and look in a mirror. You should just be able to make out your eyes. If so, you're wearing the best density lenses for driving and most outdoor activity.
● Next, look at the edge of the doorway, at the straight vertical line, and move your head back and forth. If the line wiggles, there's probably a defect in the lenses.
● Go to the front of the store and see if there's a traffic light in view. Can you distinguish the different-colored signals? Gray and brown lenses allow the truest color portrayal.
● Find out how much ultraviolet (UV) radiation the glasses block. There's been concern over the possible connection between cumulative exposure to UV and cataracts. While there is no conclusive evidence, you may want your sunglasses to block a large percentage of UV rays. If the necessary information isn't on the product tag, ask the salesperson or call the manufacturer.

Russell Wild

An Insomniac's Guide to Sweet Sleep

Sleep is death without the responsibility.

—Fran Lebowitz, *Metropolitan Life*

Keoki would rise early every morning after a full night's sleep, step outside his beachfront home in Hawaii, and run a mile down the golden sand, warm wavelets lapping over his bare, brown feet. He'd dive into the turquoise sea, cool off from the run and swim the mile back to his house. He loved life, was a picture of health, and at 72 years old was looking forward to many more full years with his wife and extended family.

But when Keoki went to see James W. Pearce, M.D., director of the Sleep Disorders Center of the Pacific at Straub Hospital in Honolulu, he was a mess. "For no good reason," says Dr. Pearce, "he suddenly couldn't sleep well. It was taking him 2 or 3 hours to fall asleep every night. He tried to put up with it for a few days but finally went to see his family doctor, who put him on sleeping pills for two weeks."

The pills didn't work. By the end of the two weeks, says Dr. Pearce, "he was frantic. He literally thought he was going to die. He wasn't running or swimming. He came to me basically panicked."

Dr. Pearce and his staff put Keoki on a rigid sleep schedule and tapered him off the medication to avoid what is known as "rebound insomnia," a symptom of withdrawal in which the insomnia the pills are supposed to relieve comes back even stronger.

They also educated Keoki about insomnia and sleep, and talked to him about how much sleep he really needed and, says Dr. Pearce, "in a couple of months he was back to his old self."

If sleep is as out-of-reach as the man in the moon, you could have an undiagnosed sleep disorder.

OPEN SEASON ON SLEEP

Sleep centers are a relatively new phenomenon, but insomnia is as old as the hills. And these days most of us just aren't getting enough sleep, say experts. The reason seems to be our modern, stress-filled life.

We move, change jobs. We get married. Just as often, we get divorced. We get jet lag. We eat at a greasy spoon or the local chili-pepper franchise, and our alimentary canal lectures us all night. Loved ones are born, they die, they get hurt, they're not home on time. We get sick, we fight, we make up, we worry, we overwork. It's a wonder we have time to sleep at all, let alone spend a third of our lives under the covers!

The need for sleep is strongly individualistic, say doctors. Yet no matter how much (or little) we need, so often our lives seem to do everything to prevent it.

And what happens when you finally slip your weary body between the sheets? That contrary mass of gray jelly at the apex of your spine begins to wake up, to rehash the day, worry about tomorrow, work up a sweat about sleep. "I'm not sleepy now," it whines; you envision its convolutions forming a willful pout. The battle of the bedroom is engaged. You have met the enemy. And you are his.

TEN STEPS TO DREAMLAND

You don't have to feel like a prisoner of war. Insomnia, after all, is a symptom, not a disease, say sleep researchers. If your sleeplessness has gone on for more than a month and you're about to go off the deep end, see your doctor or visit a sleep center at a nearby hospital. But for the temporary trouble we all experience from time to time, experts recommend these sleep-inducing tips.

Don't oversleep because of a previous poor night's sleep. "This is one of the most important rules of all," says Elliott Phillips, M.D., medical director of Holy Cross Hospital Sleep Disorders Center in Mission Hills, California. Getting up at the same time every morning, no matter how badly you've slept, resets your body's inner clock and bedtime then also becomes more regular.

If you can't sleep, stop trying. You'll just get more frustrated, the experts say. Give yourself ½ hour and then try again, suggests Michael Stevenson, Ph.D., director of Holy Cross's insomnia clinic.

Have a light snack. An empty stomach will wake you up, but so will a full one, researchers report. A snack of complex carbohydrates like crackers or cereal (not simple carbohydrates, like sugar) will hit the spot. Dieters often have a hard time sleeping because they go to bed hungry, says Dr. Stevenson. They will probably benefit greatly from a bedtime treat.

Don't take drugs. "Jus' a li'l drinkie" may help you fall asleep, but 3 or 4 hours later you'll wake up irritated, agitated and possibly with a full bladder. Also, warns Dr. Pearce, drinking to induce sleep can become addictive.

Tea, coffee, colas and chocolate all contain caffeine (unless they're labeled "caffeine-free"), a stimulant that may keep your eyes open even if consumed in the afternoon. Nicotine has the same effect.

Also, avoid sleeping pills. Prescription pills are psychologically addictive and should be used only in extreme situations, say the experts. And over-the-counter pills use the sleepiness-inducing side effects of antihistamines to get results, but they have other side-effects, such as headaches and restlessness, you may not want. "Relaxation doesn't come in a bottle," says Dr. Stevenson.

Practice relaxation techniques. Lie on your back and progressively clench, hold and relax your muscles, beginning with your hands or feet and working your way up or down your body. Breathe deeply and regularly, and imagine yourself becoming more and more relaxed. Conjure up a vision of yourself lying on a warm beach beneath a swaying palm tree (from which the coconuts have been trimmed). "After everyday practice for several weeks," Dr. Stevenson says, "you can tell yourself 'relax' and it will happen immediately." He also recommends that you practice someplace other than your bed so you don't associate insomnia with your bed.

Don't worry if you don't get 8 hours. Your daily need for sleep is highly variable, says Dr. Phillips. "There's nothing sacrosanct about 8 hours. The best guide for anybody is: The sleep you need is the sleep that provides you with the ability to be

What's Your Sleep Efficiency?

If you're sleeping only half the time you're in bed, your sleep efficiency is only 50 percent, says sleep specialist Michael Stevenson, Ph.D. That perpetuates insomnia. The goal is to achieve 90 percent—and it *can* be done.

Say you go to bed at 11:00 P.M. because you have to get up at 7:00 A.M. But instead of falling asleep, you lie awake until 3:00 A.M. So don't get into bed until 3:00 A.M., says Dr. Stevenson. You'll feel much better, less anxious, if you don't lie sleepless in bed for the 4 hours you think you should be sleeping.

After a week of sleeping well for 4 hours a night, go to bed 15 minutes earlier for a week. As you continue to sleep well, each week give yourself another 15 minutes. If it gets worse, cut time in bed by 15 minutes.

"You sneak up on it a bit at a time," says Dr. Stevenson. "Almost immediately, people begin to feel better. Ironically, you're using sleep restriction as a weapon against insomnia."

He warns, however, that this does not work for everyone. Regimented types are most likely to benefit from this exercise.

alert and go about your activities the next day." One or two nights' wakefulness won't hurt you.

Don't nap. Daytime snoozing ruins nighttime sleep, say most researchers, and plays havoc with the body's natural clock.

Have sex . . . or don't have sex. After sex, some people sail right off for the Land of Nod. Their partners, however, may be left on shore. Sex is a stimulant for some people, a relaxant for others.

Exercise early, not late. A vigorous workout raises the body's core temperature, which inhibits sleep, says Dr. Pearce. But regular exercise done earlier in the day works off nervous energy and makes for a healthier body, which promotes a good night's sleep.

Use the bedroom for sleep and sex—nothing else. When all the sights and sounds of the bedroom are associated with competing activities, you think of those things and not sleep. Therefore, don't use the bedroom as an office, a dining room, a library, a movie theater, a gym or a battleground.

In fact, if your sex life is fraught with tension, says Dr. Stevenson, "move it out of the bedroom."

THE PHILOSOPHY OF SLEEP

If you're losing sleep for a few days or even a few weeks, the main thing to remember is: Don't worry about it. You're probably not going crazy. There is an underlying cause that, once you give it some thought, can be dealt with. Even sleep researchers occasionally have trouble sleeping. Dr. Pearce says a refreshing night's sleep is something "I've probably only experienced on vacation."

And when you're tossing and turning and moaning and groaning, consider the opinion of English writer William Arthur Dunkerley: "Thank God for sleep! And, when you cannot sleep, still thank Him that you live to lie awake."

William LeGro

Beating Fatigue

Did you have to pry yourself out of bed this morning? Is your energy level as low as the stock market following the Crash of '87? Are the bags under your eyes so big they'd qualify as carry-on luggage?

When you're feeling this low, it's hard to pick up your socks, let alone to be high on life. But it doesn't have to be—you can beat the blahs and reinvigorate that energetic old you.

Below are some helpful hints from doctors on how to beat the six most common causes of the blahs.

PILLOW TALK

Do you get enough sleep? If you don't, you're obviously going to feel fatigued. Half of all Americans have trouble dozing off at some time in their lives. Sleep disturbance is a common response to changes in our lives,

from trouble at the office to serious illness. For most of us, normal sleep patterns return after the daytime problem that is the source of worry goes away or gets better.

During good times or troubled ones, experts say these three simple steps will almost always help you get better sleep.

● Don't drink any caffeinated or alcoholic beverages after dinner.
● Get to bed at the same time every night.
● Get regular, moderate exercise.

THE DOZE DIET

One factor that can run you down is a poor diet. Because "crash" diets (they don't call them that for nothing) offer so little in the way of balanced nutrition, they can turn your

muscle mass into mush and your energy reserves into empty tanks.

To get a good start on a diet that will leave you feeling fresh, bear in mind these basic rules.

● Eat a variety of foods. Avoid diet plans that force you to live on one specific kind of food.
● Don't eat fewer than 1,200 calories a day, in general, if you're a woman, or fewer than 1,500 calories if you're a man. You can't get all the nutrients you need if you eat less than these amounts.
● Don't eat big meals late at night.
● Don't skip meals.

THE UNEXERCISED BODY

If your body isn't exercised regularly, it probably doesn't use oxy-

When Tired Means Sick

If you're constantly tired, you've undoubtedly asked yourself if you have a serious health problem. Perhaps you've convinced yourself that you do.

But when is it really time to worry? To see a doctor? Maybe never. Fatigue, unless it's long-lived, very severe or associated with other symptoms, usually isn't related to any serious disease.

"Oh, my God! What symptoms? What disease?" you may ask yourself. Below, Munsey Wheby, M.D., vice chairman of the University of Virginia's School of Medicine, discusses a few diseases for which *constant, serious fatigue*

could be ... may be ... might be ... a sign. If you're without energy *and* you have any of the additional symptoms mentioned by Dr. Wheby, see your doctor, soon.

Anemia. This disease is defined as a drop in the number of red blood cells. Its symptoms usually include constant fatigue and mild shortness of breath.

Heart disease. Its symptoms can be similar to anemia. Chest pain is often present—but not always.

Mononucleosis. Often misused as a catchall phrase for long-term fatigue,

chronic infectious mononucleosis is a rare viral infection. Symptoms, aside from fatigue, may include fever, sore throat and enlarged lymph glands.

Hypoglycemia. Like mononucleosis, hypoglycemia—dangerously low blood-sugar levels—has become another catchall phrase for the blahs. It is rare. Additional symptoms may include weakness and cold sweat.

Diabetes. Victims of diabetes mellitus may experience frequent urination, unusual thirst and weight loss.

gen very efficiently. Your muscles need that oxygen. Without it, when you need muscle power, you don't get it, and you tire quickly.

What's more, even as your muscles sag, so does your self-image. Your emotional state can become a mirror image of your physical condition, adding to your fatigue.

That's why exercise benefits you in two ways. First, it improves your physical condition, enabling your body to more efficiently deliver oxygen to your muscles, increasing your endurance. Second, exercise stimulates an overall feeling of well-being.

THE PILLS YOU POP

A number of drugs—including antihistamines, pain relievers, diuretics, antihypertensives, antibiotics, oral contraceptives and anticonvulsants—can sometimes cause fatigue as a side effect.

If you are taking a drug and you think it makes you feel drowsy, the first thing to do is to call the pharmacist who sold you the product, says William N. Tindall, Ph.D., vice president of professional affairs for the National Association of Retail Druggists (NARD).

"The pharmacist will have your complete drug history and will be able to tell whether the drug you are taking is causing your drowsiness or whether two drugs in combination are having that effect. Then the pharmacist will call the doctor and, together, they'll decide the best thing to do." Don't stop taking a prescription drug without first consulting your physician.

STRESS RELEASE

It takes a lot of energy to deal with the pressures of everyday life. After expending all that energy, you may be left with a gnawing, overwhelming sense of fatigue.

Not all the stresses of life leave us feeling emotionally drained. "It takes a certain kind of stress, in which you have no choices, no options, no alternatives," says Harvey L. Alpern, M.D., a Los Angeles cardiologist.

If you're stuck in this kind of situation, there is something you can do. As a first step, Dr. Alpern suggests learning relaxation techniques and using them to take 10- or 15-minute "vacations" from your work around the home or office every day. "Doing these exercises and paying attention to your feelings can break that all-day feeling of tension," says Dr. Alpern.

THE BLUES AND BLAHS

"Many depressed people may have serious trouble sleeping," says Ralph Wharton, M.D., professor of psychiatry at Columbia University.

"The sleep disturbance is part of the depressive cycle. They'll wake up feeling tired. In fact, they've been sleeping, but they've been having very troublesome dreams, which can be as exhausting as if they were struggling during the day, digging a ditch. They're digging a deeper and deeper hole."

You can get out of this hole if you begin to understand why you feel depressed. But there's more to it than this. Once you know the underlying cause of your emotional downturn, you then have to change the way you react to the situation or, failing that, change the situation. For either option, you might need the emotional help of a trained mental-health practitioner.

Fatigue can sometimes mean physical illness. Fortunately, this is usually not the case. But if you have to drag yourself out of bed every morning, you'd better see a doctor.

A Pick-Me-Up Showdown

Don't depend on that candy bar for that boost of energy to get you through the afternoon. Take a walk instead.

This was the bittersweet conclusion of a study at California State University at Long Beach. Subjects in the study were either given a candy bar (of their own choosing) or told to take a brisk 10-minute walk repeatedly over a 3-week period. They were then asked whether they felt more energetic, less energetic or about the same.

What did they say? Immediately after polishing off their Snickers and Milky Way bars, the subjects reported feeling more energetic. As time rolled on, however, things began to change. The 18 volunteers began to feel more and more tired. An hour later and again 2 hours later, the group reported feeling significantly *more tired* than before.

The walkers, on the other hand, felt not only more energetic 1 and 2 hours after their walks, but also more relaxed. The candy munchers felt more tense. So why do so many of us still reach for candy bars?

"It's an insidious thing," says Robert Thayer, Ph.D., author of the study and professor of psychology at California State. Because the immediate effect of eating the candy bar is positive, says Dr. Thayer, "we've been conditioned to eat them."

But, he says, the study clearly shows that between a candy bar and a 10-minute walk, "there's no question which is the better choice. A short, brisk walk is a very effective energy booster."

Bumps, Bangs and Bruises

It's been another one of *those* days. While slicing your tuna sandwich in two, you also took a slice out of your left pinky. Then, while filling the dishwasher, you banged your head on the kitchen cupboard and saw more stars than an astronomer. And now those new shoes you thought were so comfortable in the store have left you with a foot the size of a Buick.

Do you just call it quits, check into the nearest hospital and sign up for a month's stay? Of course not! With a cool head and a few first-aid tips, you can learn to handle those minor ailments.

CUTTING THE WORRY OUT OF CUTS

You just took a spill on the sidewalk that registered an 8 on the Richter scale. You pick yourself up, brush yourself off and notice your knee is ripped and bleeding. According to Stephen Rosenberg, M.D., associate professor of clinical public health at Columbia University School of Public Health and author of *The Johnson and Johnson First Aid Book,* here's what to do to stop the bleeding.

● Press firmly on the cut, preferably with a clean gauze pad, cloth or your own bare hand (but wash your hand first, if possible), for at least 10 minutes.
● Put ice or cold water on the pad to help slow the bleeding and reduce swelling.
● Elevate the cut above heart level.
● Clean the cut by washing it thoroughly with mild soap and water. Gently scrub with a gauze pad, or if dirt or gravel are embedded, use a soft toothbrush.

● Cover the injury with a clean, sterile adhesive bandage.
● Change the dressing once a day or whenever it becomes wet or dirty. Keep the cut or scrape covered for at least three days.

Dr. Rosenberg says you should seek medical attention if:

● The cut is longer than ½ inch.
● The wound gapes or you cannot stop the bleeding, there is numbness or inability to move the injured part.
● You have not had a tetanus shot in the last five to ten years.

GETTING THE WOOD OUT

You take a split of wood from the pile to the fire. As you let go, you feel something that's stayed behind. You look down at your hand and see a splinter. Here's what Dr. Rosenberg says you should do.

● Wash your hands and the affected area with soap and water.
● Pull out the splinter using tweezers that have been sterilized in boiling water or held over a flame letting them cool off before you use them. Pull at the same angle that the splinter went in.
● Reluctant splinters can be worked out with a sterilized pin.

Dr. Rosenberg says you should seek medical attention if:

● The wound gets red, tender or painful. This is a sign of infection.
● You have not had a tetanus booster in the last five to ten years. Puncture wounds are particularly vulnerable to tetanus because the deeper the

How to Heal Twice as Fast

Wounds heal twice as fast when covered as when left exposed to the air, so you should always keep a healthy supply of bandages on hand. And since cuts come in all different shapes and sizes, so should your bandages.

Here's what you should have in stock.

● Square and strip adhesives in a variety of sizes. You should use the right size to cover the entire cut comfortably without limiting movement.
● Bow-tie adhesives to cover the tips of fingers or toes.

● Butterfly strips to pull the edges of a cut together to aid healing.
● H-shaped strips to go over knuckles but allow fingers to move freely.
● Gauze pads to clean a wound or to apply pressure to stop bleeding. Fastened with adhesive tape, they can also be used to cover a cut.

To remove an adhesive bandage painlessly, douse the adhesive parts with baby oil or mineral oil and let it soak in. The bandage will practically slide off.

wounds, the harder they are to clean. The tetanus bacteria grow best deep inside where there is little air.

CRUISING WITH A BRUISING

Pinch your finger in the door, slip on the ice or catch a baseball on your forehead, and you're likely to see a lovely black and blue swelling blossoming within a few minutes.

A bruise is really a cut below the surface of the skin. "When blood vessels are damaged by a blow, they can begin leaking blood and other fluids into the surrounding tissues," explains Bruce E. Baker, M.D., professor of orthopedic surgery at the University Sports Medicine Center in Syracuse, New York. "Blood looks purple below skin level. The deeper and more severe the bruise, the more discoloration there may be," he says. As the bruise heals, it changes color. The body starts to chemically break down blood products, thus accounting for the variations in hue.

Here's what Dr. Baker says you can do to minimize the pain and damage from bumps and bruises.

● Apply ice to decrease internal bleeding and swelling. First, however, cover the bruise with a moist towel; this reduces your (already minimal) chances of developing frostbite. Then apply a plastic bag of ice cubes, pressing firmly. (Do not use chemical cooling devices.) Keep the ice on for about 10 minutes at a time.
● When possible, keep the bruised area above heart level to reduce swelling of the sore area.
● If the bruise is still tender or deeply colored after two to six days, applying warm, wet compresses may speed healing.
● If you need mild pain relief, try a nonaspirin pain reliever, such as acetaminophen. Aspirin may increase the potential for further oozing of blood below the surface.

Dr. Baker says you should seek medical assistance if:

● You have any questions about the severity of an injury. Some potential injuries include damage to ligaments, tendons and bones.
● You have a head injury that leaves you with a headache and/or swelling or bruising.

NOSEBLEED KNOW-HOW

Nosebleeds may be a major nuisance but they are almost always a minor problem. Nosebleeds are usually caused by colds, allergies or irritation or by using too much nasal spray, says Dr. Rosenberg. Here's how he says you can stop them.

● Bend your head forward slightly and open your mouth so the blood doesn't run down your throat.
● Pinch your nose together firmly but gently for at least 10 minutes.
● Put a cold compress around your nose while you are pinching it.
● If it continues to bleed, place a strip of gauze or cloth (not cotton) in each nostril with the ends hanging out and pinch the nose for another 5 minutes.

Diane Fields

Ignorance Is Blisters

Shoes too big? Been working that pickax or mop too hard? If so, you've just entered Blister City.

Blisters puff up from friction. Bad judgment in buying shoes or ignoring your need for work gloves are just 2 of the things that can cause this minor inconvenience—one you just as easily could have avoided.

But you don't need a lecture. You need relief. Here's how Stephen Rosenberg, M.D., says you can treat your blister.

When possible, he says, avoid letting a blister tear; it is better to protect it and let the fluid be reabsorbed.

To protect an unbroken blister, cut gauze into little doughnut shapes and stack them around the blister, then tape an uncut pad over the top.

If you see that the blister is likely to break, try to drain it yourself. First clean it thoroughly with soap and water. Using a needle that you have sterilized in a flame (make sure you let it cool first), puncture the edge of the blister. Press gently with a sterile pad until all the fluid has drained out. Cover the blister with gauze.

To treat a broken blister, clean gently with soap and water. Cover with a sterile pad. Protect any raw, exposed skin with a doughnut-shaped pad.

Healing with Water

Few of those familiar with the peculiar antics of Blanche DuBois would deny the woman was a bit of an oddball. In fact, her brother-in-law considered her downright loony—especially when he had to put up with her irritating habit of steaming up the house on 100-degree evenings with the vapors coming from the bathroom as she soaked in a hot bath.

But Blanche was insistent: "Oh, I feel so good after my long, hot bath, I feel so good and cool and—rested."

While such a comment only stoked the already burning suspicions about the mental state of the Tennessee Williams character, Blanche may not have been as daft as others in *A Streetcar Named Desire* made her out to be—at least where her penchant for hot soaks on hot nights was concerned.

"It only makes sense that a hot soak could help you cool off, even on a summer night," says D. L. Moore, M.D., medical director at Living Springs Retreat, in Putnam Valley, New York. Why? Because a hot bath —from 100°F to 104°F—is one of the best ways to clear away the fats and salts that accumulate on the skin, especially during hot weather. And, as hot water caresses the skin, the veins dilate, allowing the heat to hasten its escape from the body. The result? You feel good, you feel cool. Just like Blanche said.

"Water is a very simple solution to many everyday ills, yet people too often think of turning to drugs instead," says Dr. Moore. "They don't even think of turning to water. Yet water has been used successfully in the treatment of more diseases than any other remedy."

So, then, what are the medicinal qualities of water that make it such a divine healer? For one, water has the enormous capacity to cause action and reaction in the three most important systems of the body: the nervous system (including the brain, spinal cord and nerves), the heart and circulatory system, and the skin. It also stimulates the metabolism.

Before we get into the glorious bodily benefits hot water can bring, heed a few words of caution. All the experts we talked to emphasized that most methods of hot soaks should be followed by a cold splash. The reason is that hot water—say, anything above 104°F—slows the movement of oxygen to the brain. And that you don't want. But a quick cool-down with cold water—30 seconds will do just fine—starts to return oxygen flow to normal. Also, anyone with heart disease, high blood pressure or diabetes is best off staying away from any extreme temperature dunks without asking their doctors first.

Now for the best of hot-water soaks, starting with Blanche's favorite.

Some like it hot. "There is probably nothing in the world better for relaxing the muscles than a hot bath," says Dr. Moore. "Whether muscle tightness is from disease, fatigue or strain, people often find great relief soaking in a hot tub." By hot we mean anything from 100°F to 104°F. Anything above that is not recommended. Prolonged use (30 minutes or more) of water that is too hot will stimulate the heart and be exhausting.

The real value of a hot-water soak is the relief it can bring to those suffering from arthritis. Physical therapists have found that gently moving the joints while soaking in a hot tub can help improve mobility. A hot-water soak is ideal for arthritics because body weight is lighter in water, making exercises all that much easier. In fact, those with arthritis find that what they can't do out of water they can do in water.

The bath that soothes. Lower the temperature a tad to about 98°F or so—our experts call this a *warm* bath—and you have the ideal climate for soothing an array of other ills, with insomnia at the head of the list.

"There is nothing in the world better for insomnia than a warm bath," Dr. Moore states flatly. He suggests 15 minutes in a warm tub right before crawling under the covers as one of the best cures for sleeplessness.

Lower the temperature a tad more, to between 92°F and 97°F, and you'll have what is called a *neutral* bath. What can a neutral bath do that a hot one can't? For one thing, a neutral bath has a more sedative effect than a hot bath. It relaxes the blood vessels of the skin. It also soothes nerve endings, helping to calm you down when you're feeling nervous. In fact, before the advent of tranquilizing drugs, neutral baths were used with great success in calming agitated mental patients.

Rub-a-dub-dub. . . . Poor Blanche DuBois. Had hot tubs been around in her day, perhaps her family and friends would have better understood her yen for a hot soak. While these oversized buckets of redwood (a family of four fits quite nicely) are touted more for their social than their therapeutic appeal, they *can* do your body a lot of good, if they are used properly and sensibly.

Anything a hot bath can do, a hot tub can do better. "The agitation of the hot-water jets against the skin can help relieve sore muscles and induce relaxation," says Dr. Moore. Better yet is the whirlpool, the stain-

The Ingredients of a Great Bath

Bath additives can spice up your tub water and turn a boring bath into a sensuous spa.

Although, for sheer convenience, commercial bath products are your best bets, you can create your own concoctions from fresh ingredients from your kitchen shelf. To keep from clogging your drain and to help keep down the buildup of residue in your tub, keep the following pointers in mind.

Place all loose and dried ingredients in a square of cheesecloth or muslin and tie securely. Let it dangle from the faucet as the water pours out. You can also use the bag as a soapless scrub for sensitive skin.

As an alternative, steep a handful of herbs or tea leaves in a teapot of boiling water for 3 to 5 minutes. Then strain it into your bathwater.

Never substitute essential oils for the herbs. Such essential oils as cinnamon and peppermint are so concentrated that adding even a drop to a tubful of water can be very irritating to the skin.

For a variety of special effects, mix several herbs together when brewing your own bath. When combining several botanicals, either in a cloth bag or a teapot, use about a tablespoon of each.

	Relaxing	Muscle soothing	Skin healing	Skin softening	Skin tightening	Stimulating
Apple cider vinegar		●	●			
Baking soda	●		●			
Camomile	●		●	●		
Comfrey			●		●	
Epsom salts		●				
Lavender	●					
Milk				●		
Sage		●				●
Salt	●				●	●
Seaweed		●	●		●	●
Tea (black)			●			
Thyme					●	●

less steel or ceramic version of the hot tub, usually found in hospitals and spas. A whirlpool has stronger action than a hot tub, which only enhances the massaging effect.

Nevertheless, it's only prudent to step into a hot tub with caution. Even though hot tubs are made to withstand much higher temperatures, a safe range is about the same as you'd want for your hot bath—from 100°F to 104°F maximum. However, most hot tub manufacturers recommend that water temperature not exceed 100°F. Pregnant women, the elderly, and those with heath problems should check with their doctors before using a hot tub.

This bath is hip. Even more than the full-body bath, the hip or sitz bath has enormous healing potential. "It is particularly beneficial in helping to clear up most infections in the pelvic area—the uterus, ovaries, vagina, bladder or prostate," says Dr. Moore. Digestive problems, irritable bowel syndrome and stomach cramps are sometimes alleviated with a sitz bath. And a hip bath is great for easing the discomfort of hemorrhoids, too. "For hemorrhoids, though, I'd alternate hot and cold sitz baths," says Dr. Moore.

To take a sitz bath, fill the tub up to the level of (but not covering) your navel. Elevating your feet on the sides of the tub or, if possible, hanging them over the tub, is recommended. The water temperature should be the same as for a hot bath.

The shower massage. "The jet spray from a warm shower beating down on a sore neck or shoulders is a wonderfully soothing way to help take away the pain," says Carole Lewis, Ph.D., clinical associate professor at George Washington University School of Medicine.

Debora Tkac

Soothing Skin Problems

Jim Matthews invested $60 in a new pair of basketball sneakers that he hoped would make him run faster, jump higher and make more baskets than the Boston Celtics.

What they did was give him a first-class case of contact dermatitis—a skin problem characterized by reddened skin, blisters or flaking, and sometimes all three. In Jim's case, the bottoms of his feet turned bright red, then dead white. His doctor suspected it may have been an allergic reaction to the glue used in the sneakers. The fact that Jim retired the sneakers and his rash never returned made the diagnosis even more obvious.

Unfortunately, getting rid of dermatitis or the myriad assortment of other itchy skin disorders isn't always so easy.

FLARE-UPS AND POISONS

There are several forms of dermatitis, doctors say. Contact dermatitis, which is what Jim had, is usually caused by a reaction to something that touches your skin. Figure out what's touched you, get rid of it, and your dermatitis should disappear. Applying a cream that contains 0.5 percent hydrocortisone—look for it at your local drugstore—may speed the process even further.

One of the most common forms of allergic contact dermatitis is poison ivy. To get rid of the poison, dab the blisters with a little calamine lotion and go about your business. Of course, if you're supersensitive to the vine, or its cousins—poison oak and poison sumac—things get a little more complicated.

"It's one of the few true emergencies in dermatology," says William Epstein, M.D., professor of dermatology at the University of California at San Francisco. "These people must get to a hospital for a shot of corticosteroids," Dr. Epstein cautions, because the skin of someone who is supersensitive will get red and itchy, then start to swell up within 4 to 12 hours—roughly four times as fast as a "normal" poison ivy reaction. Their eyes can be swollen shut by the next day and blisters will appear within 24 hours.

That's why it's so important to prevent—or at least minimize—a poison reaction. "If you think you've been exposed on a picnic, a hike or while gardening, golfing or hunting," says Dr. Epstein, "take a dip in a stream or soak yourself with a hose. You can also use rubbing alcohol. In fact, the best possible treatment would be alcohol followed by water. *Don't* use a washcloth. The cloth will pick it up and spread it around."

And keep on the lookout for a new protective spray still undergoing tests by the U.S. Food and Drug Administration. This product sprays on almost invisibly, disappears quickly and provides protection that lasts up to 24 hours.

CONTROLLING THE ITCH

Not all forms of dermatitis may be as easy to handle. *Atopic* dermatitis, for example, is an itchy dermatitis that may keep recurring—frequently from infancy—among allergy-prone people. The key here is to help keep your dermatitis under control to avoid flare-ups. Here's how.

● Avoid the urge to scratch by keeping your nails cut short.
● Avoid itch triggers. Heat, cold or rapid temperature change are three biggies.

No More Scars!

If your face is pitted and scarred from acne or chickenpox (or living at the wrong end of a fist), check with your dermatologist, suggests the American Academy of Dermatology. Scars may be improved by surgical excision, sanding (dermabrasion), steroid injections or the injection of collagen, a protein fiber found in the body.

Even faces with hundreds of pockmarks and pits can now be helped, reports Stephen A. Solotoff, M.D., in the *Journal of Dermatologic Surgery and Oncology.* Your dermatologist can use a surgical punch to remove scars and replace them with skin from behind your ear. Four to 6 weeks later, your new face is "fine-sanded" to its final form. You'll have to avoid the sun for at least the first 3 months and then wear a sunscreen every day, cautions Dr. Solotoff.

• Wash your clothes with Dreft, Ivory Snow or any other mild detergent. Double-rinse each load and avoid fabric softeners.

• Instead of regular soap, use a cleansing bar such as Dove or an oatmeal soap.

• Avoid excessive bathing.

• Avoid stress.

• Wear only cotton next to your skin. Avoid wool, nylon or polyester, which can initiate itching.

• Drink lots of fluids.

• Use white toilet paper. Leave decorator colors for your walls.

• Apply an emollient, such as Complex-15, Eucerin, Keri, Lubriderm Lotion or Moisturel Lotion, two or three times a day and after your bath. If your skin still seems a little dry, move up to a cream (Complex-15, Lubriderm Cream, Purpose or Moisturel Cream) or ointment (Aquaphor, Eucerin, Nivea or Petrolatum White). If your skin is extremely dry, you should consider an emollient that contains urea (Carmol 10 or 20, Ultra Mide 25) or lactic acid (LactiCare 1 percent or 2 percent, Aqua Lacten, Lac-Hydrin).

• Use a room humidifier or vaporizer.

• Try eliminating foods to which you may be sensitive.

• Get to know your ophthalmologist. In one 20-year study of 492 people at the Mayo Clinic, Rochester, Minnesota, 13 percent of those with severe atopic dermatitis developed cataracts.

DITCH THAT WINTER ITCH

Another type of dermatitis is "winter itch," often caused by the clash of the warm indoors with the cold outdoors. So if you get the winter itchies, dermatologist Rodney Basler, M.D., of the University of Nebraska Medical Center College of Medicine, suggests you try these methods.

• Take fewer, faster showers and baths and use tepid or cool water. If your skin is really dry, try a sponge bath every other day. But no bubble baths.

• Use a mild, cream-based soap even under the arms, on the genitals and, for women, under the breasts in dry weather.

• The less water the better. If your hands are severely damaged, use a cleansing agent such as Cetaphil lotion or Alpha Keri Moisture Rich Cleansing Bar. Wear cotton-lined rubber gloves for household chores.

• Rub an oil such as Alpha Keri Shower and Bath Oil into your skin after any exposure to water.

• Avoid cosmetics that contain alcohol and steer clear of mudpacks. Switch to water-based toners or cut alcohol-based astringents with water. Try witch hazel water as an alternative.

TREATMENTS FOR PSORIASIS

You can't *cure* psoriasis, a skin disease of unknown origin in which its victim sheds skin faster than a rattlesnake. But you can, doctors say, *control* it.

How? With any one of the various treatments or combinations of treatments involving drugs, light, vitamins and coal tar. PUVA therapy, for example, can help control psoriasis in roughly 85 to 90 percent of those who have it over less than half of their bodies. The therapy, which is usually reserved for people who have failed to respond to other treatments, such as coal tar baths or cortisone creams, takes 25 sessions over two or three months to work. Your doctor will give you a drug called psoralen (the "P" in PUVA) and then expose you to a tightly controlled ultraviolet A irradiation (the "UVA"). You'll need to return

somewhere around 30 times a year for maintenance therapy.

Why doesn't your doctor just prescribe a walk in the sun? Sunlight *does* help about 95 percent of those victims who tan easily, reports the American Academy of Dermatology. But for those who get sunburned, it must be used cautiously. In fact, sunshine can be a double-edged sword.

"Be very cautious with the sun," warns Larry Millikan, M.D., chairman of the Department of Dermatology at Tulane University School of Medicine. "Don't get burned. If you have 10 percent of your body covered with psoriasis and you go into the sun and burn another 80 percent, that injury to the skin might cause the other 80 percent to develop psoriasis."

But what about the small percentage of people for whom all treatments, including PUVA, don't work? Tegison, a drug that is chemically related to vitamin A, may be able to relieve the most severe, disfiguring and untreatable forms of psoriasis. Another drug under research is a derivative of vitamin D_3.

At the Osaka University Medical School in Japan, for example, 13 of 17 patients (76 percent) given a derivative in pill form noticed a significant improvement in their skin. And 16 of another 19 patients (84 percent) who used a cream containing another active form of vitamin D_3 also reported improvement.

And keep your eyes open for heat therapy. Scientists from Stanford University School of Medicine and Psoriasis Research Institute investigated how heat generated by ultrasound, water contact or infrared systems can be used to treat the disease. Heat *does* seem to offer varying levels of improvement, the researchers report. They note, however, that further studies are needed to develop or refine the heating system that will work best.

In the meantime, here are a few tips from the American Academy of Dermatology and other skin experts.

- Prevent injuries to your skin. They can trigger disease flare-ups or make existing plaques worse.
- Avoid irritating your skin by plucking eyebrows, using razors that are too sharp or too dull, or wearing clothes or shoes that rub or pinch.
- Limit your use of alcohol. And if you're undergoing PUVA therapy, keep it to less than five drinks a week. Anything more may be harmful to the liver.
- Use a humidifier to keep the air moist.
- Avoid detergents, harsh soaps or chemicals if you have psoriasis on your hands.
- Wear cotton-lined rubber gloves or lined plastic gloves when doing dishes.
- Try applying waterproof adhesive tape to any plaque that is bugging you. Leave it on for a week or longer.
- Try fish oil. A study at the University of Michigan revealed that 8 of 13 people (61 percent) with psoriasis showed improvement after substituting 2 to 3 ounces of fish oil for other fats in their diets. You should not attempt this, however, without consulting your doctor.
- Use a moisturizer.
- Watch out for drugs that can exacerbate or even cause a flare-up. Lithium; nonsteroidal, anti-inflammatory drugs, such as indomethacin; and some medications that are prescribed for heart disorders and high blood pressure can aggravate the disease.

PIMPLES AND ACNE

They appear the night before your big speech or the day before your wedding. It starts as a small swelling under your skin, grows with the expansive force of a miniature volcano and erupts into a big, red, ugly, awful, mortifying pimple. Yep. Zits *are* the pits. But what can you do about them?

Acne—whiteheads, blackheads, pimples and cysts—is basically a condition that is triggered by rising hormone levels during puberty. The hormones cause your oil glands, which open into pores on the surface of your skin, to expand. If the oil produced in those glands—2,000 of them per square inch on your forehead alone—mixes with skin cells and bacteria just under the surface of your skin, a blackhead develops. And if the top of the oil gland isn't wide enough, a whitehead develops, builds and erupts into a pimple.

Whether it's a single pimple or a full-blown case of acne, treatment is somewhat controversial. Severe cases of acne sometimes require antibiotics, X-ray therapy or a vitamin A derivative called Accutane, notes the academy. In less severe cases, treatment can include hormones or ultraviolet light treatment.

Whether or not you should squeeze a pimple is also controversial. Some doctors think you should keep your mitts off because you'll probably increase your chances of both inflammation and scars. Others shrug their shoulders and figure that as long as you're probably going to pick at your pimples anyway, you should learn to do it correctly. In fact, says James E. Fulton, M.D., Ph.D., direc-

Things That Go Bump in the Summer

Anytime you work up a summer sweat, you may also be working up skin problems.

"Heat rashes like prickly heat occur when perspiration oversaturates the skin, making it 'boggy'" says Rodney Basler, M.D. "The skin then swells up, closing over the sweat glands, locking bacteria and other germs inside. These trapped microorganisms cause the sweat glands to become irritated and slightly inflamed, creating a heat rash," says Dr. Basler.

"You can help prevent heat rashes and other perspiration-related skin disorders by wearing light, loose, absorbent clothing when you exercise so that moisture can evaporate from your skin," says Dr. Basler.

"Using an absorbent powder all over, and an alcohol-based astringent on trouble spots, can also help allevi-ate these itchy, unsightly summer skin conditions," adds Dr. Basler.

Inflamed follicular oil glands on the buttocks ("bikini bottom"), pose another hot-weather problem for your skin. Your posterior is affected because of the large number of oil-producing glands there that are associated with hair.

"Cover these hair follicles with a wet, tight Lycra or spandex bathing suit that promotes sweat but doesn't let your skin breathe and doesn't dry fast, and the result is apt to be a red, bumpy rash," says Dr. Basler. "This condition is also a problem for men who wear tight racing trunks.

"Drying and cleaning the area with astringent will help," continues Dr. Basler, "but it does more good to take a break and change into something dry and loose."

Relieving the Itch You Can't Scratch

Whether you're sitting on a horse, sitting at a desk or sitting on your hands, there's one itch you can't scratch in polite company. And that's the one on your bottom. The way to cure anal itching is usually the same as the way to prevent it.

Be scrupulously clean. An itchy bottom is usually caused by a rash that's a cross between athlete's foot and diaper rash, reports John Alexander-Williams, M.D., in the journal *Postgraduate Medicine*. And it's com-monly triggered by minute particles of fecal matter lodged within skin fur-rows and hairs around your anus. That's why you should bathe the area at least twice a day, and always after defecating, suggests Dr. Alexander-Williams. Use a soft, wet cloth but no soap. Or use the premoistened tissues sold to clean babies' bottoms.

Keep yourself dry. But avoid irri-tating your bottom by rubbing with a towel. Wear loose, porous clothing and avoid synthetic materials, tights, panty hose, tight jeans or jockey shorts.

Keep your hands off. Scratching your itch, even in private, is still a no-no. It can make it worse. If you tend to scratch in your sleep, says Dr. Alexander-Williams, wear cotton gloves to bed. If your itch is unbearable, check with your doctor. He may be able to prescribe some medication. Avoid local anesthetics and antibiotics, both of which can exacerbate the problem.

tor of the Acne Research Institute in Newport Beach, California, squeez-ing your pimples the right way can actually speed healing and reduce scarring. Here's Dr. Fulton's step-by-step pimple attack.

Watch for the right moment. "The best time to pop a pimple," says Dr. Fulton, "is a few days after you first notice a yellowish center developing, which indicates that pus and debris clogging your pores have moved to the surface."

Wash with plain soap and water. You can skip medicated acne soaps, says Dr. Fulton, because they're based on the myth that dirt causes acne. It doesn't. Nor do antibacte-rial ingredients work below the skin surface where acne originates.

Steam. Lean over a bowl or a basin of hot water and steam your skin for 5 minutes. Steaming softens oil plugs and makes extraction easier.

Squeeze. If you must squeeze a pimple with your fingers, make sure your fingernails are well trimmed. Wash your hands thoroughly and wrap your fingertips with tissues. If the black-head or plug doesn't pop out easily on the first couple of tries, don't force it.

Dab on benzoyl peroxide. Used for three weeks, this lotion can frequently control mild cases of acne better than antibiotics. Wash your face with soap and water, then, 30 minutes later, dab it on. Avoid wip-ing the lotion around your eyes and sensitive areas such as your nose and mouth. If you need to apply it on your neck, use a milder solution. Leave it on for 2 to 3 hours, then increase time to twice a day and overnight. Leave it on for only 15 to 30 minutes if your skin is very sensitive. And be patient. Your acne should begin to vanish within two to four months.

WARTS: THE DISAPPEARING ACT

There are many different kinds of warts, and not one of them is caused by touching a toad. They're caused by a virus that's probably passed from person to person. But, except for genital warts—which have a tendency to set up precancerous conditions if left untreated—most warts disappear within a couple of years.

Of course, if you get tired of looking like the wicked witch or you tend to develop new warts as fast as the old ones go away, you might want to buy an over-the-counter preparation to get rid of them. Or you can see a dermatologist, who may peel, cut, burn or freeze them off.

But don't be surprised if your doctor says he's going to give you an allergy. And, yes, he means an allergy. He'll make you allergic to a particu-lar chemical, then paint a diluted solution of it on your warts. Your body's immune system will go into allergic overdrive. End of warts. And a vaccine that's being developed may soon make wart attacks history.

Ellen Michaud

Join the Mole Patrol

Madonna's is making her a million, and Marilyn Monroe's certainly didn't blemish her career.

For most of us, however, moles are hardly so lucrative. Some can be downright costly. In fact, some can lead to a deadly form of skin cancer.

Moles are the darker, larger cousins of freckles and are formed when pigmented cells clump together. They come in a rainbow of colors from pink to black and may be flat, raised, smooth or hairy. They may come with your birthday suit or you may develop them later on in life.

Fortunately, most moles are harmless, and the more conspicuous ones can even be camouflaged with cosmetics.

But sometimes these spots can spell trouble and should not be ignored. "Most moles are benign and do not have to be removed, but there is a bad skin cancer that can develop from a mole," says Jean-Claude Bystryn, M.D., director of the Kaplan Cancer Center Melanoma Program at the New York University School of Medicine. "As many as 10 percent of the type recognized only within the past few years as dysplastic nevi do become cancerous. And when a mole turns to cancer, it's melanoma, the dangerous kind that can metastasize [spread]."

If that sounds alarming, it should. This life-threatening kind of skin cancer is increasing more rapidly than any other form of cancer in the United States—except lung cancer in women.

KEEP AN EYE ON YOUR MOLES

Fortunately, this black cloud of information has a silver lining. It's possible to minimize the risk of melanoma, if you act in time. Nearly 100 percent of *early* melanomas can be cured by surgery alone.

But what that means is that you'll have to monitor your moles on a regular basis. The Skin Cancer Foundation suggests that each year, on your birthday, you carefully examine your birthday suit from head to toe as follows.
- Inspect each mole. Note its location and appearance.
- Use mirrors (or a close friend) to help you catalog those hard-to-see moles.
- Record your moles on a mock-up body drawing. Note where each mole is situated (both on your front and back). Use a ruler with millimeter markings to determine size. Record the size in millimeters in the drawing. Also note the color (tan, brown, dark brown, gray, black, blue, pink, rose, white, flesh-colored) and the shape (oval, irregular, indented).
- Examine yourself monthly if you are at high risk for skin cancer (meaning you have many moles, are fair skinned or are a sun worshipper).

The Truth about Age Spots

They're splattered on your shoulders. They're sprinkled on the backs of your hands and dotted across your forehead. Just what are these little brown patches, anyway? And how did they get there?

These skin spots are the adult version of freckles, only unfortunately, at this stage, they're called age spots or worse, liver spots. The truth is, they have nothing to do with your age or your liver, but they have everything to do with staying too long in the sun.

As you get older, your skin is no longer able to protect you from harmful rays by tanning evenly. So your skin begins to overproduce pigment in patches.

How can you ban these blotches? It may be possible to lighten them with a dab of lemon juice or commercial bleaching cream. Some experts believe, however, that the creams contain bleaching agents in such small doses that they aren't likely to really get rid of the blotches.

You might also try some masking makeup. Just don't cover up any changes that may require further attention, such as enlargement, thickening or a developing crust.

Perhaps the best way to treat these "mature freckles" is to regard them as a signal that you are getting too much sun and that you need to wear a strong sunscreen whenever you venture outdoors.

First Aid for Mishaps

It's fairly easy to leave your moles alone if they are located in out-of-the-way places, like smack in the middle of your back. But sometimes it's not always you who's rubbing a mole the wrong way.

Bra straps, belts, bracelets, waistbands and harsh fabrics, for example, can rub a mole red and sore. And what should you do if, while shaving, you're constantly accidentally nicking that little brown bump on the end of your chin?

The answer is simple. Think about getting it removed.

"It's wise to have any mole removed that's become irritated, red or bleeding, whether you know what caused it or not," says Allentown, Pennsylvania, dermatologist James R. Wall, M.D. "It's just good insurance against skin cancer." The good news is that the procedure can be done in a matter of minutes, with little or no pain and, usually, without leaving a scar.

First the doctor injects the mole and surrounding skin with a local anesthetic. Next the mole and a bit of neighboring tissue are cut out, placed in a vial and sent to a pathology lab for diagnosis. The excision is stitched up and covered with a small bandage. All you may feel is a slight stinging sensation as the anesthetic wears off. In several weeks, you may not even be able to tell you had a mole in the first place.

In fact, because this procedure is relatively simple, you may not want to wait until something happens to a mole before getting rid of it. Removing it can eliminate having to keep a constant vigil on your skin spots, says Dr. Wall. "It's a procedure that may be well worth your peace of mind."

SPOTTING THE SIGNS OF TROUBLE

Moles that have the potential for being troublemakers usually give clues in the following ways and should send you to your doctor immediately.

They look different. Low-risk moles resemble each other, but high-risk moles look very different from one another.

They're multicolored. Low-risk moles are usually uniformly brown or tan, but high-risk moles show mixtures of tan, brown, black or reddish pink within a single mole.

They have irregular borders. Low-risk moles have clear-cut borders between the mole and surrounding skin, but high-risk moles often tend to fade into surrounding skin.

They tend to be large. Anything over 5 millimeters should be given especially close attention.

They occur in large groups. High-risk moles usually occur in quantities of 100 or more and appear most frequently on the back, though they may also occur in areas below the waist, on the scalp or on the breasts. Low-risk moles usually occur in fewer numbers (20 to 50) and are scattered over the body, usually on sun-exposed areas of the skin above the waist. The scalp, breasts and buttocks are rarely involved.

They change suddenly. Low-risk moles change slowly, if at all. High-risk moles may quite suddenly change in shape, size, color or texture (getting hard, soft or lumpy). They may also begin to bleed or itch.

KEEP A HANDS-OFF POLICY

You should never meddle with your moles. Instead of plucking hairs from them, try cutting the hair off close to the skin. Don't subject your moles to constant scraping from jewelry or clothing. It may be a good idea to have a mole removed if it is located in the path of constant friction, such as under a belt line or bra strap.

Try to limit your exposure to the sun, especially between 10:00 A.M. and 3:00 P.M. when its rays are strongest. According to Darrell S. Rigel, M.D., assistant professor of dermatology at New York University, it's theorized that the sun depresses the body's immune system to such an extent that overexposure may induce melanomas anywhere on the body, even in areas that are rarely, if ever, exposed to its rays.

If you do spend time outdoors at midday, make sure your skin is properly covered with a sunscreen, preferably one with a high sun protection factor (SPF). Don't forget that 70 to 80 percent of the sun's damaging rays can penetrate through cloudy haze and water, and that snow or sand can reflect 85 percent of the sun's most damaging rays. (For more information on sunscreens, see "How to Stay Safe in the Sun" on page 168.)

Healthy Teeth for Life

Before you read another word, find a mirror. Take a good look at yourself in repose. Now smile. See the difference? Like the difference between a passport picture and the real you. That's the difference a smile makes.

That beautiful smile is meant to last forever—and it can. The secret is simple: prevention.

"Dental disease is almost totally preventable by you and me," says James R. Hooley, D.D.S., professor of oral surgery at the UCLA School of Dentistry. "It's very simple. If you live in a community where the water is fluoridated, use a fluoride toothpaste, floss daily, brush at least once a day thoroughly and have periodic checkups, the odds are you that will not need anything more than routine dental work, such as cleaning and scaling and the replacement of restorations such as fillings."

But if you don't practice prevention, the odds are that you're headed for trouble.

WHERE TROUBLE STARTS

Your teeth's most dangerous enemy is the platoon of bacteria living in your mouth. There are 200 to 300 different types of germs that call your mouth home. Some of them are beneficial: They can help the body produce vitamins, generate enzymes to help you digest food and reduce the level of harmful bacteria in the oral cavity. Some of them, however, are troublemakers, what dentists refer to as plaque.

Plaque is usually invisible, but you may recognize it as "morning mouth." That's the familiar white film that collects on the teeth overnight

Hand-to-Mouth Toothache Relief

Here's a drug-free remedy to try next time you get walloped by a toothache.

With an ice cube, massage the web between your thumb and index finger on the back of your hand as shown in the illustration below. It seems to work whether you massage the hand on the same side as the pain or on the opposite side, reports Thomas Gossel, Ph.D., chairman of the Pharmacology Department at Ohio Northern University.

Apparently, "ice massage" short-circuits pain in a way similar to acupuncture.

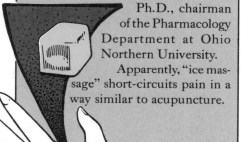

when your saliva, turned off while you sleep, can no longer rinse it off. It's actually a sticky colony of bacteria and food debris that not only gives you "the worst breath of the day" but also, if it's not removed, will produce acid that dissolves tooth enamel, infects the gums and leads to periodontal disease and bone loss.

Ten to 15 minutes after eating, the bacteria in your mouth begin producing acid, which may eat away at the enamel of your teeth.

"The damage is done quite quickly," says Rick Hoard, D.D.S., chairman of the Section of Operative Dentistry at the UCLA School of Dentistry. "In fact, it starts as soon as you stop eating. The physical act of eating is a form of self-cleansing the teeth. In addition, we produce a gallon of saliva a day, which has that washing effect on our teeth."

KEEP TOOTH DECAY AT BAY

If a cavity is formed, a cycle starts. The cavity traps food debris, which combines with the bacteria to produce the acid that digs even deeper into the tooth. As with most dental diseases, the process can be slow, insidious and painless.

"People get a false sense of security if they feel no pain," says Dr. Hoard.

A regular visit to a dentist can detect cavities early and avoid complex and more expensive dental procedures. You can also avoid cavities by following this simple home care program.

- Remove plaque thoroughly at least once a day, ideally by brushing and flossing after each meal.
- Use a fluoride toothpaste and mouthwash. Fluoride helps fight cavities by strengthening the enamel, making it resistant to acid assault.
- Have regular checkups to catch cavities and other problems while they're still small.
- Restrict sugar intake and between-meal snacks to cut down on plaque production.

FIGHTING PERIODONTAL DISEASE

Along with cavities, consider periodontal disease the gravest enemy your mouth has. Periodontal disease is an infection of gum and bone that accounts for a major proportion of all tooth loss. If you are an adult over 40, chances are you already have some signs of this insidious disease. But unless you see your dentist, you might not know.

"Your mouth can be nice and pink and beautiful looking and you may have periodontal disease," says UCLA's Michael G. Newman, D.D.S.

That's because the real damage is being wrought under the gum line. Bacterial plaque clinging to the necks of the teeth manages to dig a hole between the tooth and gum, creating a pocket that, safely out of reach, can fill with food debris, plaque and, as the infection advances, pus. At the same time, it eats away at the bone supporting the tooth.

If the plaque hardens—which it does when it combines with calcium—this resultant calculus acts "like a dirty splinter," says Dr. Newman. It irritates the gums, which then pull away from the teeth, creating more pockets to trap food debris and bacteria. Teeth may loosen and may even fall out.

There are some warning signs. In the early stages of periodontal disease, your gums may bleed when you brush or floss. They may be tender, red and swollen. These are symptoms of a condition called gingivitis. "Bleeding is not a sign of health," says Dr. Newman. "If your gums bleed, it is important to see your dentist."

The best way to fight periodontal disease is to make sure you never get it. Here's how.
● See your dentist, usually several times a year, depending on how quickly you build up calculus. Only the dental professional can remove calculus, using dental instruments.

● Brush frequently with a soft toothbrush and floss daily. A hard brush can cause gums to recede and may damage teeth.
● Use a fluoride toothpaste or mouthwash. Fluoride kills bacteria. So does your saliva, but it stops being produced at night, so make sure you brush and floss your teeth thoroughly every morning and evening.
● Massage gums frequently to stimulate blood flow and eject plaque from beneath the gum line.
● Use new antiplaque toothpastes and mouthwashes and irrigating devices as adjuncts to basic care.

HOW TO CLEAN YOUR TEETH

Cleaning the teeth is an important skill, one many haven't mastered. Here are a few simple suggestions that will help you improve your technique.

Use a disclosing tablet. As a spot check, you should occasionally use a disclosing tablet, a harmless dye available at most drugstores, to reveal invisible plaque colonies. Simply chew the tablets or, if you're using a solution, swish it around in your mouth. When you spit it out, you'll see a red stain on your teeth. Brush properly until the stain is gone.

Brush and floss. To clean teeth, angle a soft-bristled brush at about 45 degrees and jiggle or vibrate it in a circular motion. It should intrude into the gum slightly. Scrub chewing surfaces. Also brush the tongue, where bacteria lurk.

Break off about 18 inches of waxed or unwaxed floss and wind it around your middle fingers. Guide it in between teeth with your thumbs and forefingers. Don't snap it between the teeth, or you'll damage soft tissues; use a gentle sawing motion instead. Slide the floss into the space between the gum and the tooth. Hold it tightly and scrape the side of the tooth, moving away from the gum.

Denise Foley

Tooth Knocked Out? Put It Back

Would you know what to do if you or someone close to you accidentally knocked out a tooth?

A tooth has a good chance of surviving if it is pushed back into the socket within 30 minutes. Any dentist can do it. You can even do it yourself, although you'll still have to get to a dentist as soon as possible.

Here's what the American Dental Association (ADA) says you should do if you lose a tooth.

Do not disinfect, scrub or scrape the tooth. If it's dirty, rinse it gently under running water. Then push it back in its socket. Once it's back in place, press down on it with a finger or bite onto a rolled handkerchief and then head for the nearest dentist. He'll probably need to splint it in place for a week or more.

Never carry a tooth in a tissue, the ADA warns. If it's not possible to put the tooth back in its socket, you can put it in a container of milk or cool water, according to the ADA.

Thirst Alert: How to Read Your Water Level

Chances are you don't think too much about water until it's not there when you want it. Then it doesn't take long to regret having taken it for granted. After about three days without water, you'd be plenty sorry. In a week, more or less, you'd be too dried up to care.

You don't have to be staked to an anthill in the Sahara to experience dehydration, however. It is an insidious process and more common than most of us realize. It can happen if you're pregnant, sweating heavily or taking certain medications. Or, if you're older and have undetected diabetes, it can be caused by a weak thirst response or slowed kidney function.

And your symptoms may be varied. You could be weak, lightheaded, flushed, intolerant of heat, irritable or confused. If you're an athlete, you might notice your performance is lagging or that you're getting muscle cramps.

It's true that most of us need not be concerned about dehydration. If we sweat or urinate too much, our bodies quickly respond. Cells in the brain sense a drop in blood volume and an increase in the salt levels of the blood. They excrete a biochemical that makes us thirsty. At the same time, other cells put out a biochemical that makes the kidneys conserve water. We urinate a darker, more concentrated fluid.

THIRST AND AGING

In healthy, younger people, these two mechanisms work just fine to keep the right amount of water in our bodies. We drink enough to restore the normal concentration or molecules of salt in our blood. Or, if we overdrink, our kidneys soon dump the excess.

But it's also true that some people need to watch how much water they drink, because their bodies' monitoring systems are faulty. They may not be drinking enough. Or, in rare cases, they may be getting too much.

Researchers have found that healthy, older people whose bodies need water are not likely to feel thirsty the way younger people do. Deprived of water for 24 hours, older people are less likely to say they feel thirsty or to complain of a dry mouth, even though their blood samples show they are actually more dehydrated. The older folks also fill up on less when they drink again.

"These findings suggest that older people can't rely on their thirst mechanism to determine how much water they should be drinking," says the study's main researcher, Barbara Rolls, Ph.D., of Johns Hopkins University School of Medicine. Combine this with the aging kidney's inability to conserve water and you've got the potential for a real problem.

"If they are sick, in the hospital, on medication, or get diarrhea, older people face the danger of becoming seriously dehydrated because they do not ask for fluids," Dr. Rolls says.

TROUBLED WATERS

Dehydration is serious business. Our bodies are 60 percent water, which means there's water, water everywhere, from the thick jelly inside our eyeballs to the fluid in which our brains float. The initial effect of dehydration is a decrease in blood volume. The blood thickens as the ratio of plasma to blood cells decreases, the heart must pump more vigorously, and we end up with what's known as circulatory

insufficiency. We also tend to overheat, as the body's main cooling systems work to conserve fluid. Eventually, as the body continues to draw water out of the cells in an effort to restore blood volume and cool itself, we could literally dry up and die.

Mild dehydration can cause weariness, loss of appetite, flushed skin, heat intolerance, impatience, indistinct speech, stumbling and dizziness. More severe symptoms include muscle spasms, delirium, shriveled skin, inability to swallow, sunken eyes, dim vision, painful urination, deafness and numb skin. Severe dehydration ends in seizures, coma and death.

Diabetes can cause dehydration in older people. In this disease, the kidneys use up lots of water to filter sugar out of the blood. In younger people, this larger urine output produces increased thirst, a symptom that alerts doctors to check for early diabetes.

"But older people who have developed diabetes do not always report symptoms of thirst to their doctors, which may be one reason they are not diagnosed," Dr. Rolls says.

DIURETICS CAN DRY YOU OUT

Diuretics are potent drugs that draw salt and water from your body. They are often used to control high blood pressure or to relieve edema—waterlogged tissues caused by hormone imbalances or heart or kidney failure. These drugs are meant to dry you out. The problem is that the careful monitoring of dosage that is needed to avoid problems often is not provided.

"Commonly, patients are started on a high dose to relieve edema," says William Kaehny, M.D., a kidney disease specialist and associate professor of medicine at the University of Colorado School of Medicine. "Once the edema is gone, the dose should be decreased." That's not always done, and the result is dehydration.

"Blood volume and blood pressure decrease, so when you stand up you get light-headed and may even faint," says Dr. Kaehny. "You may have muscle cramps, nausea, even vomiting if your blood pressure gets low enough."

If you're taking diuretics for high blood pressure, it's important to have your blood pressure checked both lying down and standing, Dr. Kaehny says. "Your blood volume may be fine lying down, but when you stand and blood pools in your legs, it may not be enough." Check with your doctor about cutting back on your diuretic dosage.

During a heat wave, diuretics can greatly increase your risk of dehydration, warn two British researchers. They found this out when they decided to increase the diuretic dosage of an 86-year-old woman whose ankles had become badly swollen during unusually hot weather. After three weeks on the medicine, the woman became mentally confused and kept falling down.

Her condition, although serious, was easily remedied by replenishing her body with salt and water. Diuretics are frequently used by the elderly, the doctors note. They recommend diuretic dosages be reduced or stopped altogether during heat waves.

HOW MUCH SHOULD YOU DRINK?

Simply telling people to drink more water may be good enough advice for most, but it isn't specific enough for very old or ill people, Dr. Rolls says. Most people do well with 1½ to 2 quarts of fluid a day—six to eight 8-ounce glasses of liquid or less—depending on the amount of fluid they get from foods. But some need to drink more, and some get by well on less.

"People's kidneys vary greatly in how much water they conserve," Dr. Rolls says. She suggests you periodically check the color of your urine to make sure it's moderately dilute. If it seems concentrated—if the color is dark or the odor is strong—increase the amount of fluids you drink.

If you live in or visit a dry, hot climate, your water intake needs to increase dramatically. You sweat more, but since the sweat quickly evaporates, you may not notice how much water you are losing. Dry wind, hot or cold, also dries you out as effectively as it dries sheets on a clothesline.

Athletes would do well to drink ½ cup or more of water before they start their game or race and to frequently drink small amounts during their activity, sports medicine specialists agree. Muscle cramps that occur after a period of exertion are frequently due to dehydration.

Gale Maleskey

Water Cures

There are times when you'll be told to drink well beyond the call of thirst.

People prone to kidney stones are often advised to drink more water. "And it works," says William Kaehny, M.D. "Drinking about 4 quarts of fluid a day markedly reduces the formation of most kinds of kidney stones." Water dilutes the concentration of minerals that can crystallize in the kidney, forming stones.

Some drugs can also form crystals in the kidney, damaging the tiny tubules that filter the blood. Sulfa drugs (antibacterial agents prescribed for problems like bladder infections) and some chemotherapy drugs are the most likely offenders. "If the label on a drug says to drink plenty of fluids, make sure you do that," Dr. Kaehny warns. Drinking plenty of water with a medicine also allows you to absorb more of it and reduces the possibility of irritation to your throat or stomach.

Bladder infections also benefit from forced drinking. "The water flushes bacteria and inflammatory debris from the bladder," Dr. Kaehny says. You might not want to worry about getting up at night for a drink, though. Researchers have found that highly concentrated urine, like that found in the bladder after a long night's sleep, helps slow bacterial growth.

If you're recovering from a serious bout of diarrhea or vomiting, you may want to replenish yourself with a lightly salted broth or vegetable soup, says Dr. Kaehny. Such intestinal eruptions deplete sodium and other minerals, such as potassium, magnesium and calcium, which may all play roles in water balance.

Before undertaking these suggestions, you should check with your doctor. Although rare, too much fluid can lead to water intoxication, a potentially serious condition.

The Fit Foot

Along with "Hello," "Good-bye," "How are you?" and "I didn't do it," one of the most often repeated phrases in any language has to be, "My feet are killing me."

No wonder. The human foot is a complex mechanism, with more bones than a bucket of fried chicken and such an intricate network of muscles, ligaments, nerves and blood vessels that most of us have little understanding of what makes our feet work, much less how to prevent problems. Add to this the fact that more of us are jogging and running our way to better health—but neglecting our feet until something goes wrong—and it's easy to see why foot ailments are among the most common health problems in the country.

"If people gave half as much thought to foot health as they did to foot fashion, we could prevent a lot of problems," says Norman Klombers, D.P.M., executive director of the American Podiatric Medical Association. "You spend up to 80 percent of your waking hours on your feet. They affect the alignment of your entire skeletal system, and most people don't realize that foot problems can be the reason for aches and pains elsewhere."

Feet also act as a barometer for the general state of the body. Anemia, arthritis, diabetes, heart, circulation and kidney disorders and other conditions may be detected first in the feet.

Practically all of us are born with healthy feet, but 70 percent develop foot problems by adulthood. Heredity, improper foot care (including wearing shoes, socks or stockings that don't fit properly), injury, and the loss of muscle and ligament tone that comes with aging are among the most common causes of problems. Women suffer four times as many foot ailments as

men, with high-heeled shoes often to blame.

Your feet carry a heavy load and need all the consideration they can get. If you're like most people, you walk several miles daily, usually on hard, unyielding surfaces. That all adds up to about 115,000 miles in a lifetime—more than four times around the earth. The feet of most active people absorb the impact of up to five million pounds a day.

And that's a lot of pounding! So here are a few footnotes from some of the leading foot doctors on how you can alleviate the wear and tear that goes with it.

CORNS AND CALLUSES: RUBBING THE WRONG WAY

Corns are usually caused by shoe friction against a toe. The easiest way to avoid them is to wear only properly fitted footwear. If your shoes don't rub against your toes, it's doubtful you'll ever develop a corn. Soft corns can develop between toes if shoes are too narrow.

If you have a corn, don't try to cut it off with a razor blade, because bathroom surgery can lead to infections, says Marc A. Brenner, D.P.M., past president of the American Society of Podiatric Dermatology. "A doctor using sterilized instruments can do this safely and with little pain, but it's dangerous for anyone to try it at home."

He also advises against the home remedy of soaking your feet and then using sandpaper or a callus file to grind away the corn. "You can cause a more serious problem, such as an infection, and not correct the cause of the corn. Even if it works, the corn will probably reappear in three to five weeks."

Over-the-counter corn-removal medications should be avoided because they contain an acid that penetrates the hard skin surface but can burn the surrounding soft, healthy skin. Podiatrists often treat skin ulcers caused by these products.

If you wear wide-toed shoes but still suffer from corns, the cause may be a biomechanical fault, such as a hammertoe, in which the knuckle of the toe rises above its normal position and rubs the top of the shoe because of the poor mechanics of the foot. Another cause can be an underlying bone spur, a bony growth created when local inflammation is present over an extended period of time. X-rays may be needed to determine the problem, and treatment necessary if the cause is biomechanical.

If you develop a callus, a common podiatric problem that usually appears on the heel or ball of the foot, the treatment is the same as for a corn. The hard, thick-skinned callus, however, is more difficult to prevent because it's caused not by your shoes but by your foot structure and the way you walk.

"Insoles are often prescribed to reduce the friction that causes calluses," says Dr. Brenner. Orthoses, or custom shoe inserts, are designed to accommodate your calluses if the cause is an out-of-line bone that hits the ground harder than other foot bones.

It's easy to tell the difference between these two tough spots on your feet: Corns consist of a callus covering a very hard core, usually white in appearance. Although you can see skin lines through a callus, the core of a corn disrupts your skin print. If you press down on the center of a corn, it'll hurt (if you don't feel pain unless you squeeze the affected area, it's more likely a wart). Calluses—toughened skin without the core—are most often painless.

GAME PLAN FOR ATHLETE'S FOOT

Athlete's foot is a fungal infection that plays its game between your toes. It's contagious and loves to live in a warm, moist, dark environment, such as your shoes.

The best way to keep the fungi out of your loafers is to create an inhospitable environment by wearing shoes made of natural materials, such as leather and canvas, that let moisture escape and let feet breathe. Dust inside the shoes with cornstarch before and after wearing to absorb moisture. Keep your shoes dry and try not to wear them on consecutive days, because it takes a day or two for them to dry completely.

Bathe your feet at least once a day using soap and water, and be sure to dry thoroughly between your toes. It helps to change your socks twice a day, and if your feet sweat excessively, wear socks made of cotton or some "wicking" fiber, because they keep feet cooler and drier.

Another way to prevent the flaking, cracking, itching, burning skin caused by fungal infections is to apply an over-the-counter medicated powder to your shoes each day. If the problem persists, a podiatrist can prescribe a stronger medication. Also, it would help to wear thongs or other protective footwear wherever a fungus may be lurking, such as around the community pool or in the showers at the local health club.

UPROOT THOSE PLANTAR WARTS

Plantar warts are painful skin growths that occur on the soles of your feet. They are caused by a highly contagious virus that can be contracted by stepping on a wet, abrasive, virus-infected surface. Abrasion helps rub the virus into the skin on the bottom of your foot, which explains why the warts generally occur on weight-bearing areas.

A wart should never be handled with an over-the-counter medication. "Check with a podiatrist to make sure you have a wart and not a callus, corn or skin cancer," says Dr. Brenner.

A podiatrist has a wide array of treatment alternatives that may include dry ice, vitamin A injections, acid treatments, surgically removing the wart or vaporizing it with a laser. But be aware that regardless of the method used, there's 5 to 15 percent recurrence rate.

Plantar warts are slow growing. If you spot a suspicious growth on your foot, have it checked immediately, because a wart is easier to treat when small.

THE FRICTION BETWEEN YOU AND YOUR FEET

One common foot ailment that's not often misdiagnosed is a blister, an annoying sore that all shoe wearers have experienced at least once. Excessive friction and pressure on the skin are the main causes. To prevent blisters, moleskin padding can be applied to areas that, because of the shape of your foot, may rub against every pair of shoes you buy, constantly causing the sores.

Skin that's too dry or too sweaty is also prone to blisters. Apply a thin coat of petroleum jelly to dry skin before activity. If your feet sweat a lot, cornstarch sprinkled in shoes and socks helps.

"For a small blister, you only need to cover it with a sterile dressing," says Dr. Klombers. "For a larger blister, a little home first aid isn't out of order."

Sterilize a sewing needle with 70 percent isopropyl alcohol. Clean the blistered skin with an antiseptic and make small holes to release the fluid. Blot the fluid with a piece of sterile gauze. An antibiotic cream may be applied and covered with a protective pad.

"Knowing when to deal with a blister yourself is a tricky decision," says Dr. Klombers. "Generally, if you can get to it easily and it's not too severe, you can handle it yourself. If there are signs of blood inside the blister, or if it becomes infected, see your podiatrist."

BORN TO HURT

A few common foot ailments have little to do with lack of consideration

Exercises for Tired Feet

If your feet tire easily, exercise them daily and try these routines: Point your toes outward for a few seconds, then flex them inward; alternate standing on tiptoe for a few seconds with normal standing. Repeat each exercise 10 times, if possible.

Here are some other exercises for maintaining healthy feet.

● Strengthen calf and heel muscles by sitting on the floor with your legs straight ahead, then bending your feet toward you as far as possible.
● To relieve strain on the arches, rest your weight on the outer borders of your feet, then roll them inward.
● Strengthen your toes and the muscles on top of the foot by sitting in a relaxed position with your bare feet on the floor. Try to pick up a towel, pencil or marbles with your toes.

for your feet and are instead the result of inborn problems.

Bunions, for instance, are usually hereditary and aren't caused by improperly fitted shoes, although pointed shoes aggravate and accelerate bunion formation.

A bunion starts as a small enlargement on the side of the big toe and grows over the years. Because it's the result of faulty foot structure and function, there are no self-care measures or ways to prevent the condition. "Surgery is the only way to correct the bone problem," says John McCrea, D.P.M., of Beloit, Wisconsin, "and then orthoses may be necessary to control any abnormal motion. If we can spot potential bunion problems in young patients, we can design orthoses that may help prevent future problems."

An inborn structural or functional defect is also often the cause of flat feet. Totally flat, archless feet are rare, however, and most people who think they have the condition actually have normally low arches. Low or flat arches won't keep you out of the army anymore, but they can cause a strain that may lead to discomfort in the foot, knee, hip or lower back.

Collapsed arches are quite common in people in their fifties and sixties. When the arch starts to give way, orthoses can be used for support. "This should prevent the strained ligaments that lead to other problems," says Dr. McCrea.

High arches can also cause discomfort, because the ball of the foot and heel absorb the total impact while walking. Shoes with good shock-absorbing qualities are crucial, and orthoses may be needed for extra support.

THE ACID TEST

Another inborn condition that can lead to foot problems is how your body deals with uric acid. The inner workings of some people either produce too much uric acid or can't remove what's created. The result is a metabolic disease called gout, in which crystals of the uric acid accumulate in body joints, often in the big toe.

Gout attacks are sudden and very painful, and even the weight of a bed sheet on a swollen, gouty toe can be agonizing. The condition, a form of arthritis, is most prevalent in middle-aged men, and often runs in the family.

In some susceptible people, foods high in substances known as purines, such as sardines, shellfish, anchovies, liver and sweetbreads, can trigger a uric acid increase and a gout attack, as can alcohol and some medications.

Besides suggesting dietary changes, a podiatrist may prescribe an anti-inflammatory medication or one that controls uric acid levels. In rare cases, repeated attacks can leave a toe stiff, and surgery or orthoses may be required to relieve the problem.

Six Tips for Buying Shoes

"Most people don't know how to buy shoes," says Norman Klombers, D.P.M. "Most women buy them to please their eyes, not their feet, with thin soles that offer little to no protective cushion."

Here's what you need to know.

● Allow a thumb's width between the end of the big toe and the tip of the shoe when buying footwear.
● Have your feet measured while standing and, since almost everyone has one foot that's bigger than the other, fit the larger one.
● Always try shoes on before buying, since manufacturers' sizes differ.
● Buy your shoes in the afternoon, because your feet swell a bit during the day.
● Don't buy those you "need to break in." Shoes should feel comfortable when you first try them on.
● Buy only leather or fabric shoes— they let your feet breathe and conform to the shape of each foot.

NAILS YOU SHOULDN'T POUND

Your toenails are protective devices that occasionally cause discomfort if not properly cared for. Ingrown toenails are the most common and painful nail condition, occurring when the side of the nail digs into the skin. Improper nail cutting is generally the cause, although a toe injury or fungal infection can also trigger problems.

Ingrown toenails can be easily avoided by using good, clean clippers designed to cut the nail straight across — not rounded to match the shape of the toe, and not too short. Many ingrown nails result from picking or ripping the nails, which usually leaves a small piece, known as a spicule, to easily grow into the skin. Cutting into the corners of your nails can also lead to spicule formation.

To help relieve some of the discomfort until you can get to a podiatrist, soak your foot in lukewarm water to soften the nail, then tuck a small wisp of cotton between the offending nail edge and the skin. "This provides temporary relief but does nothing to cure the problem," says Dr. Brenner. "It also doesn't do any good to cut a V in the center of the nail. The nail won't grow toward the center and away from the ingrown edge, as some people believe. All nails grow from back to front only."

Over-the-counter remedies that contain tannic acid may help toughen the skin on the side of the nail and resist ingrowing in some cases. Avoid those that contain other kinds of acids, because they often are too harsh.

Injured toenails are just as common because so many people drop things on their feet. The nails turn black and blue, and the pressure from blood collecting under the nail is quite painful. While there are several home remedies that have been around for years, consult a podiatrist, who'll use an electronic needle or drill to safely relieve the pressure.

An Open-and-Closed Case for Surgery

If you go to a podiatrist and find that surgery is in order, you'll also find that there are 2 distinct techniques currently being used.

One is conventional foot surgery, in which the surgeon makes an incision that opens up the area. It's usually performed in hospitals but may be performed in an office or ambulatory-care setting, and it is used in correcting major foot deformities, such as replacing joints or remodeling bone structure.

The other approach, known as minimal-incision surgery, is often performed in a doctor's office. A small incision is made and a tiny dental-type drill is used to grind off bone. Unlike conventional "open" surgery, where the surgeon can see the area in question, the minimal procedure is considered "closed" because the surgeon can't view the bone. It's reserved for less complex procedures, such as removing bone spurs on toes. The patient saves time and money, there's no overnight stay in a hospital, and the recovery time may be shorter.

Regardless of the type of surgery, keep these things in mind.

● Most foot surgery is elective. Agree to an operation only after more conservative therapies have been exhausted.
● Avoid having surgery on the same day a problem is diagnosed. Go home and think about it and get a second opinion if you prefer. The only type of surgical procedure that should be performed during an initial visit is one to resolve an acute condition, such as removal of an ingrown toenail.
● Consider surgery primarily for pain relief or to correct deformities to help you walk better.

WALK YOUR FEET TO HEALTH

How do your feet shape up? The stronger your feet, the better your chances of warding off problems.

Any good foot self-care program should include walking, one of the best ways to strengthen and keep feet in shape. "Walking is great for the feet and the total person," says Gary Gordon, D.P.M., of Glenside, Pennsylvania, whose specialty is sports foot injuries.

If you're starting a fitness regimen that includes walking, Dr. Gordon advises that you begin slowly. "If you have no history of medical problems, walk for 30 to 60 minutes four times a week. After three months, if you're ready, increase your workout time."

In general, take a brisk walk with long strides. Wear good walking shoes that support and cushion your heel. Use soft, thick socks and allow your shoes to dry thoroughly between walks. Try walking barefoot occasionally on sand or grass, but be careful of sharp objects.

Tom Shealey

For Women Only

With tending to a house, career, kids, a husband, three square meals a day, sessions at the health club and a full social schedule, it's no wonder a woman's work is never done.

Health problems? Forget it! There just isn't time in a day to get sidelined by these bodily malfunctions that nature unkindly labeled "for women only." So how do we cope? Simply by avoiding them in the first place. Here's how.

COPING WITH CRAMPS

Some women sail through their menstrual cycle without skipping a beat. Others have to skip out on their regular routine to deal with the pain and misery of menstrual cramps.

What causes cramps? One theory is that some women produce excess amounts of prostaglandins (hormone-like substances made from essential fatty acids) at the onset of their periods. The prostaglandins stimulate excessive uterine contractions, which in turn cause the pain. Here's what doctors say you can do to relieve the discomfort.

Reach for pain relief. If your cramps are on the mild side, you need only reach for one of the familiar over-the-counter cramp medications such as Midol. Midol contains plain old aspirin, a known inhibitor of prostaglandin production.

If your cramps are the type that bring tears to your eyes, you probably need something stronger. Ask your doctor to prescribe a nonsteroidal anti-inflammatory drug like Motrin (which contains strong doses of ibuprofen) or Anaprox (a form of naproxen). In one study comparing the pain-relief power of aspirin versus prescription ibuprofen, the ibuprofen brought relief to 61 to 84 percent of the cramp sufferers, while aspirin helped in only 21 to 30 percent of the cases.

Many doctors recommend that you wait to take these pills until the first sign of bleeding, because cramping could be a sign of pregnancy.

Have a backrub. According to women's athletic trainer Bill Prentice, Ph.D., of the University of North Carolina, a massage can rub away minor cramps. Ask a friend to use fingers or thumb and firmly rub in circles at the midsection of your back, just right of the third bony vertebra up from the base of your spine. The pain may disappear in less than 5 minutes.

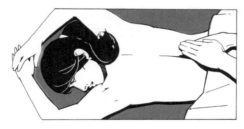

Curl up in a ball. The yoga position known as the "child's pose" can be a great way to stretch out cramp spasms, suggests Susan Lark, M.D., author of *Premenstrual Syndrome Self-Help Book*. All you do is sit back on your heels, with your arms limp at your sides. Bring your forehead to the floor, stretching the spine as far as possible. Close your eyes and hold as long as comfortable.

PMS: THE EMOTIONAL COLLISION

Do your menstrual miseries start days or weeks before your period even makes its appearance? Your breasts might become tender, your back throb, your ankles swell—your whole body feels fatigued. Or maybe your hunger goes out of control or you feel like you're stuck on a never-ending emotional roller coaster ride—angry one moment, dissolving into tears the next.

This collection of mental and physical symptoms has been widely publicized as premenstrual syndrome, or PMS. While 25 percent of premenopausal women report at least one or more of these discomforts, only about 3 to 7 percent have enough symptoms to be clinically diagnosed as having *true* premenstrual syndrome, says John Steege, M.D., associate clinical professor of obstetrics and gynecology at Duke University Medical Center. And, he says, research still hasn't found why PMS plagues some women and not others. "One thing we do know about PMS," Dr. Steege says, "is that women with a history of depression seem more prone to the disorder."

Another thing they know is that there is no clear-cut solution to relieve the symptoms. Although the hormone progesterone is commonly prescribed for PMS, it has not been proven totally successful. Women have, however, reported varying degrees of success by adopting some of these lifestyle changes.

Get off your stress cycle. Make a chart of your symptoms and note what else may be going on in your life that may be causing you anxiety (a fight with your spouse, car trouble, you name it). Studies show that outside stressors can be magnified at the time of your menstrual cycle.

Consider taking vitamin E. In a recent study, women who took 400 international units of vitamin E for three months had a reduction in breast tenderness, weight gain and abdominal bloating, depression, anxiety, fatigue and cravings for sweets. (This level of vitamin E should be taken only with the approval and supervision of your doctor.)

Limit caffeine. For caffeine-sensitive women, doing without can mean less anxiety, fluid retention and breast tenderness.

Don't sit on the sidelines. When you were a schoolgirl, you probably, at least once, used your period as an excuse for not attending gym class. But you may have been better off remaining active, says Dr. Lark. Walking, tennis and swimming improve breathing and blood flow, which helps to prevent fluid retention and swelling.

Control your cravings. No one knows why some women get the premenstrual munchies and crave sweet and salty foods. Still, one way to put the brakes on your monthly binging, Dr. Steege says, is to eat well all month long. Choose low-sugar, low-fat, high-complex-carbohydrate foods as part of your balanced diet.

FIGHTING VAGINAL INFECTIONS

Most of the time, the vagina keeps itself healthy with its very own maintenance system—secretions and "good" bacteria that have just the right acid environment to keep most fungi, viruses and "bad" bacteria safely at bay.

There are some things, however, notes Long Island gynecologist Penny Wise Budoff, M.D., in *No More Menstrual Cramps and Other Good News,* that can cause this self-cleaning system to go on the fritz. And before you know it, you've got an environment that could invite vaginal enemies such as yeast infections. You may wind up with a maddening itch, an irritating odor, or something more serious.

Fortunately, assures Dr. Budoff, you can help protect yourself from infections. Here's how.

Don't overuse feminine hygiene products. Frequent use of feminine hygiene sprays, bubble baths and alkaline soaps can irritate vulval tissue or vaginal walls and upset the acid balance.

Wear cotton underwear. Avoid tight jeans, panty hose or synthetic underwear, which create a moist environment especially inviting for yeast infections. Choose clothing with ventilated cotton crotches.

Avoid overusing antibiotics. Doctors have observed that these drugs can upset the vaginal bacterial balance and promote yeast growth.

Wipe from front to back. This prevents intestinal bacteria from entering the vagina.

Use the least absorbent tampons you can. Alternate with sanitary napkins to allow your vagina to naturally flush itself. Use sanitary napkins during the night.

Use barrier birth control. Spermicides used with condoms or diaphragms can help prevent sexually transmitted infections.

Marcia Holman

The Six Best Disease Fighters

Develop these healthy habits today to help prevent disease tomorrow.

● Pass up the butter and other fats. Low-fat meals help fight breast, ovarian and colon cancer.
● Shed excess weight. It helps avoid diabetes, heart disease and varicose veins.

● Exercise regularly. Regular weight-bearing exercise helps prevent osteoporosis, the brittle bone disease that strikes 1 in 4 women.
● Treat yourself to a cup of yogurt, as well as some skim milk or low-fat cheese. These high-calcium foods keep bones strong.

● Slather yourself with sunscreen. It's the number one defense against skin cancer.
● Practice early detection. Monthly breast self-exams done at the same time every month help detect breast cancer early. Yearly Pap smears can protect you from cervical cancer.

For Men Only

Some things in life are more common among men than among women: Camel cigarettes, Corvettes and Budweiser, to name a few. So, too, are certain health problems.

If you've ever wondered or worried about prostate problems or hernias or testicular cancer, then, Bud . . . this here's for you.

THE TROUBLE WITH PROSTATES

Normally a chestnut-sized gland whose primary known function is to supply the liquid part of a man's ejaculate, the prostate can swell up to the size of an orange. Since it completely surrounds the urethra, or urinary exit pipe, it's not hard to understand what happens when it swells. (Two men were sharing a hospital room, the story goes. "W-w-w-what's your tr-tr-trouble?" one asked. "Prostate," the other replied. "I used to pee the way you talk.")

Benign prostate hypertrophy (BPH), or noncancerous enlargement of the prostate, is a common problem. It's not clear what causes it, but it's so widespread among older men that it's thought that age-related hormonal changes are a major factor. Another potential—and preventable—culprit: fatty diets. Autopsies of enlarged human prostates have shown an extraordinarily high cholesterol content compared with normal prostates.

Research suggests that reducing dietary cholesterol may reduce the size of a swollen prostate.

A survey of the sexual histories of over 400 older men offers another possible prostate-saving measure, or at least one that may reduce your chances of developing prostate cancer: *sex*.

A simple questionnaire consisting of two impudent questions was answered by 274 men with prostate cancer and 149 men without, all of them over age 60. The two questions were "How many different sexual partners have you had in your lifetime?" and "During the sexually active part of your life, how frequently did you ejaculate every week?"

"The average ejaculatory frequency in those with prostatic carcinoma was significantly lower than in the control [cancer-free] group," reports Anjan K. Banerjee, M.B.B.S., of the Manchester Royal Infirmary. In other words, a good sex life may help prevent cancer of the prostate, the third most prevalent cancer among men.

HELP FOR THE HERNIA

Hernia is a general term that describes what happens when a body part goes where it isn't supposed to. In most cases, it means that a corner of the peritoneum, a sac that envelops the intestines and abdominal cavity, has slipped into one of the openings that leads from the abdomen to the chest or legs. (Imagine a tire with a hole in it. Then picture the inner tube poking through the hole and forming a bubble. The "inner tube" is the peritoneum, and the "bubble" is the hernia.)

Male Nutrition: Four Important Sources

By now, we all know that certain nutrients are very important for women. For example, we know that women need more iron than men. But what are some of the most important nutrients for men? Here are 4.

● Magnesium. This mineral plays an important role in keeping the heart muscle beating rhythmically. Magnesium may help men not only avoid a heart attack but also survive one should it occur. To boost your magnesium levels, eat more seafood (particularly shrimp, clams and crab), spinach, whole grains, peas, beans and corn.
● Vitamin C. This vitamin may help to prevent heart disease in several different ways. It also can help protect the body against pollutants. Good sources of vitamin C include citrus fruits, green peppers, brussels sprouts, broccoli, cantaloupe, cauliflower and strawberries.
● Zinc. Male sexual maturity and fertility depend on adequate zinc. Zinc also has a profound influence on the body's ability to resist disease. Foods high in zinc include seafood, liver, mushrooms, sunflower seeds and soybeans.
● Fiber. Getting adequate fiber in your diet will lower your risk of colon cancer, coronary heart disease, diabetes, obesity and high blood pressure.

Fiber can be found in many whole grains, such as bran and oats, and a variety of fruits and vegetables.

Blame evolution for hernias. They might be the price we pay for walking upright. While you can't do anything about your evolution, there are measures you can take to reduce your chances of getting a hernia.

● Lose weight. Being overweight, though it will not create a hernia, can make matters worse. Obesity stretches the peritoneum like a balloon, making it more likely to pop.

● Strengthen abdominal muscles. Weak abdominal muscles probably raise the risk of hernia because they don't act as a natural truss the way strong muscles do.

● Don't strain. Heavy lifting, coughing, and straining to move the bowels are other kinds of stress that can increase intra-abdominal pressure and trigger a hernia.

TESTICULAR SELF-CARE

Cancer of the testicles is pretty uncommon, actually. Accounting for less than 2 percent of all malignant tumors in men, it doesn't really make the statistical big leagues. Still, it's nothing to mess with: Among men in their 20s and 30s, it's the biggest cancer killer of all.

Treatment has improved in recent years to the point where in all but the most advanced cases, you stand an 85 to 90 percent chance of a cure. Still, the earlier it's detected, the better your chances. And that's where most young guys screw up. One random sample of 90 college-age men at the University of Vermont, for instance, showed that 75 percent of them had never even heard of testicular cancer, and not one knew how to do the simple self-exam described below.

To nip this potentially deadly cancer in the bud, the National Cancer Institute recommends that young men do this self-exam once a month.

After a hot bath or shower, when the scrotum is fairly relaxed, just gently roll each testicle between your thumb and middle finger. You may feel something a little bit spongy on the back side of each testicle. That's the epididymis, a collection of sperm-storage ducts (they're normal). What you're looking for and hoping not to find is a small, hard, usually painless lump or swelling. If you do find one, don't hesitate to see a urologist.

CAMELS, CORVETTES AND BUDWEISER

The fact that men die younger than women may be partly genetic, but men, it's largely your own fault. Men drink and smoke more, and drive faster than women. They're also more likely to be Type A's (see the box, "Are You a Type-A Guy?"). Moral: Take it easy. Slow down. Okay, Bud?

Stefan Bechtel

Are You a Type-A Guy?

Well, are you? The main exterior signs of Type-A behavior are aggravation, irritation, anger and impatience. They're overt but still often hidden from the Type A. Generally, Type A's are great at spotting Type-A behavior in others but awful at detecting it in themselves.

So if you're a Type A, how can you accurately assess your own behavior? Be honest with yourself, says Meyer Friedman, M.D., a San Francisco cardiologist who, along with Ray Rosenman, M.D., Menlo Park, California, first studied Type-A behavior (he coined the phrase) and offered evidence hinting that it may hurt your heart enough to kill you.

Here are some of the questions you should ask yourself (and the people who know you).

● Do you have a compulsion to win at all costs, even in trivial contests with children?
● Do you clench your fist during ordinary conversation?
● Do you have easily aroused irritability or anger, even in minor matters?
● Do you sigh frequently?
● Do you have trouble sitting and doing nothing?
● Do you detest waiting in lines?
● Do you eat, walk or talk fast?
● Do you often angrily defend your unshakable opinions?

● Do you grind your teeth?
● Do you nod your head while speaking (rather than while listening, as many people do)?

"Few Type A's exhibit all the Type-A signs," Dr. Friedman says. "But most Type A's have several. We have found that exhibiting even one of them (mild Type A) increases your risk of having a heart attack before age 65."

If you fail the test, Dr. Friedman suggests you start to slow down, stop occasionally to smell the roses, learn to relax. Your life may depend on it.

Laughter Is Good Medicine

A man deliberately leaves a nickel in the coin-return slot of a telephone booth—and lurks nearby to secretly share the excitement of the person who will discover the treasure. Nurses collect humorous books in a wicker picnic basket and keep the basket at the ward desk, to let patients and staff check out the contents whenever they please. Corporate executives bring baby pictures of themselves to work, pin them to a bulletin board and mischievously ask visitors, "Hey, wanna see a naked picture of our vice president?"

Have these adults gone mad? On the contrary, by deliberately adding fun and laughter to their lives, they are behaving in an eminently sane way.

These days, more and more experts are recognizing that play and laughter can enhance our physical and emotional well-being, help us handle stress better and open new lines of communication with our fellow human beings.

GOOD FOR THE HEART AND SOUL

While emphasizing that fun is hardly a cure-all, the medical establishment is showing an increasing interest in the effects of the positive emotions on health, says Alison Crane, R.N., founder and executive director of the American Association for Therapeutic Humor, headquartered in Skokie, Illinois.

A good laugh, notes Crane, changes blood pressure (blood pressure rises during laughter, but lowers *below* the starting point afterward), reduces muscle tension, improves digestion and—if you laugh so hard that you cry—releases tears that contain bacteria-killing agents. Research also indicates that laughter may trigger the release of catecholamines, hormones that increase alertness.

Perhaps even more important than the physical effects, says Crane, are the psychological benefits of humor and laughter. Reduction of tension and anxiety is one of the most important.

Laughter improves communications between people, notes Crane. "A colleague of mine once noted that shared laughter creates community. If you're trying to create a cohesive group in business, with friends or family, laughter can facilitate that sense of belonging." Fear, loneliness and isolation disappear in shared laughter.

"There are so many people in our culture walking around tied up in knots because they won't give themselves the release of laughter and play, they won't permit themselves that healing embrace," says Matt Weinstein, Ph.D., corporate consultant and founder of Playfair, of Berkeley, California, a company that teaches adults how to have fun.

A common excuse, Dr. Weinstein says, is, " 'I am busy. I am under pressure here. I don't have time for that stuff.' The truth is, that's the time when people need it most. Laughter and play is a total life philosophy, not just a good-time philosophy."

Rx FOR FUN

How can you add more laughter to your life? By taking the time for fun and play, say the experts; by opening your eyes to the humor around you. Here's how.

Take a laugh break. Buy a portable cassette player, get some comedy tapes and listen to them three or four times a day, suggests Dr. Weinstein. "Force yourself to take a laugh break. Who cares if people walk by your office and see you laughing for no reason?" It only adds to the fun.

Or, suggests laughter expert Joel Goodman, Ed.D., director of The HUMOR Project at the Saratoga Institute in Saratoga Springs, New York, and editor of *Laughing Matters* magazine, take a break to browse through humorous books, articles or cartoons you've clipped—anything that makes you laugh. "I have books of 'Herman' cartoons next to my bed," Dr. Goodman says. "Usually, if I'm down in the dumps, literally within 2 minutes I'm laughing out loud."

Develop your comic vision. Dr. Goodman also recommends getting in the habit of casting a bemused eye on the world around you. "I interviewed the comedian Steve Allen, who told me, 'Nothing is funnier than the unintended humor of reality.' If you put that principle in practice, humor will be waiting to greet you. Keep your eyes and mind open. We can be intentional about humor. We don't have to leave it to chance."

For example, reading the morning newspaper can be changed from a depressing ordeal into a search for the sunny side, says Dr. Goodman. "Some people say, 'I don't like to read the paper; I don't need to take on the burdens of the world and get more depressed.' I'd suggest, if you look for them in any daily paper, you'll find at least five things that will tickle your funny bone."

Find a funny friend. "One man told me that Rodney Dangerfield was his favorite funny guy," says Dr. Goodman. "Whenever things got tough, he would say, just to himself, one of Rodney's famous lines: 'Look out for number one, and don't step on number two.' That helped him 'keep on trucking' on more occasions than he cared to remember." Enlist your

How to Tickle a Funny Bone

We all know that laughter is good medicine. But how do you fill the prescription for someone else? After all, it's not all that easy to humor someone who's not in the mood for it.

"The key points are realizing that humor is not always appropriate and, whenever possible, to invite humor from the other person rather than impose it on them," says Joel Goodman, Ed.D.

"Rather than saying, 'You need to laugh, I'm going to tell a joke now,' observe the person. See what makes him laugh or brings joy to his eyes, and then try to invite the occasions for that to happen on a regular basis."

If you know, for example, that your friend loves Bill Cosby, provide him with Cosby audio tapes or videos. Ask his family or friends about favorite games and toys. Consider investing in a stuffed animal—even adults respond to them well. Other suggestions:

● Encourage an older person to reminisce about happy memories or funny stories.

● If you know the person well, don't hesitate to go wild. "I have a number of friends who have been hospitalized, and have had mimes deliver balloon bouquets or silly telegrams," says Dr. Goodman.

● Share your own humor. Lend funny books and tapes from your own collection.

---

own funny friend. Pick someone you think is hysterically funny—be it Woody Allen, Erma Bombeck or the wisecracker down the street.

"Use that person as an 'internal ally,'" says Dr. Goodman. "The next time the going gets rough, ask yourself the following questions: 'How would this person see this situation I'm in? What would this person do or say if he or she were in my shoes?'"

Delight yourself. There's more to fun than a pile of laughs, says Alison Crane. "A better expression than 'sense of humor' is 'sense of delight.' I'm so happy when I watch Fred Astaire and Ginger Rogers dance. Here are people doing something you know is tremendously hard, and they make it look totally effortless. The delight is in the difference between what you perceive and what's actually happening—that's fun, it's so nice to see."

Make a point of delighting yourself several times a day. One good way to start is to make a list of 30 things that you love doing—anything from taking a shower to watching Fred and Ginger dance to hoofing it yourself.

The last laugh should be on you. "I strive to take my work seri-. ously but myself lightly," says Dr. Goodman. One simple exercise that Dr. Goodman recommends for not taking yourself seriously is drawing—with a little twist.

Draw a picture of something that's causing you stress—but use the wrong hand, or do it with your eyes shut. Inevitably, when you open your eyes, you will smile at the results. "You can turn this exercise into a 1-minute-a-day humor break," says Dr. Goodman.

Spread the wealth. "I think that if good luck happens to you," says Dr. Goodman, "you'll make good things happen to others." That's why he does his bit by leaving a nickel in the till after making a telephone call. "Then, if I have time, I hang out in the vicinity," he says. "The reaction when someone finds the nickel is incredible. It's like they just won the state lottery."

There are plenty of other ways to share laughter. Dr. Goodman tells of a man who has collected funny cartoons for 30 years; every month he sends some of the cartoons to people on his goodwill list. Another man, an executive, photocopies cartoons or jokes on stationery to be used as office memos.

ALL IN THE FAMILY

"A lot of people have grown up learning not to use humor," says Dr. Goodman. "Parents say, 'Wipe that smile off your face,' 'Get serious,' 'Grow up,' 'Act your age.' All these subtle and not-so-subtle messages discourage kids from using humor." So encourage children to laugh and be spontaneous, and don't discourage their ideas. Keep funny games and books around the house that both children and adults can enjoy.

If you own a video setup, use it to make funny films. "Actions speak louder than words," says Dr. Goodman. "If parents want to help themselves as well as their children, they should encourage laughter whenever it's appropriate."

Dr. Weinstein has a slightly more elaborate suggestion for a do-it-yourself home-humor project. "Buy a bunch of bananas, bring them home, take a razor blade and slice one open, take the banana out, put a hot dog in there, seal it up again, put it in the refrigerator, and *deny everything!*"

Cathy Perlmutter

Body Gremlins: Getting Out the Knocks and Pings

You know your body. You know when something is wrong. You know if your temperature soars to 111°F, you lose 35 pounds overnight and your heart feels like it's caught in a vise, it's time to see the doctor—fast. But what about those little things, those "body gremlins"?

Things like "floaters" in the eyes, spontaneous sneezing fits, momentary dizziness and eyelid twitches affect just about all of us at one time or other. Are they reason for concern? Fortunately, usually not. Just the same, you want to know what the heck causes them and how to get rid of them.

Getting the right answers, however, can be tough. For one thing, it isn't always easy to ask about them without blushing. And for another, body gremlins, as you would expect, don't get much attention from medical researchers. Nevertheless, medical people do understand more about these physiological phantasms than you think.

We introduce you here to the common body gremlins and what they mean. Say hello to . . .

THE "SOMETHING FLOATING BY" GREMLIN

Ever wonder about those tiny specks that seem to promenade across your eyeball at idle moments? Are they animal, vegetable or mineral?

They're neither bugs nor dirt nor phantoms. "Floaters, as they're called, happen to just about everyone," says Andrew J. Philips, M.D., an ophthalmologist and an assistant surgeon at Wills Eye Hospital, Philadelphia. "They are essentially cells or tiny fibers that have broken away from the retina or from the structures making up the transparent gel inside the eyeball. Most often, the natural aging process causes the breakup, and we see the

debris drifting, following the direction of our eye movements.

"Though this degeneration is accelerated somewhat in people with myopia [nearsightedness] and certain other eye problems, the process is generally harmless. If you experience a sudden increase in floaters, however, you should visit an ophthalmologist."

THE "ROYAL PAIN-IN-THE-SIDE" GREMLIN

Maybe you call it a stitch in the side, or maybe you don't call it anything—you just flinch. It's a sharp, temporary pain, and it usually befalls people when they're walking or running. Despite the momentary agony, it's not cause for alarm and certainly isn't the beginning of a heart attack or appendicitis.

"The pain is caused by a spasm of the diaphragm muscle," says Ben E. Benjamin, Ph.D., a muscle therapist and author of *Listen to Your Pain* and other books about muscle therapy. "If the diaphragm isn't properly warmed up before exercise, or is strained more than usual, it can go into automatic involuntary contractions—the so-called painful stitch. If you let up on your activity a bit or take a rest, the spasm usually disappears."

THE "GESUNDHEIT" GREMLIN

Out of the blue it hits you: a fit of thunderous, annoying, 21-gun sneezing. And then silence. Where does this gremlin come from?

"Sneezing is an ancient reflex," says Selig J. Kavka, M.D., student of the phenomenon and internist at Mount Sinai Hospital, Chicago. "It's the body's way of clearing the nasal passages of irritants and allergens, though it can be triggered by things that have nothing to do with airborne matter. For example, strong emotions —including sexual excitement—can launch a volley of sneezes."

And so can, of all things, sunlight. People have been known to walk into the light of day and suddenly start sneezing their heads off, as though they were allergic to sunshine. One researcher called this reaction the photic sneeze reflex and found evidence that it's more widespread than anybody guessed. Exactly what causes it, though, is a gremlinological puzzle.

Another mystery is how sneezing fits can conform to patterns. "Some people sneeze only twice in any one episode," says Dr. Kavka. "Others may explode into great sneezing salvos before stopping. And, oddly enough, such patterns may actually run in families. If the parent sneezes only four times, for example, the child may

maintain the same response."

So how do you exorcise the sneeze gremlin? There's no standard ritual, though people have tried everything from sniffing garlic to pressing the upper lip to a hundred forms of distraction. If the cause of the problem is allergens, irritants or emotions, dealing with these factors can only help.

One thing that won't help, though, is trying to stifle a sneeze by holding your nose or clenching your mouth shut. Containing the explosion like this is likely to damage nasal membranes.

THE "MERRY-GO-ROUND" GREMLIN

Ever hop up from your chair to find the room spinning like a leaf in a gale? Many people have, and often the cause of this fleeting dizziness is nothing more malevolent than the gremlin known as postural hypotension.

"This malady—essentially a drop in blood pressure when you change postures—is very common," says Daniel P. Marshall, M.D., a Memphis physician and coauthor of *Staying Healthy without Medicine.* "Your blood pressure is constantly adjusting to your body's positions. When you lie down, your blood pressure goes up. When you stand up, it goes down. When some people stand up, however, their pressure drop is too rapid, causing a transient lag in blood to the brain,

and thus temporary dizziness.

"This chain of events is generally not worth worrying about. But people who find it especially distressing or those taking blood pressure medication should check with their doctor."

THE "BIG-EYED, TWITCHING" GREMLIN

Just as you get ready to cast a longing look toward your beloved, your eyelid twitches. And twitches. Is it a sign of true love? No, just myokymia, the jerky contraction of muscle fibers.

"Myokymia can happen at several points in the body," says Dr.

Philips. "But it's especially disconcerting in the small muscles of the eye and face. The twitching there can be caused by a temporary imbalance in nerves or blood flow, and it happens most frequently when people are under stress or when they overtax their eyes or facial muscles. The phenomenon, fortunately, is not serious and soon goes away."

THE "OPEN UP AND SAY 'A-A-A-AH' " GREMLIN

You wake up in the morning, stick your tongue out at the bathroom mirror and cringe. The dreaded coated tongue strikes wonder and loathing in the hearts of humans.

Loathe all you want, but wonder no more. That coating is not just food debris from the preceding evening's meal—it's also millions of dead cells. "There's a tremendous amount of cellular growth on the tongue's surface," says Samuel Dreizen, D.D.S., M.D., chairman of the Department of Oral Oncology at University of Texas Health Science Center. "That means each day the tongue has to slough off vast numbers of dead cells."

And though a dramatic change in the tongue's color may indicate disease, the color or texture of any coating is insignificant. "The coating could be any color," says Dr. Dreizen. "But the clean, uncoated, healthy tongue should be pink." None of which makes a green morning tongue any prettier. But a few facts always make a body gremlin easier to live with.

Lewis Vaughn

A Guide to Stop Smoking

Is smoking harmful to your health? Can Frank Sinatra carry a tune?

No medical subject has been so exhaustively studied. "Cigarette smoking is the chief single avoidable cause of death in our society and the most important public health issue of our time," stated Surgeon General C. Everett Koop in one of his reports on smoking. Nothing has ever been more conclusive.

Wising up, many smokers have quit or are quitting: The proportion of adult smokers in the United States has dropped from 42 percent in 1965 to 30 percent in 1985, and fewer young recruits than ever are getting sucked into the smoking habit.

That's the good news. But roughly 50 million Americans still cough themselves through the day, fidgeting and fumbling constantly with their cigarettes and ashtrays, scorching holes in friends' (often ex-friends') sofas, and warding off disapproving stares from the no-longer-silent majority. Sound familiar?

If you smoke, you've probably tried to stop—most smokers have. Don't feel bad if you haven't yet succeeded. An estimated 40 million former cigarette smokers in the United States are living proof: *You can quit.*

Garland DeNelsky, Ph.D., director of the Cleveland Clinic Foundation's Smoking Cessation Program and an ex-smoker himself, likens smoking to "an old friend putting poison in your coffee every morning." Giving up smoking is "the best gift you could give yourself," he says, "but it takes some planning and effort."

EXPECT THE UNEXPECTED

Many people who try to quit smoking are most often lured back during times of stress or when exposed to cues associated with smoking, such as parties and pool rooms. If you smoke, you must learn to recognize these cues, says Dr. DeNelsky, and, perhaps more important, you must expect the unexpected.

Like hikers taking off on a cloudy day, he says, "smokers attempting to quit must consider the possibility of a thunderstorm." This would be an occasion such as the death of a loved one, a wedding or a beach vacation, when even the most resolute of quitters can be thrown off guard and reach for a cigarette.

At the Cleveland Clinic, doctors are experimenting with a variety of techniques to help you handle both the daily cues and the occasional "thunderstorm." The most effective weapons, says Dr. DeNelsky, are "active coping strategies."

"Some people, when they feel the desire for a cigarette, will jump in the shower," he says. "Some will walk around the block, some remind themselves of why they're quitting . . . these are active coping strategies." The trick is to find one or more that work for you.

Dr. DeNelsky himself jingles a pocketful of old ignition points from his 1973 Oldsmobile when he gets the urge to smoke. It's worked for eight years.

Such methods, including hypnosis, which Dr. DeNelsky says can also be helpful, are aimed at breaking the mind's addiction to tobacco. But the body also develops an extremely nasty dependence. Researchers at the Cleveland Clinic and elsewhere are looking for the best ways to help you set both mind and body free.

ZEROING IN ON A "CURE"

"We're gaining more insight into the factors that control smoking and that make it difficult for people to stop," says David P. L. Sachs, M.D., director of the Smoking Cessation Research Institute in Palo Alto, California, and clinical assistant professor of respiratory medicine at Stanford University Medical School. "The more we understand what's going on, the better targeted our treatments can be."

Treatments to date that have proved most successful, says Dr. Sachs, involve attacking the psychological and the physical addiction to tobacco at the same time.

At the same time is the key. Nicotine polacrilex, also known as nicotine gum, currently the only drug on

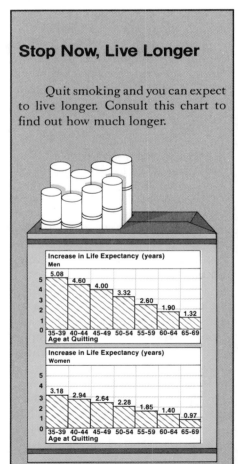

Stop Now, Live Longer

Quit smoking and you can expect to live longer. Consult this chart to find out how much longer.

Increase in Life Expectancy (years)
Men

Age at Quitting	35-39	40-44	45-49	50-54	55-59	60-64	65-69
Years	5.08	4.60	4.00	3.32	2.60	1.90	1.32

Increase in Life Expectancy (years)
Women

Age at Quitting	35-39	40-44	45-49	50-54	55-59	60-64	65-69
Years	3.18	2.94	2.64	2.28	1.85	1.40	0.97

the market for smoking cessation, can be very effective in a structured program or under a doctor's close supervision, says Dr. Sachs. But used by itself, without guidance, the medication will likely be "a waste of time and money."

Nicotine is, of course, the addictive ingredient in tobacco, and nicotine polacrilex can satisfy the body's craving without the inhalation of cigarette smoke and its many other noxious ingredients. (Nicotine polacrilex itself can cause such problems as upset stomach, hiccups and nausea.)

Other classes of medications, such as the blood pressure regulator clonidine, may interfere with the addiction itself and are showing promise in clinical studies, says Dr. Sachs. So are new ways to use nicotine, such as in a nose spray.

But, Dr. Sachs adds, "The smoker shouldn't be anticipating that if he waits five years there will be a magic bullet that will make him stop smoking. These new drugs will only potentially be better tools to help the smoker."

HIGH-TECH ANSWER

One such helping tool, introduced to the market in February 1987, is a computer.

LifeSign is the brainchild of a psychologist and two computer experts. It's small enough to fit into your pocket and carry with you throughout the day. It beeps. It buzzes. It flashes messages. It tells you when you can smoke, when you can't and when you *must* (the more inopportune the moment, the better), tailoring a tapering-off schedule to meet your level of addiction.

Experiments have shown LifeSign is effective "from 18 to 28 percent of the time—similar to what you get in a clinic," says Lee W. Frederiksen, Ph.D., vice president for development of Health Innovations, in Herndon, Virginia.

The "portable clinic" is available through many doctors and hospitals, says Dr. Frederiksen, or you can

Follow the Path of Mark Trail

Mark was a heavy smoker, puffed a pipe for nearly 40 years—since the day he was born, in fact.

The day he was born?

If you read the funnies, you probably know Mark as the brave and handsome Mark Trail, guardian of the Lost Forest. His adventures, and pipe usage, date back to 1946.

Breaking old habits isn't easy, but when he read a letter from 9-year-old Daniel Kahn of Atlanta, asking that he drop the pipe because "smoking is bad to your health and it pollutes the air wicth [sic] could hurt the birds," Mark knew what he had to do.

Actually, Jack Elrod knew. "Mark had been smoking since the strip began; it gave him a macho image and helped the reader to identify him," says Elrod, who both writes and draws the serial. In 1950 when Elrod first teamed up with the strip's originator, Ed Dodd, who is now retired, the perils of tobacco were not well known.

In past years, they've become known not only to young Daniel but to many other *Mark Trail* readers as well. Perhaps Mark's smoking was bad for the birds—it was undeniably bad for his health. So Elrod had him kick the 38-year habit. Cold turkey.

"I feel great . . . . I stopped smoking, and I feel like a new person!" Elrod had Mark spontaneously announce to his cartoon buddies one December morning in 1983. Since then, says Elrod, "I've gotten a lot of favorable comments about Mark not smoking."

But even for a fictional character, quitting wasn't that easy.

"I'd drawn the pipe for so many years that I had to put a little note above my drawing desk that says 'Remember—No Pipe,' " says Elrod. But the no-pipe rule doesn't pertain to all the strip's characters. Says Elrod, "I still have my villains smoke."

Any chance the strip's good guy, who hasn't lifted a pipe in a couple of years now, will ever break down and light up again? "He'll have to do it behind my back," says Elrod.

MARK TRAIL   by DODD & ELROD

PRINTED WITH SPECIAL PERMISSION OF NORTH AMERICAN SYNDICATE

purchase the device directly from the company (phone 1-800-543-3744). LifeSign sells for approximately $70 plus handling.

If you're not the computer type or would simply prefer help of the flesh-and-blood kind, just pick up the phone. The American Lung Association, the American Heart Association and the American Cancer Society all offer quit-smoking programs; contact your local chapter. Smokenders, for $295, offers a six-week program (phone 1-800-828-4357). Or ask your doctor for help.

Russell Wild

Mirror Diagnosis

You usually take a peek in the mirror to fix your hair, adjust your tie, put on your makeup, or just generally check out how you look. But have you ever gazed in the mirror to see how you *feel*?

It's not a bad idea. Because that image mugging back at you contains evidence about the state of your health. So put vanity aside, slip into your birthday suit, face up to your full-length mirror, and give yourself a visual exam.

MAKE EYE CONTACT

Look yourself straight in the eyes. Are they bloodshot? Bloodshot eyes can be caused by swimming in chlorinated water, one glass too many of your favorite vino, even an infection. Persistent inflammation is more likely to be caused by infection, so check with your doctor if the problem lasts for two or three days.

Now gently pull down one lower eyelid. It should be pink. If it's white, you could be anemic. So make sure you're getting enough iron in your diet.

And what about the whites of your eyes themselves? Look on the side nearest your nose. Are there any small, yellowish bumps? These can be a sign of sun damage. Make sure you wear sunglasses that filter ultraviolet light or a hat that shades your eyes when you go outside. And ask your doctor to make sure they're not on the edge of your cornea—the transparent part of your eye that covers the iris and pupil. That can hurt your vision.

CHECK YOUR SKIN

Stand back from the mirror just a little and look at the color of your face. Do you seem pale? A yellow-white, papery complexion may just be a natural, normal consequence of old age, but check with your doctor, because pallor can also be a sign of anemia or kidney trouble.

Does your skin seem red? A ruddy complexion may be a sign of high blood pressure. Or a slightly red, purple and orange color combined with excessive wrinkles and a slight sinking of the cheeks can indicate the toxic effects of cigarette smoking.

Does your skin look tough and almost corrugated? Does your smile have a permanent sag? Those are signs of a loss of skin elasticity caused by overexposure to the sun. And if that's not bad enough, severely sun-damaged skin can develop ugly brown patches—frequently known as liver spots—or scaly gray patches, called keratoses, which occasionally develop into cancer.

If the skin on your face and hands is tough and wrinkled but the skin on protected parts of your body is smooth and young-looking, excess sun is most likely the problem. So use sunscreens faithfully and avoid the sun's hottest onslaughts.

OPEN WIDE

Move closer to the mirror again and take a look inside your mouth. Is the edge of the gum around your teeth bluish red or much brighter red than the adjacent gum tissue? That's an indication of inflammation, infection or periodontal disease that can lead to tooth loss. See a dentist, especially if you haven't seen one recently.

Next look at your teeth where they meet the gums. Are there any concave ridges? That's tooth erosion, and it can be aggravated by improper brushing back and forth with a hard-bristled toothbrush. Changing to a soft-bristled brush and altering your style of brushing may arrest the process.

While you've got yourself agape, check to see if you have any excessively worn tooth surfaces. If the point of one tooth is worn down, or if your lower front teeth are very worn down, you may have a bad bite or you may unknowingly be grinding your teeth at night. Your dentist can probably help you with this problem.

WATCH YOUR BACK

Now grab a hand mirror, turn around and take a good look at your back. It's very important to keep an eye on all of those rarely glimpsed lumps, bumps and blemishes, because changes in them are the signs that point to skin cancer.

"Melanoma, a particularly insidious and virulent form of skin cancer, often starts out from slightly raised skin lesions such as a mole or an age spot, and in the course of enlarging changes from a medium to a dark brown to a bluish or dark gray color," writes Herbert Haessler, M.D., of Harvard Medical School, author of *Bodyworkbook*. So any skin blemish that changes in size, color or texture should be evaluated professionally without delay, he advises.

There are also some things you can tell about your back from the front, so step back a little and turn sideways to the mirror. Granted, it's probably not the most flattering perspective, but it's a useful one. If your shoulders are very rounded or you seem very swaybacked, that can be a tip-off to future back problems. That's because bad posture can tire your muscles and make your back hurt.

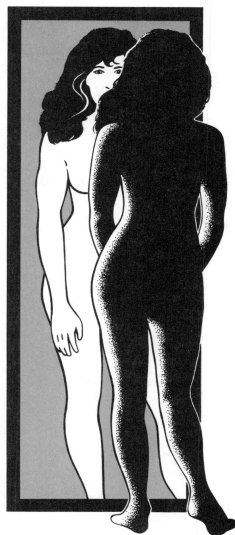

You may feel fine, but how do you look? Your mirror can sometimes be the first clue that your health is not up to par.

Unfortunately, "A potbelly or swayback may be due to weak abdominal muscles, and that can cause back pain," says Lawrence W. Friedmann, M.D., coauthor of *Freedom from Backaches*. "And if one hip is higher than the other, it means one leg is longer than the other. That causes you to limp, stressing the muscles on one side." It can also cause scoliosis. Fortunately, says Dr. Friedmann, it's easily corrected by inserting a lift into the shoe worn on the foot of the shorter leg.

"An extremely rounded upper back in the elderly can be a symptom of advanced osteoporosis," says Vicki Kalen, M.D., former director of the Spinal Diseases and Trauma Clinic at Stanford University Medical Center. "But it doesn't happen overnight. Those patients have probably been calcium deficient since early adulthood. The bones slowly get so weak they get squashed—it's called compression fractures. And surprisingly, there may be no pain. Doctors sometimes prescribe large doses of calcium, vitamin D, fluoride and estrogen to improve bone mass, but it doesn't always work." The best medicine for osteoporosis is prevention—in particular, making sure you get plenty of calcium.

ON YOUR FEET

Now lower your gaze and take a look at your feet. Do they point outward? Do your ankles appear tipped inward?

"If not treated, your feet may point out more and more over time, and your arches may become flattened," says Richard H. Baerg, D.P.M., former director of podiatric service for the Veterans Administration.

"It's something that should be assessed professionally. The abnormal motion this condition causes can contribute to the early onset of osteoarthritis in the small joints of the foot. It might also cause excessive strain on the ligaments, leading to long-term problems such as joint inflammation. Treatment with an orthotic device (a shoe insert) can properly align the bones and alleviate the problem."

But what if your knees and feet *both* point outward? Then you may be headed for a hip problem, says Dr. Baerg. "It's common in older people. The muscles around the hip become less active and there's no natural swing to their gaits. They seem to shuffle. It's a matter of allowing time to overtake your body." Engaging in a variety of muscle activities can prevent that from happening, says Dr. Baerg.

Wearing high heels for long hours over a long period can also cause leg problems. "If you look at your legs from the side, the line from the calf to the heel should have a natural curve, with an indentation above the heel," says Dr. Baerg. "If yours is more of a straight line, your calf muscles may be shortened." Exercise, stretching and gradually reducing the size of your heels can help reverse the problem.

Well, that's it. You can put your clothes back on now. Just make sure to catch a glimpse of yourself in the mirror before you go out—you may have a hair out of place.

THE TOTAL PERSON

Now face forward and look at the whole you. Are you overweight? Where? Researchers at the Medical College of Wisconsin found that women who carry their extra fat around their waists are more likely to suffer from diabetes, high blood pressure, menstrual abnormalities and gallbladder disease than women who carry their extra bulk on their hips. And a study of Swedish men found that the bigger their waists in comparison to their hips, the higher their incidence of stroke and heart disease. The researchers conclude that the distribution of fat may be a better predictor of cardiovascular disease than the amount of fat.

Does your shape tell you you're at higher risk for certain diseases? If so, follow your doctor's instructions and reduce the risk by losing weight and cutting your salt, fat and sugar intake.

Susan Zarrow

Top Tips from Top Doctors

Mothers, brothers, aunts, uncles, so-called friends. There are probably more people than you care to think about who are ready and willing to tell you how to run your life.

So, let them run your life if you like. But not your health! When it comes to your physical and mental well-being, there's no room for secondhand knowledge. Listen to the experts instead.

We went to the top doctors, seeking their best advice on matters of health. Here's what they had to say.

DON'T PANIC!

Bruce Janiak, M.D., doesn't hesitate when it comes to giving advice about emergency situations. Dr. Janiak is director of the Emergency Center at Toledo Hospital, Ohio, and past president of the American College of Emergency Physicians. His top health hints are:

● If you are unsure about whether or not to go to the emergency room with your problem, call your doctor or the emergency room and ask.
● If your child has a fever, don't panic. A fever is the body's normal response to illness; in fact, it's part of how the body heals itself. If a child has a fever of 102°F or 103°F, it's probably nothing to worry about. But watch for any changes. Call your doctor or the emergency room first before rushing to the hospital.
● Anytime you feel a sudden chest pain with shortness of breath that you aren't used to, get help immediately. Don't bother to call first, go right to the emergency room.
● If you suspect that you or someone else has accidentally swallowed poison, don't panic. Most "poisonings" aren't that dangerous. Call an emergency room or a poison control center for first-aid instructions.

LIFE WITH LESS STRESS

Emmett E. Miller, M.D., Menlo, California, specializes in helping people manage their stress. He's widely known for creating some of the first self-help tapes ever available. His are called "Software for the Mind." Here he offers some tips that will help keep you healthy in this stressful modern world.

● Find a mental island of peace at least once a day, every day, whether it's with your first cup of coffee, on your lunch break, or after dinner. Focus on how you're feeling at the moment—don't plan for the future or worry about the past.
● Do some vigorous exercise for at least 20 minutes, three times a week. The definition of vigorous exercise depends on the person; it could be walking up and down the hall or it could be running 5 miles.
● Take the time to take it easy. Periods of stress should always be followed by periods of relaxation.
● Experience love on a daily basis. It will do wonders for your heart. Don't just know that you love someone, actually feel it. You'll understand the difference if you give it a little thought. And feel your love in the presence of the other person, if possible.
● Take periodic inventories of your level of self-esteem—your self-respect, self-acceptance, and self-confidence. Be sensitive to what's happening. If you feel like you're lacking in one area, take action to correct the imbalance. Everyone knows what they need to do to have better self-esteem, but most people don't follow through on improving it. You should.
● Check your breathing periodically during the day. If it is shallow or restricted, you are tense and need to relax. If it is labored, you are exhausted. If you're breathing evenly, you are feeling good and relaxed. Enjoy it.
● Prevent back pain by building stomach muscles. About 17 percent of all Americans will develop a back disability in their lives, and 25 to 30 percent will suffer back pain at some time. Stomach exercises are the best means of prevention and cure.
● Realize what is important to you. Ask yourself, "If I were to die today, what would I want to be remembered for? What am I willing to die for?" Having a strong sense of purpose in life stops depression.

BRUSH UP ON YOUR BASICS

Care for your teeth and they should last a lifetime, says Jay Watson, D.D.S., associate dean of clinical affairs at the University of California School of Dentistry. Here are his basic tips for healthy gums and teeth.

● Brush and floss at least once a day, and after every meal if you can.
● Eat sugar only moderately, if at all, to cut down on plaque.
● Use a fluoride toothpaste and mouthwash to fight cavities, and have your teeth cleaned professionally.

TAKE IT TO HEART

The heart is perhaps the most important organ in the body, and Aram V. Chobanian, M.D., knows what makes it tick. Dr. Chobanian, a member of the Joint National Committee on the Detection, Evaluation and

Treatment of High Blood Pressure and director of the Cardiovascular Institute at Boston University Medical Center, offers these hints for a healthy heart and good blood flow.

● Keep your weight within 10 percent of your ideal weight.
● Eat less than 3 grams (1½ teaspoons) of sodium a day.
● Eat more fish and poultry than red meat and dairy products.
● Get regular exercise daily from an early age on.

THOUGHTS ON FOOD

Maria Simonson, Ph.D., Sc.D., is famous for her work with weight control and eating disorders. As professor emeritus at the Health, Weight and Stress Clinic at Johns Hopkins Medical Institutions-Good Samaritan Hospital in Baltimore, Dr. Simonson has had quite a bit of experience with people's perceptions of food. She has some good advice for everyone.

● Eat to live, but don't live to eat. That means good nutrition and balanced meals—no fad diets.
● Keep active—both mentally and physically.
● See yourself as you want to look and then try to live up to it. Because every person is governed by their body image, you should try to form a positive one.

LISTEN UP!

Ear specialist Robert A. Dobie, M.D., believes that what you hear is what you get. He's seen plenty of people damage their ears with too much sound. Dr. Dobie, a professor of otolaryngology at the University of Washington Medical School and chairman of the American Academy of Otolaryngology Subcommittee on the Medical Aspects of Noise, gives these hints for healthy ears.

● Anytime you have to raise your voice to have a good conversation, you're in an environment that's noisy enough to damage your hearing in time. Stay away from these situations, or at least protect your ears with earmuffs or earplugs. Remember, too, that noise risk isn't just loudness; it's loudness multiplied by duration. The longer you're exposed to a noise, the more dangerous the noise is.
● See a doctor if you experience any of these signs of ear disease: hearing loss, tinnitus (ringing in the ears), pain or drainage, vertigo (dizziness), facial paralysis (because the facial nerve runs through the bone of the inner ear).
● Don't put anything smaller than your elbow in your ear. That means don't use cotton swabs anywhere in your ear besides the lobe and the entrance to the canal. For earwax problems, buy an over-the-counter earwax irrigation system.
● To soothe itchy ears, put baby oil or mineral oil in your ear with an eyedropper. Itchy ears are usually caused by dry skin. Baby oil can help relieve dryness.
● If you have a problem clearing water from your ears, try putting rubbing alcohol in your clogged ear canal with an eyedropper. This will make the water evaporate. It shouldn't hurt. If it does, consider it a sign that you've got an infection or abrasion in your ear and see your doctor.
● If you are prone to ear problems when you fly in an airplane, take a decongestant an hour or so before descent. Or pop your ear by taking a deep breath, pinching your nose, closing your mouth and blowing gently toward your nose to unblock your eustachian tubes. Don't do this too hard or you'll pop your eardrums. If your face turns red, you're blowing way too hard.

GET IMMUNE TO BAD ADVICE

With all the concern these days about immune system problems, immunologist James F. Jones, M.D., says it's easy for people to fall prey to unproved methods for "boosting" the immune system. Dr. Jones, who is a member of the National Jewish Center for Immunology in Denver and associate professor of pediatrics at the University of Colorado School of Medicine, offers these sound tips for keeping your immune system healthy.

● Use common sense to keep your body healthy with good diet, exercise and self-care, and your immune system will have a better chance of staying strong.
● Be wary of diets and other regimens that are touted as sure-fire ways to boost your immune system.
● Have regular immunizations. Many adults don't think they need them, but they do. Check with your doctor for the ones that apply to you. If you have children, make sure that they are also protected.

A LONGER LOVE LIFE

Richard E. Berger, M.D., co-author of *BioPotency: A Guide to Sexual Success*, associate professor of urology at the University of Washington Medical School and director of the reproductive and sexual medicine clinic at Harborview Medical Center in Seattle, offers this advice for staying sexually healthy.

● Wear seat belts. Too many car accident victims injure their genitourinary systems because they don't follow this simple advice.
● Always use a condom when having sex to limit your exposure to sexually transmitted diseases.
● Don't smoke. It can reduce fertility and also male potency, and it is a leading cause of bladder cancer.
● Drink only moderately and don't use recreational drugs. It'll help preserve male potency.

Stephen Williams

chapter two

FOOD AND NUTRITION

Foods That Heal

It seems endless sometimes, the list of things you shouldn't eat. Your entire childhood rang with gustatory prohibitions:

"You can't have that, it's too sweet."

"No, don't eat that, it'll spoil your appetite."

"Candy's for *after,* not before—and maybe not even after if you don't straighten up and fly right, young man."

"You want your hand back, you put that soda down *now.*"

It seems a wonder that any of us can even *look* at food, let alone eat it, after our mothers get through with us. But we do, and giving credit where credit's due, our mothers probably have a lot to do with most of us keeping our teeth beyond age 40.

We, on the other hand, can take full credit for something else—the belly sticking out over our taut leather belts is entirely and absolutely *ours.*

But not to worry: Food isn't *all* bad. It keeps us alive, after all. And it can even do more than just keep the candle burning. The right foods can help us fight off a disease before it gets a foothold, and beat it back when it does.

FIGHTING DISEASE

"Foods really can't be used to *cure* most major diseases, but they can be very effective in *preventing* a wide range of them," says Brian Morgan, Ph.D., acting director of the Institute of Human Nutrition at the College of Physicians and Surgeons of Columbia University.

"Nutrition is incredibly important, really. One obvious example of the relationship between food and disease is the high-fat diet, which puts you at high risk for cancer and heart disease. A diet low in saturated fats, on the other hand, will reduce your risk of heart disease significantly, while a low-fat diet across the board—cutting back in quantity on all the different fats normally in your diet—will reduce your risk of colon, breast and uterine cancer," he says.

Low-fat eating may do more than just cut the risk. One study at the University of Southern California School of Medicine indicated that through drugs and a low-fat diet, heart disease could, in some cases, be *reversed,* something many cardiologists considered impossible.

"This study demonstrates that we now have the wherewithal to turn heart disease around in its early stages," says David Blankenhorn, M.D., the physician who served as the study's chief investigator.

THE IDEAL DIET

Here is Dr. Morgan's prescription for healthy eating.

Use proportion control. "Everyone should try to arrange their food intake so that about 15 to 20 percent is protein, 50 to 60 percent is complex carbohydrates and 20 to 30 percent is fat, he says. "The easiest way to achieve this balance of foods is just to make sure you eat balanced meals containing fresh fruits and vegetables, poultry and fish rather than just a 'meat and potatoes' diet."

Get your fiber. "It seems clear that a high intake of insoluble fiber will reduce your risk of colon cancer and, less seriously, uncomfortable things like constipation," he says. Good sources of insoluble fiber are wheat bran, nuts and green vegetables like cabbage, broccoli and brussels sprouts.

Eat your vegetables. Vegetables containing beta-carotene, that is. "Anything that's red, like a tomato, orange, like a carrot, yellow, like squash, or dark green, like broccoli, has a lot of beta-carotene in it," says Dr. Morgan. "Beta-carotene is a substance your body uses to manufacture vitamin A, and it appears that a diet high in beta-carotene will help protect against most types of cancer."

In fact, researchers at the State University of New York at Buffalo compared the diets of 450 people with lung cancer to the diets of over 900 healthy people. They found that the people afflicted by lunger cancer had a significantly lower beta-carotene intake than that of the healthy group.

Play it safe with antioxidants. "It's starting to look like certain types of cancer are caused by free radicals, which are very active molecules that may act as irritants powerful enough to cause cancer," says Dr. Morgan. "Antioxidants—the most powerful is vitamin E, followed by vitamin C—which help prevent free radical formation, should probably be well represented in the diet."

Good food sources of E and C include wheat germ oil and sunflower seeds for E, citrus fruits and brussels sprouts for C. Beta-carotene, incidentally, also soaks up free radicals, although it's not known if that's the major cancer-prevention mechanism involved in its effects.

Eat fish on more than Fridays. "The omega-3 fatty acids found in fish oils appear to be protective against heart disease, probably by cutting

Health Food—Or Fraud?

Some of the all-time classics of the health food industry may not be class acts at all, says nutrition expert Brian Morgan, Ph.D.

Honey. "This is just fancy sugar, made from 2 molecules instead of 1. It has absolutely no special advantages over regular refined sugar. People mention trace elements, but they're present in insignificant amounts."

Brewer's yeast. "It is a good source of B-complex vitamins (except B_{12}) and it has a significant amount of chromium, but it produces gas—lots of it—and tastes pretty rough."

Carob. "This is a good source of fiber, but it's not so good in another way. If you're going to give your child sweets, it's better to give them chocolate instead of carob, because chocolate has cocoa bean oil in it, which protects the teeth from acids. Carob doesn't."

Kelp. "Vastly overrated. We get most of the iodine we need from other sources just as effectively. It might contribute some fiber, but it's otherwise not very useful."

---

blood cholesterol and triglyceride levels—both significant risk factors for heart disease," says Dr. Morgan. "A small number of studies also indicate that it may help alleviate arthritis and other inflammatory diseases of the joints by reducing inflammation."

Daily doses of fish oil led to modest but significant improvement in the symptoms of rheumatoid arthritis patients studied at Harvard Medical School and Albany Medical College. These were the first studies to show definite clinical effects of fish oil on an inflammatory disease.

But you don't have to eat a lot of fish to get the benefits. The evidence we have now seems to indicate that someone who eats fish about three times a week gets the maximum protection, says Dr. Morgan.

SPECIFIC FOODS

Here are recommendations from Dr. Morgan for foods with healing potential.

Broccoli. A good source of fiber and beta-carotene that's also high in vitamin C (the cancer-fighting antioxidant).

Pectin-rich fruits, such as apples, grapefruit and oranges. "The various pectins have been shown generally to help reduce blood cholesterol levels," says Dr. Morgan. And although citrus fruits are the best natural sources, you have to be willing to eat the pith, or white parts lining the skin. "Realistically," says Dr. Morgan, "the most effective way to get enough to do you any good is to add it to desserts." If you want to try his suggestion, you can find pectin in the supermarket under the brand names Sure-Jell and Certo.

Oats. Oats in any form are an excellent source of fiber that have been shown to have a significant impact on blood cholesterol levels.

Peppers, all sorts. They are incredibly high in vitamin C.

Potatoes, including the sweet potato. Potatoes are basically a starch, without much fiber unless you eat the skin. They are, however, good sources of vitamin C, and the sweet potato is high in beta-carotene. And they may also help protect you against stroke.

Garlic and onions. "Garlic and onions may have the ability to lower blood cholesterol levels, but the evidence isn't overwhelming," says Dr. Morgan.

Low-fat yogurt. "It's a good source of calcium that's also very low in fat," says Dr. Morgan. So, what's so great about calcium? Well, it helps build stronger bones, for one thing.

And two Dutch studies have confirmed the findings of at least three earlier ones. They found that more calcium in the diet correlates with lower blood pressure.

Leafy, dark green vegetables. They're high in beta-carotene and have significant amounts of iron and fiber.

Liver. "Liver's great, lots of B-complex vitamins, lots of iron and good protein," says Dr. Morgan. "The only problem with liver is that it has lots of cholesterol. Avoid it if you know you already have a problem with high cholesterol levels. If not, and you like it—enjoy."

Soybeans and soy products. "A great source of protein, soluble fiber, and B-complex vitamins (except B_{12})," notes Dr. Morgan. For vegetarians, soy can be important: It's a complete protein all by itself.

Soybeans have one of the highest concentrations of protease inhibitors of any food. There is some evidence that these compounds may help cells in a precancerous stage revert to normal. Cells stay normal even after the protease treatment is stopped. Once a cell becomes cancerous, protease inhibitors can no longer help, however.

Kim Anderson

A Dieter's Guide to Easy Weight Loss

If Aladdin's lamp found its way into your hands, would you include losing weight in your list of three wishes?

The rub with losing weight is that we're usually better at wishing for slimness than attaining it. And sometimes we even try too hard, going on a rigid reducing regimen that eventually leaves our resolve limp as a rag. Here's a suggestion with a lot less potential for backfiring: Take it easy.

"Your extra weight is the final result of many small behavioral acts, things like eating between meals or driving to places only two blocks away," explains Kelly Brownell, Ph.D., co-director of the Obesity Research Center at the University of Pennsylvania. "So you can lose weight by making many small, clever changes—in diet, exercise and attitude."

For slow but sure weight loss, draft into your daily habits as many of the following little ways to lose weight as you can. We say little because any single one probably won't make much difference. But together they can change your behavior just enough to get you eating better, moving more— and losing more!

The "Am I Hungry?" Rating System

"I'm hungry."

We say this for the oddest reasons: because it's noon (lunchtime), because we're at Mom's (her meals make us feel loved), because we're feeling harassed (cookies help us cope). What do the clock, Mom or frustration have to do with your feelings of hunger?

Nothing, says Judy Wardell, author of *Thin Within*. The "I" of "I'm hungry" is your conscious self responding to external cues. What you feel is appetite, a psychological urge. Real hunger is physiological; it's your body's way of requesting more fuel. Hunger is the only cue you should respond to.

To eat when you're hungry and to eat only as much as your body needs, use a "0 to 5 eating scale," Wardell urges. "On a scale of 0 to 10—0 being empty, 5 being comfortable and 10 being stuffed—at what level of hunger is your body right now?" she asks.

This is your first hunger reading. Keep it in mind. From now on, you're going to start eating only when you're at 0, and you're going to eat only to 5—the point of comfort. "Instead of listening to everyone else about your weight problems," Wardell says, "listen to the wisest authority of all—your body."

1. Go grocery shopping on a full stomach. Nacho chips, doughnuts and other tempters won't have half the allure they would if you hunted through those aisles hungry.

2. Shop from a list of necessities. Allow yourself only one purchase that wasn't preplanned.

3. Take only a limited amount of money to the grocery store as an extra reinforcement against buying high-calorie foods.

4. Invite your spouse or housemate into the kitchen with you when you're preparing meals and cleaning up to keep you from sampling as you go.

5. Don't eat foods out of their original containers. You may think you're having "just a tad," but you'll probably consume more than if you had dished out the food in a measured portion.

6. Don't keep your "weakness food" in stock. Present yourself with the hassle of going to the store for single servings if you can't fight off a craving. This way you'll either get some exercise (especially if you walk to the store) or you'll decide the snack isn't worth the bother after all.

7. Remove food stashed in inappropriate places. Get the candy bars out of your desk drawer and remove the nut bowl from the coffee table.

8. Downscale your brand of ice cream. If it'll be a cold day in Key West before your freezer doesn't have a carton of this confection waiting for you, buy the least expensive or a reduced-fat brand. Your intake of fat and calories will be considerably lower than if you eat the gourmet kind.

9. Eat only at scheduled times in scheduled places.

10. Use good plate psychology. Don't use place settings with intense colors such as violet, lime green, bright yellow or bright blue; they're thought to stimulate the appetite. The same goes for primitive-looking pewter and wooden plates. Instead, appease your appetite with elegant place settings in darker colors. Choose plates with broad decorative borders and concave middles. You can fit less food in them.

11. Have someone else serve you, and ask for smaller portions.

12. Police your eating speed by putting your fork down between bites. You will have eaten less food by the time you feel full.

13. Establish a time-out routine halfway through your meals. One trick: Put a large pot of water on the stove when you sit down to eat. When it boils (in about 10 or 15 minutes), get up and make a pot of herb tea. When you go back to the table, you probably won't feel like eating much more.

14. Chew each bite of food at least ten times to really taste it and to make yourself eat more slowly.

15. Use whipped or softened butter or margarine. You'll spread the flavor around using a lot less than if it were hard and you had to scrape it on.

16. Share desserts if skipping them is unthinkable.

17. Leave the table as soon as you're finished eating instead of lingering over the last bites.

18. Don't skip meals. You'll only overeat later.

19. Swear off elevators and escalators. Take the stairs.

20. Forget about hiring a house-cleaner and do the work yourself. Depending on your body weight, studies show you can burn 195 to 305

Fiery Foods Cremate Calories

Here's one of the easiest weight-loss tips you're likely to ever come across: Spice up your diet. According to one study, foods that burn your mouth also burn up extra calories.

After eating any food, your metabolic rate rises. But hot spices boost postmeal metabolism by an extra 25 percent, say researchers at Oxford Polytechnic in England.

They figured this out by feeding 12 people 766-calorie meals. The meals were the same, except that some were spiked with 3 grams each of chili and mustard sauce. Those who ate the spicy food burned up an extra 45 calories in 3 hours, on the average. Some people burned as much as 76 extra calories!

"It's an exciting observation, that hot foods have the potential for increasing metabolic rate," says the principal researcher, C. J. K. Henry, Ph.D. She cautions, however, that the findings warrant more study. She also points out that not all hot spices seem to burn more calories—ginger, for example, has no effect on metabolism.

calories for each hour you spend washing windows, mopping floors and doing other tasks.

21. De-automate your housework and make your body work harder. Wash dishes, mix batters and open cans by hand, hang your wash on the line instead of using a dryer.

22. Exercise during television commercials. Those 3-minute spurts will keep you out of the kitchen.

23. Go out dancing, miniature golfing, bowling—anything active—if

you normally sit around and play bridge or watch television. The most calories you can burn in an hour playing cards is 95, but waltzing can whisk away 195 to 305 for every hour on the floor, and an hour of square dancing can stomp away 330 to 510 calories.

24. Drink no-calorie sparkling waters when you're out, instead of alcoholic beverages.

25. Get rid of those degrading signs and pictures on your refrigerator—no 300-pound women in bikinis or pink pigs on beach blankets to shame you into not eating. Your will power will be stronger from encouragement, not belittlement.

26. Learn that it's okay to say "No, thank you" when other people offer you food.

27. Hold a conference and explain your weight-loss wish to family, friends or doughnut-bearing co-workers. Ask them to understand if you turn down their dinners or candy.

28. Set a realistic goal for yourself. "Take it one day at a time and don't punish yourself for slipping," says Suzann Johnson, a registered dietitian and nutritionist with Weight Watchers International. "You'll be more successful if you remember to be your own best friend."

Maria Mihalik

Blood Pressure Control

Go hug a farmer. Why? Because the prescription to keep your blood pressure down may be growing in his fields and orchards. Or grazing in his pastures.

Potassium, abundant in fresh fruits and vegetables, and calcium, found largely in dairy products, may be science's latest dietary one-two punch in the fight against hypertension.

Researchers have found that people whose diets are potassium-rich — vegetarians, for example — have a low incidence of hypertension even if they're genetically disposed to the condition and don't control their salt intake.

On the other hand, researchers have also found that people with high blood pressures don't seem to get much calcium in the form of dairy products — and it's hard to get much without them.

In one test, for example, people who were mildly hypertensive and had lower levels of serum calcium experienced a moderate but consistent drop in blood pressure when they were given oral calcium supplements. The biggest improvement was seen in those people who had the lowest levels of calcium to start with.

How do these nutrients regulate blood pressure? The exact mechanisms continue to evade researchers. But scientists suspect that they help the body slough off excess sodium and assist in controlling the workings of the vascular system.

A DIET THAT'S EASY TO SWALLOW

As important as these two nutrients are, it's nice that they're so easy to work into a menu. You can even get them — deliciously — in the same dish. Or build a diet around the foods they're in. All it takes is a little knowledge and a lot of ingenuity.

Getting potassium isn't tough because it's in almost everything. Fruits, vegetables, beans, fish, poultry and lean cuts of meat are loaded with it. But getting calcium is not quite as easy. Unfortunately, the foods that contain the most calcium also tend to contain a fair amount of fat and sodium, which can spell trouble for hypertensives on fat- and salt-controlled diets.

But difficult does not mean impossible. Here's the way experts suggest you design your own antihypertension diet.

Exercise your ingenuity. Look at the lists of potassium- and calcium-rich foods in the accompanying table. Keep in mind that dairy products — milk, cheese, yogurt — are great sources of calcium. (Since dairy products are high in fat, though, look for low-fat choices.) Now let your mind start combining familiar foods: low-fat milk with bananas, canned salmon with potatoes and broccoli, raisins with yogurt. Imagine half a cantaloupe filled with a scoop of ice milk or ricotta cheese. Think about a summer cooler made in the blender from orange juice, bananas and nonfat dry milk. Before you crack open a cookbook, experiment with your own combinations.

Go to the library. Look for low-calorie, low-fat and low-sodium cookbooks. Regular cookbooks are fine if you're the kind of inventive chef who knows how to substitute low-fat products for high-fat ones and doctor high-salt recipes so the taste doesn't vanish.

If you're not, your best bets are cookbooks whose authors have controlled the amount of fat, calories and sodium for you. Three of our favorites are *The Calcium Bible*, by Patricia Hausman, *The New American Diet*, by William E. Conner, M.D., and Sonja L. Conner, and *The Lose Weight Naturally Cookbook*, by Sharon Claessens and the Rodale Food Center.

Double your pleasure. Not only can you get potassium and calcium in the same dish, you can get them in the same food. Here are a few of the foods that are high in both nutrients: sardines, skim milk, broccoli, canned salmon with bones, buttermilk, whole milk, soybeans, blackstrap molasses, navy beans, almonds, ice milk and yogurt. If you're exercising your ingenuity, you can probably put together a whole meal literally from soup to nuts using just a few of these double-duty foods.

Stock up on low-fat yogurt. Not only is it low in fat and relatively low in sodium, it's high in calcium and potassium and can be used for everything from salad dressing to dessert. To get an even higher shot of calcium, nutritionists suggest, look for low-fat yogurt to which the manufacturer has added nonfat milk solids, thus adding considerably more calcium and no more fat. You can also zip up plain yogurt by adding potassium-rich foods such as frozen orange juice concentrate, raisins, sliced fresh fruit or shredded raw vegetables.

If you're not a yogurt fan, you can get all of its benefits by hiding it in cold soups and blender shakes. Add fresh fruit and a little honey and blend them all together.

Add nonfat dry milk wherever you can. Two tablespoons of nonfat

Foods That Fight Hypertension

Lower your blood pressure with these potassium-rich foods.

Food	Portion	Potassium (mg)
Potato, baked	1 med.	610
Avocado	½	602
Raisins	½ cup	545
Orange juice	1 cup	496
Banana	1	451
Apricots, dried	¼ cup	448
Squash, winter, cooked	½ cup	445
Cantaloupe	¼ med.	413
Milk, skim*	1 cup	406
Sweet potato, baked	1 med.	397
Buttermilk*	1 cup	370
Milk, whole*	1 cup	370
Great Northern beans	½ cup	344
Sirloin, trimmed of fat	3 oz.	342
Haddock	3 oz.	339
Round steak, trimmed of fat	3 oz.	336
Salmon fillet, fresh, cooked	3 oz.	319
Sardines, drained, with bones*	3 oz.	319
Apricots, fresh	3	313
Perch	3 oz.	293
Flounder	3 oz.	292
Pork, trimmed of fat	3 oz.	283
Leg of lamb, trimmed of fat	3 oz.	274
Tuna, drained	3 oz.	267
Turkey	3 oz.	255
Tomato, raw	1	254
Cod	3 oz.	208
Beef liver	3 oz.	200
Chicken	3 oz.	198
Broccoli, cooked*	½ cup	127

SOURCES: Adapted from Agriculture Handbook Nos. 8-1, 8-5, 8-9, 8-11, 8-13, 8-15, 8-16, 456 (Washington, D.C.: U.S. Department of Agriculture).

*Also high in calcium.

dry milk added to half a glass of skim milk boost the calcium from 150 milligrams to 255 milligrams. Add a banana, and you've got a supercharged potassium/calcium breakfast.

Substitute with ricotta cheese. While cottage cheese and fruit may be a favorite lunch, you can substantially increase the amount of calcium in the meal by substituting ricotta. Though it also has more fat and calories than cottage cheese, ricotta has about 260 milligrams of calcium in ½ cup, compared to only about 80 milligrams in cottage cheese. You can cut out some fat by using part-skim ricotta or by mixing it with low-fat cottage cheese. It's great with high-potassium vegetables, too.

Try a stir-fry pizza. Make your own pizza dough—or buy it ready-made—but don't go for the usual toppings. Try vegetables like carrots, onions, peppers and broccoli, either stir-fried in a bit of oil or steamed. Top with part-skim mozzarella and bake as usual.

Try canned pink salmon. Salmon is high in potassium and calcium —because of the tiny bones you eat— and mixes well with cheese and vegetables. Served hot with vegetables or as the star of a cold vegetable-pasta salad, salmon can become a staple of your blood pressure diet.

Use tofu and beans. If you have to restrict your dairy intake, soyfoods such as tofu and some cooked beans can provide a modest amount of calcium. Tofu in particular can be used in place of cheese in many dishes. It has 232 milligrams of calcium per 4-ounce serving. And it also comes packaged as Tofutti, which looks and tastes a lot like ice cream.

Denise Foley

Cooking for a Healthy Heart

Heart disease used to be something that just "happened" to you. You could blame it on genes, getting older or just about any other handy excuse, but there wasn't a whole lot you could do about it. These days we know better. We know that smoking, inactivity and, especially, poor food choices may multiply our risk many times over.

In 1961, the American Heart Association (AHA) delivered its first dietary guidelines to an overweight public, and the organization has since encouraged Americans to cut back on cholesterol, salt, saturated fats, total fats and excess calories and to fill up on the goodness of whole grains, vegetables, fruits, low-fat dairy products, lean meats, fish and poultry.

THE HEART FACTS

Here, AHA experts guide you through the essentials of a heart-healthy diet.

Cut back on fat. Total fats should account for less than 30 percent of all your calories, experts now say.

This figure represents a decrease from previous recommendations of 30 to 35 percent. Since the average American still gets about 40 percent of his daily calories from fat, 10 percent of the calories you would normally eat as fat (200 to 270 calories) should probably be either cut out or replaced by other sources, such as carbohydrates.

Limit—above all—saturated fats. Not all fats are created equal. Saturated fats are the most likely to lead to heart problems; they should make up no more than 10 percent of your total calories. For most people, this means cutting their saturated fat intake in half. A man eating 2,700 calories a day, for example, should keep his saturated fat intake to 30 grams, the equivalent of about 2 tablespoons of pure saturated fat. For a woman eating 2,000 calories a day, that's 22 grams of fat or about 1½ tablespoons.

You can probably meet this requirement by cutting back on fatty red meat, butter, dairy fats and highly saturated vegetable fats like coconut and palm oil, found in processed foods such as nondairy creamers, and baked goods.

Of the remaining 20 percent of fat calories, less than half should come from polyunsaturates (like safflower oil and corn oil) and the remainder should come from monounsaturates (like olive oil).

Save the eggs for Easter. Cholesterol intake should be less than 100 milligrams per 1,000 calories, not to exceed a total of 300 milligrams per day. Most people get that much cholesterol now in the meat, dairy and baked products they eat. Since even one egg has almost 300 milligrams of

Say Sayonara to Cholesterol

Tofu or not tofu? It's often hard to tell.

Grab another bite of that hot dog. Another smidgeon of that manicotti. Swallow. Now tell. Is it real beef? Real mozzarella? Or are you being snowed by that winter-white oriental master of disguise, tofu? Your palate may be fooled, but your heart can tell the difference.

Tofu is one of several foods from around the world that health-conscious Americans are starting to incorporate into their diets.

Medical researchers at the University of North Carolina now say that if you haven't discovered the Japanese import yet, perhaps you should— especially if your blood cholesterol level is higher than it should be. They base their recommendation on a recent study comparing the soy-derived jack-of-all-trades to the cow-derived Monterey Jack.

In a recent study, 12 vegetarian men were asked to change their normal diets in only 1 way: no cheese; tofu instead. The results? "Pretty dramatic," says Michael Liebman, Ph.D., one of the study's authors. Abstaining from cheese while feasting on tofu manicotti, tofu omelets and grilled tofu sandwiches, the men saw their cholesterol levels drop an average of 11 percent over a 3-week period.

That's not to say you should scrap your new cheese grater. Dairy products are important, and not all cheese-eaters have elevated cholesterol levels, says Dr. Liebman. But if you do, says Carolyn Dunn, coauthor of the study, then "substituting tofu for cheese could result in a significant drop" in your cholesterol level—and in your risk of heart disease.

Low-Fat Eating: Get on Target

"Low-fat" has become practically synonymous with "health"—and for good reason. High-fat diets have been implicated in a host of diseases, including heart disease.

The American Heart Association suggests eating no more than 30 percent of your calories as fat. But what does a diet of 30 percent fat look like in the real world of steak au poivre and créme caramel?

Here's a start. The target pictured here shows high-fat foods at its outer edges and lower-fat foods toward its center. If your buying habits lean mainly to outer-limits foods, you can assume your diet's going to be on the outer limits of fat content. But if your buying hovers toward the center, you can trust you're in territory that's going to make for a healthier lifestyle.

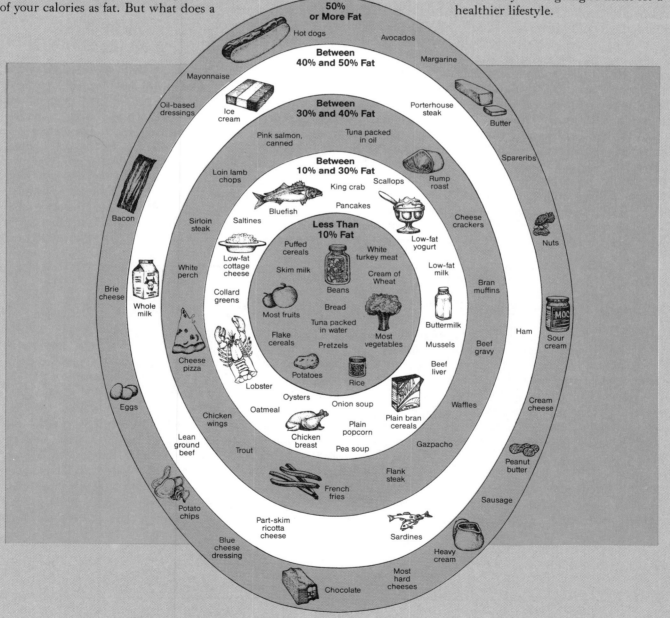

50% or More Fat
Hot dogs · Avocados · Margarine · Mayonnaise · Porterhouse steak · Oil-based dressings · Ice cream · Butter · Spareribs · Bacon · Nuts · Brie cheese · Whole milk · Cheese crackers · Eggs · Ham · Sour cream · Cheese pizza · Cream cheese · Potato chips · Peanut butter · Lean ground beef · Sausage · Blue cheese dressing · Heavy cream · Chocolate · Most hard cheeses

Between 40% and 50% Fat

Between 30% and 40% Fat
Pink salmon, canned · Tuna packed in oil · Loin lamb chops · Rump roast · Sirloin steak · White perch · Chicken wings · Trout · Part-skim ricotta cheese · Sardines · Flank steak · Gazpacho · Waffles

Between 10% and 30% Fat
Scallops · King crab · Pancakes · Bluefish · Saltines · Low-fat cottage cheese · Collard greens · Most fruits · Flake cereals · Lobster · Oysters · Oatmeal · Chicken breast · French fries

Less Than 10% Fat
Puffed cereals · White turkey meat · Skim milk · Cream of Wheat · Beans · Low-fat yogurt · Low-fat milk · Bread · Tuna packed in water · Most vegetables · Buttermilk · Pretzels · Mussels · Beef gravy · Beef liver · Potatoes · Rice · Onion soup · Plain bran cereals · Plain popcorn · Pea soup

cholesterol, eggs are obviously something to limit—to about two whole eggs per week.

Note that cholesterol and saturated fat are not the same thing. Although these two substances very often occur in the same foods, this is not *always* the case. Some foods that are high in cholesterol are low in saturated fat, and vice versa.

A classic example is shellfish. Lobster, scallops and oysters have been blacklisted by doctors for years because they contain about twice as much cholesterol as red meat or poultry. But they also contain virtually no saturated fat. If you take *both* cholesterol and saturated fat into consideration, shellfish are a better dietary choice than even the leanest red meats.

Don't be concerned about protein. "High in protein!" many food commercials boast. In fact, protein intake should be approximately 15 percent of calories and, for the average American, this figure is just about right. Unless you're a professional bodybuilder or are under doctor's orders to up the protein, there's little reason for concern.

Crank up the carbohydrates. Carbohydrates should make up 50 percent or more of calories, with emphasis on increasing intake of complex carbohydrates like whole grains, beans, vegetables and fruit. Right now most Americans get about 40 percent of their calories from carbohydrates, and about one-third of that is from sugar.

Sprinkle no salt. Sodium intake should be reduced to approximately 1 gram per 1,000 calories, not to exceed 3 grams per day (that's 1½ level teaspoons of salt). This is far less than the 6 to 8 grams a day the average American consumes. Not using salt in cooking or at the table and avoiding high-salt foods can help you cut sodium intake back to 2 grams.

Cut the booze. Alcoholic beverages should be limited to no more than two beers or two glasses of wine a day. People who have more than three drinks a day experience a significant increase in blood pressure. Even moderate drinking can pile on the calories.

Eat a varied diet. A wide variety of foods should be eaten. The more varied your diet, the better your assurance that you get all the vitamins, minerals and other essential nutrients you need. Keeping your food selections varied and interesting also helps you to stick with your new health-promoting diet. Also, restricting total calories to what you need to maintain your ideal body weight should be part of your eating program.

HOW TO BE A SMART SHOPPER

Now that we've covered the basics, take a stroll down the cool, fluorescent-lit, linoleum aisles of a typical supermarket with dietitian, author and American Heart Association volunteer Leni Reed Riley of Dallas. Be forewarned, though: If you usually fill your squeaky metal cart with Fritos, Dr. Pepper and Slim Jims, your shopping habits are going to have to change.

Riley conducts her Supermarket Savvy Tour in a well-stocked grocery

A Lesson from the Eskimos

By all rights, the Eskimos of Greenland ought to be prime candidates for coronaries and strokes before their 40s, but they aren't. Besides their remarkably low incidence of heart disease, they don't have the skyrocketing blood cholesterol levels that in Western man lead to atherosclerosis, a condition responsible for 1 out of every 2 deaths in the United States. In fact, a Greenland Eskimo is almost as likely to die of a nosebleed as of a heart attack.

One reason for this enviable good fortune may be something called eicosapentaenoic acid, abbreviated EPA.

It's what's known as an omega-3 fatty acid, and it's plentiful in the oily, cold-water fish the Eskimos love.

Studies have found that EPA may lower blood cholesterol considerably—even more than polyunsaturated fat does. It also triggers a major drop in triglycerides, another blood fat linked to heart disease.

While you're unlikely to get a doctor's prescription for mackerel or salmon—the 2 fish highest in EPA—eating fish once or twice a week could reduce your heart attack risk.

What if you don't like or are aller-gic to fish? Nutritionists now tell us that there are *plant* sources of omega-3 fatty acids. They're abundant in walnuts, soybeans, tofu, many common beans, wheat germ oil and rapeseed oil. The lettucelike vegetable purslane appears to be especially rich in omega-3's. Used extensively in soups and salads in some Mediterranean countries, the vegetable is thought by some scientists to be one of the reasons that rates of heart disease in these countries are so low.

store. Her tour is an aisle-by-aisle course in reading labels, interpreting advertising claims and learning which foods contain reasonably low amounts of fat, salt, cholesterol and calories.

Riley, president of a supermarket consulting firm, emphasizes that "there are ways to cut corners and time and still eat very nutritiously."

Here's how it's done.

Pick a peck of pita. Choose among these bread products: For *little to no fat*, pick pita bread (preferably whole grain), rice cakes or unfried corn tortillas. For *low fat*, buy whole grain or partially whole grain breads, sandwich buns or English muffins. Other low-fat breads include Italian, French and water bagels (not egg bagels).

Flip away fat. For low-fat pancakes and waffles, choose whole wheat or partially whole wheat mixes. Then, according to directions, add a polyunsaturated oil and substitute two egg whites for each whole egg. Cook on a nonstick skillet or waffle iron, greased with just a little bit of an acceptable oil, such as olive or corn.

Plan a healthy morning. Choose cooked cereals that you can make without salt (grits, mixed grain, oatmeal, rice and wheat) or cold cereals such as puffed rice, puffed wheat or shredded wheat. Avoid instant cereals, because they generally contain sodium.

Note that granola cereals often have at least twice as many calories as most other cereals. Avoid those granolas made with coconut oil, palm oil or vegetable shortening—the catchall term for vegetable oils, be they polyunsaturated like soybean and corn or saturated like coconut and palm.

Make soup simple. Make a can of low-sodium broth (beef or chicken) into a quick, healthy meal by adding fresh or frozen vegetables, cooked chicken chunks or diced tofu, fresh or dried herbs and a little sherry, freshly grated ginger and/or hot pepper sauce.

Dilution is the solution. Delicatessen items, usually high in fat and salt, can still be adapted to a healthy menu. With chicken or tuna salad, for instance, add more vegetables and pasta or rice to dilute the mayonnaise.

How low can you go? When you see labels that say "lower" or "reduced" fat, salt or sugar, "you should ask 'lower than or reduced from what?' " Riley says. A package of chicken franks, for instance, says "lower fat," but the label shows that 72 of the 90 calories in one frank are from fat. "Since that's lower fat, you can imagine what regular is like. Sliced boneless breast of turkey or lean ham would be a much better choice.

"You can rinse much of the salt and sodium nitrite off the ham with cold water," she says. Be sure to use the ham immediately, however, because the salt and sodium nitrite act as preservatives.

Let's be frank. Don't assume that all-beef hot dogs are made from lean beef. All-beef hot dogs actually contain just as much fat as regular hot dogs.

You needn't desert dessert. Most frozen yogurt desserts are much lower in fat than frozen tofu desserts, which may contain corn, palm or coconut oil. But don't expect frozen yogurt to be much lower in calories than most ice creams. What they lack in fat, they make up in sugar. The new fruit sorbets are a delicious, low-calorie alternative to ice cream.

Check the jar. Look for no-salt or lightly salted peanut butters without hydrogenated oils added to them.

Pick up some of these spicer-uppers. Your supermarket stocks little items that can easily substitute for the butter, oil, sugar and salt that we typically add to our diets for a little extra taste. Try these.

● Hot spices. Tex-Mex and Cajun cooking adapt well to low-fat, low-salt methods because the strong spicy flavors need no help.

● Mustard. Brush on broiled fish or chicken. Add a little paprika, red pepper or parsley.

● Pineapple, mandarin oranges or other fruits. Use in chicken dishes. Try orange juice concentrate on broiled fish or chicken. Instead of piling on the mayo, add mango, papaya, a few pine nuts and a little honey to chicken salad. A fruit salad dressing of pureed bananas, yogurt, poppyseed and orange juice contains only 30 calories a tablespoon.

● Extracts. Known by names such as coconut, almond, vanilla and rum, these can boost the flavor of that cake, pie or pudding while you cut back on salt, fat and sugar.

● Cinnamon and fruit butters. On hot cereals they make a sensible alternative to butter and milk.

You can still have an occasional bag of Fritos, and maybe even a Slim Jim from time to time, but for a healthy heart, fill your cart with the nutritional products you'll only find off the junk-food aisle.

Stocking the Healthy Kitchen

We like to think of our kitchen as a warm, inviting hearthstone—the center of good feelings, good smells, good tastes and, best of all, good health.

The secret of it all, of course, is in the food—food that conjures up thoughts of memorable meals and happy times. Good food means good home cooking. And that starts with your kitchen tools.

Today's tools have come a long way from the iron and stainless steel your mother and grandmother used when they cooked for you. A lot of modern gadgets are designed to cut down on fats and calories, which contributes to a healthy body. Others are made to cut down on time, which contributes to a healthy mind, as in: "Hey, I don't *mind* cooking!"

Equipment for a healthy kitchen can be as minimal as a steam basket, a wok and two or three heavy pans (preferably nonstick for fat-free cooking). But with space, budget and taste allowing, your kitchen collection can expand to include those simplistic to high-tech items designed (sometimes unintentionally) to make your food preparation more nutritious.

Here's the best in healthy cookware, recommended by the experts.

1. Blender—Its multiple functions make it practical to have on hand, especially for pureeing vegetables or soups or for whipping up low-calorie drinks.

2. Cast-iron pans—Everyone needs iron in their diets, and using cast-iron pans is one easy way to help you get a little extra. Make sure you have at least one ridged pan that allows accumulated fat to collect in its grooves instead of in the food's fibers.

3. Coffee grinder—Sure it grinds coffee beans, but it can also chop fresh spices, garlic and shallots.

4. Double boiler—Yes, this utensil is good for more than melting chocolate. It helps warm up leftovers, like potatoes, vegetables or meat casseroles, without using butter or oil. It is also handy in making the lighter sauces that are part of the healthy cook's repertoire.

5. Electric juicer—Anyone who's ever tasted freshly squeezed orange or grapefruit juice knows what a wonderful device this can be. But its importance to the healthy cook goes beyond good taste. By squeezing your own juice, you'll retain some of the all-important fiber that is strained out of commercial brands. There are some juicers made to handle heavier tasks, like turning such things as apples and carrots and other vegetables into drinkable health.

6. Fat skimmer—This handy little gadget, which somewhat resembles a miniature mop, lifts the fat from soups and stews as they cook, making for leaner meals.

7. Fish poacher—This piece of cookware might seem a bit extravagant for anyone but the true fish-lover. But buying fish fresh and cooking it whole in an aromatic poaching liquid just might be the key to turning finicky eaters into fish fanciers. Poaching needs no fat and keeps fish moist. And anyone tuned into nutrition doesn't need to be told the healthful potential of adding fish to your diet at least three times a week.

8. Food processor—It cuts food preparation time by more than half! It is especially good for slicing, chopping and shredding such things as cabbage, carrots, onions, mushrooms and the numerous assorted vegetables you'll want to use to add fiber and nutrition to meals and to cut down on the need for meat in stir-fries and stews. When possible, process vegetables after they're blanched to minimize vitamin loss.

9. Food scale—Is that 3 ounces of meat you're adding to that stir-fry, or is it more like 10 ounces? Looks can be deceiving, especially for those whose stomachs are bigger than their eyes. A food scale measures exactly how closely you're sticking to your food plan.

10. Gravy skimmer—An essential measuring cup that separates fat from the natural juices emitted during long roasting. It leaves you with a healthier, fat-free base for gravies and sauces.

11. Hot-air popcorn popper—No oil goes in this electric popcorn maker, which can turn out a hot, wholesome and low-calorie snack in a matter of minutes. And it takes up less room than a can of pretzels or a bag of potato chips.

12. Immersion blender—It's a hand-held blender/beater/whipper. This new-age appliance will puree vegetables into an instant sauce or dressing right in the bottom of the salad bowl; make low-cholesterol mayonnaise right in the jar; whip low-fat, creamy sauces right in the sauce boat; beat up low-calorie, high-calcium yogurt shakes right in the glass; puree soups right in the pot or make baby foods right in the jar.

13. Meat loaf pan—We don't mean the one passed down to you from Grandma. The modern version has an inner pan that is ridged and perforated to let fat drain into an outer pan as it cooks. What you get is a meat loaf with less fat and fewer calories.

14. Microwave oven—It's almost a health necessity! Used properly, it goes a long way to preserve nutrients and cut back on fat in cooking. (To discover the many healthy uses for your microwave oven, see "Healthy Microwave Cooking" on page 88.)

15. Nonstick pans—You should have at least two. These pans allow you to sauté without the addition of any fat.

16. Pastry brush—It's good for much more than pastry. Use it to spread a thin coating of unsaturated fat on breads and muffins for browning or for dabbing meats and fish with no-fat marinades to add moisture and flavor.

17. Peanut butter machine—If you have children who seem to live on peanut butter, this is the machine that will help ease the guilt of spreading out that creamy (and fatty) richness. By making your own, you can avoid the sugars and hydrogenated fats that are often added to commercial brands.

18. Polyethylene cutting board —This surface is nonabsorbent, odorless and will not blunt knives or chip or crack. It can be sterilized in the dishwasher and will not hold bacteria as wooden cutting boards do.

19. Pressure cooker—Pressure cookers have been around for a long time, and for good reason. Pressure cooking is healthy because it retains more nutrients than conventional

cooking. It's fast because it can cook soups, stews, pot roasts and potatoes in half the time of conventional cooking. The state-of-the-art version offers even more—it's quiet and has built-in safety mechanisms.

20. Refrigerator thermometer— Protect your foods from spoilage by keeping the freezer temperature at 0°F and the refrigerator at about 40°F.

21. Roasting rack—If you're a meat-lover, you shouldn't be without one. Placing your meat on a rack in the roasting pan allows the meat to sit above rather than in the fat that's seeping from the meat. For chicken, there is a vertical roaster that permits heat to penetrate from all sides for a crisper, moister, lower-fat bird.

22. Rolling mincer—For those little jobs. The five sharp, circular blades in this hand tool quickly mince fresh herbs and parsley.

23. Salad spinner—There'll be no more soggy salads when you use this. The salad spinner dries your greens with centrifugal force without bruising. It might even encourage you to start your own spinach patch!

24. Steam basket—A great way to keep vegetables at their healthiest. Steaming helps keep nutrients in; boiling allows the nutrients to leach into the water.

25. Tender Cooker—This is a small pressure cooker that fits into your microwave. Whereas the microwave tends to rob moisture, the Tender Cooker seals it in, making roasts and whole chickens a natural for fast and healthy microwave cooking.

26. Toaster oven—This is important to those who use a microwave heavily. It helps in last-minute browning (a shortcoming of most micro-

waves). Get one with a warming feature to help those hectic near-meal moments when you're getting together a multiple-course meal.

27. Vegetable brush—No smart cook would be without at least two. Use them to scrub such things as carrots so you can cook them in their skin. Peeling only scrapes away vitamins.

28. Wok—The authentic and still the best tool for stir-fry cooking. The real Chinese woks are made of tempered steel, and age like fine wines. With proper care, the more you use them, the less fat you will need. For the wok works, buy a bamboo steamer basket insert. It'll make your wokery more versatile than ever.

29. Yogurt maker—Why buy yogurt when you can make it, especially when you can make it better and with fewer calories?

Debora Tkac

Keeping Food Safe

A meal is only as fresh and nutritious as the ingredients that go into it, yet most of us don't always have time to shop for ingredients the same day we plan to use them.

Don't despair if your refrigerator is beginning to look like a cross between a biology experiment and an old-age home. Follow the table on these pages, and you'll never have to throw away brown apples or green meat again. Since we know how easy it is to lapse when life gets hectic, you'll also find information on how to revive certain foods when they've just passed their peak.

Most perishable foods should be stored in the refrigerator, where cold temperatures help stop or slow the aging process. The optimum temperature to halt ripening is between 38°F and 40°F. Check your refrigerator thermostat to make sure it's doing the best job possible.

Keeping food fresh comes down to three basic principles.

- Buy the best you can afford.
- Wrap and store it promptly and properly.
- Use it as soon as possible after you purchase it.

This table will help you do all three.

Lock In the Freshness

Food	Store	Use Within	Tips
Fruit			
Apples	In refrigerator in perforated plastic bags	2 weeks	Delay browning of apple slices by coating with lemon juice.
Bananas	At room temperature (ripe bananas can be refrigerated, but their skin will turn black)	2–3 days after green disappears	Dip slices in lemon juice to slow browning.
Grapefruit	In refrigerator, uncovered	2 weeks	Skin imperfections do not affect the quality of the fruit.
Grapes	In refrigerator, unwashed and uncovered	4–6 days	Grapes are highly perishable and should not be halved, seeded or washed until ready to use.
Lemons and limes	In refrigerator, uncovered	10 days to 2 weeks	To revive shriveled fruit, soak in boiling water for 10 minutes.
Oranges	In refrigerator, uncovered	2 weeks	Skin imperfections do not affect the quality of the fruit.
Pears	At room temperature until ripe; ripe fruit should be stored in refrigerator crisper	3–5 days	If cooking or baking pears, choose underripe fruit. If slicing, dip in lemon juice to slow browning.
Tangerines	In refrigerator, uncovered	2 weeks	Skin imperfections do not affect the quality of the fruit.
Vegetables			
String beans	Refrigerate in perforated plastic bags (washing before storage will help maintain moisture)	2–5 days	Avoid beans with seeds that are visible from the outside.
Beets	Covered in refrigerator, unwashed	2 weeks	Removing green tops will prolong freshness. Save greens and cook as you would spinach.

Food	Store	Use Within	Tips
Broccoli	Refrigerate in perforated plastic	2–3 days	Broccoli blanched until bright green will keep for about 5 days.
Cabbage, Chinese cabbage and brussels sprouts	Refrigerate wrapped in plastic or keep in crisper; do not wash	2 weeks; Chinese cabbage, 1 week	Chinese cabbage will stay fresh longer if you mist its leaves.
Carrots	Remove tops; refrigerate in plastic bags	2 weeks	Remove green tops before storing. Avoid storing near apples, because their ethylene gas will make carrots bitter.
Cauliflower	Refrigerate in perforated plastic bags	5–7 days	To prevent spotting, store without washing.
Celery	Trim off leaves, rinse and shake off excess moisture; refrigerate in plastic bags	2 weeks	If root is brown, remove before storing. Celery will become mushy if it's stored too cold so keep it on the upper refrigerator shelves.
Eggplant	In cool place or in refrigerator; keep in plastic bag to retain moisture	2–4 days	Shriveled skin means bitter taste.
Leafy greens and Lettuce	In refrigerator in perforated plastic bags	3–5 days	Single-leaf greens, like beet and turnip, should be stored unwashed, refrigerated, flat in a damp towel. Lettuce-type greens should not be separated from their stems or they'll dry out.
Peppers	In refrigerator crisper drawer in plastic bags; wash and dry before storing	5–7 days	Once cut, wrap tightly in plastic and use as soon as possible. Green peppers will keep longer than sweet red ones.
Potatoes	In a cool (45°–50°F), dark, dry place with good ventilation; light causes greening; high temperatures cause sprouting and shriveling; in paper, not plastic bags	2 months (if storing at room temperature, use within 1 week)	Do not store below 40°F (potatoes will darken and develop an unpleasant sweetness). Do not store near apples because apples give off ethylene gas, which will cause potatoes to rot.
Winter squash (acorn, butternut, crookneck, hubbard)	At cool room temperature (60°F) or in root cellar; do not refrigerate; keep dry	1 week (if storing in root cellar, 2 months)	Acorn squash keeps particularly well.
Tomatoes	In a cool place, out of the sun; refrigeration destroys flavor	1 week	For longer storage, wrap individually in newspaper and store at cellar temperature for up to 6 weeks, checking twice weekly.
Poultry	In coldest (lowest) part of refrigerator; if purchased in plastic wrap, remove and wrap loosely in waxed paper to allow air to circulate; wrap and store giblets separately	1–2 days	To preserve moisture, don't peel off skin until ready to cook.
Meat	In coldest (lowest) part of refrigerator; remove store wrap and wrap loosely in waxed paper to allow air to circulate	1–3 days	Lean meats keep longer than fatty ones.
Fish	In coldest (lowest) part of refrigerator, wrapped loosely in waxed paper to allow air to circulate	1–2 days	Fish (fillets and whole) will keep for about 4 days if blanched for a few seconds before refrigeration. Fish must be absolutely fresh for this method to be successful.

Food Fibers: Nature's Single Best Medicine

Good health grows on trees! It hangs from apple-laden boughs and courses through crinkly spinach leaves. It hides in carrots growing beneath the soil and flows in those amber waves of wheat.

And all of this good health is yours for the picking. Every morsel of food that you get from plants—luscious fruits, crisp vegetables, flavorful grains—contains fiber. Researchers are finding fiber has remarkable power to preserve your health and prevent disease.

The list of credits so far? Fiber may help prevent heart disease, diabetes and obesity, research shows. It may even play a role in preventing cancer, some studies suggest. And curing constipation with fiber may be the oldest medical trick in the book.

THE MANY FACES OF FIBER

Fiber is the term for the parts of plants that your body can't digest. The first step toward using the health power of fiber is knowing that there are actually several different kinds, each with its own unique ability to keep you well.

There's cellulose (the most prevalent fiber, the one that made bran famous), hemicellulose and lignin, fibers found in whole grains, fruits, vegetables and beans. There's pectin, the fiber that puts the gel in jelly. And finally, there are gums, which are sticky fibers you eat without even realizing it. These plant-derived thickening agents are used in foods as different from one another as bologna and ice cream.

One way to keep all of these straight is to think of them as falling into two categories: insoluble, those that do not dissolve in water, and

Ease into Eating Fiber

Has the fiber revolution been passing you by?

If you're ready to give it a try, you may want to take it easy on your system and get started in a gradual way. It takes a little while for your innards to adapt to a high-fiber diet. Of course, you won't hurt yourself by jumping right in. It's just that you might feel a little uncomfortable at first (What's all this rumbling and grumbling in my gut?) and you don't want to be discouraged right off the bat.

So try phasing it in over a week or more, until you find a level that's comfortable for you. And here's another tip: If you add bran to your diet, drink more water to keep things humming along.

soluble, those that do. The insoluble fibers, cellulose, most kinds of hemicellulose and lignin, are best known for their ability to ease constipation. The soluble fibers, pectin and gums, are making their name as cholesterol- and diabetes-fighters.

LOWER CHOLESTEROL

Water-soluble fibers found abundantly in fruits and vegetables have been shown to lower cholesterol, and that can lower your chances of heart disease.

The fiber called pectin is an old-timer in the ranks of cholesterol-fighters. As long ago as 1961, a study showed that eating pectin reduced blood cholesterol significantly. No less

than 15 studies have confirmed those early results in the years since. Pectin has the much-sought-after ability to lower low-density lipoprotein (LDL) cholesterol, the undesirable kind, without touching high-density lipoprotein (HDL) cholesterol, the kind thought to be beneficial.

Studies have shown that a fiber called guar gum is equally as effective as pectin. And research by the U.S. Department of Agriculture (USDA) is showing that other gums lower cholesterol, too. In one study, Kay Behall, Ph.D., a research nutritionist at the Human Nutrition Research Center, Beltsville, Maryland, investigated the effects of three different gums—locust bean gum, karaya gum and carboxymethylcellulose—in 12 volunteers.

The results were similar to those seen with pectin. Total cholesterol was lowered significantly in the weeks that the gums were eaten. Levels dropped from an average of 200 (not very high to begin with) to 170. And as with pectin, HDL cholesterol was unaffected.

Oat bran and dried beans are the only good food sources of gum that you can buy at the supermarket right now. The other gums are available only on a commercial basis.

But pectin is readily available—in fruits and vegetables. Studies show that the amount necessary to lower cholesterol is 8 to 10 grams a day—the amount in four oranges, for example.

FIGHTING DIABETES

Fiber can help control diabetes, and possibly prevent it in the first place. More than 15 studies in the last ten years have shown that pectin flattens the rise in blood glucose following a meal. Less glucose in the blood means less insulin is needed to bring it down.

"It's my opinion that fiber acts primarily to prevent glucose from entering the bloodstream as rapidly as it would if there were no fiber present," says Sheldon Reiser, Ph.D., research biochemist and research leader at the USDA's Human Nutrition Research Center. "It forms a gel that acts as a 'diffusion barrier' in the intestine. The glucose has to go through this additional 'membrane' to be absorbed, so it's slowed down. The glucose level doesn't rise as fast or as high, and the insulin level doesn't rise as high."

FIBER FIGHTS FAT

Even if you overindulge in high-fiber foods, you almost can't help but lose. Here's why.

● Most fiber foods are not calorically dense. That means that you can indulge in an orgy of eating fruits and vegetables without getting many calories.
● Fiber foods take up a lot of room. You'll feel full on fruits and vegetables before you take in a lot of calories.
● Fiber foods sneak calories out of your body. In a study by June Kelsay, Ph.D., a research nutritionist at the Human Nutrition Research Center, men on a high-fiber diet excreted 150 calories more per day than men on a low-fiber diet of equal calories.

A MOVEABLE FEAST

If you have a problem with constipation, adding fiber to your diet will almost certainly help. Study after study has shown that fiber speeds the movement of stool through the intestines. Why? Fiber has the ability to attract and hold on to water. It makes the stool softer and easier for your intestines to move along.

If constipation is a problem for you, look to the insoluble fibers to do the trick: cellulose, hemicellulose and lignin. This means you should eat whole grains, fruits, vegetables and dried beans.

FIVE EASY FIBERS

Here are some suggestions to help you add more fiber to your meals.

● Think brown when you think of bread. Whole wheat (or other whole grain) bread should be the rule.
● Eat potatoes and other vegetables with their skins.
● Eat vegetables that have edible stems or stalks, such as broccoli.
● Eat fruits that have edible seeds, such as raspberries, blackberries and strawberries.
● Try brown rice, corn tortillas, bulgur wheat or whole wheat pasta. Whole grain doesn't have to mean bread or cereal.

Susan Zarrow

Are You Getting Enough Fiber?

How often do you eat these foods?

● Several servings of whole grain breads, cereals, rice or pasta.
● Several servings of vegetables.
● Several servings of whole fruit, such as berries, apples and pears.
● Legumes, such as dried beans and peas.

Your answer for all of the above should be "almost daily." "If you're doing that," says Sheldon Reiser, Ph.D., "you can't miss getting enough fiber."

The studies that have shown the benefits of a high-fiber diet seem to point to a recommendation of 20 to 35 grams per day of "total dietary fiber" —all kinds combined in sort of a lump figure. For practical purposes, a good "guesstimate" of the optimum amount is up to 30 grams per day.

The best strategy is to eat a wide variety of fiber-containing foods. That way you'll hit on all the different types of fiber and reap all of the benefits that fiber foods have to offer.

Cutting the Fat

We all know by now (or at least we should) that too much fat in our diet is not good for us. Yet most Americans still get some 40 percent of their calories from fat—twice what most experts believe is best for optimum health.

One big reason for this high percentage is that many of us still believe adding fat to food is the only way to add taste. We sauté in butter and oils and add heavy cheeses and cream to our soups, stews and casseroles. But that "fat-is-flavor" theory is yesterday's thinking.

COOKING LEAN

There are tons of wonderful ways to cut back on fat in food preparation and cooking (a big chunk of the 40 percent mentioned above gets inserted at the stove), without cutting corners on flavor. Consider these tips from the clever cooks at the Rodale Food Center.

● Trim visible fat from all meats—roasts, steaks and chops—and remove the skin and visible fat from chicken and other poultry before cooking. This can cut the fat content by up to one-half.
● Use nonstick pans or a nonstick vegetable spray (a well-seasoned pan makes it even easier) for frying eggs, pancakes, crepes and similar foods. It really works!
● Sauté meat, poultry and fish in a little seasoned stock or liquid instead of in oil or butter. Stock can be frozen in ice-cube trays for use on an as-needed basis. Or, sauté chicken and fish in flavored vinegars or leftover cooking liquid from steamed vegetables.

● Oriental sesame oil and extra-virgin olive oil or walnut oil are excellent choices in cases where a little oil is absolutely indispensable as a seasoning agent. These oils have highly concentrated flavors, so you need only a few drops of any one to add taste to any dish—soups, salads, vegetables and sauces. Never fry with sesame or walnut oil. Instead, stir a few drops into the dish just before serving.
● If a soup recipe calls for sautéeing vegetables in butter or oil, you can do one of two things: Either steam-sauté the vegetables using a little of the soup liquid in the covered pot or simply omit this step and allow the vegetables to cook along with everything else in the soup.
● Poaching is an ideal, tasty cooking method for most firm-fleshed fish and boned chicken, and it's quick. Heat fish or vegetables in three parts water and one part lemon juice. A blend of four parts water and one part soy sauce is nice for chicken, vegetables and red meat. You can season the poaching liquid with vegetables and herbs.
● Use stock, herbal tea or juice instead of oil in marinades. If you're baking, cover the pan to keep the food moist. This is an ideal method for fish, vegetable casseroles and meat loaf.
● Spit-roasting is an excellent way to cut out the fat. This type of slow cooking allows the meat to expel much of its fat. Don't coat the food with high-calorie sauces, though (a high calorie content often signifies a lot of fat). Rather, baste the meats in their own juices.
● Stewing, or braising, is also ideal because slow cooking allows the meat to give off its fat, which can be skimmed off.
● The best way to defat soups, stocks and stews is to refrigerate them for a few hours, then skim off all the

congealed fat that forms on the top. Just reheat the dish to serve.
● Cook roasts, chops, steaks, meatballs, hamburgers and other meat patties on a raised broiler pan in the oven so the excess fat will drip away into the lower pan.
● Use aromatic foods such as tomatoes (fresh or pureed), onions, garlic, mushrooms, peppers, leeks, fresh parsley, basil and thyme to add flavor to sauces instead of butter, cream or cheese. Small amounts of such flavor concentrates are all you need.
● When preparing dishes with milk, yogurt or cheese, always use nonfat, low-fat or skim dairy products (like low-fat yogurt and cottage cheese, nonfat milk, and part-skim mozzarella and Swiss cheese).
● In recipes that call for ricotta cheese, substitute with 1 percent low-fat or

dry-curd cottage cheese. You can reduce the calories by as much as 50 percent. If you want a smoother texture, cream the cottage cheese in a blender or food processor first.

● To cut even more dairy calories, you can substitute mashed tofu—a low-fat, high-protein, cholesterol-free soyfood—for ricotta and cottage cheese in recipes. Since tofu is milder in flavor than the dairy cheese, you may want to add a little more seasoning to the recipe. Taste and see.

● If you're hooked on high-fat sour cream, try this instead: Process 1 cup of part-skim ricotta cheese in a blender or food processor until smooth. Stir in 1 cup of plain, low-fat yogurt. Chill. Fat content is less than one-quarter that of sour cream.

● Buttermilk and plain, low-fat yogurt can be substituted for milk and light cream in sauces and soups, cold or hot. To avoid curdling when you heat them, first mix 1 teaspoon of cornstarch into 1 cup of the buttermilk or yogurt. You can also remove the pan from the heat and stir in the yogurt or buttermilk just before serving.

● You can make a baked potato flavorful with a few drops of soy sauce or Worcestershire sauce or an herb-and-spice blend. Or mash tofu with a little low-fat (imitation) mayonnaise. Add curry and herb seasonings to taste.

● Save the meat renderings in the bottom of the broiler pan to make a natural gravy without added fat or starch. To degrease the renderings quickly, place them in a heat-proof measuring cup. Then submerge the cup in ice water three-quarters of the way up. The fat will rise to the top and begin to thicken so you can skim it off easily. Reheat the remaining juices and season them with bouillon or herbs and spices to taste.

● To reduce the fat in salad dressings, replace at least two-thirds of the oil in a basic vinaigrette dressing with pureed cucumber or plain, low-fat yogurt.

● Choose tuna (or other canned fish) packed in water rather than oil.

Here's the Beef

While most supermarkets use standard names for cuts of beef, restaurants use many aliases. And since there is no beef-eater's thesaurus, you need a guide. Here are a few of the more common pseudonyms.

Chateaubriand. This is a tenderloin, sometimes called filet mignon. This is always at least a choice cut and it might be prime—both are high in fat.

Surf 'n' turf. You can ask the waiter wishfully if this is haddock and round steak, but typically this is a shellfish (usually lobster) and a tenderloin cut of beef that by itself would be filet mignon—relatively high in fat.

London broil. Your best bet: This is a flank steak, highly recommended at home or out. It's less expensive than many other cuts and from a nutritional standpoint is one of the best cuts of beef.

● Instead of frying corn tortillas for Mexican dishes, steam-bake them in the oven. Wrap the tortillas securely in foil and bake just until hot and pliable, about 10 minutes at 375°F.

● Avoid *any* packaged or processed foods where oil and butter are listed in the top three ingredients.

EATING LEAN

Here's a set of guidelines for eating meat the healthful way.

Go lean. Order naturally lean cuts of beef, pork and lamb. The popular flank steak—otherwise known as a London broil—is a respectably lean cut of beef. A pork roast, made from pork loin, is also lower in fat, as is a leg of lamb.

Trim the fat. A 6-ounce T-bone steak, untrimmed and without the bone, contains 552 calories and lots of fat. Trim away all the visible fat, and you've got a 364-calorie steak with almost half the fat eliminated. Don't be shy about asking the restaurants and supermarkets you frequent to do the same thing for you. In order to make an appreciable difference, the fat has to be trimmed before the meat is cooked. Besides, it's easier on your will power if you don't have to do the trimming.

Eat smaller portions. Again, this isn't easy to do, but if you can think of meat less as the star attraction on your dinner plate and more as an ensemble player along with more healthful vegetables, it helps.

A word on hamburger. It's true that ground beef—even the so-called lean kind—gets around 64.5 percent of its calories from fat. But there's an alternative: Ground round gets only 57.7 percent of its calories from fat. Try it, you'll like it.

Debora Tkac

The Low-Stress Diet

There's stress, and then there's *stress*.

There's the chronic stress you encounter when you're doomed to listen to your husband suck his teeth till death (or divorce) do you part.

And then there's acute stress, the type we all encounter every once in a while: Tomorrow you're making your first speech—to 2,000 nitpickologists . . . your boss is doing his best George Steinbrenner imitation . . . and you have to fly across country, relying on a pilot who just may have been last in his class at flight-training school.

Do days like these have you nibbling on your nails? Try something tastier. Like food.

Nutrition experts say the right food at the right time can help you live with—even relieve—the stress modern life dumps at your door as regularly and plentifully as junk mail.

BRAIN CHEMICALS THAT OUTSMART STRESS

Perhaps no one knows this better than Judith Wurtman, Ph.D., a researcher at the Massachusetts Institute of Technology who has written a book on the subject called *Managing Your Mind and Mood through Food*. Dr. Wurtman's program is based on eating the foods that promote the brain's production of three mood-altering neurotransmitters, brain chemicals that pass information from brain cell to brain cell. The three are called dopamine, norepinephrine and serotonin, and here's what they do.

Dopamine and norepinephrine are the energizers. Your brain manufactures them from the amino acid tyrosine, which is found in protein foods. Serotonin acts either as a tran-

quilizer or an aid to concentration, depending on the time of day it's present in the brain. Carbohydrates encourage serotonin production by increasing the brain's supply of the amino acid tryptophan.

(*Note:* Don't take tyrosine and tryptophan in pill form, Dr. Wurtman warns. You could develop some potentially harmful side effects: Tyrosine could alter blood pressure, tryptophan can cause extreme drowsiness, and each can block the other essential amino acids from getting to your brain.)

Dr. Wurtman's research shows more than which foods produce which brain chemicals—she's discovered exactly which foods to eat to create the brain chemistry that can help counter specific types of stress.

PREPARING FOR "SCHEDULED" STRESS

What should you do when you know ahead of time that you're going to be under stress? That meeting. That speech. That exam. That interview. You need to be alert but not nervous. You have to think fast, not frenetically. Here are some preperformance hints from Dr. Wurtman.

Make it light. This means low in calories, carbohydrates and fat. Favor low-fat protein foods like lean meats or fish. This will ensure a high level of brain-energizing neurotransmitters.

Normalize your body's caffeine level. Don't go cold turkey to avoid the jitters: Drink what you typically drink or you'll end up with withdrawal symptoms like headache and fatigue. And if you normally don't use caffeine, don't try it as a special pick-me-up. You'll be so "up" they'll have to scrape you off the ceiling.

Use little or no alcohol on the big day. If social circumstances seem to dictate that you must have a drink, make sure you're a teetotaler for at least 3 hours before your performance.

Time your meal. If you can, eat about 2 hours before the big event to ensure that the part of digestion that takes blood away from your brain will be completed.

Don't try to perform on an empty stomach. Hunger is distracting, and when combined with tension it may make you feel queasy or give you a headache.

DEALING WITH SUDDEN STRESS

All this is fine when stress is on schedule. But what do you do when it arrives unannounced?

Eat everything you always wanted to. Candy, cookies, pie, cake, ice cream, jams, syrup, soft drinks, crackers (or, if you're feeling virtuous, rice, potatoes and corn). We're talking calming carbohydrates here, which is probably the exact kind of food you'll be craving anyway.

"Nature has a way of guiding us to sweets and starches when we are feeling stressed," says Dr. Wurtman. "The right food at the right time in the right amount is as effective as a tranquilizer."

There is, however, a serious, important method to this delicious madness.

● You need to be on a well-balanced diet.
● If you have any serious mental or physical problems, this program won't cure them. If you are hypoglycemic (have a tendency toward low blood

sugar), Dr. Wurtman advises that you get your doctor's okay before following her program. If you're a diabetic, don't use the program at all.
● The program is for short-term use only.
● No pigging out. You'll just put on weight, Dr. Wurtman warns. "It's always the first one or two cookies that initiate the production of serotonin," she says. (Serotonin, remember, is the brain chemical that produces the calming effect.)

And here's some other anti-anxiety advice.

For the first response, eat your carbohydrates with as little protein as possible, because protein can impede the production of serotonin. Digestion has to take place before serotonin is produced. For speedy digestion, stay away from fat, which slows the process.

You also need to be selective about the kinds of carbohydrates you eat. Eating fructose (found in fruit) won't cause the changes in your blood that lead to serotonin production. You want carbs that change as fast as Clark Kent changes into Superman; those foods take an hour getting out of the phone booth. Dr. Wurtman also says that leafy greens and bright-colored vegetables don't supply enough carbohydrates to activate serotonin production.

So it's devil's food cake and Fig Newtons. But not the whole cake and not the whole box. Just 30 grams—or 1½ ounces—of pure carbohydrate. "That's 2 ounces of gumdrops, 3 ounces of jelly beans, or 2 cups of Cheerios," Dr. Wurtman says gleefully. Or 1 Sara Lee yellow cupcake, 2 fudgsicles, 6 gingersnaps, 10 vanilla wafers, 16 animal crackers. Don't let your conscience be your guide.

And if you're overweight, you may need more sweets and starchy foods, because the extra fat in your fat cells slows down the carbohydrate-to-serotonin process. You may need up to a 2-ounce dose of pure carbo. It is not necessary to eat more than the prescribed dose. As with medicine, the correct dose will make the stress go away.

How fast does it work? This is *medicine*, and that means fast relief: about 20 minutes. Dr. Wurtman says the most effective way to get carbohydrates into your system is to drink them—and she doesn't mean alcohol. Try putting 2 tablespoons of sugar into a cup of herb tea. Or sip instant cocoa made with water or skim milk. Or grab a can of regular soda.

A few more words to the wired.

● Eat your carbo tranquilizer in a calm setting.
● Eat or drink slowly. No wolfing or gulping. You'll eat or drink too much.
● Take a few minutes to do something relaxing while you take your carbo fix, Dr. Wurtman says. "This helps boost the mood-altering effects of serotonin as it is being synthesized in your brain."

William LeGro

The All-Day Nibble Plan

Today you have an all-day meeting to choose the new president of the Garden Club. You know it's going to be a tough day. There's dissension between the zinnia and marigold factions, petunias aren't speaking to pansies, and bulbs are threatening to boycott unless a lily is the next leader. How are you going to get through the day with your dignity, sense of humor and purpose intact?

Judith Wurtman, Ph.D., suggests her All-Day Nibble Plan. It's very simple.

Skip meals; snack instead. "Constant nibbling under stress is practically universal human behavior," Dr. Wurtman says. But if you eat regular meals, too, you will acquire a bulbous shape.

Nibble on low-fat or no-fat carbohydrates. This will make a good amount of nerve-calming, mind-focusing serotonin available to your brain. Air-popped popcorn, rice cakes, dry breakfast cereals, miniature marshmallows are good choices.

Don't forget oral gratification. This effect dates from infancy: Whether it's sucking, chewing or sipping, the hand-to-mouth activity is soothing. "Lay in a good supply of sucking foods," Dr. Wurtman advises: lollipops, popsicles and sourballs. Sipping is similar: fruit juices, iced tea and club soda. Chewing can calm you: crunchy vegetables (*after* you've begun to feel the relaxing effect of serotonin from sweets and starches) and dried fruit rolls.

Caution: This diet breaks all the rules of good daily nutrition, Dr. Wurtman says. But it won't hurt for a day or even 2 days, especially if you take a good multivitamin and mineral supplement each morning.

Nutrition to Go

Dining out tonight?

Eating out most often means turning over control of your (we hope) normally healthful diet to some sauce-and-cream-, cholesterol-and-fat-, salt-and-sugar-crazed chef. Right?

Not necessarily.

These suggestions from the Society for Nutrition Education and other diet experts will help you make fast, informed food choices when you're dining out. They're based on U.S. Department of Agriculture Dietary Guidelines, which emphasize eating a variety of foods, maintaining your ideal weight, controlling fat, sodium and sugar intake and eating foods with adequate fiber.

PLAN AHEAD

First, do your homework on how the chefs at various restaurants do *their* work. Your city or the area you're traveling in may offer a dining guide prepared by the Chamber of Commerce, area Cooperative Extension Service, local American Heart Association chapter or hospital dietitians. This might list which restaurants offer leaner sauces, fat-free cooking techniques and other healthier preparations.

If restaurant phone numbers are included, you might call ahead to find out how foods are typically prepared. This can eliminate the unfortunate surprise of, for example, going to an oriental buffet and unexpectedly finding that all the food is fried.

Once you've selected a place that has both the ambience and attention to health that you want, keep in mind that you aren't sentenced to just plain fish and salad with a stingy squeeze of lemon juice. Although you know it's best to choose lean foods like skinned chicken or fish, the finest delights from the kitchen are in your realm as long as you remember the key rule: portion control.

SET YOUR LIMITS

Your waiter or waitress can help with this. "Tell the waiter, 'I'm controlling the fat (or sodium, or calories) in my diet for health reasons. I can do that if I have less than the normal-size portions,' " says Carolyn Lackey, Ph.D., foods and nutrition specialist with the North Carolina Agricultural Extension Service. "Most people will be receptive to you." There are several ways to manage this.

If your heart's set on a truly decadent dish—buttered, breaded, creamed or cheesed—ask if it's offered in half-or smaller-size portions. (This option frequently isn't listed.) Or tell the waiter to bring you half of the regular serving anyway. "Some will try to appeal to your economic sensibilities and tell you it'll cost the same," Dr. Lackey notes, "but be firm—you're better off." Or, if it doesn't trigger the guilt siren, eat only half of a full entrée and have the waiter immediately take away the rest.

Other alternatives: Choose one or two appetizers for your meal. Order items a la carte for less total food. Share desserts.

ORDER WISELY

Dr. Lackey discovered a good way to avoid salad-bar sinning while working late one night in a restaurant. A waiter saw her with papers spread out on the table and asked if he could save her some time by getting a salad for her. He brought a bowl of fresh greens and crisp vegetables.

"I realized I didn't have to go over and be drawn to the marshmallow-puff fruit salad," she laughs. Now she asks the waiter for this favor often. Here are some other tips.

● Watch out for menus peppered with cooking terms, especially those in foreign languages, that translate into "fat added." *Sauté* also means add butter. *Tempura* means fried in batter. *Au gratin* indicates the dish has cheese sauce. And even *broiling* falls from grace when it's done in butter. If a term is unfamiliar, don't be embarrassed to ask what it means.

● Request that no salt be added to anything during preparation.

● Ask if fried entrées can be broiled instead. This works well with fish, shrimp and chicken.

● Have your vegetables steamed or microwaved to keep nutrients in, and fat and sodium out.

● Banish butter at 100 calories per tablespoon and switch to sour cream at 26 calories per tablespoon whenever possible. Better yet, ask the waiter for a small dish of cottage cheese or yogurt as a topping for your baked potato. These have less than one-eighth the calories of butter or margarine, plus calcium and protein.

● Having salad dressings served on the side is a popular request—but did you know you can request the same for sauces and gravies? You can then give your food a flavorful splash instead of the chef giving it a swim.

● Choose these excellent appetizers: fresh seafood items like oysters on the half shell, seafood cocktail with a lemon wedge, and fresh fruits and vegetables. Avoid pâté, caviar, fried hors d'oeuvres or high-fat dips.

● Gazpacho, vegetable or bean soups get your dining off to a healthier start than do high-sodium broths and consommés or high-fat creamed soups.

● If you want french fries, order the thicker steak fries instead of skinny fries. They soak up less fat.

PICK OUT THE BUZZWORDS

Learn these additional buzzwords. According to the American Heart Association, avoiding high-fat, high-cholesterol, high-sodium dishes, and finding healthful ones, is largely a method of learning a few menu buzzwords. These terms and phrases telegraph *low-fat* preparation: Steamed, in its own juice, garden-fresh, roasted, poached, in tomato juice and dry-boiled (in lemon juice or wine).

Be aware that some low-fat, low-cholesterol preparations are high in sodium. Watch out for foods that are pickled, smoked or in cocktail sauce or broth.

Menu descriptions that warn of saturated fat and cholesterol preparation may also indicate high sodium. Avoid foods that are buttery, buttered, in butter sauce, fried, pan-fried, crispy, braised, creamed, in cream sauce, in its own gravy, hollandaise, parmesan, in cheese sauce, escalloped, marinated (in oil), stewed and basted.

With a little practice, experimentation and trial and error, there's no reason that dining out can't be a healthful experience.

Maria Mihalik

A Fast-Food Review

No-fault fast food—no such thing? Not quite. The food we get from those quick visits to the drive-up windows no doubt will never win any awards from nutritionists.

An occasional burger is no great setback as far as your health goes. But if you rely on fast foods fairly regularly, you need to make more careful choices to avoid fat, sodium and cholesterol problems.

Here are some options.

Do some foraging. Select restaurants offering salad bars, soups, baked potatoes, juices and low-fat milk. "If you opt for the traditional items, be aware that french fries may actually be 1 of the items lowest in sodium," says Carole Bisogni, Ph.D., associate professor in nutritional sciences at Cornell University. "And once fish and chicken are deep-fried and sauced, they're no better than specialty burgers as far as fat content goes."

You can bypass these problems by choosing a lightly dressed (or undressed) salad with fresh, crisp vegetables and by limiting portions of bacon bits, croutons and creamy salads such as potato and macaroni. A baked potato (if it's not buried in rich toppings), milk (preferably skim) and citrus juice are other good bets.

Hold the sauces. Burgers and specialty sandwiches aren't the worst food in the world if you ask that fatty sauces not be smeared on. Without cheese sauce or extra juice, lean roast beef sandwiches are acceptable. You might try to find a place that pressure deep-fries chicken and fish. This involves less time in the fat—less time for the food to soak it up. Even better, remove all of the skin and outer crispy layer yourself.

Reach for balance. If you're seduced by the fried-food aroma and find yourself eating a burger, shake and fries, make your other meal of the day light and include vegetables, fruit and whole grains. This will help make up for the essential nutrients you may miss with a fast-food meal, as well as keep your day's calorie intake from going through the roof.

Fast-food breakfasts offer fat and sodium posing as croissants, egg sandwiches, sausage and biscuits. Choose orange juice, pancakes and plain toast or muffins instead.

Healthy Microwave Cooking

If you're part of a busy family, you're probably already sold on the incredible convenience of a microwave appliance. But did you know that microwaves can actually help you improve the nutrition and healthfulness of your meals?

Microwaving preserves vitamins and minerals because the shorter cooking time means fewer nutrients are lost to heat. Then too, microwaves work especially well on fresh, high-water-content foods like fish, poultry, vegetables and fruit. This means you can emphasize low-calorie, low-fat foods in your menus without sacrificing nutrition or time.

Finally, a 1984 U.S. Department of Agriculture study found that microwaved meat contained less fat and fewer calories than meat cooked by electric broiling, charbroiling, roasting, convection heating or frying, regardless of how much fat the raw meat contained.

As you can see, microwaving offers busy people much more than speed. It's also a convenient way to lower fat, reduce salt, preserve vitamins and minerals and keep high-fiber foods in your diet without spending a lot of time in the kitchen. Here are the latest hot tips for cooking quick, healthy meals with your microwave.

Instead of sautéing fish and vegetables in butter, reduce saturated fats by microwaving them using fragrant lemon and herbs.

Salting simply dries out microwaved foods. Enhance flavors by substituting provocative aromatics such as ginger and scallions with chicken, or grated lime peel and garlic with shrimp, for example.

Reduce salt and fat in your recipes by marinating. This will take very little time if you microwave the marinating food for 1 to 2 minutes on the lowest power before you cook it.

Make it easy to include low-calorie, fresh shellfish in your diet with this timesaving trick: To cook clams and oysters, place six in a circle with their opening edges facing the center. Microwave on full power for about 4 minutes or until all shells are open.

You can cook eight medium shrimp in their shells to perfection. Set your microwave on full power for about 30 seconds. Let the shrimp stand another 30 seconds before serving.

Fish oils help preserve your heart's health, so put more fish in your diet. Get the most flavor and the best texture from microwaved fish by bringing it to room temperature for 1 to 2 minutes on low power. If the fish is too cold, you'll overcook the outside before the inside is done.

Lean fish such as flounder fillet microwaves very well. Try

Art Micro: Cookware with Style

You can now empty that shelf that you've stuffed with those disposable "microwave-safe" containers and, while you're at it, toss out those tacky plain white plastic bowls and microwave plates. Style has come to microwave cookware.

"Microwave cookware is getting high design," reports Judith Benn Hurley, author of *Healthy Microwave Cooking*, "There are some nice ceramics from France and Germany. American companies have come up with some microwave cookware that is pretty chic-looking. What this means is that if cooks are excited about a particular pot or pan or microwave cooking dish, they will use it more and be more imaginative with it."

You won't have to use your imagination anymore to see what's going on inside the pot, either. "Corning has microwave cookware called Visions. It's an amber-colored pot that goes on the stove or in the microwave or oven," says Hurley. "It's good for microwaving

because it allows for participatory cooking. Normally with microwaving you can't get in and sniff and pinch the food because it's tucked away in the unit. Now, with this see-through cookware, you can peek in through the window and see what's going on." Hurley says there are other innovations to watch for.

● Browning dishes. These flat, pie-shaped dishes have metal in the bottom. They sear food to give it a different texture rather than the poached or stewed texture and are good for fish and chicken dishes.
● Space-age cookware. New containers made out of the same material as rocket nosecones will let you microwave food, then seal it up and freeze it, all in the same container.
● Healthier popcorn poppers. These new ones are made in a funnel shape, bigger on top and smaller on the bottom, that encourages the kernels to pop, and you don't have to use oil.

smothering the fish with chopped tomatoes and basil, then microwaving, covered, on full power for about 4½ minutes per pound.

With a little help from your microwave, you can afford the time to cook lean, healthful poultry. When microwaving chicken legs, arrange the pieces in a circle with the meaty parts facing the edge. This way, the microwaves will reach the meatiest parts first, so the pieces cook more evenly.

To preserve maximum nutrition in vitamin-packed vegetables, cook them quickly but evenly. Broccoli and asparagus should be arranged in a circle with the tender buds facing the middle. This exposes the tough stalks to more intense cooking.

Whenever you cook more than one kind of vegetable at a time, cut all vegetable pieces the same size. Combining vegetables that have similar textures also helps. Cook root vegetables together, for instance.

When you want to peel fresh tomatoes for soups or sauces, microwave them on full power for approximately 1 minute (adjust this time according to size and ripeness).

When you want to remove the skin from a fresh pepper, you can skip the traditional long-roasting method. Simply microwave it on full power for 3 minutes, turning the pepper three times. Then wrap it loosely and place it in the freezer until cool. The skin will peel easily.

For a fast, nutritious, low-calorie dessert, bake an apple. Peel the top third to prevent the insides from bursting through the skin as the heat expands them. Cover the apple and cook on full power for 3 minutes. Serve with yogurt flavored with maple syrup and cinnamon.

Dried fruits are packed with vitamins and minerals. To plump rai-

Cooking Fiber Fast

Keep these long-cooking, high-fiber vegetables in your diet by cooking them fast in a microwave.

Vegetable	Preparation	Cooking Time
Artichokes	Cover loosely	5 min., full power
Acorn squash	Split and cover tightly	7 min., full power
Eggplant, medium	Cover tightly	8 min., full power
Spaghetti squash	Puncture in several places	8 min., full power

sins and other dried fruit, lightly sprinkle 1 cup of dried fruit with juice or water. Then cover and microwave on full power for 1 minute, stirring after about 30 seconds. Let the fruit stand about 4 minutes before using it in baking, on cereals, in compotes or as a snack.

Nuts are a fine concentrated source of protein, vitamins and minerals. To shell nuts easily, place a handful in a covered dish with enough water to cover them. Microwave on full power for 4 to 5 minutes. Drain, let them cool and dry, then shell. Shell chestnuts by slitting the shells, then microwaving a handful, uncovered, on full power for about 45 seconds.

Baking bread at home ensures nutritious loaves. One timesaving trick to check if your yeast is live: Mix it with the recipe's sweetener, the liquid and ¼ cup of the recipe's flour. Cover with vented plastic wrap, then microwave on lowest power, for 1 minute. Look for pops or bubbles.

If you're ready to bake but some of your ingredients are frozen, don't invite unwanted microbes by defrosting them slowly. Instead, bring them to room temperature in the microwave.

To preserve nutrients in your sauces, cut down on cooking time. Microwaved sauces cook faster in a measuring cup than in a shallow dish.

Researchers have found that microwave cooking is less effective than conventional cooking for destroying salmonella and staph organisms in meat. You're better off cooking a turkey, say, in a brown-in bag. But if you must microwave your bird, remember that it must maintain an internal temperature of 170°F for at least ½ hour. You will need to use your conventional oven to do this.

If you microwave meat and poultry prior to grilling, you can slash overall cooking time and retain natural juices. Start with a 2½-pound chicken. Remove all skin. Place pieces bone side up on a microwave drainer, with the meatiest portion facing out. Cover with waxed paper and cook on high power for 4½ minutes. Turn and cook another 4½ minutes, or until juices run clear when meat is pierced with a fork. Transfer to grill and cook for 5 minutes on high heat, basting often.

Health Secrets from Vegetarians

Time was when vegetarians were viewed by some as second-class diners, sitting at the lunch counter of life nibbling carrots, tofu and nutburgers while all around them, carnivores indulged in a riot of meat and gravy.

But the excellent health of many vegetarians has been opening eyes and changing attitudes. Studies indicate that vegetarians are less prone than meat-eaters to some serious health problems, including heart disease and certain cancers.

But do you have to be a total vegetarian to reap some of the rewards of a vegetarian lifestyle? Not at all.

Frank Sacks, M.D., a nutrition researcher at Harvard Medical School, says "reducing your intake of meat and fatty dairy products to only a few times a week will help. If the whole country did this, there'd be a marked decline in heart disease."

As the American beef and pork industries know all too well, the whole country *is* starting to do this. And this may be just the right time for you to go with the flow.

FEWER ANIMAL PRODUCTS, FEWER HEART PROBLEMS

It's proven: Eat more grains and vegetables, and you can lower your cholesterol and blood pressure, trim your waistline and, as a result, lessen your chance of heart disease.

Lower your blood pressure. One study looked at Seventh-Day Adventists, most of whom are vegetarians, and found their blood pressures to be significantly lower than that of omnivores. Adventist men's and women's systolic blood pressures (the upper number) were almost five points lower than nonvegetarians', and the average diastolic blood pressure (the lower number) was four to five points lower.

It apparently doesn't take long to realize the effects of vegetarianism. A group of omnivores who became experimental vegetarians for a few months realized a decrease in systolic blood pressure of almost seven points and a three-point drop in diastolic pressure. When they resumed eating meat, their blood pressures returned to pretest levels after several weeks.

Lower your cholesterol. Researchers from Harvard Medical School fed vegetarians ½ pound of beef a day and watched their pulse rates increase as their cholesterol levels rose 19 percent. The meat portion each vegetarian ate was close to that of the average American, only leaner. They regained their low cholesterol levels ten days to two weeks after resuming their meatless ways.

Lower blood pressure and cholesterol levels can mean fewer heart problems. In fact, when English scientists tracked almost 11,000 carnivores and vegetarians for seven years, they found just this: Vegetarians succumbed to heart disease less often.

MORE THAN YOUR HEART WILL BENEFIT

Certain cancers, gallstones, diabetes and osteoporosis are all less likely to befall you if you are a vegetarian, studies indicate.

Cancer less likely. The body of a meat-eating woman processes the female hormone estrogen differently from that of a vegetarian woman. Researchers from the New England Medical Center, in Boston, and Tufts University School of Medicine found that vegetarian women excrete two to three times as much estrogen as meat-eaters. The more estrogen lost, the lower the levels in the blood. Scientists believe that the recycled estrogen traveling through the bloodstream may have a cancer-linked effect on the breast.

Men can lower their risk of another kind of cancer. Researchers at Loma Linda University School of Medicine have found that vegetarian Seventh-Day Adventist men have lower levels of the male hormones testosterone and estradiol. The scientists also note that vegetarian Adventist men eat twice the amount of fiber and have low risks of hormonal-type cancer. Their theory is that the high-fiber diet may help rid the body of these hormones, which have been linked to prostate cancer.

Gallstones stay away. Researchers at the University of Oxford in England report that vegetarian women are less likely to develop gallstones. They examined more than 700 women aged 40 to 69 over the course of several years and noted that the meat-eating women were almost twice as likely to experience problems.

Diabetes: meat ain't sweet. A 21-year project that followed the health of more than 25,600 Seventh-Day Adventist men and women found that their risk of dying from diabetes is half that of the general population. Looking even closer, researchers found that, especially for men, diabetes was listed more often on the death certificates of meat-eating Adventists than on those of vegetarians.

The study's authors offer these theories: Meat or saturated fat may interfere with insulin metabolism, or the relatively low amounts of fiber and complex carbohydrates consumed by meat-eaters may enhance their risk of diabetes.

Make no bones about osteoporosis. A study of Adventist women also suggests that their vegetarian diets could play a role in preventing the bone-degenerating condition known as osteoporosis that afflicts many postmenopausal women. Medical researchers found that women 50 to 89 years of age who were on a vegetarian diet that included milk and eggs had lost 18 percent bone mineral mass, while women who ate meat had lost 35 percent.

Since there was little difference in the amount of bone-strengthening calcium the two groups of women consumed over the years, the scientists speculate that, for some unexplained reason, meat may cause loss of minerals in older women.

WHAT'S A POOR CARNIVORE TO DO?

In light of all this, a meat-eater who can't bear to part with roast beef may wonder what to do.

Remember, "you don't have to adopt a total vegetarian philosophy or lifestyle in order to become a healthier you," says Harvard's Dr. Sacks.

Realize that there are several factors that come into play when considering the health status of vegetarians. They generally are concerned about their health and don't smoke or drink to excess, which has a positive effect. And many of the scientists who've conducted meatless research are quick to acknowledge that lifestyle can play a powerful role.

Whether you decide to change your whole lifestyle or simply sacrifice a few servings of meat a week in the name of better health is up to you. Take note that some people should

A Guide to Going Meatless

Whether you're contemplating a total vegetarian diet or just considering meatless meals a few times a week, a bit of menu planning is in order. Nonmeat sources of certain nutrients that are usually obtained from animal foods are listed below.

Nutrient	Sources
Protein	Legumes; grains; nuts and seeds; dark, leafy greens; eggs; dairy products
Calcium	Dairy products; dark, leafy greens; legumes; most nuts and seeds; molasses; figs; apricots; dates
Iron	Legumes (especially soybeans and soy products other than oil); dark, leafy greens; dried fruits; whole and enriched grains; molasses
Zinc	Eggs, cheese, legumes, nuts, wheat germ, whole grains, some kinds of brewer's yeast
Riboflavin (B)	Dairy products; eggs; whole and enriched grains; brewer's yeast; dark, leafy greens; legumes
Vitamin B	Dairy products, eggs, nutritional yeast, foods fortified with B supplements
Vitamin D	Fortified milk, fortified soy milk, exposure of skin to sunshine

take extra care when considering a vegetarian-type diet, according to the American Dietetic Association. They include:

● Pregnant and lactating women. Lacto-ovo vegetarian diets (which include dairy foods and eggs) provide all the required nutrients. Iron, folate and zinc supplements may be needed by strict vegetarians.

● Infants and children. Lacto-ovo and ovo (eggs allowed) vegetarian diets meet the protein requirements for growth, but iron and zinc levels should be watched. Infants on a strict vegan diet should be given fortified soy milk for energy. Deficiencies of calcium, vitamin D, B_{12} and riboflavin easily occur.

● Adults with special health problems. Anyone with a diet-related problem, such as lactose intolerance, should consult a professional dietitian for meal planning.

But if you're an average person, and you think a meatless diet just couldn't supply you with enough protein (or calories, or something), and therefore wouldn't be healthy, think again. Ask your doctor. He can easily fall back on the scientific data and politely tell you, "Bull."

Tom Shealey

The Anti-Cancer Diet Plan

SCENE I: You've been behind the wheel for several hours now, and you can think only of rest and food. Through the night fog ahead you make out a glowing neon sign. It reads: "The Anti-Cancer Café." You turn into the lot, park and head for the door. You're greeted by a maître d' in white; stethoscope and wine key hang side by side around his neck. "Table for one—nonsmoking, of course?" he inquires. "This way, please." You're led to your table. Moments later, the waiter appears.

WAITER: Welcome to the Anti-Cancer Café. Tonight we offer a number of potent anti-cancer specials.

YOU: Do you mean there are foods that fight cancer?

WAITER: Most certainly. No one can guarantee that you won't get cancer if you eat a certain diet, but almost all experts agree that you can significantly reduce the risk.

YOU: Oh, yeah? How do they know that?

WAITER: Lots of studies have been done on animals. Even more impressive, there have been many surveys on human population groups. Did you know that stomach cancer is quite rare in the United States, yet fairly common in Japan, and the only reasonable explanation is the different diet?

YOU: Well, no, and I'm sort of interested, but . . . I'll bet your menu is full of weird things like, uh, doo-hickey beans in soy jelly, huh?

WAITER: Nope. The anti-cancer diet is full of variety and tasty things.

YOU: Like brussels sprouts, I suppose.

WAITER: Like *all kinds* of vegetables, *and* fruits, *and* grains, *and*, well . . . Why don't you look at the menu? I'll be back.

You open the menu. The lights fade.

SCENE II: You look over the dietary guidelines. The waiter returns. You look perplexed.

YOU: This menu is enormous.

WAITER: Yes, it is—but you'll notice that the dessert section is minuscule. In fact, the café offers very few high-calorie foods because one of the American Cancer Society's dietary guidelines for reducing your chances of getting cancer is to avoid obesity. When the Cancer Society did a major study of obesity in humans over a 12-year period, it found an increased incidence of uterine, gall-bladder, kidney, stomach, colon and breast cancers among the obese. Of those 40 percent or more overweight, the women showed a 55 percent greater risk and the men a 33 percent greater risk of cancer.

YOU: Wow. So *whatever* I order, I shouldn't overdo it, huh?

WAITER: Right. You'll also notice that our menu offers dishes that are low in fat—nothing fried, just lean meat, no butter. Americans consume about 40 percent of total calories as fat. That's too much. Less than 30 percent is ideal. Did you know that eating too much fat raises the odds you'll get breast, colon or prostate cancer? One 1986 study shows a striking correlation between fat consumption and breast cancer mortality rates in various countries. Where people eat lots of fat, like in the Netherlands, the risk of dying from breast cancer is many times higher than it is in a country where people eat little fat, such as Guatemala. By the way, there's a graph on your menu. (See the accompanying box.)

YOU: But how do we know that the Dutch just aren't inclined to get

breast cancer? Like maybe it's in their genes or something?

WAITER: Good question. But this cancer appears to be diet-related. It turns out that people who move from, say, a rice-and-vegetable culture to a hamburger-and-bun culture soon wind up running about the same higher risk of certain cancers as their new neighbors. For example, one study shows that Japanese women in Los Angeles have breast cancer incidence rates four times higher than Japanese women in Osaka.

YOU: Why?

WAITER: The Japanese diet was not only low in fat, it was also high in fiber. And consuming fiber may significantly reduce the risk of some kinds of cancer. Scientists aren't sure if it's the fiber itself or if it's because diets high in fiber are typically low in fat. But this shouldn't really concern you —if you eat 25 to 30 grams of fiber a day, you're better off; on this, there's little disagreement.

YOU: Gee, that sounds like a lot of fiber.

WAITER: It is. And that's why our menu offers a wide selection of vegetables, whole grains and fruits. These foods should make up a considerable part of your diet.

YOU: Okay. I'm ready to order now. I'd like a salad to start, and the turkey breast with broccoli. Wait. Maybe I'll have ham instead.

WAITER: Sorry, sir. We seldom offer salt-cured, smoked or nitrite-cured foods. Where such foods are most common, such as in Japan, we find the highest rates of stomach cancer. Smoked foods, you see, often contain some of the same carcinogens that we find in tobacco, and nitrites in food can form cancer-causing substances.

YOU: So, no hot dogs, sausages or bacon for me—huh?

The Cancer/Fat Connection

Not much fat in the diet, not much breast cancer. Lots of fat, and breast cancer may be a problem. There certainly seems to be a link. In Guatemala, for example, where people eat only about 40 grams (roughly 1.4 ounces) of fat a day, the risk of dying from breast cancer appears to be less than one-tenth what it is in the Netherlands, where about 180 grams (roughly 6½ ounces) of fat are gobbled up daily. It seems a correlation exists between these two factors the world over.

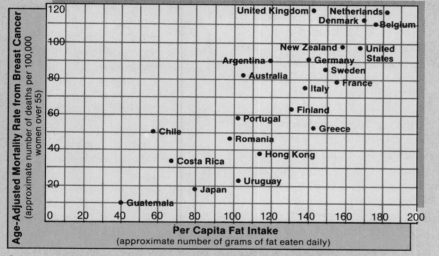

SOURCE: Adapted from "Diet and Breast Cancer in Causation and Therapy," *Cancer*, October 15, 1986 (Supplement).

WAITER: Everything in moderation.

YOU: Good advice. I'd like a bottle of good wine to go with the meal.

WAITER: May I suggest a *glass* of our best chablis. Doctors have long had reason to suspect a link between certain cancers and heavy drinking, so our wine servings are by the glass. One recent study at the National Cancer Institute raised eyebrows by showing that women who down as few as three alcoholic drinks a week may increase their risk of breast cancer by as much as 50 percent.

YOU: *(Gulp.)* Maybe I shouldn't order a drink at all?

WAITER: Only you can decide. Before you do, ask yourself if you're in the high-risk group—female, overweight, with a history of breast cancer in the family. For the rest of us, an occasional cocktail seems to present no serious risks. Now let's move on to our vegetable selections. We specialize in foods rich in vitamins A and C and cruciferous vegetables.

YOU: Cruc-if-wha?

WAITER: Cruciferous vegetables —brussels sprouts, broccoli, cabbage and cauliflower. Studies on animals suggest these can inhibit certain cancers, particularly of the digestive and respiratory tracts. But doctors rec- ommend you eat a variety of vegetables, not just cruciferous ones—and fruits. This will ensure you lots of vitamins, especially vitamins A and C, both thought to fight cancer.

YOU: I hate brussels sprouts.

WAITER: Then order one of the other vegetables. And allow me to suggest that for a good source of vitamin A, you eat leafy green vegetables, like spinach or kale, or a yellow-orange vegetable such as pumpkin, sweet potatoes or carrots. Citrus fruits, of course, are a great source of vitamin C.

YOU: What if I just pop vitamin pills?

WAITER: Well, remember that fruits and vegetables also provide essential fiber and nonfatty calories.

SCENE III: You and the waiter exchange some final words.

YOU: Hey, I'm hungry.

WAITER: Just one more thing you should know: A recent report by the National Research Council concluded that pesticide residues in our food clearly warrant concern. So, here at the café, if we can't find naturally grown produce, we at least wash everything really well.

YOU: Gee, I guess I should do that at home, too. Say, there are no prices on the menu, and it doesn't say if the tip is included.

WAITER: The anti-cancer diet doesn't cost much—it's mostly common sense. As for the tips—don't worry about it—here at the Anti-Cancer Café, we give *you* the tips. Use them in good health.

Curtain.

(Special thanks to the American Cancer Society and Sidney Weinhouse, Ph.D., professor emeritus of the Temple University School of Medicine and member of the board of the American Cancer Society for providing technical information.)

Russell Wild

A Guide to the Best in Beverages

Quenching our thirst has never been more complicated. So many different beverages vie for our attention that when someone asks, "What will you have?" we can't always make up our minds. Should it be a diet or regular soft drink? Whole milk or skim? Mineral water or sparkling water? And which choice would be the healthiest?

Before you go looking for a drink, it might help to know more about what you're drinking. Listed below are some of the latest facts about the most common beverages available.

SKIM MILK: THE CHOICE OF A SMART GENERATION

Perhaps because it is one of our first foods, we regard milk as one of the healthiest. Indeed, expressions like "the milk of human kindness" and the "land of milk and honey" testify to the affectionate place that milk holds in the human heart. But whole cow's milk doesn't always make the human heart healthier. It's rich in saturated fat—the kind that clogs arteries and causes heart disease.

As you probably already know from television jingles, whole milk contains only 4 percent fat. But that measurement is by weight. The true, meaningful measurement of fat is actually percentage of calories from fat, and *48 percent* of the calories in milk come from fat. That makes it a fattier food than many cuts of beef. "Low-fat," or "2 percent," milk isn't much leaner. Fully 34 percent of its calories come from saturated fat. But skim milk has only 5 percent of its calories from fat.

To minimize your fat intake, give skim milk a try. Fortified skim milk contains as much calcium, vitamin D and vitamin A as whole milk—without the saturated fat.

THE BOTTOMLESS CUP

If Americans suddenly gave up drinking coffee, an awful lot of mornings would start with a whimper instead of a bang. But a few years ago coffee drinkers were urged to do just that. The reason: A wave of evidence, percolating from research labs, blamed coffee for irregular heartbeats, breast cysts and bladder cancer.

Since then, moderate use of coffee has been cleared as a health threat. But coffee-lovers would be wise to heed the following.

● Drinking more than four cups of coffee a day can cause "caffeinism," a disorder easily mistaken for anxiety neurosis.
● *Most* adults can tolerate three cups of coffee—which contain about 100 milligrams of caffeine each—without experiencing such adverse symptoms as diarrhea, headache, heartburn, palpitations, nervousness or insomnia. But some can't.
● Anyone with anemia, heart disease or gastrointestinal problems shouldn't drink a lot of coffee. As an alternative, try decaffeinated coffee or drink café au lait. (That's coffee diluted with steaming hot milk.)
● Black tea contains about 60 milligrams of caffeine per cup—about half as much as a cup of brewed coffee.

SOFT DRINKS: THEY'LL SOFTEN YOUR MIDDLE

What fuel does America run on? If you said petroleum, you'd be only half right. As a nation, we're also powered by carbonated soft drinks. Our cars may guzzle gasoline, but we guzzle soda pop at the rate of 42 gallons per year. That's an average of 486.2 cans a year for every man, woman and child. In fact, we drink more "pop" than any other beverage, including water, of which we drink only 41 gallons a year.

Regular and diet cola is what Americans choose 69 percent of the time. Lemon-lime sodas run a distant second. Diet colas account for 23 percent of all soda sales. As for decaffeinated colas and sodas with added fruit juice—they may well be the wave of the future.

Turn On the Juice

Aside from pure water, the healthiest fluids are often those stored inside the skin of everyday fruits and vegetables. Natural, home-squeezed juices contain none of the excess sugar, artificial color or caffeine so common in soft drinks. Nor are they heavily processed. By pressing your own juice, you're going right to the source.

Making apple cider can be expensive—the press that's required to shred the apples and squeeze the pulp can cost several hundred dollars. By contrast, you can start squeezing oranges with a $2 hand reamer. Electric juicers and juicer attachments for food processors can give you almost endless possibilities for making fruit and vegetable juices.

Grape juices may be the easiest to make at home. Simply wash, de-stem and crush the grapes, then squeeze them through cheesecloth and refrigerate the liquid overnight. In the morning, use the clear juice off the top and leave the sediment behind.

What's wrong with drinking soda? In a word: sugar—at the rate of about 3 grams per ounce. Yes, sugar can provide energy. But soda delivers sugar without the B vitamins that enable the body to turn it into energy. Also, the calories in soda, like those in candy, are "empty" calories. You have to eat more food at other meals to make up for the nourishment that the sugar in soda pop lacks. And that can add inches to the waistline. Here are a few more facts that don't usually pop out.

● Orange soda and root beer tend to be the sweetest sodas (up to 198 calories per can), while ginger ale and tonic water are usually the driest (as few as 120 calories).
● A 12-ounce can of cola contains about 36 milligrams of caffeine. That's less than half the caffeine content of a cup of coffee. If you started your day with a mammoth 32-ounce container of cola from the convenience store, you'd be drinking about 100 milligrams of caffeine, or the equivalent of about one cup of coffee.

BOTTLED WATER: NO GUARANTEE OF PURITY

In 1986, we drank 280 million gallons of bottled water. We have it delivered in cardboard crates. We buy it in plastic gallon jugs at the supermarket. But bottled spring water isn't necessarily any healthier than city water. An investigation by *Consumer Reports* found that Los Angeles and New York City have excellent municipal water, and there's no guarantee that even rural aquifers are untainted by pesticides or landfill seepage. Tap water can sometimes be just as good as well water.

Imported bottled waters have become popular in recent years as a low-calorie substitute for soft drinks. They go by different names and, depending on the source, they'll be carbonated, rich in minerals, flavored or all three. Here are a few of their names and definitions.

Liquid Calories: A Comparison

Beverage (8 oz. unless indicated)	Calories
Milk	
Whole	150
Skim	86
Fruit and vegetable juices	
Coconut milk	552
Grape juice	155
Apricot nectar	141
Orange juice	111
Tomato juice	42
Soft drinks	
Cola (12 oz.)	151
Fruit punch	112
Grape drink, canned	112
Diet cola (12 oz.)	2
Beer, wine and spirits	
Dessert wine (3½ oz.)	161
Regular beer (12 oz.)	146
Whiskey sour (3½ oz.)	144
Light beer (12 oz.)	100
Red table wine (3½ oz.)	74
White wine (3½ oz.)	70
De-alcoholized beer (12 oz.)	65
Sports drinks	
Ultra Energy	200
Vitalade	86
GatorAde	50

SOURCES: Adapted from Agriculture Handbook Nos. 8-1, 8-9, 8-11, 8-12, 8-14 (Washington, D.C.: U.S. Department of Agriculture).

● Mineral water. Water that usually contains sodium, magnesium and calcium; in some states, it must have at least 500 parts per million dissolved mineral solids to be labeled "mineral water." It is usually carbonated.
● Sparkling water. Carbonated water in which the gases that are dissolved in the water are "captured" before they can escape, resulting in the tell-tale fizz.
● Club soda. Artificially carbonated tap water to which minerals have been added.
● Seltzer. Artificially carbonated tap water that is frequently flavored and/or sweetened, making it high in calories.

DRINKING: A MIXED REVIEW

For those who wish to drink safely, *moderation* has always been the rule. But what constitutes moderation? Doctors offer the following guidelines.

● Don't go over two drinks a day. Two drinks a day—the equivalent of two beers, two glasses of wine or a double whiskey sour—is considered by some the upper limit of prudent drinking for any healthy person under 60.
● Remember the "55 rule." As long as a person's blood alcohol level remains under 0.055 (half the amount that constitutes drunk driving), alcohol won't cause physical or psychological harm, say Roger E. Vogler, Ph.D., and Wayne R. Barts, Ph.D., authors of *The Better Way to Drink.* To obey the 55 rule, don't drink more than two drinks an hour.
● Even moderate drinking, however, may be detrimental. Tests given to men who drank an average of two or three drinks 12 times a month (and women who drank two drinks 7 times a month) revealed measurable deficits in mental performance.
● For pregnant women, even moderate drinking can result in mental retardation or physical abnormalities in the infant.

So, if you toast to good health, don't get burned.

Kerry Pechter

Foods That Boost Your Brainpower

Look, up in the sky!

It's a flying frontal lobe!

No! It's a mighty medulla oblongata!

No! It's Superbrain!

Superbrain! Faster than a speeding algebra problem . . . more powerful than a dual disk drive . . . able to leap tall mental obstacles at a single bound! And who, disguised as Clark Cranium, fights a never-ending battle for Truth, Justice and the Intellectual Way!

Now don't turn that page, folks. Stay right here and you too can learn how to become another Superbrain—just like your favorite comic-book hero.

It's simple, it's easy and because, as the old saying goes, you are what you eat, it's healthy, too! That's right, you can improve your mind—become more alert, even increase your memory —all by knowing the correct foods to eat.

MOOD FOOD

If we are what we eat, it is then safe to say that we also think what we eat, for as studies now show, our diet affects the way our mind operates.

Think of it this way. The next time you skip lunch and gobble down a candy bar instead, you're sending sugar, fats and a whole assortment of unnatural ingredients through your bloodstream. It might work in giving you a quick (but short-lived) jolt of *physical* energy, but when it comes to mental energy, it's a lot like pouring water into an empty automobile gas tank. It'll fill the tank, but the car's still not going anywhere.

On the other hand, says noted nutrition researcher Judith Wurtman, Ph.D., of the Massachusetts Institute of Technology, if your diet consists of fresh foods, especially those high in protein, you're supplying your body with the proper amino acids, which will produce the chemicals needed to stimulate your brain, keeping it energized and alert.

Simply stated, if you want to be smart you have to eat smart.

Why Heavy Drinking Is Dumb

SCENE: A dimly lit bar.

DRUNK: This time make it a double.

BARTENDER: Hey, Sam, do you know that a recent study in the *British Medical Journal* stated that abusing alcohol actually shrinks brain cells in number and size and makes your brain smaller?

DRUNK: Did you say something about rain in Britain?

BARTENDER: No, Sam . . . brains. A medical study proved that heavy drinking can shrink the size of your brain.

DRUNK: You mean smaller raindrops?

BARTENDER: Aren't you listening to me, Sam? Brains. Heavy alcohol drinking shrinks a type of brain cell called a neuron that makes up nerve tissue in your brain's cerebral cortex. And even if you stop drinking, your brain tissue won't completely go back to its original state of health. Now what do you think of that?

DRUNK: Zzzzzzzzz.

BARTENDER: I rest my case.

BRAIN DRAIN

When we eat carbohydrate-laden foods with little or no protein, our bodies produce a chemical known as serotonin, referred to as the calming chemical, explains Dr. Wurtman, author of *Managing Your Mind and Mood through Food*. When serotonin increases in the brain, we become emotionally relaxed, calm, even a bit drowsy, especially late in the day. Some people actually react by feeling sluggish and dull, especially if they have not eaten any protein for a long time.

That may be fine if your day happens to revolve around lying in bed, watching television and eating bowls of potato salad. But a carbohydrate-induced feeling of mental drowsiness may not be the best idea if you happen to be spending the day at work, interviewing for a job, driving through heavy traffic, or planning to climb up on your roof to repair that wobbly TV antenna.

"Carbohydrates eaten straight release insulin into the bloodstream, causing amino acids in the blood to leave rapidly and enter muscles and other cells in the body," says Dr. Wurtman. "One amino acid, tryptophan, leaves more slowly and during that time can enter the brain to immediately manufacture serotonin. At this point you begin to relax."

DON'T BE A FATHEAD

Make a mistake, do or say something stupid and someone may call you a "fathead." According to what Dr. Wurtman says, there may be good reason.

"During the long, drawn-out digestive process that follows a high-fat meal, relatively more blood is diverted to the stomach and intestines and away from the brain," she explains. "Mental processes are slowed, the mind is dulled, and the result is sloppy thinking. . .or no thinking at all.

"Foods high in fats can have a disastrous effect on your ability to concentrate. If at any point during the day you need to think clearly, you'd better stock up your body with proteins; otherwise you'll find yourself feeling mentally slow, using poor mental judgement and becoming easily distracted."

BRAIN GAIN

Whenever you eat protein, more of the amino acid tyrosine will enter your brain. Tyrosine is converted by the body into dopamine and norepinephrine, also known as the alertness chemicals.

"When the brain is receiving the alertness chemicals, people begin to think more quickly, react rapidly to stimuli and feel more attentive," says Dr. Wurtman. "Their minds feel more motivated, alive and energized."

Dr. Wurtman refers to this as being on a mental roll. "Problems, even big ones, often seem more manageable because of the heightened brainpower brought on by eating foods high in protein."

THE BRAINPOWER MENU

Foods containing very little fat, almost no carbohydrates and very high protein are best bets to keep your mind energized and alert, says Dr. Wurtman. These foods are shellfish, fish, chicken (without the skin), veal and very lean beef (meaning all the fat is trimmed away).

Some low-fat, high-protein dairy products are also good for keeping the brain powered. Although vegeta-

Caffeine for a Smart Start

Caffeine-free cola. Decaffeinated coffee. Herb tea rather than a caffeine-filled tea bag. These days it seems we spend more time dodging and ducking sources of caffeine then we do actually enjoying its substitutes.

"Caffeine is controversial at the moment, but the hard truth of the matter is this: There is very little scientific evidence that drinking coffee and other caffeine-containing beverages in moderation will have harmful, long-term effects on health," says Judith Wurtman, Ph.D.

In fact, a study conducted by Harris Lieberman, Ph.D., at the Massachusetts Institute of Technology shows caffeine improves mental performance and plays an important role in elevating morning brainpower, reports Dr. Wurtman.

It seems that in the morning, brain cells are more sensitive to caffeine because of the overnight fast. The caffeine effect will get you in gear in a matter of minutes and keep you alert and mentally energetic for hours. Thus, that first cup of coffee—or tea—in the morning can give you a powerful jolt of alertness, says Dr. Wurtman. Some of you may need two cups, but you should stop there. Save that third cup for the late afternoon, when you may need another caffeine pick-me-up.

ble protein sources are often high in carbohydrates and low in fat, they are not particularly good sources of high-quality protein.

Many foods are high in both protein and fat and should be avoided when trying to keep your brain alert. Lamb, pork and pork products, liver, hard cheeses, whole milk and regular yogurt will slow the mind down.

BREAKFAST IN BED

If you start your day by eating a high-fat, high-carbohydrate breakfast, like sausage and pancakes, you may as well order it in bed and plan on staying there the rest of the day. Your brain will be sluggish and unable to concentrate, says Dr. Wurtman.

Eat some protein in the morning, such as eggs, low-fat yogurt, cottage cheese or a slice of wheat toast topped with low-fat cheese, to keep your brain energy at pace with your body during the first part of the day. Carbohy-

drates will be useful for the latter part of the day when you want to unwind, decrease stress and relax. So after work, try eating some pasta or other high-carbohydrate foods for dinner.

Richard Dominick

Getting the Most from Your Nutrients

If you eat three square meals a day or take vitamin supplements, you might think you're getting adequate nutrition. But you could be wrong.

Nutrition isn't that simple or direct. Your body doesn't always make the best use of all the vitamins you take in, either in food or in supplements. Some nutrients never get to where they can do the most good. Others sail through your system without being absorbed.

YOUR DIET INSURANCE

But there are ways to help ensure that you're getting what you need.

You can multiply your intake of vitamins and minerals, without spending extra money on supplements or foods, by making a few simple, economical changes in the way you shop and prepare meals. These hints will help you get the most nutrients for your food dollar.

Choose the best. Not all fruits and vegetables are created equal. In general, the darker the food, the more nutrients it contains. For example, pink grapefruit contains more than 30 times the vitamin A of white grapefruit. Romaine lettuce has twice the calcium and iron, 8 times the vitamin C, and more than 10 times the vitamin A of iceberg lettuce.

One of the most nutrient-packed vegetables you can eat is broccoli. Other top contenders are spinach, brussels sprouts, lima beans, peas, asparagus, artichokes, sweet potatoes, carrots, red bell peppers and winter squash.

Go easy on the processed foods. They have more calories and less nutrients than their natural counterparts. Raw nuts have far more thiamine and vitamin B_6 than roasted nuts. Whole

wheat bread and brown rice are higher in nutrients and fiber than their processed white counterparts. Even if the processed food is "fortified," it usually doesn't provide the same range of nutrients as a natural, whole food.

Eat food fresh. And we mean *very* fresh. Even a day or two in the refrigerator can rob a fruit or vegetable of precious nutrients.

Why? Because produce is virtually *alive*—its cells are still consuming oxygen and burning fuel to produce carbon dioxide and heat. This uses up nutrients. Fruits and vegetables can lose half their vitamin C after two or three days in the refrigerator, and they lose it even more quickly at room temperature.

Cover and refrigerate produce as soon as you bring it home. And if you can't buy your produce fresh, buy it frozen; freezing retains most of the nutrients.

Store it right. Heat, light and exposure to air or water destroy certain nutrients. Follow these steps to maximize nutrition and storage life.

● Refrigerate greens in an airtight container such as a vegetable crisper. Or use plastic bags, punching a few holes for drainage to prevent sogginess. (Exceptions: cucumbers, peppers and eggplant go soft in bags).
● Don't wash or cut fruits and vegetables before storing them, and never soak or store them in water. Leave green peas and lima beans in the pod until you're ready to cook them.
● Store dried foods in dark, dry places and sealed against air. Dried fruits can also lose vitamins A, C and E if exposed to oxygen. Fresh fruits should be stored in an environment that conserves moisture.

Minimize cutting. Chopping produce and exposing the cut surface to air causes oxidation, which destroys certain nutrients—especially vitamins A, C and B_6, thiamine and biotin. So wait until the last minute before chopping, opening cans or thawing. When you do cut produce, cut it in big chunks to minimize nutrient loss. For example, you lose more vitamin C by mincing peppers than by slicing them.

Eat the whole thing. The outer layer of a plant is usually where most of the nutrients are concentrated. So use a scrubber instead of a peeler on carrots and potatoes. The skins protect against vitamin loss during cooking, too. This principle holds for fish as well. Sardines—especially the inexpensive kind, with tiny edible bones—far outscore salmon steaks and haddock filets in vitamin A, calcium, phosphorus and iron.

Cook it right. Fast cooking at relatively high temperatures is the best method. Cook in pans with tight-fitting lids to minimize exposure to air. And the less water you use, the better.

In general, stir-frying is the best method for retaining nutrients, followed by pressure cooking and steaming. Boiling is one of the worst, as is deep-fat frying.

Whenever possible, cook in iron pots. Food cooked this way may contain three to four times more iron than food cooked in glass.

MAXIMIZING ABSORPTION

Even when you eat a balanced diet and take all the proper supplements, you may not be absorbing the bulk of the nutrients you take in. For example, even under the best conditions, calcium uptake rarely exceeds 50 percent of intake, and maximum iron absorption from certain foods may be only 5 to 15 percent.

How well you absorb nutrients depends on many factors, including:

● How much exercise you get (a fit body metabolizes vitamins and minerals more efficiently).

● How well you handle stress. The digestive disturbances that often plague the emotionally stressed can interfere with nutrient absorption.

● What kinds of nutrient-robbers you live with. The continual use of stimulants like caffeine can take its toll over time.

● Whether you consume the nutrient in a bio-available form. The body metabolizes certain forms of a nutrient better than others.

But for the majority of healthy, active people, the primary factor in nutrient absorption is diet. Not so much what you take in—although that's obviously important—but when and in what combination.

Here are some other tips to help you make the most of your carefully collected nutrients.

Eat small, nutritious meals and snacks. All the nutrients your body takes in at a big meal can be hard to swallow, says John Pinto, Ph.D., associate professor of nutrition and medicine at Cornell University Medical College and assistant member at Memorial Sloan-Kettering Cancer Center in New York City.

"Many of those nutrients won't be absorbed," Dr. Pinto says, "because it's easier for the gastrointestinal tract to absorb nutrients from small amounts of food over a small period of time."

Swallow your fat-soluble vitamins with foods containing fat. Vitamins A, D and E are absorbed in the intestine in the presence of fat.

Consequently, if you take your fat-soluble vitamins on an empty stomach, you might flush out most of the vitamins before they can be absorbed.

What about those of us on a low-fat diet? Not to worry, says Cedric Garland, Ph.D., a professor of community and family medicine at the University of California in La Jolla.

"From a practical point of view, a diet containing 15 to 20 percent fat would still be sufficient to absorb fat-soluble vitamins," Dr. Garland says.

Take your supplements with food. Food helps improve the absorption of nutrients. "It's best that nutrients be consumed with a meal," says Dr. Pinto. "The very sight of food begins to stimulate the appetite, triggering the release of various enzymes. Intestinal blood flow increases, preparing to help transport food through the body and move nutrients from the intestine into the bloodstream."

Multiple Choice: Four Tips for Picking a Supplement

Taking a multivitamin and mineral supplement as nutritional insurance makes sense for many of us, but picking a good multi from the hundreds on drugstore shelves can be intimidating. The following tips from nutritionists may help.

Check the formula for balance. If it says 100 percent after each nutrient, it's balanced. Reading the label also lets you check for specific nutrients—extra calcium, for example—in amounts you want.

Decide how much you want. If your goal is insurance, a multiple that provides 25 to 100 percent of the U.S. Recommended Daily Allowance will do it. An exception is vitamin D, which should not exceed 100 percent.

Decide what you can swallow. Check pill size before you buy. Some manufacturers cram everything into a once-daily at the expense of your esophagus.

Understand that more is not better. You may be tempted to think that if your multiple at its suggested dosage isn't good enough, you can just take it more often and not bother to switch to some better-balanced product. You may want more calcium, for instance, but need to take 3 pills, rather than 1, a day. Taking an unbalanced supplement 3 times a day still does not provide the recommended doses of some nutrients, but you may end up taking too much of other nutrients, throwing things even further out of balance.

Anti-Aging Antioxidants

Your deepening wrinkles—or the gray hairs that almost seem to pop up overnight on your head—may be the visible signs of your aging. But the aging that goes on *inside* your body actually has more far-reaching consequences.

Much of the internal damage that accumulates over a lifetime, and the diseases that go with it, may be linked to mischievous molecules inside us called "free radicals." So says Sheldon Hendler, M.D., Ph.D., author of the book *The Complete Guide to Anti-Aging Nutrients.*

But we don't have to accept passively what the years dish out. "Free radicals are something we can identify, measure and do battle with," says Dr. Hendler.

RADICALS ABUSE YOUR BODY

Free radicals are as wild as they sound. "Actually, they don't like being 'free,' at least in the sense of remaining single or unattached," he says. They are typically substances with unpaired electrons, and that puts them in a "desperate tizzy to get hitched to almost anything they can grab onto."

When they latch onto something, it's known as oxidation. And oxidation can "rust" the body almost as it does metal. This oxidation occurs most readily in fats. So cell membranes, which are rich in fat molecules, are prime targets. A free-radical attack on the cells could kill or severely damage them—leaving them vulnerable to cancer or other diseases.

"Given the fact that fats account for more than 40 percent of the total calories in the typical American diet, it is not difficult to see how we might be exposed to extensive free-radical activity," says Dr. Hendler.

Free radicals, which are created by the body's normal metabolism, as well as by radiation, ozone exposure and cancer-causing chemicals, do have a purpose, however. Some play a role in the body's enzyme reactions and help kill invading bacteria. But the extras are bad guys. They leave not only destruction in their path but also their imprint, an age pigment called lipofuscin.

THE "NUTRITIONAL FOUR" TO THE RESCUE

"The details of how free radicals cause disease are not really fully known, but they do," says Denham Harman, M.D., Ph.D., of the University of Nebraska School of Medicine. "There is a great deal of data indicating that, when all is said and done, free radicals are the major cause of many diseases."

So far, free radicals have been implicated in a long list of problems that accompany aging. Included among them are cancer, atherosclerosis, high blood pressure, Alzheimer's disease, osteoarthritis and immune deficiency, says Dr. Harman.

But there is good news. Substances called antioxidants can neutralize free radicals by pairing up their electrons. And vitamins C and E, forms of vitamin A, and the mineral selenium are known to be antioxidants that, along with antioxidant enzymes produced by the body, help to protect the body's cells.

Researchers have found that vitamins E and C can decrease the level of free radicals in the blood. One hundred people, aged 60 to 100, were given vitamin E (approximately 200 international units) or vitamin C (400 milligrams), or both, daily for a year. The vitamin E alone decreased the free radical level by 26 percent. The vitamin C decreased it by 13 percent. And the group taking both E and C decreased their levels 25 percent. (This level of supplement intake should be undertaken only with the approval and supervision of your doctor.)

Other evidence is surfacing that suggests that dietary antioxidants may be able to prevent free radical activity—and some of its unpleasant side effects—throughout the body. Here are some examples.

Cataracts. Research on animals has shown that vitamin C may protect the lenses of the eyes from the constant bombardment and damage by light and oxygen that makes them vulnerable to cataracts.

In a study conducted at Tufts University, the animals were fed either high or low doses of vitamin C. Those taking the higher doses got three to five times as much vitamin C in their lenses. Their lenses were then artificially aged by exposing them to ultraviolet light. They found that those with more vitamin C in their lenses were better able to withstand the photo-oxidative stress that was used to artificially age them.

Respiratory diseases. "Ozone is one of the strongest oxidants known, so it has the potential for doing tremendous damage to the lungs and to the entire body when you breath it in smoggy air," says William A. Pryor, Ph.D., director of the Biodynamics Institute at Louisiana State University. Ozone weakens the body's ability to use oxygen for energy metabolism. The effects can be subtle or they can kill.

Numerous studies have shown that susceptibility to lung damage from ozone may be reduced by adding vitamin E supplements to animals' diets —and animals given vitamin E live appreciably longer than vitamin E-deficient animals when exposed to ozone.

Cancer. Vitamins A, E and C and selenium may play roles in preventing some cancers, says Ronald Ross Watson, Ph.D., of the Department of Family and Community Medicine at the Arizona Health Sciences Center in Tucson. Studies have concluded that:

● Areas with low selenium in the soil and water have more deaths from cancers of the esophagus, stomach and rectum.
● Vitamin A deficiency may increase the risk of cancers of the lung, larynx, bladder, esophagus, stomach, colon, rectum and prostate.
● Vitamin C reduces the risk of cervical dysplasia, a precancerous condition.
● Vitamin E may have a role in reducing the risk of lung cancer, according to researchers at the Johns Hopkins School of Hygiene and Public Health.

Immune deficiency. "We know that immune function declines with age," says Jeffrey Blumberg, Ph.D., of the U.S. Department of Agriculture Human Nutrition Research Center on Aging at Tufts University. "And we've found in our animal studies that high levels of vitamin E are capable of reversing this decline. Not totally reversing to levels comparable to those in younger animals, but partially."

Our immune systems play an important role in resisting diseases. "If the immune system is less vigorous, then disease has a much greater chance of winning," he says.

Senility. "It hasn't been proved, but many people have suggested that senile dementia has its origin in free-radical damage," says Dr. Blumberg. "We don't know how free-radical damage might cause senile dementia, but one way it could do that is by damaging nerves in the brain.

Foods That Fight Aging

Research has shown that antioxidants—namely vitamins A, C and E and the mineral selenium—often help each other out, having even more power together than they have alone.

So including the foods listed below in your diet might help boost your body's fight against free radicals.

Outstanding food sources of vitamin A are:

● Broccoli
● Cantaloupe
● Carrots
● Spinach
● Sweet potatoes

The best food sources of vitamin C are:

● Broccoli
● Brussels sprouts
● Cantaloupe
● Grapefruit juice
● Green peppers
● Orange juice
● Oranges
● Papayas

The best food sources of vitamin E are:

● Almonds
● Hazelnuts
● Pecans
● Raw wheat germ
● Sunflower-seed oil
● Sunflower seeds
● Wheat-germ oil

The best food sources of selenium are:

● Broccoli
● Cabbage
● Onions
● Seafood
● Whole grain cereal and bread

The amounts of selenium in foods may vary according to the level of the mineral in the soils where they were produced. In general, soils in the West contain more selenium than those in the East.

"We have shown in our study that free-radical damage occurred in the brain more readily in old animals than in young animals," he says. "We also found that vitamin E protects against that damage. When we gave the animals vitamin E-deficient diets, the damage was much greater. The effects were similar in the liver, but we were mainly interested in looking at the brain."

Life extension. It is reasonable to expect that we can stay healthier and increase average life expectancy (now 74.8 years) 5 or more years while possibly increasing the maximum life span slightly beyond 100 years, says Dr. Harman.

The probability of developing any one of the "free-radical diseases" may be decreased by eating a diet rich in natural antioxidants, such as vitamins E and C, and low in total fat (including unsaturated fats) and by not overeating, says Dr. Harman.

Free radicals are by-products of our metabolism. The more you eat, the more free radicals your body creates and has to contend with, he says. By doing all you can to put the lid on free radicals, you'll be helping to preserve your youthfulness where it really counts—inside.

Heidi Rodale

Be Sure with B

Could there have been an Abbott without a Costello? Laurel without Hardy? Lewis without Clark? Koufax without Drysdale?

Could any group of 25 men have won the 1969 World Series, or did it have to be the amazin' Mets?

Did Fred Astaire and Ginger Rogers have that "certain something," or could Fred have danced with Moe Howard just as elegantly?

Would the Beatles have made it as John, Paul, George and Luigi?

Whether it's a singing group, nine men on a field or an entire corporation, teamwork is what makes it click. Great teams must work hand in hand, one helping the other. Like Burns and Allen, Batman and Robin, thiamine and riboflavin.

Thiamine and riboflavin? Are they that new juggling act from the Ukraine?

No. They are part of the B-complex vitamins, perhaps one of the greatest teams of all time.

THE TEAM SPIRIT

Whatta team! Separately, each B vitamin's function is important, but taken together, as a team, they become even more potent. B vitamins are essential for good blood circulation and helping the heart stay healthy. They also keep the correct hormone balance in your body, and they play an important role in keeping your immune system strong. *And* they help

keep you mentally alert and emotionally stable, improve your energy and help you deal with stress.

How can you be sure you'll get the right amount of B vitamins in your diet?

"Relax," says Jack M. Cooperman, Ph.D., director of nutrition at New York Medical College. "If you eat a balanced diet every day, your body will be receiving all the B vitamins it needs to keep it in perfect running order. The beauty of Mother Nature is that everything our bodies need for good health is given to us in our foods. Eat balanced meals every day and you will be getting all your B vitamins."

PLAYING BY THE RULES

Your body will let you know if it isn't receiving enough B vitamins in your daily diet. If you can't shake off a cold or you're always getting infections, if you're having trouble sleeping, concentrating or keeping up your appetite, if you feel sleepy after meals, have low energy or frequent constipation, chances are your daily diet is lacking in the B complex.

Individually, each vitamin has an important position in the B-team. According to Dr. Cooperman, here's what they do.

Thiamine (B₁). Why is thiamine an important part of the vitamin B-team? It promotes growth, aids in digestion, improves mental attitude and keeps your nervous system, muscles and heart in good running order.

Good sources of thiamine are whole grain cereals, pork products, brewer's yeast, green peas and other legumes, beef kidney, beef liver and sunflower seeds.

Niacin and Your Heart

After a 9-year study, scientists at the Maryland Medical Research Institution have found that niacin just may be an answer to battling heart disease.

It all began when the researchers were doing a follow-up to the well-known Coronary Drug Project. Initially, the study's results showed that people who each took 3 grams (3,000 milligrams) of niacin had about 27 percent fewer nonfatal heart attacks than people taking other drugs or a placebo. What it didn't show was a drop in the rate of fatal heart attacks—that is, until several years later when the scientists did a follow-up to their study.

The group that had been taking

niacin was found to have 9 to 13 percent fewer deaths—from heart disease or from any other cause—than the other groups, including those treated with a then-popular cholesterol-lowering drug called clofibrate.

The Recommended Dietary Allowance for niacin for an adult male is only 18 milligrams. When used in such large doses as in this study, it is considered to be a drug and should be administered only under the care of a physician.

Research continues on the benefits of niacin in preventing heart disease, but many scientists have found it to be efficient in cutting cholesterol levels.

Riboflavin (B_2). When riboflavin enters the body as part of the B-team, it promotes healthy skin, nails and hair, stops eye fatigue and is essential for converting protein, fats and carbohydrates into energy.

Good sources of riboflavin are milk, beef and chicken liver, beef kidney, brewer's yeast, Swiss cheese and enriched flour and bread.

Niacin. Niacin is crucial for the proper maintenance of healthy skin. It works in tandem with riboflavin to convert carbohydrates, fats and protein into useful energy. A deficiency may even cause dementia.

Good sources of of niacin are liver, lean meats, poultry, peanut butter, beef kidney, legumes and salmon.

B_6 (pyridoxine). This member of the B-team helps prevent skin and nervous disorders and guards against infections. It helps slow down aging and prevents restless sleep. It can even work as a natural diuretic.

Such foods as whole grain cereals, liver, beef kidney, white meats (chicken and fish), potatoes, avocados, bananas, egg yolks and sunflower seeds contain an abundance of B_6.

B_{12} (cyanocobalamin). If there were no B_{12}, there would be unhealthy nervous systems, bad mental concentration, memory and balance, no red blood cells, irritability galore and a planet full of insomniacs.

But don't fret! There's plenty of B_{12} around—but only in animal products. It can be found in meats, liver, kidney, milk, Swiss cheese, salmon and eggs.

Folate. Folate, or folic acid, is needed by your body to produce the genetic factors RNA and DNA, thereby making it essential for the manufacture and repair of all cells. It also prevents anemia and infections and aids in the development of the immune system.

Good sources of folate are wheat germ, beef and chicken liver, beef kidney, brewer's yeast, mushrooms, oranges and orange juice, asparagus, broccoli, lima beans, bananas, strawberries, sunflower seeds, cantaloupe and some legumes.

Pantothenate. Pantothenate, or pantothenic acid, is necessary to build complex molecules like fats and hemoglobin. Without it, the body's ability to carry out certain chemical functions would be diminished.

The term *pantothenate* is derived from the Greek word *panthos,* meaning "everywhere." Although pantothenate is found in many foods, certain processing methods, such as flour milling, destroy it. It is found in particularly high amounts in organ meats, whole grain cereals and most fish.

DO YOU NEED SUPPLEMENTS?

Unless you are under a doctor's care and eating less than 1,200 calories a day or not eating a balanced diet, you needn't worry about getting enough B vitamins, says Dr. Cooperman. "But remember," he says, "the body cannot store the B complex, making it essential that you eat a balanced diet every day."

So speak with your doctor. If you aren't eating a balanced diet, he may prescribe a multivitamin supplement.

Richard Dominick

Riboflavin Does It Again

Attention all women! Jump off those rowing machines, turn off that stationary bike, slip out of those aerobics costumes—and increase your daily intake of foods high in riboflavin first!

That's right. A report at an annual meeting of the Federation of American Societies for Experimental Biology revealed that older women on a regular exercise program need more riboflavin.

A group of 14 women between the ages of 50 and 67 were placed on a regular exercise program. One-half of the group were given diets containing riboflavin at the Recommended Dietary Allowance (RDA) level, while the other half were taking riboflavin at 1½ times that level. The women rode stationary bikes for 30 minutes a day, 6 days a week for 4 weeks. At the end, the group receiving the RDA levels showed evidence of a significant depletion of riboflavin.

One of the best sources of riboflavin is dairy foods. Although this study dealt with only older exercising women, all women should consider adding more yogurt, milk and cheese (all low-fat, of course) to their diets.

Vitamin C to the Rescue

People today try to get extra vitamin C in their diets for just about anything and everything that does or might ail them: to treat or prevent colds, heart disease, cancer, flu, arthritis, infertility and cataracts; to build up their immune systems; or if they've been exposed to pollutants or toxins. You name it, someone is making an attempt to get vitamin C for it, whether in a side dish of broccoli or a supplement.

Is it worth it to focus your attention on foods rich in vitamin C? Scientific studies seem to say yes.

O-o-o-h! Don't eat that. It causes cancer. We've all heard that about almost everything we eat, and we dismiss it and keep on eating, or worry about it . . . and keep on eating. After all, cancer's all around us, right? And no one's actually proven a link between cancer and what we eat, right?

Wrong! There is conclusive proof that nitrites and nitrates, used to preserve many processed meats, especially pork and beef products, are transformed in our own mouths and stomachs into potent cancer-causers (carcinogens).

Like the Lone Ranger, vitamin C rides again. It hates tumors like that masked man hated stagecoach robbers. A British study found that oral supplements of vitamin C significantly reduced cancer-causing activity in stomach juices.

And at least five studies on three continents have shown a lower incidence of stomach cancer when the diet includes plentiful fresh fruits and vegetables containing vitamin C.

There's a catch: Vitamin C has to be in your tummy at the same time as the nitrites. You've got to eat your C-rich fruits and vegetables or take your daily C supplement just before or at the same time you gobble your nitrites. Vitamin C can't unmake the cancer-causers once they've been formed. Fortunately, manufacturers are now adding vitamin C to their nitrite-preserved foods.

No smear campaign. A research team at Albert Einstein College of Medicine and the Bronx Municipal Hospital Center unexpectedly found that all 46 women in their study who had positive or suspicious Pap smears were ingesting low or deficient amounts of vitamin C. A follow-up study found significantly lower vitamin C levels in women with cervical lesions.

It's everywhere, it's everywhere! Pollution, that is. And vitamin C. It's now widely accepted that C markedly affects the toxic and cancer-causing properties of more than 50 common pollutants in our air, water and food. The vitamin can affect the toxicity of the pollutant, or the pollutant can affect levels of vitamin C in the body.

Get to the heart of the matter. Guess what? Vitamin C may help your

Supplements and the Safety Zone

Vitamin C is one of the safest nutrients. Researchers have fed thousands of milligrams daily to subjects, who experienced no serious ill effects. Their most common complaint? Diarrhea. But as with all nutrients, there can be adverse side effects for some people. The form of vitamin C that probably affects the greatest number of people is the chewable tablets. It's been reported that the tablets can dissolve tooth enamel in a matter of months.

While anyone who takes supplements should do so with their doctor's approval and supervision, you must check with your doctor about taking C supplements if you have sickle cell anemia or G-6PD (it affects about 10 percent of American black males), hemochromatosis (iron overload), folate deficiency, leukemia or kidney disease or stones.

Vitamin C may reduce the effectiveness of the tricyclic antidepressants, including Elavil and Sinequan. It may also alter the results of several blood or urine tests for a wide range of ailments. It's essential to check with your doctor before dosing yourself with vitamin C if you fall into these categories.

heart stay healthy, help prevent atherosclerosis and cut cholesterol levels. And there's evidence that this workhorse vitamin reduces triglycerides, blood fats now considered to be as important as high cholesterol in the development of heart disease.

In one experiment, 1 gram of vitamin C also helped reduce blood clots in healthy men after consuming 75 grams—almost 3 ounces!—of artery-clogging butter. Such clotting is called thrombosis, and it can lead to a heart attack or stroke. The researchers at Tagore Medical College and Hospital in India said vitamin C may prove to be an effective anticlotting agent without the possible serious side effects of current drugs.

Researchers at the USDA Human Nutrition Research Center on Aging, at Tufts University, studied almost 700 people over age 60. They found that a higher level of vitamin C in the blood correlated with a higher level of HDL cholesterol (the protective kind). But the level of total cholesterol was not higher, an indication that LDL cholesterol (the kind that blocks arteries) was reduced by vitamin C. (When the researchers checked vitamin C intake instead of blood levels, they found the same effects.) Studies by other researchers with other age-groups have shown similar results.

In the Tufts study, the effect of vitamin C was strongest in people between 60 and 69 years old, and decreased gradually in older people. The researchers aren't sure why, but they think it may be because the older people had higher HDL levels to begin with.

The researchers estimate that an intake of about 1 gram (1,000 milligrams) of vitamin C per day could increase HDL by 8 percent. "Given the magnitude of effect observed in the current report, the potential impact on a large population in terms of [coronary heart disease] is quite signif-

Do You Need a Supplement?

"Food is an important part of a balanced diet," writes author Fran Lebowitz, "[and] gives real meaning to dining room furniture."

Vitamin C researchers would probably say there's a little more to food than that. Many say you don't need supplements of the vitamin; just eat right. Despite the finding of Albert Einstein College of Medicine researcher Seymour Romney, M.D., that women with suspicious or positive Pap smears had low-C diets, he doesn't want women to rush out and buy vitamin C supplements, thinking they can prevent cervical cancer this way. "It's too simplistic," he says.

It's clear, says Dr. Romney, that sound nutrition involves an interaction of multiple nutrients, eating habits, food preparation and consumption, and lifestyle. No one says vitamin C can prevent cancer all by itself; it needs to work in concert with other nutrients.

Significantly, however, vitamin C's anti-cancer abilities are proven sufficiently for the American Cancer Society to recommend that people eat C-rich foods.

And like many vitamin C researchers, Dr. Romney's diet reflects his findings: "I enjoy lots of good oranges," he says. University of Michigan pharmacology professor Vincent Zannoni, Ph.D., who studied the effects of vitamin C on alcohol metabolism, says he never takes a supplement. He just eats enough fruits and vegetables to ingest between 500 milligrams and 1 gram of C a day.

Anthony Verlangieri, Ph.D., however, doesn't believe the Recommended Dietary Allowance (RDA) is nearly high enough. Since diabetics are especially prone to cardiovascular disease, Dr. Verlangieri recommends they take 2 grams of vitamin C a day, while healthy people who want to main-

tain cardiovascular fitness should take a gram daily. (This level of vitamin C should only be taken with the approval and supervision of your doctor.)

Your vitamin C doesn't have to come from supplements, Dr. Verlangieri acknowledges, and he notes there has been a large drop in deaths from heart disease at the same time consumption of fruits and vegetables has risen. But he wonders about the ability of modern Americans to consume enough properly prepared fruits and vegetables to do the job effectively.

While not recommending a hike in the RDA, Edward Calabrese, Ph.D., of the University of Massachusetts Division of Public Health, wants a reexamination of the RDA to take into account the fact that we are exposed to a great many toxic pollutants in our daily lives, some of which C has been proven able to disable.

icant," they say. "An added benefit is the relative ease and safety with which [vitamin C levels] can be raised."

Vitamin C also appears to keep blood vessel walls intact. If there's not enough C, the cells in the walls break loose and LDL cholesterol—the "bad" kind—gets a toehold and invites more LDL to join the clogging party. High blood pressure, stroke or heart attack can be the outcome of this party. Diabetics are especially prone, says University of Mississippi heart researcher Anthony Verlangieri, Ph.D. His large three-year study using monkeys (like humans and guinea pigs, monkeys can't make their own vita-

min C) supports his previous findings of C's beneficial effect on blood vessel walls.

Immune squad, front and center! This elite squad comprises a specific group of white blood cells, scientifically known as lymphocytes. They are the body's first line of defense against infection; some carry around, and others produce, antibodies that fight infection. And guess what? They're chock-full of vitamin C—40 to 60 times the concentration in the blood plasma itself. When disease—or trauma—strikes, they lose much of their vitamin C. With clues like that, it's no wonder researchers study the

vitamin's role in immunity. Here's what they're finding.

● Though not everyone agrees, it now seems clear that vitamin C lessens the severity of the common cold, and maybe the frequency, duration and complications.
● Large doses of vitamin C have been shown to inhibit the flu virus's ability to prevent the growth of lymphocytes into infection fighters.
● A number of studies have shown vitamin C can increase the movement of hungry little bacteria killers called neutrophils. This effect is both upon

C Hangs Out in Joints

Without vitamin C, your body can't make collagen, the protein that forms your tendons, ligaments and cartilage. These connective tissues literally "glue" your body together.

Rheumatoid arthritis is called a collagen disease because it occurs throughout the body's connective tissues. It's a cruel and deforming illness: One theory holds that the immune system literally turns traitor and ravages its own body—swelling, inflaming and immobilizing joints. So important is vitamin C to collagen formation that the collagen connection is to vitamin C researchers as the Holy Grail was to Sir Gawain.

Pennsylvania College of Podiatry professor Robert H. Davis, Ph.D., concocted a cream of vitamin C, aloe vera and ribonucleic acid (RNA). All three are known to work against inflammation and arthritis, and vitamin C's collagen-producing properties make it a prime candidate for an arthritis

treatment. In test rats, the cream not only inhibited massive arthritic changes but reversed them, including apparent remodeling of damaged bone, a feat researcher Dr. Davis called "major dramatic changes."

Dr. Davis was looking for an alternative to steroids and synthetic drugs, which can have side effects worse than the disease. There haven't been any clinical trials with humans to follow up his prize-winning study, and Dr. Davis says people with severe arthritis still should be treated by a doctor. But since progress in testing his formula in humans has been slow since his study— for reasons, he says, having to do with money, bureaucracy and official skepticism, not for medical reasons—should sufferers try to make up their own application?

"If you could get fresh aloe plant gel, or the bottled kind, and mix in a little ascorbic acid and apply it, I'd say yes," says Dr. Davis. His formula is 5

parts aloe to 1 part ascorbic acid and 1 part RNA (which is present in all living cells); he says the RNA may not be necessary. And, he adds, the new ester form of vitamin C seems to penetrate the skin better and faster than ascorbic acid. All of the ingredients, he notes, have been approved for topical application by the U.S. Food and Drug Administration. (Use this formula, however, only with the approval and supervision of a doctor.)

Meanwhile, researchers in England used vitamin C to treat 3 vitamin C-deficient rheumatoid arthritis patients who suffered bruising. Rheumatoid arthritis patients' skin is often fragile and bruises easily. Bruising is also a product of vitamin C deficiency.

The doctors gave each of the patients 500 milligrams of vitamin C daily; the bruising disappeared and didn't return. (Again, this level of vitamin C should be used with your doctor's approval and supervision.)

neutrophils' random movement as they scour the countryside, as it were, sniffing for a scent of bacteria, and upon their ability to home in like bloodhounds on a bacterial trail.

● Vitamin C has been found to be an infection fighter due to its ability to enhance the immune system.

● Vitamin C is also known to stimulate production—in mice—of what was touted a few years ago as the body's own wonder drug, interferon. This is actually a messenger sent out by cells under viral attack, warning other cells to man the barricades before the enemy arrives.

● Benjamin V. Siegel, Ph.D., professor of pathology at Oregon Health Sciences University, says vitamin C also activates T-cells, which are believed to be the best cancer-cell killers our bodies possess. These T-cells have multiple duties, including regulation of the immune response itself.

The eyes have it. Vitamin C, that is. It's highly concentrated in eye fluids and lenses. Eyes, especially those that have seen many years, can cloud over with cataracts, which are caused by oxidation. Studies with laboratory animals—and human lenses in test tubes—show vitamin C's powerful antioxidant properties may help prevent or delay the onset of cataracts.

Moving on to your mouth. Vitamin C has been shown to alleviate bleeding gums in the early stages of gingivitis. Gingivitis is an inflammation of the gums which, if left unchecked, can lead to periodontal disease. It is due to the poor dental hygiene that your dentist never tires of warning you about.

With all that biting and chomping going on, the gums need a constantly replenished supply of collagen, that omnipresent supportive protein, which is dependent upon vitamin C for its production. While a C deficiency hasn't been found to *cause* periodontal disease (which can result in tooth loss),

---

A Cure for Infertility?

When it comes to sperm and fertility, it's not together we stand, divided we fall. When sperm stick together, they can't wiggle their way to the egg very well.

Researchers at the University of Texas gave vitamin C-deficient subjects with clumping sperm and resultant infertility a gram of vitamin C a day for a month. In 3 weeks, says Earl B. Dawson, Ph.D., clumping was way down and sperm count way up. But other infertile men who were given 200 milligrams a day achieved the same results, although their improvement was not as quick in the first week.

Dr. Dawson advises caution. There are many reasons for infertility, and vitamin C may not be the answer to your problem. Always check with your doctor before assuming you know what the problem and the cure are.

---

good vitamin C nutrition can help keep early stages of the disease at bay.

Love your liver. A University of Michigan study found that guinea pigs on a diet of guinea pig chow, alcohol and low vitamin C developed liver damage resulting from an infiltration of fatty acids and/or death of liver cells—both steps that can lead to cirrhosis—while those on a diet high in vitamin C didn't.

Wounds heal faster. One study showed that bedsores healed faster when patients were given high doses of vitamin C. Physician Anthony N. Silvetti, M.D., from Melrose Park, Illinois, puts a blend of C, amino acids and complex sugars right onto bedsores, and he says it works well, even in wounds that hadn't healed for 30 years.

Also, because postoperative patients have been found to have low levels of vitamin C, some researchers feel that supplementation can help guard against complications in surgical wounds. One researcher reported that at least 200 milligrams a day is needed to maintain normal levels of the vitamin.

In studies of both humans and mice, large doses of vitamin C helped burns heal. In humans, vitamin C alleviated pain, shortened the healing period and reduced the time interval needed for grafting.

Also, at least in the human studies, levels of C have to be very low indeed for the wounds to heal improperly. The stress of injury, however, could be enough to drop those levels to the point where supplementation is needed.

If you smoke . . . You probably need more vitamin C. Smokers have lower levels of the vitamin in their blood. No one knows why, but the implication is that their bodies need more C and thus are using more.

William LeGro

Striving for Stronger Bones

Image one: The old woman moves slowly along the sidewalk, stopping occasionally to let the quicker and more agile young people around her pass by.

Her most noticeable characteristics are the color—a glowing steel gray—of the carefully brushed, well-cared-for hair wrapped in a bundle at the top of the slender neck. And the curve, in the once-elegant back, of a spine now bent and warped in the infamous widow's hump.

Image two: The older woman moves briskly along the sidewalk, casually dodging around her slow-moving peers and passing many of the younger people out strolling on this fine afternoon.

Arms pumping, she accelerates as the park comes into sight. Her head comes up—eyes flashing, small streams of sweat running down from the glowing gray hair—and she breaks into a slow jog.

Her back is absolutely straight.

Most women, given a choice, would prefer to enter old age like the woman in image two: Moving with the grace and physical élan of a gazelle—aging, admittedly, but nonetheless a gazelle.

The sad fact of the matter is that many women enter it looking more like the woman in image one—stooped and bent, moving more like turtles than African antelopes. Some estimates put the present number of women suffering from this condition (known as osteoporosis) at close to eight million in the United States. That's sad, because there's a lot women can do to keep from turning out like image one.

PREVENTION STARTS YOUNG

"There's a lot we can do to alleviate or slow the progress of osteoporosis," says Paul Saltman, Ph.D., professor of biology at the University of California in San Diego and author of *The California Nutrition Book*. It starts with preventive measures.

"When I say prevention," Dr. Saltman goes on, "I'm talking about a whole range of things, but primarily three of them: nutrition, exercise and hormone replacement therapy for women.

"And in this regard, it's important to make two points: One, prevention is not just a women's issue. Thin, Caucasian women, 50 or older, who've experienced early menopause are at highest risk, but a number of studies indicate that for every five to eight women who develop it, one man does—a significant number.

"And two, it's not a disease of age, it's a disease of youth. To protect yourself from the effects of osteoporosis, it's clearly better to start young and maintain good bone-building practices throughout life."

Gregory Mundy, M.D., concurs. Dr. Mundy is a professor of medicine and chief of the Endocrinology Department at the University of Texas Health Science Center.

"You can certainly accomplish a great deal more toward preventing the onset of the disease if you begin early, preferably in the teenage years," says Dr. Mundy. "Clean living, in the sense of eating right and getting enough exercise, is also one of your best defenses against the disease, and I think good habits established early are more likely to stick."

Straight Talk about Calcium Supplements

You've decided to start doing what you can to fight back against osteoporosis. One obvious step is adding calcium to your diet. But when it comes to supplements, what's best? Or does it make any difference at all?

There are 6 different forms of calcium on the market: carbonate, lactate, phosphate, chloride, gluconate and chelated calcium. They differ in the material the calcium is attached to (carbon in carbonate, lactic acid in lactate, and so on), in cost (carbonate is usually cheapest) and in calcium content (carbonate has the most).

"But I really don't think any one form is superior to another," says Paul Saltman, Ph.D. "Food sources, of course, are preferable, but in over-the-counter supplements I think calcium carbonate is fine. People should stay away, however, from so-called natural sources like dolomite and bone meal: Toxic levels of lead have been documented several times in supplements made from these sources."

So, what do you have to do to make sure *your* bones are as well built as they can possibly be?

STEP ONE: EATING THE RIGHT FOODS

"This is critical," Dr. Saltman says. "You need enough of the right foods in the right amounts to make sure that you're getting calcium, the nutrient most important to bone strength; that you're getting vitamin D, the nutrient that helps your body use calcium; that you're getting fluoride, which makes your bones denser and that you're getting enough trace minerals—zinc, copper and manganese, for example—which can affect the formation of bone at the cellular level."

The foods highest in calcium, of course, are dairy products such as milk, cheese and yogurt. Salmon and sardines with bones and dark green, leafy vegetables (mustard greens and broccoli, for example) are other calcium-rich choices. So are tofu and legumes. Dr. Saltman also recommends supplementing your diet with a modest dosage of extra calcium, especially if you avoid dairy products.

"I practice what I preach," he says. "I'm personally taking 500 milligrams a day, and I've got my wife taking 1,000 milligrams." And for someone who already has osteoporosis, he advises 1,500 milligrams in conjunction with hormone replacement therapy monitored under a doctor's care.

STEP TWO: EXERCISE

This doesn't have to mean running marathons or pumping iron.

"Walking's a splendid exercise for developing strong bones, and it has the advantage over many others in that it's something most anyone can do, regardless of age," Dr. Mundy says.

Dr. Saltman agrees. "Walking's one of the best things you can do to

Booze and Coffee: Tips for the Addicted

If you're interested in maximizing your body's absorption of calcium, or if you're already suffering from thinning bones, think about cutting back on 2 things: coffee and alcohol.

"Alcohol is a diuretic, which means it increases the amount of fluid excreted by the body," says Paul Saltman, Ph.D. "The more fluid you lose, the more calcium. Coffee does the same thing.

"Alcohol, however, has another negative effect: It may reduce the rate at which your body reuses the circulating calcium released from your skeleton during the bone-rebuilding process that's continually under way."

Don't panic: You can still drink beer and sip coffee. Dr. Saltman says a dollop of milk in every cup is all it takes to replace the calcium lost drinking coffee, while a supplement will support moderate social drinking (2 drinks a day).

build and keep strong bones. Which is not to say you can't run marathons or lift weights if you want to. It's just that you don't *have* to," he says.

"The important thing to remember is that, yes, exercise builds bones, but it's not something that works overnight. We recycle our bones about every seven or eight years, so you need to make exercise a regular part of your life for a long period of time to derive any skeletal benefit from it."

An important note: All the evidence isn't in, but research indicates that exercise may not only help prevent the onset of spinal osteoporosis—it may even stop its advance and in some cases reverse it.

Consider the following results from a Danish investigation, which measured the bone mineral content of women who exercised against that of women who didn't. The exercisers (ages 50 to 73) did moderate 1-hour workouts twice weekly, for eight months.

At the end of the study, "lumbar [lower] spine bone mineral content of the exercise group *increased* 3.5 percent, whereas that of the [nonexercising] control group *decreased* 2.7 percent," the research team writes. "The data suggest that physical exercise can inhibit *or reverse* . . . bone loss from the lumbar vertebrae in normal women."

An interesting point here: Although all the women were considered healthy, they all had experienced a Colles' fracture of the forearm, a type of fracture traceable to osteoporosis.

STEP THREE: HORMONE REPLACEMENT THERAPY

Women, like men, experience a slow loss of bone after reaching age 30, but the rate accelerates greatly with menopause. The decrease in estrogen production is largely responsible, and both Dr. Saltman and Dr. Mundy advocate sensible hormone replacement therapy for women.

"It doesn't appear to do much to reverse the process in women over the age of 60, but it clearly either stops it or slows it down significantly in women between 50 and 60," Dr. Mundy says. "I'd suggest it primarily for women aged 50 to 60. After that, it doesn't seem to make much difference."

Kim Anderson

Keeping in Sync with Copper and Zinc

It begins in the earth: A microscopic quantity of mineral is worn from the larger mass by the shearing forces of earth plate movement.

Water from thunderheads far overhead percolates down through the earth and washes the mineral into the waiting embrace of a plant's underground network of roots. The thirsty plant absorbs the water and the mineral begins its journey to the surface—and into the bodies of the animals who will eat the plant and the people who will eat the animals.

But once there, the real drama begins—the linkage of mineral with body in an almost endless interplay that affects nearly every part of the human being, from heart and lungs to immune system and brain.

MINUTE BUT MIGHTY

Zinc and copper are two of those minerals. Scientists call them trace minerals, meaning the body needs only small amounts. For a healthy adult, the Recommended Dietary Allowance (RDA) for zinc is 15 milligrams. For copper, there is no RDA, although 2 to 3 milligrams is considered the "safe and adequate" range.

The role of these two minerals in human health, however, is an enormous one that seems to grow larger with each new scientific inquiry—especially with zinc.

"Zinc is very, very important," says Ananda S. Prasad, M.D., professor of medicine at Wayne State University and an internationally recognized authority on zinc's role in human health. "It is involved in more than 200 enzyme systems affecting almost all body functions, in growth and development and in certain immune system functions—immune responses to viral, parasitic and fungal infections and wound healing."

Copper is equally important. The body uses it to make red and white blood cells and collagen, the connective tissue that holds us together and is important for the formation of bone. It helps to make melanin, which helps us tan, and the myelin sheathing wrapped around our nerves as insulation. It also helps to regulate cholesterol metabolism and the heart.

A shortage of either mineral may have health impacts ranging from minor to major, even life-threatening ones. But zinc deficiency develops more often.

"Copper is very important, no question about it," Dr. Prasad says. "It's just that a copper deficiency doesn't happen quite as often as zinc deficiency, which is actually fairly common."

So what happens if you don't get enough zinc?

A mild shortage can produce numbing of your sense of taste and smell, skin changes (dryness, rashes), weight loss, fatigue and mental lethargy. More severe shortages, although almost unheard of in the

A Zinc Food Sampler

Food	Portion	Zinc (mg.)
Oysters, raw	4 med.	51.00
Chicken heart	3 oz.	6.00
Calves' liver	3 oz.	5.20
Beef liver, braised	3 oz.	5.16
Ground beef, lean, broiled	3 oz.	4.56
Lamb, lean	3 oz.	4.20
Pumpkin seeds, roasted	¼ cup	4.20
Clams, steamed	6 med.	4.12
Beef round, trimmed of fat, broiled	3 oz.	3.98
Turkey, dark meat	3 oz.	3.80

SOURCES: Adapted from Agriculture Handbook Nos. 8-1, 8-5, 8-8, 8-11, 8-12, 8-13, 8-15, 8-16 (Washington, D.C.: U.S. Department of Agriculture).
"Provisional Tables on the Zinc Content of Foods," by Elizabeth W. Murphy, Barbara Wells Willis, and Bernice K. Watt, Ph.D., R.D., *Journal of the American Dietetic Association,* April 1975.
McCance and Widdowson's The Composition of Foods, by A. A. Paul and D. A. T. Southgate (New York: Elsevier/North Holland Biomedical, 1978).

American diet, can result in impaired growth, delayed wound healing, less resistance to disease, infertility and even death.

Dr. Prasad says that not enough information is available to estimate the magnitude of milder forms of zinc deficiency in the United States. But certain groups are at special risk: the elderly, pregnant women, nursing mothers, alcoholics, the still-growing young, those on a low-calorie reducing diet and anyone else who eats poorly. Vegetarians are a special case: Their diets eliminate meat, a rich source of zinc, and often include large amounts of cereal grains, which contain phytate, a compound that binds with zinc and partially blocks its absorption.

Similar unpleasantness occurs if you don't get enough copper in your food. Experimentally documented effects of copper deficiency include anemia, weakened bones, increased cholesterol levels, degeneration of the central nervous system, weakness of arterial blood vessels and enlarged heart.

Where to Find the Copper

Food	Portion	Copper (mg.)
Crab, boiled	3 oz.	4.08
Beef liver, broiled	4 oz.	3.16
Cashews, dry-roasted	¼ cup	0.76
Sunflower seeds, dry-roasted	¼ cup	0.59
Whole wheat flour	½ cup	0.30
Dried prunes, uncooked	¼ cup	0.17
Dried apricots, uncooked	¼ cup	0.14
Navy beans, cooked	¼ cup	0.13
Banana	1 med.	0.12
Raisins, seedless	¼ cup	0.11

SOURCES: Adapted from Agriculture Handbook Nos. 8-5, 8-8, 8-9, 8-11, 8-12, 8-13 (Washington, D.C.: U.S. Department of Agriculture).
"Copper Content of Foods," by Jean C. Pennington, Ph.D., and Doris Howes Calloway, R.D., Ph.D., *Research*, August 1963.
McCance and Widdowson's The Composition of Foods, by A. A. Paul and D. A. T. Southgate (New York: Elsevier/North Holland Biomedical, 1978).

MEETING YOUR DAILY REQUIREMENT

What's the best way to make sure you're getting enough zinc and copper? The experts agree: Eat enough food from all four basic food groups and include those foods high in zinc and copper.

"The best source for both of these minerals is red meat, and organ meats in particular," says Paul Saltman, Ph.D., a professor of biology at the University of California at San Diego and author of *The California Nutrition Book*.

Shellfish, particularly oysters, are also rich in zinc and copper. "But more important, the minerals in shellfish are readily assimilable—your body can use them easily and efficiently," says Dr. Saltman.

TOO MUCH IS TROUBLE

Dr. Prasad advises against zinc supplements providing more than 15 to 30 milligrams daily.

"If one is taking very high dosages —approaching or above 50 milligrams or so a day—it might pose a hazard," he says. "I don't recommend that except in special circumstances—where a therapeutic effect of zinc is needed—and then only on the advice of a physician."

The dangers of too much zinc include anemia, a suppressed immune system and impaired copper absorption, with all the consequent risks to health posed by copper deficiency, such as increased cholesterol and cardiovascular disease.

Too much copper can be dangerous, too, producing damage to the brain, central nervous system and kidneys. The red metal can also reach toxic levels more quickly than zinc because the body needs less of it. But overdosing on either mineral is practically impossible unless one gulps supplements with total disregard for suggested daily doses.

"The best defense against too much or too little of *any* trace mineral," notes Dr. Saltman, "is to maintain a varied diet and, when prudent, take a multimineral supplement.

"I'm a great believer in good eating habits, in consuming a wide variety of food in reasonable amounts from all four food groups," he says. "If you do that, and if you eat meats, you'll get what you need of copper and zinc."

Kim Anderson

Iron: The Mineral with Strength

SCENE: Two blood cells are sitting around, talking.

HEMO: Wanna go out tonight and pick up some corpuscles?

GLOBIN: Nah, I'm too tired.

HEMO: Come on, let's go out and paint the blood red tonight!

GLOBIN: Maybe tomorrow. *(yawning.)* Can you open a window and get some oxygen in here?

"Tired blood" may be a Madison Avenue ploy, but it's also a real condition brought about by lack of iron in the blood.

Without iron, there would be no hemoglobin, one of the body's most essential proteins. Red cells are what makes the blood red, but hemoglobin is what makes the red cells red. Hemoglobin's job is to carry the oxygen from the lungs to the rest of the body. When iron is deficient, hemoglobin is reduced. What results is a decrease in oxygen being transported to the brain and muscles. Headaches, constant fatigue and shortness of breath set in as the lungs try to pump more oxygen into the body. When this happens, you are suffering from iron-deficiency anemia, better known from television commercials as "tired blood."

WHO NEEDS IRON?

Women usually do, that's who. Men usually carry enough iron stored in their bodies to last up to three years. Women, on the other hand, often lack a natural reserve of the mineral. Pregnant women need an extraordinary amount of iron, and women with a normal menstrual flow need twice the amount of iron in a month that men do.

Vegetarians, infants, and people on certain weight-reduction diets also have a difficult time getting enough iron.

A Swedish study that appeared in the *American Journal of Clinical Nutrition* also suggests that people on an extremely high-bran diet may also be in need of more iron. So may school-age children.

IRONING OUT SCHOOL PROBLEMS

When you read your child's report card, do the teacher's comments include "short attention span" or "inattentiveness"? If so, a lack of iron may be the culprit.

"The newest information suggests a connection between cognitive performance in growing children and a lack of iron," says James Cook, M.D., head of the Division of Hematology at the University of Kansas Medical Center. "An iron deficiency may cause the child to have a hard time concentrating."

One study has shown that children with even a mild iron shortage have poorer memory and learn less quickly than kids with adequate iron. In other words, an iron deficiency can lead to an impaired memory. "Children with a subclinical iron deficiency *can* learn—they won't be retarded—but the deficiency will interfere with what they learn," says Thomas F. Massaro, Ph.D., of Pennsylvania State University.

If you believe this may be the case with your child, feed him more iron-rich foods. "Preferably, all vitamins and minerals should be gotten from our foods," says Jack M. Cooperman, Ph.D., director of nutrition at New York Medical College. "For the average person, a balanced diet is all we need to supply our body with enough iron and other minerals."

Vegetarians: Check Your Intake

Since liver, roast beef and lean ground beef are excellent sources of iron, is the vegetarian cursed to a life of tired blood, headaches and shortness of breath?

"Not necessarily," says James Cook, M.D. "Since vitamin C greatly increases our body's absorption of iron, adding foods rich in vitamin C can supply the vegetarian with sufficient levels of iron.

"Eating oranges or tomatoes with nonmeat foods high in iron can help the vegetarian's body increase its absorption of iron into his system," he says.

Iron-rich foods palatable to the vegetarian include blackstrap molasses, lima beans, sunflower seeds, soybeans, prunes, apricots, cooked broccoli and spinach, almonds, peas, beet greens, raisins, and endive.

For vegetarians who occasionally use poultry or fish in their diets, cod, haddock, tuna and the dark meat of turkey and chicken are all excellent sources of iron. Like vitamin C, these foods promote iron absorption.

But getting that balance isn't always so easy, especially where iron's concerned.

THE IRONY OF IRON

For example, in order to stay healthy we are told to exercise and avoid saturated fats. But ironically, while doing so, you may be depleting your body of its iron supply. Studies show that strenuous exercise and heavy sweating can cause losses of this precious metal. Meat, which has plenty of saturated fats, is loaded with iron. The more we exercise and avoid meats, the less iron our body may be receiving.

Even when we eat enough iron, we may not be absorbing enough. What we absorb is influenced by what we eat along with it.

HEAVY-METAL FOOD

Here's how to get iron that your body can use.

● Vitamin C will double the amount of iron absorbed by your body. Adding orange or tomato juice, half a grapefruit or strawberries to your meals will increase your iron intake. Include vegetables rich in vitamin C, such as tomatoes, green peppers, broccoli, radishes and leafy green vegetables.
● Eat breads, cereals and pasta that have been iron fortified. Check the label on the package to find out.
● Use blackstrap molasses as a partial replacement for sugars and other sweeteners in your confections. It's an excellent source of iron.
● Cook with cast-iron pots and pans. By simmering ½ cup of spaghetti sauce for 3 hours in a cast-iron pot, you can raise its iron content from 3 milligrams to 88 milligrams—that's more than eight times the Recommended Dietary Allowance for men and postmenopausal women!
● Eat red meats. They are among the few foods that have high iron content. Choosing lean cuts in small portions will supply your body with plenty of iron and still keep those calorie levels down near those of fish and poultry.
● Include beef, poultry, fish, lamb, veal or game and you will multiply fourfold the iron absorbed from the rest of the meal.
● Avoid drinking coffee and tea with your meals. Tea can reduce your iron absorption by at least 50 percent and coffee by about 39 percent.

Richard Dominick

Let Your Doctor Be Your Metal Detector

"I'm taking a daily iron supplement."

"Oh yeah? Why?"

"Gee, I don't know. It said I should on television."

If that sounds like you, then cap that bottle of iron pills and go see your family doctor before swallowing another tablet.

Too often, when people feel a little run-down, they think of the "iron-poor blood" TV commercials and run out and buy iron supplements, says one U.S. Food and Drug Administration researcher. In most cases, people can obtain an adequate amount of iron from proper food selection.

If you think you're suffering from an iron deficiency, have your family doctor test your blood for its iron content. If it's low, he'll advise you what to do.

Who should be concerned about their iron intake?

Pregnant women have a high demand for iron and should decide, with their physicians' guidance, how best to meet their iron needs, says the researcher. Iron supplements are useful when a physician can clearly demonstrate that an iron deficiency may be caused by insufficient dietary intake or unusually high need. Supplements are not for people with conditions that interfere with the utilization of high body stores of iron. Since blood test results may mimic iron deficiency, it is necessary to be more fully tested to prevent misdiagnosis.

In other words, if you feel run-down, get a little extra sleep, do a little mild exercising and try eating a balanced diet before turning to iron supplements.

YOUR HEALTHY HOME

Your Home Safety Checklist

Do you wear a hardhat inside your house? Maybe you should. In one recent year, more than 20,000 people were killed in home accidents. In all, over three million people suffered injuries. With figures like that, you should probably strap yourself into your easy chair with seat belts.

"Most people aren't knowledgeable about the possibilities for accidents around their own houses," says Frank Vilardo, Dr.P.H., of the Indiana University Transportation Research Center. "People tend to think more about safety in the workplace because there are regulations that must be enforced and supervisors to make sure the standards are followed. When they get home, they relax and feel safe in a comfortable environment where they don't feel they have to look for potential accidents."

This doesn't mean you need to trade in your slippers for a pair of steel-toed work boots. You can make your home sweet home a home safe home by following this blueprint for safety. So get your hardhat and we'll go room by room and give you tips from the National Safety Council and other safety experts on how to make your home a safer place to live.

KITCHEN

● When using a knife, cut away from, not toward, your fingers.
● Always use a cutting board when cutting meats or vegetables.
● Never try to catch a falling knife.
● Don't use knives to pry off jar lids or open cans.
● Keep knives sharpened. Dull knives are ineffective and require more force when cutting.
● Do not store knives in the same drawer as flatware.

● Group knives together in dishwasher silverware racks with the points down.
● Wear close-fitting clothing when using your kitchen range; loose sleeves are easily ignited by burners.
● Use potholders, not towels or paper tissues, to remove pans from the range. Towels and paper may come too close to the burners and ignite.
● Keep curtains away from the range. A draft could blow them onto the burners and start a fire.

LIVING ROOM

● To help prevent falls, keep rugs flat and smooth. A simple wrinkle is enough to trip someone. If the corners of a rug start to curl, secure them with carpet tape or turn the rug so the curled edge is out of the walkway.
● Keep traffic lanes straight and uncluttered. People should be able to walk through the room without detouring and squeezing past obstacles and around furniture.
● Keep magazines and newspapers on tables or in racks.
● Have light switches near doors so no one has to cross the room in darkness.
● Don't put electrical wires across traffic lanes. Also, don't put them under rugs or carpets.

● Make sure all your furniture is firm and solid. Fix or get rid of chairs and tables with wobbly legs.
● A lamp itself can be damaged by heat from the bulb. A large open shade is needed so that most of the heat will escape through the top. A lamp with an enclosed, small, metal shade will block heat from escaping, which is why you should never use a stronger watt bulb than the manufacturer recommends.

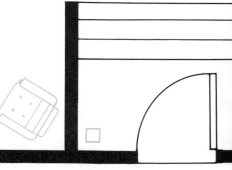

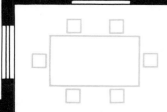

• Use the proper size burner. Don't put a small pan on a large burner, because the exposed part of the burner could ignite your clothes.

• Turn handles to the inside or back of the range to reduce the risk of hitting the handles and spilling the hot contents on yourself or children.

• If there is a grease fire in a pan, turn off the burner and cover the pan with a lid or other flat object. Don't pick it up and carry it anywhere; this will only fan

• Electrical cords may eventually dry out and become brittle. At the first sign of deterioration, replace them.

• The ventilation opening in a television set should not be placed close to a wall or piece of furniture or be covered with cloth or paper. This can cause heat inside the cabinet to build up and start a fire.

• Don't install a television set in a built-in bookshelf unless the appliance has sufficient clearance on all sides to allow for proper ventilation.

• All glass doors should be made of safety glazing material. To make the glass more visible, place decals or pressure tape on it at two levels: the adult's eye level and the child's eye level.

the flame, making it burn more fiercely.

• If a grease fire starts in the oven, close the oven door and turn off the heat.

• Major appliances should be grounded using a three-hole grounded outlet.

• Turn off the garbage disposal unit before trying to retrieve an item in it or unjamming it.

• Don't use a fork or other metal instrument to remove bread from the toaster. Also, unplug it before removing lodged food.

• Don't plug in a mixer and then insert the beaters. The same goes for inserting a blade into an electric knife.

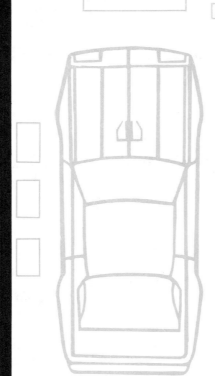

GARAGE

• Keep your garage in order with tools in place, the floor clean and flammable liquids stored in safety cans that bear the label of a nationally recognized testing agency.

• Electric garage-door openers can be hazardous, especially to children. (Children have been killed when caught beneath closing doors.) While newer models stop or reverse the door when an object is encountered, older models may not have this safety feature, which means the controls should be out of reach of young hands or locked inside the car.

• If you open your garage door by hand and it's the type with several folding sections, handles should be on each section so fingers won't be mashed while closing the door.

(continued)

BATHROOM

- Keep all electrical appliances out of the bathroom. If they must be used, keep them in a place where they cannot accidentally fall into water. If possible, choose battery-operated appliances.
- All bathtubs and shower stalls should have grab bars. Fasten them securely into the wall studding with long screws, not merely into the plaster tile or wallboard.
- Use a good soap container, preferably one built into the wall. It will help avoid bathtub falls caused by slipping on the soap.
- Put a nonslip surface or a device such as a suction-type rubber mat or safety strips on the bottom of your tub or shower.
- Use only bath rugs with rubberized backing for the bathroom floor so the rugs won't slide.
- Bath and shower doors should be glazed with safety glass or plastic, not just ordinary glass.
- Install a thermostatic regulating control valve to prevent scalding; hot running water can present a serious burn hazard in the tub and shower.
- Use plastic or disposable cups; glass drinking tumblers can break when dropped on a hard surface.
- All clothes hooks on the backs of doors and elsewhere in the bathroom should be located above eye level to prevent face and eye injuries.

BEDROOM

- To make the bedroom safer, arrange furniture so there is a clear path from all doors to the bed. Access to the bathroom from the bed should be short, direct and clear of furniture.
- Provide a light switch at the entrance to the bedroom so there is never a need to walk into or through a dark room.
- Use a bedside light that you can turn on before getting out of bed, or off when getting into bed. If this is not possible, put a flashlight on a bedside table.
- Tidy up the bedroom before you go to bed. You may get up at night and stumble or fall over clothing or shoes left on the floor.
- If small rugs are used in the room, be sure they have non-skid backing. Smooth out wrinkles and folds and tack down loose edges.
- Be sure mothballs and crystals used in closets are hung in containers out of reach of toddlers.
- A bedside table is useful for holding medicines, glasses, water and other items. Only medication for the night should be at the bedside, and you should always turn on the light and put on your glasses (if you wear them) when taking medication at night.
- Keep bedroom doors closed at night. It can slow a fire and keep lethal gases and smoke from reaching you.

CHILD'S BEDROOM

- Windows in rooms occupied by small children should be securely screened. Youngsters should not be allowed to sit or stand on windowsills.
- Beds of young children should never be placed in front of windows.
- Put stickers on the window that will alert firemen that there is a child in the room should there ever be a fire.

BABY'S ROOM

- Never use plastic wrapping on crib mattresses.
- The crib's bars or slats should be close enough together so that a baby's head cannot fit between them.
- The crib's sides should latch securely and be up at all times when the baby is in the crib.
- Keep all pillows and articles of clothing out of the crib.

Wallpaper: A Burning Discussion

B. F. Goodrich has introduced a wallcovering that can give you early warning in the event of a fire. Designed to work in conjunction with any ionization-type smoke detector, the vinyl wallcovering emits a colorless, odorless and harmless gas when the wall temperature reaches 300°F.

The gas sets off the smoke alarm much earlier than it would go off ordinarily. The new paper is especially useful in sensing smoldering fires that are caused within walls by faulty wiring.

All B. F. Goodrich wallcoverings (except a model called Tiffany Suede) are treated to sense fires. The brand names to look for are Koroseal and Cosmos. The prices are comparable to those of other wallcoverings.

HOME WORKSHOP

● When they're not in use, put all tools and materials away in their proper places.
● Check to make sure extension cords are the right capacity for the wattage of the tool and that they are free from frayed or damaged insulation.
● Keep the floor free of oil, grease, chips, sawdust and scraps.
● Keep a UL- or FM-labeled, multipurpose (ABC) fire extinguisher in your workshop area.

BASEMENT

● Provide a light on the basement stairway to illuminate the whole length of stairs. Install a light switch at the top and bottom of the stairs.
● Make sure handrails are installed on stairways and that the rails are strong and convenient to grasp.
● Paint the bottom basement step white to make it easier to see.
● Install a smoke detector at the top of the basement stairwell.
● All electrical appliances should be located far enough away from water faucets and other metal construction features so that it is impossible to touch the appliance and the grounded metal object at the same time.
● Never enter a flooded basement when the water is high enough to have reached appliance motors or any electrical equipment. Call the electric company and have them shut off the power in the basement.
● Frequently check your dryer's lint trap for accumulation; it could be a potential fire hazard.
● Don't store boxes, magazines, old rags or clothes out of the way beneath the basement stairs. Some organic materials, particularly oils, are subject to spontaneous combustion as they oxidize.
● Gasoline should be kept in safety cans that bear the label of a nationally recognized testing agency, and they should be stored outside the house in a locked shed or detached garage.
● If the basement is used for recreation, have ceilings of fire-resistant materials, such as drywall, plaster or acoustic tile.

Don Barone

The Home Medicine Chest: Keeping Stock

Go open your medicine chest and blow off the dust that's accumulated on the shelves. Now look and see what's inside.

You'll probably find a few empty prescription bottles dating back years, one or two Band-Aids, a nail file and a hoard of useless odds and ends.

Most times when you go to your medicine chest it has everything—everything but what you need. Why is it you never break a nail until after you've misplaced the nail clippers!

It doesn't have to be that way, though. Start by thinking of your medicine chest as another household appliance. After all, you don't just wander up to your refrigerator and expect the food you need to be in it. You've got to stock it. The same holds true for your medicine chest.

YOUR BASIC STOCK

Robert Warren, Pharm.D., director of pharmacy services at Valley Children's Hospital in Fresno, California, believes in preparing for the inevitable—those normal, everyday health problems that affect everyone at one time or another. "Prepare for fevers, flu, colds, scratches, cuts, headaches and the normal aches and pains."

That doesn't mean you have to buy out your local drugstore. According to the Columbia University College of Physicians and Surgeons *Complete Home Medical Guide* and other health experts, here is what you should have in stock.
- Aspirin/acetaminophen, to reduce fevers and relieve minor aches and pains.

- Antacids containing aluminum hydroxide and magnesium hydroxide.
- Antihistamine/decongestant, for cold or allergy symptoms.
- Cough syrup with expectorant.
- Mild laxatives.
- Antidiarrheal medication with pectin or bismuth subsalicylate.
- An emetic, like syrup of ipecac, to induce vomiting.
- An antiemetic, for controlling vomiting.

Once you have everything you need, however, it doesn't mean you can keep them there—unused—for years. There's a matter to consider that's known as shelf life.

MEDICINAL AGE CARDS

Shelf life is not the measure of how much time it takes to fill up the shelves in your medicine chest. It's the measurement of how long the medicine you've placed on those shelves will remain potent and safe.

And when it comes to storing medicine, we could write a new Murphy's Law. Something like: Find the worst possible place to locate a storage space, then do your best to make that the standard site.

This seems to be how it was done in deciding where to put the medicine chest. It should *not* be in the bathroom. Interior decorators put it there, not pharmacists. Dr. Warren says the bathroom is the worst place to store medicine. "It's the most humid, warmest place in your house. Almost every drug is adversely affected by humidity."

Take aspirin, for example. Dr. Warren says in a warm, humid environment, like your bathroom, it changes to acetic acid real fast. "In fact, you can smell it when it does," he says. "Take the cap off the bottle and smell it. If it smells acidic or like vinegar, it's gone bad."

Diamonds are forever . . . drugs are not. Everything is affected by time. Here are some rules that pharmacists and doctors recommend concerning the shelf life of the more popular medicines.

- Antibiotics shouldn't be kept for more than a year.
- Ointments that turn hard or separate should be thrown out.
- Alcohol will in time evaporate from solutions.
- Liquids, such as cough syrups, are no good if they change color, look cloudy or separate and form a solid mass at the bottom of the bottle.

And who among us doesn't save a couple of pills out of a prescription, just in case "it" should come back someday? It is now required that all drugs show their expiration dates on the label. When the date arrives, it means they're starting to lose their potency. Throw them out. If you have drugs that don't have date labels you should consider them already too old. Throw them out.

Here are some other ideas from experts that will help ensure a healthy life span for your medications.

- Keep your medications in small containers so that you can replenish the supply fairly quickly. This is especially true if you keep your medications in the bathroom.

● Buy medications wrapped individually in foil when possible. This type of packaging is effective in keeping out the humidity, and the medicine will retain its potency longer.

Some medications don't belong in the bathroom at all, note the experts. Items that break down in heat, like insulin or vaccines for allergy, should be stored in your refrigerator. They are usually nontoxic on ingestion, so it's a good place to keep them. Nevertheless, keep them out of the reach of children.

But medications aren't the only things that belong in a well-stocked medicine cabinet. Those little accidents can—and do—happen.

● Bandages—one box of assorted or six 1-inch and six 1½-inch strips.
● Roll of tape—paper or cloth, 1 inch wide.
● Sterile gauze pads—individually packaged squares.
● Cotton balls.
● Ace bandage.
● Cotton tip applicators.
● Scissors—sharp enough to cut cloth, but blunt-edged in case a child finds them.
● Antiseptic—such as rubbing alcohol (70 percent solution).
● Eye wash—with eye cup.
● Antibiotic cream—a tube containing bacitracin or polymyxin.
● Anti-inflammatory/anesthetic ointment—containing 0.5 percent hydrocortisone cream.
● Antipruritic—an anti-itch lotion or spray containing calamine with phenol, for poison ivy or insect bites.
● Petroleum jelly.
● Ice bag.

● Hot-water bottle or heating pad.
● Tweezers and sewing needles—for removing splinters.
● Teaspoon or small calibrated plastic cup.
● Oral thermometer.
● Flashlight.
● First-aid manual—the *Standard First Aid and Personal Safety* manual from the American Red Cross is a good choice.

Joan Handler says that while first-aid supplies may be out of sight, they shouldn't be out of mind. "Pick the month of your birthday and use that date to annually check your first-aid supplies and replenish them as needed."

Also check for crinkles and broken seals on the bandages or gauze. "If they're broken, the sterile quality is no longer intact," says Handler, "and the item should be thrown away."

Don Barone

THE FINEST IN FIRST AID

Ouch! That word is usually followed by a few thoughts about finding first aid, quickly. But the time to think about first aid is not when you're standing in front of the bathroom mirror looking at the blood seeping through the toilet paper you've stuck on your cut. The time to think about first aid is pre-ouch.

The best advice for dealing with first-aid supplies is that old Boy Scout motto: "Be prepared."

"Have everything dealing with first aid in one place; that way when an emergency arises you won't have to run all over the place searching for the first-aid supplies that you may need," advises Joan Handler, a health services specialist for the American Red Cross.

According to the *Complete Home Medical Guide*, here's what else you should have on hand.

The Pantry Pharmacy

You don't always have to go to the drugstore to stock your medicine chest; you can get some of the supplies right from your pantry.

Baking soda (sodium bicarbonate). Sprinkled into a tepid bath, it's good for soothing sunburn. Mixed into a thin paste, it can soothe poison ivy or insect bites. Used as a mouthwash, it will help relieve canker sore pain.

White vinegar. Good for preventing swimmer's ear. Prepare a solution by adding 30 drops (2 cc) to an ounce of boiling water. Allow the mixture to cool. (Caution: Do *not* use it hot!) After swimming, put 2 drops in each ear. The acid will kill the bacteria that may be present in any water left in the ear.

Plain tea. It soothes mild burning and itching. Soak a compress in cool tea and apply it to the skin.

Coke syrup. The syrup—not the soda—can be used as an antiemetic to help stop vomiting. One tablespoon straight up should do the trick. One pharmacist says he always keeps a small supply on hand for when his children get sick.

Clearing the Indoor Air

It was a dark and stormy night.

He took one step into the smoke-filled room and got a faceful of almost 1,500 known chemicals, including aluminum, formaldehyde and outlawed pesticides. To escape the cigarette smoke, he hightailed it into a closet and almost collapsed from inhaling 100 percent para-dichlorobenzene oozing from the new box of mothballs his wife had left open on the shelf. He quickly made it to the bathroom, where he thought he was safe, and slammed the door. Chemicals such as butanols, xylene, and toluene rose up from the new, soft-vinyl floor tile and entered his lungs. As he turned, ammonia and phenols drifted up his nose from the bar of deodorant soap sitting in the soap dish.

"I can't take it any longer," he screamed before collapsing on the bathroom floor.

Sound like an excerpt from a dime-store horror novel? Hardly. Human ecologists estimate that we spend 90 percent of our time indoors —most of it in our homes—where we are bombarded with thousands of household chemicals, gases and pollutants that we breathe, touch or ingest daily.

COMMON SCENTS

If you can smell it, and it's not on the stove, chances are it isn't good for you. Recent studies conducted by the Environmental Protection Agency (EPA) show that in many cases, air pollution is heavier—and unhealthier —indoors than it is outdoors.

Poor ventilation is a contributing factor. Don't keep your home sealed like a tomb, letting the stray chemicals, dust, fumes and cigarette smoke hang heavily in the air. Open the windows and let the air escape. You'll feel better and breathe easier, too.

But the *main* cause of indoor air pollution is the sources of the chemicals themselves. Remove as many sources as possible.

Head for Tobacco Road. If someone in your house smokes tobacco, for example, tell them to snuff the butt out in the ashtray or hit the road. Cigarette smoke can linger in your house for weeks, filling the air with hundreds of pollutants, including benzene, which is a known cancer-causer. The major contributor of benzene was once thought to be gasoline vapors, until EPA testing showed that people's heaviest exposure comes from being near cigarette smokers.

All in all, cigarette smoke contains over 1,500 known chemicals, none of which do you any good. Even if you are a nonsmoker but you live or work with a smoker, you are being exposed to these chemicals on a daily basis.

If someone in your family hasn't yet kicked the tobacco habit, force them to light up outside, or at least by an open window or exhaust fan so some of the harmful pollutants can escape.

Let them "freshen" the trash can. Can't smell the fish frying through the wonderful scent of pine trees drifting through your kitchen? Wrong. You can't smell the fish frying through the unhealthy levels of para-dichlorobenzene floating out from your solid and aerosol air fresheners.

"There is no reason to keep air fresheners in your house," says EPA

The Insulation Blues

"Boy, my eyes are irritated."

"Oh, yeah? Well, I have a scratchy throat."

"Big deal. I get headaches every day. Sometimes twice a day."

"So what? I'm nauseated all the time."

"That's nothing. My sinuses drain faster than the Mississippi River."

Are we overhearing a family conversation at The Hypochondriacs? No. This might be dinner conversation at your house if it happens to be overinsulated.

"Too much insulation may save you money on your heating bill, but it doesn't do a lot of good for your health," says Richard Hartle, industrial hygienist at the National Institute for Occupational Safety and Health.

"Fresh air cannot get into the house, nor can air circulate when your home is too well insulated. What happens then is harmful pollutants cannot escape, causing the air quality in your own home to lower."

How much is too much insulation? It depends on the size, shape and age of your house, but one thing is certain—when planning to insulate your home, speak to an energy efficiency expert first.

If you do suffer from any of the symptoms listed above and you and your doctor are reasonably sure they're from insulation, then either open a few windows and let the fresh air in or consider installing a central air conditioning unit to help keep the air pollution down and your home's air quality up.

research scientist Lance Wallace. "All they do is send a concentrated level of a cancer-causing chemical into the air. To be safe, throw your air fresheners out."

You can open windows or use recirculating central air conditioning units to keep your house smelling fresh without risking your health by inhaling harmful chemicals designed to smell like a pine forest.

It's a gas. Natural gas combustion leaking out from our home heating and cooking systems is a major source of indoor air pollution, says Michael Lebowitz, Ph.D., associate director for environmental programs and professor of internal medicine at the University of Arizona College of Medicine.

"Many people don't realize they must keep their kitchen exhaust fan or some exhaust fan in the house — even if it's in another room — running while cooking at their gas stove. Otherwise, they are doing themselves harm by breathing in nitrogen dioxide."

Proper ventilation is essential for homes that use gas for heating or cooking, stresses Dr. Lebowitz. Without it, nitrogen dioxide, nitrogen oxide, carbon monoxide, formaldehyde and a host of other hydrocarbons may begin circulating first through your home, then through your lungs and bloodstream. Dr. Lebowitz also warns that an unvented kerosene heater is extremely dangerous. Sulfur dioxide, a toxic gas, can accumulate.

Have a professional check your natural gas heating and ventilating system at least once a year, suggests Dr. Lebowitz, and in between, if you happen to catch a whiff of gas, call the gas man immediately.

DUST TO DUST

The EPA now believes that 20 percent of our exposure to lead comes from dust particles floating around the rooms of our house.

"We track lead into our homes on our shoes," says Wallace. "It gets picked up in the dust and floats

Radon: An Age-Old Menace

It's invisible, odorless, tasteless and deadly. It's been here for billions of years and it will be here for billions more. It's called radon, and it is a radioactive gas that rises to the surface of the earth from uranium formations and creeps, slithers and seeps into millions of homes nationwide. The National Cancer Institute says radon may be responsible for up to 30,000 lung cancer deaths a year. It is the leading cause of lung cancer among nonsmokers.

What can you do to stop this menace? Michael Lafavore, author of *Radon: The Invisible Threat*, suggests buying a home testing kit at any leading home center store. "They cost anywhere between $10 and $25 and are simple to use," he says. If your home's radon level registers high, retest at least once to be sure.

"Opening basement windows to get cross-ventilation is a good short-term way to clear your home of radon," says Lafavore. "Investing in a home ventilation system is also a smart idea."

Sealing basement cracks and openings will also help keep radon from entering your home.

After all that, if radon levels still test high, contact a contracting company to have your home professionally sealed against the gas.

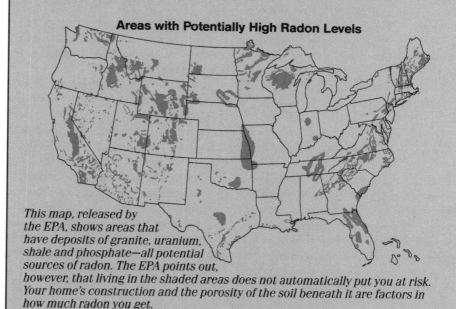

Areas with Potentially High Radon Levels

This map, released by the EPA, shows areas that have deposits of granite, uranium, shale and phosphate—all potential sources of radon. The EPA points out, however, that living in the shaded areas does not automatically put you at risk. Your home's construction and the porosity of the soil beneath it are factors in how much radon you get.

throughout the house, where we can inhale it. Babies crawl on the floor, get it on their hands, lick it off and ingest it.

"Maybe we should take a lesson from the Japanese and take our shoes off every time we enter the house. Doing that would keep many pollutants outside of the home."

We should also dust and vacuum frequently. Don't allow dust to accumulate.

"Better ventilation can improve the air quality in your home up to 20 percent," states Wallace. "But removing the unnecessary sources can improve it enormously."

Richard Dominick

Healthy Housekeeping

A healthy housekeeper is a good housekeeper, right? But what's a good housekeeper?

Is it someone whose windows sparkle in the sun? Someone whose kitchen gleams so brightly you need sunglasses to eat your eggs? Someone for whom dust is the most disgusting four-letter word?

"Every community and culture has its unspoken standards," explained the late globe-trotting Mennonite missionary Doris Janzen Longacre in *Living More with Less*.

"In Indonesia you swept the packed earth around your house at least once, if not twice, a day. Thirty years ago in North America it was the way you did the washing. Laundry was a real job—remember bluing, starch, tubs and wringers? To accomplish it properly required skill and dedication."

THE BRIGHT TORNADO

Today, of course, we have permanent press, bleach, spray starch, fabric softeners, washing machines and clothes dryers. Wringers are sold in antique shops, washtubs are filled with flowers and bluing is something you put on the gray in your hair that makes it shine like the cutlery in your silver drawer.

So what's a good housekeeper today? A *smart* housekeeper. It's someone who can put housework in its proper perspective and get it done *fast*.

"Housework is so you don't die of germs," says Don Aslett, head of a professional cleaning company, cleaning consultant to major corporations and author of several books on the subject. "It's for survival, for health." It should take between 4, 5 and 11 hours per week, depending on how

many knickknacks, slobbering babies and salivating dogs you have. And, of course, how many rooms you have.

But as Aslett lectures around the country, people tell him of 30- and 40-hour cleaning weeks. Does a house require that much care? No. Not unless you have four or five kids, says Aslett. Otherwise that amount of time should be your cue to reevaluate what—and whom—you're cleaning for.

CLEAN, CLEANER, CLEANEST

Are you cleaning too much? Have you got your priorities mixed up? Have you become compulsive about cleaner, whiter and brighter?

Very possibly, reports Doris Janzen Longacre. In fact, wrote the missionary, "If our culture buried people with their favorite tools, some North American housekeepers would go to their final rest with a paper towel in one hand, an aerosol disinfectant in the other, and a deodorant laid at the feet."

But how much house cleaning is too much? G. Terence Wilson, Ph.D., professor of psychology at Rutgers University, used this analogy: "I like what the late Supreme Court Justice Potter Stewart said about pornography," said Wilson. " 'It's impossible to define. But you know it when you see it.' "

Similarly, you'll know it if you're overcleaning. "A clinical compulsion is very obvious," the psychologist says. "You've lost control. You cannot stop doing something even though the consequences are severe—time is wasted, life is disrupted." If that describes you, he adds, you need to see a professional counselor.

DON'T BE A NEATNIK

But for those of you who regard housework less as a compulsion and more as a cross to bear, how can you get it done—fast?

Well, one woman hires herself—just like a cleaning lady—on Saturday morning from 9:00 A.M. to 11:00 A.M. When her time's up, she stops. If the wash isn't done, that's tough.

Eugenia Chapman, who works as the head housekeeper at a historic mansion in Salt Lake City, advises getting rid of all your junk. "Box it up, garage-sale it or give it to the Salvation Army," says Chapman, "but get it out of your house."

And Don Aslett, who has cleaned everything from a log cabin to an industrial high-rise, says the fastest way to clean a house is to prevent as much of the dirt and dust as possible.

Large mats inside and outside every door will keep out 80 percent of the filth you'd normally spend your life dusting and vacuuming, he says.

Enclosing your knickknacks in a glass case means you only have to dust the case, not 47 Dresden shepherds.

And a comforter can serve as a bedspread. Then all you have to do is shake it out in the morning—not spend 15 minutes tucking, pulling and straightening.

DON'T LET A CHORE BE A BORE

But even the fastest housekeeper can get bored with housework. How can you keep it interesting? Try these tips from Aslett.

Compete. Race yourself to see how much faster you can do a chore every time you have to do it. If you scrubbed the bathroom floor in 4 minutes last week, aim for 3 this week.

Eliminate. Ironing socks and folding underwear is unnecessary. Don't do it. And think about what other jobs you do because you "should."

Delegate. God gave everyone in your family two hands. Not just you.

Make it social. Help a friend clean windows, then have him help you do yours. You'll spend so much time chatting about kids, cousins, aunts, uncles and in-laws, the windows will seem to clean themselves.

So what's a good housekeeper? Why, the person who knows when to clean and how to clean, of course. And when to put away the mop.

Ellen Michaud

Health Notes on Household Cleaners

Those household products that line the shelves of your supermarket promise to make your life easier. But what about healthier?

The fact that a household product makes it to the marketplace is no guarantee that you won't have a bad reaction to it. In fact, new research suggests that there's a connection between everyday household products and depression, headache, loss of alertness, insomnia, chronic fatigue and, in some cases, even brain damage.

Wonder which ones affect *you*? Here's a guide to some of the more common household cleaners and some of their potential side effects.

Substance	Toxic Effects	Symptoms	Alternative Methods
Caustic cleaners, such as oven and drain cleaners	These highly corrosive chemicals can cause severe skin and eye damage.	Slow-healing chemical burns formed rapidly.	Use baking soda for scouring ovens. For baked-on grease, put ¼ cup ammonia in oven overnight to loosen; scrub with baking soda. For drain cleaners, pour ½ cup salt down drain, followed by boiling water. Flush with hot tap water.
Wall/floor cleaners	All toxic, especially cleaners containing petroleum distillates. Some depress the central nervous system and cause liver and kidney lesions.	Headache, drowsiness from inhalation.	Use mild detergents to clean large areas, then rinse.
Solvents, such as paint, varnish, furniture and shoe polishes	Breathing vapors or accidental drinking can be harmful, even fatal. Long-term exposure to some solvents may cause liver or kidney problems, birth defects, central nervous system disorders and cancer.	Headache, drowsiness from inhalation, nausea.	Furniture polish: To make a nontoxic polish, melt 1 tbsp. Carnauba wax into 2 cups mineral oil. For lemon oil polish: Dissolve 1 tsp. lemon oil into 1 pt. mineral oil. Shoe polish: Use polishes that do not contain methylene chloride, trichloroethylene or nitrobenzene.
Spot removers and drycleaning substances	Carcinogenic; toxic if inhaled, eaten, or absorbed through skin. Repeated exposure may cause liver and kidney damage.	Nausea, drowsiness.	Hand-wash fabrics when possible to remove stains.
Mothballs	Possibly carcinogenic.	Vapor irritating to skin, eyes and throat. Nausea, headache, anemia, seizures.	Sachet of dried lavender, equal parts rosemary and mint, dried tobacco, whole peppercorns and cedar chips, soaked in real cedar oil. Store and maintain woolens correctly.
Disinfectants	Toxic, corrosive.	Ingredients can cause chemical burns to all tissues and can be absorbed through the skin. Ingestion may result in nausea, paralysis, coma and death from cardiac or respiratory collapse.	Rubbing alcohol, soap and detergent are alternates. Avoid products containing phenol or cresol.

A Bug-Free Environment

It happened the day your mother-in-law stopped in for tea. Unannounced, no less.

She notices everything. The eyes never stop moving. They take in the curtains, the floor, the countertop. They even see the tiny space behind the refrigerator where nobody ever cleans.

And you passed. Almost. All you did was pick up the napkin holder, and that's when this ugly, black "thing" decided to stroll across your kitchen table.

It's time to get serious. Who's it going to be? You—or the pests?

THE PESTS

Good choice.

Fleas, roaches, ants, spiders, termites. Prepare to meet your match. Experts say when it comes to the battle of the bug, your best strategy is to meet the enemy on its own turf . . . or rose bush, as it may be.

"In most insect control cases, we suggest that you cut them off outdoors; stop their entry in the first place," says Carlton Koehler, Ph.D., an urban entomologist at the University of California, Berkeley.

Annihilate the ants. "In cases of ants coming indoors, you need to get rid of the aphids that are on the plants just outside of your house. When their source of food dries up, the ants will go looking for something else. Treating your roses or trees with something like an insecticidal soap will solve the aphid problem and thereby reduce your ant problem."

You'll stop the ants, but what about their relatives—those fleas, cockroaches, termites and spiders? If the whole gang is showing up at your home, there are ways *not* to be the perfect host.

Foil the fleas. Scratching more lately? Feel like "flea-ing" your house now that it's quickly becoming overrun with the little pests? Lisa Lemke, an entomologist for the U.S. Department of Agriculture, Household Insect and Fly Division, Gainesville, Florida, says if your house has fleas, you should get the itch to vacuum.

"Before you begin treatment with any type of insecticide, you should vacuum thoroughly. This will get up some of the larvae and a few of the adults." But it won't get rid of the problem. You'll also have to treat your pet—who's probably harboring as many (if not more) fleas as your carpet—at the same time that you treat your house. "It's a three-process thing that should be done closely together," says Lemke. You've got to treat the house, the environment where the pet lives, and then treat the pet itself. "If you wash your pet with just regular soap or shampoo, you will, a lot of times, decrease the number of fleas. Detergents break their surface tension, causing them to come off and drown in the bathwater." (For more information on treating flea-plagued pets, see the box, "Put a Stop to Fleas and Ticks," on page 349.)

For those fleas that can swim or have taken up boarding privileges in your carpets, beds and upholstery, Lemke recommends using a fogger with an insect growth regulator (IGR) made up of methoprene. "It's called Pre-Cor commercially, and it's very safe. It works on the larvae so that they don't develop into adults." If you can't find it in a pet shop, check with your vet.

Kill the cockroaches. Declaring war on cockroaches means using combat tactics. "Use Combat bait trays. They're very safe and effective, and they're child resistant," says Lemke.

"If you live where you don't have a high humidity problem, use boric acid. It works well. Just spread it where they will walk through it, and it will take care of your cockroach problem."

Calling in the E-Team

Visitors: The Pests, 1
Home team: You, 0

If you're on the losing end of a battle to regain your home turf, you may need an exterminator on your team.

But hiring a professional to spray some chemicals all over your furnishings and floors should not be undertaken lightly, says George Rambo, Ph.D., director of research, education and technical resources for the National Pest Control Association. To start, he recommends "looking for someone who is a member of a state or national association, because they generally have more training."

Dr. Rambo also suggests that you learn as much as possible about the specific pest that is bothering you; don't just say you want to get rid of the yucky black things under the cabinets. "Ask the pest-control person questions that you already know the answers to. That way you can judge how knowledgeable he is."

Rambo also says, "Ask questions about the type of pesticides they plan to use. Good pest-control operators will discuss their pest-control program with you and work out what will be best for you."

And, hopefully, what's worst for the pests.

Snakes Alive! How to Evict Creepy Critters

You can't step on a bat. Snakes won't run away from a can of Raid. Mickey Mouse belongs in Disneyland, not in your pantry!

Not all household pests are of the insect variety. Mice, rats, bats, snakes and squirrels can also drive you nuts, and cause a good amount of damage, to boot. But there are reliable ways to give these varmints an eviction notice. John Chapman, an entomologist and manager of technical services for the pest-control company Terminix International, has some advice on how to rid yourself of these menaces.

Mice. "Prevention is the best thing. Keep the area around your home clean, keep your foods in sealed containers, keep trash and garbage removed from the home rather than right at the back door and don't let it accumulate for more than a week."

Chapman also advises that you make sure there are no cracks and crevices around your house. If there are, seal them up—even the tiniest of holes. "A mouse can get through a round hole the size of a dime or a flat crack ¼ inch in width, so if your doors are not fitted properly, they can come right in."

If they do get in, Chapman recommends using a baited snap-trap, put out of sight and out of reach of children and pets, or a new childproof trap that uses a tube to catch the mouse and seal it inside.

If killing the poor little critters is more than you can handle, try getting a cat. There are country folk who swear by them.

Rats. "Rats are more cautious than mice. They're harder to entice with bait," says Chapman. "Use a glue board, which is just a sticky surface that the rat will adhere to and not be able to get off of. Find out their paths, which are usually next to a wall surface, and put the glue board where they walk. If possible, create a hallway effect with boards or cardboard to entice the rats to walk over the glue boards." If you want to free the rat, take the trap (and the rat) outside and pour vegetable oil on the glue board. This should release the rat.

Bats. "Keep your eaves, vents and chimneys screened. If you do get an infestation of bats, watch the structure in the evening, right after sundown, and note the openings they come out of, then seal them up. If one or two get left behind, take a mousetrap and nail it on a pole or broomstick with the trigger side toward the end of the handle. Then set the trap, reach up and touch the bat with it, and you'll catch it." Chapman advises wearing gloves when doing this and having a plastic trash bag handy to dump the bat into.

Snakes. "If the snake is out in the open, get a cold-type fire extinguisher and give it a good blast. Snakes are cold-blooded animals, and they will get very sluggish and weak, if not frozen stiff. Then, using a stick or shovel, you can put the snake in a burlap bag to dispose of it."

To deter snakes from making your home their own, Chapman suggests that you "eliminate debris and keep woodpiles, rocks and boards away from your home. Keep weeds down and seal up cracks."

Squirrels. "Get what's called a live trap (Havahart). It won't hurt the squirrel. Place fresh nut meats inside the trap to lure the squirrel in. Then when you catch it, take it to a park and let it go."

THE FAR SIDE

"Well, heaven knows what it is or where it came from—just get rid of it. But save that cheese first."

Lemke also says not to have standing water around, or leave food out, because that's what cockroaches are attracted to.

Terminate the termites. "There's very little you can do at home for termites," says Lemke. "You need to call a pest-control operator. You need special tools and special insecticides, things you can't even get over the counter." Lemke doesn't believe, though, that a homeowner is totally helpless in dealing with these pests. "Keep an eye out in your cellar for evidence of termites. Look for tubes on the surface of the wood and, if you're going to build a deck onto your house, use pressure-treated wood. Termites are less likely to harm it. Or, if you're building a house, treat for termites before you put in the foundation. Prevention is the best control."

Smash the spiders. "Generally speaking, if you have spiders outside, under your eaves, around woodpiles or garbage cans, you'll have them inside your house, too. Knock down their webs with a broom when you see them, and then spray the area with an insecticide containing Dursban," says Lemke.

Don Barone

Home Heating Hints

It's 6:00 A.M. on a winter morning in Killington, Vermont. The temperature is way below zero. It's dark. It's snowing. And you'd like to stay snuggled under your quilts.

But you can't. So you leap out of bed, run down the hall, push up the thermostat, run back to your bedroom and take a flying leap into your nest of flannel and feathers. There you huddle—shivering, heart pounding, the tip of your nose turning blue—to wait for the ba-OOM of your furnace as it roars into life.

But all you hear is silence. Then a kind of PZZzzzz.

When was the furnace last tuned?

NO CLEAN, NO STEAM

The truth is that oil- and gas-fired systems should be tuned every year, experts say. Otherwise you're liable to end up frigid and frozen. Maybe even charred and broiled.

Oil and gas checkups are pretty much the same—just as the furnaces themselves are similar. For a gas furnace, says Phil Runge, manager of utilization and engineering services at the American Gas Association, you should ask your local gas company's service representative or heating contractor to clean your filters, check the ductwork for leaks, adjust your furnace's fan belts to the proper tension, check the flame's stability and look for cracks in your heat exchanger—a chamber in the heart of your furnace where cold air is warmed before being returned to your house. Every two or three years, he might also vacuum dust out of the burner area.

"Have him check the chimney and vent as well," says Runge. "Make sure the chimney's clear—no bird's nests—and the vent cap's not distorted.

Chimneys: Facts on Fire

Chimney problems are the most common cause of house fires in the United States, says John E. Bittner, executive director of the National Chimney Sweep Guild. Here's how to avoid them.

Check for creosote. Get in the habit of inspecting the flue at least every 2 months during the heating season—more often if you use a wood stove frequently. Use a mirror and light to look up the flue through the clean-out opening or fireplace damper. If you see ¼ inch of crusty, flaky deposit, it's time for a cleaning.

Make sure your chimney is properly lined. A missing, cracked or deteriorated liner can allow smoke or condensation to leak from your chimney.

Keep insulation away from your chimney. Insulation can cause heat to collect around the chimney and can ignite nearby wood. Pull insulation at least 2 inches away from the chimney and build a "dam" to keep it away.

Install a chimney cap. A good chimney cap should have a mesh screen to keep birds and animals from building nests that can block the chimney.

Wind, storms and ice can damage the cap since it's so lightly constructed," he explains. "And just a little distortion—sometimes just ¼ inch—can block the flue."

What can you do yourself? Check, check and double-check, says Runge. Here's his list.

Check the draft diverter. The draft diverter is a hooded opening into the furnace room from the flue pipe. Its purpose is to draw in enough air from the furnace room so that a constant draft is maintained—and unaffected by the outside air temperature or wind factor. "Otherwise a cold temperature outside would provide too much air pressure at the burners and heat would be wasted up the chimney rather than transferred through the heat exchanger," says Runge. Want to guess what that would cost?

An easy way to check the diverter is to take a match, blow it out and hold it at the opening of the diverter while the furnace is operating, says Runge. If the match's smoke is drawn up into the opening, your flue's okay. If it's not, shut the system down fast and call your gas company and a certified chimney sweep. You've got a blocked flue with potentially deadly results. If gas exhausts can't be vented to the outside, three guesses where they're going to go.

Check for rust. Rust is a symptom of inadequate drafting, says Runge. It appears because the exhaust gas in your furnace has been cooled too much, and water—which is inherent in any combustion process—is condensing out and wetting the cool metallic surfaces on the inside of your furnace. So look over the flue and see if you can spot any rusty brown patches. If you've got corrosion on the outside, ten to one it's on the inside as well.

Check for leaks in the flue pipe. Look carefully for any holes that could be causing a leak, especially if you've got rust. Leaks mean you aren't getting good venting, says Runge, so carbon dioxide gets into your house and displaces the air. Then there's less oxygen for your furnace to burn its gas.

The result? "Even a small drop in oxygen—as little as 2 percent—and your furnace starts producing carbon monoxide," warns Runge. "And that's a killer."

BURN, BABY, BURN

Heating with wood is a cozy, practical and patriotic alternative to traditional gas- and oil-fired systems. But is it safe? Yes, experts say, if you follow these easy rules.

Maintenance checks are very important. Replace the catalytic combustor in your catalytic wood stove. Your stove should be inspected once or twice every year. The catalyst should be replaced every two to three years.

Not all wood is created equal. Nothing but seasoned firewood should be burned in your wood stove, says Runge. Otherwise, there will be an increase in emission wastes and pollutants, which can have a poisonous effect and ultimately lead to a catalytic meltdown.

Establish a 3-foot "danger zone." Your wood stove may be a safe 3 feet from walls and furniture, but that margin of safety can go up in smoke if you leave newspapers, wood, children's toys or anything else flammable within reach of your stove's intense heat. And build a barrier if you have to, but keep your kids out of the danger zone as well.

Keep a gas fire extinguisher handy in case of an emergency. It's more practical and effective than sand if the fire is in the chimney. Water thrown on a hot fire explodes into steam, scatters hot ash everywhere and can crack cast-iron heater parts.

Never wear loose-fitting clothing (flowing nightclothes especially) when tending a fire. Some of the new synthetic fabrics are as flammable as they are fashionable.

Put ashes in a metal container. Hot coals can linger two or three days after the fire's out. A cardboard box can be turned into a cardboard bonfire in seconds.

Put trash in a landfill. Never burn trash, Christmas wrappings, newspapers, painted wood, chemical chimney-cleaners, fire colorants or lighter fluid. Chemicals in these materials can destroy catalytic combustors and give off harmful pollutants.

Never burn artificial logs in a wood stove. They burn hotter than your stove is equipped to handle and contain waxes that can clog your chimney just like creosote.

Install smoke detectors on each floor of your house. A single detector installed upstairs may not respond to first-story smoke signals in time to save your life.

SPACE-HEATER SAFETY

Once in a while you may want to take the chill off a room without activating your house's entire heating system or stoking up a roaring fire. That's where a space heater comes in handy. But space heaters were responsible for an estimated 20,000 visits to an emergency room for treatment of burns—and about 200 deaths due to carbon monoxide in one year alone. Most were associated with improperly operating heaters. How can you use them safely?

According to fire safety experts, here's what you should do.

● Keep a window open if you're using an unvented fuel-burning heater.
● Never completely fill a heater with oil or kerosene, because the fuel will expand as it warms, then spill and cause a fire.
● Never use flammable liquids around a space heater, since their vapors can flow from one part of the room to another and be ignited by any open flame, even a candle.
● Never use an unvented heater in a room where you're sleeping.
● Use only a heavy-duty extension cord with the same rating as your electric heater.
● Don't touch any electrical switches if you smell gas in a room heated by a gas heater. Just turn off the heater if it's on, open a window and run next door to call the gas company.

And one last tip from the American Gas Association's Phil Runge: Don't fool around with the oxygen depletion sensors (ODS) on the new generation of gas heaters. If your heater keeps shutting down, open the window a little more instead of disturbing the sensor. "That ODS is saving your life," says Runge. Your heater's shutting down because it doesn't have enough oxygen. And that means neither do you.

Ellen Michaud

Water
Fit to Drink

What you don't know can hurt you—especially if it's in your drinking water.

In Fallon, Nevada, it was arsenic. In Woburn, Massachusetts, it was TCE. And in Scranton, Pennsylvania, it was a minute organism called *Giardia lamblia* that made the municipal water supply undrinkable.

The statistics are even scarier than the stories. According to the Environmental Protection Agency (EPA), 45 percent of the large public water systems served by groundwater are contaminated by organic chemicals, and 63 percent of all rural residents—that's nearly 39 million people—drink contaminated and possibly unsafe water.

An overwhelming problem? That's an understatement. Hopeless? Not so, say the experts. "I know of few situations that aren't treatable," says Don Saltman, president of Suburban Water Testing Laboratories, Temple, Pennsylvania, and a member of the board of directors of the national Water Quality Association, an organization of dealers, manufacturers and suppliers of water-treatment systems.

And many people are doing something now. The EPA estimates that millions of Americans are buying drinking water-treatment units for their homes.

PINPOINTING THE PROBLEM

"If the taste or odor of your water changes, or if you live in close proximity to a potential source of pollution, such as a landfill, you might want to have it tested," suggests Victor Kimm of the EPA.

But you might want to test even if you live hundreds of miles from the nearest landfill.

"In some places the 'system' is little more than a pond and a chlorine feeder to kill bacteria," says Richard C. Stump II, vice president and laboratory director for Suburban Water Testing Laboratories. "They take the pond water, add chlorine and send it down the hill, unfiltered. Sometimes there are no full-time employees. Somebody goes up once a day or once a week to check on the system to see if it's still working—or still there."

If you do decide to test your own water, using a local laboratory or a mail-order service, here are a few of the most common contaminants you will probably want to look for.

Coliform bacteria. These bacteria aren't ordinarily harmful by themselves. But they signal the presence of other, more dangerous bacteria in your water. The U.S. government guidelines call for an average of 1 or less per 100 milliliters of water.

Nitrates and nitrites. The government guidelines stipulate a maximum contaminant level of 10 milligrams per liter of water, which is aimed at preventing a sometimes fatal condition that diminishes the oxygen-carrying capacity of the blood in infants. Nitrates and nitrites are also associated with stomach cancers, although there has been no clear link to nitrates and nitrites in drinking water.

Toxic chemicals. TCE (trichloroethylene), PCB's (polychlorinated biphenyls), carbon tet (carbon tetrachloride)—they're the too-familiar nicknames for some of the more common man-made poisons in our drinking water. Many have been found to cause cancer and genetic changes in laboratory animals.

Trace metals. You don't want to see large amounts of mercury, cadmium or chromium in your water. In areas with soft, acidic water, lead—which is especially dangerous to children—has been leaching out of the pipes and turning up in drinking water. Less harmful but still a nuisance: iron and manganese, which can stain laundered fabrics.

H₂O First Aid

Here are two emergency measures to give you clean drinking water until the water-quality professional arrives.

● If you suspect metal in your drinking water, let your water run for 3 to 4 minutes before you use it, says Jean Briskin of the Environmental Protection Agency's office of drinking water. This will help flush out any lead, cadmium, zinc or copper that may be lingering in the pipes. But don't let the water go to waste. You can use it to water your plants.

● For any kind of microbacterial contamination, boil water (uncovered) for at least 20 minutes before using it. This removes bacteria and some organic chemicals.

Trihalomethanes. The water disinfectant, chlorine, has given us a possible Sophie's choice: cholera or cancer? Chlorine, which kills bacteria in drinking water, also apparently reacts with other substances in the water to form compounds called trihalomethanes. One such trihalomethane is chloroform, which has been shown to cause cancer in laboratory animals and may be linked to some human cancers.

SOLVING THE PROBLEM

If your water's bad, it's time to do something. But how do you pick from all the options in water-treatment equipment? To help you make a decision, here's a scorecard of the major water-treatment systems.

Activated carbon. A method older than Plato, this system is effective at removing chloroform, chlorine, some pesticides, organic chemicals and bad taste and odor. The contaminants cling to the porous surface of the carbon, which is usually contained in a replaceable filter. But carbon, or charcoal, filters have one serious drawback: They require vigilant maintenance. Most experts agree that granular carbon is the best, and that frequent changing is essential. In laboratory tests, under-the-sink models were more effective in the long run in removing chloroform than the faucet models, which are usually less expensive.

Distillation. This is a simple method of treatment. Water is heated until it turns to steam and then the steam is condensed into water. Theoretically, this removes all bacteria and contaminants from the water. But theory isn't practice. Distillation systems don't necessarily remove chloroform and other organic chemicals, which can vaporize with the water and recondense. Using an activated-charcoal filter with a distiller will increase its organic-removal rate to over 90 percent. You may need pretreatment if your water is extremely hard or full of iron, which fouls the device.

Reverse osmosis. Used to turn saltwater into drinking water, the reverse osmosis system can remove turbidity, dissolved solids, bacteria, viruses, pyrogens (fever-causing substances), hydrocarbons, asbestos and most pesticides and other chemicals. It doesn't remove chloroform. Many reverse osmosis systems contain three different membranes, which rely on water pressure to help remove pollutants. The cellophanelike membranes vary in characteristics and price. The condition of your water should determine which one is best for you.

Installation is usually not a do-it-yourself project, and the membrane cartridges have to be replaced every one to three years. You may have to have your water treated if it's hard or full of iron. And if your water pressure isn't sufficient, you may need to add a small pump, all of which increases your cost.

Ultraviolet radiation. Some water systems use ultraviolet (UV) systems to kill bacteria and reduce the amount of living organisms in treated water. UV radiation doesn't add anything to the water, as does chlorine, but it can have its drawbacks. It's not effective on some viruses, for instance, and energy costs can be high. Also, this system does not prevent recontamination. Doubling up with another filter to eliminate sediment increases the UV system's effectiveness, in part because it doesn't work well in cloudy or dirty water.

If you haven't found the one treatment device to solve all your problems, don't be alarmed. Some water problems require two or more units, says Douglas Oberhamer, chief executive officer of the Deep Rock Water Company, Denver.

Help for Private Wells

What about those of us who get our water from private wells rather than public systems?

By and large, the major problem that individual well owners find is bacteriological. In one study sponsored by the Virginia Department of Health, for example, 58 percent of the individual wells sampled were contaminated with coliform bacteria, organisms that frequently indicate the presence of more serious bacteria such as typhoid.

But remember, what kills bacteria in swimming pools? Right — chlorine. So if bacterial contamination turns out to be your problem, says Lucius Cole, technical director of the national Water Quality Association, you should have a pump installed that will inject measured amounts of chlorine into your water system as it enters your home.

"You may find you need a prefilter, an activated carbon unit and reverse osmosis system or some other combination to take care of your water troubles," says Oberhamer. "A professional will be able to help you design the best system for you."

Denise Foley

Lawn and Garden Care

Taking care of your lawn and garden is usually no risk and a lot of pure pleasure. But there *are* hazards—some serious, some not so serious—that the informed homeowner needs to be aware of.

THE ALLERGY GUARDS

Let's start with a common problem—allergy—and see what the experts say you can do to make it more bearable.

Your lawn—or more specifically the pollen released from it to the wind in spring—is one of the biggest sources of things that make you snort and sneeze against your will. But possibly the best single defense against a blooming lawn is also one of the simplest: Keep it clipped.

"If you let a lawn grow freely, eventually it's going to literally go to seed, start flowering and releasing pollen," says Eliot Roberts, Ph.D., executive director of the Lawn Institute in Pleasant Hill, Tennessee.

"You can prevent that just by keeping it clipped. A few varieties of grass can flower even when they're cut to ¼ inch, but the kind most people have won't, if you keep it trimmed at the recommended height—1½ inches."

Mowing the lawn can significantly reduce your risk of an allergy explosion the next time you step outside, but it can't eliminate it, simply because, as James Thompson, Ph.D., pollen allergy expert and senior botanist at Hollister-Stier Pharmaceutical Company in Monmouth, Oregon, points out, most pollen blows in from somewhere else. Dr. Thompson says a typical vacant lot left uncut can generate almost 22 *pounds* of pollen in less than a week, most of which blows away.

So what can you do?

One simple solution recommended by Dr. Thompson: Wear a mask, or what the professionals call dust and mist respirators. These uncomplicated fiber shields—Dr. Thompson uses the version marketed by the 3M Corporation—fit snugly over your nose and mouth. They screen out all airborne particles larger than 1 micron. The smallest pollen particles are seven times that size.

One caution: Check the particle size your mask permits. So-called painter's masks, for example, keep paint out but let pollen in. And don't reuse masks: Pollen almost always collects on the outside surface and falls inside when you take the mask off—a sure prescription for sniffles and sneezes the next time you put it on.

INSECT WARFARE

Pollen is tough, but at least it doesn't have wings. Have wasps, bees, hornets or other top guns in nature's annoying air force decided to annex your patio as their practice range? Here's some anti-aircraft advice.

One solution, of course, is the use of pesticides—spraying around your home to eliminate bothersome stingers and biters. If you have a life-threatening or severe allergy to a particular insect or bug, this may be the way to go.

"I'm as reluctant to commit mass slaughter of another species as anyone, but I'm also competitive," says Cornell University entomology professor Edgar Raffensperger, Ph.D. "If it came down to me or the insect, I'd take whatever steps were necessary to ensure my own survival."

Pesticides, however, are dangerous substances. Dr. Roberts strongly encourages hiring a professional exterminator—affiliated with either the Professional Lawn Care Association of America or the Professional Grounds Management Society—to do the work. But if you insist on doing it yourself, take the following precautions.

● Wear protective clothing. "The gear available to the homeowner probably won't do the job as well as the expensive equipment the pros use, but it's better than nothing," Dr. Roberts says. Suggested items include a respirator, rubber gloves, long-sleeved shirts and long pants to minimize skin exposure.
● Wash thoroughly afterward. "You don't want this stuff to sit around on your skin," Dr. Roberts says. "People should clean their equipment, then clean themselves and change their clothes. Remember to wash those clothes separately."
● Read the label. "This is critical," says Dr. Roberts. "That label gives you a reasonable idea of what you safely can and cannot do with that particular product. It should be adhered to religiously."

All of which makes *not* using pesticides that much more attractive: It's so much simpler. And there are other steps you can take to reduce your risk of being stung. Here are Dr. Raffensperger's suggestions, based on a career spent around bugs and insects.

● Wear light, neutral-colored clothing, which many insects find less appealing. Don't, in other words, dress in colors that make hummingbirds think you're dinner; the bees might agree.

● Avoid scents of any kind. Smelling like a rose might please the nose but it invites unnecessary conflict with the insects who like the aroma, too.

● Stay away from likely places for insects, but if you can't avoid it, use a good repellent, essentially any product containing DEET (diethyltoluamide). Spray it on exposed skin *and* parts of clothing where insects might enter (for example, pants cuffs and shirt collars). Bees aren't bothered by it, but biting insects—chiggers, ticks, mosquitoes and others—are.

CLIP LAWNS CAREFULLY

The most dangerous member of the backyard gang isn't alive. Power equipment accounts for most major accidents related to lawn and garden care. The two leading offenders: The walk-behind power mower and the riding mower. Each year, the first produces an estimated 38,000 injuries that require emergency room care, says the U.S. Consumer Product Safety Commission. And the riding mower is involved in an estimated 75 deaths every year.

"The manufacturers have almost gone overboard trying to make their equipment safe," says Dr. Roberts. "There's no reason these accidents should be happening, but they keep happening anyway. People have *got* to be more careful."

The following guidelines for making sure you don't become a statistic were drawn from Dr. Roberts and from Outdoor Power Equipment Institute publications.

● Always push your mower at a walk; never run.

● *Push* the mower. Pulling increases the risk of slipping and pulling the machine over your feet.

● Mow across slopes with push mowers. If you slip, you'll slide away from the mower.

● Mow up and down slopes with a riding mower. You're less likely to flip the machine.

● Avoid mowing on wet grass. Wet grass is slippery and dangerous.

● Never carry passengers.

● Always check visually before backing up.

● Handle gas carefully. Store it in the right kind of container and keep it away from cigarettes and other smoking materials.

● Keep hands and feet away from moving parts. Translation: Turn equipment off before making adjustments; don't leave it running. You should also take the wire off the spark plug when cleaning the blades.

Kim Anderson

The Bent-Back Syndrome

You bend over to pick things up, you bend over to reach things, you bend over to get underneath a wayward tree branch. All that bending can cause pain in the body part doing it—your back. But Michael Wolf, Ph.D., president of International Fitness Exchange in New York City and a nationally known exercise consultant, says the following tips can make your back's contribution to home lawn and garden care easier.

● Warm up before gardening. This is an obvious but uniformly ignored first step. "The same guy who warms up for 30 minutes every night before he lifts weights doesn't think twice about picking up a 100-pound sack of fertilizer cold," says Dr. Wolf.

● Use your legs to pick things up, instead of your back. Kneel, grasp the object, keep the back straight and then stand up.

● Get help when you need it. But if it can't wait, try dragging heavy bags instead of carrying them. Or sled them on a sheet of cardboard.

● Take your time. "I think quick, fast movements may be responsible for more back injury than anything else," Dr. Wolf says.

Organize and Save Time

"What time should I be there?"
"Any time."
"Do you have the time?"
"Time out!"
"At the tone, the time will be . . . "
"Time is money."
"It's about time."
Time . . . Time . . . TIME!

Time is everywhere. On our wrists, hanging on the kitchen wall, listed in our TV schedules, illuminated on our VCRs. We live by time, work by time, arrange our lives around time and, if we don't manage it correctly, we waste time.

"Getting organized and not wasting time is one of the keys to getting our lives in control," says Brunswick, Maine, psychotherapist and stress-management expert Allison Herman-Basile. "If our surroundings are out of control, cluttered, and our time mismanaged, our everyday life will be in the same disarray, causing stress to strike.

"Organization and proper use of time is a good way to keep our mental and emotional selves in order."

So, if a hike to the North Pole seems easier than getting your household in order, perhaps our stress expert's timesaving hints can help.

DON'T GET CAUGHT IN THE STUPORMARKET

A baby screams.

Something cold and metal slams into the back of your legs.

An inhuman voice, like chalk on a board, screeches over the loudspeaker.

Hours have passed. The frozen dinners are now lukewarm soup, the milk sour, the lettuce limp.

Are you having a nightmare?

No. You are just supermarket shopping during peak hours.

You can save yourself time and aggravation by either shopping first thing in the morning or last thing at night. The crowds are thinned out, the checkout lines are a breeze, the crazed cart-pushers are at home.

"Crowded supermarkets can put you in a stupor," says Herman-Basile. "You can waste time and energy, only to come home and find you forgot a half dozen items. If crowds get you down, make you uncomfortable or give you stress, do *all* your shopping—food, clothing, whatever—during off-peak hours. You'll save time and be more relaxed."

BUYING TIME

Everyone gets a little tired around 4:00 in the afternoon, especially after being on the go all day. For a mother, it may even be worse.

"Give yourself a break from the kids for an hour or two and pay a neighborhood girl to watch the children," suggests Herman-Basile. "It'll cost you a few dollars, but you'll be buying a little time for yourself to

Write On Schedule

What's the latest Yuppie craze? Gucci odor-eaters? Stocks-and-bonds wallpaper?

No. Organizers, that's what!

What exactly is an organizer? Well, they come in different sizes, some are bound in vinyl, others in leather, they may cost anywhere from $14 to $500 and, if used correctly, they can help you get organized and pinpoint exactly how you're wasting your time.

An organizer is a logbook. You write down everything you want to accomplish that day, then check it off as you do it. You also jot down anything else you might have done that's not on your schedule.

"At the end of the day, you will know how you spent your time, who or what is wasting your time and how to organize yourself better in the future," says a spokesperson for Daytimers, one of the many suppliers of organizers.

Besides being a logbook, an organizer is also a convenient way to carry and keep credit cards, checkbooks, cash receipts and important papers. They can hold such items as a calendar, telephone and address directory, fold-out yearly project planners and assignment sheets.

Organizers are not only for the busy executive. They can help the frazzled housewife get her daily chores done on time, keep a log of bills to pay and keep her on schedule during her busy day.

All Moms Are Created Equal

What's wrong with this picture?

Pop's watching the ball game. Junior is in the backyard building a tree house, while little Sally is on the front stoop playing with her dolls. The teenagers, Biff and Happy, are upstairs playing records and talking on the telephone. And Mom? She's all over the house, preparing dinner, washing clothes, scrubbing the bathroom and waxing the kitchen floor.

If this sounds familiar, maybe it's time you stood up for your rights, says John Ravage, managing editor of *WIN* magazine, a publication devoted to achievement through self-management.

"It's about time housewives stood up and shouted, 'I am not a servant! I am a manager!' " says Ravage. "And like all managers, they must begin delegating some of the work around the house.

"After all, organization is the key to a properly run household, and what better way to get organized than to start assigning chores to the family and take some of the burden off yourself?"

Ravage suggests getting one of the older children to take care of washing the clothes on Saturday, another one to tackle scrubbing the bathtub, the younger ones to perhaps answer the telephone and take messages. As for Pop and his ball game? Get him working as well. A wife has more responsibility than a husband, notes Ravage. Even if they're both bringing home the bacon, she usually has to do everything else, including be cook, nurse, chaplain, accountant and maid.

either relax, get to some chores that you need a clear head to perform, like check writing, or make a few uninterrupted phone calls.

"You'll be surprised at how much you can get done and how much better you'll feel just getting an hour or two to yourself."

WAKE AND SHAKE

To save time and energy around the house, don't put things off. As soon as your feet hit the floor in the morning, make the bed. After the last bite of food is eaten at a meal, wash the dishes. This will save you from backtracking all day trying to catch up with your ever-increasing housework.

BILL ME LATER

You can drive yourself crazy and waste time if you sit down once a month to pay a mountain of bills, says Herman-Basile. "Why overwhelm yourself spending hours tackling the job all at once, when a little organization can make the job easier?"

She suggests taking each bill as it comes in, writing the due date on the front of each envelope and placing it in the stack according to its urgency.

Once a week, grab the top couple of bills and pay them. Doing it 5 minutes a week can save you hours of aggravation at the end of the month.

CATCH THE WAVE

SCENE: A typical home at the end of the workday.

HE: Honey, I'm starved.

SHE: We'll be eating soon. I just put the meat loaf in the oven.

HE: Good. How long? A couple of minutes?

SHE: Two hours.

HE: A-A-A-CCKKK!

Cooking in a microwave oven can save you countless hours of wasted time a week. No more rushing home to get dinner in or on the stove 3 hours early.

Being able to prepare and cook a meal an hour before dinner is not only a time-saver, but it can also relieve the stress of cooking 365 dinners a year.

DECK THE MALLS

What's worse than a shopping mall on Christmas Eve, packed to the rafters with mad, last-minute shoppers all fighting for the last box of bath beads? You having to join them, that's what.

"Being organized can make holiday shopping a breeze," says Herman-Basile. "Why wait until December to begin shopping? Make out your Christmas list early, like in August, and begin shopping then.

"By Thanksgiving, when the shopping panic strikes, you'll be finished and can enjoy the Christmas season in peace."

Another good bet is shopping through a mail-order catalog. You can cross off everyone on your list by simply sitting at your desk at home. No malls and no maddening crowds to put up with. What's even better, many mail-order houses will even send your presents already gift-wrapped. All you have to do is place them under the Christmas tree.

Richard Dominick

Making a House a Home

Home. Some people prefer a one-room apartment in the big city, while others want a few acres, an old farmhouse and a pond. Still others put their down payments on a brand new split-level in the suburbs or a rambling old home near the town square.

But how do you turn that collection of wood, cinderblock, siding and furniture you call your house into a bona fide, where-the-heart-is home?

LIFE ON MEMORY LANE

For a house to become a home it must reflect your personality, says Marjorie A. Inman, Ph.D., associate professor of interior design at Purdue University. Not your interior decorator's personality, or the going-out-of-business department store's, or the Joneses' who live next door. So, where do you find the design that's stamped "you"?

Start by going down Memory Lane.

"Photographs are very important to have around, even if you don't look at them very often," says Dr. Inman. "They are a good link to the past, and even just stored in the closet, they can be very comforting." Your whole house doesn't have to be based on the past, she says, but it should contain some articles that give you comfort. A beat-up easy chair, your favorite childhood stuffed animal or just something you like to hold or look at can help in extending that homey feeling.

A personal connection to the past is especially important when moving from one place to another or planning to redecorate from top to bottom. According to Dr. Inman, unfamiliar surroundings, such as a new house or all new furniture, is one of the leading causes of modern-day stress.

THE PERSONAL TOUCH

Still, it takes more than memories and mementos to make a house a home. Photos of your family going a century back aren't going to mean a thing in a house decorated with please-don't-touch furnishings. Turn-of-the-century settees, Chinese figurines and pale Persian rugs aren't going to fit into a family whose members like to eat in front of the television and entertain the neighborhood hounds.

Experts say that people who really know what they need and what makes them feel good will create the most successful home environments.

New York interior designer Joan Wolf suggests planning what you intend to do in each room when considering a new house or renovating your old one. You should think in terms of *practical* and *livable*.

For example, if your family tends to congregate in the living room for just about every occasion, including meals and homework, don't fill it with expensive and uncomfortable furniture just because you happen to think it looks good. Comfort and convenience should coexist with aesthetics.

"You should know everything you want from your furniture or new home before you buy," says Wolf. "Decide what you want to do in each room and buy accordingly. Do you want a piano in the living room? Which room will you entertain your guests in? Which room will be the family gath-

---

Green with Serenity

You walk into your home after a hard day's work. Who should be there to greet you? Your spouse, the kids, the family dog?

How about a potted plant?

"They may not be giving you a hug at the door, cheering or wagging a tail, but it's very soothing and relaxing to come home to a houseful of thriving, beautiful plants," says Brunswick, Maine, psychotherapist and stress-management expert Allison Herman-Basile.

"Recent studies prove that keeping plants in your house adds a calming effect to the environment. In short, they are pleasing to the eye, add beauty to the room and make you feel more at home by giving it a personal touch," she says.

Herman-Basile suggests placing a large potted plant by the entrance of your home to greet you and your guests. In fact, an assortment of different plants, both hanging and potted, add a warming welcome to any room.

ering place? If you like to cook or spend time sipping coffee and chatting in the kitchen, make sure you give it the 'I'd like to hang around' appearance; do something like moving in your favorite easy chair."

You should also:

● Give yourself a quiet, soothing, uncluttered room suitable for quiet meditation.
● Make sure everyone in the family has his own space—a private place to keep things and escape to.
● Plan your lighting carefully. Lighting plays an important role in setting the mood of the room.
● Give considerable time and thought to selecting suitable colors and color combinations.

YOU AND YOUR HUE

Color, in fact, is the most important decorating decision you'll make.

Some fashion designers believe that our skin tones place each of us in a general color category and that once we know our "season," we'll be able to choose the colors that suit us best. Interior designer Lauren Smith, author of *Your Colors at Home,* has adapted the idea to decorating and believes that people not only look their best but also feel their best when they surround themselves with their colors.

"If we feel good wearing certain colors, we will feel good living with those same colors," says Smith.

In other words, by picking the wrong color in rooms and furniture, you can end up feeling as out of place in your home as a Siberian husky in Florida. If you always wear autumn colors, like browns and muted yellows, then be sure not to paint your bedroom in summer colors such as pink or blue. The wrong color schemes may cause you to feel out of place in your own home, adding to the stress of your new environment.

"The most reliable way of determining your season is to find a professional color consultant and have your colors done. It takes about an hour and costs around $50, but it is a lifetime investment," says Smith. "After all, you're ahead of the game if it stops you from buying a house with expensive wall-to-wall carpeting in a color that makes you feel ill at ease."

So what happens if autumn colors make you feel comfortable and relaxed, yet depress your spouse and children?

"There are color alliances between seasons," adds Smith. "By studying the palettes of everyone concerned, you and your consultant can find colors that will be good for everyone living in your home."

The Color of Homey

Psychologists know that certain colors have a certain effect on behavior. Warm colors like orange, red and yellow can stimulate the appetite; light earth tones can calm and comfort anxious people; and kids have been found to learn better in brightly colored rooms. So it only makes sense that the colors you use in your home will have some sort of effect on its occupants.

"The colors you choose for a room will definitely affect what gets done there," says Maria Simonson, Ph.D., Sc.D., a behaviorist who works in color therapy at Johns Hopkins Medical Institutions-Good Samaritan Hospital in Baltimore.

If you want a room, such as a living room, to have a soothing effect, use off-white, antique white, soft greens, blues or silvers or earth tones. Stark white can make a room look sterile and depressing.

Gray can be cold but is relaxing in combination with other, warmer colors. Bright-colored accents will make you feel perky.

Here are some color guides you might want to consider when planning your decor.

● In the family room, use warm earth tones or pale, golden yellow. They can be accented with bright, warm or cool colors.

● For the dining room, use off-white, pale gold, tan or beige in cool climates and cool blues and greens in warmer climates. They relax.
● In the bedroom, pale blue, pale green and beige make for optimal sleeping conditions in hot climates. Pale pink, lavender and mauve are good for cooler climates.

If you're planning a bar for your home, says Dr. Simonson, stay away from the bold, dark colors you often find in lounges and hotel barrooms. They encourage you to drink more. If you're using wallpaper, make sure it's not too overpowering.

The Good Neighbor Policy

America's best-known, bloodiest neighborhood dispute supposedly got started over a stolen pig. The famous feud between the Hatfields and McCoys fought in the 1800s on the Kentucky/West Virginia border was triggered when the one neighbor penned up a hog belonging to the other. It wasn't long before the hog owner's family took revenge by killing someone in the hog thief's family.

And, for the next several years, the Hatfields and McCoys continued taking turns getting revenge for one trivial incident or another until the neighboring hillsides were dotted with graves.

Undoubtedly, your relationships with your neighbors are not quite as deadly as the Hatfield/McCoy vendetta. Maybe it's just that you've stopped speaking to the guy in back because he never returned the saw he borrowed. Or the woman next door's been ignoring you ever since you painted your side of the fence purple.

Or maybe you don't have much to do with your neighbors simply because you don't know them. As one working mother put it, "I'm so busy commuting and juggling commitments that I wouldn't know my neighbors if I saw them on TV."

A HEALTH ASSET

If that sounds familiar, you may be missing out on a healthy slice of life. Neighbors can be good for body and soul, say experts. Studies in developing countries where people maintain close neighborly ties show that they have less heart disease than people in urbanized countries with less neighborly contact. "It appears that people who are more socially isolated are less able to cope with the everyday

stresses and strains of life," says researcher and behavioral scientist William Dressler, Ph.D., of the University of Alabama School of Medicine.

A good neighbor may be anyone, from the guy you share small talk with on the elevator ride to your apartment floor to someone who shares the secrets of your soul. As reported by Letty Cottin Pogrebin, author of *Among Friends: Who We Like, Why We Like Them, and What We Do with Them,* up to 45 percent of us name one or more neighbors among our three closest friends.

Yet, writes Pogrebin, "even when neighbors are not dear to one another, they often are important for mutual help and protection." For example, your neighbor watches over your house or pets while you are away. You help your neighbor dig out of a snowbank or pick up her prescription at the drugstore.

"Neighbors are a form of insurance, just as valuable as property, fire or health insurance," adds Stephen Glaude, executive director of the National Association of Neighborhoods in Washington, D.C.

TAKE SOME NEIGHBORLY ADVICE

So how do you keep the homefront friendly? "You have to work at it," says Glaude. When you first move into an area, for example, start taking walks around the neighborhood. Some people find that it's easier to strike up conversations with strangers if they have a pet or child in tow. Ask about the best dry cleaning store or where to have your car serviced.

Don't expect, however, that your neighborly relations will always be as close as they were between the well-

Building Block Harmony

There's a part of the North Meadow Street neighborhood in Ithaca, New York, that looks like it's been built by kids—it has a curving slide and brightly colored, upended rubber tires.

This is no ordinary playground. It's the combined work of children, parents and teachers who together designed and built a kid's dream with donated lumber, volunteer labor and a good deal of cooperative spirit.

The playground project is just one example of what can be achieved when neighbors pull together. Want the corner lot cleaned up? A community garden? You can achieve these things for your neighborhood, says Marla Anderson, training director of National Association of Neighborhoods, as long as you make your goals immediate, specific and realizable.

Once you have an idea for making your block better, here's how to make the dream come true.

● Knock on doors. Invite your neighbors to attend a brainstorming coffee hour to discuss plans.
● Hold a meeting. Ask a speaker from another neighborhood to share similar solutions.
● Develop support. Involve local clubs—like the Kiwanis or the Boy Scouts.
● Raise money. Have bake sales, shovel snow, mow lawns. Enlist a local foundation or community-minded corporation to donate money and materials.

matched Ricardos and Mertzes on the "I Love Lucy" show. Many neighbors have divergent personalities and divergent styles of living.

Most of the time, notes Glaude, it's a matter of overlooking your neighbors' idiosyncracies. If you think your neighbors are littering their lawns with tacky lawn ornaments so it looks like a bad imitation of Disneyland, there's not much you can do about it but exaggerate your separateness. Try to make your property look distinct with tasteful landscaping.

"The important thing to remember about neighbors is that we are all interdependent," Glaude says."No matter if your neighbor has different tastes, religion or color, we all want the same thing—a safe, clean, quiet place to live. We need each other to achieve that."

That's especially important to keep in mind if more serious problems arise. "Where safety is a concern, you may need to speak up," says Glaude. "But you can still be neighborly about it."

An old junk car left rusting in your neighbor's yard, for example, could attract rodents and become a health hazard. "Try not to threaten or put the other person on the defensive," says Glaude. "Instead, say something like, 'You know, that car could be dangerous—I'll help you get it towed.' "

BE THE DIPLOMAT

Always keep in mind that "an ounce of goodwill is worth a pound of confrontation," says Glaude. Besides, "goodwill is more contagious.

"Diplomacy is best," he says. "It keeps the aura of neighborliness alive. Once conflict gets started, there goes the neighborhood."

Here's how to spread goodwill among your neighbors, especially in sticky situations.

Give the benefit of doubt to the borrower. Your neighbor might have legitimately forgotten that you lent him the widget for the garden hose last summer. Don't hold a grudge—or your tongue. Kindly ask for your possession. If your neighbor perpetually forgets to return things, stop lending.

Discuss common property up front. If you plan to put up a wooden fence that straddles both properties, talk about it before construction. Mention that it's going to need painting every year and suggest that you take turns with the maintenance. That way you both air your plans and expectations.

Don't ignore unshoveled sidewalks. A snow-covered walk can be treacherous. Offer to shovel your neighbor's sidewalk or to pay the kid who shovels yours to shovel his, adding, "this time it's on me." You'll make him conscious of the problem and probably stir his pride enough to make him take care of it himself next time.

Marcia Holman

When Nosy Is Neighborly

It's a fine line you're crossing between nosiness and niceness when it comes to keeping an eye on your neighbors. But where do you cross the line? If you see or hear the following, don't hesitate, say the experts. Butt in. It's the neighborly thing to do!

Violence against a person. You suspect someone is being beaten or you see a child with suspicious bruises. "Don't think it's meddling to call the cops," says Steven Glaude, executive director of the National Association of Neighborhoods. "It's better to be safe than sorry." Or call 911 if your area is hooked into the emergency system.

Pet abuse. If the people next door have left poor, skinny Fifi howling in subzero temperatures, call your local chapter of the humane society, SPCA or animal control department. Let them judge if there's been abuse.

Health hazards. If your neighbors leave rotting garbage and junk strewn around and you can't seem to work the problem out between you, call the local health department. If you don't have a health department, contact local municipal officials.

In the following situations, it's best to check with your neighbors *before* contacting the authorities.

Suspicious-looking vehicles. The moving van parked at your neighbor's may actually be a front for thieves. First, call the neighbor's house. If there's no answer, try to contact them at work and mention that you noticed the van. If you can't contact the neighbor, get the license number of the van and watch for suspicious behavior. Consider it a tip to tip off the police.

Wild teen parties. Go to the kids directly and ask if their parents are aware of their party. Mention that the noise may be upsetting other neighbors and that it could get them into trouble. If the noise persists, call the cops.

Low-Stress Moving

Think of the country of Spain. Its total population is 38.8 million people. Now imagine them all picking up and moving, then doing it again the next year. And the next.

Seems silly, right? Well, that's just what Americans *are* doing. Thirty-nine million of us move every year, says the Census Bureau.

Looked at another way, that number translates into 2.5 million tons of household belongings moved interstate every year—and an equivalent amount of emotional baggage. China *and* hearts can break in a move.

THE MEMORIES OF OUR LIVES

Ashley took her first steps in this kitchen . . . Those pencil marks on the wall show how Johnny grew year by year . . . Remember when we planted that tree? Now the realtor just calls it a shady lot . . .

How do you say good-bye to a home? To memories? Moving, it seems, can be a moving experience. "It's more traumatic than people think," says Mark Stone, Ed.D., dean of the Forest Institute of Professional Psychology in Des Plaines, Illinois, who's done studies for realtors on the subject of relocation.

"As the day approaches, many people ask themselves, 'Why did I do this?' Individuals, as the time gets near, think they've done something impetuous. They get second thoughts."

MEMORIES TO GO

You can end those second thoughts by taking the tree you planted with you. You don't have to uproot it when you uproot, just take a cutting and plant it at your new house.

"Bring your memories of the home with you," says Dr. Stone. "Bring things that will stand for your memories of the house. They could be pictures, a piece of furniture you bought specifically for the house, flowers from your flower garden, even a dried leaf from the tree you planted."

"SALE-A-BRATE"

Dr. Stone says another way to feel better about moving is to party when the "Sold" sign goes up. "Make it more of a celebration than a going-away. People have housewarming parties when they move in; there's no reason not to have one when you move out. Leave on a positive note."

Be Prepared: Your 30-Day Moving Plan

Don't wait until the week before to start getting ready for your move. Preparation, say the moving experts, takes a good month. Here's a 30-day moving countdown that will help make your bon voyage a pleasant one.

30 days before moving day:

● Fill out change-of-address cards. Notify the post office, magazine subscriptions, your creditors and your friends and acquaintances of your new address.
● Take inventory of all your household goods.
● Round up your medical, dental, insurance, tax, school, auto and credit records and store them in a place where you can get at them quickly.
● Make all your travel plans and hotel reservations.
● Start using up the food in your freezer.

Two weeks before the big day:

● Have your bank transfer your accounts and release your safe deposit box.
● Notify local utilities and cable companies of disconnect dates and arrange connect dates with new utilities.
● Have a garage sale. If you're moving to a warm climate, this may be the time to sell the snowshoes.

One week to go:

● Start packing your suitcases and get everything back from the cleaners.
● Dispose of all flammables. Movers will not ship pressurized containers.

One day to go:

● Empty and defrost your refrigerator and freezer and let them air out. Put baking soda or charcoal inside to keep them fresh.
● Clean and air your stove.
● Finish packing your personal items.

Well-thought-out planning far in advance will allow you to avoid the stresses that can come with a move.

Not all professional movers are equally responsible.

● Know what type of insurance you have, the value of your furniture and how much it would cost to replace it.

● Take a good inventory of your personal belongings. Petty says a good way to do this is to take photographs of every room with everything in place. Open up the drawers and photograph what's in them, too.

● Have a professional appraise your valuables. This will make it easier for you if you have to substantiate their worth for a claim.

● Realize ahead of time that most furniture is not made to move and that repairability is a problem. Pack your valuables well.

person in charge of packing fragile artifacts. She's had to move Egyptian glass made *thousands* of years ago. That's B.C. — Before Corning Ware.

She has a special tip for moving fragile belongings, whether it's a vase from the Ming Dynasty or one from the first floor at Macy's. "We put things into a polyurethane foam that you can buy at your local hardware store. We lay the object on it, trace it out, then cut a cavity in the foam. We do that for a top piece and a bottom piece. Then when we put them together it forms a cushion of foam around the artifact." Or your souvenir teacup from Niagara Falls.

Don Barone

U-HAUL OR U-DON'T

After the psychological lift, the next step is figuring how you're going to physically lift and load your belongings. Should you do it yourself or have someone else do it for you?

Diane Boschian, public information director for U-Haul International, Phoenix, Arizona, says 65 percent of the people moving today move themselves.

If you're trying to decide whether to do it yourself or not, she says, "Take a look at how much you want to spend, how much time you have, if you're physically able to do it, how big your family is and how many rooms you need to move."

Gary Petty, vice president of the National Moving and Storage Association in Alexandria, Virginia, has a few other tips you should know about before you move.

● Get bids. This is especially true for interstate moves because prices will vary greatly among shippers.

● Get references from the shippers.

PACK THE SMITHSONIAN WAY

You think your stuff is fragile? Talk to Greta Hansen, a conservator of the Smithsonian Institution's Museum of Natural History and the

Should Your House Retire with You?

If you're trying to decide about moving somewhere else once you retire, Shirley Waldrum of the American Association of Retired Persons (AARP) has some advice that may help you decide.

"Consider your lifestyle. Do you want a large house to take care of, a lawn to mow? Can you afford the upkeep of the house? Can you afford to heat it?

"Make a list, one for the husband, one for the wife. List what's impor-

tant to you. Do you need your family, friends, doctors? Do you like your present climate? List whatever's important to you. Then compare the lists. That will give you an accurate picture of what's best."

She went on to say that AARP figures show that the majority of retired people do not move and that those who do move within the same city, usually from a large house to a smaller apartment nearby.

chapter four

WORKING HAPPY

Hassle-Free Commuting

SCENE: A four-lane highway, bumper-to-bumper traffic. The camera closes in on one particular car. It's filled with carpooling businessmen. They are all uncomfortable, disheveled and annoyed. They've been stuck in traffic for over an hour with no hope of moving soon. In the back are three businessmen. The one in the center, weighing close to 300 pounds, is speaking.

FATTY: You boys will have to excuse me this morning, but my wife made beans and cabbage last night and . . .

The camera pulls away from the car, back to miles of bumper-to-bumper traffic. It slowly approaches a man standing at a bus stop. It is Rod Serling.

ROD: Mr. and Mrs. Average American. Every morning up by 5:00 A.M. to shower, dress, swallow a cup of coffee and a doughnut and head out into the world of stalled traffic, late trains and subways and "left lane ends, 500 feet" signs. It used to be they only hated their jobs. Now they hate getting there and coming back home, too. So what do they do about it? Nothing. They put up with it five days a week, year in and year out. Meanwhile, the daily stress of commuting is slowly weakening their mental and physical health. Every day, blood pressures and pulse rates are skyrocketing. People get to their destinations hurried and harried, each one a step closer to an ulcer, stroke or heart attack.

Is there an escape from this maddening way of life without packing it in and dragging your family to a soybean farm in Iowa? The answer is yes.

Be a Big Wheel: Try Cycling to Work

Riding a bike to work, darting in and around heavy traffic, you're bound to hear the following:

"Get a horse!"

"Got a paper route?!"

"Hey, Beaver! Where's Wally?"

Once at work, 10 minutes ahead of your officemates who either drove or took the bus, you might hear such astonished remarks as:

"You mean you rode your bike all the way across town?"

"Are you nuts?"

"What's the matter? Can't afford a car?"

Well, don't fret. If they knew what you know about bicycle commuting, they might be out there as well.

Most people simply don't know how to use a bike for transportation. They rode bikes as children, and maybe even do a little recreational riding as adults. But commuting to work? They haven't the slightest idea of what equipment to use, how to stay dry in wet weather or how to drive safely in city traffic. Bicycling may look less convenient, but it can get you there faster and keep you in shape doing it. While your fellow workers are caught in traffic jams, delayed by late buses or subways or waiting on the side of the road for the tow truck, you can be breezing through the traffic on time and on schedule.

Here are a few tips from the editors of *Bicycling* magazine to help you become a well-equipped, knowledgeable bicycle commuter.

● Many people start by jumping on their bikes the way they did when they were kids, and then complain about the rain, traffic and hills. Nonsense! Read *The Complete Book of Bicycle Commuting*, join a bike club or go on a long ride with an experienced bicyclist first to learn the ropes.

● Don't turn your bike into a second car with a thousand accessories. Get a basic bike with a good set of accessories—helmet, lights, rain gear, rack, bike bags, pump and tools. Be sure the bike has aluminum alloy rims or a hub brake for wet braking.

● Think like a driver. Ride according to the rules of the road. Ride with grace, style and a confident, competent posture. This will earn you the motorists' respect.

● Have your route to work mapped out in advance and know the streets and turns. Know all the stop and yield signs, all the lanes of traffic that merge, which roads are or will be under construction. If you alter your route, mark it on your map and memorize it.

Sit back as we now show you how to escape from . . . the Commuting Zone.

MIND OVER MUTTER

If you find yourself late for work, stuck in traffic, and your blood pressure rising, it's okay to start talking to yourself, says Allison Herman-Basile, a psychotherapist from Brunswick, Maine, who specializes in relaxation and stress management. "Whether you're carpooling, sitting on a crowded train or sitting alone in your automobile, start muttering to yourself. Convince yourself you are still in control of the situation and that no matter what happens, you will not allow anxiety to set in. You'll find you'll begin to relax almost immediately."

The key to convincing your mind that everything is all right is to mutter before the signs of stress hit. "Once stress strikes, your body takes over your mind and begins to do itself damage," adds Herman-Basile. "Your heart begins pounding, your blood pressure takes off, your palms become sweaty, lactic acid is released from your muscles, the liver secretes sugar that had been stored, adrenaline begins pumping through your system, and you may suddenly feel dizzy. Years of this will do extreme damage to your physical and mental well-being."

So, before your body takes over, close your eyes, take a deep, slow breath and, in a soft, calm voice, reassure yourself everything is under control.

COMMUTING CAN BE A BEACH

Another way to calm yourself from the stress of commuting is to close your eyes and put yourself in another environment. "It's called visionalization," says Herman-Basile. "Just close your eyes and begin imagining yourself wherever you're most comfortable."

Most people imagine themselves alone on a beach. They visualize the waves crashing on the shore, the sound of the seagulls, and the cool wind against their faces. Before long, their heartbeats slow, their blood pressures lower and they are once again relaxed.

DON'T MOAN—PHONE!

When early-morning traffic is crawling over the bridge, the subways are backed up, the train left minutes ago and someone who just had a garlic bagel with onions decides that the best place to breathe is right in front of your face, stress is probably a step or two away. "Rather than concentrating on all the bad things happening to you at that moment," says Herman-Basile, "quickly begin solving your immediate problems."

For instance, if that morning's commute is backed up, forcing you to miss an important meeting, there's nothing you can do about it. Instead of dwelling on the problem—solve it. Plan to pull off at the next exit and get to a telephone. If you happen to be on a train, get off at the next stop and use the station's public telephone. By calling and explaining the commuting delay, the stress is released.

ORANGE JUICE GLAD YOU'RE A COMMUTER?

A good way to beat the commuting blues is to start the day off with a good breakfast. If you're standing in the middle of a train aisle, the temperature is 90°F and the guy behind you keeps poking the tip of his umbrella into your foot, coffee and a doughnut are just not going to make it.

A balanced breakfast is your best defense in combating commuter stress. According to Peter G. Hanson, M.D., author of *The Joy of Stress*, the best diet for stress is one that provides the

right number of calories to maintain your ideal body weight, is eaten at a reasonable pace and is balanced.

Orange juice, whole grain cereal and a slice of buttered high-fiber bread is a good example of a breakfast that will give the commuter a greater chance of arriving at work calm and relaxed.

ALONE AGAIN

When you finally arrive at work, wrinkled, headachy and harried, don't jump right into the business day. Take a minute or two for yourself, suggests Herman-Basile. The day waited this long for you, it can wait another couple of minutes. Head for the washroom and clean up.

Once at your desk, sit down for a moment and take a few deep breaths. Stretch the tightened muscles in your neck and back. What went on during your commute is over now, and the tension, stress and anxiety it brought upon you should be left outdoors.

"Start by sitting at your desk with your eyes closed," suggests Herman-Basile. "Begin at the top of your head, contracting and then releasing each muscle, and slowly work your way down to the bottom of your toes. This will release any tension buildup inside your body, ease your muscles and send a calming sensation throughout your body."

And whatever you do, don't let the stress of the business day get to you, because when it's over, the stress of commuting is still outside, waiting to take you back home.

Richard Dominick

The Low-Stress Office

Your "in" basket just appeared in a *National Geographic* pictorial on mountain climbing. You're so behind, the bottom memo makes reference to the Liston-Clay fight. The lighting in your office is so bad, at times you wish you were radioactive and could read by the light of your own head.

They pipe music into the office now, something by Black Sabbath hummed by the Mormon Tabernacle Choir backed by the All-Bagpipe and Barking Dog Band. The new phone system isn't working either. The last time you dialed your secretary's extension, you found out it was 57°F at the Singapore airport.

Are you working in the Office from Hell?

Is your blood pressure graph higher than your sales chart?

Do you hear voices even when your intercom is turned off?

If any of the above sounds like your situation—relax. You are just part of the working world, where stress is as common as the 10:30 A.M. coffee break.

EIGHT DAYS A WEEK

Henry Thoreau once wrote, "The mass of men lead lives of quiet desperation." Today, that quote might read, "The mass of men and women in offices lead lives of loud desperation."

"I need that report now!"

"Why weren't you at that meeting?!"

"Hackenbush! You're fired!"

Will Rogers once said he never met a man he didn't like. That may be true, but he never worked in an office from 9:00 A.M. to 5:00 P.M., five days a week, with a boss whose emotional stability rates below that of the Boston Strangler.

Time-wise, work dominates our lives. Most of us spend 2,080 hours a year on the job alone, not counting the hours it takes getting there and back. When stress strikes in the office, we take that stress home, where the yearly total of hours donated to our jobs continues to rise. So, you might ask, why then do we work? To eat, provide, clothe and, in many cases, to pay off huge mortgages and five-year car loans, to build that pool in the backyard, to join that tennis club and to keep up with those crazy Joneses who just moments ago placed a solid gold flamingo on their front lawn.

So if we must grind away at our jobs for more than 2,000 hours a year, doesn't it make sense to go about it in the least stressful way?

PLAN OF ATTACK

"Make out a daily plan of how you will tackle your work and you will immediately begin to feel less stress about it," says Allison Herman-Basile, a Brunswick, Maine, psychotherapist specializing in stress management and relaxation. "Lack of organization and control is probably the main cause of self-generated stress in the workplace."

In other words, rather than sitting at your desk in the morning wondering where and how to start, come in prepared with a daily routine.

"Keeping lists, timetables and a diary will keep you organized and help control the chaos and confusion

Sick and Tired of Work?

SCENE: A secretary picks up a ringing telephone.

SHE: Good morning. Ross, Ross and Ross Advertising.

HE: Hello. Is Mr. Ross in?

SHE: Sorry. He's too tired to pick up the phone right now.

HE: All right. Is Mr. Ross in?

SHE: He's vomiting at the moment.

HE: Okay. How about Mr. Ross?

SHE: They just took him away in an ambulance.

HE: I'll call back.

This is an exaggeration, of course, but office workers should be aware that their fatigue, headaches, nausea, stuffy noses, chest pains, dizziness, sore throats, blurry vision and itchy skin may be symptoms of the Sick Building Syndrome.

How's that again?

When modern office buildings are too well insulated, they can seal in harmful pollutants that cannot escape, says environmental health expert Richard Hartle from the National Institute for Occupational Safety and Health. "Everything from copying machine chemicals, building adhesives, carpet-cleaning chemicals, cigarette smoke and organic compounds from furniture and paints can become trapped inside the air of the office building," says Hartle. "The office worker has no choice but to inhale these pollutants."

Hartle suggests fighting for a no-smoking policy at the office, opening windows, installing ceiling fans to help circulate the air, regulating room humidity and asking for an adequate ventilation system to be installed, if there isn't one already, as a way of combating the Sick Building Syndrome.

when your work is mounting at your desk. When you have control over your workload, you begin lessening your stress," adds Herman-Basile.

BOSSZILLA

Your immediate supervisor at work is: (*a*) crazy, (*b*) probably wanted by the FBI, (*c*) half man, half some type of life form from Pluto, (*d*) wearing a goalie's mask and carrying an axe or (*e*) all of the above.

No one said it would be easy, but when your supervisor's scream has been known to shatter safety glass, no one said it would be this hard either.

So what do you do?

"The first thing is not to take it personally," says M. J. Irvine, Ph.D., psychologist at Toronto General Hospital. "Most times it is not you but an outside force responsible for the supervisor's behavior. If the situation doesn't change, don't get flustered. Remember, he is under more stress than you and may just be overreacting to it."

Dr. Irvine suggests perhaps approaching your supervisor at a quieter moment and asking to talk about the situation.

"The key to stopping stress is to be in control of the situation. Your employer is not yelling at you, he is yelling over company matters. Take a deep breath, count to ten, smile and go about your work."

THE YAWNING OF A NEW DAY

Day in and day out. Tote that barge. Lift that bale. Note that charge. Lift that sale. If the overwork and monster bosses don't get you, the monotony and boredom will. So how do you make day 947 seem as fresh as day 1?

"Put priorities first," says Neal Sofian, a corporate health specialist for Health at Work in Seattle. "Remember, it is only a job, and your physical and mental health comes first."

He suggests exercising as a way of keeping your mind and body strong. "The mind and body are connected," he adds. "If you can't change the mind, change the body. Better physical health will keep your mind strong and able to tolerate the boredom of work. You can't solve a boring job, but exercise will help make you feel better about it."

CHRISTMAS IN JULY

It's 100°F in the shade, but you wouldn't know it. Ice is forming on your keyboard and your tongue has frozen to the telephone receiver. In January, while the world outside your office is encased in a solid block of ice, your co-worker is dressed like a hula dancer, and you've hired your neighbor's kid to fan you all day with a large palm leaf.

Are you crazy? No. You're just a victim of the Phantom of the Heating/Air-Conditioning Unit—and there's nothing you can do about it.

"When environmental stresses such as adverse heating or cooling, office noises or overcrowding strike, one must always remain calm," says Dr. Irvine. "In most cases you cannot change your environment, so you must try to create a more pleasant setting for yourself."

If your office is too hot, try a portable clip-on fan. Too cold? A hand warmer and comfortable sweater may be just the thing. The copying machine makes more noise then the Yucca Flats plutonium bomb? Try headphones, assuming your job and supervisors allow them.

"The key to cutting down environmental stresses is to not allow the distractions to wear you down," adds Dr. Irvine. "If they become too bad on any given day, get away from your desk awhile and relax. Take a coffee break. You'll feel better."

Richard Dominick

The Executive Stressretary

We take you now to one of the busiest offices in the publishing business. We are visiting the *Globe* in Boca Raton, Florida, where a new edition of a 48-page magazine has to be written, edited, laid out and printed every week. There, in the middle of this madhouse of editors, reporters, photographers and graphic artists, sits one of the executive secretaries, Rita Tucker.

"My desk is piled a mile high with reporters' copy, my phones are constantly ringing, there is noise everywhere, people are always shouting, and no matter what I'm doing, an editor finds 6 more things for me to do immediately," says Tucker.

So how does she get through the day without her head exploding from all this stress?

"When things get bad I walk around the office a lot, take a stroll down the hall and take several deep breaths," she says. "When it's real bad, I count to a hundred. I also keep small toys all around my desk. They make me feel better, keep me relaxed and make me feel like this is my own personal space. Some of them are made from rubber and I squeeze them instead of losing my temper.

"At the end of the day I go home and take a hot, soothing shower," she adds. "That seems to take all the stress out of my body and gets me ready for another hectic day."

Savvy Sitting

Sit down, please.

Now look what you've done!

When you sit to take a load off your feet, that load has to go somewhere. Right? Your back (despite your first thought) is the most common victim of this shifting of physical responsibility.

The body works in strange ways. The load that may have been merely annoying to your tired feet when you were standing is actually heavier and more threatening to your back after you sit down.

When you stand, the forces pressing on the disks in your spine are relatively equal. When you sit and thus bend your spine, the balance is uneven. That creates a vulnerability, especially if you sit in a way that leaves your back unsupported.

Your legs fare no better. The sluggish circulation that results from sitting too long can be annoying; for some (those with varicose veins or blood-clotting problems), it's even possibly dangerous.

Add to these problems the general achiness of shoulder and neck muscles that have gotten into the rut of sitting and you're describing one unhappy body.

What can you do if you're shackled to a desk all day and your body is crying out for help? Well, there are several things you can do *to* your chair, *in* your chair and *out of* your chair.

FIX THAT CHAIR

How do you know you have a good office chair? Basically, because you can ignore it. "Curiously, the most appropriate (or comfortable) chair is hardly noticed," says Marvin Dainoff, Ph.D., an expert in ergonomics, the science of applying human biomechanics to the design of the things

people use. "As long as it provides proper support, it's usually ignored."

If you're stuck with, or are particularly fond of, a particular chair, there are a few things you can do to make things more comfortable.

● Add a lower-back cushion (called a lumbar support) or a seat wedge to your chair. Both of these items can be purchased at stores that sell back-care products (or make your own from a towel). When it's positioned at the small of your back, the lower-back cushion supports the natural curve of your spine (your back will seem slightly arched). The seat wedge, which you place on your chair seat, rises slightly higher in the back to help tilt your pelvis forward and create the same natural curve in your spine.

● Look underneath the seat to see if your chair has any adjustable features. Many chairs do. See if it will move up and down, tilt forward and backward or allow you to adjust the backrest. Try different positions until you feel comfortable.

If you're looking for a better chair for yourself, here's what to look for.

● Adjustable features, such as those described above.
● A backrest that helps you maintain the natural curve in your spine, in much the same way lower-back cushions and seat wedges do.
● A seat that's 25 percent wider than your buttocks and ends with a scroll or waterfall edge that won't cut into the thighs and inhibit circulation.
● An armrest that allows your arms to share some of the load of sitting. An armrest also makes it easier to get into and out of your chair.
● A five-blade pedestal for the best chair stability.

Stretches for the Sedentary

To unkink your body after long hours of sitting, try these exercises.

Shoulder circles. Circle your shoulders backward in a wide arc.

Head circles. Circle your head slowly and gently, first to the left, then to the right.

Back arch. Place your hands in the small of your back and arch gently backward. If you have trouble with an excessively arched back, don't do this exercise. Most people, however, need to arch their backs more than they do. For safety's sake, do these standing up.

Upper-body stretch. Stand in a doorway. Grab both sides of the doorway, with your hands behind you at about shoulder level. Let your arms straighten as you lean forward. Hold your chest up and chin in.

Body curl. Push your chair away from your desk, lean forward and touch your toes. Unwind and sit back up, allowing the spine to uncurl one vertebra at a time.

Leg and foot stretch. Extend your leg, circle your ankles, and flex and point your toes.

● Casters that allow your chair to roll, to help give your legs some exercise when you push yourself from desk to filing cabinet, for example.

SIT WITH FINESSE

Once you have a good chair adjusted to your needs, you may think the battle is nearly won. In fact, it's just begun. How you sit in that chair is crucial. Here are some simple tips, culled from doctors, physical therapists and workplace experts.

● Don't slouch! Pity your back, shoulders and neck. If you're forced to sit at work, pull your chair up as close to your desk as possible. Try to sit directly over your work. If you must lean forward, try to bend from your hips, rather than rounding your back and shoulders. Use a book rest that holds things upright so that if you need to read, you won't have to bend over your work. Or else hold the reading matter up at face level while resting your elbows on the desk. Keep your head centered over your body.

● Keep a small footstool or phone book under your desk. Prop one or both feet on the stool to help relieve pressure on your lower back.

● Try to sit on both hips at the same time to distribute your weight evenly.

● Wriggle around a lot. Forget everything your parents told you about sitting still and not sitting forward on the edge of your chair. You should move around a lot, and sitting forward takes the stress off your lower back. You should also forget the taboo about resting your elbows on the table —that position takes some body weight off your spine, too.

● Try not to cross your legs, which nearly doubles the stress on your spine and muscles.

TAKE FREQUENT BREAKS

When you do have the freedom to leave your desk, you should take it and run—literally. A brisk walk or regular running program (or any other aerobic exercise that keeps your legs moving) can do wonders for your circulation as well as for your tired, unused muscles.

If you don't have time for daily exercise, at least be sure to get up once an hour and walk around. You might want to invest in a stand-up desk that guarantees you'll still get your work done even while you're standing. Remember, the more often you change positions in and out of your chair, the better.

An Unusual Back Support

What promises you excellent back support, is portable so you can take it anywhere and looks like a giant slingshot? It's the Nada-Chair.

You loop one strap around each knee, as if they were the prongs of the slingshot, and you stick your lower back where you'd normally put the stone.

"At first it's a little awkward with all the buckles and adjustments," says one reviewer, "but it's basically straightforward and very comfortable."

"It allows you to really relax in the cross-legged position on the floor and gives excellent lower-back support in a chair," says another.

And, says a third reviewer, "On special occasions, such as canoeing or watching a concert on bleacher-type seats, it might come in handy."

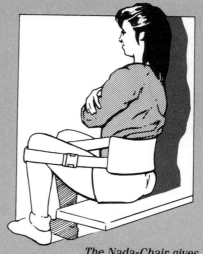

The Nada-Chair gives comfort without back pain.

Coping with Co-Workers

Pity poor Wendell. Every day he goes to work at the monkey house. Oh, yes, it's all happening at the zoo.

Wendell's boss is making whoopee with Wendell's new secretary—and the company isn't even in the cushion business.

The office gossip grapevine has a mouth and appetite that make the plant in the movie *Little Shop of Horrors* look like a petunia—and it's really developed a taste for Wendell-burgers.

Everyone else assiduously practices what they learned in Manipulative Maneuvering and Corporate Brown-Nosing 101, while Wendell refuses to dirty his pinkies in office politicking.

So Wendell watched woefully as the promotion he should have gotten plopped right into Gordy's lazy lap.

Milo dragged himself into the office late for the ninth time in two weeks, and fed-up Wendell reported him to Personnel—and now nobody's talking to Wendell.

Except Suzy Creamcheese, who in fact leans against Wendell's desk and jabbers like a one-woman cocktail party.

Wendell, Wendell, Wendell. These people give work, and thus your life, all the appeal of a vacation at the Funny Farm. But the solutions, Wendell, are all up to you.

THINK POSITIVE

International career-management consultant Richard Germann, author of *Working and Liking It*, says the positive approach to people works best. "Look at all your relationships at work without stereotyping people," Germann says. "Avoid developing hostility toward the person who's bother-ing you. Hostility makes you powerless. When you take the positive initiative, you're giving yourself power."

Start by making a list—"as silly as it sounds," says Germann—of the person's positive qualities. (If you have to, start with a negative list to get it off your chest.) Then keep the positive list in mind in your dealings with him or her—no matter what the problem.

THE CAST OF TYPES

You shouldn't expect utopia, least of all at work, say the experts. It takes all types to make work go 'round, so here's a rundown of the most common characters and how to deal with them sanely and effectively.

The workaholic. Marilyn Machlowitz, Ph.D., a Manhattan management consultant, says workaholics have a bad reputation that may not be deserved. Instead of blaming them for making you and others look like featherbedders, she says, "Ask yourself, 'Hey, am I doing what's required in this job? Are the workaholics getting opportunities I'm not?'"

But if you know you're meeting or exceeding the requirements, make sure the people who matter know your performance is up to par. Says Germann, "It's not an issue of defending yourself against a person you think is making you look bad."

The politician. "There's an unduly negative connotation" to office politics, says Dr. Machlowitz. You should be able to do your job and let the right people know what you're doing. Don't isolate yourself; it's not good for you or the company. Learn the rules, then play the game.

The backstabber. This is a situation you have to meet head-on, says Germann. "Don't go tit-for-tat. Don't try to analyze where the relationship went wrong. Draw a line through the old relationship and make a conscious decision that you will have a good one." Forget the past, start anew. Don't fake it; be honest. And keep trying. The person won't be able to resist a persistently positive approach.

"No one says it will be easy," says Germann, "but the alternative is worse. A negative trend feeds on itself and leads to complete severance of the relationship." This, of course, can make your work uncomfortable at the least and maybe impossible.

The slacker. If he's interfering with your work, says Germann, "you could blow the whistle and try to get rid of him. But the mature way is to try to help him." Realize that person "probably isn't terribly motivated. He may hate his job." While you're not a job counselor, you can talk to him—at the proper time—about what he likes to do; find out what his strengths are. "Base the relationship on that," says Germann, and eventually you may even help him find a position he does like.

The rumormonger. You can harvest wine or vinegar from the office grapevine. What you hear can be right or wrong. It can help you, but it can also sink your morale and—even if you don't hear it—damage your reputation and maybe even your future.

Dr. Machlowitz says the best rule of thumb is "to listen but not to dish. There's a bad connotation to be known as a gossip but a good connotation to be known as being in the know."

If the grapes are gossiping about you and the stories are false, you must try to find the source, squelch the rumor and prevent future ones, says Hendrie Weisinger, Ph.D., author of *Dr. Weisinger's Anger Work-Out Book.* As you trace the rumor, stop along the way and ask people to stop spreading it because it isn't true.

If you find the source, ask why he started it. Don't get mad, don't argue, but let the rumormonger know how you feel and ask him to put himself in your place. Provide a way to save face by telling him what the facts are and saying something like, "I know you wouldn't want to spread false rumors."

BLOWING THE WHISTLE

Despite all you do to accommodate contending forces at work, you may be forced to call a halt to severe abuses. This is a difficult position to get yourself into, but sometimes you have no alternative. "You have to do it in a way that hurts the fewest people," says Germann, "because it can backfire."

If you do it right, you can help the person whose behavior you want to change. Examine your motives first. Do you really just want to get rid of the problem-maker to make life easier for you? Or maybe get her job?

With pure motivation, develop a plan of action. Then approach a trusted higher-level contact in the company and bounce it off him in confidence. "Your attitude has to be: How can we help him, and the company?" says Germann. You're probably not the only one who's noticed the problem, but because you know the person you may be able to lend insight.

William LeGro

Stupid Cupid

A lot of people spend more time with their co-workers than with their spouses. Two-people offices, 2-people projects, long working hours and even longer happy hours throw co-workers into close contact.

The contact can get too close, despite everyone's best intentions. And it can be destructive, says career-management consultant Richard Germann.

Co-working lovers usually end up excluding other co-workers, who are left to wonder if their work is getting done or if one of the lovers is being favored over others. It can lead to gossip, jealousy and bad morale.

This doesn't mean that all office romances are wrong, says Germann. They sometimes do work. But the risks are great. If someone else's affair is interfering with your work, he says, react rationally. Approach the person positively, tell him or her you need help in your work or ask if you can help him or her. *Then* bring up the relationship as a possible factor in work problems. If that doesn't work, you may have to work around the affair until it runs its course, which it almost always does.

You can also make sure the same thing doesn't happen to you. Tom McGinnis, Ed.D., a psychologist in Fair Lawn, New Jersey, who helps men and women deal with this common problem, has this advice for stopping trouble before it begins.

● Send clear signals that you don't approve of extramarital affairs.
● Stay out of tempting situations.
● If someone's giving you the eye, be frank in saying you're not interested, and ask him or her if you're unconsciously leading him or her on.
● Talk to your spouse about an attraction you're feeling. Do it lightly, humorously.

Guide to a Good Boss

If you work outside the home, you know the importance of getting along with the boss. Perhaps next to the nature of the work itself, nothing so much determines how much you like your job—and how well you do—as whether you and the boss see each other as chums or bums.

All other considerations aside, since you may spend more time with your boss than you do with your family, the relationship had better be a good one, for the sake of sanity alone.

In business schools and among human relations experts, the subject of how to deal with bosses is being studied and discussed. The area has become known as "managing up." Here are some tips from the experts on how to hone your boss-managing skills.

KNOW THE BOSS

Managing up requires that you possess highly sensitive social and psychological antennae. This means literally diagnosing your boss, finding out what his personality traits are and mapping out a common ground between his style and yours. John Darling, Ph.D., a former professor in the business school at Texas Tech University, calls the ability to do this "style flex."

There are four kinds of people, says Dr. Darling. There are Mike Wallaces (assertive), Liza Minnellis (expressive), Ollie Norths (analytical) and John Denvers (amiable). Whatever your boss's disposition, "flex" in his direction, says Dr. Darling.

Similarly, there are two basic kinds of bosses: "listeners," who like verbal briefings, and "readers," who want written reports. Whatever their likes or dislikes may be, humor them, says Darling. If you have trouble diagnosing the boss, try drawing a chart and writing down both your boss's and your own "style." Then plot your behavior-modification strategy.

KNOW THYSELF

The flip side of diagnosing the boss is diagnosing yourself, and this can be a notch harder. It's not unusual, says Harvard's Gabarro, for energetic young managers to feel disproportionately hostile or frustrated when confronted or thwarted by an authority figure. The smart subordinate recognizes his or her anger and backs off before boiling over. The biggest mistake is failing to know yourself and failing to recognize the emotional elements in a professional relationship.

TALK TO THE BOSS

Be willing to communicate. Ask dumb questions—instead of making dumb mistakes. Volunteer information before the boss asks for it. Be candid even if it means relaying bad news. Managing up means having the moxie to speak up when the boss's intentions aren't clear.

"Sitting and waiting produces the most stress and the least results. It's a fact of life that the squeaky wheel gets the grease," says Mary Ann Allison, a manager at Citicorp and coauthor with her husband, Eric, of *Managing Up, Managing Down.*

Another expert, John Gabarro, D.B.A., of the Harvard Business School, says that those most effective in business "make a point of seeking the information and the help they need to do a job instead of waiting for their bosses to provide it."

Everyone Needs a Mentor

Effective managing up means being politically astute, knowing the right people in the organization and finding a mentor. In their book *Managing Up, Managing Down,* Mary Ann and Eric Allison recommend studying flow charts to find out who does or doesn't have power.

This usually means cultivating an immediate supervisor, but it might even mean cultivating the boss's secretary or even people in lateral directions who can potentially stall your projects. It also means befriending managers, possibly higher up on the ladder than your boss, who might serve as your mentor.

"In a corporation," says business author Tom Friedman, "mentors are more senior managers willing to guide, counsel and protect their juniors. They are now considered required equipment for the ambitious corporate climber."

How to find a mentor? Walk up and talk to one. "Pick someone you like," says Eric Allison, "then just ask. Say something like, 'I really respect your skills as a manager and admire the way you handle people. May I ask for help or feedback from time to time?'" You'll be on your way to having that all-important mentor.

KEEP PERSONAL ISSUES AT HOME

Tom Friedman, author of *Up the Ladder,* stresses the importance of knowing how to read a complex situation and to distinguish personal issues from professional issues. "You have to separate how you feel about your life, about your family, about your career, from the specific boss/employee relationship," he says. "You can get into awful trouble with your boss if you're defensive or angry about something that has nothing to do with work."

The tricky part is that the boss/employee relationship attracts trouble. "It's a lightning rod," says Friedman, "especially if you spend all of your time working together."

THE BOSS IS HUMAN

According to human relations experts, the really mature subordi-

Drawing by Whitney Darrow; © 1976 The New Yorker Magazine, Inc.

"Mr. Edwards, this is your secretary, Melissa. When you have a moment, would you run down and get me a regular coffee and a pineapple Danish?"

nate understands—above all else— that bosses themselves are fallible, that they are concerned about their own performance and that they welcome all the support they can get from their staff.

Being predictable in performance is important, too. The successful employee delivers consistent results, not results that are brilliant one day and mediocre the next. A neat appearance and a well-organized office also help build the image of a rising star.

If you're wondering how managing up differs from apple-polishing, business school professors say that managing up has the interests of the whole team in mind. "Brown-nosing is more self-serving," says Dr. Darling, "but style flex is an effort to facilitate the achievement of individuals as well as organizations."

Ultimately, the best argument in favor of managing up is that it makes life at the office less stressful, makes the boss trust you more and supervise you less, and offers the satisfaction of being appreciated by an authority figure. All told, proper managing of the boss is probably going to be worth all the effort you put into it.

Four Signs of a Bad Boss

Let's face it. Not all bosses are created equal. Some are great; others, well, they're somewhat less than great. Particularly if yours falls into the "less than" category, you may want to share the following information.

Mark J. Tager, M.D., coauthor of *Working Well: Managing for Health and High Performance*, interviewed workers all over the country, asking them to think about the worst boss they'd ever worked for. Then he asked what the boss did that made him or her so bad, how the boss's behavior made the employees feel and how it affected motivation, commitment to the job and desire to go to work. Finally, he asked what were the mental and physical effects of working for a bad boss.

Although answers varied, Dr. Tager found that there was a Top 4 list of management "techniques" that most commonly drove employees up the wall and made them sick.

Being unpredictable. This seems to make everyone sick. Being a predictable boss doesn't mean stagnation or boredom at the office. Employees simply want to know that a certain action will produce a certain outcome. Good work will merit praise; mistakes will earn a reprimand.

Whittling away at self-esteem. Bad bosses seem to make an effort to chip away at their employees' self-esteem. How do they do it? Among the most common ways are humiliating employees in front of colleagues, doling out unwarranted criticism, deny-

ing the employee recognition, promotions or awards, and taking credit for work the employee has done.

Creating win/lose situations. Stress often results when managers set up win/lose situations (in order for the manager to win, the employees must lose). Employees become distrustful, sensitivity and empathy are stifled, authority conflicts become frequent, new ideas are discouraged, deadlocks are created and decisions are delayed.

Providing too much or too little stimulation. Some bosses just don't know the people who work for them. One employee can take a lot of stimulation and thrive; another would be exhausted keeping up. The same goes for too little stimulation. Good bosses know what makes their people tick.

Your Health and Your VDT

If you sit in front of a computer all day, basking in the warm green light of your video display terminal, staring at little luminescent figures on a glowing screen, you undoubtedly know all about tired eyes . . . not to mention back and shoulders. But the torso is a discussion on its own (see "Savvy Sitting," on page 148). Here we'll deal specifically with those two poor, overworked, mistreated peepers.

Fortunately, there's a lot you can do to start treating them right.

Here are some tips from optometrist R. Anthony Hutchinson, author of *Computer Eye-Stress, How to Avoid It; How to Alleviate It,* and from the Optometric Extension Program Foundation in Santa Ana, California.

WHAT YOU AND YOUR EYES CAN DO

● Have your eyes checked once a year by a vision specialist (every six months if you wear contact lenses). The prime candidates for VDT fatigue are people with untreated eye problems. Your doctor can prescribe special stress-relieving lenses designed specifically for VDT users, if your condition warrants it.

● Take a 15-minute break every 2 hours that you use a VDT. If you're an extremely heavy user, take a break once an hour.

● Don't forget to blink! It sounds elementary, but lots of video-users forget to blink for fear they will miss something rolling by on their screens. Dry eyes are susceptible to fatigue. In addition to blinking, eyedrops can help keep eyes moist. Use the "artificial tear" kind rather than the "gets the red out" kind.

● Learn exercises that strengthen your eye muscles to keep them from getting so fatigued. Your doctor should be able to prescribe some or recommend a specialist who will do so. Dr. Hutchinson's book includes a series of simple eye exercises.

FINDING A USER-FRIENDLY SCREEN

● Get the best resolution screen you can find. If you're shopping around, sit at various computers in the showroom for several minutes each and note any differences in readability. Ask the salesperson how many "scan lines" the monitor uses. Scan lines are the horizontal image-makers across the screen that determine clarity. The higher the number, the better. Don't accept fewer than 700.

● Choose a monochrome (single color) screen for most computer work. Some monitors will allow you to do graphs and displays in color and then switch to a single color for writing. Amber and green are the easiest colors for your eyes.

● Be sure the capital letters at least ⅛ inch high. The size of the screen isn't

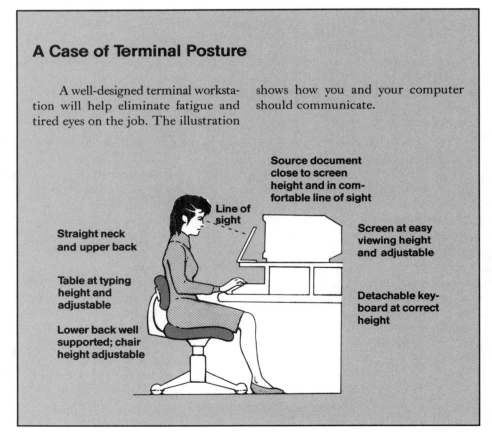

A Case of Terminal Posture

A well-designed terminal workstation will help eliminate fatigue and tired eyes on the job. The illustration shows how you and your computer should communicate.

Straight neck and upper back

Table at typing height and adjustable

Lower back well supported; chair height adjustable

Line of sight

Source document close to screen height and in comfortable line of sight

Screen at easy viewing height and adjustable

Detachable keyboard at correct height

so important; the size of the characters is.

FINE-TUNING YOUR SCREEN

● Make sure that you can easily adjust the brightness and contrast on your screen. The overall room illumination should be three to four times the screen background, and the characters on the screen should be five to ten times brighter than the screen background. (Ask the computer maintenance people to help you determine this.)

● Find out if your monitor is protected with an antiglare coating or screen. If it isn't, see if you can get an add-on filter (available at computer stores). Another way to reduce glare is to tilt or swivel your monitor. Try not to face toward windows or bright light sources.

● To detect glare, sit with the computer off; whatever you can see reflected in the screen is going to be in the way when you're using it. If you have trouble detecting where a bright light is coming from, move a book or paper around in front of the screen and observe when the glare is blocked out. Keep in mind that a light-colored shirt might make *you* a glare source.

● Clean your screen regularly — it attracts and accumulates dust.

● If you can, adjust the overall room illumination to the equivalent of the light given off by a 60-watt bulb in a small room. Then use a small adjustable lamp to light up whatever document or paperwork you may be using.

ADJUSTING YOUR WORKSTATION

The VDT screen should be slightly below your horizontal line of sight (see the box, "A Case of Terminal Posture"). The viewing distance between your eyes and the screen should be about 18 inches.

If you are working with printed material ("hard copy" in computer-speak) while using a VDT, the copy should be placed at the same height and distance as your screen. This will help your eyes by minimizing head movement and change of focus as you look from screen to paper.

Russell Wild

Radiation and Pregnancy: Computing the Facts

If even the word *radiation* makes you shudder, rest assured that the radiation produced by your VDT will *never* form a mushroom cloud around your computer, not even a little one. For one thing, says Michele Marcus, Ph.D., assistant professor of epidemiology at New York's Mount Sinai Medical Center, VDTs produce a different kind of radiation than do bombs, power plants, or even X-rays.

VDTs produce *electromagnetic* radiation, as opposed to the much more nefarious *ionizing* radiation. But does less nefarious mean absolutely harmless?

The general agreement among experts is that there's no danger for most of us. For pregnant women, however, "we're just not sure," says Dr. Marcus. Several reported "clusters" of miscarriages and birth defects among some women doing full-time computer work, she says, "could be attributable to a number of factors." It could be radiation. It could be the stress of the job. It could also be chance.

Several studies have indicated chance. But one recent Swedish study using pregnant mice indicated radiation. Pending the results of more studies — including one by researchers at Mount Sinai that will look at thousands of VDT-using women — Dr. Marcus suggests that pregnant women, most especially those in their first trimesters, limit the time they spend in front of a computer.

Preventing Burnout

Sniff, sniff. Do you smell something burning? Or should we say, *someone* burning?

Do you light cigarettes with your business cards? Have you started tossing the food across the table to your customers? Do you need a tow truck to get you out of bed in the morning?

Are you wishing you had six years of personal days accrued? Do you make faces at the phone after you hang it up? Have you sent a picture of your boss to a company that can make it into a dartboard?

If you've said yes to any of the above, you may be suffering from job burnout.

RUNNING ON EMPTY

"Burnout happens when you have utilized all your fuel," says Stefan A. Pasternack, M.D., clinical associate professor of psychiatry at Georgetown University School of Medicine. "You have depleted your resources of energy, and you've got nothing left."

Zippo! Coasting on fumes, it seems like you've gone to the well that moves you, and the well is dry. "Burnout is a destruction of motivation," says Beverly Potter, Ph.D., a psychologist who studies all aspects of work including burnout, and author of *Beating Job Burnout*. "It's a complete destruction of whatever it is that moves and drives a person to work and perform well."

WHERE THERE'S SMOKE, THERE'S SIGNALS

It seems the more driven you are, the more likely it is that you may run out of fuel. "People who are prone to job burnout often work in esteemed settings where high levels of dedication and achievement are expected," says Stephen P. Weinstein, Ph.D., clinical professor of psychiatry and human behavior at Jefferson Medical College. "They have a deep need to be considered effective and responsible, often investing too much of their egos in

"Go away! I'm peopled out."

RICHARD GUINDON

their work, to the point where all gratification comes from their jobs."

If you think you're smelling smoke from burnout, there are smoke signals you can look for. "Insomnia, fatigue, anger, frustration, unhappiness, lack of enthusiasm for your job, and avoiding work are all warnings signs," says Dr. Pasternack.

Other signals may take on a more physical form. Dr. Weinstein adds, "People who may have burnout can suffer from headaches, stomach upset or chronic back problems. If they have these symptoms, they should have them evaluated by a physician."

DOUSING THE FLAMES

You don't have to melt under burnout, experts agree, but only *you* can cool the flames. Here's what you can do to prevent burnout fires.

Don't play with fire. "Know your strengths or weaknesses psychologically so you can deal optimally with

Overcoming the Overtime Blues

Do you get your 40 hours in by, say, Wednesday? If so, "9 to 5" may signify your odds of burning out.

If you know ahead of time that you're going to be working a lot of long hours, Abby Ginzberg, associate director of the Institute for Labor and Mental Health in Oakland, has some tips that might help you prevent overtime burnout.

● Reduce the other pressures in your life. Make sure, for example, that your spouse understands why you're working late and that it will only be short-term.
● Make sure other duties are delegated to other people so that they don't pile up.
● Make sure you get enough sleep so you're not exhausted.
● Eat well-balanced meals to keep your energy up.
● When it's over, take a couple of days off and recover. Use that as a reward to get through the overtime period.

what gets under your skin," says Dr. Pasternack, "and, if possible, avoid it."

Keep your cool. "Pace yourself properly to avoid extreme fatigue," adds Dr. Pasternack. "Stay rested, well exercised, properly nourished, and have good motivation."

Avoid workaholism. Workaholics are more susceptible to burnout, according to Dr. Weinstein. "A lot of people put all of their eggs in one basket, with that basket being work. They don't develop any other interesting sides of their lives. When and if they become tired of what they're doing, they have no place to turn. There's no other source of pleasure in their lives. It's real important that people develop more than just one aspect of living."

If you can't take the heat, go on vacation. Dr. Weinstein's advice: "Vacations are important; getting away is important." He points out, though, that a vacation should not be a working vacation. Nor should you make your vacation seem like work. By this he means don't box yourself into a schedule of things you must do, like be at the beach from 1:00 P.M. to 3:00 P.M., go to dinner at 6:00 P.M. "Go on vacation to relax and get away from your job. Don't set strict goals for yourself while you're on vacation."

Ah, but what if after taking all this advice, you don't want to come back from your vacation? How do you answer the *big* question: Should you quit your job?

ADIOS OR NOT?

Before you rush off to have 50 copies of your resumé typeset, take some time to clear your head and do some rational thinking, says Dr. Weinstein. "Evaluate the situation; think of what you could do differently at work, where you could expand." He has some other tips you should consider before you decide to leave your job.

Help for the Help Professionals

Job burnout affects people in all professions, but according to Beverly Potter, Ph.D., people who work in the so-called helping professions are at higher risk of helping themselves to a case of job burnout.

Counselors, teachers, nurses, doctors, police, social workers—all those people who help other people—need to help themselves from burning out. Dr. Potter says people in the helping professions need to develop what she calls "personal power" to avoid job burnout, and for them she has 8 tips that will lead them on the path to developing personal power.

Practice self-management. Give yourself rewards for accomplishments. Keep in mind that you're doing something worthwhile.

Learn to manage stress. Know how to separate work from home; learn how to relax and regroup.

Build a support system. Develop some friends who know what you're experiencing, and talk to them. Use them for encouragement.

Build personal skills. Identify skills that will help you function better in your job and then go out and get them.

Modify the job. Don't work solely with one aspect of the job. For instance, work part of the time with patients and part of the time with paperwork.

Change jobs. Don't change careers, just change location. Don't leave the profession, because chances are you actually enjoy the work.

Learn mood management. Alter how you think about the job—don't think negatively. Don't expect to be a miracle worker; be more realistic. Look at all the positive effects you have had on people.

Detach concern. Says Dr. Potter, "Somebody once said to Mother Theresa, 'You work with sick and dying children all the time, how can you stand it?' She replied, 'We love them while they're here.'" That's detached concern. While you're helping people, you do everything you can, you're totally committed. But when they die or leave, you let them go.

● Find new ways to contribute at work. What can *you* do to make your job more interesting?
● Ask for feedback from your boss and co-workers. You may be underestimating how well others view your performance.
● Look into areas of possible future growth. Is there room for a possible promotion?
● Don't neglect interests outside of work. Find activities that give you satisfaction and enjoyment.
● Lessen exposure to stressful aspects of the job by changing the format of your day. For example, if your job requires extensive phone work, set aside 2 hours of each day for paperwork to give yourself a breather.
● Schedule personal time. This could be one day a week or an hour a day to do with as you please.
● Enjoy yourself.

Don Barone

Effective Business Meetings

Your coffee mug is dry. You look at your watch. Tick. Tick. You look at your notepad. Your afternoon's doodles could fill the Sistine chapel. You look up.

Jack from accounting is explaining —in detail—why marginal pre-tax revenues projected over the next three fiscal periods will blah blah the shareholders and blah blah blah . . . "And now," says Jack, pausing for effect while fidgeting with the slide projector, "if you'll all be so kind as to look at the screen, we'll just dim the lights a bit . . . "

That's your cue—and you're out. When the lights come back on, you shake your head, crawl out of the conference room, drag your way down the hall, plop into your chair and think, "I hate Jack."

Next week, it's your turn. "What can *I* do differently?" you ask. "What can I do to make *my* business meeting both as productive and as painless as possible? What can I do so that my colleagues don't wind up hating *me*?"

CALLING ALL COLLEAGUES

Former management-development specialist Joanne Ruetsch has been asked this question before. As a past member of the corporate training and development team at Blue Cross and Blue Shield of New Jersey in Newark, Ruetsch taught executives the structure behind a well-run meeting. Not surprisingly, the seminars were among the most popular seminars the department conducted.

Here are the points she says you should consider.

Is this meeting necessary? That's a crucial first question that's often overlooked, says Ruetsch.

What's my objective? Why do you want to see all these people face-to-face at the same time? Do you need to reach a decision about something? Do you want to share information? Do you want to have a discussion around a problem—and do you plan to resolve the problem at that meeting? Is this merely a fact-finding conference?

What are the alternatives? Once you've established an objective, it's important to ask yourself what alternatives there are to a full-blown meeting. Could you disseminate the information in a memo? Could you make a few quick phone calls?

THE THOUGHTFUL AGENDA

If, once you've asked yourself these questions, it looks like a meeting is unavoidable, then it's time to start planning an agenda. "This is the most critical part of planning a good meeting," says Ruetsch.

What goes into a good agenda? There are four key steps.

Get to the point. Make a list of the items you want to discuss. Be sure to keep it brief and specific—one line should be enough for each item.

Decide which person at the meeting will be responsible for each item. "Never ask someone to a meeting without having a reason why you want him there," says Ruetsch. It may be to handle an agenda item; it may be that you need him there for political reasons. Just make sure you have a reason.

Decide what process you'll follow in handling each item. Do you just want to give out information? Do you want to solve a problem with the item? Do you want to reach some sort

of decision about an item? If you just want to discuss something but don't want to reach a decision at this point, tell your meeting attendees that and explain why.

Set a time limit for each agenda item. "This is also essential," says Ruetsch. Be sure you're realistic though—don't give 5 minutes to a controversial item you know everyone's going to have an opinion on. With few exceptions, no meeting should be planned for over 2 hours in length. If your meeting must last longer than that, provide rest breaks every 60 to 90 minutes. "That's about as long as people can go before they'll start getting up themselves and going for coffee or whatever."

PERFECT TIMING

What's the best time to schedule a meeting? Ruetsch says it's probably from 9:30 to 11:00 in the morning. "That gives people time to get organized at their desks, answer phone messages and clear out their "in" boxes before they come to the meeting," she says. "They've had a chance to plan their days, chitchat with colleagues and drink their first cup of coffee. Then they're ready to sit down and concentrate with clear minds."

If a morning meeting isn't possible, Ruetsch says the second-best time is from 1:30 to 3:00 in the afternoon—as long as the meeting ends on time. "You should always leave people time at the end of the day to go back to their desks and clear things up before they go home," she says.

"Of course, all these are just guidelines," she says. "If your corporate culture is one in which people meet regularly at breakfast, lunch or in the late afternoon, then go with that."

You should also start the meeting when you said you'd start it—no matter who isn't there, advises Ruetsch. "If you keep waiting for people to show up, it makes the on-timers angry, and people get the idea that it doesn't matter if they're late for your meetings —you'll wait for them. If you close the door and get started on time, it shows you mean business. Then if people know they're going to be late, they'll call you in advance. You can either tell them that's okay or you can advise them to try and be there on time, since you need them for a particular agenda item."

Stick to the agenda you've prepared—especially in terms of time limits. You can lay down ground rules at the beginning, regarding interruptions, diversions and other agenda crunchers. Then go by your rules.

"You'll be surprised at how people will mimic you or follow your lead— most of us don't realize how much power we have in these situations," says Ruetsch.

Another problem are speech-makers. "One of the most effective ways" to handle a long-winded participant, says Ruetsch, is "to ask what he or she wants to do with the information offered." If this fails and the speech-maker is still going strong, Ruetsch advises that you acknowledge how strongly the person feels about the particular subject and then make plans to meet with him or her privately at some other time to discuss the matter.

TIE UP LOOSE ENDS

At the end of every meeting, it's a good idea to summarize each item

and the action that was taken. If you send meeting minutes, make them brief. Write down the item, the action taken and by whom. Send minutes out as soon as possible after the meeting.

After the meeting adjourns, sit down by yourself for 5 minutes and evaluate your performance, advises Ruetsch. Was anyone there who truly didn't need to be? Did you handle speech-makers effectively—and what will you do the next time the situation comes up? Were your time limits realistic? "Five minutes of your time right now saves you a lot of time in the long run," says Ruetsch.

"In fact, all the preparation for meetings may seem like a lot when you're very busy. But when you think about the hours and hours you waste in inefficiently running meetings, isn't it worth it?"

Jack may not think so, but you know better.

Lunch without the Punch

Remember the last time you hosted those clowns from Monkey Business? How Susan from marketing jumped up on the dais and started to sing the national anthem? How Jack from accounting passed out on the bathroom floor?

Company business lunches rarely end up as rowdy as the company Christmas party, but one too many at a bottled business lunch can leave you wishing you hadn't opened your big mouth— for more reasons than one. Believe it or not, there are ways to discourage

yourself from drinking on the job, even if you're the odd man out.

Here are some good suggestions.

Make an exercise date. If you're having a meeting that involves a lunch where liquor is usually served, schedule an exercise session for that afternoon, such as tennis or handball.

Loosen up without liquor. One of the reasons people like to drink at business functions is that it loosens them up. If you can find a substitute, you're home. If you have beautiful grounds around your company, try taking your

clients for a walk. If you work in a city, try an art gallery, museum, park or a zoo.

Drink without alcohol. Make your nonalcoholic drinks sophisticated and exciting. Order imported water or fresh fruit juices with mint leaves and fruit garnishes. Or order nonalcoholic beers and wines, which are becoming increasingly popular.

Meet early. Try holding your business meetings at times when liquor is not expected, like during breakfast.

Coping with Shift Work

Og would retire after a tough day of foraging berries and chasing woolly mammoths. In his cave, he'd sleep soundly, not daring to venture out lest he encounter a saber-toothed tiger shopping for its dinner. Limited night vision and man-eating cats, the theory goes, obliged Og to work by day and sleep by night, or, as some would say, to live as a *diurnal*, as opposed to a *nocturnal*, animal.

Over the centuries, Og's descendants tilled the land, constructed shelters and even domesticated cats—all by day. Oh, sure, a few shepherds and camp guards occasionally had to work after the sundial quit, but generally speaking, while Rome may not have been built *in* a day, it was certainly built *during* the day.

Then came Thomas Edison, working, of course, by day, to invent the light bulb—and the next thing you know, bosses discovered shift work. If you are one of the several million Americans who sometimes work the same hours that saber-toothed tigers once spent roaming the land, you undoubtedly know what came next.

MIDNIGHT BLUES

Surveys indicate that if you work at night, you are likely to have more problems sleeping and suffer more upset stomachs. Also, you may abuse drugs more frequently than your diurnal colleagues. Cops working nights tend to be more aggressive, doctors more careless and—as federal officials found when they sprang a surprise visit on Pennsylvania's Peach Bottom nuclear facility—power plant operators less alert (several were found asleep on the job).

Nuclear families also suffer. According to one survey, shift workers are almost twice as likely as nine-to-fivers to feel that their work interferes with their family life.

But you say you're independent, you don't run a nuclear plant, and anyway, you've always preferred the crickets' chirp to the roosters' cock-a-doodle-doo? Yes, some people are night owls, but such birds are rare.

"We're not meant to be up at night—it's as simple as that," according to Harvey Goldstein, Ph.D., a Washington-based behavioral science consultant for federal agencies such as the FBI and the Secret Service. The whole concept of shift work, he says, "bucks a pattern that developed over hundreds of thousands of years.

"We have people in law enforcement out on the street at night walking around like zombies," says Dr. Goldstein. "You wouldn't believe the amount of coffee some of these guys consume."

Drinking 20 cups of coffee is one way to make it through a night's work, but there are better, healthier ways. Here are a few.

Get regular, quality sleep. Always go to bed at the same hour. That sounds easy enough, but it's often much easier for nine-to-fivers than it

Keep Beat with Your Circadian Rhythm

A flower opens its petals by day and closes them by night. The flower has adapted itself to the earth's rotation. It has developed a *circadian*, or daily, rhythm.

So have you.

A number of your bodily rhythms operate on roughly 24-hour cycles. Your body temperature, for instance, starts to rise shortly before you do. If, one particular day, you awaken later or earlier than usual, your temperature, as well as your blood pressure and heartbeat, will be out of adjustment.

While your body gropes to figure out what's going on, you're likely not to feel so hot. It's a common problem for shift workers who must constantly rearrange their schedules.

Joseph LaDou, M.D., acting chief of the Division of Occupational and Environmental Medicine at the UCLA School of Medicine, thinks getting to sleep and waking up at the same hour every day could mean a major boost to our physical and mental well-being.

"I suspect that the next major popular health movement will be absolute regularity in lifestyles," says Dr. LaDou. "Variations between weekdays and weekends throw a lot of people off."

is for night workers. Especially on weekends, many who work at night are inclined to keep, or try to keep, the same hours as their day-working friends.

Take good care of yourself— and laugh. A good diet and exercise are important for a healthy mind and body—any doctor will tell you that. Unfortunately, these are often missing in the topsy-turvy lives of many shiftworkers, especially—ironically— those of many young doctors, who often work grueling hours and radically shifting schedules. It's common for many to labor from noon to midnight, get several hours' sleep, then return to work for another 12 hours.

Allan J. Schwartz, Ph.D., clinical psychologist and chief of the Mental Health Section of the University of Rochester's Health Service, counsels medical interns faced with such schedules.

To perform as well as possible, he advises them to watch their junk food intake, limit sugar and fat intake, and exercise. But they're doctors; they know that. He also advises them to appreciate the importance of a factor that may not be as evident—laughter.

Perhaps you saw the "60 Minutes" segment where a medical intern was chuckling about GOMERs (Get Out of My Emergency Room!)—a term interns frequently use for their patients. Dr. Schwartz is quick to defend this crude talk behind the emergency-room door.

Under the strain of shift work, he says, "humor can provide a virtually necessary psychological buffer." Doctors laugh about patients the same way night-driving truckers might snicker about highway cops and highway cops might snicker about truckers, says Dr. Schwartz.

He suggests you get together with your nocturnal colleagues to talk, make jokes and laugh at the problems you're sure to have in common.

Talk it over. It's important, as well, to talk to your spouse. Relation-

Who-o-o Are the Night Owls?

The U.S. Bureau of Labor Statistics says 11.6 million Americans, or 15.9 percent of all full-time salaried employees, work something other than regular daytime hours. Approximately 9 percent have steady night or evening jobs, 4.3 percent work rotating shifts, and the remaining 2.6 percent work other schedules such as split shifts (say from 8:00 A.M. to noon, then 3:00 P.M. to 7:00 P.M.).

According to the U.S. Bureau of Labor Statistics, the following job areas involve the highest percentages of shift workers.

- Protective service—60.8 percent.
- Restaurants and bars—47.6 percent.
- Food service—43.1 percent.
- Health services—36.1 percent.

All Full-Time Employees

Daytime workers 84.1%
Shift Workers 15.9%
Night or evening work 9.0%
Rotating shifts 4.3%
Other schedules 2.6%

- Entertainment and recreation—33.4 percent.

ships are the first victims of shift work, says Dr. Schwartz. It is important for your spouse who's left alone most nights to understand the nature of your work, so as not to misinterpret your absence for a lack of interest (or worse).

ARE YOU ADAPTABLE?

Experts agree that not all shifts are created equal, nor are all employees equally capable of handling shift work.

Several industries have found that people are better off working rotating shifts that move clockwise rather than counterclockwise. That is, your body can cope more easily when this week's day shift becomes next week's evening shift and the following week's graveyard shift, rather than moving backward from a night shift to a day shift.

These shift changes should happen slowly, giving the body a little time to cruise before having to shift gears again. Shift changes every other week are better than weekly ones. Daily changes can be pure agony.

Some workers are always going to be just plain miserable doing shift work. You may be one. Doctors say that elderly workers, epileptics, diabetics and people with digestive disorders and chronic sleep problems are most likely to fall into this group.

If you're not coping well with shift work, if you've tried the tips suggested here, if you've talked to your boss but he just won't listen, then, says Dr. Goldstein, you might consider one last resort: Quit. Go find a good day job . . . like Og.

Russell Wild

Ways to Wind Down after Work

Tick.

4:30 P.M.: The computer is down, and today's figures haven't been entered yet.

Tock.

4:40 P.M.: Six incoming phone lines, and they're all blinking.

Tick.

4:50 P.M.: The afternoon mail is late, but it still needs to be read.

Tock.

4:55 P.M.: Deadlines, the end of the quarter is tomorrow.

Tick.

5:00 P.M.: Finally, today's work-day is over . . .

. . . but you're still wound up. What you need to do now is wind down. But how? How?

THE WAYS OF UNWINDING

"Winding down is a two-stage process," says Robert Eliot, M.D., director of the Cardiovascular Institute at the Swedish Medical Center in Denver and internationally renowned stress expert. Dr. Eliot advises, "First get some natural glucose in your brain. After work, drink some fruit juice, eat an apple, some cherries—even a bran muffin is good. The glucose will help your brain metabolism and help you wind down naturally."

The next stage is a one-act play. "Once you get home, take 20 minutes, by yourself, and relax," he says. "Take some personal time, meditate, take a walk; in fact, a walk is the best thing for you. The father of cardiology, Paul Dudley White, M.D., said, 'Walk your dog, whether you've got one or not.' It's great exercise, and you don't need any special equipment to do it."

How the Famous Hang Loose

Everyone needs to wind down after work, even if your work does make you famous. Take Ronald Reagan, for instance. According to his personal physician, John E. Hutton, M.D., he winds down by "going to the exercise room every day and working out for ½ hour. When he's at his ranch in Santa Barbara, he winds down by chopping wood, clearing brush and horseback riding."

Everybody has their own way of winding down. Here's how some other famous folks do it.

● Baseball superstar Reggie Jackson, after hitting home runs, goes home and winds down by tinkering with his collection of 60 automobiles.

● Actor Mickey Rooney winds down from his latest movie or stage performance by going to the racetrack.

● Singer Martha Raye says watching soap operas hits a responsive chord when she wants to wind down.

● Journalist Hugh Downs pulls up his anchor role and winds down by soaring as a glider pilot.

● Author Mickey Spillane says winding down with a beer tastes great. (Or is it less filling?)

● Author Alistair Cooke winds down by never doing any work later than 6:00 P.M.

● Real estate developer Donald Trump winds down by winding up another deal or by developing his backswing on the golf course.

Change your pace. You can walk at any pace, as long as when you want to wind down, you do a change of pace. Janet Lapp, Ph.D., a clinical psychologist in Fresno, California, says, "Do something completely different from what you normally do. The more of a contrast it is, the more it seems to help you. If you do book-work all day, you don't go home and do book-work. You exercise, walk, jog, lift weights."

Be "like-wise." *Like* is the key word here. When considering what to do to wind down, it's wise to do what you like.

"Look at your past," advises John Neulinger, Ph.D., director of the Leisure Institute, Dolgeville, New York, and professor emeritus at City College of the City University of New York. "Look at what you do over a stretch of time and judge all your activities in terms of how you feel when you do them. You may find out that you enjoy certain activities over others, and you just never realized it before. Those are what you should do to relax. Don't do something because it may be the 'in' thing to do."

Do what turns you on. Within reason, of course. One way to relax might be to turn on some music. It seems any tune will do. According to a recent biofeedback study completed by Dr. Lapp, "We found that when people listened to music that they like —whatever kind of music that may be—they relaxed more. We also found that when they listened to music that they _didn't_ like, it caused a terrible reaction to their nervous systems. Blood pressures went up, pulses went up."

That might explain why it may be hard to relax at home when you like to hear Bach and the kids like rock 'n' roll. Dr. Lapp also says that if you _do_ like rock 'n' roll, you can listen to that and relax, too.

SOME PROVEN RELAXERS

The key to unwinding, say the experts, is to find your own _individual_ way to relax. We asked harried workers how they slow down after work and found that the solution can be quite simple.

Exercise. Listen to music. Some people like to go home and play with their children, or their dog or cat. That works, too.

So does doing nothing. Some people relax by watching sports or game shows on TV.

Others relax by cooking or chopping vegetables. Some do it by growing vegetables; gardening is a popular way of winding down.

There are lots of ways to wind down, some normal and some, well, judge for yourself. One person responded, "I go home, grab a box of cookies—has to be Lemon Coolers—and then I lie down on the floor and take an hour's nap. Works great."

To each his own. However you do it, all the experts recommend that you do it. Wind down, or, they say, you'll wind up sorry.

Don Barone

Getting the Get-Up-and-Go

Yawnnn . . . ah, please pardon. For some of us, winding down isn't the problem. Winding up, on the other hand, is.

At 11:00 in the morning and after 4 cups of coffee, are you still in the ozone? It's kind of tough to get going in the fast lane when you're stuck in neutral. Here are some tips for those who need a jump-start in the morning.

Exercise. Barry Sultanoff, M.D., a physician who specializes in education and self-care in Bethesda, Maryland, says you need to get oxygen flowing through your system. Oxygen is energy, so take a brisk walk, do yoga or go jogging.

Eat a balanced breakfast. Brian Morgan, Ph.D., an assistant professor at the Institute of Human Nutrition at the College of Physicians and Surgeons of Columbia University, recommends, "The best breakfast to eat to get going in the morning is one consisting of whole wheat cereal with either skim or 1 or 2 percent milk. That will give you a very balanced meal of protein and carbohydrates, plus a good amount of the essential vitamins and minerals."

He also says to limit your intake of coffee and sugar in the morning, because those will only give you a quick burst of energy, and after that you may actually feel even more tired.

Choose to be awake. Dr. Sultanoff says it's possible to re-educate your subconscious so that you can actually _want_ to get up.

Dr. Sultanoff teaches a seminar developed by Robert Fritz called Technologies for Creating. In the seminar, he tells people to notice the current reality—for example, you're history till noon—and then choose how you really want to feel. He says to say to yourself, "I choose to be awake, relaxed, alert and full of vitality in the morning." Write it down and read it before you go to bed. Then visualize that result. He says that over time the technique will change the way you feel in the morning by giving you the new belief that you can get going.

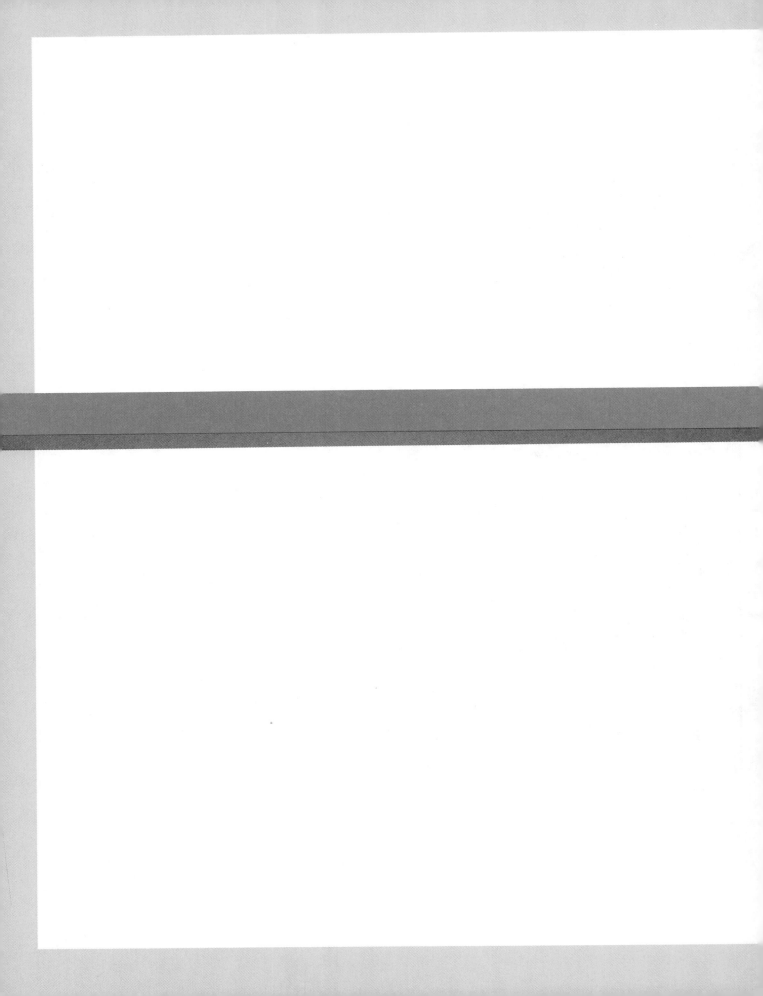

SEASONAL WELLNESS

Dealing with Heat Waves

It was so hot, cold cream bubbled. It was so hot, lawns got steam-cleaned. Steering wheels gave burns and Popsicles never had a chance. There was no place to hide, because there was never enough shade.

We're talking serious heat wave here. Deadly serious. The National Weather Service estimates that about 175 people die every year due to the effects of summer heat.

Older people, those over 60, are much more likely to feel the effects of a severe heat wave, especially if they have any preexisting medical condition. "Anyone who is frail from other disease problems, such as diabetes, heart and circulatory diseases or lung or kidney disease, should be particularly careful about overexposure during a heat wave," warns T. Franklin Williams, M.D., director of the National Institute on Aging.

Robert E. Windom, M.D., assistant secretary for health in the U.S. Department of Health and Human Services, also advises caution during heat waves for people taking diuretics, sedatives and tranquilizers, anticholinergic drugs and some heart and blood pressure medications that alter the person's ability to sweat. They should discuss possible effects of the heat with their physicians.

You *need* to sweat; that's how your body cools itself off. When it comes to sweating, though, humidity is the worst medicine.

THE HUMIDITY FACTOR

Humidity is a problem because it retards the skin from allowing moisture to evaporate into the atmosphere, says Austin Henschel, Ph.D., a physiologist at the National Institute for Occupational Safety and Health who has studied the effects of heat on individuals.

Evaporation is a cooling process, but when it is very humid outside, the moisture—sweat—can't evaporate as rapidly—it has no place to go. There just isn't any room because the air is already totally saturated with moisture. What happens then is the sweat just pools on the skin, retarding any further sweating. Because you can't get rid of the heat you feel hotter and hotter.

And hotter. And still hotter, putting you at risk for heat exhaustion.

Heed the Signs of Heatstroke

Heatstroke is a serious, life-threatening medical emergency that requires immediate medical treatment. "When heatstroke happens, the person becomes basically like a cold-blooded animal instead of a warm-blooded animal," says Carey Wallace, M.D. "Your body temperature is controlled by the environment you're in, rather than your own regulatory mechanisms."

Dr. Wallace adds that heatstroke has vastly different warning signs from those of heat exhaustion. "With heatstroke, the person will *not* be sweating. Their skin will be hot and dry. Often they will have a temperature of 106°F or higher." The pulse may be rapid and strong. The victim may be unconscious.

Heatstroke can also affect a person's behavior. "Anytime you see someone acting strangely or inappropriately belligerent when it's hot, you need to check them right away to see if they are sweating or not. If they are not, get them medical attention immediately," says Dr. Wallace.

While you're waiting for that medical attention, there are some first-aid techniques that the American Red Cross suggests that you do.

● Make sure the person is breathing and you can feel a pulse. If not, perform cardiopulmonary resuscitation (CPR), which you can learn at the local chapter of the Red Cross or the American Heart Association.
● Take the victim out of the source of heat.
● Rapidly cool the person. Undress him and repeatedly sponge his bare skin with cool water or rubbing alcohol, apply cold packs continuously, or place him in a tub of cold water until his temperature is sufficiently lowered.
● Use fans or air conditioners, if available, because drafts will promote cooling.
● If the victim's temperature starts to go up again, start the cooling process once more.
● Do not give the victim anything by mouth.

THE SIGNS OF HEAT EXHAUSTION

In Alabama, heat waves are as familiar as the Crimson Tide. Carey Wallace, M.D., an emergency room physician at AMI Brookwood Medical Center in Birmingham, has seen his share of heat-related illness. Dr. Wallace says that dehydration is the main cause of heat exhaustion. "The person is sweating profusely and losing a lot of body fluids and electrolytes."

Symptoms of heat exhaustion are

fairly easy to spot in comparison to those of heatstroke, according to Dr. Wallace. "Usually a victim will get tired and light-headed. Often his skin will be pale and clammy. Sometimes he will have nausea and vomiting and a headache, but he won't develop a fever; his temperature will stay approximately normal. Finally, as the victim gets extremely dehydrated, he will get very weak and will develop a fast heart rate."

If heat exhaustion is not treated promptly, the patient may progress to the life-threatening illness heatstroke. The American Red Cross has some basic first-aid tips for taking care of someone who is suffering from heat exhaustion.

● Move the victim to a cooler place.
● Apply cold, wet compresses to the extremities and behind the neck. Fan the victim lightly.
● Give small amounts of water as tolerated, if the victim is alert. Watch for nausea and/or vomiting. If this occurs, discontinue water immediately. If tolerated, increase the amounts given. Saltwater solutions consumed by the victim may cause vomiting.
● Have the victim lie down and rest. Raise his feet 8 to 12 inches.
● Get in touch with your emergency medical service as soon as possible. It's important that the person receive proper medical assistance.

Don Barone

It's Only as Hot as You Feel

The thermostat says it's 90°F but to you it feels more like 106°F . . . and it probably really is.

The National Weather Service has developed a Heat Index. That's a measure of how hot it really feels when relative humidity is added to the actual air temperature.

To find how hot it *really* is when the heat is on, check the Heat Index Chart below. The air temperature is on the left side of the table and the relative humidity is at the top. The point at which the temperature and relative humidity columns intersect indicates how hot it really feels. For example, if the temperature is 85°F and the relative humidity is 80 percent, it will feel like 97°F.

The chart at the right tells how that truer temperature may affect your health.

Heat Index	Possible Heat Disorders
130° or higher	Heatstroke highly likely with continued exposure.
105° — 130°	Heat cramps, starting in the legs or stomach, or heat exhaustion likely, and heatstroke possible with prolonged exposure and/or physical activity.
90° — 105°	Heatstroke, heat cramps and heat exhaustion possible with prolonged exposure and/or physical activity.
80° — 90°	Fatigue possible with prolonged exposure and/or physical activity.

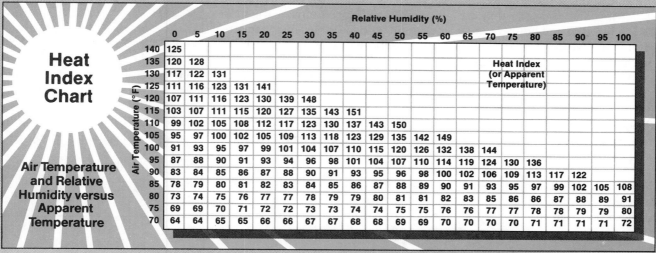

Heat Index Chart

Air Temperature and Relative Humidity versus Apparent Temperature

Heat Index (or Apparent Temperature)

Air Temperature (°F)	Relative Humidity (%)																				
	0	5	10	15	20	25	30	35	40	45	50	55	60	65	70	75	80	85	90	95	100
140	125																				
135	120	128																			
130	117	122	131																		
125	111	116	123	131	141																
120	107	111	116	123	130	139	148														
115	103	107	111	115	120	127	135	143	151												
110	99	102	105	108	112	117	123	130	137	143	150										
105	95	97	100	102	105	109	113	118	123	129	135	142	149								
100	91	93	95	97	99	101	104	107	110	115	120	126	132	138	144						
95	87	88	90	91	93	94	96	98	101	104	107	110	114	119	124	130	136				
90	83	84	85	86	87	88	90	91	93	95	96	98	100	102	106	109	113	117	122		
85	78	79	80	81	82	83	84	85	86	87	88	89	90	91	93	95	97	99	102	105	108
80	73	74	75	76	77	77	78	79	79	80	81	81	82	83	85	86	86	87	88	89	91
75	69	69	70	71	72	72	73	73	74	74	75	75	76	76	77	77	78	78	79	79	80
70	64	64	65	65	66	66	67	67	68	68	69	69	70	70	70	70	71	71	71	71	72

SOURCE: NOAA's National Weather Service

How to Stay Safe in the Sun

When was the last time you sunbathed? You think it probably was last Labor Day weekend at the beach? Or that warm Indian summer day at the lake? Well, think again.

Have you taken into account the morning you shoveled an overnight snowfall out of your driveway? Or the hour you spent shopping at the outdoor flea market? Or the late fall afternoon you sat at the tot lot watching your children at play? You didn't think of those times, did you? Most people don't. And those may be just the occasions when you don't realize you're spending too much time in the sun—and that you're exposing your vulnerable skin to an extra dose of ultraviolet light that could lead to skin cancer.

"I have a patient, a schoolteacher, who told me she didn't spend much time in the sun," says Henry E. Wiley III, M.D., assistant professor of medicine at the University of South Florida and a dermatologist in private practice. "I could tell that wasn't the case by the tan on her forearms. It turned out she spends 45 minutes every school day supervising the children at recess. She thought that because she wasn't playing tennis at midday, she wasn't getting any sun. We may be exposed to hundreds of hours of incidental sun that we don't count."

In the United States, dermatologists and other skin cancer experts have their work cut out for them. Despite the fact that skin cancer is epidemic—with roughly half a million new cases a year—most Americans still consider tanned skin a sign of health.

Yet acquiring a tan could signal the start of a serious problem. "Tanning is nothing more than the skin trying to protect itself from the sun's damaging rays," explains Arthur R. Rhodes, M.D., assistant professor of dermatology at Harvard Medical School and director of dermatology at the Children's Hospital in Boston. "We all know that a sunburned skin is a damaged skin, but a suntan is also a sign of damaged skin."

Put another way, tanning is just another word for melanin, the dark skin pigment. People who have olive or dark-skinned complexions have more melanin and are believed to be less vulnerable to skin damage than their fairer counterparts.

THE CONSEQUENCES OF TOO MUCH SUN

No matter what your skin tone or how dark you get, you won't necessarily be shielded from the harmful effects of the sun's most sinister ultraviolet rays, known as UVB's. These short-wavelength UVB rays are most prevalent between 10:00 A.M. and 2:00 P.M. (11:00 A.M. and 3:00 P.M. daylight saving time) and are responsible for causing most basal cell and squamous cell carcinomas—the most common and curable skin cancers. Supposedly, say doctors, these UVB rays scramble your skin cells' DNA, their vital genetic material, causing cancer to develop.

The deadliest (and increasingly prevalent) form of skin cancer is malignant melanoma and, until recently, scientists weren't sure that the sun's radiation had much to do with the disease. Now there is some convincing circumstantial evidence that sun exposure—particularly the shorter, more intense exposures of the recreational sunbather rather than the long-term occupational exposures of, for instance, farmers and fishermen—may be linked to the disease.

Take the Sizzle out of Sunburn

The warning signs were clearly posted, but you chose to ignore them. "I *never* burn," you said to your traveling companion as you set out for the warm, tropical sun and warm January breeze on the tiny island of Bonaire. "Besides, it's winter, it doesn't feel that hot, and I still have a layer of tan left over from the summer."

But by early evening, you were lying in bed in agony, looking a lot like the cooked lobster you were planning to savor at your evening meal.

What can you do when a scheme to squeeze in too much sun goes sour? To treat sunburn, Robert S. Stern, M.D., suggests the following.

● To soothe the pain, take a tepid or cool oatmeal bath using a commercial product such as Aveeno Bath. Follow the directions. Do not use oatmeal from your cupboard; the flakes are too large.
● To counteract the dryness, slather on moisturizer.
● To alleviate discomfort, take aspirin or ibuprofen or an alternative analgesic.

"If that doesn't do it, it's time to see your doctor," says Dr. Stern.

Melanoma patients tend to be much younger, by 10 or 20 years, than patients with the more common basal cell carcinoma, which tends to develop after age 35 from the effects of a lifetime of sun exposure. According to studies conducted by Arthur Sober, M.D., of the Harvard Medical School, and Robert Lew, Ph.D., of the University of Massachusetts Medical Center, people who have had blistering sunburns as adolescents were twice as likely to develop melanoma—with poor tanners at highest risk.

Unlike a tan, the harmful effects of ultraviolet waves don't fade away at the end of the summer. They accumulate. "That's why," says Dr. Rhodes, "heavy sun exposure in the first two decades of life is potentially the most dangerous. Even though there might be a delay of 10, 15 or 20 years, the effects may eventually show up as cancer."

SUN-WORSHIPPERS LOOK OLDER SOONER

Cancer isn't the only damage done when you cook too long in the sun. It's now a well-established fact that those who worship the sun get older-looking skin to show for it.

"The sun causes premature wrinkling of the skin and atrophy and changes in blood vessels," Dr. Rhodes says. This happens because the infrared and ultraviolet rays from the sun penetrate to the deeper layers of the skin and ruin the skin's elasticity. After many exposures it begins to sag.

There is also evidence that sun damage may be more than skin deep. "There's data showing that sun exposure—even excessive weekend sunbathing—may have a suppressive effect on the immune system," says Dr. Rhodes. No one knows for sure yet what effect this can have on health. But, says Dr. Rhodes, he "wouldn't be surprised" if it makes some pre-

disposed people more vulnerable to certain diseases.

Let Your Skin Type Be Your Guide

Here are some general guidelines for choosing a sunscreen appropriate for you.

Type of Skin	Appropriate Sunscreen
Fair skin that never tans and always burns	Sunscreen should have an SPF of at least 15
Fair skin that develops a faint tan and burns occasionally	Sunscreen should have an SPF of 6 to 10
Dark skin that tans well and burns only occasionally	Sunscreen should have an SPF of 4 to 6
Dark skin that tans well and never burns	Sunscreen should have an SPF of 2 to 4

A New Way to Revitalize Sun-Damaged Skin

You say you're a lifelong sun-worshipper and all you have to show for it is a tanned hide? Take heart. There's a skin cream that may help you correct your past sun sins. It's called Retin A, and it's been shown to actually alter the cell structure of skin, making leathery, sun-damaged skin look smoother, younger and softer.

The active ingredient in the new cream is tretinoin, a derivative of vitamin A that's been successfully used to treat severe acne. In controlled studies, the cream has proven to be capable of at least partly reversing the structural damage of excessive sun exposure, and

it may be useful in slowing down the photoaging process.

Test subjects who applied the cream every night for 6 to 12 months reported that the mottled, leathery look of their skin began to disappear. "Patients frequently said that their skin had a new glow," the researchers observed, perhaps because the cream boosts blood flow to the skin's surface.

"This is not the fountain of youth," comments Alejandro Cordero, Jr., M.D., of the Medical School of Buenos Aires, "but it can improve photoaged skin without adverse reactions."

SUN SMARTS

All is not lost if you were a sun-worshipper in your younger days, assure doctors, as long as you start protecting yourself from the sun as an adult from now on. Here's what you can do.

Always wear a suitable sunscreen. According to studies conducted by Robert S. Stern, M.D., of Beth Israel Hospital, Boston, and Harvard Medical School, your risk of developing a nonmelanoma skin cancer may be reduced by 88 to 91 percent if you avoid the sun or use a sunscreen now.

Sunscreens are creams and lotions that contain chemicals that absorb and filter the sun's harmful radiation. The higher the product's sun protection factor (SPF), the better the protection. (See the table, "Let Your Skin Type Be Your Guide," on page 169 for guidelines for choosing a sunscreen.)

It works this way: If your unprotected skin normally takes 20 minutes

Bronzing without Burning

"There's no tanning without some injury to the skin," says Frederick Urbach, M.D., professor of dermatology at the Temple University School of Medicine. "A purist would simply say, 'Don't tan,' but I'm a realist and to say 'Don't tan' in this day and age is just not a practical prescription. It's much more sensible to teach people how to tan while causing the least amount of injury to their skin."

Here's how.

Start in early spring. "A problem arises when people who have 1 week's vacation in July try to get their tan in that week," says Dr. Urbach. "They don't realize that it takes 5 days for the skin to even begin showing the kind of tan that indicates a protective thickening of the skin. Instead, the color that these folks turn indicates they've cooked themselves until they're burned. Next they just peel."

So use a sunscreen daily and build your tan slowly, with repeated exposures. Never try to get a tan all at once—your body simply can't acceler-

ate its production of melanin in time to protect your skin.

Go at a snail's pace. Begin by spending 15 minutes sunbathing on the first day and add 5 minutes each day thereafter. Avoid sunbathing at midday.

Consider your skin tone. Whether you burn or bronze depends on the amount of melanin, or tanning pigment, in your skin. Melanin protects your skin from the sun's ultraviolet rays, which can cause skin cancer. The more melanin, the less your risk of the disease. If your eyes are dark brown or hazel, you probably have a good supply of melanin. If your eyes are blue or green, your body probably contains less melanin.

Your natural skin tone is another clue—olive-tone skins have more melanin, fair skins less. And since exposure to sunlight increases melanin production, you can stay in the sun for progressively longer periods of time as your tan darkens. And if you use a tanning preparation—a sunscreen—you can lengthen that time.

Apply sunscreen before stepping outside. Smear it on about 45 minutes to an hour before you head out into the sun so that the active ingredients have time to soak into your skin. "It's amazing how many people sit at the pool and forget about vulnerable areas like the tops of ears, feet or hands —and then say that their sunscreens don't work!" says Dr. Urbach.

"Or they'll walk 15 minutes on the beach, spread out their towels, check the water, get out their radios or books and, only then, put on a sunscreen. By that time they've been out in the sun for half an hour. For unprotected skin, that's plenty of time to get sunburn," he says.

Choose temperate vacation spots. Avoid vacationing during spring and early summer—May through July —when the sun is strongest in North America. Remember, too, that the ultraviolet rays from the sun grow gradually more intense the nearer you are to the equator, because that's where the sun strikes the earth most directly.

to become red in the full sun, a sunscreen with an SPF of 10 will allow you to stay out in the sun ten times longer—3 hours and 20 minutes— before you become red. The most potent sunscreens contain derivatives of para-aminobenzoic acid (PABA), which shield you from the harmful UVB rays.

Keep in mind that the SPF is only an approximate number. Heat, humidity, perspiration, reflective surfaces and wind are among the factors that can reduce safe exposure time.

And sunscreens do permit some ultraviolet rays to get through to the skin. So it's not a good idea to stretch sun time to the limit without reapplying the lotion.

Don't be skimpy. For best protection, be sure to cover those forgotten areas like the tips of your ears, your lips and the tops of your feet. Remember to apply sunscreens every time you go out into the sun—not just when you intend to bask on the beach. In temperate zones, this means from May through October, says Dr.

Rhodes. In the Sun Belt, it means year-round.

Don't expect water to protect you. It won't. In fact, almost 90 percent of the ultraviolet rays penetrate the top 3 feet of water. So wear a sunscreen when you sweat or swim and reapply afterward (even if your sunscreen is supposed to be waterproof).

A block may be better. If your nose, cheeks, lips or shoulders are particularly burn-sensitive, you might try dabbing on zinc oxide, an opaque, pasty-looking substance that totally

The Secret to Tanning without the Sun

You can have a year-round golden glow without baking in the sun. Now there's a whole new generation of sunless tanning lotions on the market, and they're light-years away from the old ones that left you streaky and orange.

With these products, color is achieved when the ingredients in the lotion interact with amino acids present in the skin to safely create a natural-looking tan.

The drawback with this type of artificial tanning product is that it can rub off on collars and cuffs. Also, you have to reapply the lotion every few days.

Still, you can have a fine-looking "funtan" if you use these products as follows:

● Apply lotion thinly and evenly; for a darker look, repeat the application the next day rather than applying one thick layer.
● Allow lotion to dry thoroughly before going to bed or putting clothing over it, so it doesn't get rubbed off.
● Remember, if you use the lotion on your face, also apply it to your throat if you'll be wearing an open-necked blouse or shirt.
● Use only a very small amount around knees, ankles and elbows; you need less in those areas.
● Always use a sunscreen over the sunless tanning lotions when you're outdoors. Neither the lotion nor the resultant skin darkening is meant to provide protection from the sun's rays.

blocks out the sun. It's most often seen on the noses of sunbathers.

Le Zink is an eye-popping variation of traditional zinc-oxide cream plus the sunscreening ingredient homosalate. It comes in a variety of neon colors, giving a fashion flare to a health-protecting benefit!

Beware of glare. You may think you're being shielded as you sit beneath your beach umbrella or big-brimmed hat, but sunlight is very tricky. If there's sand or light-colored concrete around, chances are you're being zapped by reflected light. Remember, too, that white-painted surfaces and aluminum reflect more UV light than sand: 70 to 90 percent compared to about 25 percent. Always wear your sunscreen (even beneath your chin) with this in mind.

Don't count on clouds. You shouldn't feel safe from sunburn just because clouds have rolled in. As much as 80 percent of the sun's burning rays can find their way through a cloud cover that may appear downright gloomy. Nor is wet clothing or water much of a match for the sun's penetration power: People have been known to suffer sunburn through wet T-shirts and while swimming laps.

Skip perfume, evaluate drugs. Some perfumes can exaggerate the sun's burning powers immensely. Certain prescription drugs like the antibiotic tetracycline also can amplify the sun's harmful effects, so check with your doctor to see if the drugs you're taking can cause a so-called photosensitive reaction.

Be a moving target. A body in motion takes in only about a third as much sunlight as a body flat on its back —a good reason to mix a little fitness into your desire to appear fashionable.

Wear clothing cover-ups. As a rule of thumb, cotton clothing tends to be more protective than synthetic fabrics, dark shades more effective than light. A white cotton shirt, for example, gives an SPF of 7 and a pair of jeans has an SPF of 1,700. How do you choose the best hat? "Hold it up to the light," suggests Dr. Wiley. "The more you can see through it, the less protection you're going to have."

Don't get zapped in the snow. Take some sunscreen to the ski slopes.

The snow's reflective properties are compounded at high altitudes: The sun's ultraviolet radiation intensifies approximately 4 percent for every 1,000 feet above sea level. Snow and ice will reflect up to 99 percent of sunlight, and that makes your skin twice as likely to burn than if the ground were bare.

Drive defensively. For years doctors have remarked that skin cancer and solar keratoses (skin growths that often portend the development of cancer) seem to occur more frequently on the left side of people in the United States and the right side of people in Australia and Great Britain (where the steering wheel's on the right). They think it's due to the greater amount of sunlight people are exposed to when they drive with the window open.

So don't drive without your seat belt—or sunscreen.

The Bites and Stings of Summer

Getting bugged—and bitten—by insects is a warm-weather hazard. Nearly any outdoor activity between April and October exposes you to an army of flying, buzzing or crawling creatures. A camping trip yields a dozen mosquito bites. A peaceful afternoon of gardening ends when you get in the way of a honey bee.

How can you cope with the bites and stings of summer?

PLAN YOUR COUNTERATTACK

Instead of swatting and scratching, take some steps to *avoid* bites and stings. C. Stanley Williamson, a health services specialist with the American Red Cross, urges common sense.

Williamson says people aren't cautious enough and don't teach their children to be careful. "There's a difference between grabbing candle flies or lightning bugs and trying to catch yellow jackets," he says. "But I've seen kids try to do that. Or children will take a wasps' nest and shake it, or hold it up to their ears to hear the buzzing. At least that's what one little girl's parents told me she did, and she had the two stings on her ear to prove it."

Here are ways to prevent an insect attack.

● Use mosquito netting over an infant's crib or carriage.
● Place a heavy blanket or mat on the ground before you sit down.
● Don't go barefoot or wear sandals in the grass.
● Choose long sleeves and long pants for outings.
● Pick light-colored clothing, not black or loud prints.
● Avoid shiny jewelry.

How to Handle a Snake Attack

Just *seeing* a snake is enough to rattle most people. But what should you do if you're actually bitten by one?

Keep your cool and act quickly, warns Jana Knutson, a certified poison information specialist at the Arizona Poison and Drug Information Center in Tucson. No matter what kind of snake bites you—poisonous or nonpoisonous—you should seek medical help immediately, she says. A bite is a puncture wound and can lead to infection.

What you shouldn't do is what you see in the old cowboy movies—incising the wound and sucking out the blood.

What should you do? On your way to the emergency room, you can apply a light constricting band above the wound—but it should be loose enough to slip a finger under. To keep the venom localized, keep the bite at heart level, if possible, and stay as calm and still as possible. Do not apply ice.

Also, get a good look at your attacker. Being able to identify the snake will help the medical experts in treating the bite. If possible, bring the snake with you—but only if you can do so without risking harm to yourself. "Even if you cut the snake in half, it can still bite you," says Knutson.

The very least you should do is get a look at its head. Heads that are triangular shaped indicate a poisonous variety; the heads of nonpoisonous snakes follow the lines of the body, much like a worm. One exception is the coral snake, but it has a different identifying characteristic: colorful rings encircling the body.

● Do not use perfume, hair spray or scented soap if you're going to be outdoors.
● Keep car windows closed when you are parked. Check for insects before driving. If assaulted while driving, stop before trying to get rid of an insect.
● Use insect repellent on clothes, not skin.
● Avoid insect-infested areas, such as swampy areas, orchards, marshes, outdoor privies, garbage dumps.
● Do not swat at bees or make quick, jerky movements. Bees do not sting when unprovoked, Williamson says, adding, "All they want to do is land, collect pollen and take off."
● Hire a professional to remove hives and nests near your home.

THE BIG STING

What do you do to ease the discomfort if you do end up with an ugly, itchy welt? It all depends on the severity of the reaction, says Williamson.

Reactions to bites and stings fall into three categories: local reactions, toxic reactions and life-threatening reactions, also called anaphylactic reactions. Most people experience local reaction, with irritations such as itching, swelling and burning. Here are ways to ease the minor discomforts.

Remove the stinger. Don't use tweezers to remove a bee's stinger: that only squeezes more venom into the wound. Use a knife blade, spatula or fingernail to flick it out.

Pack on the ice. Apply a commercial cold pack, ice bag or ice cubes in a plastic bag that has been wrapped in a towel or washcloth. This reduces pain and swelling and prevents the venom from getting into the bloodstream as rapidly.

And here are some home remedies to help ease discomfort.

Use some lotion. Ease the itch from bites by applying over-the-counter preparations such as calamine lotion.

Head for the kitchen. Get out the meat tenderizer and make a paste by adding a little water to the powder. Apply it to the sting. The purpose isn't to make you tender as a T-bone. The tenderizer, notes Williamson, contains enzymes that reduce swelling, lift out the venom and reduce inflammation.

TICK TALK

Ticks are small, flat, mostly brown, eight-legged creatures that attach themselves to humans by burrowing into the skin. They usually hang out in tall grass, in trees, on sand dunes and on the edge of the woods. When in any of these areas, you should check your skin and scalp for them frequently.

There's nothing particularly painful about a tick bite, although they often do imbed their heads in your skin and swell with your blood. The danger, although remote, is tick-borne diseases like Lyme disease and Rocky Mountain spotted fever. Not all ticks carry these diseases, but they are all parasites, which is reason enough to get rid of them right away.

The signs of Lyme disease are a blotchy skin rash, flulike symptoms and pain in the joints. Those infected may later experience chronic arthritis or nervous system disorders such as facial paralysis. Signs of Rocky Mountain spotted fever include headache, backache, fever and red spots, which begin on the extremities.

To remove ticks quickly and safely, try these techniques.

● Cover the tick with a heavy oil like mineral or salad oil. This clogs the tick's breathing pores, causing it to retreat. If it doesn't come off to the touch, leave the oil on for 20 to 30 minutes and remove the tick carefully with tweezers.
● Make sure the *entire* tick is removed. If the head is left in, it could lead to an infection. Do not crush or pop it. Wash the wound with soap and water.

Vicki Jarmulowski

Bee Careful: An Allergy Can Be Deadly

Any reaction to a bee sting is an allergic reaction of sorts. But those with severe sensitivity to stings have a life-threatening problem—and one they may not know about until stung. Multiple stings may yield similar symptoms in the nonallergic.

Symptoms of an allergic reaction to a bee sting can include some or all of the following: severe itching; weakness; hives or hivelike rash; coughing and wheezing; swelling and redness around the site or around the lips, eyes and tongue; sweating; abdominal cramps; nausea and vomiting; difficulty breathing and possible collapse.

If any of these symptoms develop, or if a person has a history of such reactions, get medical help immediately, says American Red Cross official C. Stanley Williamson. Don't wait to see if they get worse. Here are some things you can do to ease discomfort, but they are *not* meant to replace a doctor's care.

● If the bite is on a limb, apply a lightly constricting band—not a tourniquet—between the bite and the heart. The band should not cut off the blood flow and should be loose enough to allow you to slip an index finger underneath.
● Have the person lie as still as possible. Keep the bite lower than the heart.
● Apply ice, wrapped in a towel or in a plastic bag, to slow the flow of venom into the circulatory system.
● Kits are available for self-injecting an antidote to bee and insect toxins. Allergic persons should consult a doctor about getting and using one.

Hay Fever Relief

There's an old saying that if you get a cold in summer, it will last until autumn's first frost. What the saying refers to isn't really a cold, it's hay fever. And what the term hay fever refers to isn't really caused by hay, and it isn't really a fever, either.

"I would define hay fever as seasonal allergic rhinitis," says John A. Anderson, M.D., head of the Division of Allergy and Clinical Immunology at Henry Ford Hospital in Detroit. *Rhinitis* means inflammation of the mucous lining of the nose. And *seasonal* refers to the fact that hay fever comes at certain times of the year, depending on what part of the country you're in, when pollen and mold spores are floating through the air.

Obviously, not everyone is allergic to pollen and mold spores—most people never get hay fever. Some experts think that the tendency toward hay fever is often inherited. But inherited or not, hay fever seems to build up over a period of time. After a sensitive person is exposed to the pollens and molds over and over, the body starts to produce antibodies that end up making you sneeze, tear and tire. In other words, you feel plain lousy.

Pollen is so small that about a quarter of a million grains of it stacked one on top of the other would tower only about 1 inch high.

In early spring, the pollen that causes hay fever usually comes from trees like elm, maple, birch, poplar, beech, ash, oak, walnut, sycamore, cypress, hickory and alder. In the later spring and early summer, you get hit by pollen from grasses such as timothy, orchard, red top, sweet vernal, Bermuda and some types of bluegrasses. Weeds that cause pollen include sagebrush, pigweed, careless, plantain, spring amaranth, tumbleweed, Russian thistle, burning bush, lamb's-quarters, sorrel, cockleweed and marsh elder.

One plant that is often blamed for hay fever is goldenrod, but goldenrod doesn't release much pollen into the air. It's only a problem if you get really close and decide to see whether or not it has a pretty smell.

No, the plant that's most likely to cause your hay fever—at least while you're in the United States—is ragweed. Not only does it put a lot of pollen into the air during the late summer and fall, it also seems to have a personality problem: a lot of people are sensitive to it.

There's No Escape

If ragweed is such a problem, why don't we just burn it off the face of the earth?

That might be a nice fantasy for hay fever sufferers, but it's far from possible. It grows all over the United States, and it doesn't do any good to plow it under. Ragweed seeds can survive way down in the earth for years, only to germinate and grow after being dragged to the surface when a foundation is dug or a road built.

You might want to clear the ragweed out of your backyard, however, to get some relief. Studies show that if the ragweed around your house is cleared, your periods of peak exposure to airborne ragweed pollen will be less severe. Just remember, ragweed pollen has been shown to float on air currents for up to 250 miles. It's hard to escape.

AVOIDING POLLEN

It's hard to avoid pollen in the United States; depending on the wind and the type of pollen you're allergic to, it's pretty much everywhere, says Dr. Anderson. You can check with your doctor to see if he can suggest a part of the country you could visit when your hay fever is at its worst. But for the majority who can't escape, Dr. Anderson offers these tips for avoiding pollen.

● Stay in an air-conditioned room that's pretty well sealed from outside air. There will be less pollen in the room than outside, and you'll have fewer problems.
● Get a central electronic or solid-phase air-filter system for your house. They'll clean the pollen out of the air. Room units aren't as good as central units, because most houses have so many openings where air can circulate that the smaller units can't handle all the pollen.
● Use your air conditioning and keep your windows up when you're driving your car, especially in the country. It's possible to pass a field of ragweed and have the wind carry so much pollen through the window that the pollen will be more concentrated inside the car than in the air outside.
● You should shower, wash your hair and wash your clothes as soon as you go inside if you are exposed to a lot of pollen by doing something like walking through a field of ragweed.
● Take a trip to Europe. While there have been a few reported cases of hay fever in Europe recently, the continent is still considered to be largely free of the ragweed pollens that cause the condition.

The Asthma and Allergy Foundation of America offers this information that might help you avoid pollen.

● There is more pollen in rural and suburban areas than in cities.
● There is less pollen near large bodies of water.
● The pollen count is at its lowest at night.

UGH, MOLD!

With all the talk about ragweed during pollen season, it's easy to forget that mold can also cause hay fever—and not just during the warm months, either. Molds that cause hay fever grow easily on grains, like wheat, barley, corn and oats; on dead leaves, grass and other plants; and in the corners of basements.

Hay fever from molds is a problem all over the United States, but it is more of a problem in dry regions of southwest California and the Northwest, and at higher altitudes. The mold will grow indoors or out, and the season is long—from April to November in some areas.

There are more mold spores after a rain, and the peak mold season is usually fall, when the ground is wet and covered with leaves and other debris, especially in the Northeast. You can also get a lot of mold in the winter or spring after a thaw.

Dr. Anderson offers these tips for avoiding mold spores.

● Keep your house dry. Moisture is especially a problem in basements. It's a good idea to use a dehumidifier if your home is damp.
● Stay away from mold sources like leaves. Don't rake or mow the lawn without protection. (For more on lawn care and allergies, see "Lawn and Garden Care" on page 132.)
● Be aware that there might be a lot of mold in your summer cottage when you first open it after a long winter. Try to dry the cottage by airing it out.
● Avoid piles of hay. While the hay itself doesn't cause a problem, the mold that grows on it might.
● Learn to love winter. You're relatively safe from outdoor mold spores in the winter when the ground is frozen and covered with snow.

STOPPING THE SYMPTOMS

Even all these precautions probably won't keep you completely free from hay fever. When it does strike, you'll want a way to ease the symptoms. You might want to turn to your local drugstore for help.

"Over-the-counter antihistamines are safe, as long as you follow the directions on the package," says Gregory W. Siskind, M.D., head of the Division of Allergy and Immunology at New York Hospital/Cornell University Medical Center, New York City.

"They're good even if you use them season after season," adds Dr. Anderson. But be aware that some antihistamines cause drowsiness, and some work better than others. And don't give antihistamines to any child under the age of six without a doctor's approval, even if they are over-the-counter brands. Ask a pharmicist about trying different ones until you find one that works best for you.

While antihistamine pills are okay, Dr. Siskind says you shouldn't rely on nasal sprays to relieve your hay fever symptoms. "They should be avoided because they cause a rebound effect. At first they work a little, but when the medicine wears off, your problem will be worse and you'll have to use more and more nasal sprays or nosedrops. They're much more of a problem than they're worth. Your doctor may ask you to use them in certain cases, but don't prescribe them for yourself."

MEDICAL CONTROLS

If over-the-counter antihistamines don't work, you should see a doctor to get some more effective relief, suggests Dr. Siskind. "You'd be needlessly disrupting your life if you kept searching for other types of relief without a doctor's help. Hay fever is relatively easy to treat these days with different drugs."

"The first line of defense these days are localized inhalers," says Nicholas Chiorazzi, M.D., professor at Cornell University Medical College and chief of the Division of Clinical Immunology and Rheumatology at North Shore University Hospital in Manhasset, New York. These medicines are inhaled through the nose. Some of them are steroids that reduce your body's release of chemicals such as histamines, which are released when you come in contact with the allergens. Other types of inhalers actually keep the body from releasing the histamines in the first place. "Generally, these are used together, and the success rate is good," says Dr. Chiorazzi.

But not everyone will respond to the inhalers. So doctors still use a more old-fashioned type of treatment, immunotherapy. "With this you give injections of the substance that the person is allergic to," says Dr. Chiorazzi. "You start out with small doses and build up over a period of time. No one is exactly sure why these injections work, but they can be effective for certain people." There are no major side effects to the injections, other than the fact that they are expensive and a person must sometimes keep getting them for years.

And the net effect is good. "Between avoiding the allergens and either using the inhalers and/or getting injections, hay fever symptoms can be a thing of the past for most people these days," says Dr. Chiorazzi.

Stephen Williams

Survival
in the Cold Zone

You trudge your way from the front door to your car. It seems so far. You think of Mexico and beaches. Of Tahiti and palm trees. Of Morocco and desert sand. Nothing helps. You're still cold.

Standing where you are, knee-deep in snow, you watch your breath escape and sail away, listen to the whirling of your neighbor's wheels on ice, and wonder: Is this what life is like on Pluto?

Nancy Sachs, M.D., an emergency medicine physician in Chicago, has never been to Pluto, but she's been to one of the coldest spots on earth. Dr. Sachs served as resident medic for the U.S. South Pole research base on Antarctica—during winter. She is an authority on cold.

Extreme cold can be unpleasant; it can also be dangerous. But, says Dr. Sachs, if you know how to prepare for it, next winter's cold wave can be a breeze—even if that breeze gusts to 60 knots and the temperature falls to −100°F, as she and her colleagues experienced at the South Pole.

Below, Dr. Sachs helps you glide through those icy days.

BEWARE
THE WINTRY THREESOME

As warm-blooded animals, we humans must maintain a regular body temperature of about 98°F. The greatest danger of cold weather is a condition known as hypothermia, where the body expends more calories than it has available and its temperature drops.

The surest and quickest way to fall victim to hypothermia is to expose the body not only to cold but to wind and moisture as well. The wintry three-

some can cause rapid evaporation of heat from the body.

No single fabric can keep you dry, supply warmth and block the wind, so dressing in layers of different materials is the only real guaranteed protection against the wintry threesome. Each layer of winter clothing should have a function.

Undies should whisk away moisture. The bottom layer is to keep you dry. Some fabrics, such as cotton, absorb your sweat and hold it. Others, much better choices for winter innerwear, allow your perspiration to pass through, keeping your skin dry. These

include silk and some modern synthetics, such as polypropylene.

Put insulation in the middle. The materials that probably come to mind when you think of dressing for winter *are* the best choices: wool or down. Both elements breathe (allowing the moisture from below to evaporate) and do a good job of trapping your body's heat.

The outer layer is a shield from the wind. Here your best choice will probably be a synthetic, such as polyester; leather's okay, too. If the winds are carrying snow or freezing rain, make sure your outer shell is waterproof.

Taking the Bite Out of Frostbite

Frostbite, just like a heat burn, is a thermal injury to the skin, although serious cases can go deeper. Fortunately, frostbite can be avoided. Nancy Sachs, M.D., tells you how.

Not all body parts, or even all bodies, are created equal. The body parts most vulnerable to frostbite are your fingers, toes, ears, nose and cheeks.

Keep an eye on these body parts, especially for pain, numbness or a change in skin color—to either red or white. In severe cold it makes sense to use a "buddy system" for keeping an eye on each other's face for any color change.

If you sense trouble in your fingers or toes, wriggle, but *don't rub them.* If the skin is frozen, this can damage the blood vessels. Don't breathe on them either, as the moisture you exhale will only add to the problem. The best

measure is to bury your fingers in your armpit—or someone else's.

Keep your ears covered. To the extent possible, keep your nose covered, too. Carry a handkerchief and wipe your face often. The cold can make your eyes and nose run, wetting your skin. Beware of metal eyeglass frames —they can get mighty nippy, burning the skin underneath.

If you suspect frostbite, head indoors. If you've experienced pain and the pain disappears, *rush* indoors. Take aspirin to improve circulation. Soak your hands or feet in warm water— but test the water first, as your frostbitten appendage may be numb. If blistering occurs or if the natural color of the frostbitten area doesn't return within 2 hours, see a doctor.

Cover that head! The old saying that if your feet are cold, cover your head, makes sense. A hat is a top priority on a frosty day. It matters not if you've got an impressive mane—human hair is not the same insulator to you as fur is to an animal.

Protect those extremities. The parts of your body most vulnerable to the cold are those that jut out from your main frame—the feet and hands, especially the toes and fingers. The same layering principles outlined above make double sense where these body parts are concerned. The best mittens (mittens are toastier than gloves) come with three layers. Two pairs of socks, one inner for dryness, such as silk or polypropylene, and one outer for warmth, such as wool, are better than one.

Hang loose. With all your clothing choices, from socks to hat, let the fit be loose. For one thing air is one of the best insulators—the more of it between layers, the better. Second, tight clothing can restrict circulation when you need it most. Steer clear of snug jeans and stiff shoes.

WINTERIZE YOUR BODY

Dressing for the outdoors is only part of your winter self-care program. Here's what else you should do.

Have a cup of soup. Liquid intake is just as important on Christmas Day as it is on Independence Day. Remember that your body still perspires in the winter—and because the air is drier, you can dehydrate. Hot liquids, such as soup and tea, serve the dual purpose of hydrating the body and providing warmth.

Don't overheat your house. Your body has a built-in thermostat that allows you to deal better with harsh winter weather. You can help keep your body's thermostat tuned by keeping your house thermostat set low, say below 72°F. (In Antarctica, says Dr. Sachs, the indoor thermostats are typically set below 68°F.)

Practice temperance in low temperatures. A lot of toasts aren't toasty: alcohol dilates blood vessels so that you lose body heat more quickly. And the only thing warming about a cigarette is the match: Smoking constricts blood flow and increases your chance of getting frostbite.

Keep the blood flowing. Exercise is a fast way to create heat, so doing a few jumping jacks can warm you up. But exercise expends energy. You don't want to overdo it. If you're out shoveling snow, don't let your laboring hide the fact that it's cold. Dress properly and have a good breakfast before going out.

Russell Wild

Secrets of a "Polar Bear"

He says he hasn't had a cold, a flu or a virus in . . . well, he can't remember the last time. He says he feels as vigorous, as energetic, as healthy as ever. What is 73-year-old Alex Mottola's secret?

He's a polar bear.

Actually, he's president of Coney Island's Polar Bear Club. Polar bears young and old (the youngest member is 12) can be seen every Sunday afternoon splashing in the surf off Coney Island—come rain or shine, come snow or hail.

Mottola much prefers the beach in January to August. For one thing, "there's more room." But he and his 40 fellow polar bears *like* the water cold. The colder the better.

On a typical 30-degree January day you can find Mottola and friends at the beach for 3 to 4 hours, frolicking about in swimsuits, jumping in and out of the surf (a total of about 5 minutes for the day), drying off without the help of towels. It is this activity to which Mottola, a retired businessman, attributes his good health. "I'm no doctor, but I think this kind of exercise helps build up a tolerance to cold germs," he says.

Mottola says his fellow bears are as healthy as he is, including one 86-year-old woman who, on snowy winter days, arrives at the beach on skis. In her bathing suit. "She skis right up to the water, takes them off, jumps in for a swim, and then skis off when she's through," says Mottola.

Dealing with Winter Woes

The winter sun was barely above the horizon when Robert Sleight left his Virginia home for an early-morning appointment. A light rain had fallen during the night, and temperatures had dipped to just below freezing. Sleight hurried across the parking lot toward his car, eager to be on his way. But the next thing he knew, he was flat on his back, seeing stars, wondering what had toppled him. A moment later he realized—he'd been waylaid by a nearly invisible sheet of ice.

"The trick is to be alert, and I obviously wasn't," says Sleight, who is—ironically—director of the Walking Association and chairman of the National Safety Council's Committee on Fall Prevention. "I was preoccupied, walking too fast for conditions and not paying attention to the ground."

WAYS TO STAY UPRIGHT

But how could he have avoided falling even if he was paying attention? Here are a few suggestions for staying upright.

Try the short-step shuffle. The same techniques beginning skaters use to stay upright will work for people who unexpectedly find themselves in a slippery spot, says Justine Townsend Smith, executive director of the Ice Skating Institute of America.

"Take short steps, always keeping your knees bent slightly, and hold your arms in front of you at waist level," she says. Your body weight should be over the balls of your feet and your arms should be providing balance.

Bite the ice. Eskimos wear mukluks, sealskin bootees worn over several pairs of socks. Oil-rig workmen wear thick-treaded rubber boots. Penguins sport rough-textured orange flippers. Obviously, practicality is the key to good winter footwear. But smooth-soled shoes can be as slick as ice skates, and high heels have the additional disadvantage of throwing you off balance.

"We recommend a substantial overshoe with tread," says Nina Morose, program manager of public safety for the National Safety Council. Sole composition isn't as important as its surface texture. "For maximum traction, you want a thick tread that looks like a snow tire," she says.

Such shoes work well on packed snow and help on rough ice. But on smooth ice, no tread is going to work very well.

Break the ice. Shoveling won't remove ice, of course, so you'll need to chop it up, cover it with cinders or sand, or use a de-icer. One study done by a chemical company found that the same de-icer many road crews use, calcium chloride pellets, melted ice twice as fast as rock salt, and was even more effective at temperatures below 20°F.

Expect the unexpected. A heavy freezing rain, where the entire landscape turns into a beautifully jeweled booby trap, might seem like the most likely scenario for a fall. But people expect it to be slippery, so they're very careful and avoid going outside if possible, says Walter Zeltmann of the International Weather Corporation in Brooklyn. A forensic weather specialist, Zeltmann will reconstruct for court proceedings the conditions that existed during a car, plane or body crash.

A more likely slip-and-fall setup is freeze-and-thaw weather, when snow on the ground melts during the day and freezes at night, leaving thin, clear sheets of ice on pavements. People hurrying to work in the morning, before the sun has had a chance to warm things up, hit these patches with all the panache of a tipsy giraffe. Add a light powder of snow to hide the ice, and you've got the ultimate hazard.

That's why you should scan the surface ahead for glare, white frosted areas and "anything that doesn't look quite right," Zeltmann says. If you know where water normally puddles

No Skidding!

Which way do you turn the wheel in a skid?

It all depends on what kind of car you have. If your car has rear-wheel drive, says Willard A. Alroth, a traffic engineering consultant in Skokie, Illinois, keep your feet off the brake and accelerator and turn the wheel in the direction of the skid. In a car with front-wheel drive, keep your foot off the brake, accelerate slightly and try to steer out of the skid.

The small amount of traction your car can generate is divided among braking traction, steering traction and acceleration traction, he explains. And in a skid your car needs all its traction in one place: the steering.

up around your home and in your neighborhood, expect to find ice there in the wintertime.

And don't forget that winter falls can follow you indoors, too. Snow that drops off people's shoes in busy entranceways can create super-slippery floors. Take your time negotiating these areas.

Avoid metal surfaces. Metal surfaces can surprise you because they freeze faster than concrete or bare ground. "Sometimes you see steel plates laid over holes at construction sites," Zeltmann says. "They usually have a little tilt to them. You hit one and it's like an unexpected ride on a sliding board. Down you go."

Trade in your slippers. No one plans to fall, least of all on their own front porch, but it's best to be prepared, Sleight says. At least exchange your slippers for a decent pair of shoes and put a winter coat on over your bathrobe. "Don't be casual about going outside, even for just a few seconds," he says. And use the handrail you should have on your porch and steps.

Aim for the buns. If you feel gravity pulling, go with the fall. Bend your knees, tuck your arms in to your sides and kind of collapse to one side —landing on the softest part of your seat, says Smith. As instinctive as it may be, try not to put out your arms. A stiff arm used to break a fall is often a fractured one afterward. If you must use an arm—if you'd otherwise fall flat on your face, for instance—bend it slightly to use as a shock absorber, Sleight says.

Open your mouth. It was still sleeting when Carolyn Kyra of Catasauqua, Pennsylvania, stopped for groceries. "I crossed the street with no problems, but as soon as I stepped on the curb, I fell," she says. Both bones in her lower leg were badly broken. "I have five kids at home and was laid up for three months, so this was a real crisis for us," she says. She lost her suit against the store because the law in her town only requires that people clear their walks within three days after a storm. "I think that's ridiculous," she says. "I think any time a store is open, the owners should be liable for having a safe passageway in front."

"I'm amazed at how quickly they get out and clear the streets," Sleight says, "and at how long it takes for walkways to be cleaned." So complain if you have to—to the store owner, homeowner or town council. Then maybe *you* won't be Mother Nature's "fall guy."

Gale Maleskey

Winterize Your Car's Emergency Kit

One snowy day it's going to happen. Your car will run out of gas, slide into a snowbank, refuse to start. And you'll be stuck—probably in the middle of nowhere.

What do you do? Avoid the temptation to walk for help unless you're sure shelter and a telephone are a short distance away, recommends the National Safety Council. Stay with your car, put the hood up and turn on your flashers. Then make use of your winter emergency kit, which should include the following items.

● Two flares or reflective triangles to be put 5 and 120 paces behind your car.

● A bag of cat-box filler to throw under your wheels for traction.
● A windshield scraper and brush.
● A flashlight.
● Two wool blankets for warmth.
● Two large plastic trash bags. If you start to get cold, poke a hole in the bottom seam for your head and slip the bag over your body.
● A coffee can, candle and matches. You can melt snow for water and put the candle in the can to warm your hands and feet.
● Some nonperishable food. And don't forget an opener for canned food.

Beating the Moody Blues

All right, when is this going to end? You celebrated the autumn leaves, Halloween, Thanksgiving, Christmas and New Year's—or at least muddled through them. You knew winter had arrived, yet there were things to do in the early going that staved off your winter blues. Now it's late January, February, early March; you've had quite enough, thank you, but winter doesn't care. Low, gray clouds scud across a leaden sky; a sharp, frigid breeze slaps your face. "Too bad," winter sneers. "I'm here, and my specialty is making you miserable." And irritable, sleepy, bored, restless, resentful and impatient, not to mention hard to get along with.

There are ways to put winter in its place—out of your mind and heart. We asked psychologists who have heard it all what they recommend and followed that up with an informal survey of people who get winter blues and have developed methods of coping.

WHAT TO DO, WHAT TO DO?

The main thing, says Ethan Gorenstein, Ph.D., assistant professor of clinical psychology at Columbia University, is to "do something that gives you as an individual a sense of accomplishment, something that seems manageable, no matter how small, and will distract you." It's better to start small and simple, Dr. Gorenstein says, because just contemplating a big project when you're already feeling down often dooms you before you start.

So here's a list of simple "somethings" to do.

Exercise. A Norwegian study linked depression relief to the increased absorption of oxygen that exercise produces. Several studies have noted that depressed people felt better and scored lower on depression tests after exercising. Morris B. Mellion, M.D., of the University of Nebraska Medical Center College of Medicine, says that since depression can be viewed as a person's response to loss of control (in this case, over the weather), "exercise becomes a form of mastery or a way of regaining control of one's body."

The benefits don't stop there. Dr. Mellion says, "The positive effects of being successful in an exercise program spill over into other realms of life."

Play. One anthropologist wrote that play is "a stepping out of 'real' life." In the midst of winter, what more could you want?

Create. Draw, paint, write poetry—but not with the goal of winning a Pulitzer prize. Improve your career skills. "I do much more design work on a freelance basis to keep my mind off winter," says one artist.

Shop. A common response in our survey. Buy things that will make you feel better, or something you've long needed. But don't get manic about it; stay within your budget or you'll feel worse.

Get a hobby. "I tackle major home projects, like furniture refinishing and painting," says one respondent. Take a night class. Join a choir.

Colorize. Wear bright colors, put them on your walls (whether you paint the walls or hang pictures on them). Surround yourself with green plants, vivid flowers.

Break your routine. Take a day trip into the city or out to the country. Take in a show, a museum, a nice restaurant dinner. Take a train instead of driving. One woman says she goes to a beach in the off-season: "It's usually desolate, but the walk along the coastline is refreshing and lots of memories of summer poke through."

Consider the future. One respondent plans her garden layout. "I plan for the months ahead," says another, "deciding dates for vacations, picnics, parties. The time passes quickly when there are nice things to dream about."

Take a trip to a warm place. For a while, it can make you forget and sink into luxurious relaxation. (The only problem is that you have to come back and face the music.)

Eat right. Winter seems to bring out the carbo-loader in us. Eat healthier by not overdosing on sweets, which can send your blood sugar haywire and your weight soaring—both guarantees of more depression.

Think positive. Remember, the days start to get longer on the first day of winter. One survey respondent adds, "I try to immerse myself in the season's natural beauty."

WHAT NOT TO DO

Along with the positives, there are some negatives—things that can make winter harder to endure and that you should avoid if you're prone to the winter blues.

Avoid alcohol and drugs. "They provoke only momentary relief that keeps you from tackling your problems," says Dr. Gorenstein.

Avoid sad things. Sad music, sad books, sad movies "keep you in the depressed cycle," says Dr. Gorenstein.

Avoid self-pity. "It's better to tell yourself, 'Pull yourself together. Be realistic. There are a lot of things out there you can do to feel better'," says Dr. Gorenstein. Don't wallow in your misery.

Light Shines on SADness

"I don't want to get fired this winter," Betty told doctors when she came to the National Institute of Mental Health (NIMH). She had reason to be worried. The 37-year-old accountant was on probation for making mistakes, which she said were caused by her tendency to get sleepy on winter afternoons and become unable to concentrate.

Since adolescence, Betty had suffered from winter depression. This meant daytime lethargy, craving for sweets and a consequent addition of 10 to 20 pounds of fat, sadness, irritability, social isolation and decreased sex drive. She was taking many sick days, and she had suicidal thoughts. Her depressions always began in late fall and lasted until spring.

During spring and summer Betty became a dynamo. "That's when I've received all my promotions," she said. It's also when she lost her winter fat layer.

The doctors sat Betty down in front of a panel of bright, full-spectrum lights (mimicking the sun's natural rays). Within 3 days, Betty's depression had lifted, and her concentration, sleep, energy and appetite returned to normal.

Because of therapy like this, people like Betty can now switch on their light boxes (professionally manufactured to exacting NIMH specifications), sit down to read the paper, sip their juice and bathe for ½ in the glow of their own private sun. As long as they use their light box at the time, intensity and distance prescribed by their doctors, they don't get the winter blues.

Betty was a victim of seasonal affective disorder—SAD. SAD is the latest field of psychological inquiry; therapy is drug-free, talk-free. The treatment is heavy doses of bright light, more than office light but less than that on a sunny beach. First described in 1981 by Norman E. Rosenthal, M.D., of the NIMH, SAD tends to be "a milder form of depression than that seen in a full-blown clinical depression," says Paul Gaist, program coordinator of the Seasonality Studies Program at NIMH, "but it can still be quite devastating."

SAD and light therapy (phototherapy) are so new that there are differing theories as to why the therapy works. NIMH researchers believe the body is yearning for the full-spectrum rays of the sun, not obtainable from ordinary fluorescent bulbs. A team at Oregon Health Sciences University thinks that in some people who are more sensitive to changes in their body clocks—their circadian rhythms—SAD is caused by fewer hours of daylight in the winter; these researchers say the crucial issue is *when* you sit in front of a light box, not the type of bulb. Other debated questions include how much light you need, how far to sit from it, and the long-term effect on your eyes.

As if winter SAD doesn't pose enough questions, summer has its own version of SAD, called reverse SAD. Gaist explains that during hot summer days, many people practically live behind tinted glass—in air-conditioned offices, cars and restaurants—again depriving themselves of natural light.

Further, SAD—winter and summer—seems to be part of a continuum of depression: 90 percent of the SAD patients in the NIMH studies were diagnosed as having a manic-depressive profile, and phototherapy has been shown to be effective in 80 percent of the cases.

But winter woes and summer slump aren't reserved just for diagnosed depressives. Both Gaist and David White, Ph.D., of Oregon Health Sciences University, agree that most, if not all, people could have some of the SAD symptoms without the full-blown syndrome. In fact, nondepressed SAD researchers themselves are using phototherapy, says Dr. White, and they report feeling more energetic.

If you suffer from the winter or summer blues, Dr. White recommends that you see your doctor first for a checkup to rule out illness. Phototherapy should be done under a doctor's guidance: If it is improperly done, says Dr. White, you don't benefit, and may sink further into a funk. Researchers advise against trying to make your own light box—the construction must be precise. Manufacturers are now marketing light boxes for about $300 and up.

A cheaper method may be just to get up and take an early morning walk—if you live in a place that gets adequate morning sunlight.

A NIMH information packet on SAD is available if you write to the NIMH Office of Public Inquiries, Room 15/c05, 5600 Fishers Lane, Rockville, MD 20857.

William LeGro

Bloom in the Spring

Nobody looks forward to spring more than those who live in Greenland. Nobody. You think your winters are bad? Try shoveling your sidewalk when it's, say, −40°F or −50°F, with winds up to 200 knots.

That is, if you can see your sidewalk. In Greenland during the winter, it's nighttime 24 hours a day. It's dark when you get up for work, dark when you come home from work. It's as dark at noon as it is at midnight. Electric light bulbs live short lives here.

But spring *does* come. In fact, you can see it coming. "In spring, the light starts creeping over the hill," says Master Sergeant R. Devan Calvert. "It stays light here for about 10 minutes a day. Every day it stays lighter by 20 minutes or so, until finally it's light 24 hours a day in the summertime."

That's when Calvert can see where he is, which is the U.S. Air Force base in Thule (pronounced *Too-lee*), Greenland: population 1,200, located 700 miles *north* of the Arctic Circle.

Chaplain (Major) David Mills also lives in Thule, which he says in the springtime looks a bit like upstate New York with glaciers. "In springtime when the sun comes out, it's nice and warm, 30°F or 40°F, and the wildflowers and grasses start to grow on the tundra. In fact, it's very beautiful to walk down to Baffin Bay and watch the icebergs float by."

All of Thule celebrates the coming of light, and spring. Calvert says people from all over get on their

Flower Power—in February

It's the first day of spring. The temperature's 20°F, the wind's howling and there's a 90 percent chance that Mother Nature's going to dump another helping on the patchy cakes of snow that have been around for all too long.

But even though it may *feel* like winter, it can still *look* like spring—if you've planted spring bulbs around your house. In fact, the first sightings of spring usually begin when the snowdrops (so appropriately named) pop through the hard earth each February.

If you want to watch spring spring to life, all you need to do is plant your spring bulbs in the fall. Here's a bloom list that will get your spring off to a flowering start.

February/March: Snowdrop, anemone, crocus, narcissus, species tulips, spring snowflake, trumpet daffodil.

April/May: Grape hyacinth, hyacinth, crown imperial, hybrid tulip, other daffodils, ornamental onion.

Daffodils

Snowdrops

Anemones

Thoughts That Turn to Spring

Do you get tongue-tied trying to put your feelings into words? Then relish the expressive springtime verse of great poets and writers.

Hard is the herte [heart] *that loveth nought
In May.*
Geoffrey Chaucer

In the spring a young man's fancy lightly turns to thoughts of love.
Alfred, Lord Tennyson

*A little Madness in the Spring
Is wholesome even for the King.*
Emily Dickinson

*The trumpet of a prophecy! O Wind,
If winter comes, can spring be far behind?*
Percy Bysshe Shelley

A change in the weather is enough to renew the world and ourselves.
Marcel Proust

Autumn arrives in the early morning, but spring at the close of a winter day.
Elizabeth Bowen

*The world's favorite season is the spring
All things seem possible in May.*
Edwin Way Teale

dogsleds and come to Thule to play. "They play Mukluk hockey. It's kind of like playing soccer on ice. The Danish people, and the Americans from the Air Force base here, pull on their parkas and then get together for some fun." For them, as for so many people anywhere, spring is a time for rejuvenation. For new beginnings. For blossoming.

LIGHTEN UP

As the gloomy days of winter give way to the sunny days of spring, people everywhere seem to brighten up.

Karl Doghramji, M.D., assistant professor of psychiatry and human behavior at Jefferson Medical College, has studied the effects of light on people. He says people feel more hopeful with the coming of spring, and he feels one reason could be related to the length of the "photoperiod," or the light cycle during the day. He believes people have an actual physical reaction to the weather lightening up.

"We have evidence to show," says Dr. Doghramji, "that when people are exposed to greater amounts of darkness, such as found in the winter months, they start getting depressed. Exposure to simulated daylight reverses their depression. There is definitely a positive change in mood when spring comes. Spring is a tonic in a very real sense."

TONICS, TEAS AND ELIXIRS

Don't just spring-clean your house this year, spring-clean your body. How? With whatever makes you feel good. Find your own spring tonic or try some folk traditions.

The Europeans, for example, specialize in body spring-cleaning rituals once a year in April or May. They select certain foods or herbs and use them to help get winter out of their systems. For a whole week they "take" a specific food "remedy." They consider it spring medication.

In France, artichoke elixirs are taken in the belief that they will help clean out the liver.

In England, people make a traditional pick-me-up drink that is imbibed throughout the first week of spring. It consists of equal amounts of celery juice, beet juice, carrot juice and sarsaparilla.

Closer to home, American garden writer Jeff Cox recommends a rejuvenating spring herb tea. "We make the tea from burdock root, a few violet leaves, stinging nettles (boiling them removes some of the irritating principle in their leaves), mustard leaves or flower shoots, dandelion leaves, and wild onions," he writes in *The Gardener's Almanac.*

CELEBRATING SALAD DAYS

"We will serve no dandelion before its time." So say the Pennsylvania Dutch. Every spring you can see them out in their backyards weeding out a salad. Maundy Thursday, the Thursday before Easter, is a day set aside for the tradition of gathering wild greens for a pre-Easter meal.

Dandelions, those plants that keep lawn-care folks in business, are harvested and used in a springtime salad. And they're darn good for you, too. One cup of raw dandelion greens provides 1½ times an adult's Recommended Dietary Allowance (RDA) for vitamin A. The greens also contain a third of the RDA for vitamin C.

Don Barone

Falling for Autumn

As steaming, sweltering, sultry summer sizzles toward its sticky end, it occurs to you that there most certainly *is* a cure for the summertime blues, at least one: It's called autumn.

> Ahhh, autumn
> The days turn crisp, cool, and clear
> Bees, flies, and wasps disappear
> Multicolored leaves scrunch at your feet
> Harvest brings its fruit so sweet
> Overhead, birds move in flocks
> Ripened burrs gum to your socks
> Ahhh, sweet autumn

Some people can't even think about this time of year without suffering a brutal attack of poetitis. Just what is it about autumn?

A TIME OF INSPIRATION

"It's change, movement toward death and rebirth, and a beauty and a loss that drives one into oneself," says Peter Cooley, Ph.D., poetry editor of *The North American Review*, English professor at Tulane University and author of four books of poetry. (The poetic effort above is *not* one of his!)

Dr. Cooley says autumn is undoubtedly the most inspirational of seasons, not only to him but to many a fellow poet. Two of his favorite poems about this season are Shakespeare's 73rd sonnet:

> That time of year thou mayst in me behold
> When yellow leaves, or none, or few, do hang,
> Upon those boughs which shake against the cold . . .

and John Keats's "To Autumn":

> Season of mists and mellow fruitfulness
> Close bosom-friend of the maturing sun . . .

A TIME TO PLAY

Autumn is a time to romp and play in the great outdoors. "In this part of the country, visitors are often attracted by the spectacular foliage, but there's so much more that autumn offers," says Jonathan Hyde, a spokesman for the Massachusetts Office of Travel and Tourism.

"The crisp, sunny days, the color in the air—everything brings a sense of energy," he says. "It's a wonderful time of year to be active, to take a ride in a hot-air balloon, canoe, hike, row, take a train ride, visit the beach with a softball or a Frisbee, enjoy a nature trail, try hang-gliding, discover the many fairs."

A TIME TO RELAX

Autumn is a time to relax; there's never a need to fret about such horrors as frostbite and heatstroke. "Fall is probably my favorite season to dress," says Catharine Hartnett, a spokeswoman for L. L. Bean in Freeport, Maine. "It's not so cold that you have to bundle yourself up in winter woolies, yet it's never so hot that you suffer," she says.

For those autumn days that go from nippy mornings to warm afternoons and back to nippy nights, Hartnett recommends the three-layer approach: underwear, preferably of silk; a cotton jersey, maybe turtle-neck; and for the outermost layer, a thick cotton or wool sweater (which can be removed at midday).

A TIME TO REJOICE

Autumn is, perhaps above all, a time to rejoice, a time of festivals. "I don't think there's any time of year as rich in festivals as the fall," says Jasper Ingersoll, Ph.D., professor of anthropology at the Catholic University of America.

The notion of giving thanks to God, or the gods, around the time of the harvest did not originate (as American folklore has it) with the first meeting of the Pilgrims and Indians. "It has roots that go back to the beginnings of agriculture in Mesopotamia, perhaps 10,000 years ago," says Dr. Ingersoll. And from the old Middle East the tradition traveled around the world.

Similarly, he explains, today's Halloween evolved from pagan rites many thousands of years ago, in which priests of ancient northern Europe would honor the Lord of the Dead.

A TIME TO HIT THE ROAD

North America is rife with harvest-related, Halloween-related, and just plain old fun festivals all through the autumn months.

Here are but a few.

Grape Jamboree. The last full weekend of each September, the organizers of this 25-year-old festival in Geneva, in northeastern Ohio, promise you two jam-packed days of grape exhibits, grape-stomping, parades and a variety of delights such as grape pies, grape ice cream and grape cotton candy. You'll also find fresh-picked grapes and freshly squeezed grape juice. For information, call (216) 466-JAMB.

Goose Festival. Each fall, 600,000 Canada geese pass by Fenville, in southwestern Michigan, on their way south. Around the time of the festival—the third weekend in October—at least 10,000 or so can usually be seen hanging around. Come and participate in the Great Lakes goose-calling championship and the Wild Goose Chase 10K run. There are also mule wagon rides, a wildlife art show and pancake breakfasts. For information, call (616) 561-2720.

Brussels Sprout Festival. "What can be thrown, eaten, is thought to prevent cancer and is celebrated in October?" Ask the organizers of this annual event, which is held the second weekend in October in Santa Cruz, California. Here in central California, which boasts 90 percent of the country's brussels sprout production, you can enjoy sprout kabobs, sprout pizza, sprout ice cream and sprout chip cookies. Shake hands with Mr. Sprout, see sprout jugglers and listen to greengrass music (bluegrass with added sprouts). Win a trip to Brussels. For information, call (408) 423-5590.

Lumberjack and Bluegrass Jamboree. Come to Mullens, West Virginia, the second weekend in October and see (or participate in) the crosscut, horizontal cut and power cut competitions. Or enjoy the axe throw and bolt-splitting championships. Also enjoy bluegrass music, hayrides, clogging and a special visit by Smokey the Bear. For information, call 1-800-CALL WVA.

Haunted Happenings Week. Spend a bewitching Halloween in the coastal village of Salem, Massachusetts, famous for its sorcery. Each year, in the last week of October, the public is invited to tour haunted houses, participate in a witches' ball, sit for psychic readings, see chilling exhibits and witness a reenactment of an old witch trial (no one is executed!). For information, call (617) 744-0004.

Anniversary of the Signing of the Constitution. For a moving patriotic experience, visit Washington, D.C., on September 17 and see the original Constitution on display, a naturalization ceremony, a celebrity speaker and a band concert. All events are at the National Archives. For information, call (202) 523-3097.

Anniversary of Lincoln's Gettysburg Address. Each year on November 19, this celebration in Gettysburg, Pennsylvania, features memorial services, period costumes and a parade (on the closest Saturday). For information, call (717) 334-6274

Russell Wild

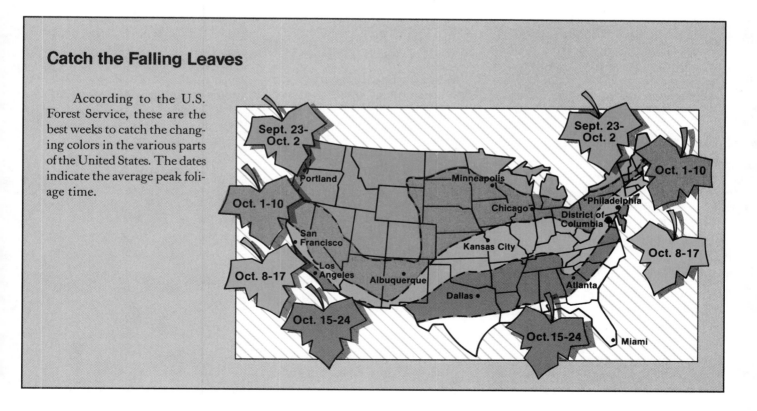

Catch the Falling Leaves

According to the U.S. Forest Service, these are the best weeks to catch the changing colors in the various parts of the United States. The dates indicate the average peak foliage time.

Happier Holidays

'Tis the season to be jolly.

Away in the closet, the presents are stacked. But you may have the feeling that everything's stacked against you. For some people, psychologists say, the holidays have more potential for being a drag than just about any other time of the year. They predict that the annual festivities may inspire sadness and longing, fear of family conflict and both financial and physical fatigue in countless weary celebrators.

"There are a number of reasons why people get the 'holiday blues,'" says Robert Oresick, Ph.D., assistant professor of psychology and counseling at the College of Basic Studies, Boston University. "One of the main ones is that the holidays serve as a marker in time. You don't notice the passage of time on June 8 or February 18 unless one or the other happens to be your birthday.

"But around the holidays, the amount of time that has gone by really hits you. In looking back, many people become dissatisfied or disillusioned, realizing how many of their dreams have fallen by the wayside."

But others don't let themselves get twisted around, groping for cast-off dreams. They create new ones instead. Their dreams are within easy reach—it just takes a bit of holiday-inspired creativity to know where to look. Here are a few ideas to get you started on a new, happier track.

START A NEW TRADITION

Jeff and Diane have plenty of charitable spirit, but between rushing to fit in visits with both sides of the family and worrying about buying just the right gifts for everyone, they often find that, around the holidays, they don't have much chance to exer-cise it, let alone do anything else. One year, though, they decided to take advantage of all the energy that's in the holiday air and get involved with something they would enjoy.

"One of our neighbors mentioned she was getting a group of people together to sing Handel's *Messiah* in a community concert at her church," Jeff says. "We've both always been able to carry a tune, and we both love music. So the opportunity seemed perfect.

"The chorus became more important than anything else that went on during the holiday and, as a result, made everything else better. It may not have alleviated the usual problems of the holiday, but it sure made them seem trivial. We hope to make singing in the chorus a family tradition," he says.

GIVE THE GIFT OF YOUR TIME

When it comes to giving to other people, the holiday season is the traditional time to do it. And there's nothing that feels better than knowing you've helped somebody.

The Kelly family of Colorado has been bitten by the helping bug. "For the past few years, we take some time during Christmas to make up baskets of toys and food for a few poor families who live in an area near our home," says Susan Kelly. The family members like this kind of interaction because it helps them get beyond the commercialism that often invades the season. "It's a time when you're given license to give without an ulterior motive," explains Susan. "It's not a 'what's in it for me' type of exchange."

Besides their own love of giving, the Kellys are eager to teach their children what they've already learned through years of such work. Susan says, "I want them to know that people aren't stupid because they are poor or don't speak English. And giving the baskets has helped—I've noticed a greater sensitivity on their part."

CELEBRATE WITH SOMEONE NEW

Perhaps the best celebration is the one that keeps you happy throughout the rest of the year. That's one that creates strong new friendships. And often, the holidays provide just the right atmosphere to do that.

Bob and Cindy Maynard live in Vermont, running their business, the Vermont Country Cyclers, and raising their two children, Megan and Tyler. Every year since they've lived in Vermont, Bob and Cindy have strapped on their cross-country skis and gone out to the woods the day before Christmas to chop down their tree. One year, that expedition became the highlight of the entire holiday.

"We've known and been friendly with five other couples since we moved to Vermont," says Bob. "But we just hadn't been that close. That year was the first time we all had young children, and that prompted us to spend a little more time together around Christmas. Now we're really glad we did. The 12 of us put our children on our backs and skied out to the woods. The air was very still and the snow had barely been disturbed. It was beautiful."

MEET YOURSELF

Getting in touch with old friends and making new ones can be rewarding holiday experiences, but this year you might also want to spend some time with another very important person. Who? Yourself, of course.

Debbie, a Pennsylvania attorney, used the holiday as a time to really know and learn about herself. "One year, I went to the Kripalu Center for Yoga and Health for a three-day health holiday weekend over New Year's," she says. At the yoga community in Lenox, Massachusetts, Debbie participated in group meals, meditation and exercise, as well as celebrations. "There, the nonjudgmental atmosphere makes it a lot easier to reflect on yourself."

That environment was perfect for the kind of holiday Debbie wanted to have. She explains, "I think a lot of the way we set up our holiday now encourages withdrawal from yourself and disregard for your own needs. The pressures of socializing, the high expectations, and all the high-intensity, high-speed activities—that's not the way I want to spend a holiday."

Alexis Lieberman

Take the Glitches Out of Gift Giving

Sure, you *care* enough to send the very best. The problem is, you don't have the money. So you end up, like so many others, on a last-minute Christmas Eve shopping spree, buying what you really didn't want to get for someone who doesn't want it, and spending more money and aggravation than it was worth.

Here's how to avoid such mayhem.

Plan Christmas in July. As you wander through flea markets or outdoor arts and crafts shows throughout the year, buy interesting items you know will make great gifts. Don't worry that you have no one particular in mind. You can match gift to person later.

Capture casual hints. If your mother wistfully eyes a handbag while window-shopping, discreetly jot this gift idea down in a notebook. Go back the next day and buy it or call the store and ask that it be sent.

Give "gifts of love." Priceless gifts can be a coupon for a massage, a week of exotic meals, a promise to keep the bathroom cleaned.

Suggest experiences. Your favorite couple may enjoy a bottle of exotic liquor, two glasses, a candle and a note instructing them to "share a special moment together." A new mother may appreciate some special bath soaps with a note inviting her to take a luxurious soak while you babysit.

You can also avoid the pressure of giving presents if you remember that not all your gifts will receive rave reviews.

Keep in mind, too, that 'tis sometimes better to receive than to give. So, if your friend gives you a present but you did not get him one, graciously accept the gift and allow him to feel the joy of giving.

REST AND RECREATION

Massage
Your Cares Away

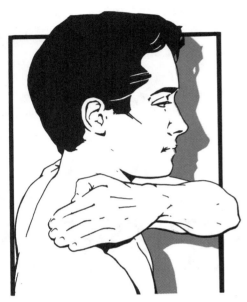

Warning: This section is rated "R"—"R" for Relax.

If you've been feeling tense lately and need to unwind, then lay this book down in front of you and prepare to give yourself a terrific massage. It doesn't matter where you are. You'll need no special equipment or tools. Soft music is optional. Just follow certified massage therapist Marilyn McAfee's simple instructions that follow, and you can't go wrong!

Has tension made a home for itself in your upper back and neck? Here's the eviction notice: Reach across your chest and over the opposite shoulder. Now firmly knead those upper back muscles over as large an area as you can. Get both sides.

Headache-prone? Try this 1-minute "cure": Warm your hands by briskly rubbing them together. Place both hands gently over your eyes and hold for 30 seconds. Slip your palms to the sides, and slide circles over both temples for another 30 seconds. Be very gentle—you're not waxing a car!

Next: Push your fingers (not your nails!) onto the top of your head. Now try to rotate your scalp in as many directions as you can. Apply fairly strong pressure—you want to move the skin against the bone. Adjust all ten fingers several times to cover the entire head.

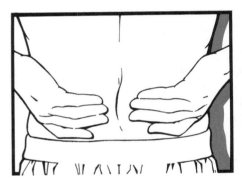

Been standing a lot? Here's the answer: Reach behind you and press your fingers firmly against the lower back muscle. Make short deep circles, moving your hands slowly up, as far as they will go. Leave an inch on either side of the spine.

Your arms deserve attention, too. Start at the wrist and work your way up, squeezing with your opposite hand. Allow the palm to create the pressure and the fingers to stabilize the movement.

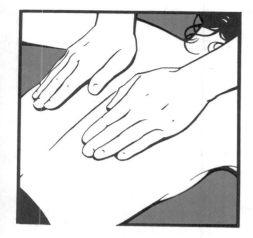

Now it's his or her turn. Below, follow McAfee's instructions and you'll learn to give a massage like the pros. Oil is recommended—try sesame seed, safflower or almond oil mixed, if you like, with a dab of aromatic clove, musk or lemon oil. A little soothing instrumental background music is always a nice, relaxing touch. Make sure to set the thermostat on warm. You're all set to go. Oh, one more thing . . . You'll need a friend for these!

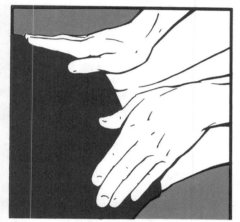

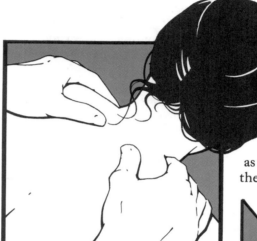

Next, from the same position, run your hands across your partner's back in horizontal sections. Pull with your right hand as you push with your left, covering the width of the back entirely as you slowly work your way from the shoulders to the buttocks.

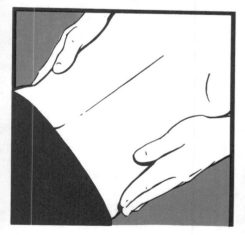

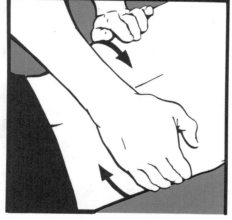

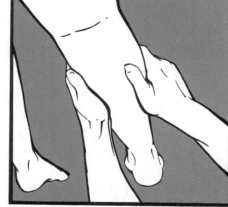

Have your partner lie face-down on a firm surface (a carpeted floor covered with a towel is the next best thing to a professional massage table). Stand or kneel on the floor near your partner's head, then lean over and drape your hands over the shoulders. Now push gently down the back on either side of the spine. When you reach the buttocks, roll your hands outward and bring them back to you along the side of your partner's body.

Now move to a position where you can easily grasp the upper shoulders, and knead the muscles between your fingers and thumbs. Do this for a minute or so, or longer if your partner is particularly tense in this area . . . You'll know!

If your partner's been on his or her feet all day, you'll get a big thanks for this one: Positioning yourself at the feet, press firmly with your thumbs into the calf and then the thigh muscles, skipping over the back of the knees. Circle your thumbs outward as you move up each leg.

Now, slip your hands under this book, pass it to your partner, and convince him or her that it's *your* turn!

Russell Wild

Super Stress Busters

Stress. It's no secret that too much of it, for too long, can collect in your body and make you sick. The trick is to learn to live with stress today to minimize its effects tomorrow.

Often what's needed to combat stress isn't elaborate exercise programs or expensive escapes to some South Seas island. At times you need effective stopgap solutions to help you deal with stress right now—when you are toe-to-toe with the tensions of everyday life. That's why we've put together these quick and easy stress releasers that diffuse stress and keep you from buckling under the crunch. Find which techniques work for you.

Take a hike. When pressures mount to the boiling point, don't just sit there and stew; get up and take a walk. A brisk 10- to 15-minute walk is a good safety valve that has been shown to relieve muscular and nervous tension, reports Herbert deVries, Ph.D., former professor of the physiology of exercise at the University of Southern California.

Have a "cuppa" tea. Herb tea, that is. Says California herbalist Nan Koehler: "Even the ritual of preparing tea—holding the warm cup in your hands and feeling the steam—can be tremendously soothing and relaxing." Camomile is the most common calming tea. Other herbs noted for their soothing properties include basil, catnip, hops and valerian.

Let it all out. Bottled-up anger can boost your blood pressure, give you headaches and possibly lead to ulcers. A healthier response to stress is to calmly confront conflicts head-on. Discuss problems in a detached manner. Go ahead and groan once in a while, too. Some experts believe a good groan vibrates the body, relaxes the muscles and sort of "massages you from the inside out."

Another effective pressure valve is to have yourself a good cry. Tears may help relieve stress by ridding the body of potentially harmful chemicals produced in stressful times. Or you might just want to laugh at life a little—or a lot. Laughter diffuses tension and restores perspective.

Breathe easy. Your breathing becomes rapid and shallow when you're overwrought. Slow it down and you discharge stress. Try filling your lungs slowly in 7 seconds, then take 8 seconds to exhale. Train yourself to deep-breathe to certain triggers—a red light and a ringing telephone are two good triggers.

Do a slow stretch. Make your muscles relax by gently and slowly stretching a specific set of muscles until you feel a tug. Hold for 10 to 30 seconds and release. This is a good tension releaser to try when stuck in traffic: Grasp the top of the steering wheel with both hands, making sure your forearms are also resting on the wheel. Place your buttocks and lower back against the back of the seat. Now hunch your upper body forward and arch your back like a frightened cat.

Shut out "shoulds." Trying to live up to certain imposed images and standards can add to your stress load. Be aware of the stereotypes surrounding you and the pressure to conform—the perfect parent, or the superwoman with the Cosmo-girl figure. Think of your real self, not your ideal self. Try

How to Keep Butterflies Out of Your Stomach

Ever get that fluttery feeling in your gut just when you have to give a speech, take a test or go to a party at the boss's house? Sometimes the "butterflies" are more distressing than the actual event.

"That's referred to as anticipatory anxiety," says Robert Kerns, Ph.D., assistant professor of psychology at Yale University School of Medicine. "It's not so much doing the task that's so anxiety-producing, but the anticipation of it—the ruminating about it. We tend to think about the event in ways that provoke intense anxiety. The result is butterflies in the stomach."

What can be done about it?

"A good strategy is to realize that you are responsible for what you're doing to yourself and that you have the ability to control those feelings," says Dr. Kerns. "You can say, 'It's not the situation—it's my thinking about it that's generating the anxiety. I'm responsible, I'm in control and I'm able to do something about it.'"

Relaxation techniques (see "Relaxation Techniques That Work" on page 200) also help, as does mentally rehearsing the anxiety-producing upcoming event in your mind until you begin to feel comfortable with it, says Dr. Kerns.

not to be perfect. Think: "This is who I am, not who I should be."

Get a little help from your friends. Peer support systems—both at and away from home—can keep you sane through stressful situations and help you find solutions to problems. They will also keep you healthy. Research indicates that social ties can lower your risk of heart disease, cancer, digestive disorders, even accidents.

Give yourself good P.R. Progressive relaxation—tensing muscles and then slowly releasing—is a good way to banish stress from your body. First, lie down and close your eyes. Make a tight fist and tense the muscles in your wrist and forearm. Hold for 5 seconds, feeling the tension, then unclench and let the tension drain from your forearm, wrist and fingers. Note the difference between the feeling of tautness and the pleasure of total relaxation. Now repeat this tension/relaxation sequence for your left hand, then for your shoulders, neck, face, legs, feet and toes. Soon you'll be able to perform it anytime and anywhere you find yourself in a stressful situation.

Touch your toes. No, not that way. We're talking about a gentle foot rub that can make you feel good and relaxed all over. Start by applying pressure with your thumbs to your soles, then massaging every square inch. Work your toes by moving them from side to side, then forward and back.

Head for the hills. Or the ocean, open fields or desert. "Being in a natural surrounding is good for relieving stress," says psychiatrist Aaron Katcher, M.D. "Watching the surf or the clouds roll by is a form of meditation. Our thoughts are focused on the rhythm of things, and they're not occupied with problems or worries." Some experts say that a drive to the country or a stroll in the park is as effective as tranquilizers or biofeedback.

Repeat a relaxing word. Studies show that saying the same word over and over—preferably one ending in an "m" or "n" sound, like warm or sun—can help quiet the central nervous system, slow the heart rate and lower blood pressure.

Marcia Holman

De-Stress Your Home Life

Every day, the world bombards us with stress. That's why your home should be a haven, a place to relax and recharge your batteries. But that won't happen if your home life is also stressful.

That's why we asked Paul I. Rosch, M.D., president of the American Institute of Stress, and other experts in the field for a few tips to de-stress your home life. Here's what we got.

Respect privacy. If Junior needs time to brood to Bon Jovi, let him. But let him know that you need your private time, too. Privacy for children can help develop personality; for adults it can help rest personality.

Respect individuality. Individuality is as important as privacy. If a family member is presenting an image you don't see eye to eye with (providing it's not blatantly in poor taste), try hard to be open-minded. Being overly judgmental can not only start a fight but also stifle a family member's development and sense of self.

Guide, do not steer. If you have goals for your children or your spouse, remember that those goals are yours and not necessarily theirs. Try encouraging the kind of development you would like to see, but if that doesn't work, back off. You risk making a monster of yourself by keeping too tight a grip on the reins, and you also risk losing the very control you're trying to gain.

Have definite rules and stick to them. Ruling with a light touch doesn't mean being a wimp, however. Clear-cut rules are your safeguard against chaos. That goes for everything from curfews to dish duties. Stress can be greatly eliminated if all members of a household know their responsibilities and know, too, the penalties for not sticking to them. It's those gray areas that make for gray hairs, so keep things as black and white as possible.

Demand a time and place to relax. It should be as central as your home's heating system: a quiet spot where you can do what you want when you want. All family members should have such a place and such a right. If your home is small, it may require some cooperation, but the results should be worth it. Even if it's just 15 minutes alone in a warm bath, quiet time can mellow kids and adults alike.

Garden Therapy

Plant a few seeds and you'll grow more than just zucchini in your garden. That's right. Along with flowers and vegetables, you'll harvest a healthier and happier you. You can turn to your garden for resistance to stress, to lower your blood pressure and to get stretched out and toned up. What's more, growing and eating a variety of crisp, fresh vegetables and fruits adds needed fiber and nutrients to your diet and may boost your resistance to heart disease, cancer and other disorders.

Clearly, there's more to gardening —the top-ranked outdoor leisure activity in the country—than meets the eye. When you escape from your revved-up, high-tech world and find refuge in the primitive peace of your garden, experts say, you can rejuvenate your body and soul in scientifically measurable ways.

BUDDING BENEFITS

One leading researcher who has measured physiological responses to green, living things is Roger Ulrich, Ph.D., associate professor of geography at the University of Delaware and an expert in the fertile field of plant/ people relationships. He's also a gardener who knows the value of close personal contact with the environment.

"We benefit emotionally and physiologically," says Dr. Ulrich, "both by direct, active involvement, such as gardening, or in a more passive way, such as viewing nature."

Dr. Ulrich's studies showed that fairly substantial physiological and emotional changes occurred when people were exposed to plants. Their blood pressures lowered, their muscles loosened and their heart rates slowed. There was even a shift toward more positive states in the way their skin conducted electricity.

The link between gardening and a healthier heart is a bit more tentative. But the evidence is growing. Researchers in the Netherlands, for example, have found that people who lovingly tend their plants have significantly fewer heart attacks than those who never stop to smell—or grow— the roses. Gardening lowers blood pressure and increases the body's resistance to stress, the researchers concluded.

As good as gardening may be at hardening your resistance to heart disease, experts say, the physical exertion of gardening might also harden your bones.

If you're a woman and your idea of exercise is pushing 50, your skeleton is very likely losing calcium with every passing year. But you may be able to slow down or halt that process altogether by tugging at obstinate dandelions, lugging bags of manure or waltzing a wheelbarrow across bumpy rows of raised soil.

Gardening offers the added benefit of safe, sensible aerobic exercise, says Peter Jacobson, M.D., an orthopedic surgeon at the University of North Carolina at Chapel Hill School of Medicine. "It's like going for a steady walk."

But aside from the physical workout and the nutritional benefits of growing fresh-as-can-be food, what do gardeners get out of the virtually endless cycle of growth and harvest? The answer appears to be emotional regeneration, a restored sense of control over the often uncontrollable events of life.

A GUIDE FOR GREENIES

Gardening is easy, even if you've never grown anything before. You can fill your yard with flowers and harvest a good-size crop of vegetables. Here are a few tips to start you on your way.

Plan summer in winter. While it's still cold outside, you should begin planning what you want to grow—and order your seeds—for a bountiful garden later, according to Warren Schultz, horticultural editor with the National Gardening Association.

You should plan to start many plants in small containers, indoors, 6 to 8 weeks before the last expected frost date in your area. You can then transplant to the garden when warmer weather arrives. A few examples are tomatoes, lettuce, peppers and eggplant. Some plants, like cabbage, parsley and broccoli, can be planted outside earlier and should be started indoors as early as 12 weeks before the last frost date.

Have your soil checked. "That's really the basis for a healthy garden," Schultz explains. "If the soil's not in good shape (too acid or too alkaline for what you plan to grow), nothing you plant will do well, and you'll never know what you've done wrong."

To have your soil tested, contact your county Agricultural Extension Service. The agency might charge you a small fee, but it should be worth the cost. Soon you should be able to boldly grow where no plants have grown before.

Curl up with a good book. Before you get dirt under your fingernails, thumb through some gardening references written for rank beginners. A good place to start is

Square Foot Gardening, by Mel Bartholomew. But browse in the bookstores and ask other gardeners for advice. The shelves are brimming with gardening books by many experts.

Start small. "You ought to start with maybe no more than a half dozen types of vegetables or flowers growing in the garden," says Schultz. "It's easier to keep track of things, to make observations on the plants and how they grow, without setting yourself up for discouraging experiences." A window planter might be an attractive option if you live in the city. Window boxes, however, tend to heat up more rapidly than backyard plots, says Schultz, so they need more water and ample drainage, along with more frequent fertilization.

Plant surefire crops. Why sow seeds of discontent? If you've never grown exotic plants, don't plant orchids and bananas. Instead, plant tried-and-true vegetables—beans, carrots, cucumbers, tomatoes, broccoli or cabbage. Try sowing hearty flowers like snapdragons, nasturtiums and marigolds.

Jeff Meade

The Healing Garden

If you plant fruits and vegetables, you might be growing disease-fighters right on your own doorstep.

Behold, for example, the carrot. It may look like just another salad-bar munchie to you, but the spindly root conceals within its crunchy orange flesh a leading anti-cancer contender—beta-carotene, found in almost ridiculous abundance in the carrot and in other yellow and leafy green vegetables.

Beta-carotene against cancer. Studies in the United States and elsewhere strongly suggest that we would have less lung, colon, stomach, cervical and prostate cancer if we consumed more fresh fruits and vegetables rich in beta-carotene.

Recommended: Carrots, spinach, kale, mustard greens, sweet potatoes, red peppers and cantaloupe.

Pectin fights cholesterol. Another disease-preventer might be pectin, the fibrous "glue" that holds cells together in plants. Numerous studies show that pectin reduces cholesterol. People who eat fruits and vegetables, the studies suggest, have less artery disease.

Recommended: If you live in sunny climes, any citrus fruit with a white rind. If not, try growing tart apples, sour plums, Concord grapes and gooseberries.

Vitamin C against cancer. Links have also been found between vitamin C, found in many fruits and vegetables, and a reduction in the incidence of cancer of the colon, bladder, stomach, rectum and esophagus.

Recommended: Brussels sprouts, sweet green peppers, cauliflower, tomatoes, broccoli, strawberries and cantaloupe.

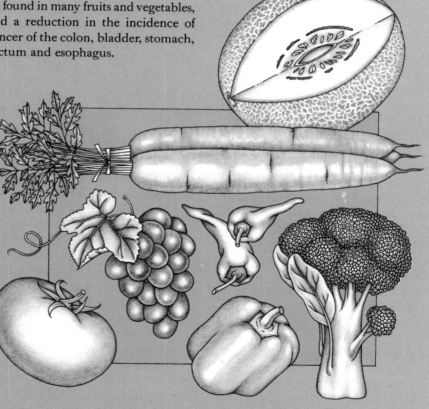

Reading, Writing and Relaxation

There's no reason to read or write anything these days—TV and telephones can take the place of old-fashioned books, paper and pencil. But should they? TV may be fun and the telephone may be fast, but the experts say that reading and writing will not only help you relax, they'll improve your mental and physical health, too.

Writing, for example, lets you express yourself and get to the heart of what might be keeping you uptight and bothered. What better way to relax than by getting what's bothering you off your chest!

While it might seem difficult to scientifically prove the health value of writing, James W. Pennebaker, Ph.D., of Southern Methodist University, did just that. He headed a study that found that writing about issues confronting you may help boost your immune system. Dr. Pennebaker and his colleagues asked 25 college students to spend 20 minutes a day for four days writing their thoughts about unimportant topics. Another 25 students were asked to write for the same time period, describing their feelings about problems they couldn't fix. Blood tests showed that the students who wrote about their problems had an increased lymphocyte response, which means they had a stronger immune system. The other students showed no such improvement.

WRITING ERASES WOES

Because writing is a private act, it has advantages for people who have trouble expressing themselves to others. And by writing, rather than talking about a problem, you are able to look back at what you've written and examine what you were thinking.

Writing about something can be seen as the first step toward going public with it—without taking a risk. "Writing something about yourself, say in a journal, is a transition between keeping it to yourself and telling it to someone. You know, or at least hope, that someone will read it someday. But you don't have to risk telling someone right away," says Irwin Rosen, Ph.D., a psychologist and director of the Adult Outpatient Department at the Menninger Foundation in Topeka, Kansas.

"This is true of literature, too. Every poem, every novel, every short story, is somewhat autobiographical. It has to be, because everything the writer writes is based on something he knows," says Dr. Rosen.

A BEGINNER'S GUIDE

Okay, writing is good for you. But how are you going to write if you've never done it before?

Don't stifle yourself. The main obstacle facing many writers is self-censorship, says Fran Clifton, Ph.D., a psychologist in private practice in New York City. Self-censorship is what's at work when you sit down to write something and start worrying about who's going to read it, whether you're doing it "right," and even who's going to publish it.

One key to help you avoid self-censorship when you're writing for pleasure is to "remember that you're writing for therapeutic reasons, and not to win the Nobel prize," says Dr. Clifton.

"You should concentrate on the process, not the product," says Mary Murdock, Ed.D., assistant professor at the Center for Studies in Creativity, Buffalo State College. "Compare yourself only to yourself, not to 'successes' you read about. Everyone has to start somewhere. We must realize that professional writers struggle with their words just like everyone else. Hemingway sometimes wrote badly—he just didn't publish it."

Do what comes naturally. "When you write, put yourself in a nonthreatening situation," says Dr. Murdock. "Because writing requires so much concentration, you want to work in a place that gives you privacy and quiet—although there are exceptions to this. Some people thrive in more chaotic environments."

Don't be timid. If you're afraid someone will read what you wrote, just rip it up and throw it away when you're finished, says Dr. Murdock. But eventually you may want someone to see it.

"Even those who want to communicate with others are often afraid, thinking the other people might be too judgmental," says Dr. Murdock. "If you do start showing your writing, make sure you choose a knowledgeable, understanding person."

One way to find a good audience is to take a writing class with other people who are learning. Check with local colleges to find one.

Start with a journal. The experts agree that you should start by writing about whatever topic comes to you most easily. In most cases, this will mean keeping a journal.

"You can't fail or make a mistake writing a journal," says Patricia Hample, who teaches English, poetry, fiction and autobiographical writing at the University of Minnesota. "With a journal you can write whatever you want. There is no beginning, middle, or end. You don't need to fit any form."

If you have trouble finding something to write about, you might try an exercise that Dr. Clifton sometimes uses. He has people start recording a dream as soon as they wake up, and write down not only what happened during the dream but also continue writing about the dream as though it were still happening. "This can help you solve your problems and can also lead to some very creative writing," says Dr. Clifton.

READING: THE GREAT ESCAPE

While not everyone is cut out to be a writer, everyone is cut out to be a reader. Fiction, nonfiction, poetry— they all can be used as a cushion between you and the stresses in your life, say the experts. Reading *is* relaxation.

"Everyone has to escape once in a while," says Dr. Clifton. "If you can get away from it all for a little while by reading, that's good." But truly getting away from it all often depends on *what* you read.

"There are people I know who have never read a novel, yet they might be great readers," says Edna K. Bauer, a therapist in private practice in Binghamton, New York. "It's just that what they read is always practical and work related. That just makes them more tense."

But reading great literature can be a source of anxiety, too, if it's not what you want to read. "I have to confess that I can't read Shakespeare," says Bauer. "It makes me more tense trying to get through it. When I'm tense I read spy novels. Junk novels. Bringing papers home from the office and reading them after dinner, for

How to Pen a *poem*

Here's what 3 experts say you should know about writing poetry.

Galway Kinnell, Pulitzer prize-winning poet and recipient of a MacArthur Foundation "genius" award:

● Write about what is most important to you.
● Don't worry about the form the poem takes.
● Work at it. Writing poetry isn't easy.

Patricia Hample, author of several volumes of poetry, including *Resort, and Other Poems:*

● If you want to write poetry, you should read poetry. A problem these days is that many people want to tap dance, but no one wants to be in the audience.

● Reading as a writer is not a spectator sport. You have to be active. Keep a notebook while you read. Mark up the book you're reading. Find out what it is about the poem that moves you.

Philip Schultz, winner of the 1984 Lamont Poetry Selection award for his volume of poetry, *Deep within the Ravine:*

● At the beginning, you should write for the pleasure of writing. Don't bring any critical judgment to it.
● Write on an emotional level. Write what you feel. Don't worry about how it looks on the paper.

instance, wouldn't be a very good way to relax. People who are reading to relax should choose pleasurable things to read."

Dr. Murdock agrees. "Give some thought to what you like to read. Aren't there certain types of things that are more relaxing to you than others? Sometimes you might want to read a book that really makes you think. Other times you want to read a book or magazine that lets you almost doze off, and escape."

Reading can be a good way to become less obsessed with yourself, at least for a little while, says Dr. Clifton. "We are at our best when we are not aware of ourselves. The world really starts to expand when you read. You develop empathy for others."

Reading or writing can create a self-awareness and pleasure that will help you relax and improve your health. "Language is as tactile and malleable as clay," says Hample. "Words aren't just little functional units of communication. Words are alive."

Stephen Williams

Games
Happy People Play

The wide-screen TV is blank, the radio off, the CD player unplugged. A couple sits in a dimly lit den, huddled over black and red geometric shapes. Their concentration is so intense you could literally hear a pin drop—if it weren't for the muffled thud of dice rolling over the shapes. The object of their intensity is backgammon, a game that has enthralled players as far back as the Middle Ages.

Despite our super stereos and 100-channel television sets, we're still entertaining ourselves with games. As one historian of games put it: "The games impulse is a universal one."

LEARNING THE GAME OF LIFE

What's the great allure of games? The obvious answer is that—whether you are playing solitaire, Monopoly, hopscotch, charades or tug-of-war—games are good, old-fashioned fun. And fun just never goes out of style.

But there's another, slightly more serious side to games. "Games have a practical application," explains Ritch Davidson, who calls himself the senior vice emperor of Playfair, a business management consulting company in Berkeley, California. "They teach us how to play the game of life." In fact, sometimes they teach us how to play the war game of life.

"Japanese soldiers," writes Canadian games historian R. C. Bell in *Games of the World*, "were once required to play shuttlecock (a game similar to badminton) for agility and speed; in a very different culture, American Indian youths developed their marksmanship by throwing darts through a rolling hoop."

But not all games function as a playful boot camp. Peacetime skills are cultivated, too. "Even participating in a simple card game teaches us valuable lessons in how to take risks, be patient, plan ahead and react quickly," says Elliot Avedon, Ph.D., professor of recreation and leisure studies at the University of Waterloo in Ontario, Canada.

"Games bring back the personalized, active aspect of learning," says David Sleet, Ph.D., of San Diego State University. "They're a vehicle for getting people to interact with each other, to make decisions and to rehearse different kinds of behavior before they try it out on the real world."

The best part about all this is that learning is turned into . . . well, a game. "Games minimize the difficulty of learning because they're fun," says E. David Wilson, senior vice president of Milton Bradley Company.

THE SELF-IMPROVEMENT GAME

Still not game? Here are two more good reasons to have a good time.

Games make you smarter. "When you play games," writes Marco Meirovitz, coauthor of *Brain Muscle Builders: Games to Increase Your Natural Intelligence*, "you are actively exercising your thinking skills." Playing a card game can teach you deductive logic—how to put together separate but related facts, eliminate irrelevant information and reach a conclusion.

Want to sharpen your skills in decision making, concentration and strategy? Then make like a king and move one—play chess. Games histo-

rian Bell says that kings used this imaginative reconstruction of a battlefield to prepare for war and that it still provides excellent tactical training—maybe for corporate takeovers and other executive maneuvers. (Why do you think they call the top position chairman of the *board?*)

And if your mind seems a little scattered, take our word for it: Scrabble.

Actually, that's the advice of behavioral psychologist K. Warner Schaie, Ph.D., professor of human development and psychology at Pennsylvania State University, who says that crossword puzzles and games like Scrabble increase your verbal and memory skills and can keep your mind sharp.

Games improve your relationships. When you play a game with one or more partners, especially games that involve verbal interaction, you can get to know others better. Some games are even designed to enhance communications. A recent board game called Scruples involves asking players provocative and revealing questions about morality, personal values and sex. Questions like "Would you pose nude in a national magazine for $10,000?" can certainly spark some interesting conversations.

And the so-called new games like earth ball, where large groups of people toss around a gigantic rubber ball, have been used to help groups learn to work toward mutual goals.

LET ME ENTERTAIN ME

Some people think games are for kids; they haven't played one since they heard their last recess bell. These are usually the people who tend to take life too seriously, says Dr. Avedon.

But put games back into your life and you can feel like a kid again. Here are some "rules" for getting back in the game.

Play for the fun of it. Winning isn't everything. Pleasure and challenge should be your goal.

Expand your skills. If you always play word games, try playing poker. If you always play board games, try more active games like darts.

Be aware of what games teach you about yourself. Notice if you always let the other guy win or if you become nasty playing Pinochle. Not wanting to experience those feelings may be what's keeping you from games.

Play games regularly. Don't wait for the TV to go on the blink before getting out the old game board or deck of cards. You just may find a *better* source of entertainment.

Marcia Holman

How to Heal a Sore Loser

Poor Joey. Nobody wants to play games with him. When he was little, it was because he would purposely smudge the hopscotch grid when he stepped on a line. And now, when he misspells a Scrabble word, he tosses his tiles on the floor and stomps off. Some say he even cheats at cards.

It would certainly appear that Joey is a bad loser. What isn't so apparent, though, is that Joey is not having any fun in the first place. Joey's simply in the wrong game.

"Different games suit different personalities," explains games expert Elliot Avedon, Ph.D. Some people are more comfortable with pure chance games like Parcheesi, while others prefer strategy games like chess. Some like a combination of both.

By the same token, some people may be put off by games that use certain objects (like cards) or certain situations (like horseshoes) or involve playing with partners.

So what can you do for the sore loser? Help him discover games more suited to his personality. And if that doesn't work, teach him to play solitaire!

Relaxation Techniques That Work

What a morning.

The car wouldn't start. The dog got loose. You spilled coffee on your lap during the drive to work. And then your briefcase popped open in the parking lot—important papers everywhere in a mini-hurricane of swirling white bond.

You're so mad you could eat a crowbar, and the idea of getting anything done before lunch—hey, come on, you're only human. It'll take that long just to calm down. Right?

Wrong. The techniques described here can calm the most frazzled nerves in minutes. They can help you the next time the fates conspire to rain on your parade.

A SHIELD AGAINST STRESS

"For a technique to be effective, it has to elicit what I call the relaxation response," says Herbert Benson, M.D., author of *Beyond the Relaxation Response* and chief of the Department of Behavioral Medicine at New England Deaconess Hospital in Boston.

"That's a condition, not a technique, in which the individual displays lower metabolism, slower breathing, slower heart rate and reduced blood pressure and experiences feelings of peace and tranquility." And virtually every common technique—including those mentioned below—has been shown to produce this response."

So, okay, it can be done, and if you do it, you'll feel better for the moment. But does it really *change* anything?

You bet it does.

"The relaxation response effectively protects people from the harmful effects of stress," Dr. Benson says.

"Anxiety and hostility often will disappear, and you will be more open to changes of any sort, including viewing the world differently."

And since stress has been identified as a contributor to many major illnesses, fighting back with relaxation might do more for your health than all the pills in your medicine cabinet.

"Stress produces changes in a host of body parameters that includes adrenaline production," Dr. Benson says. "A number of studies have shown that adrenaline *impairs* immune function, while others have demonstrated that relaxation *enhances* it."

HOW TO RELAX

How do you achieve those benefits for yourself? It's simple. Just pick a technique from those listed below and start practicing now.

Try peaceful concentration. Meditation comes in a variety of disciplines, some of which require skill and dedication. Here's one Dr. Benson says you can practice on your own.

Find a quiet place (you can even use your office with the door closed), sit down and close your eyes. Relax your muscles. Concentrate on your breathing, keeping it slow and natural, and start repeating a focus word or phrase with each exhalation. The focus word simply acts as an anchor for your attention and can be a prayer, an affirmation ("I'm a great guy") or something as simple as the word *one*. Use the same focus word each time to build an association in your mind between relaxation and repetition of the word. Maintain a passive attitude and discard stray thoughts as they arrive.

And here is another tip from Dr. Benson: "Don't worry about whether or not you're doing it 'right' or not. Worrying about how well you're doing kills it right there."

The following techniques were suggested by relaxation expert John Curtis, Ph.D., author of five books on relaxation and currently professor of health education at the University of Wisconsin.

Take a deep breath. This is a simple exhalation exercise. Sit down, close your eyes and focus on your breathing. With each exhalation, concentrate on feeling the body sinking down and loosening up, becoming more relaxed on each exhalation.

"The body has a pace of its own, and if you encourage the mind to pay attention to that inner rhythm, it will gradually match paces," Dr. Curtis says. "You'll slow down substantially."

Think yourself calm. In sequential relaxation, you pick one end of your body and work your way to the other, relaxing one body part at a time by first tensing the muscles and then relaxing them.

"The nice thing about this one is that it keeps the mind active and involved," Dr. Curtis says. "It requires you to pay attention—you *can't* think about balancing your checkbook because you're busy doing the technique."

Put your senses to work. With sensory awareness, you find a comfortable position, close your eyes and simply start scanning the body from one end to the other, looking for sensations—heat or cold, tension or relaxation, comfort or discomfort. Find out what's happening and where it's happening. In this technique, your body's own feedback serves as the mind's anchor.

"This one's excellent for unwinding at home," Dr. Curtis says. "You'll often fall asleep. And like progressive relaxation, it's good for the so-called Type A personality, the guy who has a hard time sitting still, because it involves the mind a little more actively than meditation."

Sit down, close your eyes and do absolutely nothing at all. "Just sit and close your eyes, listening to yourself breathe—nothing else—and in a couple of minutes you're going to get very relaxed," Dr. Curtis says. "Any time you focus your attention within the body, you're going to end up relaxed, because the body operates more slowly than the mind. You're sort of *boring* the mind into relaxation."

Try the nontraditional. These techniques require either equipment, more time, or money: biofeedback, saunas/hot tubs, weekend vacations, and plain old exercise.

"It really doesn't matter which technique you choose," Dr. Benson says, "as long as it meets two criteria: It's in some fashion rhythmic and it in some way breaks the chain of your normal train of thought. A weekend vacation works fine *provided* that it breaks that loop, that you don't take your normal train of thought with you. Leave work at the office, in other words."

Dr. Curtis says much the same thing. "It's been documented time and time again that all of these techniques produce essentially the same result—the relaxation response. But

it's important that you choose one that you're comfortable with. Take biofeedback, for example. It's clear that you don't need a machine to relax, and we encourage our students to wean themselves away from them. But if you believe in them, heck—go ahead and use them."

Dr. Benson sums it up: "The more comfortable you are with a technique—the more you believe in it—the better it's going to work. The important thing is to break that everyday cycle of thought, and whether you do that with a walk or meditation doesn't matter as long as you *do* it."

Kim Anderson

Tranquility in Motion

Think of it as anti-aerobics—exercise that *doesn't* make the pulse pound, sweat pour and muscles ache. It's there, it's real, it works—it makes you relax, in other words—and it's mostly oriental in origin.

"It's been documented that T'ai Chi and Chi Kung (originally oriental martial arts) produce exactly the same physiological response as passive relaxation techniques like meditation," says Herbert Benson, M.D. "Practiced properly, they are thoroughly relaxing."

T'ai Chi and Chi Kung share characteristics (gentle, fluid movements performed in synchrony with slow, carefully controlled breathing) with another Eastern contribution to Western relaxation, yoga.

A system of physical exercises derived originally from Hindu scrip-

tures, yoga relaxes its practitioners through formal stretching exercises and breathing/concentration drills similar to those outlined in the text.

"It all becomes so simple, once you understand the underlying principle," Dr. Benson says. "Anything, yoga included, that breaks that attention loop I keep talking about will elicit the relaxation response."

To de done properly, all 3 of these techniques require instruction from an expert and practice. To find out about classes near you, contact your local YMCA, martial arts academy or health club.

Happier Happy Hours

Where do you live? Or, more important, where do you drink? If you drink in Alaska, Arizona, Hawaii, Indiana, Kansas, Maine, Massachusetts, Michigan, Nebraska, New Jersey, Ohio, Rhode Island, Texas or Virginia, you might be *un*happy to know that these states have laws or regulations concerning happy hours.

Those of you in other states, stop chuckling. You may be next. Other states are considering putting controls on happy hours.

HARD TIMES FOR HARD LIQUOR

The laws seem to be having an effect on our drinking habits. According to Impact Databank of New York City, consumption of alcoholic beverages has risen only slightly, up to 6.6 billion gallons in one year, compared to previous, bigger jumps.

And *what* we're drinking is also changing. People are drinking an average of only 1.63 gallons per person per year of liquor, down 17 percent in one decade.

But wherever and whatever you drink, the key is to maximize the personal and social pleasures and stay away—far away—from abuse. To do that, you need to drink *smart*.

No, "smart" isn't the latest low-alcohol beer. It's an attitude, a way to add an ounce of caution and judgment to whatever you're drinking. Here are a few smart tips from Roger E. Vogler, Ph.D., author of *The Better Way to Drink*.

Drink to enhance, not escape. Alcohol should be used for making good things better, not bad things okay. Using alcohol as a "cure" is the first step toward making drinking a disease.

Avoid drinking every day. Daily drinking can lead not just to habituation but also to increased tolerance to alcohol, necessitating the use of more to achieve the same effect. Taking even just one or two days off a week can prevent this.

Drink slowly. Many people wind up overdrinking for the simple reason that they don't give their drinks enough time to take effect. It takes 20 to 30 minutes for a drink (12 ounces of beer, 4 ounces of wine or 1¼ ounces of 80-proof liquor) to do its thing, so wait *at least* that long before pouring yourself another.

Consider drink substitutes. Whether they know it or not, many people drink for reasons that have little to do with the effects of alcohol. They enjoy making the drink, holding the drink, hearing the ice cubes jingle. These associated factors impart as much if not more pleasure than the actual booze they're drinking. These people should try drink substitutes: drinks containing either very little alcohol or no alcohol at all (see the table, "How Low Can You Go," at right.

Obey the "55 Rule." Whether it's with blood alcohol levels or with a car, the key to safety is not to exceed the "speed limit" of 55. With an automobile this is 55 miles per hour, of course, but with alcohol it's the percentage of alcohol in the blood. For most people, this means roughly two drinks in an hour—a point beyond which the positive effects of alcohol begin to diminish and the negative ones increase.

Strain on the liver, loss of physical coordination, loss of emotional control, increased likelihood of accidents and hangovers—all these negative consequences begin to increase

How Low Can You Go?

If you like to drink but don't like to get drunk, here's the lowdown on the amount of alcohol in some common beverages found on the bar.

Beverage	Alcohol by Weight (%)
Most hard liquors (bourbon, Scotch, vodka, gin)	40–50
Cordials and liqueurs	18–30
Fortified wines (sherry, port)	18–20
Table wines (rosé, chablis, burgundy, sauterne)	11–14
Light wines (alcohol-reduced)	7–8
Wine coolers	5–6
Regular beer	4–5
Light beer	3.5–4.3
Low-alcohol beer	1.7–1.8
Alcohol-free beer	0–0.5

beyond a blood alcohol level of 0.055, while alcohol's positive effects (stress relief, feelings of optimism and well-being) begin to decline.

LESS IS MORE

No question about it—there are times when a cold beer, a glass of fine wine or a well-made mixed drink is among life's greater pleasures. But there are a lot of other times when business or social occasions leave you drinking almost perfunctorily, just because a lunch partner or waiter keeps urging you to have more.

If you find yourself in a situation where you're almost expected to drink but you don't want to get drunk, here are some tips from Richard Basini, author of *How to Cut Down Your Social Drinking.*

Stop early. "Cocktail hour" is a misnomer—most of them last nearly two, if not longer. Set a cutoff time for yourself, or stop when you start to feel the effects. Drink only nonalcoholic beverages after that.

Switch on and off. An alternative to stopping: Follow every drink you have with a glass of water. You'll always have something in your hand to sip, but you'll be getting half the liquor and calories.

Dilute your drink. Start out with a regular drink, but when it's half gone, add water or soda to it. Every time your glass is half empty again, add more water or soda.

Sip slowly. A warm martini, flat gin and tonic or diluted bloody Mary isn't very appealing. The longer your drink lasts, the less you'll feel like finishing it.

Cheers!

Know Your Limit

You're at a family barbecue. It's hot, you're thirsty and the beer's on tap—cold and foamy. You guzzle down a mug fast. That helps. Now you're on your second, going a little slower. By the end of the third mug, someone says the hamburgers are almost ready. Just before you sit down to eat, your cousin asks you to drive home and get the volleyball net you forgot to bring. It's only a 3-mile drive, but when you stand up to go, you feel a little unsteady. Should you get behind the wheel or send someone else?

The answer—emphatically—is, *send someone else!* Check out the accompanying table and you'll see that for most women and men, there will be some impairment of driving skills after only 2 drinks. You'd have to weigh a hefty 180 pounds or more to be unaffected by that amount. Sure, you might pass a breath test if you were stopped by the police, but do you really want to take the chance of causing an injury to yourself or others because you weren't at your sharpest?

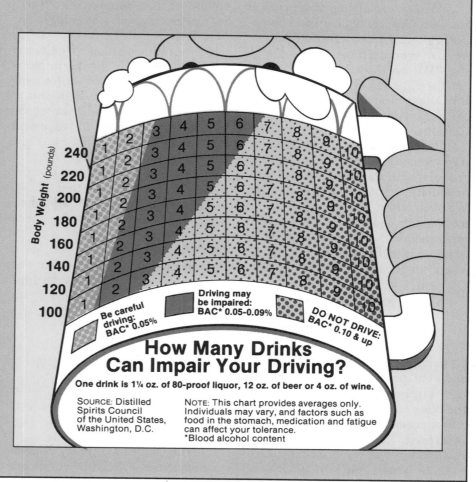

How Many Drinks Can Impair Your Driving?

One drink is 1¼ oz. of 80-proof liquor, 12 oz. of beer or 4 oz. of wine.

Be careful driving: BAC* 0.05%

Driving may be impaired: BAC* 0.05-0.09%

DO NOT DRIVE: BAC* 0.10 & up

SOURCE: Distilled Spirits Council of the United States, Washington, D.C.

NOTE: This chart provides averages only. Individuals may vary, and factors such as food in the stomach, medication and fatigue can affect your tolerance.
*Blood alcohol content

Spectacular Spectating

People were made to be spectators. What else could have possibly led us to invent chairs with hinged seats!

We *need* cap nights, bleachers and box seats. We *need* popcorn and pomp, Carnegie and Candlestick. And yes, we may even need the Mets.

"We are brought up as social creatures," says J. Wilbert Edgerton, Ph.D., a professor in the Department of Psychiatry at the University of North Carolina.

"We appreciate events from the standpoint of being a member of a group. It's one way of not feeling lonely or solitary, sort of like a shared mind. We need others to share with us, and we need to share what we see with other members of the audience. Being a spectator is almost like belonging to a support group."

PART OF THE IN-CROWD

"Gentlemen, start your engines!" "The Cubs have won the pennant, the Cubs have won the pennant!" "Ladies and gentlemen, Barbra Streisand!"

The race, the game, the concert, the place to be. Dr. Edgerton says we also spectate so we can be part of the in-crowd. "Nobody wants to be excluded. We all want to be included, to know what's going on. That's also why we spectate."

And it seems that almost no one is being excluded. According to researchers at Northeastern University's Center for the Study of Sport in Society, 19 percent of the American public—35 million people or so—consider themselves ardent spectators, going to more than 20 events a year. And 70 percent—or more than 120 million of us—consider ourselves to be "moderate" spectators, going to only 20 or less events a year.

Spectating also spurs our emotions. "When we yell 'kill the umpire!'" says Dr. Edgerton, "We don't really want to physically kill him. But by being a part of an audience we can legitimately feel anger and express it. It gives us an outlet for exercising hostilities."

How many times have you personally won the World Series? Or been in perfect key singing an aria at the Met? Or the first to pass the checkered flag at Indy?

"We identify with the people who play the game. Every mistake they make hurts us, and every triumph they have, we triumph with them," says Dr. Edgerton.

A SPECTACULAR VIEW

There isn't a bad place to view the Grand Canyon from. Unfortunately, most teams or concerts don't play there.

They do, though, play in places that have steel poles, tiny scoreboards miles away, and something called "loge seating."

There's no use trying to sit where all the best plays will take place, because they will always happen on the other side of the field. But there is a way to get a good seat: Check out where the game or event is taking place—ahead of time.

Take it from a man who knows how to buy tickets. William Schmitt is president of Ticketron in New York City, where about 60 million tickets are sold each year. He has a unique method for trying to get the best seat.

"What I did when I wanted to buy New York Jets tickets was to go over to the stadium during the day and look around," he relates. "I tried to find a good seat before I bought the

Did You Damage Your Hearing?

The last notes have been played, but your ears are still ringing. Have you damaged your ears at the latest concert?

One way to help you find out is to call Dial-A-Hearing-Screening-Test. When you call the national information center at 1-800-222-EARS, an operator there will give you the number in your locale. When you call the local number, you'll hear 4 tones and a message. If you hear all 4 tones, your hearing is fine. If you don't, you may have hearing problems, and you should have it checked out by a physician.

The hotline is not for children's hearing or for diagnostic purposes.

Tailgating in Any Weather

Tailgating in Pittsburgh in the wintertime is not for the meek. Bob Garritano is known to Pittsburgh Steelers followers as the team's number one fan. This is what he says he packs to help stay warm when it gets to be 10 or 20 degrees below zero.

"You've got to have a big crock of chili, the spicier the better. Then some seafood soup and definitely a big huge pan of macaroni spiced with Italian sausage. We also have a wide variety of breads for insulation and some white pizza. Then we wash it all down with a bloody Mary, hot toddy or hot chocolate."

Is 110°F to 115°F hot enough for you? That's not the temperature of the food but how hot it can get outside when the Arizona State University Sun Devils play in their stadium in Tempe, Arizona. Ron and Helen Wunderley go to every game, and while their tailgates may be hot, their menu is not.

Helen says, "Appetizers start with a cold, 10-layer bean dip with guacamole, then we have a 7-foot-long submarine sandwich with lean meat, tomatoes and greens. We also serve cold marinated mushrooms and cold marinated cherry tomatoes with a cold pasta salad. Then for dessert we have lots of cold fresh fruit in a fruit salad or Popsicles."

wear heavy socks, then stick your feet in plastic bags, then put your boots on. It keeps your feet dry. We also wear snowmobile suits and parkas. Now we even have seat pillows that warm up when you sit on them."

The spectators in Miami, on the other hand, don't have quite the same problem. Al Bellamy, a trainer for the University of Miami Hurricanes, says sometimes spectators watch the games in 95°F to 100°F heat. For hot-weather spectators he advises, "Wear light-colored, loose clothing."

Drink lots of nondehydrating liquids like water and juices. Stay away from alcohol, which can be dehydrating. And wear something to protect your head, like a hat or cap.

SPECTATOR SURVIVAL KIT

If you don't want to make a spectacle out of yourself, here's a list of other things that you might want to bring with you to the event.

● Radio—It's a little hard to hear the stadium announcer with thousands of fans screaming and stomping their feet. Bring one with an earplug and listen to the play-by-play.
● Television—Some of the newer, smaller models fit in the palm of your hand. If the game is sold out and being broadcast in your area, bring one of these and you'll get to watch all the replays. You'll be the most popular person in your section.
● Cushion—The players wear padding, so you should, too. Some of the newer cushions actually hold beverages in them. So on cold days, fill your cushion up with hot coffee.
● Binoculars—We all can't sit in the first row. Binoculars will help get you out of the cheap seats.
● Tickets—Ah, yes, the time to check to see if you have them is when you're in your driveway . . . not in their parking lot.

tickets. Seating arrangements don't show you everything. This way I knew what the place really looked like, and I had a better chance of getting a good seat."

SAY WHAT?

Okay, you've got good seats. You can see everything. You watch the band come on stage, pick up their instruments, turn them on—then blast you back a few aisles.

According to audiologist Stephen Roberts, Ph.D., in Fresno, California, rock concerts can wreck your ears. "In fact, many of the musicians have noise-induced hearing loss. Some of them even wear an earplug in one of their ears to protect the hearing in one ear while monitoring their voices in the other."

For frequent rock-concertgoers, he recommends following the musicians' lead and then going one better. "Put earplugs in both ears to protect your high-frequency hearing. Any time you leave a concert and you have a ringing in your ears, you have trauma-tized your ears. To protect against this, go buy a set of earplugs. Buy the kind that will expand in your ear once they are in place. Or get a pair custom made by an audiologist. You will still be able to hear the concert, but the noise won't be as loud and your ears won't be traumatized. It'll bring the music down to a level that's comfortable to listen to."

OUTDOOR SURVIVAL

From earplugs . . . to earmuffs. Here's a fact of life. It only snows in NFL cities on Sundays between 1:00 P.M. and 4:00 P.M. If there's overtime, it snows longer.

You can fight back, though. Cold weather does not stop the spectators in Green Bay from watching the Packers. Shirley Leonard of the Green Bay Packers public relations department remembers one time when it snowed 14 inches during one game.

She says Green Bay Packer spectators come prepared, with "electric socks and gloves that keep your hands and feet warm. A good thing to do is

Don Barone

Dance
Your Troubles Away

The place: a playpen. Inside its mesh walls, a toddler moves to a tune on the radio. Her bundled bottom dips down, then up. Her pudgy arms flap like a chicken. Soon her whole body is wiggling and she gurgles with delight. This baby has just performed her first dance.

The place: A park bandshell. A group of senior citizens is listening to a rousing rendition of "Stars and Stripes Forever." Their heads start swaying, their toes start tapping. The folks in the back get up and start moving; no one can sit still to this music.

You don't have to look far to see people of all ages dancing. In fact, you don't even have to leave home. Just flip on the TV and wait for a commercial. You'll see a bunch of people high-stepping their way across your screen, waving soft drinks, cereal bowls or hamburgers, or shimmying around some shiny new car.

"There isn't a society in the world that doesn't dance," says dance therapist Susan Singer, director of activity therapies at Friends Hospital in Philadelphia. Dance is a part of every culture, from primitive fertility rites to debutante balls.

And people are doing more every-day dancing, too, especially since watching John Travolta hustle his white-suited body across the lighted dance floor in the film *Saturday Night Fever.*

The reason for such dedicated dancing? "It lets you feel your alive-ness," says Tara Stepenberg, move-ment studies teacher at Naropa Institute in Boulder, Colorado. But perhaps another dance instructor puts it best when she says, "Dancing. It's like someone put every single aspect of life, living and exercise into a bucket and poured the contents into the dance studio. It's a great feeling."

THE BENEFITS OF DANCING

For some people, however, the last time they danced was when Miss Fern *made* them dance way back in the seventh grade. Remembering the sweaty palms and the two left feet, they now figure, Who needs it?

"Society has all kinds of ways to separate us from our bodies," says Carol Kahn Presant, communications direc-tor for the American Dance Therapy Association based in Columbia, Maryland. "There are taboos about moving our bodies as adults. It's the notion that if it feels good, it must be bad."

Choosing the Best Step for You

With so many dances, how to choose? The simplest way is to watch different dances until you find one that makes you say, "Hey, I want to do that, too." Here are some other guidelines.

● For strength and control, try ballet. It's disciplined, structured and can help you get in touch with your body.
● For shaping up, your best bets are belly dancing, dancercise or anything with continuous aerobic movement that uses lots of muscle groups.
● For self-expression, jazz and mod-ern dance are earthy and will help you feel emotionally balanced.
● For socializing, Fred Astaire fans will find ballroom dances—from the rumba to the foxtrot—glamorous, grace-ful ways to hold someone close. But if square dancing or folk dancing is more your style, you're bound to find lots of people contact with little pressure. "Because you come to dance, you're not under pressure to initiate a ro-mance," says dance instructor Edith Jason. "You release and have a darn good time. If perchance you find romance, that's a fringe benefit."
● For letting yourself go, head for a place with a live band or a great juke box. Imitate what others are doing or invent your own dance.

But people who succumb to that taboo are missing out on the whole point of dancing. "The idea is to get back to that authentic movement—back to that sensation we felt as toddlers, when dancing made us feel strength and control, and at one with our body."

Dancing can keep you healthy in other ways, too. Let's take a look.

It keeps you fit. Dancing can keep you limber and put roses in your cheeks and sparkle in your eyes. You might even shed a few pounds.

Dance makes for a painless aerobic workout, according to internationally recognized folk dance instructor Jules Bender from Plainview, New York. "You experience increased respiration and circulation, deep breathing, a fresh supply of blood and oxygen to organ systems, improved metabolism and digestive systems and better neuromuscular coordination."

Ballroom dancing, says Shari Goldstein, spokesperson for the Arthur Murray dance studios, offers such an excellent, low-impact aerobic workout that one dancer "had to take up jogging to maintain her stamina and energy levels during national dance competitions!"

It lifts your spirits. "When I focus on moving my body," says Steven Wistrich, head of the dance program at United States International University, "the troubles in my head slip away."

The idea that the body can often help solve the mind's problems has not gone unnoticed by the mental health profession. A growing form of counseling called "dance therapy" is based on the theory that moving the body can sometimes help people express and work out troubling feelings better than words.

"When you are down and out, just moving helps," says Singer. "Dancing is a step in the right direction. You won't dance away your troubles, but your stress will be reduced."

Your body becomes your friend. Dancing can help you learn

Shake Up a Storm This Vacation

Retired attorney Jules Bender, 72, says that his tense, anxious, typical Type-A personality brought him nothing but a heap of heart trouble. Then he discovered folk dancing.

"My body felt cleansed and restored physically, mentally and emotionally," says Bender, who is now an internationally recognized folk dance instructor. "It's just what the doctor ordered, a nonverbal, noncompetitive fun activity in a social setting."

And now he doles out this particular brand of medicine to others on a regular basis. Each summer, he and his associate Edith Jason conduct Wellness Week Vacations and folk dancing weekends where they teach various activities, including dance, among the serene mountains of Massachusetts and New York. Participants dine on various ethnic cuisines, then take a dancing trip to places from Italy to Israel without the hassle of customs and airports.

You're no Gene Kelly, you say? No sweat, says Bender. "If you can walk, you can dance." The steps are easy to imitate, not taxing and can be picked up by people of all ages and skill levels. More information can be obtained by writing to Bender at 42 Gilbert Lane, Plainview, NY 11803.

If you'd rather kick up your heels than put them up, try one of the several dance getaways offered in your area. Contact People's Folk-Dance Directory, P.O. Box 8575, Austin, TX 78713.

When you dance regularly, you increase body awareness, adds Presant. You become sure-footed and free of the fear of falling. You may soon find yourself climbing and trying other kinds of movement.

It makes you feel young. "Movement is the essence and secret of healthier, happier aging," writes Raymond Harris, M.D., medical consultant to the President's Council for Physical Fitness and Sports.

Dance can keep you up and about, independent and happy. Square dancing, for example, forces you to listen and respond to a caller's commands; it forces you to interact with the outside world. "Physically, it's excellent, and mentally, you've got to be alert because you're always listening to the caller. In Florida, there are a lot of older people who do this, and it keeps these people alive," comments one enthusiastic square dancer.

It brings people together. "It feels very good to be dancing and moving and looking at smiling faces in a circle," says Edith Jason, who teaches international folk dance. "When you hold hands in a circle, you feel the energy of others, an appreciation of culture, a natural urge to be in harmony."

DUST OFF YOUR DANCING SHOES

If your dancing feet are a bit rusty, try the following suggestions.

● Practice solo dancing. Put on your favorite music, close your eyes and go with the rhythm—just like you did when you were a toddler. Try tossing a few scarves or balloons around. They're great dance inspirations.
● Join a dance class. Look for instructors who pay attention to how movement feels, include warm-ups and cool-downs and have a well-ventilated room with inspiring music.

to like the way your body moves, says psychotherapist Bunny Dickerman, a member of the Academy of Dance Therapists Registry. "You see your body not as a focus of problems but as a source of satisfaction."

Marcia Holman

Music Therapy: Melodies That Mellow

"My clients' hang-ups were affecting my ability to sleep," says Charles S. Russ, Jr., president of a consulting firm in Kansas City, Missouri. "I was lucky to catnap a few hours a night."

Finally, Russ turned to Janalea Hoffman, one of an estimated 4,500 registered music therapists in the United States who use music to relieve distress. After only two sessions, he found himself sleeping much of the night. Laughs Russ, "Most of the terminated executives who come to me are wound tight as springs. I make them see Jan while we work together. I decided what was good for the goose is good for the gander."

Why is music so effective in relaxing muscles and minds? "No one knows exactly," says Alicia Clair Gibbons, Ph.D., director of music therapy at the University of Kansas and past president of the National Association for Music Therapy. "Music somehow influences our heart rate and breathing. It also helps release emotional stress in a nonthreatening way."

MUSIC TO YOUR EARS

If you're going to try music, what type should you choose? Whatever works, most experts say. Dr. Gibbons explains, "What helps you sleep may agitate or depress me. The 'right' music depends on our cultural background, our preference and our mood."

Still, many therapists agree on certain rules of thumb. Slow music sedates us more often than fast music. Strings and woodwinds are more soothing than trumpets and trombones. Music lacking the percussion of rock or the syncopation of jazz is easier to relax to than music with an intrusive beat.

Avoid lyrics, say the pros. Either we keep ourselves too busy trying to understand the words or we visualize what the singer looks like. These activities ruffle our minds. For the same

Tunes Build Muscle Tone

If you're a shower-stall serenader or a housecleaning crooner, keep it up. A study reported in the *American Journal of Nursing* suggests singing may be good aerobic exercise.

Twenty opera singers were compared with a group of nonsingers and, sure enough, the singers had more cardiorespiratory pizzazz.

"Singing is a conditioning exercise of the muscles of respiration," the researchers concluded. "It very efficiently tones up the chest wall muscles in a manner similar to swimming, rowing and yoga."

reason, it's a good idea to avoid music that summons up memories, pleasant or not.

TUNING IN TECHNIQUES

Professionals use music in a variety of ways to help their clients sleep. A sampling of four suggested techniques follows. Give yourself up to two weeks to get expected results.

Respondent conditioning. "It works for me!" says Shira Kaskowitz, a music therapist at Washington Hospital, Fremont, California. As Pavlov's dogs learned to drool at the sound of a bell, so we can learn to sleep by hearing the same music each night. Here are the steps to follow.

● Listen to various pieces of music to find one that seems most restful to you.
● After turning out the light, turn on the piece of music you selected. Listen to it over and over until you fall asleep.
● Listen to this same selection each night when you're ready to sleep, but don't listen to it any other time. Eventually the music will stimulate a "time to sleep" response, and you'll drift off before it has hardly begun.

What music does Kaskowitz use for her own respondent conditioning?

An extended version of the Pachelbel Canon in D, on the album and tape *Timeless Motion*, by Daniel Kobialka. She also recommends Kolbialka's *Fragrances of a Dream*.

Calming disquieting thoughts. Here are the steps psychotherapist Mark Stanford, Ph.D., who is in private practice in San Jose, California, suggests taking when your mind is racing.

● Turn on the light; fix something soothing to drink.
● Get comfortable, turn on music that makes you feel good, close your eyes a moment and listen. The music provides a focal point to help you feel in control.
● Write down in a notebook whatever thoughts the music suggests, no matter how little sense they seem to make. Keep listening and writing until you feel sleepy.
● The next day, read over what you wrote and share it with a counselor or friend.

Following this regimen will help keep your mind clear at night, allowing you to sleep, according to Dr. Stanford.

Tonal massage. By visualizing tones massaging our bodies, we relax muscles and promote inner harmony. The more harmonious we feel, the more easily we fall asleep. Janalea Hoffman, who is in private practice in Missouri, suggests taking the following steps.

● Turn on the music and concentrate on the sounds while clearing your mind of regrets and worries.
● Imagine that the tones, starting at your feet, are moving up your legs and into your abdomen like the fingers of a masseur or masseuse.
● Imagine how your heart looks, with its valves and vessels, then imagine how your lungs look with their air sacs and branches. Visualize the tones relaxing these organs, slowing down and regularizing their rhythms.

● Visualize the tonal fingers working on your shoulders and neck, then on your jaw, eyeballs and temples.
● Visualize the tones entering and tuning your glandular system, especially the lymph nodes, pancreas and liver. Imagine how the glands begin to work together, at an appropriate pace.
● Visualize your muscles, organs and glands as a complex machine with all the parts interacting in harmony. Your increasingly slow, even breathing lets you know that you are about to fall asleep.

Breathing away muscle tension. After he retired, Howard developed tinnitus, a whistling in his ears that kept him awake most of the night. Medication was suggested, but clinical psychologist Stephen Kibrick, Ph.D., in Calabasas, California, urged him first to try breathing and meditating to music. In four weeks, the tinnitus vanished. Here's how to do it.

● Put on some appropriate music, like *Relax Yourself Music*, a tape Dr. Kilbrick produced with Jean Hattem, R.N., with music by Fred Caban.

● Think about nothing except your breathing. Say to yourself something like this: "I am relaxing, breathing slowly and rhythmically. With each easy breath I feel more and more relaxed."
● Breathe in and out several times as you focus on successive groups of muscles. Start with your toes and ankles, move to your legs, then to your buttocks and lower back, your abdomen, your hands and wrists, your chest, your shoulders and neck, your face and scalp, your jaw. Feel each muscle group grow heavy and relaxed.
● Picture in succession three numbers appearing on a blackboard. Take a deep breath as you conjure up each number. For example, the first number, 3, is your symbol for complete body relaxation. The number 2 is your symbol for complete mental relaxation. The number 1 is your symbol for oneness of mind and body.
● Drift with the music for a few minutes longer until you fall asleep.

Michael Scofield

The Anti-Headache Harmony

Can you get in harmony with your headache? One study group seemed to have tuned out their migraines when they listened to music.

In a follow-up survey done at California State University, Janet Lapp, Ph.D., a clinical psychologist and former professor of psychology, found that a group that listened to music reported significantly fewer and less intense migraine headaches than other no-music groups who had participated in the same study.

"I was surprised," said Dr. Lapp, "But in fact, they reported their headaches were reduced from a frequency of 2 to 0.3 migraines in an average week."

Dr. Lapp says that the relaxation skills that the group had learned were enhanced by listening to music. Whenever they heard music throughout the day, it served as a cue to practice their relaxation and visualization techniques.

Television: Keeping It in Focus

You flip on the 6:00 P.M. news and before you know it, your spouse is saying goodnight and you realize you've just devoted 6 precious hours of your day to the old boob tube—again.

Is it a sign that you're a television addict?

"Television is a wonderful medium, and there's certainly nothing wrong with watching it," says Frank Palumbo, M.D., a member of the task force on children and television of the American Academy of Pediatrics. "You've had a long day, you come home, you want to watch the news or one or two shows you really like. It's very enjoyable. But if you find yourself spending 6 hours in front of the set every night, something is probably missing in your life. As with any other addiction, you need to look at it and see how it's affecting you."

HOW TO CONTROL YOUR HABIT

"The amount of TV people watch is really related to their total style of life," says George Gerbner, Ph.D., professor of communications and dean at the Annenberg School at the University of Pennsylvania. It doesn't matter what the programming is. As people have less and less to do, they watch more and more TV because it's very attractive. It relates them to places and people from around the world. Here's what you can do to keep viewing time in check.

Expand your interests. "If you want to change your viewing habits, make sure you don't just deny yourself," he says. You need to find activities and interests that are more exciting to you than watching TV.

Make TV a planned activity. Choose in advance the programs you want to watch and watch only those programs. Make your selection by checking a TV guide rather than by flipping through the channels. Make sure you have another activity to pick up when the program is over. Most important, turn the set *off*.

Fight inertia. It's easy to slip into a "TV trance" when your eyes are planted on the screen for an hour or more. No wonder the hours slip away. Refocus your thoughts by turning off the sound during commercials. Talk. Read. Do ten push-ups. Use the break to ask yourself, Is this really what I want to be doing tonight?

Keep your set in an inaccessible place. If all your living room furniture is arranged to face the set or if the TV is the first thing you reach for when you walk in the door, you're likely to watch it too much. Move it to an out-of-the-way spot, such as the corner of the room or the spare bedroom.

ARE YOU RAISING A COUCH POTATO?

Kids from ages 2 to 12 watch approximately 25 hours of TV a week—more time than a student spends in the classroom, according to the American Academy of Pediatrics. And the negatives of heavy viewing are heavyweight: It has a deleterious effect on schoolwork, encourages snacking (which can lead to obesity) and conveys unrealistic messages about drugs, alcohol, tobacco and sexual relations.

Also, according to the academy, numerous studies show that children and teenagers can imitate the violence they see on television. Children's shows are six times as violent as adult shows, and the average child sees over 12,000 acts of violence on television every year, according to the academy. Cartoons contain an average of 20 violent acts an hour.

"We're the only civilized country in which the schlockiest, cheapest material is given to children. What we're doing to the children of this nation is a disgrace," says Dr. Gerbner, who suggests that parents pressure their legislators to improve children's programming. You can also join the efforts of Action for Children's Television (ACT), a nonprofit member-

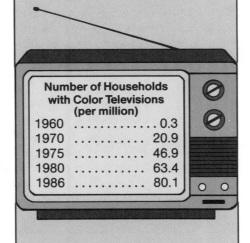

Color It Real

"What color was the world when you didn't have color TV?" a 10-year-old asked her father. It's a question that startled the father, who was born about the same time as TV, and one that is likely to come out of the mouth of any youngster today. As the following chart shows, our priorities in viewing have changed dramatically since 1960.

Number of Households with Color Televisions (per million)	
1960	0.3
1970	20.9
1975	46.9
1980	63.4
1986	80.1

ship organization working to improve the quality of children's TV experiences. For information, write ACT, 20 University Road, Cambridge, MA 02138.

In the meantime, however, there's plenty you can do right in your own home to keep your kids from becoming "vidiots."

Set a time clock. Have your kids keep a record of how much TV they actually watch—you may both be dismayed. Together, set a maximum time limit. Many experts suggest that 2 hours a day is the most a child should watch TV. Be flexible, however. A child may grow resentful if occasional exceptions cannot be made.

"Don't be afraid to turn off the set after a couple of hours," advises Dr. Palumbo. "They may scream and tell you you're horrible, but you'll probably find that within 10 or 15 minutes, they're doing something else."

Parents, unite. Arrange a meeting with parents of your kids' friends to discuss your TV-time campaign. They may want to join you. This way, your child can be part of a group rather than feeling like the odd kid out.

Teach discriminating viewing. Watch your kids' favorite shows with them, then discuss the programs. If you find a program objectionable, tell them why you don't want them to watch it again.

Suggest they go through the viewers' guide at the beginning of each week and select the shows they want to watch. Discuss the selections with them. Have they chosen a variety or do they have a heavy concentration of police shows or cartoons?

Watch and discuss. If your kids are hooked on violent shows, watch with them and discuss other, better, ways of expressing anger or disagreement. What would happen in real life if people behaved as they do on "Miami Vice"?

Make them aware of TV stereotypes, particularly in afternoon reruns of old shows. What roles do women

and minorities play? Is everyone on TV thin and gorgeous?

Discuss TV values. Are the successful heroes and heroines ruthless, corrupt and power hungry? Do their cars cost more than your family's home?

Help them understand commercials. Ask your kids: "How do advertisers lure viewers? What's really in those cereals and those candy bars? Can those toys really perform like they do on TV?"

To help cut quantity time to quality time, experts also recommend these dos and don'ts.

Is There Life after TV?

Suppose, just as an experiment, you unplugged your TV set for 30 days. Would your family just shrivel away, starved for electronic nourishment? Or would you all grow and prosper?

The citizens of Farmington, Connecticut, launched a campaign to find out just what would happen. Their Big Turnoff was the brainstorm of Nancy DeSalvo, children's services coordinator at the town's public library. She was appalled at the poor listening skills of elementary school children who came to the library. The kids couldn't understand a story without a picture to accompany the words. She found out they were watching an average of 24½ hours of TV a week!

The library council decided that January would be a good month to inaugurate the first Turnoff and scheduled a full calendar of events to compensate for TV.

"The first week, there was a certain amount of withdrawal," says DeSalvo. "They didn't know what to do with themselves. At first, they just moped around. Then they started talking to each other and many other good things came of it."

Circulation of children's books in the libraries went way up, reports DeSalvo. Grades went up, too, particularly for kids in the C and D range.

"Teachers also noticed a great decrease in aggression," says DeSalvo. "Three-quarters of the kids in one kindergarten class, for example, watched 'The A-Team' every Tuesday night. Their teacher reported there was a lot less pushing around in the playground on Wednesdays when they hadn't watched the show."

Families went to sporting events together, played board games and outdoor games and did arts and crafts. One boy reported that his basketball skills improved considerably.

After the Turnoff, many families reduced their viewing hours permanently. "We don't recommend that people turn it off forever," says DeSalvo. "It'll always be with us. But if a child watches more than 12 hours a week, grades will go down."

The Farmington Library Council has prepared a "TV Turnoff Kit" to help other communities plan a similar event. To order, contact Nancy DeSalvo at the Farmington Library, P.O. Box 407, Farmington, CT 06032.

● Use a video cassette recorder to make your kids' schedule more flexible and cut down on sibling squabbles. This way, a favorite show can be recorded when homework needs to be done.

● Don't use TV as a punishment or reward. You don't want to give it that kind of importance.

● Don't put a TV in the child's room. Remember, you want to be able to participate.

Diane Fields

Shopping: A Great Release for Stored-Up Stress

It's lunchtime. You've been in meetings since 10:00 A.M. You've had it with the broncos, the stallions, the bulls and every other form of galloping ego. Clearly, you need a break. You need to zap your level of stress before it zaps you. And before you have to deal with the same herd of critters *after* lunch.

What you need is a 60-minute vacation. But how? And where?

The answer—at least for many women—is at the mall. Or the department store. Maybe even the corner bath boutique. And if that sounds strange, well, international retail consultant Bill Huckabee, president of C. W. Ress & Associates in Columbus, Ohio, says he believes that shopping as a form of rest and recreation—R & R—is far from unusual.

ME-CENTERED SHOPPING

That's because Huckabee is a marketing whiz, a student of how people respond to various situations and why they do what they do. Just as a scientist puts cells under a microscope, Huckabee puts groups of people under the penetrating gaze of marketing experts who are dedicated to figuring out why they buy, when they buy, and how they can be encouraged to buy more.

His results are intriguing. Basically, Huckabee says, his groups have shown that there are two kinds of shopping. There's routine shopping for the kids' shoes, the husband's tie, the groceries. And then there's a kind of me-centered shopping that seems to be either a vacation for your mind or a reward for doing all the things that you're supposed to do.

"Look, lady, if it's trendy you want, Bloomie's is at Fifty-ninth and Lex."

Drawing by Geo. Price; © 1982
The New Yorker Magazine, Inc.

"We did a recent group interview in the Chicago area with a home-decorating–type store," Huckabee recalls. "Women in the group said they'd go shopping in this particular store after they'd finished their food shopping, which was boring and tedious.

"We asked them why, and the answer we got was, 'It's therapy. I can go into a trance. I love the quiet atmosphere, the soft music in the background. And I may or may not buy anything. But I get pictures in my head of how it might be used in my home, how I might get it as a gift.'"

The result? A relaxed woman at peace with the world.

But wait. Can't men use shopping the same way? Well, maybe they can, Huckabee says, but most don't. It doesn't seem to come naturally to them. "Except in hardware stores and bookstores," the retail consultant observes, "men want to get in and get out."

YOUR SHOPPER'S LIST

Forget the men. They're still underprivileged. Focus on you. How can *you* make shopping a mini-vacation? Here are a few fun-oriented tips from Dallas-based Neiman-Marcus, a store famous for catering to expensive and one-of-a-kind tastes.

Choose a store that knows you. That means a store with wide aisles and an uncluttered look. Why? Cluttered stores haven't figured out who you are and what you want, so they overwhelm you with choices rather than allowing you the luxury of space.

Shop when nobody else does. That means avoid the weekends and noon lunch hours. Take an early or late lunch or begin your browsing after 7:00 P.M.

Look for stores that maintain client lists. The sales associates at some better stores actually maintain a list of what you buy. So if you want a yellow blouse to go with that daffodil skirt you bought last spring, your sales associate can check her list and tell you right away whether or not they have one in stock that will match. Or, since they know the exact shade and dye lot you're talking about, they can suggest alternatives. A pearl white blouse with a hint of buttercup might work just as well, for example.

Know when your store starts stocking seasonal merchandise. Start shopping for swimwear in April, fall coordinates in July, holiday dresses in October and cruisewear in November. The best choices are at the beginning of a season; the best sales are at the end.

Find a store that does alterations. When you try on a dress, the dressing room assistant can mark the hem and send it off to the sewing room right away. That saves you at least two trips and a fitting at the tailor. And *that* saves wear and tear on the nerves.

Organize. You can keep shopping relaxed by avoiding the frenzied shopping for last-minute presents. Keep a list tucked in your bag or pocket that itemizes upcoming needs—the wedding present in November, the birthday present in July—and check it just before you browse.

Lunch with a purpose. Lunch at an in-store restaurant when there's a fashion show to preview the latest fashions.

Use the store's gift service. Don't race around from department to department looking for that perfect gift. Go to the gift service for suggestions. They're accustomed to the wildest requests. At Neiman-Marcus in Dallas, for example, one client wanted to send his friend a cashmere sweater. Nothing unusual about that. But the client wanted a sheep to go with it. So the gift service called a local animal group, got the sheep, draped the sweater preppie-style around its shoulders and delivered the —uh—package as instructed.

THE PLEASURE IS MINE

Here are more ideas from New York City's famous Bloomingdale's on how to make a shopping trip enjoyable.

Squeeze a puppy. You thought toys were for kids? No way. Especially not at Bloomie's. Stop by the toy department and squeeze one of their lush, plush toys. Puppies and pandas and bears and lambs and kittens and frogs are silky and feel so cuddly.

Sniff the potpourri. Drift by the perfume counter and let the scents of apple, cinnamon, rose or your favorite perfume envelop you.

A Picture's Worth a Thousand Dollars

Does it seem as though dollars float out of your pocket when you shop? Or credit cards offer themselves to salesclerks?

You may not be far wrong. A study by Richard A. Feinberg, Ph.D., at Purdue University has discovered that the very picture of a credit card on a cash register actually stimulates people to buy.

How? "You see a commercial on TV in which someone uses a credit card," Dr. Feinberg says, "and then something good happens." Maybe he gets a toaster oven. Or something he's always wanted. Then you see him get it over and over as the commercial is broadcast again and again and again.

"Next thing you know," Dr. Feinberg says, "all you have to do is see the card on the register and you'll spend. And spend more than if you'd paid cash."

It's totally outside your awareness, the researcher adds. It's caused just by the association of 2 things in time. A credit card. And happiness.

How can you break the connection? "This kind of reaction is not as dramatic as getting drunk or stoned," says San Francisco psychiatrist Carla Perez, M.D. "But it's still an addiction. If you can't control it, get rid of the cards." At the very least, leave them at home.

Use the store's personal shopping service. Many department stores have a group of personal shoppers who can find you almost anything. If you call ahead at Bloomingdale's, for example, your personal shopper will put on a pot of coffee or tea. You'll sit down, get to know one another and share personal preferences in color and style. Then, whether it's a dress, a suit or a set of sheets to go with your new pink bedroom, your personal shopper will take you around the appropriate department and fetch a selection of merchandise that fits your specifications —all while you sip your tea.

Limit your time. Shopping longer than 2 or 3 hours is *not* recreational.

Be comfortable. Low-heeled shoes and support hose may sound unromantic, but they keep you on your toes.

Use the catalogs. Sunday supplement and mail-order catalogs will give you a preview of what's available. Use them the way you would a travel guide.

Test the couches. Rest your feet for just 5 minutes and you can shop for another 20.

Stop off at a tasting bar. Feeling parched? In need of reenergizing? Nibble a delicacy or imbibe the spirit of grapes past. L'chaim!

Get to know the salespeople. They'll let you know when a new edition of your favorite porcelain comes in.

Make the food department your last stop. And no, we're not talking meat and potatoes. Do you eat meat and potatoes on vacation? No. You eat fresh salmon, Sardinian tomatoes and an imported smorgasbord of nuts, figs, dates and other international delicacies. Or at least you'd like to, wouldn't you?

Don't forget the bath oil. Please. Because when you're back at the office butting heads with the herd, you can think ahead to your *next* mini-vacation: a long soak in the tub.

Ellen Michaud

Computer Networking: The Meshing of Minds

You've cheated on your diet twice already today and now you're just about ready to give it all up and sit down to a TV movie with a container of chocolate-chocolate chip. Where do you look for support?

You've just read a fantastic science fiction book and want to share the experience. Where do you turn for fellowship?

You've got an Edsel for sale. You want to trade your house in Maine for an apartment in Pasadena. You've got ideas to share on animal welfare, religion, arms control or Sherlock Holmes. You want information on medical matters, how to slow the aging process, college scholarships, or divorce. You need a job. You want someone with whom to play chess or Dungeons and Dragons. You're an angry wife looking for a forum to let off steam. You're searching for a date, a mate or just a few jokes.

Where do you turn? To your computer! That is, of course, once you've (very simply) hooked your computer into a system that can reach out all over the country to find who or what you need.

HOOKING INTO THE MAIN LINE

Whether it's for business or pleasure, you can make this new trend in personal communication and interaction part of your lifestyle by subscribing to one of the national on-line systems such as BRS after Dark, CompuServe Information Service, The Source and General Electric Network for Information Exchange.

When you subscribe, you will be given a local number for your computer to call; that number will connect you with the national system. You will be charged an hourly rate for using the system. The rates (like telephone rates) are lower in the evening and on weekends than they are during business hours.

A lot of the information available through national systems is for businesspeople, but more and more systems are expanding their offerings to general consumers. Once you join, you will be able to:

- Send a letter to another subscriber.
- Chat with other subscribers who share your special interests.
- Look up information in any of hundreds of journals, encyclopedias and other reference works.
- Sell or buy anything from antiques to yachts.
- Get the weather or the latest news.
- Join group discussions.
- Leave and read messages.
- Play computer games.
- Book travel reservations.
- Take college courses for credit.

You say you don't have the money to spare? Or the need for such a specialized system? Well, you may still be able to hook into a computer network.

ELECTRONIC BULLETIN BOARDS

If you've ever read the personals column in your local newspaper or scanned the message board at the supermarket, you have an idea of the resources you'll be able to tap when you start calling bulletin-board systems (BBSs). Unlike national systems,

Drawing by Stevenson; © 1983 The New Yorker Magazine, Inc.

"Here's the story, gentlemen. Sometime last night, an eleven-year-old kid in Akron, Ohio, got into our computer and transferred all our assets to a bank in Zurich."

most BBSs are free (unless you're calling long distance, of course).

"There are bulletin boards everywhere," says Jeffrey Frentzen, review editor at *PC Resource* magazine. "It's unbelievable how many there are—some are very complicated with several phone lines and several different special interests, some are very bare-bones local systems. You just have to try them out—read the bulletins, see what they offer. And you don't have to be a computer nut to get into a BBS.

"Some are very specialized. I found one that deals with comic books—fans get together and talk. Others deal with computer interests. They're always changing. People usually have several favorites they'll call up every day to see what's happening—maybe there will be an expert on-line, or a conference. Maybe someone leaves a message that looks like it was just for you. Some BBSs are run professionally, others are run by crackpots.

"You connect with a lot of people over great distances or locally. Of course, talking to someone by BBS is even more removed than talking to someone you don't know by phone. But there's still an avenue of communication there that's unique. You can talk to someone at your convenience without having to have them there."

If you don't find an SIG (special interest group) that fits you right away, leave a message on the BBS—"Does anyone know a BBS that specializes in the rights of hospital patients?" Someone very well may. If not, you can organize your own SIG or even your own BBS. That should keep you out of the chocolate-chocolate chip.

GETTING STARTED

To go on-line, all you'll need is a telephone, a computer, a modem and the software program.

A modem is the device that connects your computer to the phone and translates the computer's digital language into audio signals that can be transmitted by phone. A modem on the receiving end will translate those signals back into computer talk. The kind of modem you buy will depend on the kind of computer you have. They range in price from $100 to $1,000.

A telecommunications software package tells the computer how to use the modem to talk on the phone. These programs run $50 and up and are available with numerous different options. For advice, check Mike Cane's invaluable guide to using on-line systems, *The Computer Phone Book*.

Diane Fields

Home Tasks Made Easy

You bought your computer 3 months ago and all you've done with it so far is write a couple of letters? It's time to bring the computer out of the office and put it to work in every room of your house. Once you take the plunge into basic programming, you'll be able to:

● Organize a fingertip phone directory so you never lose another number.
● Keep a log of long-distance calls so you can verify your phone bill.
● File away brief descriptions of magazine articles you may someday want to refer to.
● Track your ever-changing schedule.
● Organize a carpool or babysitting co-op. The computer will never forget that you filled in for Julia last Wednesday or that she worked 2 hours with 1 child at night compared to your 3 hours with 4 kids in the afternoon.
● Set up a family message center.
● Assign chores to all family members.
● See exactly how your room will look before you rearrange your furniture.
● Set up a monthly budget so you can see very clearly just where your money is going.
● Keep handy, easily updated and annotated files of recipes, videotapes, records, warranties on new products and other important "papers."
● Keep track of bills due and compute gains and losses for an extra-income home business.
● Balance your checkbook.

● Register all information about car maintenance, tune-ups and repairs as well as owner's manual information and warranty expiration dates.
● Keep a complete home inventory for insurance purposes.
● Keep a medical record for each member of the family: Inoculations, illnesses, treatments, and children's growth rates can be available for future reference.
● Set up a calendar of important events so you never forget another anniversary.
● Plan menus a week in advance; the computer will help you keep track of nutritional requirements.
● Track your kids. Register your kids' marks and achievements each term—you'll have a historic record to show grandchildren.

Volunteerism: The Great Escape

Who in his right mind would work for no pay? Nearly half of all Americans, that's who.

Whether you've given time and energy to your local hospital, senior citizens' home, arts center, school or soup kitchen; whether you're a teacher's aide, a volunteer firefighter or a door-to-door canvasser for the Elect John Doe Committee, you're in good company: approximately 89 million Americans volunteer, according to a Gallup survey.

The "spirit of volunteerism," President Reagan once said, "flows like a deep and mighty river through the history of our nation."

From where, then, does this river get its depth and might? The classic definition of altruism—an unselfish devotion to the welfare of others—certainly has much to do with why people volunteer, but that's only half the story.

"People who help other people seem to get helped themselves at least as much as the people they help," says Steven J. Danish, Ph.D., chairman of the Psychology Department at Virginia Commonwealth University.

Dr. Danish and others in his field talk of the enormous self-esteem, the pride and the many emotional benefits that can come from volunteering. And that's to say nothing of the job-related skills and professional contacts you can acquire as a volunteer. In some cases, such as pushing a wheelchair, building a cabin in a national park or tending to antelopes at the zoo, volunteering can even be great exercise.

GENERATIONS OF THE GENEROUS

"Anyone who volunteers, whatever the reason, is likely to get hooked," says Rebecca Gurholt, assistant dean of campus life and advisor to Volunteer Emory, a program at Emory University that involves more than 2,000 students and staff in volunteer projects.

Many of the so-called Me generation seem preoccupied with cars and cash but, Gurholt says, many youths "feel a real sense of responsibility. And many others, given a taste of volunteer work, will discover within themselves a capacity to share that will influence the rest of their lives."

Toward the other end of life's spectrum, the benefits of volunteering are only greater, according to Nancy Chapman, Ph.D., acting director of the Institute on Aging, Portland State University. Dr. Chapman has been involved in a number of programs involving older people in volunteering, and many are the times, she says, that participants have told her, "This has really changed my life."

Take an Unvacation

One summer Bill Wilcox, a 68-year-old Washington, D.C., professional, spent his 10-day vacation "working like a dog" in Kentucky's Daniel Boone National Forest. He enjoyed it so much, he decided to go back for more.

Wilcox is 1 of the nearly 300 volunteers who sign up each year with Volunteer Vacations. They spend their summer breaks—voluntarily—breaking their backs. Wilcox heartily recommends it.

Whether it's clearing a path, building a cabin or any of the other chores involved with maintaining our national parks and forests, Wilcox says that the work the volunteers do is "constructive . . . something different . . . great exercise (you'll lose a few pounds) . . . fun . . . and very satisfying."

Teenager Scott Morley, of Battle Creek, Michigan, labored 1 year with his mom, a teacher, and the next year with his dad, a rehabilitation counselor, blazing a trail in Michigan's Manistee National Forest. "You look at it after you're through and you think 'Gee—I made that!'"

Kay Beebe, director of the nonprofit Volunteer Vacations, says the participants range in age from their teens to their 70s and include "doctors, lawyers, physicists, longshoremen, students, farm laborers—all kinds of people."

Board is provided, and you carry your bed (sleeping bag and tent) on your back. Travel expenses are on you.

Interested? For more information, send a business-size, self-addressed, stamped envelope to AHS/Volunteer Vacations, Box 86, North Scituate, MA 02060. Or, for a chock-full-of-information directory, *Helping Out in the Outdoors*, send $3.00 to the American Hiking Society, 1015 31st Street NW, Washington, DC 20007.

"The more active and involved and committed people are, the more they have some kind of goal to work for or someone to work for who needs them, it seems the more likely they are to remain healthy," says Dr. Chapman.

THE PERSONAL REWARDS

Helping others is good medicine at any age, says Robert B. Cialdini, Ph.D., professor of psychology at Arizona State University. Especially when you feel blue, he says, helping someone else can make your spirits soar.

Dr. Cialdini has a theory. He believes that just as Pavlov trained his dogs to react to the tinkle of a bell, so are we humans trained, or conditioned, to feel better when we're helping others.

"By getting rewarded in our culture whenever we have been helpful—the pat on the head, compliments, praise, and so on—helping someone becomes a reward in itself . . . because it gets associated with social rewards in the past," says Dr. Cialdini.

And by no means is there any reason for you to think that your feeling good about helping others in any way diminishes what you are doing, he adds. "Helping makes us feel good . . . there's nothing ignoble about that at all. It is a very positive form of motivation."

It's no coincidence that our society rewards helping behavior, says Dr. Cialdini. "It's very helpful to a society to have people around who are unselfish and generous. So one thing a society does to increase the likelihood of that is to reward such people through esteem, prestige and social approval."

And just how much do volunteers contribute to our society? Statisticians at Independent Sector, a nonprofit group in Washington, D.C., have estimated a dollar value for the volunteer efforts contributed in 1985 by all Americans 14 years of age and older. Their estimate? *$110 billion!*

Russell Wild

A Special Man, A Special Talent

The kid's got the flu, the boss wants that report, and you've got to get that muffler fixed one of these days. Who has any time to volunteer?

Danny Kaye had a pretty busy schedule, too. For nearly half a century, he was one of the most celebrated—and busiest—entertainers in the world. People felt they knew him—and they loved him. Kaye brought his enormous talent to Broadway and Hollywood, radio and television; he was also an accomplished chef, a symphony conductor, an airplane pilot, a husband and a father. But that wasn't all.

The star of such film classics as *Hans Christian Andersen* and *The Secret Life of Walter Mitty* was also a dedicated volunteer. Kaye, for the last 34 years of his life, traveled the world to bring laughter to thousands of underprivileged children as official International Goodwill Ambassador for the United Nations Children's Fund, UNICEF.

In 1975, over a period of 5 days, Kaye piloted the UNICEF ONE plane to 65 U.S. and Canadian cities as part of the "Trick-or-Treat for UNICEF" fund-raising campaign. He is listed in the *Guinness Book of World Records* as the World's Fastest-Flying Entertainer.

Kaye died on March 3, 1987, at age 74. U.N. Secretary General Javier Pérez de Cuéllar called him "a champion for children in every continent."

The champion for children also conducted orchestras for benefit performances, which raised millions for musicians' pension funds. For such humanitarian efforts he received awards from the Prime Minister of Great Britain, the Queen of Denmark and the President of the United States, among others. But the awards were just icing.

"Daddy had a lifelong involvement in giving," says Dena Kaye, the star's daughter. "He would recount his experiences with children and musicians and you knew that they had a lasting impression on him and gratified him in a very special way.

"In giving, he used the very unique talents he had," Dena says of her father. For anyone wishing to volunteer, she adds, "I suppose the important thing is to recognize what your own talents are and to use them. And don't worry if your talents seem less exalted than my father's. He was unique."

I.H.T. CORPORATION
REPRINTED BY PERMISSION

Danny Kaye

chapter seven

CAREFREE TRAVEL

Traveling with Health Problems

Sunny Caribbean beaches, the green glaciers of the Rockies, the noble museums of Italy and Hawaii's lava-floored craters. Exotic locales like these used to be out of reach for people with disabling health problems.

To the heart patient, the kidney patient or the person with emphysema, traveling implied at best an anxious separation from a cardiologist, a dialysis machine or an oxygen tank. It was simply too scary. As a result, the handicapped suffered not only from their disabilities but were also deprived of the pleasure of exploring the world.

But today, as one doctor puts it, "There are fewer and fewer reasons to stay home." In recent years, travel has become much easier for people with partial disabilities. There are organizations that can plug you into a worldwide network of doctors. There are companies that will print your medical history on a wallet-size card. There are oxygen tanks, wheelchairs and specialized meals waiting for you on most commercial airliners. And much, much more.

The following useful pieces of information are designed to make the ill feel more at ease while traveling.

DON'T PLAY FOOTBALL WITH YOUR HEART

They call it airport angina, and if you're an over-40 businessman with a heart condition, it might be your worst travel nightmare. It starts when your limo from downtown gets caught in traffic and arrives late at the airport. To catch your plane, you have to dash across the concourse like O. J. Simpson. Before you know it, your heart pounds, your shoulder tingles and you're reaching for a nitroglycerine tablet.

Preventing airport angina is simple: Just leave plenty of time to catch your plane. Arrive early, check in and settle down with a magazine.

If you wear a pacemaker, remember to write down its make and model, as well as the type of electrode it uses and the date of implant. Make sure your batteries are fresh, and carry your cardiologist's phone number. Airport security devices won't harm the pacemaker.

Also, test your physical strength before your trip. If you can either walk 100 yards or climb a flight of stairs (that's 12 steps) without getting winded, you can probably withstand the stress of air travel. If you have high blood pressure, be wary of unfamiliar beverages. The bottled waters that are sold in many countries as "mineral water" sometimes contain high levels of sodium. If you're traveling with a companion, encourage him to learn cardiopulmonary resuscitation (CPR).

KEEP YOUR BLOOD SUGAR ON AN EVEN KEEL

Long-distance journeys across several time zones can disorient even the perfectly healthy traveler. But for the person who suffers from insulin-dependent diabetes and needs regular injections, such journeys require advance preparation. Intercontinental travel can disrupt the careful schedule of meals and insulin injections

"Cabin Fever" at 35,000 Feet

We take it for granted that modern airliners have pressurized cabins, but it's not widely known that the cabin pressure in most planes is considerably lower than the air pressure at sea level. In fact, cabin pressure can range anywhere from the pressure at Zermatt, Switzerland (5,346 feet) to that at Machu Picchu, Peru (8,052 feet).

That poses a problem for people with a respiratory disease. Before flying, those with emphysema, bronchitis or asthma should test their lung capacity by walking 50 yards without stopping. If they can't do that without getting out of breath, they should call the airline well in advance and ask them to provide oxygen. Written permission from a doctor is usually needed and there is an extra charge. Passengers aren't allowed to bring their own oxygen aboard.

Air travel can complicate a variety of physical conditions. Doctors often recommend that patients refrain from flying for a month after a heart attack and for at least 2 weeks after major surgery. Colostomy patients should consult their doctors before traveling by air. Those with glaucoma or a history of migraine headaches may be adversely affected by the reduced air pressure on planes.

Most major airlines will accommodate a passenger's need for a special diet, such as a low-fat, gluten-free or kosher diet, if contacted in advance.

that keeps a diabetic's blood sugar level on a safe and steady course.

Although changes in insulin dosage should be made only under the supervision of a private physician, specialists offer a few basic rules of thumb for the diabetic traveler.

In general, trips eastward require less insulin, while trips westward require more. Some physicians advise diabetics to use "finger sticks" to test their blood sugar levels every few hours on long flights and to adjust their intake of short-acting insulin accordingly. When they arrive at their destination, they can synchronize with local time. Doctors also make the following recommendations.

● To prevent insulin from being exposed to sunlight and extreme temperatures, insulate the insulin between several layers of clothes to keep it stable.
● Because insulin varies worldwide, carry a spare bottle in the event of loss or theft.
● Carry extra carbohydrate or protein foods such as cheese, crackers, fruit, raisins or candy bars with you in case your in-flight meals aren't served at the best time for you.
● Sight-seeing can cause foot problems. Wear comfortable shoes and check your feet for blisters. Always keep your feet clean and soak them as needed.

DON'T BE A PILL: KEEP MEDICATION HANDY

It happens quite frequently: A traveler packs all of his medication in his suitcases only to discover upon arrival in Bogotá that the airline has sent his baggage to Paramaribo. For people who take drugs for chronic conditions like diabetes, heart disease or depression, being separated from their medication for even one day is like a myope losing his only pair of eyeglasses—or worse.

Hotlines for Help

Do you have a question about traveling with a disability? These sources may have the answers you need.

● International Association for Medical Assistance to Travelers (IAMAT), 417 Center Street, Lewiston, NY 14092 (716) 754-4883. The organization maintains lists of American and English-speaking physicians abroad who agree to provide medical care at low rates.
● American Diabetes Association, 1660 Duke Street, Alexandria, VA 22314 (1-800-ADA-DISC; in Virginia or the District of Columbia, 703-549-1500). The organization offers advice for travelers who have diabetes.
● Society for the Advancement of Travel for the Handicapped, 26 Court Street, Penthouse Suite, Brooklyn, NY 11242 (718) 858-5483. This group offers help for those who won't let a disability keep them at home. When inquiring, send a self-addressed, stamped, business-size envelope. Dues and membership required.

To avoid spoiling your trip, always pack vital medication in your carry-on luggage. If possible, bring enough to last your entire trip, since the brand you take may not be available in more remote parts of the world.

Here are other tips for those who take drugs on a daily basis.

● If you plan to cross several time zones but need to take a pill, such as an oral contraceptive, at the same time every day, carry a cheap watch and keep it set on the time back home. That will help you remember when to ingest the drug.
● Certain narcotics, tranquilizers or sedatives might arouse the suspicion of customs officers. If your drug is a controlled substance, such as a barbiturate, keep it in its original vial and carry a letter from your physician explaining why you need it.

CARRY A CARING CARD

Imagine a situation like this: You've been standing in a hot, crowded, foreign airport for 3 hours, stranded by a cancelled flight. Suddenly you feel light-headed and slump down to the floor. Dozens of people hover over you, but they can't understand a word of your half-gasped English. Even the doctor who elbows through the crowd to assist you has no clue to your medical history and doesn't know where to begin.

When this happens, carrying a card or wearing a bracelet describing your personal health status could save your life. Several sources offer inexpensive, universally recognized metal jewelry or a piece of microfilm embedded in a plastic card that explains your specific condition. There are several sources for these special IDs.

● The Heart Chart, P.O. Box 221, New Rochelle, NY 10804 (914) 632-3388, and William Pinsky, M.D., 2363 North Broad Street, Colmar, PA 18915 (215) 822-2400, are two sources for cards that contain copies of your electrocardiogram.
● Medic Alert Foundation International, Turlock, CA 95381-1009 (1-800-ID ALERT), markets bracelets and necklaces identifying your medical condition and offers a worldwide toll-free number to call for your medical history. Cost: $20 to $38.
● DataVue Products, P.O. Box 3559, Abilene, TX 79604 (915) 698-3712, offers a card containing your medical history on microfilm with a built-in magnifying glass. Cost: about $10 with postage.

Kerry Pechter

Put a Stop to Motion Sickness

The huge, reinforced metal doors overhead swing open slowly and the sky appears—absolutely black and full of stars so bright they hurt your eyes.

You give a slight kick and your ponderous, white-armored body lifts off the sparkling deck and begins a long arc up toward the black sky framed by the open hatch.

Getting through the Spin Cycle

Paris surrounds you from horizon to horizon and you exult for a brief moment: finally, France. Finally, the Eiffel Tower. Over there, the Seine, and *there*—the Louvre.

And then it starts to spin—the sky and the tower and the whole beautiful city swirl around your head. You fall to your knees, sweating and shaking.

Motion sickness? No, according to Charles Kimmelman, M.D. It's classic vertigo.

"True vertigo is defined as the subjective sense of movement—the environment's or yours. When you stagger and throw up on a moving boat, that's motion sickness. But when the sky or the city start spinning, that's vertigo."

The best remedy for vertigo: Sit down, close your eyes, breathe deeply and stay as motionless as possible. Usually it will pass within an hour or so.

What causes vertigo? Many things, says Dr. Kimmelman: "Usually it's a disturbance in the inner ear." But it could indicate something more serious, so if vertigo is new to you, see your doctor.

In the absolute silence, you're suddenly aware of the *sound* of the suit—small clicks, and the soft whisper of air circulating as you breathe in and out.

Your head clears the hatch, the gold-tinted visor polarizes into blackness instantly in the brilliant sunlight, and you stare astounded at the beauty of the white and blue globe swirling through space miles and miles away—until your boot clips the edge of the hatch and everything begins to spin.

In that brief second of whirling stars and tumbling universe, you feel bitterness coming from the back of your throat—but only for a moment. The custom-tailored space motion-sickness medication you swallowed before launch does its job beautifully.

You mouth a silent thank you to the physicians who just saved your life.

"Motion sickness, or what we at NASA prefer to call zero motion sickness (different from the ground-bound variety) affects roughly 75 percent of our astronauts," says Mike Bungo, M.D., a staff scientist at NASA's Space Biomedical Research Institute in Houston. "Twenty-five percent throw up, 25 percent feel like it and another 25 percent have other symptoms, like dizziness. The problem with that? Well, remember—our people, unlike the guy taking a European cruise, *have* to work, sick or not. And if they were sick in a space suit outside the shuttle—well, it could be fatal."

You don't have to walk in space to experience motion sickness. According to the American Academy of Otolaryngology, the symptoms—nausea and vomiting—appear whenever the central nervous system receives conflicting signals from the systems your body uses to keep its balance: the inner ears, pressure and motion receptors in skin, muscle and joints, and the eyes.

"You can think of it as a sort of neural short circuit," Dr. Bungo says, using seasickness—the nautical version of motion sickness—to make his point. "You have perceptual conflicts, signals that don't match one another: One part tells you you're moving, the other part tells you your feet are standing still on the deck of the ship, but then your ears tell you you're rolling back and forth.

"The brain can't figure out what's *not* right, so it short-circuits. The signals it sends out when that happens produce sweating, a clammy feeling, paleness and vomiting—a.k.a. motion sickness."

MELLOWING OUT MOTION SICKNESS

Take heart, those of you who tremble at the thought of mountain roads and recoil in horror from friendly suggestions of sea voyages to help you relax.

"Almost everyone will suffer from it at one point or another in their lives," says Charles P. Kimmelman, M.D., associate professor of otolaryngology at New York Medical College. "But it's not something you need to worry about. It rarely lasts for more than an hour or two at worst, and, unless you're unusually sensitive, whatever causes the problem will usually stop bothering you completely after two or three days of exposure."

Good news for ocean cruisers and NASA shuttle fliers, but what about the rest of us? The ones who want something to get us through the occasional bumpy plane ride or 30-minute ferry trip across the sound?

For most people, the answer is pills. Over-the-counter medications available without prescription include Dramamine, Bonine and Marezine. Stronger prescription medications—something to consider if you know you're sensitive—include tranquilizers like Valium ("Very good," says Dr. Kimmelman) and another drug called scopolamine.

"Scopolamine's a different class of drug, an anticholinergic," Dr. Kimmelman says. "While the majority of motion-sickness drugs act by turning off the symptoms, scopolamine acts directly on the central nervous system. It blocks the symptoms. It's very good at preventing nausea and vomiting."

It must be: NASA uses it, albeit mixed with another drug that combats the drowsiness scopolamine often produces. To combat motion sickness, scopolamine is only available commercially as a transdermal patch—an adhesive strip, usually worn behind the ear, that releases minute amounts into the skin continuously.

"All of these medications work best if they're administered just *before* the trip," Dr. Kimmelman says. "They don't work instantaneously, so if you want to avoid the problem—take the medication ahead of time."

But popping pills isn't the only thing you can do to combat the effects of motion sickness. The American Academy of Otolaryngology offers the following tips for minimizing travel-related upheaval.

● Always ride where your eyes will see the same motion that your body and inner ears feel. On a plane, for example, look out the window. On a boat, stare at the horizon.
● Don't read while traveling. Your eyes won't see the motion your body feels, with unpleasant results.
● Don't watch or talk to someone in the throes of motion sickness. The stimulus might push you into a matching condition.
● Avoid strong odors and foods that don't agree with you. Anything that starts the stomach churning could just

as easily end in full-blown motion sickness.
● And whatever you do, *don't drink.* One of the worst things you can do while feeling motion sickness is to drink alcoholic beverages. "Alcohol's a drug that has an adverse effect on the inner ear," says Dr. Kimmelman. "That's why a drunk staggers and falls on a perfectly flat floor—his inner ear is misinterpreting the signals it gets. So don't take a drink when it's already overstimulated."

WHEN ALL ELSE FAILS

If you end up sick anyway, there is something you can do to minimize the agony. Dr. Bungo suggests that you close your eyes to minimize signal conflicts. Don't let your head move any more than it has to. And stay quiet, moving as little as possible.

Kim Anderson

Try Ginger for What Ails You

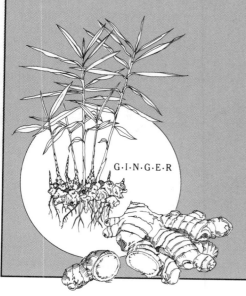

G·I·N·G·E·R

Can't stand the notion of motion, but can't stand drugs either?

Never fear, ginger's here. This common root may, in fact, outperform that old traveler's standard, Dramamine.

In a study of 36 college students who identified themselves as highly sensitive to motion sickness, researchers from Brigham Young University and Mount Union College evaluated the effects of Dramamine (dimenhydrinate), a placebo (dummy pill) and powdered ginger root.

The students were divided into 3 groups and given a capsule—medication in one, placebo in another and ginger

root in a third. The students were then blindfolded and given a ride in a tilted revolving chair. The results were surprising.

Zingiber officinale (powdered ginger root) was superior to dimenhydrinate in preventing the symptoms of motion sickness, the researchers reported.

Dramamine works by suppressing the symptoms of motion sickness. The scientists suspect powdered ginger root may work by increasing gastric movement and absorbing and neutralizing toxins and acids in the stomach, thus blocking upset.

Sensible Driving: Tips for the Long Haul

Going on a long-distance car trip? Here's how to have a healthy, safe and enjoyable experience.

Start with a personal checkup. For your eyes, that is—especially if you haven't had one in several years. Why?

"A man with 20/20 vision, driving at 60 miles per hour, has 3.9 seconds to read a highway sign composed in 6-inch letters," says Merrill J. Allen, Ph.D., professor of optometry at Indiana University at Bloomington. "If his acuity is 20/40, he has only 1.95 seconds, and with 20/100 he must try to read the sign in only 0.77 second!"

What's worse, says Dr. Allen, is that a person with 20/40 by day will have less visual acuity by night. "In other words, 20/40 by day merely cuts the critical perception distance in half compared to 20/20. At night it may cut it to one-tenth or less."

That's why it's a good idea to do most of your driving during daylight hours. You need all the help you can get to see roadside hazards as well as signs, so don't take any chances with your eyesight.

Clear the air. Don't take any chances with your car's exhaust system, either. Naturally, you'll have a mechanic give your car a once-over before you hit the road. But be particularly careful about the exhaust system. A leak in the muffler or tailpipe can send carbon monoxide (CO), a poisonous gas, up into the car. Actually, CO can get in even if there's no leak. That's because during steady highway driving, the engine's exhaust follows beside and behind the car. Leaving one window open just a crack creates a negative pressure, which can suck that exhaust right into the passenger compartment.

Obviously, a station wagon's tailgate window should not be open. Instead, to ensure that fresh air is coming into your car, open wide one window or vent in front and another in back, and keep the tailgate window (if you have one) closed.

Keep your cool. If your car has air conditioning, that's another way to get fresh air in. It's true that it reduces gas mileage, but studies show that the drag created by open windows does the same thing.

Besides, air conditioning can offer another plus—quiet. For long-distance, high-speed highway driving, it's a pleasure to be able to block out a good part of the extraneous noise. It's important to still be able to hear certain traffic sounds, though, like brakes screeching, horns honking or fire and police sirens. For that reason, tape players and radios should not be played so loud that they drown out relevant noises. Likewise, those tiny stereo headsets can make driving more dangerous by filling your ears with only the sounds they generate.

While your ears are tuned in to what's around you, make sure your eyes are, too. Rearview mirrors reveal only so much, so when changing lanes, turn your head to obtain a direct view of what's in the other lane. A dirty windshield both inside and out hampers vision, too. What's more, the near-invisible film that builds up on the inside of a windshield increases eyestrain at night. A spray window cleaner and a roll of paper towels can clean it

How to Let Off Some Steam

Safe and sane driving means avoiding irritation and encouraging relaxation. One way to achieve it all is to do a little exercise on your breaks.

Walk around, jog in place and take a few deep breaths to stimulate your blood circulation.

As for stiff backs, one family found a unique solution to that problem. They kept an alert eye for "hanging" spots—places where they could grasp (above head height) and hang, swinging their feet backward. That really helped straighten out the kinks, they say.

On a well-planned trip, you really shouldn't overextend yourself. You'll enjoy the trip a lot more if you allow for a reasonable amount of mileage each day. The American Automobile Association (AAA) says don't try to crowd too many miles into one day's driving. It will take about 2½ hours to travel 100 miles, including stops for gasoline, refreshments and exercise.

If tensions do start to build up, then don't drive. Flaring tempers, "get even" attitudes, worry and anxiety can interfere with your normal judgment, leaving you temporarily heedless of danger. Driving in this condition has been shown to contribute to a significant number of traffic accidents.

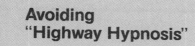

Avoiding "Highway Hypnosis"

Long trips mean long stretches of highway that seem to go on forever, with nary a change in the scenery. But keep on looking around anyway, even if there's "nothing to see." Staring straight ahead is a sure way to develop "highway hypnosis," a trance-like state in which you may experience hallucinations or lose the ability to gauge the speed at which you're traveling.

To prevent yourself from turning into a highway hypnotic, the National Traffic Safety Administration suggests you should:

● Keep your eyes moving, even if you're the only car on the road.
● Glance to the sides of the highway, check the rearview and sideview mirrors, adjust your focus to a spot about 50 feet in front of the car, look at the dashboard, then shift back to the long view.

Remember that tired eyes cause drowsiness and a smaller field of vision, and the result can be a serious accident. Still, you should realize that you can't beat fatigue forever. So be alert for these signs of overwhelming tiredness.

● Do your eyes burn?
● Are you blinking more?
● Are lights bothering you?
● Does your voice sound louder than usual or far away?
● Do you suddenly realize there's been a lapse in time that you can't account for?
● Has your foot relaxed on the gas pedal so that you find yourself going 40 miles per hour instead of the posted 55 miles per hour you thought you were doing?

Then it's time to pull over and call it quits.

To reduce fatigue, begin by learning the best way to sit while driving. Experts say you should sit high enough to see the ground 10 feet in front of the car. Your legs and feet should not be fully extended while driving. Your lower leg should rest at a 45-degree angle to the vertical when the thigh is horizontal. Even if you've pushed the pedal all the way to the floor, your leg should still be slightly bent.

Even so, sitting for long periods of time can cause compression of blood vessels in your legs. For people with any arterial disease, this can be especially dangerous. Blood clots in leg arteries have been known to occur after prolonged travel. That's one reason why it's important to remain as mobile as possible during long trips.

Another reason is that moving around is one of the most useful ways to fight fatigue. The best way to pace yourself, according to government-sponsored research, is to take 20- to 30-minute rest breaks after every 1½ to 2 hours of steady driving.

Take a snack break. When you stop for your break, it may be a good idea to have a bite to eat. Most drivers find that a meal stimulates and refreshes them. Now it has been proven scientifically that that's the case.

A group of Swedish psychologists tested the effects of food breaks versus rest breaks (without food) on motoring ability when driving long distances. The researchers found that no matter how long the pit stop, only fueling up with a meal seemed to improve driving performance.

Eileen Nechas

---

off, but in a pinch, the tannic acid that's in ordinary newspaper print does the job, too.

Think "safety first." When it comes to safety, seat belts top the list. The National Safety Council says that if all passenger-car occupants used seat belts, at least 12,000 lives would be saved each year.

Interestingly enough, one study showed that drivers who wear seat belts are the ones who take the fewest chances at stop lights, while those who don't "buckle up" are the biggest risk-takers.

Get in the driver's seat—correctly. With long-distance car trips, fatigue is one of the most common and continuous problems that crops up—and about the most dangerous. It's no surprise that falling asleep at the wheel is a factor in from 13 to 20 percent of highway traffic accidents involving fatalities.

Staying Healthy Overseas

Trips overseas are too costly, too exciting and, for many people, too few and far between to be sidelined by some "it-got-me-down" illness. Anyone who's been through the experience can tell you it's no fun falling ill 5,000 miles from home where no one else speaks English except your equally ill travel mate.

But it needn't happen to you. Even though potential health problems exist, you don't have to worry yourself around the world. The most common health problems travelers encounter on trips overseas are centered on food, water and a few infectious diseases. And worries about these problems can pretty safely be put aside if you take a few preventive measures before leaving on the trip.

THE WATER WORRIES

Water is probably one of the most important concerns for travelers. While tap water in the United States can be considered safe to drink, this is not true of many other countries, including much of Europe. W. Scott Harkonen, M.D., author of *Traveling Well*, offers these tips to help you decide which water you should or shouldn't drink (or brush your teeth with).

Don't drink:

● Tap water, unless you are absolutely positive it is safe.
● Uncarbonated, locally bottled water. According to Dr. Harkonen, restaurants will sometimes refill commercial bottled water containers with possibly unsafe tap water.
● Drinks with ice cubes, because the ice is likely to have been made from local water.
● Mixed alcoholic drinks. They can't be assumed to be free of contamination.

Here are the sources of water Dr. Harkonen recommends as safe.

● Bottled water that is carbonated, and brand-name soft drinks, as long as the bottles or glasses they are served in aren't contaminated. (The acidity found in carbonated drinks will help kill any gut-wrenching microbes that might get into your stomach.)
● Beer and wine, especially if you drink them from the bottle or can, which you have wiped dry.
● Drinks made with boiling water, like coffee and tea.
● Fresh, undiluted fruit juices.

FOOD THAT'S FIT TO EAT

Unless you are somewhere that you're *sure* the food is well prepared and won't make you ill, you should take certain precautions, says travel expert Vicenzo Marcolongo, M.D., founder and president of the International Association for Medical Assistance to Travelers (IAMAT), in Lewiston, New York. Here's his golden rule: Cook it, peel it, or forget it.

"The problems of contaminated food are worse in less developed countries in Asia, South America and Africa, but they can also be a problem in Europe, especially along the Mediterranean," says Dr. Marcolongo. He says that you should always make sure your food is served hot, not lukewarm, and for this reason you should avoid buffets.

Specifically risky foods include:

● Leafy vegetables like lettuce, and other uncooked salad vegetables.
● Mayonnaise, custard and creamed dishes.
● Raw and rare meats and undercooked fish.

● Shellfish, unless you're sure the water they are from is safe. Otherwise, hepatitis can be a problem.
● In the tropics, fresh milk should be avoided unless it has been boiled. Unpasteurized milk can spread many diseases, including brucellosis and tuberculosis. Fresh or uncured cheese should also be avoided, since it is a milk by-product.

Foods considered safe are:

● Fresh fruit you peel yourself.
● Fresh boiled vegetables and hot, well-cooked meat and fish.
● Canned vegetables, milk, soups and meats.
● In Western Europe, milk and dairy products.

Dr. Marcolongo has one other hint that might reduce your chances of suffering the consequences of bad food and drink: Eat smaller meals. Snack frequently instead of piling the food in three times a day. "The natural acids in your stomach will help kill any bad bacteria. Large meals buffer the stomach acid for too long and this allows microbes to pass from the stomach to the bowel," he says.

ADVICE FOR THE ILL

In the unfortunate event that despite all of your precautions you do get sick—diarrhea, cramps, fatigue and sometimes fever and nausea are a sure sign that you've ingested something disagreeable—don't worry. At least not immediately. "About 60 percent of diarrhea is caused by *E. coli,* a bacterium, and chances are it won't last more than three to five days. If the diarrhea continues for more than three days, there's blood in your stool, or you have very serious cramps, you should see a doctor," says Dr. Marcolongo. "You might have something serious like an amoeba or a microbe that a doctor must treat."

But if you think you are suffering from simple traveler's diarrhea, your first concern should be getting enough liquids. (See the box, "The Drink That Stops Dehydration.") "You should drink a lot of water and fruit juices to prevent dehydration, which is a problem with diarrhea. The liquids will also resupply you with salts and electrolytes you might need. Bananas and soup are good, too. Or, if you're not on a salt-restricted diet, you can buy commercial rehydration salts, which contain salt and glucose, before you leave home," says Dr. Marcolongo. "And get plenty of rest, even if it means curtailing your sightseeing for a little while."

Some people have recommended taking daily doses of Pepto-Bismol to prevent diarrhea. While it seems to prevent problems in two-thirds of the people who take it, the amount of Pepto-Bismol necessary—one large bottle a day—makes it an unwieldy preventive measure for a problem you might not experience anyway.

Some people, like athletes headed for competition and people with serious health problems, might ask their doctors to prescribe antibiotics to make absolutely sure they won't get diarrhea, but the average person should avoid taking any unnecessary antibiotics, says Dr. Marcolongo. The risk of side effects outweighs the benefits of the drugs, he says.

A SHOT FOR SAFETY

Not all travelers' diseases come from food and drink. Some are transmitted by mosquitoes and other bugs; others spread from person to person. This makes thinking about vaccinations an important part of everyone's pretravel plans.

No special vaccinations are necessary for people traveling to European countries, says Eileen Hilton, M.D., assistant professor of medicine and consultant on infectious diseases, who runs the travel and immunization center at Long Island Jewish Medical Center. "But if you are going to countries outside of Europe or North America, you can call your county health department to find out what you need. Then you can go to a travelers' clinic or see your regular doctor for the necessary shots. Some of the vaccinations, like yellow fever, however, are only available at licensed centers."

This advice is for short trips that aren't too far off the beaten path. Dr. Hilton says that anyone who is going on an extensive trip, especially in the tropics, should visit a travel clinic like the one at her hospital for counseling and vaccinations, because the risk of contracting a disease increases with the length of the trip.

The U.S. State Department Overseas Citizens Emergency Center in Washington, D.C., will give travelers up-to-date information about epidemics and travelers' advisories around the world. You can call during regular working hours and Saturday from 9:00 A.M. to 3:00 P.M. at (202) 647-5225.

Stephen Williams

Join the Chart Club

You don't have to feel like you're searching in the dark when it comes to finding specific information about the myriad diseases and problems you might encounter overseas. The International Association for Medical Assistance to Travelers (IAMAT) will send you its detailed pamphlets about health risks around the world, including charts that tell you specifically which areas of which countries have problems with malaria and other diseases. Charts detailing immunization requirements and recommendations are also available.

They'll also send you climate charts for every region of the world, listing the average temperature and precipitation, suggestions for the types of clothing you should take with you and information on whether or not the water, milk and food are safe.

IAMAT also publishes a directory of IAMAT-approved doctors around the world who are available to help travelers for fixed fees between $20 for an office call and $40 for a hotel call. You can contact IAMAT at 417 Center Street, Lewiston, NY 14092.

Overcoming Jet Lag

A few years ago, a young American couple flew to Holland, taking an early evening flight from New York. They dined on prime rib and red wine, watched the sun come up over the Azores and arrived in Amsterdam at 8:00 A.M. local time. Exhausted, they found a hotel, slept for 6 hours and woke up at dusk feeling dazed, with vaguely flulike symptoms. That night and for two nights after, they couldn't fall asleep. They were victims of the phenomenon known as jet lag. It was five days before they got over it.

Three years later, on a trip to London, the same couple again took an evening flight. This time, they politely refused the in-flight dinner, ate two whole wheat muffins instead, closed their eyes, ignored the other travelers and napped during most of the flight. When they arrived in London at 6:00 A.M. local time, they feasted on steak and eggs for breakfast and, despite their fatigue, spent the day sightseeing before retiring at 8:00 P.M. The next morning, they felt great. This time they beat jet lag, that drag-you-down reaction that includes insomnia, fatigue and stomach trouble.

Once an enigma, the cause of jet lag is now fairly well understood. Traveling through time zones disrupts our master inner-body clock, which synchronizes the hormonal and chemical cycles. When it gets out of sync, it creates a foggy and groggy condition somewhat akin to drug withdrawal or a hangover. It can steal four or five of a tourist's hard-earned vacation days, and it can interfere with an executive's or diplomat's ability to make critical decisions.

About as many cures have been suggested for jet lag as have been suggested for hangovers—so many, in fact, that it's difficult to sort out the effective ones. What works for one person doesn't always work for another. But jet lag researchers at major sleep labs throughout the country agree on certain anti-jet lag strategies that almost any traveler can put into action—before, during and after a long flight.

BEFORE YOU LEAVE HOME

Try the Ehret Jet Lag Diet. There's a diet for everything else, so why not one for jet lag? This one was invented in the late 1970s by Charles F. Ehret, Ph.D., a researcher at the Argonne National Laboratory in Chicago. The diet's goal is simple—to make you hungry for breakfast when it's breakfast time at your destination.

It's based on the idea that some foods, like proteins, make you active, that other foods, like carbohydrates, make you sleepy, and that caffeine, taken at the right time, can help shift your body clock.

Three days before your departure (that's Wednesday if you're leaving on Saturday), Dr. Ehret suggests you feast on proteins and carbohydrates. At breakfast, eat eggs, beef, cereal or other high-protein foods. At lunch, do the same. At supper, switch to high-carbohydrate foods like pasta, potatoes, and sweet desserts. On Thursday, eat very little, limiting yourself to about 800 calories worth of broth, unbuttered toast, fruit and vegetables. If you drink coffee, drink it only between 3:00 and 5:00 P.M.

On Friday, repeat Wednesday's plan, and on Saturday, repeat Thursday's. Drink coffee only between 6:00

It's West for the Weary

Most jet lag researchers focus on travel from west to east. The reason: Jet lag after eastbound travel is roughly 1½ times as severe as after westbound travel.

According to jet lag specialist Timothy Monk, Ph.D., eastbound travel requires a day of recovery for each time zone crossed, while westbound travel requires 90 minutes for each time zone crossed. For example, if you flew from Los Angeles to London, a trip which crosses 8 time zones, it would take 8 days for your biological clock to

be completely reset. However, notes Dr. Monk, you'll only *feel* the effects for about 4 days.

The human body adapts better to a longer day than a shorter day, explains Dr. Monk. Our biological clock has a natural tendency to run slow. Westbound travel adds hours to the day, making bedtime come later; eastbound trips subtract hours, making bedtime come sooner. Biologically, we prefer going to bed later than earlier. "That's why we tend to stay up late on weekends," says Dr. Monk.

P.M. and 11:00 P.M. on Saturday if you're flying east; if you're flying west, drink it only in the morning. After departure, don't eat a full meal at night. Instead ask the flight attendant to save it for your breakfast. After that, eat as you ordinarily would.

Dr. Ehret says, however, that eating alone won't beat jet lag. Exposure to light, exercise to combat oxygen debt and keeping as normal a schedule as possible are also important.

Shift your bedtime by an hour. Starting a few days before you depart, you can prepare your body for the coming time change by shifting your bedtime. If you're flying east, go to bed an hour earlier each night and wake up an hour earlier in the morning. If you're flying west, go to bed an hour later and wake up an hour later.

This will only help, Dr. Ehret warns, if you can make the time adjustment both at night and in the morning.

WHILE YOU'RE ALOFT

Turn your watch to destination time. The best way to help your body adapt to a new time zone is to start living in that time zone as soon as possible. Virtually every jet lag researcher agrees on this point. "As soon as you get on the plane," says Timothy Monk, Ph.D., a jet lag specialist at the University of Pittsburgh, "turn your watch to destination time and start behaving as if you've already arrived. Then, if your watch tells you it's time to sleep, sleep. If it tells you to eat, eat."

Skip that airline supper. If your schedule doesn't allow you to follow the first three days of the Ehret Jet Lag Plan, postponing supper on the plane until breakfast might do you almost as much good, Dr. Ehret says. In-flight suppers are tempting, especially when you're bored, hungry or anxious about flying. But they're counterproductive, because they'll

Triazolam: The Time-Relief Pill

Some doctors prescribe a short-acting sleeping pill called Triazolam to treat the sleep disruption that occurs as a symptom of jet lag. But the drug doesn't help reset the body's inner clock.

Triazolam isn't something to be taken lightly. Although it leaves the body rapidly, it may be habit-forming, and it can interact with other drugs or alcohol. Also, there are restrictions on when it can be taken.

"You shouldn't take it on the plane," says Thomas Roth, Ph.D., a sleep researcher at Henry Ford Hospital in Detroit. "If there's an in-flight emergency, you'll be impaired, and when you arrive, the drug may still be in your system. You probably won't need it for the first night, since you'll be tired from the flight. Most people wait until the second or third night to take the medication."

keep you attached to the cycles of your home time zone.

When the stewardess brings her cart down the aisle at about 8:00 P.M. New York time, just say, "No, thanks. It's only 3:00 A.M. in Paris, and I'm saving my appetite for breakfast."

Counteract cabin fever. If you've ever flown in a charter overseas, you know that the interior of the plane can look, sound and feel like a Chicago stockyard, with as many as 300 passengers crowding the cabin. It gets noisy, hot, dry and smoky, and there's no room to move. The air pressure is about equal to that in the Swiss Alps. Half of the discomfort associated with jet lag, experts believe, stems from the nausea, aching joints, headaches, dehydration and slight oxygen debt

caused by the artificial environment inside the plane. Fortunately, these are short-lived effects, lasting only 3 to 4 hours after arrival.

To counteract dehydration, drink water or juice. "The cabin atmosphere contributes to dehydration," says Dr. Monk, "so you won't want to drink coffee or alcohol. They're diuretics, and will make you even drier. The best thing to do is drink fruit juice or decaffeinated sodas." To counteract stiffness, stretch out in the aisle, or just clench and unclench your fists.

WHEN YOU ARRIVE

Don't nap on the day of arrival. If you arrive in the morning after a night flight, your body will be crying out for sleep. After all, it may still only be the middle of the night back home. But most jet lag experts would advise you to stay awake at least until the early evening and to spend as much time as possible in the sun. Exposure to daylight can actually help your body shift its clock.

"If it's early in the day," says Dr. Monk, "try to stay awake until local bedtime, even if you have to drag yourself around. Or if you have to, take a 1-hour nap—but no more than an hour." Sleeping during the day will only delay your adjustment to local time.

Kerry Pechter

Flying by Night

Imagine driving to the airport in your own car and running into no traffic when you get there.

Imagine no long lines of anxious people at ticket counters inside the terminal.

Imagine empty seats in clusters on the airplane—so you can actually stretch out and go to sleep.

Imagine all of this happening to you on your next flight to anywhere.

Stop imagining, already. It *can* happen to you—if you fly at night.

Tripping the night fantastic, experienced travelers say, can be a generic antidote to the poisons that bedevil daytime travel: airport traffic jams, lines at ticket counters, flight delays, lost luggage, overbooked planes and, yes, even fatal crashes.

The trade-off, of course, is that you give up your normal sleeping habits for a night or two, and that you be willing to arrive, with legs like Jell-O, perhaps, and with bloodshot eyes, at your destination at 6:00 A.M. But the perks of being a fly-by-nighter also include:

● Less chance of the airline losing your luggage (fewer flights, people and bags to worry about).
● Less chance of your getting intoxicated at airport lounges (they're closed in the middle of the night).
● Fewer delays, fewer late departures, missed connections and cancelled flights (less traffic in the air makes schedules easier to keep).
● And the biggie, fewer crashes.

LISTEN TO THE EXPERTS

Robert L. DuPont, M.D., clinical professor of psychiatry at Georgetown University School of Medicine and chairman of the Center for Behavioral Medicine in Rockville, Maryland, says: "Flying at night is a great way to avoid the congestion and tension at most of the major airports. Airport congestion and the tension it breeds is a major factor in a lot of people's fear of flying. There's no question that flying at night cuts it down to a minimum and actually eliminates it in some cases. It's a terrific way to travel without stress."

Virginia Black, a spokesperson for the Los Angeles Department of Airports, which operates the Los Angeles International Airport, comments on traffic at night: "No question, there's less motor vehicle traffic around airports between midnight and 6:00 A.M. than at any other time of the day or night.

"If you get a middle-of-the-night flight, getting to the airport by car, taxi or limousine is certainly going to be easier than if you get here at 8:00 in the morning, say, or 4:00 in the afternoon. No contest."

Joe Lanciotti, spokesperson for the Port Authority of New York and New Jersey, which runs one of the nation's busiest airports, John F. Kennedy International Airport on Long Island, remarks on the serenity of terminals at night: "At night, you pretty much have the whole airport to yourself—only 10 to 15 percent of the terminal is open between the hours of midnight and 6:00 A.M. All the basic necessities are open—rest rooms and cab stands and even a snack bar.

"The rent-a-car booths may not have real live people behind the counters, but they have hotline phones that'll get you a car if you want one. One thing's for sure—you never have to worry about waiting in any lines at 4:00 in the morning."

Fred Farrar, of the public information office of the Federal Aviation Administration has this to say about night traffic in the skies: "There's gen-

Wear Shoes You Can Lose

What's the best possible footwear on an airplane?

Anything you can slip off, or kick off, or slide off, or wiggle off, or peel off, or pull off an hour into the flight when your feet start sweating, or swelling, or even hurting, while cramped and curled under the seat in front of you.

Good choices: loafers, flats, sneakers with loosened laces.

Bad choices: cowboy boots or heavy construction boots.

Worst possible scenario: To be sandwiched in between a couple of Wrestlemania types, with your tray table down, half a meal still on it, and your feet starting to hurt.

A little tip: Wear smooth-fitting socks or stockings (as opposed to ribbed or ruffled ones) and your slip-off footwear will slip off—and slip back on—even more smoothly.

erally a 60 percent drop-off in the number of flights after 11:00 P.M. If you're on a commercial flight at 2:00 in the morning, you're sharing the skies with cargo and freight planes and small aircraft, carrying bank checks, for instance, from one city to another so they can be cleared in the morning.

"There's some repositioning traffic, too—planes that ended up in Baltimore the night before and need to be in Cleveland the next morning. Pilots fly them empty just to get them there so they can take off on time. No question, there's less traffic in the sky during the night."

Ted Lopatkiewicz, an information specialist for the National Trans-portation Safety Board, explains why there are fewer crashes at night: "Since July 27, 1970, according to our records, the biggest single cause of airplane crashes in the United States has been the windshear phenomenon. Wind-shear, since that date, has played a major part in 18 commercial crashes, 7 with fatalities. Windshear, as we've found out, is directly associated with thunderstorm activity . . . and the most dangerous time for thunderstorms appears to be the afternoon, particu-larly the late afternoon.

"Nobody that we know of has kept any data as to what are the most dangerous times to fly, or the most dangerous months to fly, but I'd guess both would be around the times of year when thunderstorms are most likely to strike. That would probably be in the afternoon during warm-weather months. Not in the middle of the night."

Karen Ceremsak, a specialist in corporate communications for East-ern Airlines in Miami, sums it up nicely: "When you fly at night, it's more casual, but you're getting the same service you would get during the day. Flying at night is perfect when you have an emergency and you need to travel at the spur of the moment. Just show up, pay for the ticket, get on board . . . and go."

Martin Ralbovsky

Nine New Ways to Fight Fear of Flight

Glenda Jackson and Muhammad Ali. Bob Newhart and Aretha Franklin. Gene Shalit and Maureen Stapleton. John Madden and Ronald Reagan.

What do these disparate people have in common? At one time or another in their lives, they've all been hesitant to fly in an airplane.

The reason: They were scared to death.

So you are keeping illustrious com-pany if you harbor the same very com-mon dread of traveling by air. There may come a day, though, when you will *need* to fly—then what?

You can start by listening to Cap-tain Truman W. (Slim) Cummings, who makes his living unburdening oth-erwise normal people of their acro-phobia, claustrophobia and whatever other excess mental baggage they bring with them when they board an airplane.

Cummings, a former Pan-American Airways pilot, runs semi-nars in Coral Gables, Florida, called "Freedom from Fear of Flying." Since 1974, when he began, he's helped thou-sands of people get back into planes without a worry in the world.

Here are some quick tips from Captain Cummings on how you can start conquering your fear of flying today.

● Plan a short flight to a nearby city—one where friends can be waiting for you. Or one that you've wanted to see for a long time. Give yourself some-thing to look forward to at the end of the flight.

● Take along a friend, if you must. Reserve your friend's seat right next to yours. You've got a traveling compan-ion and moral support all in one.

● Try to find an early-morning flight, so you'll have less time between wak-ing up and taking off to worry about the dreaded flight itself.

● Fly first-class. It does make people feel more comfortable. But any seat close to the front of the plane will be in smoother and quieter territory.

● Take it easy on the coffee and sug-ary foods in the hours before you fly—both have a tendency to increase your anxiety levels.

● Don't swap stories with other fear-ful fliers—their exaggerations and dis-tortions are contagious.

● Speak to a stranger—it'll be a good diversion if the stranger turns out to be interesting.

● Tell the attendants when you board the flight that you're a fearful flier—they'll respond later by doing what they can to make you comfortable.

● Wiggle your toes as the plane accel-erates down the runway. Honest. Wig-gle them even faster as the plane picks up speed; wiggling your toes keeps them—and your mind—busy at a time of high anxiety.

Your Airplane Smoke Survival Guide

Whenever the President of the United States gets onto an airplane, he keeps near him a little black box that everyone on board holds their breath over. They are hoping he'll finish the flight without using it.

Donald Stedman, Ph.D., professor and chairman of the Department of Environmental Chemistry at the University of Denver, also carries an electronic box on all of his flights. His device, however, is blue instead of black, and it is designed to help his fellow passengers breathe a little easier.

While the President's box has the potential to make a lot of smoke suddenly appear, Dr. Stedman's box measures it—smoke, that is. Especially the kind that drifts away from cigarettes and unerringly into the face and nose of the nearest person allergic to it.

Dr. Stedman takes a lot of walks while he flies. Those trips up and down airplane aisles have answered questions that nonsmokers have been asking for years.

A FIRST-CLASS PROBLEM

"It's certainly not wise to spend extra money for a seat in the first-class section if your objective is to avoid

The Peaks and Valleys of a Flight Log

Here's a graphic representation of the amount of smoke generated in the cabin of a Boeing 727 during an actual 4-hour flight.

The first peak occurred at around 6:00 when the captain turned off the "No Smoking" light. The big drop around 8:00 tells you when the smokers were served their meals, and the peak that follows shows when they finished.

Although these levels— recorded as parts per billion (ppb) of nitrogen dioxide (NO_2) in the air—were considered to be within federal standards, eye irritation was noted at readings of 12 ppb and above.

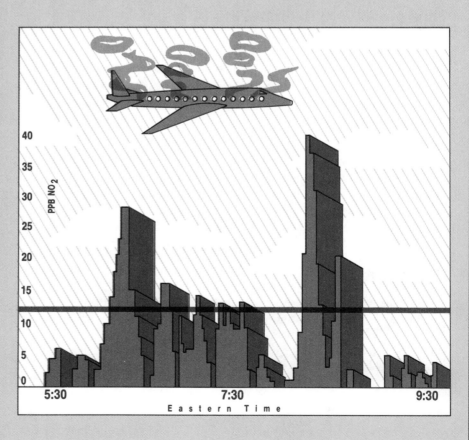

cigarette smoke," says Dr. Stedman. "The air in the nonsmoking rows in first class is actually worse than the nonsmoking rows in coach. Of course, the absolute worst air on the plane is in the center of the smoking section in coach. Every smoke-sensitive individual who's had to walk through that section to get to the rest rooms already knows that."

Dr. Stedman's machine has also defined the worst time to take that long walk: It's whenever the cabin crew is fussing with the food trays.

"Smoke levels peak just before and after the smokers are served a meal," he explains. "Generally, my machine picks up almost no readings whatsoever *during* a meal."

That makes mealtime the best time to venture through the domain of those with the stinky clothes. But why? Doesn't that haze still hang around them for hours?

"Not when the airplane is being properly vented," answers Dr. Stedman. "With a system that's functioning well, the cabin air will be almost completely clean just 2 minutes after the smoking stops. For instance, after the captain turns on the 'no-smoking' light."

WHAT FUELS THE SMOKE

But the key here is a ventilation system that *is* working well. Unfortunately for those of us who react to smoke with our sensitive eyes and noses, there's often a strong incentive for the captain to keep those vents closed tight: money.

Dr. Stedman says, "Many captains actually get a cash bonus if they can keep fuel costs down during a flight. And the easiest way to do that is to shut down the fresh air vents.

"The 'air packs' that pull in the freezing cold outside air must pressurize, warm and often dehumidify that air before it can be pumped into the cabin. It takes extra fuel to do

that," he explains, "which is why the air packs are often routinely shut *off* during long flights to save fuel. It's much cheaper for them to keep the air at an acceptable level of cleanliness if they don't have people on board adding a lot of smoke to it. I don't think that the airlines enjoy paying for the extra fuel that it takes to get rid of the combustion products those smokers are putting into the air."

"When the inside of an airplane becomes a smoke-filled haze, the first thing the cabin crew will do is turn on the recirculators," explains Dr. Stedman. "The only problem is that this system actually mixes the air from the smoking section throughout the plane, including the nonsmoking section. This type of ventilation— currently in use on almost all airplanes —would simply not be allowed under today's regulatory standards in the workplace," says Dr. Stedman.

Unfortunately, Dr. Stedman says the problem is getting worse, not better. "Airplanes are now being designed to use less fresh air and recirculate more stale air as a fuel-saving measure," he explains. "The more modern the airplane, the worse the ventilation.

"The old 727s are the best," says Dr. Stedman. "They're naturally well vented—you turn on the engine and air comes in. They don't recirculate— they literally *cannot* mix the air from smoking into nonsmoking—and their system brings in *lots* of fresh air.

"The worst are the really modern planes, like the 737, 757 and late model 747s. They rely heavily on recirculated air. Generally speaking, the wider body planes are the worst. You could almost say 'the wider the body, the worse the air.'"

ENGINEERING A SMOKE-FREE FLIGHT

In every airplane, the captain can increase the amount of fresh air entering

the cabin—*if* you complain, notes Dr. Stedman. But he adds that the person who actually has their hand on that control is the flight engineer. It's the engineer, not the captain, who directly controls the ventilation. And although the flight attendants may be sympathetic, they can't lay a hand on those controls.

Send word to the cockpit that you'd like to speak with the flight engineer. Explain that you have a medical condition, that you're having difficulty breathing and would like more fresh air in the cabin.

"The more engines the plane has, the more fresh air they're capable of pulling in," explains Dr. Stedman. "Almost all planes have variable settings for their ventilation controls— sometimes all it takes is the engineer changing that setting from low to high.

"If you're truly allergic to cigarette smoke, you should do everything possible in advance to see that your seat assignment will be in the center of the nonsmoking section," he recommends. "That's row 15 in the coach section of a 727."

That's where Dr. Stedman sits. And his little blue box tells him it's the best seat in the house.

Mike McGrath

Hotel Rooms:
Feeling Safe and Secure

The good news is: Never before in the history of the lodging business have more palatable perks been dangled like golden carrots before the noses of pampered guests.

The bad news is: Guests at many inns, hotels and motels are vulnerable to injury, stress and even death while registered at these playpens of paradise.

The litany of hotel disasters during the last decade is daunting.

● 96 dead, 140 injured after a New Year's Eve arson fire at the DuPont Plaza Hotel in San Juan, Puerto Rico.
● 84 dead, nearly 200 injured after an arson fire at the MGM Grand Hotel in Las Vegas.
● 26 dead, 38 injured after an arson fire at Stouffer Inn in Harrison, New York.
● 43 dead, 150 injured when a catwalk collapsed inside the brand new Hyatt Regency Hotel in Kansas City, Missouri.

Suffice it to say, in light of all this, that even the most chic, respectable and well-intentioned of hotels may contain certain health and safety risks, the proliferation of perks notwithstanding. After all, what good is having an exercise bike delivered to your room to help keep you in shape, or having a computer terminal at your 24-hour beck and call, if negligence on the part of the hotel could hurt you?

STAYING SAFE

Anthony G. Marshall, dean of the School of Hospitality Management at Florida International University in Miami, is one of the few people who has studied this dilemma from both sides—as a concerned consumer who frequents his share of hotels around the country, and as a hotel-management educator in charge of the students who will be running hotels in the next decade. Here are some expert tips from Marshall on how to make your hotel room healthier and safer.

Don't agree to just any room. "Some rooms at any hotel are going to be less desirable than others," Marshall says. "Rooms that are near elevators or soda and ice machines are noted for being noisy at all hours. Try to sleep when four revellers, say, after a night on the town, get off the elevator right next to your room and try to find *their* rooms.

"But the absolute worst location for a room is right above the kitchen," he continues. "You get the noise, you're right above the flames in a kitchen fire, and you're going to hear all the racket at 5:00 in the morning when workers are cleaning out the trash."

Ask before you're assigned. You have the option at almost any good hotel of at least asking to stay on a favorite floor. If you don't ask, they'll assign you a room. Make the decision yourself about which floor you'll be staying on. "My choice would be the second floor at any hotel," says Marshall. "The reason: In case of fire, it's low enough so that you can jump safely out a window. In case of intruders, it's high enough that they can't get in. The best of both worlds."

Study your room keys. The best room keys these days, safety-wise, are the plastic or metal card keys that fit into the lock the way bank cards fit into automatic cash machines. They're cross-coded this way: They say, for example, "Card No. 424," but the card really is the key for room 209. If

this card falls into a thief's hands, he'll never be able to figure out the cross-coding.

A room key with the room number emblazoned on it is a thief's dream. It advertises the very room he can now rip off. Good hotels either keep the room numbers off the keys altogether or else they use cards.

Be your own security guard. If you want to know how good the hotel security is, at least as far as the switchboard is concerned, go to the house phone, ask for yourself, and tell the operator you're not sure of the correct room number. If the answer is "He's in room 303," you're in trouble. The correct answer is "We'll connect you."

"Good security requires that the hotel switchboard not give out room

Stage Your Own Light-and-Sound Show

In Las Vegas, it is particularly funny. Glamorous and gaudy hotels on the strip leave cards in your room telling you to please conserve electricity for energy reasons: Make sure that "you turn out all the lights when you leave this room."

It's funny because Las Vegas is a city that quite possibly spends more money in a year on electric signs than some countries spend on their military defense.

When it comes to *your* personal safety, you shouldn't have to worry about saving the hotel a few pennies on its monthly electric bill, especially if you're going to spend $125 a night. So leave your lights on when you leave the room. In fact, leave your television set on, too, with the sound loud enough so that it can be heard at least through the front door.

The lights and the television sounds are two easy layers of protection from thieves, who don't usually go around breaking into rooms that seem occupied.

numbers, and the best hotels are very strict on it," says Marshall.

Watch how keys are controlled. Another good way to determine how efficient a hotel is in the area of security is to watch how hotel room keys are controlled. For example: If you're at the front desk at check-out time and there is a whole pile of room keys lying there, chances are the hotel is pretty lax. Anybody can grab a key or two from that pile. And this is particularly dangerous if the room number is embossed on the key blank.

On the other hand, if you see a maid's cart, for example, with a locked iron box attached that has a slot for room keys, you can guess that the hotel is pretty good. The maid is going to have to account for all the room keys at the end of her shift. It's her responsibility. Meanwhile, nobody has access to those keys when they're inside the locked iron box.

Be your own watchdog. A rule of thumb is to choose a concrete-and-steel hotel over an old wooden one, for obvious reasons in case of a fire. Should you select a wooden hotel because it is a famous old resort, take a room on a lower floor for ease of exit in case of an emergency. If a hotel in an urban, high-crime area doesn't have any uniformed security guards patroling it and around the grounds, you might ask the front desk why not—that's not a good sign.

Don't stay in a room in which you can't open the window, and specifically ask when you check in for a room with peepholes in the door so you can see for yourself who's knocking, and for a throw-bolt lock that can't be opened with a credit card slipped through the door.

WHAT YOU DON'T KNOW CAN HURT YOU

"Generally speaking, American hotels are still the safest and the best in the world, but that's not to say they're perfect," says Marshall. "What's come out of all the hotel tragedies over the last several years is improvements in things like sprinkler systems and internal security, things that are the direct results of a tragedy. The MGM Grand fire brought the sprinkler-system issue to a head. The rape of singer Connie Francis in a hotel on Long Island—and later winning a $2.5-million jury judgment against the hotel—made a lot of other hotels rethink their whole security operations."

What hasn't changed, however, is the law. "Hotels still are not liable by law to inform their guests at check-in time, for example, that the hotel is located in the middle of a high-crime area of the city or that the hotel recommends that its guests not take any after-dinner strolls around the block," says Marshall. "The hotel also is not obligated by law to inform you that it and its employees are in a bitter labor dispute that could turn violent and threaten your life. And the hotel is not obligated by law to tell you that the room you are staying in was the site of a bloody murder only three weeks earlier and that the killer is still at large somewhere in the city."

All the law charges the hotel with is taking reasonable care that the guests are safe, says Marshall. "If anything happens, it's up to you to prove in a court of law that the hotel didn't take reasonable care . . . if you want to collect any damages."

If you have any fears, stay at a hotel that is part of a major chain, advises Marshall. They're more expensive, perhaps, but they have far better safety and security systems than your average save-a-buck motel. Which means you'll probably be paying extra for your peace of mind.

Isn't it worth it?

Martin Ralbovsky

Camping without Complaining

Angry black clouds roll from horizon to horizon. Lightning crackles and thunder growls in the high mountain meadows, and it's hard to make out the valley below through the wall of rain hammering down out of the darkness.

The storm's brought wind with it and you're cold to the bone. The rock shelf you're hunkered under takes the worst of it, but water pools in your boots and your Levi's just won't dry out. You can't stop shaking.

You know two things: You're scared, miserable, embarrassed—and you never want this to happen again.

Well, it doesn't have to. If you follow the advice you're about to read, your next Rocky Mountain thunderstorm should be *fun* instead of frightening.

"Take your common sense with you, and camping at any time of the year can be safe, sane and enjoyable," camping expert Steve Netherby says.

He should know. He's been doing it for 30 years, works as camping editor of *Field and Stream* magazine and holds certificates from several wilderness-skills academies, including the prestigious National Outdoor Leadership School in Lander, Wyoming.

Netherby offers some tips for making sure that your next camping trip is a pleasure, not a pain.

GEAR UP— AND GEAR UPSCALE

"Good equipment is very important: It often makes the difference between a great trip and a miserable one," Netherby says. "I recommend buying the absolute best gear you can afford, for three reasons: It's going to

be a lot lighter and take up less space in your car or on your back. It's going to do a lot more for you in terms of comfort and convenience. And it's going to do it reliably and safely a lot longer than the bargain basement stuff."

Here are the items on Netherby's recommended equipment list.

A quality nylon tent with a waterproof rain fly and an exterior frame. "Nylon's probably the best material for maximum strength and minimum weight," Netherby says. "The dome is one good design that provides plenty of room with little weight.

Ground Rules on Campgrounds

Your campsite's a good one if it fits the specifications outlined below by *Field and Stream* camping editor Steve Netherby. Your spot should be:

● 200 feet or more away from water (reduces risk of water pollution and risk of animal contact).
● On level ground slightly higher than surrounding terrain (for sleeping comfort, better breeze, drainage, fewer bugs).
● Sheltered from the elements behind rocks or trees.

"One thing I'd like to see more people do is look *up*," Netherby says. "Check for dead trees or branches that might come down in a storm. They're called widowmakers, and one of them almost killed a friend of mine."

And the exterior frame gives you a little extra room inside. That's nice if you're stuck inside on a rainy day."

Netherby recommends subtracting one person from the manufacturer's rating to get a good idea of how many people can comfortably use a tent. He also says to make sure it's equipped with mesh doors and windows to keep out unwanted insects.

A sleeping bag with nylon shell and synthetic insulation such as Polarguard or Quallofil. "You should pick the shape—rectangular or fitted—that you're most comfortable with, but don't play games with the insulation: Stick with the better synthetics," Netherby says.

"Down is useless when it's wet. In fact, I think it's actually dangerous unless you're a very experienced camper who knows how to keep it dry under all conditions. The synthetics work wet *or* dry."

A good sleeping pad. "The tent will keep you dry and the bag will keep you warm, but if you're sleeping on bare floor you're not going to sleep well—and after picking the right gear, getting a good night's sleep is probably the single most important thing you can do to make sure you stay healthy and enjoy your trip," Netherby says.

His tips for sweet slumber: Buy a 1½-inch-thick, open-cell foam pad that's ribbed like an egg carton. The ribbed design resists compression, which means you sleep *over* the rocks instead of on them. And the thicker the pad, the better it insulates—important in cooler weather.

"Stay away from even the best of the air mattresses," Netherby says. "I've been trying to find the leak in one of mine for years. And that's no

Your First-Aid Checklist

Field and Stream camping editor Steve Netherby recommends that your basic first-aid kit include the following items.

- Adhesive bandages—large and small.
- Butterfly dressings.
- Triangular bandage.
- Gauze pads—large and small.
- Roll of gauze.
- Adhesive tape.
- Antiseptic cream.
- Moleskin.
- Buffered aspirin.
- Tweezers and needles.
- First-aid pamphlet.

fun at all when it happens in the middle of the night with a cold rain coming down."

Water-purification kit. "*Giardia* is probably the biggest health hazard the camping family faces," Netherby says. "You basically have to assume that all groundwater in North America is contaminated and act accordingly."

Giardia lamblia is a microscopic organism that can produce diarrhea, cramps, nausea and dehydration. The best treatment is prevention. Purify your drinking water using one of the three generally approved methods: iodine tablets, a filtration pump, or boiling. Netherby comes down slightly in favor of iodine. "All three systems work well," he says, "but there are a lot of times when it's just more convenient to drop the pills in and wait 20 minutes."

The National Park Service, however, recommends *boiling* your water for 3 to 5 minutes. Bringing the water to the boiling point is not enough.

"Iodine just isn't as reliable: You have to get the dose just right," says spokesman Duncan Morrow. "And it's easy to get the filter itself contaminated on one of the pump-filter systems. Boiling, on the other hand, works every time—no muss, no fuss."

A day pack. This is a small rucksack to carry with you when you leave your campsite to explore the woods or hike the trails. Why should you have one? Because what's in it might save your life.

"You can't predict weather or accidents," Netherby says. "Use your common sense, but remember—the stuff back in your car is no help at all 10 miles down the trail."

His suggestions for your trail pack: A first-aid kit (see the box "Your First-Aid Checklist"), sunblock (SPF 15 or above), an insect repellent containing DEET (diethyltoluamide), your water-purification system or a container to boil water in, a canteen or two, a lighter, raingear, sunglasses, a broad-brimmed hat and an extra insulation layer such as a sweater or vest and a light polypropylene jacket.

And finally—good boots. Morrow recommends a sturdy boot that gives good arch and ankle support and is as light as possible for the weight you're carrying.

THREE SPECIAL SAFETY TIPS

Morrow offers up the final piece of equipment a camping family needs to stay safe and healthy in the woods: knowledge.

"A large part of the accidents we see in the national parks are the product of a mind-set that doesn't recognize the parks for what they are—very *different* from the urban environment," Morrow says.

"People need to know that in many respects a park—any park, anywhere—is an alien environment and, like any new environment, it has its own set of rules."

Here are Morrow's tips for staying healthy in the parks.

Pay attention. Gawking at gorgeous scenery produces car wrecks and falls—the two leading killers in national parks. If you want to appreciate the scenery, pull over or stop walking and take in the sights before you continue.

Know the rules. That includes not leaving food out, not feeding the animals, not starting fires except in approved areas and not getting between a mother animal and her young. "Get between the gentlest doe and her fawn and she'll attack. When she's through, you'll look like you've been in a knife fight."

Know your own limits. "If you can't read a map, don't leave the trail. And don't assume that a hundred laps in your pool at home means you can swim the Colorado. Your pool isn't equipped with cold water, logs and rip tides."

Kim Anderson

Water Sports: It's Safety First

Whether it's Niagara Falls, a country lake, a trout pond, a winding river, a cement pool or the Atlantic Ocean, you can bet your zinc nose cream that if there's water somewhere, men, women and children in garish bathing suits, strange hats, Hawaiian shirts, water wings and suntan lotion will be there getting wet, throwing beach balls and having the time of their lives.

Come vacation time, we do almost anything we can in water, and sometimes what we do is dangerous. We overload boats, swim too far out, dive without caution, use improper gear—and sometimes we even drown.

According to figures released by the national YMCA, drowning is the third leading cause of accidental death in the United States, claiming an average of 7,500 lives each year. Of these victims, 40 percent drown while swimming in indoor, outdoor, campus or backyard pools, lakes, rivers, oceans and swimming holes. Half of these deaths occur because the swimmer was either alone or in an unguarded area. The other 60 percent of the victims are nonswimmers who had no intention of setting foot in the water. These drowning incidents include fishing, boating, sailing and canoeing mishaps, falling into backyard swimming pools and driving off bridges.

Vacation plans should include a formal family get-together where water safety is discussed, according to the YMCA. Know what you can do to prevent an accident in water and what to do if an accident does occur. Here are some tips from the YMCA to help keep your water vacations safe.

DOWN TO THE SEA IN SHIFTS

The most important rule in water safety is never go it alone. Whether you're swimming, boating, drifting in a raft or just soaking your feet off the dock, always have someone there with you.

Just think of it—if you get a cramp while swimming or accidentally slip off the boat, and you're alone, you have no rope and no helping hand for aid or comfort. If you venture too far away from everyone else, even your calls for help may not be heard in time. Anytime you're heading out in the water, try to go in a party of three or more. To go out alone is not daring and courageous—it's just stupid and dangerous!

DWI: DROWNING WHILE INTOXICATED

According to U.S. Coast Guard statistics, if you drink and have a boating accident, you have a 50 percent

I Float, Therefore I Still Am

The human body can do many things, and floating on top of water for hours upon hours is one of them. When a swimmer finds himself in trouble, he can prevent himself from drowning by simply doing 2 things: Don't panic and stay afloat.

Legs are comprised mostly of heavy muscle and bone, thereby almost ensuring us that they will not float. Therefore, when you need to float, you should concentrate on your chest and lungs. Keep your ears underwater and your chest above water, and breathe slowly and deeply. You will probably feel your legs starting to sink, but don't panic. Just keep your lower body relaxed and limp, with your back arched, and keep on breathing.

A slow, relaxed stroking motion with your hands will provide slight propulsion that will aid in keeping you alive and above water. You can stay afloat all day waiting for help if need be.

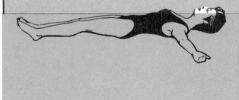 

Learning how to float is a matter of putting your head back, gently arching your back and extending your arms. In such a position, the water will begin to support the body. Different swimmers will find different positions natural, such as the horizontal float, left, and the diagonal float.

chance of drowning. Statistics show a marked increase in alcohol- and drug-related drownings during the past 20 years. The Coast Guard estimates show that for boating accidents, 50 percent of the drowning victims had blood alcohol levels above the legal level for intoxication.

So if you don't get tanked up and jump behind the wheel of your car because you know it's dangerous, don't leave your common sense at home while vacationing. If you've had a drink or two, stay out of the water. Take a nap instead, hike around your campsite or sit down to a hearty outdoor meal, but keep far away from the water.

GET IN GEAR

We do more in the water than just get wet. We sail and boat on it, thrill-seekers raft, canoe, kayak and ski on it. Some of us even para-sail high above the water, then hope to safely land on it.

No matter which water activity interests you, an essential part of your boating gear should be a U.S. Coast Guard-approved personal flotation device (PFD)—a life jacket. (Look for the label in the device, which will also specify weight restrictions.) Even the most accomplished swimmer should not venture out on a boat without wearing a PFD.

Coast Guard statistics reveal that 92 percent of people who do any type of boating do not wear PFDs. The Coast Guard estimates that of boating accident victims, 80 percent could have survived had they worn PFDs. In short, the cost of a life jacket is a small price to pay to keep you alive and floating above the water.

"WEATHER" OR NOT TO GET OUT

If you've ever been pelted by baseball-size hailstones after having your local TV weatherman forecast a

Tidbits on Eating and Swimming

Dear Gabby,

When I was 10 and on vacation with my parents, my mother told me that after I ate, I had to stay out of the water at least 3 hours or else I'd get a cramp and drown. In high school, my swimming coach said we only had to wait about 30 minutes. Now I'm a father about to take my family on their first vacation, and I'm a little confused about all this. What advice should I give my kids about eating, swimming and getting cramps?

Digesting in a Dinghy

Dear Digesting,

Despite all the myths surrounding the subject, there is no set time to wait before returning to the water after eating. According to the national YMCA, it depends on the amount of food consumed, the kind of food ingested, your general physical condition, your degree of fatigue, the water temperature and the vigor of your swimming activities.

When you swim, your blood flow is shunted away from your stomach to the muscles needing energy to keep you swimming. This slows absorption and the digestive process.

For young children, what the heck, keep them out of the water for at least an hour after eating. It couldn't hurt. As for their elders, use your better judgment. If you feel full from your meal and are sluggish, stay out of the water. Maybe take a walk along the beach to help speed up your digestion.

Gabby

mild summer day, you know how unpredictable the weather can be. If meteorologists have a difficult time analyzing and predicting what Mother Nature is about to do, the chances

that the average vacationer can accurately forecast changing weather conditions are pretty slim. Keeping an eye out for these certain known principles, however, will help you recognize hazardous weather approaching and give you ample time to reach shore.

● If cloud formations begin changing rapidly, chances are bad weather is on the way. Any change in cloud color, especially from white to gray, could signify that a storm is brewing.
● If you spot a gray line on the horizon, it's there to warn you that severe weather is just around the corner and you should head immediately to shore.
● If you hear thunder or see lightning, it's time to say goodbye to the water for a while. Water is a natural conductor of electrical current, and when your body is in the water, it too becomes a conductor. So don't take chances. If there is any evidence whatsoever of thunder or lightning, get out of the water and wait for the storm to pass.
● If you're on the ocean and the wind suddenly begins to blow stronger, head to shore. Not only does it mean a storm is approaching—stronger winds mean stronger waves, which could easily tip your boat or rough up the most experienced swimmer.
● In open-water environments such as lakes, rivers and the ocean, warmer water usually stays at the surface, but a shift in the surface temperature or sudden high winds can stir the colder water upward and catch a swimmer by surprise. Hypothermia, a condition in which body temperature dives, and fatigue could set in quickly. Whenever you feel the water temperature cool suddenly, it's a good idea to head for shore or your boat for a while, until the winds die down.

Richard Dominick

Dollars and Sense

There's no faster way to ruin a vacation than by getting robbed. It almost happened to one frequent traveler on his honeymoon in Italy. He and his wife were in Rome, staying at a luxury hotel. The day they were to leave for Venice, the new husband casually exchanged $800 worth of traveler's checks for Italian lira. On his way back to settle his hotel bill, he was surrounded by a group of dirty youngsters wearing rags and holding big pieces of white cardboard. Thinking they were begging for change, he reached into his pocket to give them something, but they started pulling at his clothes and trying to reach into his pocket.

Suddenly he realized he was in the middle of a robbery. Friends had warned him about kids who hold up bright objects and pieces of cardboard to confuse weary travelers, and then take everything they own. He shouted and kicked at the kids. They backed off and snarled at him like dogs who'd lost their dinner. The man escaped being ripped off—but barely.

Not all money losses are due to robbery, either. Some are caused by plain old lack of common sense. One traveler tells the story of the time he dropped his clothes off at a laundry in Japan. The owners couldn't speak English, and he knew no Japanese, having been there only a few days. But somehow he got the point across that he wanted his laundry washed and ironed. They let him know it would be ready the next day. What they never discussed, however, was price. When he picked it up, the bill came to the equivalent of almost $45 for one load of laundry. No, they hadn't raised the prices on him because he was a tourist. Things are very expensive in Tokyo, and at this laundry, everything was done by hand. It looked beautiful! It was the most perfect laundry he'd ever seen. But he hadn't wanted art, he'd just wanted clean clothes for the rest of his trip.

BEWARE OF TOURIST PRICES

Sometimes shopkeepers like to "earn" some extra money by raising prices for the "rich" foreigners. And it doesn't just happen in shops and restaurants. John Hatt, author of *The Tropical Traveller*, was staying in a hotel in Niamey, the capital of Niger, when he decided to telephone someone who was 12 miles away. When he hung up, the operator called him back and said the charge for the call was $25—clearly a ridiculous sum. It seems that the hotel manager and operator were operating a scheme together to rip off tourists. After 3 hours of tiresome discussion, Hatt finally got the bill down to about $6.

A woman named Diana, who works in public relations, was ripped off in a swindle that sometimes happens in foreign countries with black markets. "We should have known better," she says.

Changing money on the black market means you exchange your U.S. dollars for the local currency at a better rate than you would get at a bank or exchange house. It's tempting, because the rates offered are often many times higher than the official exchange rate. But the black market is also usually illegal, and it can be risky, as Diana found out.

"My husband and I have been to Brazil several times, and we'd always exchanged money on the black market with no problem. Well, this last time this respectable-looking guy approached us and asked if we'd like to exchange some money. We said okay and gave him $100, and he asked us to follow him a little way. Then he handed us a wad of money and took off. Once we took a look at the money, we realized we'd been taken. It was a pile of worthless money—old bills that had been devalued—sandwiched

How to Foil a Pickpocket

Rey Valdes, a detective with the Metro-Dade Police Department, which handles crime in Miami (that ever-popular destination for tourists and thieves) suggests these ways to impede pickpockets.

● Divide your money among 2 or 3 pockets. That way, if 1 pocket gets picked, you'll still have some money.
● Put a comb in the middle fold of your wallet. That way, when someone tries to pull it out of your pocket, the comb will catch on the pocket or jab you in the side, and you'll realize what's going on.
● Keep your wallet in your front pants pocket or your inside jacket pocket, and button it shut if you can.

between two good bills that were worth maybe $2 or $3. We went to the police, but we had to wait 2 or 3 hours and didn't get any help. It was a terrible situation."

FOOLPROOF ADVICE

The wise traveler takes steps to prevent such rip-offs. So here, from the U.S. State Department, are steps to follow to protect your money when traveling.

● Don't carry large amounts of cash. Take most of your money in refundable traveler's checks. Keep track of the checks you spend and keep that information in a separate place from the checks.

● Leave the credit cards you don't plan to use at home, to prevent theft. "And be sure you know what your credit card limit is," says Ruth van Heuven, public affairs adviser for the State Department's Bureau of Consular Affairs. "Some countries will arrest you for fraud if you try to charge over the limit." Keep a list of the numbers of your charge cards so you can report them if they are stolen.

● Photocopy your passport, plane tickets and any credit cards you're taking with you and keep them in a safe but separate place.

● Make advance arrangements with a relative or friend who can send you money in case yours is stolen.

● Before you arrive in the country, exchange some money so you can pay for taxis and other services on arrival. The money exchange booth in the airport might be closed when you arrive.

● Exchange money only at a bank, if possible. They offer better exchange rates than hotels and restaurants.

● Don't exchange money on the black market. If you do, you might get swindled.

Kelly Marrione, Jr., sees a lot of tourists fall prey to theft in his job as a police officer with the crime preven-tion unit of the New Orleans Police Department. He offers this advice.

● Don't carry your money in your purse, if you can help it. Keep the money in your pocket. That way, if someone tries to steal your purse by snatching it, you can let them have it. "You don't want to risk breaking your arm for a purse full of makeup."

● Keep your belongings out of view in your car. "Many people don't realize how easy cars are to break into," says Marrione. "They'll put their property in plain view in their car, like on the rear seat, and park the car and go look at the sights. Too often they'll come back and someone will have smashed the window and stolen their money and valuables. You should lock everything in the trunk."

● Keep your purse in the trunk even while you're driving, especially if you are visiting a strange city. "People in New Orleans have even smashed out the side window of an occupied car that's stopped in traffic, and taken a purse."

● If you're walking and you think someone's following you to steal your money, especially if you don't know your way around the area you're visiting, just drop your purse or wallet in the nearest mailbox. "The thief won't be able to get to it," Marrione says. "Look on the box for the next pickup time and explain what happened to the mailman. Or call the central post office. You'll get your money back."

Preventing theft of money is really just common sense, says Susan Venticinque, senior counselor for the Travelers' Aid Society office at John F. Kennedy International Airport on Long Island, New York. Here's her advice for keeping yourself from becoming a victim of crime while traveling.

● Don't leave your baggage unattended. "I always hear people say, 'But I just left for a minute.' Well, you're dealing with professionals here, and it

Calling on Uncle Sam

"We will do our best to help a U.S. citizen who's in trouble abroad, but we aren't a hotel, bank or travel service," says Bruce Ammerman, U.S. State Department spokesman. "What we would do for someone who is robbed overseas is help them with their contacts with the local authorities. And if they didn't have any money, we'd help them get in touch with someone who could send them money."

The embassies don't have slush funds they can lend to stranded travelers, but wherever possible, they will put you in touch with local agencies similar to the Salvation Army that can help you find a place to stay or eat.

"Rarely does a person end up in this situation," says Ammerman. "Usually people travel in groups of 2 or more and 1 person will have some money. But in the rare case where a person is really destitute, with no money and no plane ticket, we'll lend him or her the cost of transportation to the nearest port of entry in the United States. Government funds are made available on a strictly loan basis and must be repaid within a limited time. Loan recipients aren't able to use their passport until the loan is repaid."

doesn't take them any time at all to steal your bags."

● Only seek help or information from someone in uniform.

● Be aware of what's going on around you. "People on vacation often walk through the airports with visions of palm trees and swimming pools in their heads, and they don't pay as much attention to what they're doing as they would at home. They take extra risks, like pulling $200 out of their pocket."

Stephen Williams

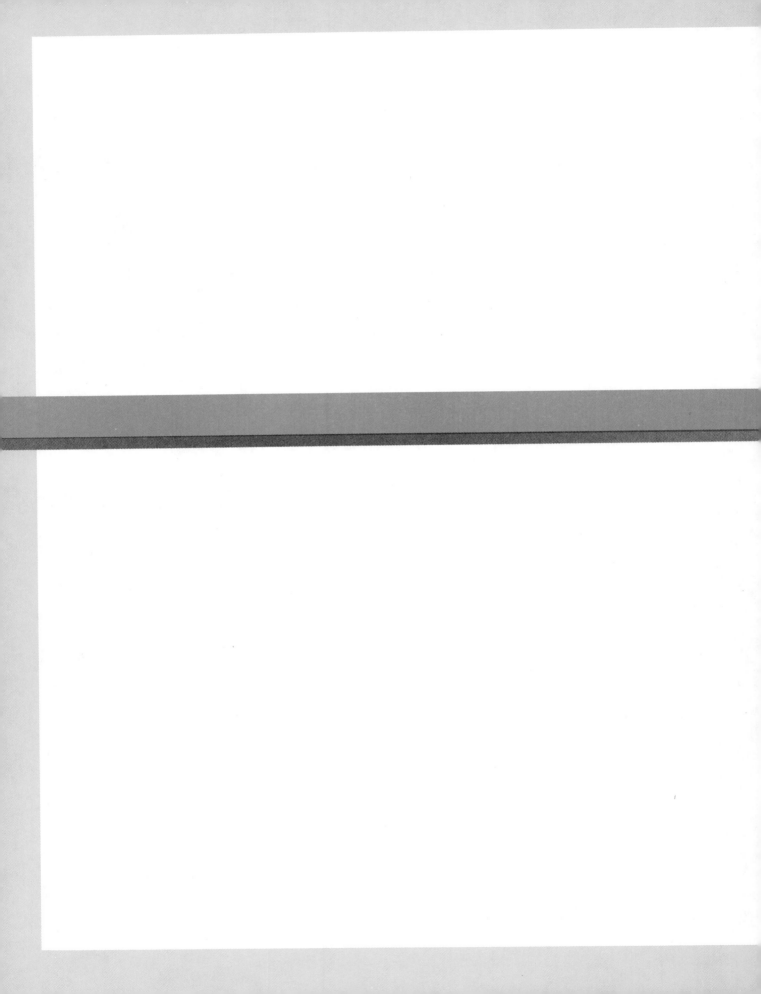

BEAUTY AND GROOMING

Anti-Aging Skin Care

You're at a high school class reunion, looking eagerly for a friend you haven't seen in 20 years. But when she approaches, you barely recognize her. Her hair and figure are fine, and she's as lively and funny as ever. But her face is lined and weathered. As you greet her, you can't help asking yourself, "Do I look that old, too?"

We judge people's age, health and maybe even their sexual attractiveness or ability to do a job right by what we see in their faces. That's why it's important to know what yours is saying about you. And if it's making you look tired or older than you feel, more than simple vanity could be at stake. Having to look at a world-weary face in the mirror every morning could erode your self-confidence and even change the way people treat you.

"I think wrinkles are a major medical and psychological problem, far more serious than most doctors acknowledge," says Albert Kligman, M.D., Ph.D., professor of dermatology at the University of Pennsylvania Hospital. "They may not be a threat to life, but the anxieties they create can spoil life. I think there are good psychological and economic reasons for that anxiety. One thing I don't tell them is that they have to accept their face the way it is. There are plenty of things you can do to smooth the wrinkles you have or to prevent more."

But first, let's take a look at why your face ages.

Why do you wind up with wrinkles? Part of the answer lies below the skin's surface. If you could peek underneath your skin, you'd see that, over the years, the supporting tissue has been damaged. This tissue, known as the dermis, contains water, fat and cells that help produce fibers. The two most important fibers are colla-gen and elastin. It's these fortifying fibers that give the skin firmness and elasticity and make it bounce back after it's stretched into a smile or a scowl.

As we age, the dermis retains less water and fat, so the skin doesn't look as firm and plump. Fewer supporting fibers are produced, so the skin is less resilient. Less oil is produced, so the skin gets drier. Cell renewal rate slows, especially in women past menopause. New cells don't develop as quickly and old ones stay longer on the surface of the skin. Fibroblast cells produce fewer supporting fibers, and those that are produced have less resiliency than in young skin. Finally, the skin receives less oxygen and nutrients as tiny capillaries beneath it close off. We begin to look old—creases appear, cheeks and neck sag, bags bulge out, spots show up.

TURNING BACK THE TRACKS OF TIME

How fast will your face age? That depends on many factors—most of which you can control. In fact, the only factor you *can't* control is the type of skin that got passed on to you from your parents.

If, for example, you are a fair-skinned blond or redhead with skin that burns rather than bronzes, you're more likely to be wearing wrinkles in your later years. If, on the other hand, you have dark, thick, oily skin, you'll probably have the least lines, because your skin's heavily pigmented outer layer protects you from the aging effects of sunlight.

No matter what your skin type, though, there's plenty you can do to ward off wrinkles and guard against looking older than you feel.

Live a shady life. Many dermatologists think the sun is the number one cause of wrinkling, pigment changes and skin cancer. "I always show women the underside of their breasts or upper arms, areas that are seldom exposed to the sun," says Dr. Kligman. "That's the way the skin on their faces would look if it had been protected—smooth, firm, unblemished."

The good news is that even if you've left your skin exposed in the past, you can gain back some of its natural smoothness if you stick to the shade and slather on sunscreen whenever you step into the sunshine.

"If you stay in the shade or use a sunscreen, you will see a reversal of many of the changes in your skin," Dr. Kligman says. "It won't become young skin again. The major changes —wrinkles, bags, sags—are going to stay. But the connective tissue underneath the top layer of the skin, the dermis, will definitely improve. The cells have a chance to make new collagen. Precancerous lesions simply disappear.

"After about two or three years of not being in the sun," he says, "you'll have what looks like a light peel, where a few upper layers of the skin have been removed, leaving the skin smoother looking."

And when you do step out in the sunshine—even for a walk in winter—wear a sunscreen. The higher the sun protection factor (SPF), the better. (For more on sun sense, see "How to Stay Safe in the Sun" on page 168.)

Combat dryness. Another dreaded enemy of your skin is dryness. You can expect some suppleness to slip away over the years as your skin cells produce less water, fat and oils.

But dryness need not be a problem. Here's what you can do.

● Wear night creams while sleeping. Apply a super-moisturizing cream to clean, damp skin. These products trap water in your skin's outer surface and plump it up with water so that fine lines seem to disappear. Your skin feels soft, moist and supple. Look for products that absorb easily into the skin. These formulations may contain a blend of emollients and ingredients like collagen or elastin. When applying, skip the oily spots and blemishes. People with acne-prone skin should avoid night creams altogether.

● Moisturize the atmosphere. In fall and winter, hook up a humidifier at home, especially in the bedroom, and at the office. Or put pans of water on top of your hot-water radiators.

● Take fewer, faster showers and baths. The more water you are exposed to, the more you invite dryness and old-looking skin. And turn the taps to warm or cool, not hot. Hot water strips away your skin's natural oils. If you prefer a tub soak, bath oil can be added to the water. Soak in the tub

How the Face Ages

Some of us age better than others, but sooner or later the telltale signs catch up with us all. Here's the natural progression of aging skin as outlined by Gerald Imber, M.D., a plastic surgeon at the Institute for the Control of Facial Aging in New York City.

By age 30: You may spot squint lines around the corners of the eyes or faint horizontal lines across the forehead. Like a leather glove, the skin becomes permanently creased into wrinkles in the areas where it's being worked into frequent expressions.

By 40: Wrinkles from other facial expressions have shown up—arcs running from the nose to the corners of the mouth and vertical lines between the eyebrows.

By 50: Wrinkles have become deeper. The skin on the cheeks and neck starts to loosen up and sag into jowls and "turkey neck."

By 60: The muscles around the eyes may have weakened, allowing fat deposits to pop through and form bags under the eyes.

By 70: Wrinkles have formed everywhere. The skin is rougher in texture and has lost its uniform color. Ovals of deeper pigmentation—liver spots—dot the forehead and temples. Both the tip of the nose and the earlobes have drooped about ½ inch or more. The skin has redraped itself over the underlying bone structure so that prominent features, like a large nose, seem to stand out even more.

Fortunately, pleasing features stand out more as well. "If you have good bone structure, you will appear to age better," says Dr. Imber. "Noticeable facial prominences like high cheekbones, foreheads and chins maintain certain highlights so that when the light hits them, they stand out and give form to the face. This constantly maintains the look of youth and vitality." And people with a right angle between the jaw and neck, he adds, will have less noticeable sagging of the skin beneath the jaw than those whose jaw and neck tend to meet in a curving line.

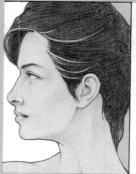   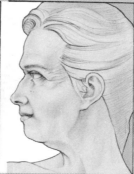 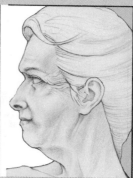

Age 30 brings on faint squint marks.

Age 40 reveals smile arcs.

Age 50 brings on the jowls.

Age 60 shows signs of bags under the eyes.

By age 70, liver spots begin to show.

for 15 minutes, then apply a moisturizer. Ban bath salts and bubble baths —they promote dryness.

● Cleanse your skin with a mild, superfatted soap and rinse well. Be careful when using cleansing and so-called clarifying lotions containing alcohol. Try a water-based toner; it may be less drying.

Avoid exposure to heat. Heat can penetrate the skin and damage connective tissues and fibers—the stuff that keeps your skin from sagging. Use handheld hair dryers, avoiding the high setting, and direct the hot air away from your face. Stay out of the hot midday sun.

Always wear weatherproofers. Don't leave home without protecting your face from the elements. Wintry winds call for wearing a neoprene face mask. A dip in the pool requires an application of a good moisturizer first to keep chlorine from being absorbed into your skin. Wear good, protective sunglasses winter and summer to prevent squinting and crow's feet.

Feed your face. Good nutrition is important for healthy, young-looking skin that's less likely to crack, peel or dry out. And healthy skin is less likely to show wear and tear.

Skin problems are sometimes the first signal of a vitamin deficiency. The B vitamins thiamine, riboflavin and B_6 are often found in lean beef, chicken, eggs, rye flour and milk, among other foods. Some B-complex deficiencies—thiamine (B_1), riboflavin (B_2), biotin—cause scaling and redness, especially around the mouth and nose.

Zinc deficiencies can cause similar conditions. And both zinc and vitamin C are important in the production of collagen, the skin's support tissue.

So be on the safe side and make sure your diet includes the vitamins and minerals for vital skin.

Antioxidants, which include vitamins A, C and E, seem to reduce the sun's damage to the skin. Synthetic forms of vitamin A have been used to help treat cancer and precancerous skin growths and to treat acne and wrinkles. Also, it increases the cell renewal rate, normalizes cell growth and stimulates blood flow and collagen formation.

Fresh fruits and vegetables are good sources of vitamins A and C, while oils, seeds and nuts provide vitamin E. Whether taking antioxidants over a lifetime will make your skin less wrinkled remains to be seen, however.

Zinc is an important mineral in the production of collagen, the skin's support tissue. Doctors at England's East Birmingham Hospital have

Breast Creams Are a Bust

Can you buy a firmer bustline? The breast cream ads would lead you to believe that you can when they claim that they'll improve the firmness and tone of women's breasts.

Sounds pretty sensational. But do these new breast creams and lotions really do what (supposedly) they say they do? Or do they simply fatten the manufacturer's pocketbook?

"They have to be phony," says Albert Kligman, M.D., Ph.D. "There's no way a cream can penetrate your skin enough to change or strengthen the tissue that supports the breast."

Perhaps the only real benefit from bust creams, adds another expert, is that they moisturize your skin.

If you really want to have a more shapely, youthful bustline, put away your pocketbook and practice the following tips.

Peel off the pounds. "Basically you're trying to combat gravity as well as age," says Dr. Kligman. "If you want to slow down the sagging of your breasts, you should watch your body weight."

Tone up muscle tissue. "Exercise can help give you better tone by developing the muscle tissue found between the chest wall and the breast," says John Romano, M.D., dermatologist at the New York Hospital/Cornell University Medical Center, New York City.

Sharon Fuchs, director and fitness consultant at Physical Dynamics in New York City, suggests:

● Work out with free weights. This type of exercise can help strengthen and tone the pectoral muscles that support the breasts.
● Practice push-ups. The modified kind where your knees remain on the floor are great.
● Stick to a series of exercises. Work on your chest and shoulders rather than doing isolated exercise for one set of muscles. Also, balance the effect by exercising the back of your body, too.

suggested that those brownish skin patches known as age spots may not be a sign of aging so much as a warning flag of zinc deficiency.

Beef and calves' liver, lean beef, lamb, roasted pumpkin and sunflower seeds, Brazil nuts, Swiss and cheddar cheeses, peanuts and dark meat turkey are good sources of zinc.

Don't make faces. A simple smile or scowl, repeated over a lifetime, can etch permanent lines into your face. So can squinting in the sun, straining to see or concentrating on something. How can we ease these expression lines?

Keep a mirror by the telephone and watch the faces you make, suggests Jeffrey H. Binstock, M.D., assistant clinical professor of dermatologic surgery at the University of California, San Francisco. Then teach yourself to systematically relax your facial muscles so that they feel heavy and warm. A gentle facial massage can help you relax and make lines less noticeable.

Also, don't bury your face in your pillow. It may sculpt your face into lines and furrows and absorb some of the vital moisture from your face.

Give yourself a break. Again and again, dermatologists have seen the connection between stress and all kinds of skin diseases—acne flare-up just before an exam, severe eczema during a divorce. There's no doubt our emotions can play havoc with our skin, but whether stress and worry can cause wrinkles is something that has yet to be verified, says Roland S. Medansky, M.D., an Illinois dermatologist.

"Compared to sun exposure and genes, I'd say stress plays a small part in aging skin," Dr. Medansky says. "But there's no question that it can cause skin to appear to age. All you have to do is look at the face of any president when he goes into office and when he comes out four years later. You might see double or triple that number of extra years on his face."

Sometimes, surprisingly, that damage might tend to reverse itself later, as ex-presidents relax and enjoy their retirement. "Remember how pasty and lined Jimmy Carter looked when he left office?" one dermatologist asks. "Well, he looks a heck of a lot better now."

RUN WRINKLES OUT OF TOWN

Know how a good brisk workout brings a healthy glow to your cheeks? Well, that blush isn't just pretty. It's a sign that the exercise is flushing your skin with blood. And the result is good news for wrinkle-watchers, says James White, Ph.D., an exercise physiologist at the University of California, San Diego, and author of *Jump for Joy*, a book of exercise programs for people concerned about their skin or recovering from plastic surgery.

Finnish researchers, for example, found that middle-aged athletes had skin that was denser, thicker and stronger than that of a matched group of sedentary people. The elastic quality that allows the skin to spring back to its original shape after being stretched was also significantly better in the athletes.

The cells in the base layer of the skin, where skin cells are formed, actually become more active with exercise, Dr. White says. More of the chemical substances that are used to produce the elastic fibers can be found in the cells of people who exercise.

In his own research, Dr. White found that people who either worked out indoors on a mini-trampoline or ran outdoors while wearing a sunblock, both for 30 to 40 minutes a day, had fewer wrinkles than non-exercisers. And the exercise group had an added bonus—the bags under their eyes vanished.

PUFF ON THIS

According to a study conducted by British physician Douglas Model, M.D., it may be possible to tell smokers from nonsmokers by studying their faces. He found that smokers had one or more of the following facial characteristics.

● Lines or wrinkles on the face typically radiating at right angles from the upper and lower lips or the corners of the eyes. We commonly know these lines as crow's feet.
● Deep lines on the cheeks or numerous shallow lines on the cheeks and lower jaw.
● A subtle gauntness.
● A leathery or rugged appearance.
● A slightly pigmented, gray tone.

What smoking does, notes Dr. Model, is deprive the skin of normal blood flow. Moreover, because smoking interferes with the healing process, it occasionally causes dangerously bad results following cosmetic surgery to smooth out wrinkles, reports Thomas Rees, M.D., a plastic surgeon affiliated with the Manhattan Eye, Ear and Throat Hospital in New York City. Eighty percent of patients who had problems recovering from their face-lifts smoked more than a pack a day. Thick layers of their skin died and fell off, resulting in larger scars and longer healing time.

A Mouth to Smile About

Getting Jon to smile is like pulling teeth. And that's just the problem—Jon could stand to have a tooth or two pulled. His top teeth are so crowded and protrude so much he could be a stand-in for Bugs Bunny. If that's not bad enough, one of his big lower teeth has turned a deep gray—a souvenir from the time he fell off his bike as a kid.

So Jon is rather guarded with his smiles. "My friends kid and call me Stoneface," he says.

But Jon's problem is no joke. He doesn't realize that by hiding his smile, he's sending the wrong signals to others. As a result, he's become somewhat of a misfit—both socially and on the job.

"If you repress your smile," explains Norman Feigenbaum, D.D.S., a New York dentist and editor of the *Forum of Esthetic Dentistry,* "you give people conflicting signals. Your words may say, 'I like you' but the lack of a smile says, 'I'm not really sure about you.' People who do this aren't getting their real message across, and yet they may never know why people aren't responding to them. This can even affect your career. In business, people trust people who seem open, not guarded."

THE POWER OF COSMETIC DENTISTRY

Few of us have picture-perfect smiles. Despite our dedication to regular brushing and checkups, our teeth may show the wear and tear of years of use. They can shift, twist, chip, crack, stain, move closer together or farther apart.

Until recently, there was little an adult could do to fix a misshapen smile except to have teeth pulled and replaced with dentures or ground down

and fitted with caps or crowns. It's no wonder people with less than a perfect smile opted to keep their mouths shut!

But all that's changed. Thanks to new cosmetic dentistry techniques, you can now have your teeth transformed—quickly, painlessly and easily.

This new cosmetic dentistry is part of the fitness movement, says Harold McQuinn, D.D.S., chairman of the Department of Dentistry at the Hollywood-Presbyterian Medical Center in Los Angeles. "People want a healthy, good-looking smile to match their bodies. That takes more than having healthy teeth and gums. Cosmetic dentistry makes teeth *look* good, too."

FIVE PROCEDURES TO GRIN ABOUT

Just what will your new smile look like? You can get a good idea by having your dentist make before-and-after wax molds of your entire mouth. But don't expect your new teeth to look totally perfect, says Dr. McQuinn. "Cosmetic dentistry should make people notice your beautiful smile, not your great caps or veneers."

With that in mind, here's a rundown of the latest cosmetic dentistry procedures.

Cosmetic contouring. This is the simplest, least expensive way to even out a slightly misshapen smile. All it takes is one visit to the dentist and a bit more money than it costs to have a few cavities filled. The dentist reshapes the teeth, much like a sculptor, filing and polishing away here, building on bits of resins there. Voila! He's created the illusion of straight, even teeth. Contouring can, for example,

file down that fanglike tooth in front or cleverly "straighten" out that overlapping one.

Bonding. Want to close that silly-looking gap or finally take care of that cracked tooth you've had since that

Lips That Create a Lasting Impression

It sometimes seems that lipstick does a better disappearing act than Houdini. Here's how to make your lipstick stay put.

● Apply foundation on your lips and follow with a dusting of loose powder.
● Outline your lips with a lip pencil. Place dots at points along the rim of your lips, then connect the dots. Soften the line with a Q-Tip.
● Fill in with a lip brush. Do not bring it all the way up to the line. Go around your entire mouth again with your lip pencil.
● Blot just a bit with a tissue.
● Reapply fresh lipstick by applying color to the center of each lip.

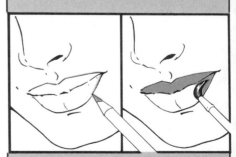

The secret to long-lasting lipstick includes outlining the lips with a pencil, left, and filling them in with lipstick applied by brush.

fateful fall from the jungle gym? Bonding may be your best bet. The dentist will etch your tooth with a mild acid gel, then apply an enamel-dentin bonding agent. Next, he'll apply a plastic veneer in thin layers, using several shades of color on one tooth. It's hardened by a handheld full-spectrum light, and the result is a tooth that looks natural in color and shape.

Bonding can be done in one sitting and costs anywhere from $200 to $500 per tooth. You'll have to repeat the procedure in three to five years, though, and steer clear of coffee, tea and berries—foods that can stain bonded teeth.

Porcelain veneering. This is the newest version of bonding for fixing chipped or cracked teeth. The dentist attaches a custom-made facade just to the front of the tooth, much as you would apply an artificial fingernail. The advantage of veneers is that they don't stain as easily as bonded resins and are much thinner, so they fit more easily and naturally into the gum line. They last five to ten years but cost about $300 to $700 per tooth and require a few visits for the fittings.

Caps and crowns. This is still the procedure of choice for fractured back teeth or if you've had extensive fillings. The problem tooth is ground down and totally covered with a cap or crown—an artificial tooth look-alike. They can cost from $400 to $1,000 per tooth but will last about seven to ten years.

Orthodontics. If you have crooked teeth, you probably already know that they can spoil your smile, cause gum disease and possibly promote tooth loss. But what you may not know is that to correct your problem you may not have to serve a term with braces.

Today, adult orthodontics take less time, money and noticeable hardware. You may, for example, be able to have "braceless braces"—retainers used along with springs, bands and wires—which are worn for several hours each day and only when you're at home. They can correct minor and moderate misalignment problems in only three to six months for a third of the cost of conventional braces.

If your teeth are severely crowded, you may need to wear the more standard braces for two to four years and pay $2,000 or more. The good news is that you could have the brackets bonded right to your teeth (which eliminates unsightly bands) and have them braced with a thin, tooth-colored or transparent wire. Or you could wear "invisible" braces that don't seem to be there at all. They are actually affixed behind the teeth.

HOW TO MAINTAIN A WINNING SMILE

Maybe you've been blessed with super-looking teeth and all you do is brush, floss and see the dentist once or twice a year. Good for you. If you want to hang onto that smile, though, you should also do the following.

● Have new cavities (or old cavities that have lost their fillings) filled with the newer, more natural-looking composite resins made of barium glass and silica particles. They are filled and bonded to your teeth (not packed in) and are less likely to chip at the edges than the silver fillings.

● Replace missing back teeth. Otherwise, the space may attract gum-disease—producing bacteria, throwing off your bite or creating gaps between your front teeth.

● Stop grinding your teeth. Worn down teeth can age your appearance, and they invite staining. Practice relaxation techniques to unclench your mouth. Or wear a mouth guard at night to keep you from grinding in your sleep (a habit known as bruxism).

Marcia Holman

Call It Mellow Yellow

Teeth become unattractively yellow as we age. That's because the enamel wears away and stains settle in. You may hasten this staining process if you regularly drink coffee or smoke cigarettes. Also, your teeth may be tinged with gray or brown if you injured them or drank heavily fluoridated water as a child, if your mother took tetracycline while pregnant with you or if you took tetracycline at an early age.

But you are not doomed to stained, dingy teeth, says Irwin Smigel, D.D.S., president of the American Society for Dental Aesthetics. A regular tooth cleaning at the dentist can sandblast most minor stains. Your dentist can bleach more stubborn ones with a strong hydrogen peroxide solution, which penetrates the tooth and whitens it.

Before you get to that point, follow these at-home brightening tips.

Don't use special stain removers. Scrubbing with abrasive toothpastes could brush away tooth enamel and let stains seep inside. Stick to regular toothpastes and brushes with rounded nylon bristles.

Limit the stain-makers. Go easy on coffee, cigarettes, tea, blueberries and red wine, as well as highly acidic foods and beverages that pit teeth so that deposits accumulate.

Don't chew ice or hard candy. It may cause hairline fractures and invite stains.

Beautiful Eyes

You're standing at the makeup counter in Macy's. And you want to look beautiful. You want to have magnificent eyes like the models in *Vogue* or *Elle* or *Harper's Bazaar.* You'd even settle for a pair of orbs like those of the woman behind the counter. She, at least, knows the difference between liner, lightener and lichen. And look at how her eyes sparkle!

But you're not really into makeup. There's so much of it, so many different kinds, so many different wands, sticks, brushes and swabs. You're worried how it'll all look on you. Yard-long eyelashes may be acceptable on a studio sound stage, but *you* have to meet your son's teacher on parents' night, and his wife at the annual candy sale.

So what should you do? Stick with that tube of dime-store mascara you bought when your youngest was born? Or pick up some shadow, ask for a little advice and maybe put a few stars in your eyes?

Right. Stars it is.

DARK SHADOWS

The first stage of your launch into a new eye look is concealer. "Almost everybody is a little bit dark under the eyes," says Glenn Roberts, Elizabeth Arden's creative beauty director in New York City. So apply a few dabs of concealer under your eye. Use one of the new, light-textured mousse formulas (one shade lighter than your skin tone) which can be applied without pulling or stretching the delicate skin around your eye. And don't apply it all the way up to your lower lid. If you look closely, Roberts explains, you'll notice that the darkness under your eye never really goes all the way up to the lower lid itself.

The second stage in a new look is an eye shadow base, which is applied from lash to brow. The base prevents any subsequent layers of color from fading, streaking, melting or creeping into the crease of your lid. Without a base, Roberts explains, the mere blinking of your eyes will cause shadow to creep.

What color shadow should you use? Make that shadows, Roberts says. Emphasize the bone just under your eyebrow with a light-colored shadow such as pink, then put a color that blends or harmonizes with your clothes on your lid. Between those two areas, use a brown, a gray, a deep plum or a darker shade of your lid color. That's where everybody over the age of 18 gets puffy, Roberts says. But if you darken the area, it minimizes the problem. It's a basic principle of art: dark colors make things recede, light colors bring them forward.

And stop the shadow before you get to the outside corner of your eye. Sweep the shadow up, Roberts advises, especially the darker shadow in the middle, and it will give your whole eye area a lift. It can, in fact, take ten years off your age by offsetting that downward droop caused by your skin's battle with the earth's gravitational pull.

The third stage of your new look is the easiest. Get a pencil eyeliner and draw a thin line under the lower lashes, Roberts says, close to your eyelash roots. Then smudge it. Don't outline the entire eye or extend your liner beyond your eye. Outlining closes up your eye, making it look small and beady, and any liner beyond the natural curve of your eye can look like an extra wrinkle. A deep one.

What's left? Only mascara. Tilt your head back, look at yourself in the mirror and use a mascara wand to stroke color onto your upper lashes. Hold the wand horizontally, Roberts says, and stroke from lid to tip on the upper side of your top lashes, then on the underside. Applying mascara this way, he says, makes your lashes fuller and thicker. It also absorbs any powdered shadow you might have inadvertently sprinkled on your lashes.

To apply mascara to your lower lashes, Roberts says, hold the wand vertically and stroke it back and forth. But make sure there's no excess mascara on the tip of your wand. You could end up looking like a reject from the circus.

They're Gonna Make Your Brown Eyes Blue

God gave you brown eyes and you wanted blue? Or green? How about aqua or sapphire?

They're all yours, says Doug Brown, product manager for Wesley-Jessen, a company that makes contact lenses that can change—not just enhance or tint—the color of your eyes.

The lenses actually mask the underlying eye color with dots, Brown explains. An artist studied how color was distributed in the human eye and then made an irregular pattern that reflected the true color of an iris. The result? Natural eye color that only your mother knows isn't real.

Who can wear colored lenses? Just about anybody who can wear contacts. And they're available both in cosmetic and corrective versions.

THE FINISHING TOUCHES

Those are the basics. You look great. And, after one glance and a double-take in the mirror, you feel great, too. Now here are a few tips on how to put that final sprinkle of stardust in your eyes from Wisconsin cosmetologist Pauline McCloud, a member of Hair America-National Cosmetology Association, who conducts makeup seminars for cosmetologists all over the country.

Wear false eyelashes. Freeze. Do *not* skip over this section, even if wearing false eyelashes seems more like something the women of Sodom and Gomorrah would do than a woman who has spent her life running backyard barbecues and school book fairs. You don't *have* to look like a streetwalker. You *can* wear false eyelashes discreetly.

"False eyelashes are always in fashion for the mature woman," says McCloud emphatically. "Eyelashes start to droop and get thinner as you get older. But false eyelashes lift the eye and give a thicker lash appearance."

The secret to avoiding the sideshow look that some women get with false eyelashes, McCloud says, is to trim them. False lashes as they come from the store are too long for the average eye, she explains. So take a pair of nail scissors and snip off a ¼ inch from the section that will be fixed to the inside corner of your eye. Then trim the remaining lashes in a gradually lengthening curve until—at the outside corner of your eye—the last few lashes are untrimmed. They're the same length as when you bought them.

Use an eyelash curler. If you decide to leave your false lashes at home one day, use an eyelash curler on your own natural lashes before you apply mascara. It will give your lashes a fuller look. Not as full as the fluttery falsies, but fuller than your own.

Stay away from dark liners. Soft purples and charcoal grays are more flattering.

Eyebrows: Getting the Perfect Trim

"The brow is like a picture frame around your eye," says the Hair America-National Cosmetology Association's Pauline McCloud. And the way to get the most effective frame is to go with the natural arch.

"People tend to get too creative," says McCloud. Don't. Keep your brows as natural as possible. Don't round them, and remember that a thin brow line will put 20 years and 20 pounds on your eye.

Just tweeze a few hairs to emphasize your natural arch, says McCloud. Or, even better, go to a professional salon and have them wax the excess hairs. Waxing pulls the whole hair out, explains McCloud, while tweezing merely chops it off at the root. So a wax job lasts longer than tweezing.

Use creams. Night eye creams and daytime moisturizers are essential for anyone over the age of 14, says McCloud. Each woman should experiment until she finds the one that works for her.

THROUGH THE LOOKER'S GLASS

But what about those of us who wear glasses? Should our makeup be any different? Yes, says Roberts. If you have a pair of lenses that magnify the world when you look through them, your eyes will be magnified when others look back at you. So soften your makeup by using a little less, a little more subtly. If you have a pair of lenses that minimize things, however, your eyes will look small, beady and ferretlike when the world looks back. So use a stronger makeup.

And if you wear tinted lenses, says Roberts, be careful of your makeup colors. A green-tinted lens over plum eye makeup or a rose-tinted lens over green shadow will make your eyes look muddy. That's why it's generally a good idea to coordinate your eye shadow color with the color of your lenses, says Roberts. If you have a blue tint to your lenses, for example, use a blue or blue-green shadow. Otherwise you may bear a slight resemblance to a bruised plum.

But what about the color of your frames? Should they match your eyes or shadow as well? No, frames should be coordinated with your hair, says Roberts. Blonds should wear frames that are beige or soft blue. Brunettes can wear almost any color. Redheads should wear tortoise or amber. And those with gray hair should wear silver or a soft blue.

But with or without glasses, Roberts says, there's no reason not to look smashing. And *just* like that model in *Elle*.

Ellen Michaud

The Mane Event: The Secrets to Healthy Hair

Remember when you were a young child, how soft and shiny and manageable your hair was? Of course you don't—you were a child. But you don't have to take our word for it. Look at just about any young child. Chances are you'll see the kind of hair you'd love to have today.

And you can have it.

Philip Kingsley, a renowned authority on hair care from New York City, says that hair suffers a number of recurring traumas: perms, colorings, sprays, bleachings, harsh shampoos, excess blow-drying, pollution and sun, to name a few.

For the sake of your traumatized hair, he recommends that you fight back with some gentle loving care. What follows is an effective fighting strategy from Kingsley and other hair-care experts.

PAMPER YOUR HAIR

If you want your hair to be shiny, it has to be clean. Hair covered with dust or dirt will look dull. You should gently shampoo every day with one lathering, using the mildest shampoo that will get your hair clean.

It's best to condition your hair after each washing. With proper conditioning, says Kingsley, even very badly damaged hair can have a shine. Most conditioners achieve this by clinging to the hair shaft, which provides a smooth surface for light reflection and also helps to fill in the irregularities.

Look for the word "quaternary" on the label, advises Kingsley. It often has a number with it, anything from 16 to 24 or more. Generally speaking, the higher the number, the more conditioning.

Beyond this, choosing the right conditioner or shampoo for your hair is very much a matter of trial and error. You may find that some products make your hair very limp; others may even dull it with a film. You may find the best thing for your hair is to mix two or three different products.

SPECIAL HAIR TREATS

Brighten your hair's outlook with an occasional (once or twice a month) conditioning treat. Here are two of Kingsley's favorite "recipes."

The egg/lemon whip. Mix together two eggs, the juice of one lemon, two half eggshells of witch hazel and a half eggshell of safflower oil. (Use more or less, depending on the length of your hair.) Work thoroughly into your hair. Cover with a shower cap for ½ hour. Remove the cap and massage your scalp for up to 10 minutes. Rinse and follow with your normal shampoo and conditioner.

The clean-as-a-whistle icing. If your scalp is oily, combine 1 ounce of witch hazel with ½ ounce of antiseptic mouthwash and 1½ ounces of distilled or purified water and apply thoroughly with a cotton ball. Don't rinse.

BRUSHING AND BLOWING

Interestingly, says Kingsley, one of the worst hair-traumatizing culprits is something that's long been recommended: hair brushing. If anything, "100 strokes a night" will roughen and dull your hair.

Dull, out-of-condition hair tends to tangle, and yanking at the tangles

---

will make them worse. Take them out carefully with a vulcanized saw-tooth comb, not a brush!

If you choose to blow-dry your hair, do so with caution. Kingsley says the trick to blow-drying without doing damage is to stop while the hair is still damp. Up until that point, there's no real harm done. So let your hair finish drying on its own.

SPECIAL TIPS FOR DIFFERENT SEASONS

Harsh weather, be it cold, hot, humid or windy, can take a toll on your hair's well-being. Here are some special tips especially for balmy summers and nippy winters.

Summertime snags. Those blond highlights your hair gets after a few weeks in the sun may make you feel like a California pin-up, but they're also a sign of potential damage.

One of the easiest and most attractive ways to shield your hair from direct sunlight is wearing a wide-brimmed hat or a scarf. Whichever you choose, be sure it fits comfortably and allows air to circulate around your scalp. Hats can also protect your hair from being whipped around and snarled by the wind.

Let the sun work for you. If you're heading for the pool or beach and a hat seems too close for comfort, you can let the sun work for you. Wash your hair with a mild shampoo, then comb a conditioner with sunscreen through your hair. Secure your hair as gently as possible with pins or combs, avoiding putting tension on your hair. When you get home, simply shampoo the conditioner out with luke-warm water, being sure to remove it completely, and presto, the warmth of the sun will have given you a free, heat-activated deep-conditioning treatment.

Winter woes. Winter in a northern climate can take a serious toll on your body and your hair. Every time you step from a dry, overheated building to the winter wonderland outdoors, your body—and your hair—struggles to keep pace.

Kingsley points out that few people eat as healthfully in winter as they do at other times of the year. The green leafy salads of summer just don't seem as appealing when the temperature plummets. But, he points out, a diet that's good for your overall health is good for the health of your hair as well. Similarly, says Kingsley, people tend to drink less water in the winter, and this is a mistake both for your overall health and your hair. Try to drink six glasses of water every day (eight are even better).

Perhaps the most common mistake made during winter is not shampooing frequently enough. If anything, says Kingsley, your hair may need even *more* careful cleansing and conditioning than in summer, because the combination of hats and overheated buildings steps up the production of sweat and oil on the scalp.

With the right year-round hair care, and a lot of TLC, youthful, beautiful hair can be yours.

How to Thicken Thinning Hair

Hundreds of millions of shiny domes around the world will undoubtedly jump together in joy when a 100 percent effective cure for baldness finally comes along. That day, however, is not likely to be tomorrow. The good news in the meantime is that you can lose loads of hair before anyone notices and before the basic look of your hair changes dramatically—especially if you know a few tricks.

Tricks? Try these, they work!

Shampoo frequently. If your hair is oily, it is heavy, so it lies down and sticks together. It then looks thin. Frequent shampooing (every day if necessary) removes excess oil. Your hair shafts will stand away from the scalp and away from other hair shafts for a fuller look.

Use conditioners. Many hair conditioners coat hair shafts, giving each shaft some extra thickness. Both RK Shampoo and Conditioner (by Redken Laboratories) and Aramis Malt-Enriched Thickening Shampoo and Conditioner (by Estée Lauder) contain body-building proteins that give your hair the overcoating it needs.

Try moving your part. Stop and take a brand-new look at yourself. After a shower, pat—don't rub—your hair dry. While your hair is damp, try wearing it with a different part. The results may surprise you. Just lowering or raising your part can make that receding hairline unnoticeable.

Cut your hair shorter. If you're bald on top of your head, you can cut your hair relatively close to the head so it is in proportion with your face (from ½ inch to 1 inch). Your hair will then look neat and natural. You may then want to consider growing some facial hair to draw attention away from the top of your head and to your face.

Pretty Hands and Feet

Remember Madge the manicurist in the TV commercial? She's the one who was always scolding beauty salon customers for their unsightly hands. "What have you been doing, hauling lumber?" she'd ask sarcastically. Then she'd plop the poor woman's hands into a bowl of dishwashing liquid. Soon after, the woman's hands would emerge looking young and soft, her nails long and lovely.

In reality, it takes a bit more than Madge's magic soak to have healthy-looking hands. That's because hands and feet that are show-off pretty require some tender loving care. Here are some tips from beauty experts that can help keep your hands and feet looking fabulous year after year.

HANDS TO BEHOLD

Your hands can look as lovely at 40 as they did at 20 if you give them the same attention you give to your face. Make the following measures a part of your routine beauty treatment.

Cleanse and seal in softness. Wash with a superfatted soap or a nonsoap cleansing bar. Rinse and pat dry. Always follow with hand lotion. (If it feels too sticky for daytime, blot the insides of your hands with tissue and leave the cream on the outsides.) Rub a little extra lotion into the cuticle areas to keep them soft.

Use a super smoothing lotion. For extra hand moisturizing, apply moisturizer over damp skin after showering. Then wrap them with plastic wrap and leave on for a full hour.

At night, apply a richer hand lotion or petroleum jelly to still-damp hands. For an intensive softening treatment, wear cotton gloves over the moisturizer while you sleep.

Treat cuticles gently. Gently push cuticles back with a washcloth when you shower. Don't cut your cuticles unless you have a hangnail. If a hangnail does develop, soften it with cuticle cream, then cut if off with sharp scissors.

Use the TLC treatment. Wear cotton-lined rubber gloves whenever your hands are in water or exposed to chemicals (even household cleaners) or any other potential irritants. Always wear gloves outdoors in harsh weather —even on short errands.

Use a sunscreen to prevent age spots on the backs of your hands.

TAKE TIME FOR A MANICURE

Your fingernails are one of the most noticeable things about you. Long, spiky, lacquered nails make you look like all you do—or are able to do—is pick up bon-bons. Ragged, uneven, stumpy nails can look like you've been using them as built-in screwdrivers and for prying open packages. What you really want to strive for is something in between.

It really doesn't take much to have nice-looking, healthy nails. One of the best ways is to get a professional manicure once a month. And in between visits, follow these simple steps.

Practice the fine art of filing. File your nails only when they are dry. Shape nails by using the fine side of a diamond dust file or emery board. File in one direction, toward the center of the nail. The sides of the nails should be straight and the tips slightly rounded. To bring up a natural shine, lightly buff with a plain chamois buffer.

Add protection with polish. Always apply polish to dry, clean nails. A base coat can add protection and help prevent discoloring from darker polish shades.

Repair minor chips with two layers of the original shade. Then go over the entire nail with another coat of that color and finish with a clear top coat.

Strip nails sensibly. Don't remove polish more than once a week if you can avoid it. Use polish remover that doesn't contain acetone, which can dry out your nails.

After removing polish, lightly scrub the nail and cuticle with a nail brush to remove the last traces of polish remover. Rinse and pat dry. At night, soak nails in lukewarm water

Nailing a Bad Habit

Nail biting is more than just a bad habit. It can disfigure a nail, break the skin and invite infections. Here are a few ways to put the bite on this bad habit.

Wrap your nails. A piece of tape wrapped around your nails will make you aware of your habit and remind you not to bite. Or try painting your nails with a nonprescription, bitter-tasting liquid.

Keep your fingers busy. Try substituting doodling or crocheting for nail biting.

Hypnosis may help. Your subconscious mind will get the message to cut out the chewing.

for 5 to 10 minutes to help replenish lost moisture. Follow with a moisturizer rubbed into the nail and cuticle.

Don't treat your nails like tools. Fingernails are not nature's screwdrivers. Don't use them to assemble bookcases, pull out staples or open packing cases.

FABULOUS FEET

If Madge's customers came in for a pedicure, she'd probably give them a lot of flak about the looks of their feet, too. Most people, it seems, spend so much time primping their fingernails that they forget to groom their feet.

"Most Americans," writes New York City podiatrist Suzanne M. Levine, D.P.M., in her book, *My Feet Are Killing Me,* "don't even care for their feet, let alone think of them as part of their beauty regimen." In other countries, though, people pay far more attention to their feet. "In Sweden, for example, 95 percent of the population take regular footbaths as part of their daily grooming practice."

With a little pampering, your feet can be as healthy and young-looking as the rest of you. Follow this beauty regimen so you can step out in style.

Beautify with a soak. A warm footbath laced with baking soda or vinegar will make the surface of your feet more acid, which will cut down on foot odor. Dry thoroughly.

Use a balm after bathing. "The feet," says Dr. Levine, "are the last area of the body to get your circulating blood supply, and therefore the skin is likely to become dry faster there than on other parts of the body." So moisturizers are a must for feet.

All creams and lotions, since they are made of basically the same ingredients (usually vegetable oils, mineral oils, lanolin and collagen), work equally well. Your preference should depend

---

Sweet Feet Therapy

Foot odor. You know you've got it when you slip off your shoes at a cocktail party and the other guests slip out of the room.

Foot odor originates in the soles of your feet where glands produce sweat. Sweat is generally a good thing, reminds Suzanne M. Levine, D.P.M. It regulates your body temperature. What makes sweat turn smelly are bacteria that act upon the secretions. So how can you combat the bacteria? Here's what Dr. Levine suggests.

Take frequent footbaths. Twice a week for about 15 minutes, try soaking your feet in a sodium bicarbonate solution—1 tablespoon in 1 quart of water. Or try ½ cup of vinegar mixed with 1 quart of water. These mixtures will make your foot surface more acidic and reduce the amount of odor produced.

Use a foot deodorant. Products that contain an antibacterial agent like aluminum chloride hexahydrate won't stop the sweat but will stop the odor. Antiperspirants will arrest wetness and odor.

Sprinkle with powders. Sprinkle your feet with products containing cornstarch, talc, borax and iodine or boric acid, all of which absorb moisture and odor.

Rotate footwear. On one pair's day off, spray them with deodorant and dust them with cornstarch. Avoid rubber-soled shoes, which don't allow your feet to breathe easily. Wear sandals in summer.

Avoid synthetics. Stick to natural fiber materials.

---

only on what packaging, scent and feel you like.

Plastic-wrap your feet. "Two or three times a week, cover moisturized feet with plastic wrap and wear socks over it, which will provide pressure and heat to help the cream penetrate into your opened pores," says Dr. Levine. This will soften your feet and keep them from drying out.

Fight friction. If you regularly run or walk a good deal, petroleum jelly on the tops and bottoms of your toes will help cut down on friction and will make your toes less susceptible to blistering.

Pretty toes need pampering. First massage in a moisturizing cream or lotion to soften and strengthen nails. Gently push your moistened toenail cuticles back. Then, using sharp nail clippers, trim your nails straight across to avoid getting ingrown toenails. For brittle nails, use lanolin or petroleum jelly daily.

Marcia Holman

A Doctor's Guide to Shaving

If this "shaving portrait" sounds familiar, you've got company. First you splash your face with scalding-hot water. Then you slap on some foam-type shaving cream—probably the same brand you've been using for the past ten years. Then, in a flash, you start scraping that cold blade across your face. To get a close shave in those hard-to-reach places, like under your neck, you draw the blade upward (even though the skin there is often irritated by ingrown hairs).

When you're done, you give your face a quick rinse and slap on some after-shave or cologne. Your skin feels squeaky clean—taut, dry, shiny—and is still zinging from the after-shave as you hustle out the bathroom door.

But your skin is not especially happy about this routine. Why? Because, whether you know it or not, you have just committed several shaving sins that have probably left your skin dried out, irritated, nicked, stretched and maybe even vulnerable to ingrown hairs.

Here's what the experts say is the *right* way to shave.

Go for a not-so-close shave. "Shaving too close," says John Romano, M.D., a dermatologist at New York Hospital/Cornell University Medical Center, New York City, "not only irritates the skin but also encourages ingrown hairs."

Ingrown hairs can develop when, among other things (mentioned later), the whiskers are cut too close to the surface of the skin. Then the razor-sharpened ends stab back into the skin itself, resulting in those familiar reddish, angry-looking welts.

So skip the new, manual, dual-edged razors. They tend to deliver a

---

A Beard That's Fit and Trim

Maybe you're sick of shaving every morning. Or perhaps you've finally given in to your wife's wishes for you to grow a beard—just like Burt Reynolds.

But unless you want to end up looking like a bum, you'll need to keep your beard in shape. Here are some trimming tips suggested by Michel Obadia of New York's Pierre Michel salon.

Pick the look that's you. Ask a professional to help you select beard length and style according to your hair type, facial features, personality and lifestyle. A fuller beard, for example, can help camouflage a weak chin. If your beard hairs are sparse, however, your best bet may be a close-cropped goatee.

Use electric clippers. They can be great for less-than-steady hands. Plus, they can be set for various beard lengths from the "5-day growth" to the full-bodied beard.

Beat the bum look. During the unsightly growing-in period, remember to keep your cheeks above your beard line and your neck shaved smooth and to trim your sideburns to the same length as the beard.

---

shave that's too close for comfort and are not recommended for anyone with even minor skin irritations.

Take your time. If losing a few seconds means saving a nick, it's well worth it, says Dr. Romano. After all, a nick—no matter how small—produces scar tissue. And in a lifetime of shaving, you can do your skin a lot of damage that way.

Wet your whiskers and wait. Thoroughly soaked skin hairs will be softer and hence easier to cut. It takes 1 to 2 minutes for them to soften up sufficiently for the kill, so it's best to splash your face with very warm water (hot water can be overdrying to the skin) before you lay on the shaving cream. Shaving after you shower can be an especially good way of assuring thoroughly hydrated whiskers. Or wet

your face, lather up, then brush your teeth while you're waiting for those little rascals to start losing their will to live.

Keep your blade sharp. Whether your razor is electric or manual, you can't get a smooth, not-too-close shave without a sharp blade. Dull blades require too much pressure, resulting in general dermatological abuse.

Choose the correct shaving cream. If your skin tends to be dry, use a rub-on cream or aerosol foam. These products provide the most lubrication and contain very little if any soap, which can be drying. If, on the other hand, your skin is oily, an old-fashioned shaving soap that comes in a cup (the kind you work up to a lather with a brush) is probably better.

You'll get a good shave plus a good cleaning.

Look for shaving products with the fewest ingredients possible, says Jonathan Zizmor, M.D., in his book *The Complete Guide to Grooming Products for Men*. Why? Whenever you shave, your skin is scraped raw to varying degrees and thereby made more vulnerable to irritation. So the fewer the potential irritants, the less risk of developing a rash or other painful sensitivity. You may find that products that contain mostly fancy perfumes, citric acids (which smell refreshingly like lemons or limes) or menthols (which are intended to cool and soothe) may be more sources of irritation than of comfort.

Prepare with pre-shaves. If you elect to use an electric razor, you need to sufficiently weaken your whiskers. If your skin is oily or normal, choose an alcohol-based lotion or plain alcohol to dry up skin oils. If you have dry skin, you are better off choosing a shaving talc or pre-shave powder that gently absorbs skin oils.

Shave with the grain. Shaving against the grain (against the direction of hair growth) can lead to ingrown hairs. What happens is that you cut your whiskers on an angle, leaving sharpened ends that stab back into the skin. So go with the grain: Draw the blade down your neck, not up.

Select an after-shave to suit your skin, not your sweetie. Many after-shaves are 40 to 50 percent alcohol—which can be extremely irritating and drying. To baby your skin, try an after-shave balm (available in lotion, cream or gel), which is basically just scented moisturizer. Or if your skin is especially sensitive, try an out-and-out body moisturizing cream.

Even plain water makes a fine face after-splash.

Work out first, then shave. The same saltiness that makes perspiration irritating to the eyes can make it irritating to freshly shorn skin. Wait to shave until after you've worked out and showered.

Shave after sunning. A freshly shaved face can be more vulnerable to the sun's burning rays. Also, some after-shave products may contain photoactive ingredients that can make you more prone to a painful sunburn.

Give your beard a break. If shaving is irritating for you, try skipping it on weekends or vacations. Your skin will love you for it.

Stefan Bechtel

Nicks, Scrapes and Other Slips

Here's some advice from Jonathan Zizmor, M.D., author of *The Complete Guide to Grooming Products for Men*, for sidestepping common shaving problems.

Nix the nicks. If your face is so dotted with bits of tissue to cover the bloody cuts that you look like a tic-tac-toe board each morning, try using a styptic pencil. It's an aluminum salt product that costs pennies but puts the pinch on bleeding.

Rub out the rashes. If you're ravaged by chronic rashes, try rubbing them with a steroid or cortisone cream, before or after shaving. It's a great way to soothe and protect the skin.

Go easy on acne. When pimples become a problem, stick to shaving with a blade. "Electric razors can cause scarring," Dr. Zizmor writes. "When you shave, make certain that you stroke your razor with the grain (the direction of hair growth), not against it. Otherwise, you'll irritate the sore areas. Your shave won't be as close, but it won't be as damaging either."

Reverse ingrown hairs. If you have coarse, curly hair, you may be subject to ingrown hairs. "What happens is that the cut-off ends of beard hair curve back when they grow, reentering the skin."

Make sure you shave with a sharp blade, that you stroke with the grain and that you don't shave too close. If the problem persists, you may want to try an epilator (usually a wax) to remove facial hair.

Perhaps the best alternative to ingrown hair hassles is to stop shaving altogether for a while.

chapter nine

STAYING IN SHAPE

Exercise against Disease

Everyone's had the thought at one time or another: Does exercise *really* do all the good it's supposed to?

It's hard to believe that something as uncomplicated as exercise—going for walks, jogging through the forest preserve—can do such marvelous things, like prevent heart attacks, stoke up your immune system, turbocharge your brain and add years to your life.

But the fact of the matter is that solid scientific research is accumulating—and at an accelerating rate—that supports the idea: Exercise, it seems, can accomplish *all* those things—and then some.

Consider the research coming out of Harvard University School of Public Health and Stanford University School of Medicine. Ralph Paffenbarger, Jr., M.D., Dr.P.H., and others examined the physical activity and other lifestyle characteristics of almost 17,000 Harvard alumni for 12 to 16 years. They measured exercise (mainly walking, climbing stairs or playing sports) by the amount of calories burned. They found that the more calories burned through exercise, the lower the death rate. Those who burned 2,000 calories a week in physical activity, for example, had a 28 percent lower death rate than less active men.

Their conclusions provide powerful ammunition for the pro-exercise camp.

"Overall, the [data] suggest a considerable gain in man-years of life for the habitually energetic alumni, especially if any avoidable adverse characteristics—such as cigarette smoking and obesity—have been minimized," the team writes. And it doesn't seem to matter what age you are. "Exercise benefits *all* types—old and young, large and small, hypertensive and normotensive, persons who smoke occasionally, ex-smokers, and light, heavy or very heavy smokers," the researchers say.

The longer life, experts maintain, is the result of an absence of health problems—problems that have been found to be preventable by routine exercise.

Aim for Optimal

They may not agree on how it works, but the experts do agree on what it takes to make an exercise program effective. To achieve health benefits, exercise must do the following things.

Stress the body. Whether walking or jogging, your exercise should be strenuous enough to push your pulse up to your target heart rate—70 percent of your safe maximum. You can figure your maximum heart rate through basic arithmetic: 220 minus your age.

Last long enough. Most trainers recommend about 30 minutes of exercise, making sure you stay within sight of your target heart rate for most of the ½ hour. The 30 minutes, by the way, should be continuous. Ten minutes 3 times a day just doesn't match 30 minutes at a shot.

Take place frequently. Again, the general consensus is that to achieve health benefits, it's necessary to work out about 3 to 4 times a week. And for weight loss, 5 times a week is better than 3.

Heart disease. "There's no study that shows that exercise *increases* your risk of heart disease, but there are lots of studies, and good studies, that show that the more activity you get, the lower your rate of heart disease," says Brown University's Paul D. Thompson, M.D.

And he's not talking small numbers. Your 90 minutes of sweat every week can buy you a lot of protection against heart disease, says Dr. Thompson.

"People who are physically active have about half the rate of heart disease of nonactive people," he says. "We've seen this result in study after study after study."

Cancer. Even here, eyeball to eyeball with one of the most feared of all diseases, exercise makes its strength felt. Recent research at Harvard University and other schools indicates exercise may lower the risk of specific cancers. They include breast cancer, colon cancer and cancers of the reproductive system.

It's not known whether the exercise itself or the relative leanness that usually accompanies it—or a combination of both—is responsible for the lowered risk. But, as Harvard's Rose Frisch, Ph.D., and her co-investigators wrote on a study of breast and reproductive system cancers in women: "The observed reduction in risk of cancer of the reproductive system associated with physical exercise has potential for public health and warrants further investigation."

Diabetes. Exercise has been found to improve the health of diabetics, even those dependent on insulin. In fact, according to one report, it may lower insulin requirements in insulin-dependent diabetics.

"Perhaps a more important role of regular exercise is the improvement of cardiovascular risk factors and prevention and retardation of its complications," notes J. Cyrus, M.D., associate professor of Medicine at the University of Louisville School of Medicine and director of the Diabetes Care Unit.

No diabetic should start an exercise program, however, without medical approval and supervision.

High blood pressure. The researchers who conducted the Harvard alumni study discovered that exercise seems to lower the risk of death in people with high blood pressure, although it *doesn't* make their blood pressures drop. And the more exercise, the better.

"Throughout [the study], death risks are reduced as physical activity is increased. The drop in risk is proportionately greater with increased exercise among the hypertensive alumni. The hypertensive alumni lowered their risk even though they remained hypertensive, meaning their blood pressures didn't go down."

Osteoporosis. This is a health threat most significant to women: It is the result of progressive bone loss that in time can cause fractures and hip problems and lead to other unpleasant consequences like the unsightly "dowager's hump." But it's less of a threat if you exercise.

A number of studies have shown that regular exercise can not only prevent this common condition but may help to alleviate it after it develops. It appears that bone, like muscle, responds to stress: The more you ask it to do, the thicker and stronger it gets.

For the bone to benefit, however, it must be loaded—forced to carry weight. Doctors at the Mayo Clinic, in Rochester, Minnesota, for example, found that women who had stronger back-extensor muscles (the muscles you use to hold your back upright) also had denser bone in their spines.

When a Healthy Habit Can Hurt

After a few workouts that left you feeling ecstatic, have you ever plunged enthusiastically into a 7-day-a-week, bop-till-you-drop exercise schedule?

If so, you're not alone. But you may be asking for trouble. That's because any time you go to an extreme on anything—even something that's good for you—you can do yourself some harm.

How does a healthy habit get unhealthy? "When you start exercising, you notice that you feel good," says Gabe Mirkin, M.D., an expert on sports medicine and author of several fitness books. "The tragedy is that the mood uplift you get from exercise lasts only from 6 to 18 hours. So you have to go back the next day and get your fix. Unfortunately, as you get into better and better shape, you need greater amounts of work to get the same uplift."

This has been called a positive addiction, but for some people it's more like a negative addiction. "Many people become attached to the mood uplift and feel absolutely despondent when they miss a workout," he says.

But when you overexercise you may also find you get frequent colds, frequent headaches, constipation, diarrhea or muscle and joint pain and swelling. You may develop an I-don't-care attitude. Women may even stop menstruating.

If you want to keep exercising for the rest of your life, doctors suggest, you should listen to your body's signals that you may be doing too much. And you should set reasonable limits. If you exercise 2 days in a row, for example, play it safe by alternating activities. Walk, run or dance 1 day—these primarily use your lower leg muscles—then bicycle, which uses mostly your upper legs, the next. Or swim, an activity that really works your arms.

But you should also step back and take a look at whether or not you really want to spend as much time on the road, in the water or hanging from a pair of parallel bars as you are. There's a great big world out there. And exercise is only a part of it.

Mental health. Stress is something we all face in life, and most of us occasionally overdose. But a significant body of research has accumulated indicating that exercise may improve your mind just as much as your body.

Researchers at Auburn University and Pennsylvania State University reported that physical fitness may act as a buffer against stress.

In general, as fitness increased "subjects were more intelligent, emotionally stable, venturesome, practical and self-confident," says Auburn's Larry Tucker, Ph.D.

If you want to stay healthy, live longer and feel good about yourself and life in general, the results are in: Start exercising.

Kim Anderson

Let's Get Motivated

The plan: Up at 5:00 A.M. and out the door, two miles out and two miles back—every day, all the way. The reality: You can barely breathe at 5:00 A.M. in the morning, let alone run.

Thinking about exercise is a lot easier than doing it—so much so that most Americans drop out of new exercise programs long before any possible health benefit can be achieved. The obvious question: What can you do to get going and *keep* going?

THE SECRETS TO SUCCESS

Obviously, the answer is self-motivation. But how do you get it? Where do you find it? The following tips were drawn from expert sources across the country.

Make a decision. Are the benefits of exercise—better health, self-image, self-esteem, longevity and general quality of life—genuinely important to you? If not, don't waste your time. Chances are you'll drop out of any program you start before it does you any good.

"It has to be important to you," says cardiologist, author and fitness expert George A. Sheehan, M.D. "You have to feel that your life in some way depends on your exercise—your energy, your longevity, your life as a creative person—and that if you stop, you're going to be diminished in some way."

Set goals. They act as psychological magnifying lenses, focusing your efforts to pick a good program and reinforcing your energy during the workout.

Determine precisely what it is that you want to achieve: bigger muscles, less weight, more strength or greater endurance. Research has shown that people who set goals that are too general ("I want to look better") typically don't achieve them. They're just too diffuse to generate any enthusiasm. But those who set challenging, very specific goals—adding 10 minutes to their runs or a specific exercise to their strength programs—frequently achieve them and consistently outperform their dreamier peers.

Reward yourself. "It's *crucial*," according to Lauve Metcalfe, director of program development at the Campbell Institute for Health and Fitness in Camden, New Jersey, the core of the soup manufacturer's large corporate wellness program. "I mean, really, who quits a program because *they're having too much fun?*"

Examples of more tangible rewards: Ice cream when you make a whole week without missing a workout, or a new pair of running or walking shoes when you knock a minute off your time in the mile. The bottom line: If it makes working out more fun—*do it.*

Take the routine out of your routine. Research has demonstrated the powerful influence of simple *variety* in keeping motivation high. Changing one or more elements in your routine may be all that's needed to recharge your enthusiasm. Appropriate changes: Runners used to jogging alone might consider running with friends. Weight lifters who work out on Mondays, Wednesdays and Fridays could shift to Tuesdays, Thursdays and Saturdays. And if worse comes to worse—take a day off.

Cross-train. This means exactly what it says. If you've run yourself almost literally into a rut, try doing something totally different. Runners

Excuses, Excuses

If at first you don't succeed, it's nice to know that 80 percent of the American population has the same problem. Here's a list of common obstacles to exercising and ways to overcome them.

● Not enough time. Recognize that you may have to sacrifice television or another favorite activity to make room. And consider combining things: Bicycle to work, for example.
● Not enough money. The local YMCA is a useful alternative to expensive health spas. Consider an exercise like walking or jogging for the ultimate economy: Neither requires expensive equipment.
● Boredom. Fight back by picking something that's fun to start with—tennis, maybe, or karate. Cross-training's another option: If you're tired of running, try swimming instead.
● Loneliness. Enroll in a group class. And if the family misses you, enroll them, too.

might take up bicycling, bicyclists might consider running, weight lifters can take up tennis and tennis players can start judo classes.

Control your fears. It's hard to go after anything if you're afraid of what might happen along the way. Success scares some people, too. Make sure you're not one of them by keeping a firm grip on your imagination. And use it intelligently—in visualization

—to invigorate your workouts with positive, achievement-oriented images.

Reality-check the body. One of the most common obstacles to maintaining a workout schedule is simple fatigue—feeling too tired to get up and run in the morning or hit the gym after work. Sports psychologist Jerry Lynch, Ph.D., director of the Center for Optimal Performance in Santa Cruz, California, suggests that you make sure that fatigue is not just mental. Often, a brisk run will leave you feeling significantly less tired than when you started.

Try competition. Competition, as Dr. Lynch defines it, isn't simply trying to be better than other people. It's an opportunity to learn about your particular activity or sport and to test yourself against others while you're learning.

"I have a very Eastern [oriental] view of competition. That simply means that I don't view it as an and/or situation, but a process: It's the race that counts, not whether I win or lose."

Dr. Lynch says that if you're careful not to overreach yourself, competition builds self-confidence, self-respect and, consequently, motivation.

Count the benefits. When things get tough—your legs ache, there's sweat in your eyes, and you haven't even started yet—remind yourself of what it's all about: Improving the quality of your life. On this point there's no debate. By almost every measure, regular exercise generates good things. They include:

- More energy.
- More resistance to illness.
- More resistance to stress.
- Less susceptibility to injury.
- Less anxiety.
- Lower risk of some degenerative diseases (heart disease, colon and breast cancer).
- Stronger bones (and control of osteoporosis).
- Stronger, more efficient heart and lungs.
- A better self-image.
- More self-confidence and sociability.
- A sharper mind.
- Longer life.

THE GOOD NEWS

It doesn't take a huge investment of time *or* money to reap these benefits, remind the experts. A brisk 30-minute walk each day can be as good for your health as the marathon runner's daily miles are for his. You're more likely to do it, on the one hand, and less likely to injure yourself, on the other.

And the best news: You *don't* have to wear those glow-in-the-dark tights.

Kim Anderson

See It and *Be* It

You can feel the sweat and see it—a glittering film of saltwater running in rivulets over the corded muscles of your arms and legs. With each heelstrike and rock of your arms, a fine burst of spray shakes itself loose to make new dark patterns in the brown dust on the edge of the road.

You're getting the rhythm now—a fine blend of body and breath, mountain and motion. You accelerate as the old logging road levels out but your breathing relaxes—it's getting easier with every stride. The sense of *work* fades. A feeling of play begins.

Sound familiar? For most of us, it isn't: Mountain runs are work. But *imagining* that it isn't is one of the most powerful ways for making it happen, according to Jerry Lynch, Ph.D.

Here are some of Dr. Lynch's tips, from his book, *The Total Runner*, for incorporating visualization into your own training.

- Believe it. You *can* do what you see yourself doing in the mind's eye.
- Want it. Desire is the fuel that sustains effort of any kind.
- Expect it. Just the way you'd expect water to flow when you turn a faucet on.
- Relax. A quiet mind is important for effective imagery practice.
- Feel it. The greater the detail you can visualize (the sweat in your eyes, the sound of your feet striking the trail), the more effective the image will be.
- Be specific. Runners should imagine good runs; martial artists, perfect punches.
- Be positive. Use images and words that won't confuse the body. Don't say, "I'm not tired." Instead, tell yourself "I'm full of energy," and then picture yourself brimming with vitality.

Walking: The Best Exercise

The point was made the day the turtle finished ahead of the hare: Walking is a winning exercise.

"If you're looking for a fitness activity capable of improving you in virtually every way, walking is it," says Fred A. Stutman, M.D., author of *Walk, Don't Run: The Doctor's Walking Book* and *Walk, Don't Die: How to Stay Fit, Trim and Healthy without Killing Yourself.* "It's the perfect exercise."

That might seem like a pretty tall claim for an exercise as easy as walking, but walking fills the bill. Research shows that the ease of walking is the secret to its advantages. It gives you the benefits of more strenuous forms of exercise—but without the beating.

"All this emphasis we've been putting on 'no pain, no gain' has been missing the point," Dr. Stutman says. "Consistency, not intensity, is what's important. The fitness activity that you can turn to regularly and enjoyably is the one that's going to do positive things for you."

IMPROVEMENT FROM HEAD TO TOE

Walking is not wimpy; in other words, it is wise. (Hippocrates didn't call walking "man's best medicine" for nothing.) Research shows that a regular walking program (at least 30 minutes a day, five days a week) can benefit the body in all of these important areas.

The head. You're no dummy to make walking your fitness activity, because research shows walking can stimulate thought by increasing the brain's supply of oxygen and boost spirits through the release of natural, mood-elevating brain chemicals called endorphins.

The lungs. Walking might not make you huff and puff, but it's still pumping up your lung power. Studies show that a regular walking program can:

● Increase VO₂ max (the ability of the cardiorespiratory system to use oxygen).
● Strengthen muscles of the diaphragm.
● Reduce symptoms of chronic emphysema and bronchitis.
● Reduce the desire to smoke (now there's something to walk a mile for).

The back. Many runners suffer from low back pain because of the stress to spinal disks created by running's pounding. Walking, however, puts no more stress on spinal disks than standing (and considerably less stress than sitting), and it actually may help relieve back pain by strengthening and toning muscles that make the spine more stable.

The bones. Bones need exercise, too. They respond to weight-bearing exercises (such as walking) by taking on more calcium and becoming thicker, stronger and more resistant to osteoporosis—a weakening of the bones associated with aging.

The feet. For the same reason that walking is kind to the back, it's kind to the feet. Walking:

● Subjects feet to forces no greater than standing.
● Strengthens muscles and tendons in the feet, so they may hurt less often.
● Reduces risk of stroke by keeping the blood flowing freely and by keeping the arteries of the brain elastic.

● Forestalls senility by keeping blood vessels in the brain free of blood-blocking plaque.
● Reduces the discomforts of headaches by increasing circulation to both the brain and scalp.

The heart. Walking's not strenuous enough to provide a good cardiovascular workout? Don't believe it. Walking benefits the heart by:

● Lowering resting pulse.
● Reducing blood pressure.

The Road to Slimness

To get yourself on the road to lifelong slenderness and good health, begin by following this easy 12-week walking program. After 12 weeks, stick with the level of exercise you've achieved at that time.

Minutes Spent Walking

Week	Day 1	Day 2	Day 3
1	10	10	10
2	12	12	16
3	15	15	20
4	15	20	25
5	20	25	35
6	30	25	45
7	35	35	50
8	40	40	60
9	45	45	60
10	45	45	70
11	45	45	80
12	45	45	90

● Decreasing levels of artery-clogging blood fats.
● Encouraging the development of "safety-valve" blood vessels capable of redirecting blood flow should a heart attack occur.

The stomach. A regular walking program doesn't just help your stomach work better (by aiding digestion) but also helps your stomach look better (by aiding weight control). Studies show that walking can:

● Burn nearly as many calories per mile as jogging.
● Step up the body's metabolism in a way that burns calories even during rest.
● Help curb appetite.
● Reduce the number of calories absorbed from a meal by as much as 5 to 10 percent, if done within 30 minutes of that meal's completion.

● Boost the self-confidence that an effective weight-loss program needs to succeed in the first place.

The legs. Walking is a step in the right direction not just for more attractive legs but also for healthier ones. Walking can:

● Slim down heavy legs.
● Build up skinny legs.
● Discourage the onset (as well as progression) of varicose veins.

PROSPECTUS

Walking's great attraction is that we all know perfectly well how to do it. Because it is a low-impact exercise, it is a good choice for anyone who is overweight and underexercised.

It won't unduly stress your joints or ligaments, but it will strengthen your heart and lungs, tone your calf

and thigh muscles and burn plenty of calories. A nice, leisurely stroll, in which you cover a mile in an hour, burns about 100 calories per mile. Speeding things up a little—to 2 miles per hour—will help you burn 200 calories, while a brisk walk—3½ miles per hour—burns 330 calories an hour.

Another nice thing about walking is that you can begin your new walking program right now. The sport requires no advanced instruction and little equipment, beyond willing legs and a pair of sturdy shoes.

Walking has two other advantages: It can be done anywhere, under any conditions, and it is a very social sport. Simply grab a few friends and turn your daily coffee-and-doughnut break into on-the-road conversation time. You'll soon be entranced by the beauty of the outdoors and by the emerging beauty of the inner, thinner you.

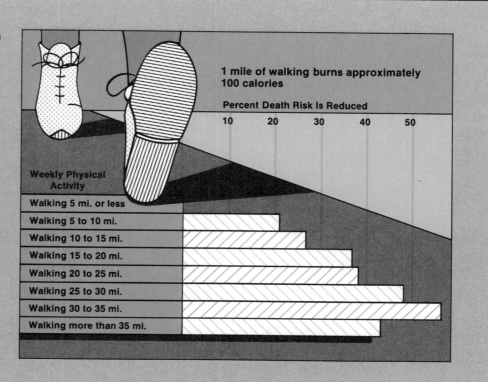

Invest in a Longer Life

Walking regularly and often is like putting money into a new kind of bank account, a lifetime health account, where the time you put in pays off interest in added time to your life. In fact, for every hour you walk, you can expect to live that hour over and 1 or 2 more hours as well, says Ralph S. Paffenbarger, Jr., M.D., one of the authors of an ongoing study of Harvard alumni.

1 mile of walking burns approximately 100 calories

Percent Death Risk Is Reduced

10 20 30 40 50

Weekly Physical Activity

Walking 5 mi. or less
Walking 5 to 10 mi.
Walking 10 to 15 mi.
Walking 15 to 20 mi.
Walking 20 to 25 mi.
Walking 25 to 30 mi.
Walking 30 to 35 mi.
Walking more than 35 mi.

Preventing Sports Injuries

The sun's hot overhead in a clear blue sky. Far below, the Rio Grande sparkles in the summer light and ravens circle in the dry desert air.

You're running in sand on the edge of a mesa, mind focused on the burn in your legs, the sweat in your eyes and the simple effort of trying to pull in enough air to keep going.

It's all-involving, this body-watching, and holds your full attention —until the primitive beauty of a single white cloud sailing across a blue sky breaks your concentration for a single, critical moment.

You don't see the rock half-buried in the sand. Your leather-and-nylon-armored foot hits the oblong piece of weathered lava, rolls—and you're sud-

denly the newest name on the roster of Americans injured in pursuit of sport and physical fitness.

Curled up in the sand with your damaged foot braced on the other knee, it may be some comfort to know that you're not alone. In a single recent year, according to Consumer Product Safety Commission studies, American hospitals logged nearly three million injuries attributable to recreational activities and sports. And, with more than 90 percent of the population participating in at least one outdoor game or sport, that number's probably going to keep growing.

But that doesn't mean *you* have to help it along. The experts all agree: Many sports injuries can be prevented

if the people involved take a few commonsense steps to protect themselves.

THE RULES OF THE ROAD

The first rule of common sense is heeding the message of pain. In the words of veteran runner, author and nationally known sports medicine expert Gabe Mirkin, M.D.: "Pay attention to what your body tells you, and if it starts to hurt—well, *stop.*"

Beyond the obvious, though, what else can you do to make your workouts safe and injury-free? Quite a bit, as it turns out. The consensus that emerges from talking to many authorities is that safety is the result of many

How to Detect a Good Doctor

"Most physicians don't know a thing about sports injuries, and some of the worst culprits are guys who call themselves sports medicine orthopedists," says sports medicine authority Gabe Mirkin, M.D.

"Your best bet is to find a physician who participates in your sport. But if you can't, find out who treats the most people in your sport or activity. Or, if that's not possible, the guy who treats the most local athletes."

H. Winter Griffith, M.D., sports medicine specialist and author of the

book, *Sports Injuries: How to Treat Fractures, Bruises, Sprains, Strains, Dislocations and Head Injuries,* has this to say about getting the best possible care if you're forced to go to an emergency room: "Most of us are interested in the patient's well-being and honestly do the best we can, but I'll admit competency does vary enormously from city to city and even from hospital to hospital within the same town.

"If the emergency room physician is 45 or older or didn't do his residency in the last 10 years, chances

are good he'll miss the boat on appropriate diagnosis and treatment.

"The emergency room can be an intimidating place with all that goes on there," says Dr. Griffith, "but you do have rights: It's perfectly acceptable to ask for a different doctor— someone who's certified in sports medicine—and they're obligated to try and get one for you. They're usually young and interested and often they'll come right over."

things, some of which vary from sport to sport and person to person. But making the following practices part of your training will probably cut your risk of injury.

● Warm up thoroughly.
● Stretch thoroughly.
● Condition the body for better strength and endurance.
● Cool down thoroughly.
● Learn more about your sport or exercise and your body, and how they affect each other.
● Use good equipment.
● Select a sport that makes sense for someone with your particular physique and physical capabilities.

Warming up. Is a warm-up necessary? Wouldn't a light stretch do the job just as well? Really, it can't possibly make sense to deliberately get hot and sweaty *before* your workout. Or can it?

The authorities consulted for this book agree: A good warm-up, one that lasts at least 10 minutes, does help prevent injuries.

"I've known people and coached several highly conditioned athletes who performed excellently without injury and without warming up, but that's lunacy for the general population," says Michael Wolf, Ph.D., president of the International Fitness Exchange in New York City.

His recommendation for the average man or woman: The best preparation for exercise would be a distinct, separate warm-up (take a brisk walk, ride a stationary bike, do push-ups or sit-ups—anything that will make you break a light sweat), then a stretch, and then 10 minutes of *easy* performance of the activity.

Stretching. Stretching after a warm-up is safer and easier because warm-up exercise raises the temperature inside your muscles, which in

turn makes them more elastic—easier to stretch and harder to injure, Dr. Mirkin says.

Women, according to Dr. Wolf, are a special case: They're often so naturally flexible that (especially given the limited amount of exercise time most people have) they can safely make do with just a light run-through of the activity. Men—victims of their heavier musculatures—need to stretch thoroughly.

But the basic rules of stretching are the same for everyone. Dr. Mirkin's guidelines: *Never* bounce. Go slowly. Stay relaxed. Hold each stretch for a silent 10-count, relax and then do it again—up to ten times. (See the box, "Stretch for Relief," on page 273 for more stretching instructions.) And always remember that most important principle of safe training: If it hurts, *stop.*

Conditioning. "Generally speaking, I think when we look at the prevention of injury, conditioning the body to prepare for activity is the most important thing," says Marjorie Albohm, a certified athletic trainer and associate director of the International Institute of Sports Science at the Indiana University School of Medicine.

"When we're talking about conditioning, we're talking about flexibility, muscle strength, muscle endurance and aerobic endurance, all of which are very different but equally important. Someone, for example, who's very flexible but does not work on the other areas of conditioning will be more prone to injury because he or she doesn't have the muscle strength or the endurance to withstand the activity."

Albohm recommends a balanced package for conditioning: aerobic exercise for the cardiovascular endurance needed to resist general fatigue and the injury-causing loss of control that may result; strength training for

improving muscular power and endurance, useful for absorbing shocks and maintaining control; and regular stretching to make sure you can use your strength and endurance without damaging yourself.

"If you put all this together in a balanced program, you're going to be okay," says Arthur Pappas, M.D., medical director for the Boston Red Sox and professor and chairman of the Orthopedics Department at the University of Massachusetts Medical School.

"Where you put the most time depends on which component needs the most work—your flexibility, your endurance, your strength—to bring it up to par for your activity. But weight training is very important—not to *bulk* but to develop good movement ability."

Cooling down. Proper cooling down—letting the body return to a resting state *gradually*—can save your life.

"It's very, very dangerous to just sit down or stand still after vigorous exercise," says Steve Farrell, a research scientist at the Institute for Aerobics Research in Dallas, Texas. "You often find in deaths involving joggers that they did an improper cool-down, which put them into cardiac irregularity."

The mechanism: So much blood pooling in the legs combined with high adrenaline affects the heart. The simple solution, according to Farrell: "Just keep moving for 5 or 10 minutes. Walking is a good way to cool down."

Knowledge. "It's hard to overestimate the ignorance of the average American when it comes to physical activity," Dr. Wolf says. "Laypeople who want to survive exercise need to learn more—from books, from certified exercise professionals, from health and medical experts—about their bodies, and they need to understand what particular activities or sports *do* to those bodies."

People with bad knees, for example, probably shouldn't ride bikes or go climbing, and those with bad backs probably shouldn't use a rowing machine, which puts enormous stresses on the lower back.

Dr. Wolf said fitness buffs interested in training safely and intelligently need to learn a little bit about everything, from how long to exercise and which exercises work which areas of the body to safe ways to perform those exercises and how to pick the ones that best suit your body and goals.

"I think that in many cases, knowing what you're doing makes the difference between injury and no injury," Dr. Wolf says. "Warm-ups, flexibility, strength, technique—I think that many times good, solid knowledge can be more important than all four."

Equipment. Is gear important? This depends largely on your sport: A swimmer's equipment—swimsuit and possibly goggles—just isn't as important as the football player's helmet and pads. The one's a matter of comfort, the other of life and death.

But if you're a runner or anyone else who uses the legs hard—like tennis players and squash buffs—the *shoes* you select can make a difference.

"The force of your footstrike at a 6-minute-mile pace is three times body weight," Dr. Mirkin explains. "If that shock is transmitted up your leg to your hips and knees, it can break bones and tear muscles. But a good shock-absorbing shoe will markedly diminish the force of that strike." And possibly save you a great deal of pain in the process.

Selecting a sport or activity that fits. The experts concur that people starting conditioning or sports activities regularly try to do too much, too soon. In the process, they also regularly hurt themselves: A workout that left you sore at 19 might leave you injured at 50.

Points of Injury

What parts of our bodies take the biggest licking when it comes to sports injury? The illustration here pinpoints the most vulnerable parts of the fit body.

Shoulder (sprain)

Lower back (disk injury)

Knee ("water on the knee")

Hamstring (strain)

Ankle (sprain)

"People have to be realistic about this," Dr. Pappas says. "You can't say that you're going to get in condition at age 40 to do the same things you did 20 years ago. It just won't work."

Where the younger fitness buff might survive an overenthusiastic workout unscathed, he might still derail on something so basic many people forget it: genetic heritage, which in the final analysis determines everything from the color of your hair to how fast you can run the 440.

Dr. Pappas says that training can overcome only so much, and everyone needs to closely compare their physical endowments with their goals in sport or fitness to make sure they match. The big-boned, heavily muscled weight lifter, for example, probably won't enjoy marathons half as much as his lighter, faster and generally more streamlined neighbor. But he might have the time of his life in a judo class.

AFTER THE FALL

The best-laid plans of mice and men often go astray. The old saying holds true today: Despite our best efforts, despite hundreds of hours of training and study and raw sweat, we sometimes get hurt anyway. So what do we do now?

That, obviously, depends on the injury itself and how severe it is. (For information on sore muscles, see "Easing Muscle Pain" on page 272.) Dr. Pappas has the following general advice: "If it's a mild injury, use your common sense. Bandage a small cut, tape a sprain. RICE (rest, ice, compression and elevation) and sometimes support is usually all the treatment you'll need.

"If it's a moderate injury—it hurts, but you can walk and talk, you're not bleeding seriously and you're essentially functional—see how it responds in 48 hours to RICE, and if it doesn't, see a physician.

"And if you have to be carried off the court—well, come on, you'd better see a physician immediately."

Dr. Pappas makes one exception to his guidelines for self-treatment: heat injury, either heat exhaustion or heatstroke. The potential for misdiagnosis is so strong, he says, that a physician should be called upon even if only the more mild injury (heat exhaustion) is identified.

Here is an outline of symptoms and suggested treatments for common injuries, taken from the *HealthFitness Instructors Handbook.*

Sprains. Injuries that result from stretching or tearing a ligament, sprains come in three varieties: first, second and third degree. First degree is a mild injury with range of motion unlimited, minimal tenderness and no swelling. RICE is all you need.

Second-degree or moderate sprains display limited function, tenderness, possible muscle spasms, painful range of motion. Swelling and discoloration will probably develop unless RICE starts immediately. See a physician for moderate sprains only if function is still marginal after 24 to 72 hours, depending on how bad it is.

Third-degree sprains are bad news: loss of use in the affected body part, much pain and tenderness, swelling and discoloration. Apply RICE but call a doctor immediately.

Strains. Overstretching or tearing a muscle produces a strain. Follow the same guidelines outlined for sprains above.

Bruises. Bruises (contusions) are the products of any impact—from stick, bat, ball or other person—that results in bleeding beneath the skin. Treatment varies in line with the guidelines for strains and sprains above, the most important guideline being function: If it hurts so much you can't continue or still hurts enough to bother you three days later, you should probably see a doctor.

Heel bruises. Caused by sudden damaging impacts on the heel, these bruises produce severe pain, immediate disability—you can't walk on the foot—and they may become chronic if care isn't taken to protect the heel. RICE is suggested here, with the use of a heel pad when you start putting weight on the damaged part again.

First Aid for Shinsplints

Shinsplints. They're something everyone who exercises gets at one time or another and it's usually the result of just too much exercise or too much too soon. Its symptom is pretty obvious: A burning pain up and down the sides of your shins.

"So many people have this problem at any one time that I think if they all went to see a doctor that's all we'd be doing—treating shinsplints," says H. Winter Griffith, M.D., a Phoenix, Arizona, sports medicine specialist.

The word "shinsplints" is actually a catchall phrase that encompasses a variety of aches and pains in the general area of the shin. "The important points to make here are that inflammation is what's causing the pain, not disease. And two, shinsplints are not associated with the bone itself—the tibia—but with the muscles and tendons around it and occasionally the membrane covering it."

Warming up before exercise, of course, and being in shape for your sport play important roles in making shinsplints part of someone else's sports history. Wearing good shoes, however, is probably the most important step you can take to prevent them.

"A shoe that cushions well will do a lot to keep shinsplints from developing, but it also helps if you run properly —sort of flat-footed, so the entire foot takes the weight instead of just the toes," Dr. Griffith says.

As for treating shinsplints, Dr. Griffith recommends rest. Take a week off, self-treat with a mild anti-inflammatory drug like Advil—aspirin isn't as effective and acetaminophen doesn't work at all—and massage the painful spots with ice, he says. Whirlpool baths also help, if you can find one.

"Rest is probably the single best thing you can do," Dr. Griffith says. "And if you won't do that, at least switch to a softer surface like grass or soil."

Fractures. All fractures require immediate care by a physician, but recommended on-site first aid includes controlling any bleeding, treating for shock, protecting the wound—*don't* move bones if they're exposed—and protecting the victim from further injury.

Lacerations. Cuts of any sort. Treatment depends on severity. Again, use your common sense. But if it's just a nick, wash it in an antiseptic like hydrogen peroxide, clean it with soap and water and apply a bandage or dressing. See a doctor immediately if it becomes infected.

Abrasions. These occur when you scrape yourself—going after that ground ball or sliding into home plate.

They should be handled according to the guidelines for lacerations. But remember, any time you introduce dirt or other foreign matter into a cut or wound, a tetanus shot may be needed.

Kim Anderson

The Fit of Fitness

The wind's blowing, the snow's falling and you're preparing for your morning fitness walk.

The heavy cotton long johns go on first, with the denim jeans. You pull on the heavy leather parka—you're starting to sweat, this is *work*—and pull a wool cap down around your ears.

You're ready to walk, right? Wrong—unless you *like* being cold and uncomfortable. In fact, the only thing you've done right is put on the wool watch cap.

COLD CONTROL

"You lose an incredible amount of your body heat through your head," says Steve Farrell, a research scientist at the Institute for Aerobics Research in Dallas, Texas.

"It's hard to pin down the exact amount—estimates put it anywhere from one-third to one-half of your total heat output—but it's large enough to be life-threatening in the winter. We recommend that people exercising in the cold *always* wear a hat."

Putting on a cap helps, but it isn't enough unless the rest of your body is properly insulated, too. And here the classic advice on wintertime weatherproofing still holds: Wear several separate layers instead of a single thick one.

"That's one of the nice things about cold weather—you can dress for it," says Murray Hamlet, D.V.M., director of the cold research program at the U.S. Army Research Institute for Environmental Medicine in Natick, Massachusetts. "If you overheat, you peel a layer off. If you get cold, add one. You can have almost total control of your personal temperature in

cold weather. In hot weather—well, short of air conditioning, you're just stuck with being hot."

FACTS ABOUT FABRICS

Despite what you may have heard about wool and other natural fabrics, the synthetics—polypropylene in all its incarnations, and the Gore-Tex family of vapor-permeable, waterproof fabrics—win hands-down when it comes to dressing for a rousing round of sweat in the snow.

Cotton, in fact, is about the worst thing you can wear. The fibers in this natural fabric hold moisture instead of moving it away from the body. That extra water held against the skin dangerously accelerates cooling.

"Anybody who's the least bit of an outdoorsman knows that getting wet in the winter is death," says Bryant Stamford, Ph.D., director of the Health Promotion and Wellness Center at the University of Louisville. "You have to stay dry to stay warm. But get cotton wet and you can't get dry and you can't stay warm."

A fabric that's gaining in popularity for winter undergarments is silk—an elegant, traditionally expensive fabric that is now available at relatively low cost from mainland China. Silk works, but it has its drawbacks.

"Silk's fine while you're nice and dry, but get it the least bit wet with perspiration and it feels, well, really unpleasant to most people," Dr. Hamlet says.

And wool? It's a good insulator but it has its drawbacks, too. It's heavy and scratchy, and some people are

seriously allergic to it. And it doesn't warm you as efficiently as the new fabrics.

Polypropylene, for example, absorbs no water at all and moves sweat away from the skin quickly: You stay warmer longer. Gore-Tex lets air and sweat vapor out but won't let water in: You stay drier, and that means warmer.

"The synthetics work, and they work well," Dr. Hamlet says. "They're lighter and more comfortable and generally perform better all-around than the natural alternatives available today."

SUMMER COOLERS

The sun's hot in a cloudless sky, and the cool blue of the Atlantic sparkles in the foreground. It's pretty—but staying cool is getting harder and harder.

Sweat glitters on your face and arms. Your headband's soaked, your white, form-fitting T-shirt is glued to your chest and waist and the excess moisture is running off your arms in a steady trickle. Hey, maybe this lunchtime walk on the beach wasn't such a good idea after all. Really now, *sweating* on your vacation?

Even beach bums have their problems. But a little knowledge can make the hottest of summer days—and tourists—a lot less uncomfortable.

"It's absolutely amazing how bundled up some people will get even in the summertime," says Dr. Stamford. "The key to staying cool in the summer is ventilation, and they're not getting *any*."

Consider the tourist above. He could have made his life considerably easier by practicing Dr. Stamford's guidelines for maximum-comfort summer dressing.

Wear as little as possible. The tourist could have managed with a little sunblock instead of a T-shirt.

"You can cool off in a lot of ways, but one key element in the summer cooling equation is sweat," Dr. Stamford says. "Sweat has to evaporate for cooling to take place, so you want as much skin surface as possible exposed to the air. *Any* clothing interferes with that."

Wear loose clothing. The tourist made two mistakes—wearing a tight T-shirt and tucking it into his shorts.

"Again—ventilation is the key in most situations," Dr. Stamford says. "Tight clothing impedes air movement across the skin, which in turn impedes evaporation. You want to wear loose, flowing sorts of clothes. They let the air move around your body."

Wear the right kind of clothing. The tourist screwed up again: His cotton T-shirt (okay) was so tight (bad) that it held water against his skin, blocking the air circulation needed for cooling to take place. A fishnet pullover would have served better.

"Fishnet works very well," Dr. Stamford says. "Cotton's fine if it's loose, but it tends to hold water against the skin, which isn't so good. When the skin's covered with water, sweating stops. You can lose cooling on your whole torso with a tight, wet T-shirt."

Another good choice: Loosely woven nylon, like that in running shorts, doesn't absorb moisture and lets air penetrate for evaporative cooling.

Wear light-colored clothing. This is the only thing the tourist did right—he wore a white T-shirt that reflected sunlight. Dark colors absorb it—and you get hotter.

"The sun's your single biggest source of heat," says Dr. Stamford. "The more light your clothing reflects, the cooler you'll be."

Hats, incidentally, don't seem to make much of a difference unless they have a wide brim, says Dr. Stamford.

The message, then, on summertime style: Keep it loose, keep it light—and if you don't *have* to wear it, don't.

Kim Anderson

Sole Survivors: Finding the Best Shoe for You

Shoes—they're the only items of athletic apparel that are appropriate for both winter *and* summer. And they can make the difference between enjoying a sport and hating it. The following tips for choosing the right shoe were drawn from an expert in sports podiatry—the art and science of doctoring the active foot.

Make sure it fits your foot. "Good fit is the single most important thing in any shoe," says Bruce Friedlander, D.P.M., a former Nike consultant who now practices sports podiatry in New York City. "If it doesn't fit, it won't do the job it's supposed to: You could get hurt."

Good fit means more than simply getting the right size. Dr. Friedlander says it's important to make sure your particular shoes are made on a *last* that fits well, too.

"The last is the form (a very expensive, very sophisticated shoe tree of sorts) that all the major manufacturers build their shoes on," Dr. Friedlander explains. "It's one of the critical differences today. All the major brands are essentially well made and well designed, so it's the design of the last that sets them apart. You want to hook on to a maker with a last that best fits the shape of *your* foot."

Women have heels that are narrower in relation to the balls of their feet than the typical man's. Trying to wear a shoe made on a last designed for men almost guarantees sloppy socks and blisters. Some men, however, have heels that are just as narrow—they need shoes made on a men's last that resembles the women's model, for the same reasons. The best way to find the right last: Try on lots of different shoes.

Make sure it fits your activity. "The shoe needs to fit the sport," Dr. Friedlander says. "You really shouldn't try to make one design work for everything—running and racquetball, for example.

"Running shoes chiefly cushion the foot, but are unstable from side to side. Racquet shoes have very little shock absorption but brace and stabilize the foot so you don't turn your ankle. Workout and aerobic shoes do a little of both.

"The main risk from trying to make one shoe do everything is injury: Play tennis with a running shoe and you could almost literally fall off your shoes—they're not designed to handle that kind of side-to-side motion."

Easing Muscle Pain

It was the national collegiate wrestling championships, and everything was on the line. The crowd was loud and enthusiastic, spurring on its favorites to displays of muscular strength, physical agility and mental concentration. Donald Cooper was one of the tournament physicians, closely watching the young, determined competitors giving it their all.

"This student just bent over double from pain," Dr. Cooper says. "He had real bad cramps in his arms and legs, and he couldn't move. I went over to him and grabbed him to get his attention, and I said, 'Listen! I'm going to pinch your upper lip. Just hold on.' He probably thought I was a little crazy. But I pinched his lip between my thumb and index finger, and the pain began to subside almost right away. That kid went ahead and won his match."

That was 12 years ago. Dr. Cooper is still the director of the Student Health Center at Oklahoma State University and the school's varsity team physician. Oddly enough, he learned about acupinch in a letter from a man who had told him he "learned" of the technique in a dream. Dr. Cooper threw the letter away and dismissed the idea until his own leg cramps revived his memory. He tried the technique and it worked. Now he prescribes it for OSU athletes. "It works 80 to 90 percent of the time. And anything in medicine that works 90 percent of the time is extraordinary."

TIME-TESTED RELIEF

There are less exotic and embarrassing ways to relieve muscle pain and cramps than having your lip pinched in front of 10,000 screaming fans. The most basic method, says Bryant Stamford, Ph.D., director of the Health Promotion and Fitness Center at the University of Louisville, is to forcefully stretch the muscle and the tendons that attach that muscle to the bone. A cramp contracts, stretching extends. For a calf muscle cramp, grab your toes and the ball of your foot and pull toward your kneecap. For a cramp in your biceps (the front muscle of your upper arm), extend your arm straight out with your palm up.

Here are some other tips to soothe sore muscles.

● Once the cramp is relieved, massage the muscle, says Dr. Stamford. Massage promotes increased blood flow to the muscle.
● Rest is best, many experts say. You can gently stretch the muscle, but trying to vigorously exercise a sore muscle will probably make it worse.
● Immediately following an acute injury—which can mean all degrees of muscle pulls—the best treatment is RICE: rest, ice (in a plastic bag wrapped in a towel, 10 minutes on, 10 minutes off), compression (wrapping the muscle with an elastic bandage) and elevation of the injured muscle. Never use heat immediately following an injury, says Dr. Cooper.
● An apelike swinging of the arm in ever-increasing circles from a bent-over position can relieve shoulder pain.
● Take acetaminophen (Tylenol and similar brand-name medications) for the first 24 to 48 hours following an injury, says Dr. Cooper. It helps relieve soreness. Thereafter, aspirin is the drug of choice. Take two or three regular-dose pills four times a day, says Dr. Cooper. Those with tender stomachs should take enteric-coated aspirin.

PREVENTION IS THE CURE

The best way to treat sore muscles is not to get them in the first place. So here's advice from the experts on how to prevent most, if not all, muscle pain associated with exercise or bad habits.

Easy does it. There's no doubt about it: "The biggest cause of muscle soreness is overdoing," says Herbert A. deVries, Ph.D., a former professor of physiology of exercise at the University of Southern California and author of *Physiology of Exercise.*

"If you're in poor condition," says Dr. deVries, "any given effort takes a larger fraction of your muscular capacity," whether your endeavor is as simple as getting out of bed or as strenuous as shot-putting. To avoid sore muscles, increase your exercise levels and intensity *gradually.* You've got to walk before you can run.

Warm up that cold body. It's only popular opinion, says Dr. deVries, that a warm-up helps prevent sore muscles. Still, he adds, "all that is known of muscle physiology tends to support the need for warm-up as a protective measure."

You don't want to warm up too much, or too little, he cautions. Too little and your body doesn't heat up enough; too much and you get too worn out to do whatever it is you're warming up for. Dr. Cooper recommends brisk walking. But you also can try jogging, a stationary bike, bench-stepping or calisthenics. This should be done *before* you stretch, says Frank Shellock, Ph.D., of the UCLA School of Medicine. That way you help reduce the risk of damaging your ligaments and tendons.

Warm up by sitting down. You don't always have to do much to warm up, Dr. deVries says. You can even warm up in the luxury of a hot bath or shower, a Turkish bath or sauna, or a hot tub.

How do you tell when you're warmed up enough? When you've worked up a light sweat.

Water won't cramp your style. The typical cramp is a heat cramp, caused by dehydration from profuse sweating, says Dr. Stamford. After all, athletes can lose 4 to 6 pounds of water in an hour. Something's got to give, right? So your muscles give you cramps. The solution is easy; drink 8 ounces of water for every 20 minutes of activity.

Don't worry about so-called electrolyte loss—loss of essential nutrients through sweating—unless you're taking diuretics for high blood pressure, says Dr. Cooper. One of the best things to do when you work out in the heat is to eat fresh fruit every day. If you exercise and take diuretics, your doctor may recommend a potassium supplement.

Stretch that warm body. There is a time for everything, and in exercise there are two times to stretch: In your warm-up phase and in your cool-down phase. The motions are the same, but your warm-up stretches should be less intense than those you do in

the cool-down portion of your exercise program. (See the accompanying box.)

Cool down that hot body. Most experts agree a cool-down is even more essential than a warm-up. Cramps and soreness are a common result of a failure to shift into low gear before you shut your engine off.

Cool down by just reducing the pace of your activity, and then begin to stretch. Dr. deVries emphasizes this is the crucial time to stretch to combat potential cramps and soreness.

William LeGro

Stretch for Relief

One way to ease muscle pain is static stretching—in many ways similar to ancient yoga positions and identical to the warm-up and cool-down stretching you should do to *prevent* pain. Do these stretches slowly and smoothly; there's no sense hurting yourself trying to cure another hurt. Hold each for at least 5 seconds, then alternate positions and repeat several times. *Never bounce.*

Hamstring Stretch
Pretend you're kneeling at the starting line of the 100-yard dash. Put your hands flat on the floor, stretch your left leg behind you, balancing on the ball of your left foot, with your right foot flat on the floor as far up between your hands as feels comfortable. Shift your weight back to the ball of your left foot, keeping your left leg as straight as possible.

Quad Stretch
Stand about a foot away from a solid support and lean against it with your right hand for balance. Bend your right leg up behind you and grasp it with your left hand. Gently pull your heel toward your body and hold the stretch.

Calf and Achilles Stretch.
Lean your forearms against a solid support with your head resting on your arms. Stretch your right leg out behind you, keeping it straight and both feet flat on the ground with your toes pointed straight ahead. Bend your left leg forward, keeping your heel flat. Keeping your back straight move your hips forward until you feel the stretch.

Shoulder/arm stretch.
Stand upright, hold one end of a towel in each hand and raise your arms straight overhead. Lower your left arm behind your back while bending your right arm slightly. Lower your right arm to the level of your left, and continue to move both arms downward as far as feels comfortable. Hold, then raise both arms.

Triceps/Shoulder Stretch

Stand with your arms overhead and elbows bent. Grasp the elbow of your right arm with your left hand. Gently pull the elbow behind your head and hold.

Neck/Shoulder/Arm Stretch.
Lean your head toward your left shoulder, put your arms behind your lower back and, with your left hand, pull your right arm down and across your back.

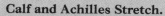

Fitness on the Road

You're a fitness buff who's been exercising for so long that missing a workout is a lot like wearing a wrinkled suit to work: It bothers you so much you can't concentrate on anything else.

So what to do when you're on the road, faced with a long stretch of sterile aircraft interiors, stale hotel rooms and rich restaurant food?

Step one: Stay calm. There are, in fact, many things the modern fitness enthusiast can do to combat the effects of long stays away from home.

"When you're on the road, you've got to play *defensive* ball," says cardiologist, author and fitness expert George A. Sheehan, M.D. "Your main concern is preserving the level of fitness you already have, not improving it. That means being very observant and cautious about what you eat and what you drink and how much sleep you get."

Gyms to Go

Runners on the road have no problem deciding what gear to take along: a pair of shorts and running shoes. But nonrunners have a problem: How to stay fit in a hotel room without all the gadgets and gear of their home health clubs.

"I recommend a blend of assisted and unassisted exercises," says Patrick Netter, a home and travel fitness consultant from Los Angeles. "You might want to combine an unassisted body-weight exercise like push-ups with an assisted exercise like sit-ups—using a foot bar that locks into your room's door."

Netter recommends the equipment below, with one caution: Stay away from the so-called stomach-buster type of exerciser, which is neither well designed nor well made. "Aerobic exercise is the *only* way to burn fat," Netter says.

Lifeline Premier Gym. Available from Lifeline USA, this set includes a lifting bar, 2 different resistance cables, an adjustable jump rope, exercise belt, carrying case, instruction book and workout chart depicting 25 possible exercises, plus a 15-minute instructional videotape.

Excel Workout Bar. This package from Excel, which also sells a system similar to Lifeline's, is a portable weight room using spin-on weights. Total gravity: 20 pounds. Carrying it with you is half the workout.

Ankle and wrist weights. Available from a variety of manufacturers, these light weights help increase the load on your body during calisthenics and other body/weight exercises.

GO EASY ON EXERCISE

Dr. Sheehan says that the typical business trip isn't long enough—more than a week—to significantly impair fitness. It's what goes with it—the irregular hours, the stress of being in strange places and the typically poor quality of travel meals—that is the true threat.

"The big problem on the road is not that you get unfit but that you get sick. There's just too much stress. You can't add the stress of increased training besides."

Runners, says Dr. Sheehan, should probably cut their mileages in half. Weight lifters and others in equipment-intensive sports typically *can't* work out while they're traveling—the necessary gear's not available. Those lucky enough to have access to the required facilities could probably work out at normal intensities, says Dr. Sheehan, since nonaerobic activities usually don't stress the system as severely. And while the East Coast cardiologist strongly encourages his clientele to exercise while traveling, he doesn't think anyone needs to *worry* about it.

"Unless you're in bed the whole time, you're not going to lose a significant amount of fitness in five to seven days. And you can maintain your level of fitness with a very small amount of training while you're on the road—it can probably be handled, as Bucky [Buckminster] Fuller put it, by carrying your own bags through the airport."

Sheehan points to his own experience as a masters-level runner to reinforce that contention. "Because of extensive traveling, for almost two months all I did was have a race on Saturday or Sunday because I was on the road all week. The trip entailed all sorts of appearances, so I just didn't have time to train. And yet, my times in those races were identical throughout all six weeks."

REST IS NUMBER ONE

The professionals who make their livings keeping corporate America fit tend to agree. Lauve Metcalfe is the director of program development at the Campbell Institute for Health and Fitness in Camden, New Jersey. In a typical month, Metcalfe's program posts 3,500 contacts with the food company's employees, including 50 or so executives bound for strange lands.

"One of the things we forget when we're talking about fitness is that a lot of people *do* miss out on sleep," Metcalfe says. "It's difficult when you travel. Different time zones, uncomfortable beds, strange places interrupt sleep. But I would encourage people, even if they can't get enough sleep, to go for a walk. Get out in the air in a nice park, let go of the stresses happening that day, and just *relax*."

Here are some other tips from Metcalfe and Dr. Sheehan for managing travel to minimize the damage and maximize fitness.

Plan ahead. Do what you can to cut the impact of travel on your fitness activities. The possibilities include regearing your home schedule to bring it into sync with your destination to fight fatigue, checking directories for hotels with fitness facilities and deciding what exercise equipment you're going to take along.

Pick a program. Put together an exercise routine ahead of time that will fit into your business schedule and/or your briefcase. Campbell executives can get a "fit kit" with a jump rope, wrist/ankle weights, one dumbbell, a floor pad and hand gripper. Metcalfe suggests actually scheduling time into your business day—under "hour with architect," for example, the architect being you—on grounds that time spent exercising is time invested: The fit executive uses the rest of the day more effectively.

Practice defensive nutrition. It's easy to drop your guard away from

Hostels of Health

Finding a place to work out in a strange city isn't as hard as it looks. The directories below list fitness-equipped hotels, health clubs and other athletic facilities across the country.

● *Fitness on the Road.* Shelter Publications, Inc., P.O. Box 279, Bolinas, CA 94294 (415) 868-0280.
● *Traveler's Fitness/Health Directory.* National Employees Services and Recreation Association, 2400 South Downing Avenue, Westchester, IL 60153 (312) 562-8130.
● *Travel Fit: The Ultimate Guide to Where to Work Out while on the Road.* Travel Fit, Inc., 9089 Shell Road, Cincinnati, OH 45236 (513) 793-7996.
● *The Rado Guide to Metropolitan Fitness Centers* and *The Rado Guide to Health and Fitness Resorts.* Rado Watch Co., Inc., 1140 Avenue of the Americas, New York, NY 10036 (212) 575-0920.
● *Meeting News Resort Finder.* Gralla Publications, 1515 Broadway, New York, NY 10036 (212) 869-1300.

home, so Metcalfe and Dr. Sheehan recommend being especially positive in your attitude toward eating away from home. Tell yourself you *will* keep a lid on your gustatory fantasies. Eat a good breakfast, and watch what you order. Steamed, broiled and poached foods are preferable to fried, battered or sauce-covered orders.

Get enough rest and relaxation. "You can't do efficient work if you're overscheduled," Metcalfe says. And Dr. Sheehan calls getting enough sleep probably the single most important tactic for protecting your health on the road. "The first thing a lot of professional teams that travel all the time do when they arrive in a new town is hit the sack."

And Dr. Sheehan says that those same athletes—despite their enormously superior physical conditioning—will often sleep *more* than the typical fitness buff and nonathlete."Sleep's a restorative, and they recognize that. A lot of them will crash for 10 hours when they're out on the road."

Special precautions: Don't exercise vigorously just before bedtime. Residual adrenaline could keep you awake half the night. Make your room as conducive to sleep as possible—television off, curtains drawn. And try to hit the sack early. Again, extra sleep can help you resist stress.

Kim Anderson

Wonderful Winter Workouts

Typical fitness buffs think winter is the worst time of the year. They can't run, they can't swim, they can't play tennis—they can't do much of *anything* they're really interested in.

What, after all, *can* you do when snow blankets the lawn, sheets of ice cover the driveway and arctic winds cruise up and down the neighborhood's streets and alleys?

A lot. Winter actually offers up a small army of unique-to-the-season fitness activities: skiing, sledding, ice skating, snow camping, snowshoeing and much, much more. And the experts agree: Wintertime outdoor exercise even has some advantages over summertime sweat.

One common myth that keeps a lot of people inside when they might be enjoying themselves outside is the notion that cold is bad for you.

"There's one population at special risk—people with coronary heart disease. But anyone else in good basic health can exercise in the cold without worrying about it," says Steve Farrell, a research scientist for the Institute of Aerobics Research in Dallas, Texas.

And freezing your lungs? Total myth, with no basis in fact. "It's nonsense," says University of Louisville Health Promotion and Wellness Center director Bryant Stamford, Ph.D. "In fact, if you've got a Viking orientation you can exercise in really *brutal* weather. Even at 20 below zero, the air you inhale is thoroughly warmed before it reaches the lungs. If you do frost your lungs, you're in the Antarctic somewhere."

COLD MELTS FAT

There is, in fact, documentation suggesting that winter workouts might even be *better* for your health than summertime sweat: Cold-weather exercise seems to burn more fat.

"An advantage of exercising in the cold is what we call mobilization of fat," says Roy Shepard, M.D., Ph.D., director of the School of Physical and Health Education at the University of Toronto. "It means that more fat is burned during cold weather workouts than in warm weather, in part because of the need to generate body heat."

"Cold-weather exercise is indeed a good strategy for getting rid of unwanted fat," Dr. Shepard says. "And it's probable—though not confirmed yet—that people could actually exercise less during cold weather than in warm weather and still lose the same amount of weight—or even more."

WHAT TO DO OUTSIDE

Okay, so it's good for you—but you can't play tennis in the snow and it's kind of difficult to run on ice. So what to do?

Not to worry: Snowtime alternatives exist that are every bit as strenuous as your summer sweat sessions—and just possibly more raw fun.

Consider the classic of classics: cross-country skiing. "It's a fantastic exercise, certainly at the absolute top of the list of stay-in-shape things you can do in the winter," Dr. Stamford says. "It works the upper and lower body at the same time, builds strength in the legs and arms, and gives the heart and lungs a superb workout.

Good old snowshoeing—a la dog teams in the Arctic and Royal Canadian Mounted Police—is right behind cross-country skiing when it comes to aerobic intensity.

"This is kind of like taking a walk with Heavyhands, ankle weights *and* a weight belt," Dr. Stamford says. "You won't cover the kind of ground you would skiing, but you'll get a good, solid workout anyway, just working against the resistance of the snowshoes and the snow."

Which brings us to probably the simplest winter fitness exercise of all—walking.

"You just can't run on ice, although I think the typical committed runner will probably try," Dr. Stamford says. "Walking in snow's a great substitute: Numerous studies have documented the extra resistance the snow generates, and it's safer than running."

WHAT TO DO INSIDE

Snow and ice just aren't your thing? Twenty *seconds* outside when it's cold is too much, let alone 20 minutes? You even suspect you're genetically programmed to go into hibernation whenever the mercury drops below 70°F?

So what do you do when it does? Simple: Take your workout inside.

"Whatever you do, you *don't* want to treat the winter as your off-season," Dr. Stamford says.

"Most Americans are a long, long way from having to worry about keeping fit—we're still trying to *get* fit. And if you want to do that, you have got to maintain a regular workout schedule year-round."

There are two ways to bring your workout inside—exercise at home or join an appropriate YMCA or health club. Dr. Stamford comes down strongly in favor of joining a club.

"Working out at home is a great way to make an hour seem like five years," he says. "I'd recommend having a stationary bike or a rower as a backup for days when you're snowed in or short of time, but I think most people do better in public gyms. It's not so boring, and the other people help make it a more stimulating experience."

The particular sport you choose to keep you in shape for summer isn't especially important, Dr. Stamford says, as long as you recognize two important facts.

● Aerobic exercise is necessary for maintaining aerobic fitness and its associated health benefits.
● Conditioning is task-specific: Performance benefits don't transfer from sport to sport.

"This is probably one of the hardest things for people to accept," Dr. Stamford says. "They ride a bike and lift weights all winter and then can't understand why their times are off when they start running again come April. The fact of the matter is this: Although you can maintain the health benefits your summer workout produced, you get *better* only at what you do. Riding a stationary bike is just not the same thing as jogging."

Which is not all bad. Dr. Stamford points out that winter is an excellent time to explore other fitness activities besides your favorite, or to work at improving basic components of fitness such as strength.

"The stronger athlete is theoretically going to be the better athlete. The thing to remember here, though, is the basic rule of thumb: The more similar the activity is to whatever you do in the summer, the more you'll get out of it in terms of improved performance."

But never forget the most basic rule of all: The best activity is the one you'll *do.*

Kim Anderson

Burning Calories: The Cold Facts

Find an activity that interests you and read the good news—the calories you'll burn every hour you're at it—in the appropriate column next to it.

Winter Activities	Calories Burned per Hour				
	105–115 lb.	127–137 lb.	149–159 lb.	171–181 lb.	193–203 lb.
Aerobic dancing, medium intensity	350	395	445	490	540
Basketball	435	495	555	615	675
Fencing, recreational	235	270	300	335	365
Ice-skating, leisure	275	310	350	385	425
Martial arts (judo or karate)	620	705	790	875	960
Racquetball	423	482	540	599	657
Rope jumping (both feet), 50–60 jumps/min.	440	501	561	622	682
Rope skipping (left foot only), 50–60 skips/min.	400	455	510	565	620
Skiing, cross country, 5 mph	550	625	700	775	850
Skiing, downhill (continuous riding, lifts not included)	465	530	595	660	720
Sledding	335	380	425	470	520
Snowshoeing, 2.2 mph	300	340	380	420	465
Stationary bicycle (resistance to get pulse rate to 130), 20 mph	700	795	885	985	1,080
Swimming, crawl, 35 yards/min.	425	480	540	600	655
Walking, 2½ mph	200	230	255	285	310
Weight training	235	270	300	335	365

SOURCE: *Maximum Personal Energy* by Charles Kuntzleman, Ed.D. (Emmaus, Pa.: Rodale Press, 1981).

Happiness Is a Health Club

The morning his paunch prevented him from reading his digital weight scale, Ted decided to join a health club. "If I have to pay to work out," he reasoned with himself, "I'll stick with it." But it turned out to be the chrome, mirrors, carpeting, wood and brass fittings—and the leotards, leg warmers and a giddy vision of heroic muscularity—that attracted him like a moth to a street light on a summer night.

So he signed the contract. The one with 4,000 words, little bitty ones, printed in light blue ink on pink paper, nearly invisible in the fluorescent glare of the Fast Track Athletic and Racquetball Club.

When he showed up to work out the next day at lunch (the only time he had free), he saw the lines at every machine, except the one marked "out of order." He bounced bravely through the aerobics class. He soaked in the hot tub, the one with ten other bodies crammed in like lobsters in a steam pot.

Four months into his program, Ted was tired: Of peeling chrome and spotted carpet, broken shower heads and hot-tub fungus, muscle aches and ligament strains. Most of all, he was tired of being ignored.

But the club beat him to it. He arrived one lunchtime to find the doors padlocked and decorated with a legal-looking document about foreclosure proceedings.

FINDING THE RIGHT CLUB

It doesn't have to be the way Ted found it. Fitness teacher, philosopher and merchandiser Jack La Lanne and the Better Business Bureau have helpful hints for finding the workout facility you want.

Critique the club. Pay a trial visit at the time you want to be able to exercise. "Question as many members as you can," advises La Lanne. "Ask them if they like the place, and what they don't like about it." Is it crowded? What kind of place do you want? Bare-bones body-building, or comfort and class, glass and chrome?

Read the report card. "There are so many fly-by-nights these days," says La Lanne. Ask for a reliability report from the local Better Business Bureau.

Read the fine print. "Don't sign any long contracts until you find out their validity," says La Lanne. Don't be pressured into signing anything right away. Take the contract home and read it over. Is everything promised written down? Is the club bonded so that if the place goes under you can claim a refund?

Scrutinize the club premises. "Cleanliness is paramount," says

---

Is Your Locker Room Bugged?

Can you get athlete's foot from your fitness facility's floor? A sexually transmitted scrunge from the toilet seat? Something terrible from the towel, putrid from the pool, sleazy from the sauna or steam room, horrible from the hot tub?

The answer is a qualified yes; when it comes to tubs and pools, the risks are small but real. Prevention is partly up to you, partly up to the club.

Studies show that the *Pseudomonas aeruginosa* bacteria get fruitful and multiply in poorly maintained tubs and pools. One outbreak in an Atlanta hotel in 1980 caught 76 people.

This bath beastie most often causes a rash from 8 hours to several days after your dip. Sink low enough and the same critter can give you swimmer's ear. Rare complications include fever, sore throat, headache, earache or nausea.

How can you tell if *Pseudomonas* skulks in your club tub? Says Jay A. Jacobson, M.D., of the Division of Infectious Diseases at LDS Hospital in Salt Lake City: "If you see green, cloudy water, leaky shower heads, if the place is obviously in poor repair," you've been forewarned. And grill the management about how they maintain the pools. But pseudomonas infections are rare events in people's lives, says Dr. Jacobson, and should not be feared.

The other potential infectious agent you might find in your health club is the herpes simplex virus. It can survive on the benches of saunas and steam rooms. These sites have never been found to be sources of infection, however, and the experts say that, overall, contagion is unlikely. It's still a good idea to sit on your own towel instead of the bare bench of a sauna or steam bath, use a toilet seat cover, and don't borrow other people's towels.

It's generally assumed that you can pick up athlete's foot from locker rooms, but since the fungus that causes it flourishes in warm, moist conditions, a prime preventive is to keep your feet dry and open to the air as much as possible. Dusting your feet with powder to absorb moisture can help.

La Lanne. Also make sure the equipment is up to date and working.

Check for quality qualifications. Instructors should have bachelor's degrees in exercise physiology or similar fields, La Lanne says, or certification by the American College of Sports Medicines.

Make sure the instructors guide you. To La Lanne, it's essential that the instructors make sure the members are reaching their goals. "The instructors should get to know the members," he says. In one study, researchers found that successful exercise programs have trained instructors who can devise the right program for you and encourage you to stick with it.

GOING BACK FOR MORE

Motivation is the key to getting the most out of your exercise program. About half the people who start an exercise program quit within the first six months. La Lanne and researchers have come up with a few ways you can make yourself stay with it.

Have fun. Variety is the key. "Never stay in a program more than three weeks," advises La Lanne. "After a while, the body doesn't respond to the same old exercise. You get bored. Do something different. You see new results, and you get enthusiastic again."

Look for a reward. Find a club that gives out T-shirts, or a month's dues, or at least a pat on the back, for reaching your goals. Or reward yourself with a special meal or other treat.

Get real. Think in terms of time spent exercising, rather than becoming the next Arnold Schwarzenegger. Meet your goals, and gradually increase them.

Keep your dates. In one study, almost half the subjects quit because they said they didn't have time. You have to *make* time.

William LeGro

The Hard-to-Hide Facts about Tanning Beds

They glow with a purple haze that burnishes your pallid skin to a tropical tint. These are the new UVA tanning beds, modern machines touted by manufacturers and salon owners as "better than the sun itself" and "worry-free" because they don't burn you.

Better than the sun? Not to worry? You'd better worry. These are beds you shouldn't lie in, claim the experts— experts such as the Photobiology Task Force of the American Academy of Dermatology, Albert Kligman, M.D., Ph.D., professor of dermatology at the University of Pennsylvania Hospital, and researchers from around the world.

The danger is ultraviolet-A, a portion of the sun's natural light spectrum. UVA, says Dr. Kligman, causes the "lax, miserable, pebbly-looking skin of older people." The new beds use bulbs that emit mostly UVA rays, which let you tan instead of burn, and some burning UVB rays. A half-hour session in a tanning bed gives you a dose equal to 2 or 3 hours in the midday summer sun. And although they don't cause a burn, they do carry certain health hazards. Here's what else the experts have to say about these tanning beds.

A + B = Trouble. Researchers have found UVA penetrates deeper and may augment the damaging effects of harmful UVB, especially in those people who tan poorly or not at all. Encouraging tumor growth, UVA does its job slowly and subtly. "There are no clues for 20 or 30 years that it's bad," says Dr. Kligman.

They're hazardous to sight. The rays can be hard on the eyes, too. Researchers have linked UVB to cataracts (cloudiness of the eye lens) and UVA to retinitis (inflammation of the retina, the portion of the eye that registers the image coming through the lens).

They're a problem for sensitive skin. The rays react badly with many drugs, cosmetics and soaps and can cause bad reactions in the form of a rash.

They cause swelling. Tanning also produces edema, where bodily fluid leaks into the skin cells and causes swelling. It might look good temporarily, but, says Dr. Kligman, it means "you've got a low-grade inflammation of the skin." This readily breaks down skin tissue because it interferes with the normal exchange of nutrients and waste products.

They're a threat to immunity. More ominous is the speculation that UVA and UVB suppress the body's immune capacity.

Despite the evident dangers of tanning beds, "we're not going to stop people from wanting a tan," says Dr. Kligman. "We recognize the imperatives" that psyche has over skin. Education is the key.

So if you're going to use them, use them *sensibly*, says Dr. Kligman. He offers this advice.

● Limit your sessions to 10 or 15 minutes.
● Use a sunscreen with an SPF (sun protection factor) of 15 or more.
● Always wear protective goggles.
● If you're taking any kind of medication, especially antihistamines, antidepressants or antibiotics, consult your doctor. It may make you photosensitive.
● Don't try to tan artificially if you don't tan naturally.

chapter ten

LOVE AND ROMANCE

Tips for a Lasting Marriage

Johnny Carson likes to joke about the miseries of failed marriages (many of them his own) in his nightly "Tonight Show" monologues. The tabloids boast million-dollar sales tattling about the fall of famous marriages. And who hasn't had the uncomfortable experience of witnessing at least one marriage ceremony that made you think, "They're never gonna make it"?

Just whatever happened to "happily ever after" anyway? For a lot of people, nothing.

Marriage is alive and well, says Florence Kaslow, Ph.D., director of the Florida Couples and Family Institute in West Palm Beach. "There are many compatible couples," she says.

"You just don't hear about them because they don't make good copy or titillating TV viewing."

Still, just because a lot of people stick it out doesn't mean they have a *good* relationship. "Longevity does not necessarily equal a quality relationship," says Herbert Zerof, Ed.D., director of the Dilworth Family Therapy and Psychiatric Associates in Charlotte, North Carolina, and author of *Finding Intimacy.* "In many long-term marriages, the partners put up with each other because they have to for economic reasons."

But, says Dr. Kaslow, it's easy to tell those who endure from those who endear. "Compatible couples are healthy couples. When they are together they seem to exude tranquility. They have an unselfish desire to please one another because there are sufficient shared paths, goals and values."

Being one of them, though—especially after decades—doesn't come easily.

"There's nothing magic about compatibility in marriage," says Robert Lauer, Ph.D., coauthor of *'Til Death Do We Part* and dean of the School of Human Behavior at the United States International University. "Compatibility is not something you have or don't have but something you must work to achieve. Otherwise, your marriage suffers from dry rot—it just slowly dies."

Partners in vital marriages realize that the marriage ceremony was not a celebration of victory but a call to a task. "They've worked at being compatible and, as a result, usually feel more compatible now than when they first married," says Dr. Lauer.

Experts believe that couples in long-lasting, happy relationships share many other common characteristics and may serve as positive marriage models for others. By practicing the following, say the experts, you and your spouse can grow more compatible.

Be like two tall trees. Married people, wrote poet Kahlil Gibran, should be like the oak and the cypress trees which "grow not in each other's shadow."

In other words, the marriages that hold up well include partners who develop separate interests. Each has time alone to read, see nonshared friends, fantasize and dream. The healthy couple, notes Dr. Kaslow, "does not seek to become Siamese twins joined at the heart."

"I Do"—Again

As the bride and groom stood before the priest, everything was nearly the same as it was when they stood there 50 years ago. About the only difference was that the bride wore a crown of white hair instead of a veil. And while the words they repeated were the same as before, the meaning was different the second time.

"This time," said the husband, "I had a deeper understanding of what I was promising." Added his new/old bride, "It was like saying if I had to do it all over again I would—because I did."

Renewing marital vows can indeed strengthen your marriage, says Philadelphia clergyman and marriage counselor Reverend Larry Hof. But it isn't just the words that make them work. Nor does it take a fancy church ceremony or the occasion of a golden wedding anniversary. Even if you renew your vows in your own bedroom on each anniversary, says Hof, they will be meaningful if you remember to do the following things.

Ask yourselves, "How are we doing?" Continually evaluate and work to improve your relationship throughout your marriage.

Say, "I forgive you." You can't make a vow for the future until you've learned to let go and forgive each other the wrongs of the past.

Allow your spouse to spread wings. If your wife wants to return to work or your husband takes up skydiving, don't fear the change. Don't be afraid of abandonment or rejection. When your spouse continues to grow and develop, you may be delighted to discover, as one husband did, that it can be like "falling in love with a whole series of new people."

Be a super sounding board. Learn how to encourage, applaud, critique or just listen to your partner. And most important, know what kind of response your spouse needs at the moment.

Don't let children intrude. Let your kids have their own activities and relationships, separate from yours. Your marriage, says Dr. Kaslow, should be "the bulwark of the family—it precedes the children and continues after the children are gone." That way, it's not likely that you will be overly doting grandparents when the kids have grown, because you have your own life to lead with new challenges.

By the same token, don't allow your parents or in-laws to drop in unexpectedly on your anniversary. "Don't let your parents intrude on your coupledom. Your commitment is to each other," says Dr. Kaslow.

Go with the ebb and flow of sex. Don't expect sex to remain at the same passionate pitch as when you were newlyweds. Sex continues to evolve and change, differing from mood to mood, year to year, age to age, says Dr. Lauer. Learn how to adapt to these changes and discuss your different needs.

Say what you're thinking. Don't expect your spouse to automatically know your innermost desires just because he or she loves you, says Dr. Kaslow. Learn to express yourself clearly and consistently. Use "I" statements such as "I feel this way" or "I don't understand." That opens the channels for resolving conflicts so that they won't fester and explode later on.

The Splice of Life: Four Symptoms of Trouble

If you're tossing the dishes at one another and bickering like George and Martha in *Who's Afraid of Virginia Woolf?* here are some other signs of trouble.

Arguments that never end. You can't agree on major issues. He wants children, you don't. She wants early retirement, you don't.

The glory days are gone. Your marriage has lost its fun and good times and there's nothing to take their place.

Sex is at a standstill. The quality and quantity has suffered for several months.

The kids have headaches. The tension is making their grades drop and their health suffer.

The good news, says Martin Goldberg, M.D., director of the Marriage Council of Philadelphia, is that, in about two-thirds of the cases, a relationship can be resurrected with professional help—but only if both partners are willing to give it a try.

How do you get a reluctant spouse to see a counselor? Remind your partner that he or she is part of the problem. "Tell them that it's a chance to air their side of the story and that the counselor is not there to judge but to teach you to solve your problems," says Dr. Goldberg.

Forget 50-50. A healthy, supportive relationship means you may need to negotiate everything from who cleans the house to who cares for the car. But don't expect it to be a 50-50 proposition. You might have to pay all the bills when your husband is laid off or cook all the dinners while your wife is working overtime. In the long run, assures Dr. Lauer, "if you give more than you expect, you'll get back just as much as you put in."

Don't nag, teach. If, for example, you want your husband to become more sensitive, try being more sensitive yourself. Or try commenting, "I admire sensitivity in a man." He'll get the message without feeling manipulated.

Be good crisis managers. When things go awry—you have an accident, the business goes bankrupt, the roof caves in—allow each other to express fury, hurt, confusion, embarrassment. Reach out to people and resources.

Remember how you coped in the last crisis. Save what worked, discard what didn't.

Know when to hold your tongue. No subject should be taboo between you, says Dr. Lauer, but that doesn't mean that it's always appropriate to talk about everything. It may be better to button your lip about the dream you had about the new guy at work or that you think your wife just did something stupid. "These may be transient feelings to you but could have a long-term effect on your partner."

Marcia Holman

Friends Are the Best Medicine

In this age of fast company, frozen embryos, surrogate parenting, quickie divorce and fleeting romance, we still cling to at least one old-fashioned relationship: friendship. And we probably always will. Why? The answer is simple. Friends make us feel good—about ourselves, about life.

When you have a friend, "The world suddenly looks different; what was commonplace yesterday is filled with magic today," writes psychologist Eugene Kennedy, Ph.D., of Loyola University, in his book *On Being a Friend.* "Friendship makes it possible to share play, exercise, or sorrow with somebody else; that is the key to the lock of life's meaning."

And now there is mounting evidence that friends can even help keep us healthy. Consider these findings.

Friends can help you live longer. In a study of nearly 7,000 adults in Alameda County, California, researchers Lisa Berkman, Ph.D., and S. Leonard Syme, Ph.D., found that people with more social contacts—whether from marriage, close friends, relatives or church—were two to five times more likely to outlive people with fewer contacts.

Friends help keep your heart healthy. According to the research of William Dressler, Ph.D., associate professor of behavioral science at the University of Alabama, people in less-developed societies who had close relationships with neighbors had lower blood pressure and fewer symptoms of heart problems and were less depressed than people in advanced societies with fewer neighborly ties.

Exactly how do friends affect us biologically? One theory is that friends share health information. The low-fat recipe that Marian gives to Jean or the "quit smoking" tip that Rob gives to Roy can have a direct effect on the friend's health.

Another theory is that friends tend to give each other emotional comfort. And that may have an effect at the cellular level. According to studies done at Duke University School of Medicine, people in tense situations have lower levels of "free fatty acids" (a risk factor for heart disease) when a friend is present.

It may be, concludes Dr. Dressler, that "friends act as buffers against stress. They modify the impact of stressful events on the body."

WHY FRIENDSHIPS FAIL

In a sense, friendship is like healthy food: It may be good for us but we may not always get enough or the right kind. "Friends are good medicine, but it isn't always easy to get the prescription filled," says Robert L. Taylor, M.D., consulting psychiatrist for the California Department of

Men and the Buddy System

Don't be fooled by all the male buddy movies. Male friendships are *not* alive and well. In survey after survey the conclusion is that most men do not have a close friend of the same sex, while most women do.

Why? "Males learn at an early age that other males are our adversaries," says San Diego clinical psychologist Ken Druck, Ph.D., author of *The Secrets Men Keep.* "At age 7 or 8, we look at a guy and think, 'Can I beat him up?' Later on, it's, 'Will my car, job or income beat his?' "

Men also fear friendships. "If we share intimacies, we may appear to be less than a man," says Dr. Druck. In fact, the only acceptable way men can relate is if there's a beer between them or a sport to share, with lots of kidding and back-slapping.

With a little work, though, these "special-purpose buddies"—guys you always do something with—may turn out to be "all-purpose friends"—those with whom you share your thoughts and feelings. Here are some important pointers.

Be selective. Learn to identify other men you can emotionally open up to.

Be a listener. If your friend mentions a problem, say "I'd like to hear more about it." Avoid remaining silent, topping it or interrupting. Don't try to fix the problem.

Be patient. Learn that friendships take work—they can survive conflicts.

Mental Health. "There's a great longing for friendship today. That's why greeting cards and soft drink commercials showing a gathering of friends are such a success—they really hit home."

It's not easy to find and keep friends when you are constantly changing location, occupation and interests. A former teacher who now drives cable cars in San Francisco has seen more than a few of his friends come and go since moving from Detroit more than ten years ago. "I have many fine acquaintances here," he says. "Most of my good friends, though, are scattered coast to coast."

Even if we do stay in one place, few of us sit still for very long. Says one businesswoman: "Between tending my toddler, going to work, exercising and housework—something usually falls between the cracks. Unfortunately, it's often my friends."

FOLLOW THE GOLDEN RULE OF FRIENDSHIP

Still, a frantic lifestyle is only partly to blame for our floundering friendships. The real problem, says Dr. Kennedy, is that we've forgotten what it takes to be a good friend.

"The first rule of friendship is to give of yourself," he says. "You can't do that if you're occupied with gratifying yourself—climbing the career ladder or jogging alone every day."

If you want to master the fine art of friendship, he suggests, follow these rules.

Be prepared to work. It's a false notion that friendships are easy, says Dr. Kennedy. "Getting through the tough times, offering encouragement when the other desperately needs it . . . the main work of friendship consists of just such homely tasks."

Make time. If friends are being squeezed out of your life, says Dr. Taylor, it's time to rearrange your priorities. Ask your friend to share an activity you usually do alone.

Seek friends outside marriage. Many of us forgo friends of the opposite sex when we take our wedding vows. Why? "The threat of sexuality is too threatening to marriage," explains Paul H. Wright, Ph.D., professor of psychology at the University of North Dakota. Even our friends of the same sex are left behind as we turn to our spouses to fill our friendship needs. "That's a mistake," Dr. Wright says. "We overburden them and limit ourselves."

Go where friends may be found. You won't find friends if you are sitting home every day. Volunteer and support groups are great ways to connect with people of like interests. Don't overlook the value of social contacts at work. And don't close out people of different ages and races. "Build a wide network of friends," says Dr. Taylor.

Share simple moments. If you must always play tennis, see a movie or do something in particular when you're together, it might not be a true friendship. "Friends are not just people with whom we share activities," says Dr. Kennedy. "They are people who, quite literally, let each other be."

Don't look for perfection. Forget the beer commercials—it's not *always* good times with a friend. There's competition and envy and times when your friends let you down. Fortunately, good friendships survive their flaws.

Marcia Holman

Test Your "Friend-Ability"

Are your friendships in trouble? To find out, answer yes or no to the following questions, then check your answers with the scoring instructions at the end of the quiz.

1. Do you forget to do things you promised?
2. Do you always try to top another's story?
3. Do you exclude others from your clique of friends?
4. Do you tell your friends what's wrong with them?
5. Do you always like to be the center of attention?
6. If you make a loan to a friend, do you let everyone know?
7. Do you often ask friends to do trivial tasks for you?
8. Do you drop in and overstay your welcome?
9. Would you drop everything if a friend needed your help?
10. Are you generally in good humor?
11. Do you easily find good things to say about others?
12. Can you keep a secret?

The correct answer for questions 1 through 8 is no; the correct answer for questions 9 through 12 is yes.

11–12 correct: You have friends because you are a friend—reliable, gracious and giving.

7–10 correct: You have friends, but some of them stick with you in spite of yourself. Hold them close, and try to make one more true friend each year.

4–6 correct: You're looking for friends but are probably unable to find them. You need to fine-tune your friendship skills.

SOURCE: Adapted from "Are You Losing Friends?" by Jane Singer. Used with permission of Singer Media Corporation, Anaheim, California.

Touch for Good Health

Think back. When was the last time you received a hug, caress, pat or tap other than during a moment of passion? Was it when you were sick? At a funeral? When you scored a run at the softball game?

The truth is, most of us would like to be touched more often. Indeed, many of us long for human contact or, as touch specialist Sidney B. Simon, Ed.D., puts it, we are "skin hungry."

"It is a hunger for the reaffirming assurance that inside our skins we are 'somebody,' that inside the skins of others, there is 'somebody' just like us," writes Dr. Simon, professor of human services at the University of Massachussetts-Amherst and author of *Caring, Feeling, Touching.*

A HUMAN REQUIREMENT

"Touch is as basic a human need as food and air," adds James Hardison, Ph.D., dean of arts and sciences at San Diego Community College and author of *Let's Touch: How and Why to Do It.* Without touch, we cannot grow properly. "Children who lack sufficient touch as infants are slower to walk, talk and read," reports Dr. Hardison. In extreme cases, a lack of touch can even lead to death.

Early studies of institutionalized infants showed that babies who were not routinely held, rocked and stroked by the nurses developed marasmus, a condition which means they literally wasted away. The infants would not respond to feeding; they became listless and had faint heartbeats and shallow breathing. Many of them ultimately died.

Dramatic? Perhaps. But more recent studies show that it's not just babies who benefit from touch. A human hand can keep us healthy later in life, too.

Professor of psychology James J. Lynch, Ph.D., reported in his book *The Broken Heart: The Medical Consequences of Loneliness* on a study of more than 300 coronary care patients and the routine event of pulse-taking. After

examining these patients, wrote Dr. Lynch, it became clear that in some patients, "pulse-taking had the power to completely suppress arrhythmias that had been occurring."

What's even more intriguing about touch is that you don't have to be sick to reap its benefits. William E. Whitehead, Ph.D., associate professor of medical psychology at Johns Hopkins University School of Medi-

The Etiquette of a Handshake

We can thank the cavemen for handing down the custom of handshakes, says Australian communications specialist Allan Pease, author of *Signals: How to Use Body Language for Power, Success and Love.* They greeted one another with arms raised, a clear message that they were not concealing weapons. Today's version of the handshake may be a bit more friendly, but it still conveys a message—about ourselves and how we relate to other people.

Unfortunately, there are still no hard-and-fast rules about handshakes, observes noted New York City management consultant John T. Molloy. And that can be especially confusing for women, particularly in business situations. "Our research shows that women seem to be most comfortable extending their hand to younger men—a gesture that is not always acceptable to older men or senior management."

Whatever the situation, though,

if you decide to give a handshake, make it a good one—firm but not annoying. Avoid these handshake styles.

● Dead fish. If your hands are cold and clammy, people may think you're weak. The opposite of this is the knuckle crusher.
● Palm down. When you turn your hand so that your palm faces the floor, you may come across as dominating. If your palm is up, you'll be seen as submissive.
● Politician. When you clasp your free hand over the handshake or your partner's upper arm, you may think you are showing your honesty and trustworthiness. But unless you know the person very well, you may raise suspicions.

cine, found that when people were touched their heartbeats slowed. "It would appear that adults may have just as much a physical need for touch as infants," observes Dr. Whitehead.

A TOUCHLESS SOCIETY

Touch may be healthy, but the fact remains that we're mostly a hands-off society. Why else would we have so many bumper stickers that ask "Have you hugged your kid today?"

The explanation? "Touching is taboo in our culture," says Dr. Hardison. We've learned that touch is okay only for very personal and intimate circumstances or to "tease, comfort or hurt others." Otherwise touch is a no-no.

At the top of the taboo list, he says, is the rule against touching ourselves (masturbation was believed to drive people mad). We dare not touch our adult friends for fear it may be construed as a sexual advance.

What's more, we limit contact with our kin to a stiff embrace because we fear incest. We're even afraid to touch our own mates in public, for fear of what others may think.

In fact, the only group that's *not* on the touch taboo list are children! Everybody from priests to politicians enjoys touching, tickling, cuddling and caressing kids. But only until the children turn ten or so. Then, says Dr. Hardison, the hugs and kisses are promptly withdrawn.

"That's when we start to give children the equation that closeness equals sex," adds Dr. Simon. "We have mixed up simple, healing, warm touching with sexual advances. So much so that it often seems as if there is no middle way between 'Don't you dare touch me!' and 'Okay, you touched me, so now we should make love.' Thus, the touch taboo is taught."

The good news is that it's possible to transcend our touching limitations and be happier and healthier as a result. How? "We must first," says Dr. Hardison, "examine our own taboos and practice new behaviors." Here's how to get in touch with touch.

Be receptive to touch. Discard old touch stereotypes. Instead of viewing that person who taps you on the wrist in a conversation as the touchy type, think of her as wanting to make genuine contact with you.

Know the types and timing of touch. A light pat on someone's knee at a meeting can get their attention. Rub or stroke their knee in the ele-

Signs That Say "Do Not Touch"

There are times when it is not right to touch. Think about the guy at a party who sidles right up to you and offers a drink. Or the new colleague who goes around slapping everybody on the back. "These people are invading our personal space," explains James Hardison, Ph.D.

Try to respect the following "zones" of personal space, as noted by Australian communications expert Allan Pease in *Signals: How to Use Body Language for Power, Success and Love.*

Intimate zone (6 inches to 1½ feet). Reserved only for lovers, parents, spouse, children, close friends and relatives.

Personal zone (1½ to 4 feet). Close enough to get friendly at social gatherings.

Social zone (4 to 12 feet). For the plumber, the postman, the new employee and people we don't know very well.

vator, however, and you could get a black eye.

Announce your touch intentions. People may be confused if you suddenly start touching them. Suggests Dr. Hardison: "If, for example, we say to someone, 'I want to hug you to wish you well on your trip,' as they are departing, the message is clear and should leave little room for misunderstanding."

Make your touch true. If you disguise loneliness or a need for attention by feigning some other message such as sympathy or congratulations, others will sense your insincerity and react negatively.

Touch your teenagers. Many experts believe that if we touch our kids more as they grow up, they will be less likely to overindulge in eating, drinking and sex. One mother of five found that she could get her kids to touch her and one another more by having them scratch each other's backs and wash one another's hair. As a result, says Tippi Bradshaw, a teacher in upstate New York, "my kids seem to do less of the typical teenage pushing and shoving."

Explore nongenital sex. Cuddle for its own sake, says Dr. Hardison. "The goal should not be to reach orgasm but to feel free in lovingly touching each other for long periods of time (20 to 30 minutes)." Verbally share what it's like to touch and be touched. You may become closer than ever.

Make contact with colleagues. Give your co-worker that literal pat on the back or tap on the shoulders—it can be a real boost for you both.

Marcia Holman

Love and Loss: A Survivor's Guide

Alone with a capital "A." That's how you feel when someone you love leaves. But you have lots of company. "I believe it's safe to say that there's a new heart broken every minute," says Debora Phillips, a behavior therapist in Manhattan and Princeton, New Jersey, and author of *How to Fall Out of Love*.

That estimate isn't so surprising when you consider that each year eight million people in the United States suffer the death of a loved one, and that about one in eight marriages will eventually break up. On top of that, there's just no telling how many romances fall apart each day.

Still, these statistics provide little consolation when the hurt happens to be yours. When love goes south or a loved one is lost, your feelings, thoughts and behavior can turn topsy-turvy, says Oregon grief counselor Alla Bozarth-Campbell, Ph.D., author of *Life is Goodbye, Life is Hello*. But she notes, this is a natural reaction to loss. You may not feel anything at first and act as though you are on "automatic." Later you may not be able to remember things or concentrate on what you are doing. Your eating and sleeping habits may be altered. In one study, 40 percent of the respondents who had lost a loved one felt as if they were going to go out of their minds.

And if that's what losing a loved one does to your mind, consider what it does to your body: You may notice a temporary loss of hair, difficulty seeing or hearing, or even feel a bit off-balance, as though you were drugged, says Dr. Bozarth-Campbell. You may have headaches, back pain, indigestion, shortness of breath, heart palpitations

The Code of the Consoler

What's the worst thing to say to someone who is grief-stricken from the loss of a loved one? "Buck up" or "You'll get over this." These patronizing words make the bereaved feel inadequate and can interfere with the normal grief process, says Milton Greenblatt, M.D.

So why do we say these things? Often it's because we can't stand the pain ourselves. His advice? "Just listen. Let the bereaved do the talking." Here are other ways to show sensitivity.

Be there. Hold a hand, give a hug, pass a tissue, cry together.

Offer assistance from afar. If you can't handle the pain of sorrow, you can help by doing small favors such as running errands and making phone calls.

Invite them out. It's especially important several weeks after the loss, when the bereaved may need encouragement to enjoy life again.

and occasional dizziness and nausea. You may even develop serious complications, like heart disease.

And for some, the consequences can be even worse—people can actually die of a broken heart. Approximately 35,000 deaths are estimated to occur annually in the newly widowed population in the United States, and 7,000 of them can be blamed directly on the spouse's death.

Grief, it seems, depresses the immune system. "What seems to happen as a result of experiencing grief," reports Milton Greenblatt, M.D., chief of psychiatry at Olive View Medical Center in Sylmar, California, "is that the immune system is depressed and the body is unable to resist diseases."

Investigators at Mount Sinai School of Medicine in New York City evaluated a group of men while their wives were being treated for advanced breast cancer and later after their wives had died. The researchers discovered a decrease in the immune activity of the men in the months after their wives died.

MENDING A LIFE TORN BY LOSS

Losing a loved one does not mean you have to lose your health. There are ways to get over a broken heart without suffering any long-term consequences, says Dr. Bozarth-Campbell. Grieving well, she explains, means understanding the nature of the loss, the impact it will have on your feelings and finding appropriate ways to release those feelings.

Here are some helpful and healthful ways to recover from losing a loved one.

Realize you'll go through phases. "It's important to realize that you may experience certain emotions while grieving the loss of a loved one," says J. William Worden, Ph.D., director of the child bereavement study at Harvard Medical School. He says, however, that the type and intensity of the emotion and just when it is felt often differ for each individual. They may include:

● Numbness. Immediately after your loss, you may feel dazed or stunned. You may deny your loss by thinking, "This isn't really happening," or "We'll get back together."

● Tears and fears. You may have crying jags or feel rage at being left alone. You may feel powerless, out of control. "It is like being mad, glad, sad and scared all at once," explains Dr. Bozarth-Campbell. "Confusion reigns."

● Nagging thoughts. You relive the good times over and over. You feel depressed, lonely and perhaps guilty, thinking you should've done more.

● Sweet sorrow. Finally, you're able to accept your loss and recall past events with more pleasure than pain. You are beginning to regain interest in activities and forge a new identity.

Express emotions. If you don't deal with the emotions of grief, you may turn them inward and get sick, says Dr. Bozarth-Campbell. "Medical research has linked emotional distress with cancer, arthritis, heart and thyroid disease and colitis."

Talk with persons you trust or express yourself into a tape recorder. Write a grief journal, which can help you sort out events that may still be too confusing to understand. Let the tears flow. One behavioral scientist has found that tears shed over the loss of a loved one differ in chemical content from other tears and may serve to restore the body's balance following stress. To trigger tears, you might try watching a sentimental movie, reading a novel or listening to sad music.

Avoid behavioral crutches. Don't rely on smoking, drinking, drugs or overeating to help you cope with your loss. Their feel-good attraction is only short-lived and may actually make you feel worse later. Instead, think healthy by eating nutritious foods and getting proper rest.

Turn off obsessive thoughts. If you find yourself continuously replaying a relationship after a breakup, try imagining that person standing on his head or in another ridiculous situation. "Silent ridicule uses humor to erode that pedestal you've so kindly built for the person you love," says Dr. Phillips.

Keep busy. Start a simple project. Help someone. Return to the activities that gave you pleasure. Share time with friends. One study found that widows, in particular, are better off if they have people to join them in activities they once shared with their husbands.

Remember, time heals. It may take at least a year or more to get over losing someone you love. But, in general, reminds Dr. Bozarth-Campbell, grieving "takes as long as it takes. Letting go too soon and holding on too long are equally dangerous."

Marcia Holman

The Life-Goes-On Support System

A broken heart can be a heavy burden, possibly too heavy for you to bear alone, says Alla Bozarth-Campbell, Ph.D. "Reach out to others," she advises. "Don't try to take care of your grief all by yourself."

If you don't have a friend, relative or clergyman to comfort you, contact one of the following resources.

Mental health therapist. Qualified counselors can help you explore unresolved feelings.

Self-help groups. Groups like Widow to Widow, hospital bereavement groups and Parents without Partners are made up of people who have been there and can provide a listening ear and mutual support.

Retreats. The best place to mend a heart shattered by a broken relationship may be at a spa. Some, like Canyon Ranch, a beautiful desert-mountain resort in Arizona, offer special programs for the broken-hearted. Guests attend self-image seminars to learn how to resolve feelings like rejection and jealousy while enjoying hearty food and healthy exercise—things that are frequently neglected when suffering emotional pain. "Retreats like this one," says Debora Phillips, Ph.D., "can help you feel good about yourself so you can get on with your life."

Restoring Potency

How do soap operas let you know a sexual relationship is souring? Well, the leading lady is shown at one side of the bed, biting her lip, while the leading man is sitting on the other side, holding his head in his hands. "Gee, this never happened to me before," he says.

It's daytime TV's way of telling us that the man is unable to get an erection—something that happens to most men at least once in their lives.

But for ten million men, this little drama is enacted over and over again. That's the number of American men believed to be impotent—meaning they are unable to achieve and maintain an erection at least once out of every four tries at intercourse.

In a soap opera, the star's potency problem nearly always seems to stem from something psychological. He's either worried about losing his financial empire or fretting about his extramarital affair. In reality, though, doctors now believe that as many as half of all male sexual problems are primarily physical.

Conditions such as high blood pressure and heart disease are frequently to blame. Also, as many as half of all diabetic males become impotent. What's more, medications used to treat these illnesses often cause the problem.

"Pinning a physical reason on potency can often make the problem easier to deal with and understand,"

says Richard E. Berger, M.D., associate professor of urology at the University of Washington Medical School, director of the reproductive and sexual medicine clinic at Harborview Medical Center in Seattle and coauthor of *BioPotency: A Guide to Sexual Success.*

WHEN YOUR BODY IS TO BLAME

Just how do you know if your body is to blame for your erection problem? One way is to recall your sexual history, suggests Albert McBride, M.D., director of the Sexual Impotence Center in San Diego. "It's a good bet that your problem is psychological if it came on suddenly or you are able to get erections when you masturbate or when you awake in the morning."

If your problem has crept up on you gradually, if you have problems urinating, or if you have numbness or tingling or burning sensations in your legs or genital area, your problem is probably physical.

Another way to tell whether your problem is physical or mental is to find out if you have erections in your sleep. Normally, a healthy man will have several erections each night while dreaming.

You can find out if you're having erections in your sleep by buying a home version of the nocturnal penile tumescence (NPT) test. A Velcro band with three connector elements that you wrap around your penis at night can show not only the presence of nighttime erections but also their rigidity. In the morning, if none of

Drugs That Can Shatter Sex

Has your doctor prescribed impotency? That's not as unlikely as it sounds. Some medications—especially when taken by men over 50—can have sexual problems as a side effect.

The blood pressure drug methyldopa, for example, has been shown to create potency problems in one-fourth to one-third of the men who take it. The solution might be as simple as getting your doctor to switch you to one of the blood pressure drugs that don't usually impair potency.

Other reported erection enemies include the ulcer medication Tagamet and the anti-anxiety drugs Valium and

Librium, plus a host of nonprescription drugs such as antihistamines (Benadryl) and motion sickness medications (Dramamine).

"Always ask your doctor or pharmacist if a medication can cause potency problems. Remember to ask about how drugs interact with each other and with alcohol," says potency specialist Richard E. Berger, M.D. "Fortunately, the negative effects of drugs on potency are almost always reversible, though it may take some time for your system to get back in gear after you quit taking the drug."

the bands has burst, it may mean that no erection took place and that a physical problem could be interfering with the blood flow that normally swells the penis.

FIRST AID FOR THE SEXUALLY STALLED

"You can take charge of the erection problem in much the same way you deal with other types of health and life problems—by getting informed and getting help," writes Dr. Berger. "You've got to take a good hard look at your habits, stresses and feelings and then decide just how they might affect your potency."

Start by examining your lifestyle for common erection saboteurs. "Sometimes your problem can be solved just by getting rid of these problems," says Dr. Berger. To start, he suggests the following.

Limit your libations. Alcohol is no aphrodisiac—all it may do is boost your desire by lowering your inhibitions. One study showed 10 out of 24 male volunteers were unable to ejaculate at a blood alcohol level of 0.09 (just short of the 0.10 needed to get you arrested for drunk driving).

Say no to nicotine. Probably because it constricts blood vessels and prevents enough blood from getting into the penis, nicotine—including chewing tobacco, nicotine gum, pipes and cigars—can make your love life go up in smoke.

Reduce stress. If your potency problem is linked to job or home pressures, Dr. Berger suggests spending the next few weeks exploring "different, nongenital ways of pleasing yourself and your partner." Later, you can progress to genital touching. Your erections may return and you can enjoy intercourse again.

Consider a specialist. "If your potency problem has persisted more than 12 weeks, you should see a physician first to make sure impotence is not your body's way of signaling an illness," writes Dr. Berger. You may be tested for diabetes and blood flow and possibly monitored for night erections.

If your problem is not physical, you may be referred to a sex therapist or psychologist. A self-help group like Impotents Anonymous may help you cope with potency problems. Write to Impotents Anonymous, 119 South Ruth Street, Marysville, TN 37801-5746 for the chapter nearest you. Enclose a self-addressed, stamped envelope.

Marcia Holman

Medical Solutions to Sexual Problems

The latest in medical technology can't make you the sexual bionic man, but it can help to restore your potency—possibly permanently. Here's what's available.

"Revascularization" surgery. The penile version of the coronary bypass is performed on men who are not getting an adequate blood flow to the penis. For men whose erections fail from an inability to keep blood *in* the penis, it's hoped that new advances to repair or remove leaky penile veins may treat the problem.

Penile injections. This self-administered injection of the drugs papaverine and phentolamine can increase blood flow and produce full, natural-looking erections lasting 30 minutes to 2 hours. One doctor reports that this treatment has produced erections in more than 76 percent of patients treated—no matter what the cause. It does, however, have its drawbacks. Some men are reluctant to "shoot up" prior to passion, say doctors. There's also the risk of developing fibrous changes in the penis from repeated injections. And then there's the ultimate (and somewhat comic) backfire: an erection that won't quit and has to be deflated with injections of another drug.

Implants. Penile prostheses get the highest marks from physicians and from patients as well—more than 90 percent of men (and their women partners) report emotional satisfaction with the results. There's a semirigid kind that stays more or less hard all the time. There's also the inflatable kind that remains flaccid until you squeeze a golf-ball-size pump (often implanted in the scrotum) that passes fluid into a pair of hollow cylinders implanted in the penis.

The best implant for you depends on your lifestyle, personal preference, health needs, physical condition and cost considerations, says potency specialist Richard E. Berger, M.D. Learn all you can about implants before surgery, since the operation is likely to end your ability to have an erection on your own.

The Second Time Around

"If at first you don't succeed, try, try again." That old familiar saying might best describe the way many Americans feel about marriage. According to statistics supplied by the U.S. Census Bureau, nearly 69 percent of divorced men and 65 percent of divorced women were remarried at the time of the last census. Eventually, they estimate, 80 to 90 percent of both sexes will remarry.

But even though the majority are willing to give matrimony another try, the question is: Will *you* succeed? If you're like Margery Curtis, a Pennsylvania travel agency owner who married her current husband, a divorcée, three years after the sudden death of her first husband, you will. "My remarriage is absolutely wonderful," she says.

In fact, despite a mind-boggling blend of nine kids in their new extended family (five are hers, four are his) many things are better than the first marriage—including sex. "We're both more experienced. Our expectations are more realistic; we know how to communicate our needs."

But the Curtises represent only half of all remarriages. The other half, according to Census Bureau officials, hit the skids. One reason? People are often not prepared for the unique problems remarriage can bring. Whether the result of widowhood or divorce, a second marriage is a whole new ball game, says Adele Rice Nudel, director of Sinai Hospital's Widowed Persons Service in Baltimore and author of *Starting Over:* "There are issues that need to be worked through that didn't exist before, and many mixed feelings around these issues."

The "second-marriage game" means a new set of players and often a new set of rules. "It's getting used to living intimately with another person when you were just getting used to living alone," writes Nudel. "It's deciding which set of in-laws to have for the Fourth of July barbecue, the ones from before or the new ones. It's learning not to cringe when your husband talks about his deceased wife to the neighbors, and you're sitting there like a lump as they're all remembering the good times together." All this gets even more complicated if two sets of kids are thrown into the equation.

So, how can you be one of the 50 percent that makes it in a second marriage? By keeping your eyes open, say the experts, and following a few simple guidelines.

Take your time. It's easy to rush into remarriage when you're stuck with a string of lonesome nights. But you may not be aware of the excess emotional baggage you could be bringing

The Prenuptial Pact

Prenuptial agreements are no longer just for the rich and famous who want to protect their fortunes against potential gold-diggers. Today, even men and women of modest means are meeting with their lawyers before their ministers to legally agree on who gets what when the marriage ends—either in death or divorce.

In fact, if you have children from a former marriage, a prenuptial agreement is definitely something you should consider. Why? Because, explains Doris Jonas Freed, L.L.D., J.S.D., chairperson and head of Research of the American Bar Association Divorce Law Committee, it prevents your spouse from laying claim to more of your estate than he or she is entitled to. "Your children are assured of their fair share of your fortune."

The drawback of a marriage contract, of course, is that such contracts are far from romantic and some couples feel that they undermine the mutual trust newlyweds are supposed to feel. What's more, these pacts can't divorce-proof a marriage.

If you're considering a marriage contract, the experts say the first thing you should do is line up 2 lawyers. That way the agreement is more likely to be "fair and reasonable" for both of you. Then find out what provisions are enforceable under your state law. Some couples want things included like who does the dishes and even where to vacation. But most states will recognize in court only provisions relating to estate planning.

along from your first marriage. "Many people enter a second marriage while they are still emotionally entangled with the first marriage," says Bruce Fisher, Ed.D., president of the Family Relations Learning Center in Boulder, Colorado.

Unless people take time to resolve their first marriages, they may be doomed to repeat unhealthy patterns of relating. "It's common for people to remarry a partner who is either exactly the same as or else totally opposite from their first spouse," explains Dr. Fisher. Someone formerly married to an alcoholic, for example, may wind up remarrying another alcoholic or a teetotaler. "That's a real clue that they haven't worked through the first marriage."

For the widowed, tying the knot before you get over grieving for your first partner could ruin your relationship with your second partner. "It takes at least a year to let go of your loved one," says Nudel. In fact, grief "usually reaches its highest peak in the latter half of the first year or during the second year." So while you may still expect to have brief sad moments on anniversaries or special occasions, "if you are still experiencing the waves of anguished grief, wait."

Learn to love yourself. The more you learn about yourself, the better your remarriage is likely to be. "When you have learned to face life alone and you are not looking for a relationship out of need, then you will be truly ready for remarriage," says Dr. Fisher. Chances are you'll find a more suitable partner because *you've* become a more suitable partner.

Learn to be giving. "Marriages often keep failing because people haven't learned to really give to their mates," says Frederic Flach, M.D., adjunct associate professor of psychiatry at Cornell University Medical College. Learn to sharpen your communication skills, make commitments,

Stop Signs to Remarriage

You could head off a ruined remarriage by gathering clues to the character of your mate. "We have been so brainwashed by the concept of romantic love, and we are often so needy, that the thought of rationally evaluating the person we are about to marry seems almost un-American," writes Philadelphia psychologist I. Ralph Hyatt, Ph.D., in *Before You Marry . . . Again.* You're wise to look for these red flags.

Spouse slurring. If your mate badmouths the last partner, ask yourself: Are you sure it was all his or her fault? You could be next on the grill.

Shrines. If your intended has a poster-size picture of the last spouse towering above the TV, consider it a sign that he or she may still be carrying a torch for the former spouse.

Rudeness. "People who are overbearing, rude or contemptuous when they can get away with it will inevitably turn that behavior on you when they feel safe enough to be themselves."

become intimate. Books can help; so can marriage counselors. A premarital class can help you learn relationship skills.

Get rid of the ghosts. "Take down the framed award your husband won. Put away your wife's golf trophies. Move the gallery of photos from the bedroom wall," suggests Nudel. "It won't be easy—you might feel some guilt—but it's a necessary thing to do in order to say good-bye. Your newly married home cannot be

a shrine to the past, not even one room. It's not fair to your new spouse."

Consider discarding old customs, too. "If you and your first spouse always vacationed on Cape Cod during the month of August, don't take it for granted that your new spouse will want to continue that custom," says Nudel.

Confide in your kids. The prospect of a parent remarrying can make children feel hurt, jealous, threatened. They may act like unmanageable monsters or sullen strangers. Help your children accept remarriage, offers Nudel, by including them in your plans and finding ways to reassure them that they will continue to be important to you. A revised will or a prenuptial agreement may help. (See the box, "The Prenuptial Pact," on page 292.)

Be a sane stepparent. You can win over his or her kids without being the wicked stepparent. Here's how.

● Don't try too hard to please them. The main focus of your attention should be on your new marriage.
● Decide on rules and discipline in advance. It's best if the biological parent acts as the house rule enforcer and backs you up when conflicts erupt.
● Let the kids set the pace. Don't expect them to call you Mom or Dad right off. Let your relationship with your stepchildren develop gradually. It helps to spend time alone with each stepchild.

Marcia Holman

Creative Conflict

"The quarrels of lovers are the renewal of love," said a philosopher of romance. In Merle and Ben Stern's case, however, their clashes were not the renewal but the near-ruin of their 17-year marriage.

"Whenever I brought up something that made me mad," says Merle, a St. Louis homemaker, "Ben would turn around and get madder." She recalls the time that their hotel room service was so slow it nearly caused them to miss a plane. "I really wanted my coffee and was furious that we hadn't ordered sooner. But then Ben got more furious and I ended up feeling I had to calm him down. I never did get my coffee. And—as usual—the problem didn't get resolved."

That was before the Sterns learned how to fight fair. "Now I know that I don't have to get so angry to discuss every problem. Ben has learned to acknowledge my feelings. Now we tackle the problem together."

Resolving problems may be one of the most important lessons couples have to learn. Why? For one thing, "conflicts are common in marriage," says St. Louis psychotherapist Doris Wild Helmering, author of *Happily Ever After*. "What you have is two people with different backgrounds and tastes trying to solve a variety of crises and agree upon a dizzying array of decisions. Couples are bound to clash frequently."

What's likely to cause the most conflict? According to a study conducted by Murray A. Straus, Ph.D., director of the Family Research Laboratory at the University of New Hampshire, marrieds get maddest over household matters. In other words, how to hang the wallpaper and what to eat for dinner is more likely to spark a spat than sex or money.

Synchronize Your Body Clocks

Shelly Barnes loves to lie in bed late—on weekends, her feet don't hit the floor until 11:00 A.M. Her husband, Jim, is a human rooster. By 8:00 A.M., he's brewed the coffee, run 5 miles and read the paper. But by 10:00 P.M. that night, Jim's agenda is sleep while Shelly is ready to dance till dawn. The result? The couple rarely has energy for the same things at the same time—including sex.

"It can be a real problem for couples if their circadian rhythms are out of sync," says Donald P. LaSalle, Ph.D., a chronobiologist at the Talcott Mountain Science Center in Connecticut. "One or the other always feels jet-lagged. They may not be able to give each other adequate companionship, emotional support or sexual intimacy."

Still, a household with a morning lark and night owl may be more peaceful. One study showed that a difference between peak energy levels between partners actually lowers conflict. "We found that if both partners are ready to do battle in the morning, it's not so good," reports researcher Carol Hoskins, R.N., Ph.D., professor of nursing at New York University.

The answer? "Be tolerant of each other's natural body rhythms. Plan things when you both are at peak. Meet often for lunch; try afternoon lovemaking."

These mundane conflicts may seem inconsequential, but they're not. "The more conflicts a couple has," reports Dr. Straus, "the more likely they are to get into physical violence."

THE ROAD TO RESOLVE

"When people go around and around about an issue, usually something has got to give. Sooner or later, someone is likely to break that cycle with a fist." Even if couples don't come to blows, though, they may try to solve repeated conflicts with verbal violence. Others may clam up and avoid the conflict altogether. Any way

THE FAR SIDE

"I'm *talking* to you! . . . You're so . . . so . . . so thick-membraned sometimes."

you look at it, says Dr. Straus, the problem won't get resolved and the marriage will eventually fail.

"The only healthy way to resolve problems is to use rational reasoning and negotiation so both parties get something out of it," he says.

The following strategies can help you resolve your problems healthfully.

Set ground rules. "Attacking—physically and verbally—is out," says therapist Edith L. Egan, a coordinator at the Northwest Center for Community Health in McClean, Virginia. Decide *before* your next confrontation that you will not tolerate this type of behavior and what the consequences may be if this happens. Share this decision with your partner.

Temper your temper. It was once commonly believed that the best way to resolve conflict was to vent your anger. But studies have found that "letting it all hang out" actually makes the situation worse—verbal aggression can lead to physical aggression. "Anger feeds on itself," says Dr. Straus.

Are you quick to boil? Find a way to let your anger dissipate. One way, suggests Helmering, is to reprogram your anger messages in your mind. "Repeat the phrase, 'I don't have to feel this angry' for about an hour or so, whenever you are driving, cleaning or doing other mindless tasks. You'll soon see that you can control your anger and you'll deal with a provoking situation more calmly."

Pick the time and place. You'll never solve your problems if you bring up issues when your mate has one foot out the door or is settling down to watch TV.

Remember, not all problems need to be resolved on the spot. Make an appointment to discuss troubling issues at a later date. Or discuss your disputes during a walk or at a restaurant. "Such public settings can keep a lid on anger and allow you to focus on the issue," says Egan.

Negotiate different styles. We learned how to manage problems from watching our parents. Maybe her family *talked* it out and his family *walked* out when things heated up. Recognize each other's inherited "conflict styles" and find ways to compromise.

Avoid "never" or "always." "I don't know of any couple where one *never* helps around the house or *always* is late," says Helmering. The other person is more likely to listen to prob-

lems if you start by saying: "In my viewpoint," or "The way I see it."

Don't make empty threats. If one of you always threatens divorce whenever you have a dispute, "it makes it too scary to bring up subjects," says Helmering. "Make a conscious decision to quiet yourself and listen when your spouse speaks."

Stick with the issue. If the conflict is over who should cook dinner, don't bring up the roast she burned last week or why he never does the dishes. Get back on track by saying, "Wait, we are off the issue." Do that and you can reduce fighting by 80 percent, says Helmering.

Knock off the name-calling. Give your spouse the same dignity you give your boss or friends, suggests Carlfred Broderick, Ph.D., co-director of the University of Southern California Human Relations Center and executive director of the Marriage and Family Program. "After all, you wouldn't call them names, would you? There's wisdom in old-fashioned civility."

Marcia Holman

The Secret to a Feud-Free Vacation

"Our Caribbean trip was a bust," said one man of his recent vacation with his wife. "I wanted to boogie; she only wanted to bake on the beach."

Sound familiar? It's not uncommon for a couple to find their vacation to paradise detoured over a warpath. Sometimes partners, like the couple above, have different expectations of how the time and money should be spent, says Paul Rosenblatt, Ph.D., professor of family social science at the University of Minnesota.

For other couples, a vacation situation is just too close for comfort. "Couples come face to face without structures or routines to distract them," says Dr. Rosenblatt. "They may fear intimacy or just not know how to handle the spontaneity. So they bicker." Disasters like missed reservations, rotten weather and lousy food can aggravate arguments.

Here's how you can help prevent your dream vacation from turning into a nightmare.

Share your expectations. Discuss what you want to do *before* you go, so you don't end up with conflicting desires once you get there.

Seek a third-party opinion. If you can't agree on where to dine, ask someone at the hotel or a local resident for a suggestion and follow it.

Build in apart time. Total togetherness can spell disaster for many couples. Why not meet up later at a romantic restaurant?

Ways to Wake Up Passion

Lucy and Craig seem to have everything. Married six years, they both have thriving careers—she's a magazine editor, he's a computer programmer. Their commitment to their marriage is strong, yet when questioned separately about their sex life, each has a surprising answer. "What's that?" is Lucy's sarcastic response. "It's great—when it happens," says Craig.

Marie and David, married 17 years, are older, but their problem is similar. David works long hours as a restaurant owner and Marie takes care of two teenagers, a toddler, the city townhouse and country bungalow. Their sex life used to sizzle. But now, says Marie, "it's a quick 10-minute tumble after the nightly news." Adds David, "Sex is about as exciting as washing the car."

Couples who complain of a stalled sex life are far from uncommon these days, say experts. For many, life in the fast lane has meant passing right by passion. "There is little question that personal dissatisfaction with sex is commonplace in our society today," write noted sex scientists William Masters, M.D., and Virginia Johnson in their book, *Masters and Johnson on Sex and Human Loving.* "Half of all American marriages are troubled by some form of sexual distress ranging from disinterest and boredom to outright sexual dysfunction."

SEX—A HEALTH REQUIREMENT

Why be bothered about sexual problems? After all, we can live without sex, right? Wrong, says Joseph LoPiccolo, Ph.D., professor and chairman of the Department of Psychology at the University of Missouri. "Sex is healthy. It helps us sleep better and feel less stressed."

If your sex life is ex-life, here are some hot tips.

Make a date with your mate. "Sex is not spontaneous—you have to plan it," says Dr. LoPiccolo. Does that mean you should sit down with your partner and pencil in passion? Well, yes. "That's not really so cold and calculating when you figure most people save sex for the last thing at night, when all they want to do is fall asleep."

So block out a chunk of uninterrupted time—early mornings, Sunday afternoons—as intimacy time for you and your partner. And don't let anyone or anything interfere—not the career, not the kids, not community projects. "Sex should not be any less important than your regular workout commitment," says New York sex therapist Shirley Zussman, Ed.D.

Add some spice. "One of the greatest threats to long-term sexual

---

Passion at 90

Is sex a fountain of youth? The latest research would indicate so. Swedish scientists found that sexually active older people are more vital, have higher levels of sex hormones in the blood and have better memories than their celibate counterparts.

These scientists found out what older people already knew. In another study called the Starr-Weiner report, 800 men and women aged 60 to 91 were interviewed. In the 60-79 age group, 97 percent said sex was a crucial part of their lives. For those older, 93 percent said it was crucial. This data strongly suggests, reports gerontologist Bernard D. Starr, Ph.D., coauthor of the *Starr-Weiner Report on Sex and Sexuality in the Mature Years,* "that not only are older people indeed interested in sex, they also think about it, desire it and engage in it when they can, with the same average frequency that [sex researcher] Kinsey reported for his 40-year-olds."

But if you are one of the seniors sitting on the sidelines, it's never too late to get in the game. "It's possible to continue enjoying sex forever," says Dr. Starr. "You already have the equipment, all you need is a little mental preparation."

First, don't try to compete with your younger sexual self. Understand that it may take you a little longer to become aroused.

Second, get rid of the "musts"—you *must* have an erection, you *must* have an orgasm, you *must* have a young body. Think of sex as a process without trying to reach specific goals. Many older adults have learned, notes Dr. Starr, that "the completion of the sexual act is the desired dessert, but the meal is also satisfying."

satisfaction is complacency—taking it for granted," say Masters and Johnson. To avoid sameness in sex, try it at different times of the day. Or change the scenery—fool around in front of the fireplace. Or check into one of those resort hotels that cater to couples (the ones with the mirrored ceilings and heart-shaped bathtubs).

Introduce new options into your sexplay, Masters and Johnson say. "This might mean experimenting with the art of sensual massage, watching erotic videotapes together, trying new sexual 'toys,' such as vibrators, or creating mutual sex fantasies which you proceed to perform."

Make pillow talk. That's the only way each of you can know what gives the other pleasure. Yet, report Masters and Johnson, some couples keep silent about sex, believing talk may spoil the spontaneity: "What we see over and over again are couples where one person doesn't have the foggiest notion of what the other wants or likes sexually, as well as couples whose well-intended caresses fall short of the mark because they're too much, too soon, too little, too light-handed, too far off the mark—all matters that could be easily corrected by a few words, discreetly murmured, at the right time."

One way to stimulate pillow talk is to make a "wish list," suggests Michael Castleman, author of *Sexual Solutions*. Write down everything you wish the other person would do for you sexually—a kiss after work, initiating sex—and rank your desires according to the ease or difficulty of fulfilling the request. You'll learn a lot about your lover and discover that negotiating intimacy is easier than you thought.

Take time to touch. You don't have to wait until you are on fire to start some sparks. "Somebody said you should have a good 20-second kiss three times a day to keep the relationship going," says Jack Jaffe, M.D., director of the Potency Recovery Cen-

---

The Newest Sexual "Disease": ISD

"Not tonight, dear." That's the common way of expressing a low libido. Now there's a clinical name for it: inhibited sexual desire or ISD, which simply means sex does not turn you on.

How can you tell if ISD is serious? "Time is the key," explains behavioral therapist Debora Phillips. If you haven't been "in the mood" for a long time, she says, you may want to see a sex or marital therapist to help you deal with any underlying psychological problems that may be causing your problem. Short-term therapy is usually all it takes to restore arousal.

Most of the time, though, ISD is a sudden, situational event, which can be traced to one of the following causes.

● Emotional stress.
● Marital conflicts.
● Childbirth.
● Loss of love for your partner.
● Illness or medications.
● Drinking, drugs.
● Inadequate sexual stimulation.
● Hormonal changes.

The good news is that a weak sex drive can usually be strengthened once these factors are resolved.

---

ter in Los Angeles. "Little things like that will eventually lead to increased libido because you'll have the supportive effort of both mates. Try for a certain amount of hugging and kissing, and later on that's going to help build up the interest." Don't forget those other all-important types of contact—stroking the hair, caressing the face, nibbling the neck.

You might even try making intercourse a temporary taboo, suggests Manhattan and Princeton, New Jersey, behavioral therapist Debora Phillips, author of *Sexual Confidence*. "Wonderful things can happen when you limit yourself to the tender touches, the long, slow kisses. When we forbid the things we take for granted, they become that much sweeter."

Adds Dr. Zussman: "Don't pressure yourself to perform." Try dancing, massage, bathing. "Remember, your only goals should be relaxation, closeness and pleasure."

Renew the romance. "The idea is to get spouses to act like lovers," says Dr. LoPiccolo. Choose sexy clothing, dreamy music, make the mood and setting special. "These things are what helped you want to get intimate with your partner in the first place," reminds Phillips.

Have fun. Sex is one of the few areas where adults are allowed to play, so take advantage of it. After all, says Phillips, "it's a romp—not an athletic competition."

Marcia Holman

Strengthening Family Ties

Remember the family of the 1950s? The Andersons of TV's "Father Knows Best" come to mind. Father, Mother, Betty, Bud and little Kathy were usually gathered in the living room or at the dinner table. Mom served the food, Dad dished out the advice. There was no problem the Anderson family couldn't resolve in ½ hour.

The Andersons of the 1980s would be quite a different clan. Mrs. Anderson might work at the office past suppertime, while Betty flips burgers at the fast-food restaurant. You might find Bud at the videogame gallery and Kathy calling up friends on her computer. As for the modern-day Mr. Anderson? Well, he might be at the gym working out. Or, possibly, not around at all until the weekends, when he has visitation rights.

Yes, the family has certainly gone through some changes over the last few decades, explains Donald Conroy, Ph.D., director of the National Institute for the Family in Washington, D.C. "Dual-career couples, changing sex roles, as well as greater mobility and the ever-increasing availability of

Family togetherness doesn't just happen. Keeping in step with relatives requires assertiveness, tender loving care and, sometimes, even a bit of sacrifice.

entertaining and intellectual stimuli outside the home have made some former family interactions obsolete. Additionally, the high-tech, or information, age that we live in has allowed us to lead lives that are bigger, faster and more colorful without necessarily bringing us closer together."

In fact, these changes have been blamed for tearing the family apart. Yet, according to nationwide polls, the family is still what most of us hold dearest in life—ahead of fame, fortune and even health.

Why? One reason, writes Nick Stinnett, Ph.D., professor of human development and family life at the University of Alabama, in *Secrets of Strong Families*, "is that we experience our most intimate relationships within the family, and these intimate relationships have great power to influence our happiness and total wellness as individuals. Perhaps we instinctively know that when we come to the bottom line in life, it's not money, career, fame, a fine house, land or material possessions that are important—it is the people in our lives who love and care for us."

IT TAKES COMMITMENT

And maybe that's why, despite all these forces of change, some fami-

Three Ways to Make Peace with Your Parents

When Ken's mother calls, his stomach turns inside out—it takes him a day to recover from a 10-minute conversation. "She's always riding me about one thing or another," he says.

At work, Ginny constantly seeks approval on every little project—because she never got it from her father. "I never felt I pleased my dad," she recalls. "If I got mostly straight A's but one B on my report card, his only reaction was that I should've gotten all A's."

There aren't any perfect parents. While we were kids, there were probably times they made us feel belittled, ignored or manipulated. And we probably resented it. But if we hold onto that anger as adults, it can poison our health, relationships and careers.

What's the solution? It's not trying to change your parents, says Harold Bloomfield, M.D., psychiatrist and author of *Making Peace with Your Parents*. You may never get Mom to quit criticizing or Dad to notice your successes. What you can do, though, is change *your* behavior. Here's how.

Rethink your resentments. Think about your parent and let out any anger you feel. Try getting it all out in a no-holds-barred, not-to-be-mailed letter.

Forgive. It helps if you write, "I forgive you, Mom (or Dad)" in a column on one side of a paper and your gut responses in the opposite column. Continue writing until you are no longer holding back forgiveness.

Become your own best parent. Build strong emotional ties with nonfamily members. "The more you take responsibility for getting your own needs met," says Dr. Bloomfield, "the more you can accept and love your parents without changing them."

lies remain intact. How do they do it? For one thing, they are committed to the family. They know when to say no to outside demands and to make sacrifices for the sake of the family. They "keep reminding themselves of what is truly and lastingly important," says Dr. Stinnett.

Also, strong families are those in which both parents share in parental leadership, children are respected as individuals, and love, time and power are balanced among all members. It's not "father knows best" but "family knows best."

If that sounds like it takes a lot of effort—it does. Says Dr. Stinnett: "People in strong families have to work at it, constantly."

Here are some of the tools you may need to build your own strong, healthy family.

Communicate. Strong families face the same problems as all families: the car breaks down, the kids stay out too late. "The difference is in the way they deal with problems," says Dr. Stinnett. "Good communication practices help to ease daily frustration levels by increasing the families' effectiveness in solving problems."

So, learn to listen. Be specific. "You never talk to me" is harder to respond to than "I wish we could have 30 minutes each evening without TV, the paper or the kids." Attack the problem rather than each other. Don't drop any bombs just because you know where the soft spots are.

One family might facilitate communication by having a tape recorder on hand so members can relay good news and gripes on the run. Another family could have a suggestion box, which is then opened at weekly family council meetings.

Plan togetherness time. Instead of rushing in to fix a six-o'clock-on-the-dot meal, sit down with the kids for a family-style "cocktail" hour or take a family stroll around the block where you won't be preoccupied or distracted.

Family Gatherings: From Enduring to Endearing

Upon learning that your family back East is planning a get-together, do you (*a*) gleefully pack your bags or (*b*) get reservations on the first flight to the Far East?

If you picked (*b*), you aren't alone. Family get-togethers are often more obligation than celebration, says New York psychiatrist Peter Dunn, M.D. "Family gatherings often make us feel stuck in old roles. Our growing up is not acknowledged, and that can make us angry and uncomfortable."

Here are 2 ways to prevent your next family affair from turning into a family feud.

Be prepared. Practice set responses to handle your brother's teasing, your father's raunchy jokes and your mother's nagging questions about marriage. Find an ally. Take a brisk walk, or scream in your car with the windows rolled up.

Plan a project. Suggest working on a family tree or having a potluck picnic—anything that puts you in an active, positive role.

Foster one-on-one relationships by forming twosomes and threesomes. Mom and son might go off to karate class while Dad takes big and little sis to the library.

Make the most of meals. If mealtime together is a distant memory in your family, try making it more festive, suggests Michael Lewis, Ph.D., director of the Institute for the Study of Child Development at the Robert Wood Johnson Medical School, University of Medicine and Dentistry of New Jersey. Limit the dos and don'ts (for example, "don't pick at your food").

Try candles or a picnic around the fireplace. Bring in ready-made complete meals. Share mealtime with the kids, then dine alone later with your spouse. "The idea is to be together for meals and to make them enjoyable for everyone."

Establish reasonable restrictions. Setting limits on behavior with intelligent enforcement teaches kids love, respect and how to survive in the real world. Experts suggest that you:

● Decide upon the non-negotiable rules. For example: Nobody hits or punches; everybody cleans their own rooms.
● Make rules clear. "You must fold your clothes, put them in your dresser and put your books back on the shelf before you can go out."
● Reward good behavior. Recognize your kids for doing the right things, says Joseph R. Novello, M.D., author of *Bringing Up Kids American-Style.* This promotes "harmony rather than hassles."
● Punish prudently. Criticize the behavior, not the child. Punish immediately after disobedience. Make it fit the crime and use it consistently.

Divide chores. Chores foster family unity and commitment—but they're also tedious and tough. One expert suggests you list all jobs, then organize them into categories, such as boring, messy, hard. Let the kids choose from each category; draw straws for leftover jobs.

Foster family fun. Traditions like popcorn on Saturday nights, backrubs before bedtime or a wall filled with family mementos promote family identity. But try new ways to discover what's special about your family. Make a video, for example, and take turns shooting, directing, acting and narrating.

Marcia Holman

The Dating Game

Just how do today's nearly middle-aged and middle-aged singles get together? Gone are the days when you could pick out your mate at the school dance or while sipping a soda at the corner drugstore. "After the school years," observes sociological researcher J. L. Barkas in *Single in America*, "it takes effort rather than 'dumb luck' to find a suitable partner."

And that's why you'll find searching singles flocking to seminars on the art and science of flirting, reading books like Ben Dominitz's *How to Find the Love of Your Life* and following the nightlife to singles bars.

But they are only deluding themselves if they follow this course, says Philadelphia clinical psychologist Judith Sills, Ph.D., author of *A Fine Romance.* "Classes and books about dating usually are about packaging yourself," she says. "But courtship is really about unwrapping—about finding out what's on the inside. That's what counts."

Nor is dating about being seen in all the right places, delivering the cleverest line, wearing the coolest clothes or having a body like Jane Fonda or Arnold Schwarzenegger. "Dating is an attitude," Dr. Sills says. "You only make contact by being emotionally ready, open, available and positive."

THINK ME, NOT THEE

You can achieve the right attitude by concentrating not on dating but on developing your life. "It's easy for people searching for suitable partners to put their lives on hold," explains Dr. Sills. "They subscribe to the idea that 'first I date, then I live.' They may delay buying furniture, taking classes or fixing up their apartments. All their energies go into the hunt."

Yet it is possible to simultaneously live your life *and* look for a mate. As odd as it may seem, people who use their energy to improve their lives instead of waiting for someone else to do it for them often end up with more successful dating experiences. They are less desperate and become more interesting to others.

Getting the most out of your job and having a variety of friends and plenty of outside interests and activities are some of the ways to make you more self-assured. Then, when you meet someone, it becomes natural to invite them to share in your life. You may, for example, not hesitate to ask someone to join you for a drink after your volleyball game or to help you hand out political flyers.

GETTING TO KNOW YOU

Here are other ways to make dating feel more like fun and less like work.

Let your calendar be your guide. Dating takes time, commitment and patience, reminds Dr. Sills. You may have to rearrange your priorities—limit your overtime hours at the office or cut back on spending

---

Computer Dating: A Calculated Risk

Today, unattached singles may become attached through a variety of means—from computer matchmaking clubs to singles cruises and adventure travel groups.

There are even spin-offs of that old standby, the singles bar: singles nights at museums, health spas, even supermarkets. (One couple wed in the produce aisle where they met. The bride carried a broccoli bouquet.)

Generally, though, these strictly-for-singles affairs work only for the super-attractive and super-confident, says Judith Sills, Ph.D.

It may be more satisfying to join groups that are organized around your personal interests and where meeting someone is secondary, advises Dr. Sills. "Choose groups that are tight enough to know everyone but loose enough to allow new people in." Good bets are coed volleyball teams, volunteer groups, beach or ski groups, church choirs and nature groups.

THE FAR SIDE

Well, here goes...If I just remember to act shy and vulnerable...

all your free time on solo activities, like tending to the garden or painting a still life. Choose hobbies that encourage companionship, like joining a bicycle club.

Don't be finicky. It's reasonable to have a few items you use to discriminate among dates (such as: must be intelligent, active, a nonsmoker). The trouble is that many people secretly have dozens of must-haves and must-not-haves. "Nobody can live up to that," says Dr. Sills. Your dating experiences become one big disappointment.

"When people complain that there are no good men or women available," Dr. Sills says, "what they mean is that there are no *perfect* men or women." These people may need to examine and adjust their expectations. Do you want someone who impresses others or who treats you well? "You can widen your dating choices considerably when you consider dating people who are less educated, less successful, less glamorous looking or younger or older than you expected," she explains.

Seek a friend, not a conquest. Go to social gatherings with the purpose of enjoying yourself and meeting new friends, says psychology professor Kathryn Black, Ph.D., of Purdue University. Talk to married people, people of your own sex, people of differing ages, people who appear to be your opposite. "You'll gain confidence talking to people while signaling to everyone else that you are there to be friendly and not desperately date-hunting. You become much more approachable."

Don't be shy. Go ahead, talk to that person who caught your eye. But spare them the clever pick-up line, says Dr. Sills. "Lines are merely artificial cover-ups for the most sincere statement, 'I'd like to get to know you.' They also invite rude responses."

Invent your own ice-breakers. One dating expert suggests women wear a feather boa or carry a *Sports*

Classified Love: Pointers for Writing Personals

DWJM.

Those letters are the kind that usually start off a personal ad, and they're the dating code of the 1980s, a kind of prematrimonial Morse code that telegraphs the basic characteristics (in this case: Divorced, White, Jewish, Male) of a potential partner.

Personal ads used to be found only in the back pages of "alternative" big-city papers—along with escort services and massage parlors. Now they grace the high-gloss pages of upscale magazines, and even small-city papers sometimes carry them.

What's the appeal of personals? They give potential daters a chance to get past the packaging, says Judith Sills, Ph.D. "Studies show that it takes about 7 seconds to decide if you want to get to know a stranger better when you first meet. Personals allow people who aren't a physical '10' an extended, better chance to present themselves."

Also, placing personals forces you to analyze yourself and the kind of person you want to date. You may not always get the date of your dreams, says Cleveland humorist Sherri Foxman, author of *Classified Love: A Guide to the Personals,* but your personals may be more successful if you do the following things.

Use proper publications. Don't place a personal in the *Village Voice* if you aren't looking for a bohemian intellectual type.

Be unique. A phrase like "weekend archaeologist" can be a great conversation starter.

Use humor. Try an eye-catcher such as, "Sincere female seeks male between 38 and death for whatever develops."

Have an honest hook. Who can resist this: "Divorced male, big house, big dog, seeks female companion—dog just isn't enough."

Illustrated magazine to catch a man's eye. It's okay to use gimmicks to get someone's attention, says Dr. Black, but "just make sure that they honestly and comfortably portray your interests."

Don't dump on your date. A sure way to make your first day with him or her your last, says Dr. Black, is to spill your guts about your bad divorce, how anxious you are to get married or how you can't wait to have a baby. There are honest and calm ways to mention these intimate things about yourself without putting inappropriate stress on a newly forming relationship.

Read between the lines. How does your date treat you when he or

she is supposedly on his or her best behavior? Does she insist on always being alone or always with a group of friends when you are out? Is he too busy with his job to make time for you? Is he more interested in one-night stands than a serious relationship? Is she married? Does he drink a lot?

"Don't believe that you can change the person as the relationship ripens," warns Dr. Black. "What you see is what you get."

Save sex for last. "It's wise to delay sex until you are sure what it means to each of you," suggests Dr. Black. And when you do have sex, make it safe.

Marcia Holman

Sex: Making It Safe

What do many Americans worry about most? Nuclear war, the environment, an alien invasion? No. According to a recent poll, women, at least, worry about getting sexually transmitted diseases (STDs).

That STDs should strike such fear into the hearts of many of us is quite understandable, says Katherine Stone, M.D., a medical epidemiologist in the division of STDs at Atlanta's Centers for Disease Control (CDC). After all, everyone can relate to sexual activity, she says. "The threat of sexually transmitted diseases hits close to home," and, unfortunately, too close to home for too many people. The number of people contracting these diseases is on the rise. According to recent CDC estimates, STDs affect 12 million Americans each year.

Why the increase? Simply put, there are more people having sex with more partners today. "Anybody who has multiple sex partners is at risk for disease," says Dr. Stone. Unless you're monogamous for a lifetime, with a monogamous partner, you're at risk. And the more partners you have, the greater the risk.

Not only are there more sexually active people, there appears to be a longer list of STDs being passed around. No less than 20 different diseases, syndromes and/or complications comprise the STD scroll today. And that's in addition to—not substituting for—the old standby STDs like syphilis and gonorrhea. Syphilis is not as prevalent as it used to be, but some strains of gonorrhea have become resistant to penicillin and can now only be stopped with other types of antibiotics.

But here's why STDs may have women, in particular, all shook up: Some infections can leave the female reproductive system in ruins. Chlamydial infection, the most frequently occurring bacterial cause of STD, affects an estimated three to four million people and is a major cause of pelvic inflammatory disease, which can lead to infertility. Venereal warts (caused by the human papilloma virus) now claim at least 500,000 new cases yearly and have been linked to cervical cancer.

THE MOST SINISTER STD

The STD that is causing both sexes the most worry is AIDS (acquired immune deficiency syndrome). One recent survey revealed that people were more concerned about it than about heart disease and even cancer. And for good reason: There is no cure for AIDS; it always leads to death.

AIDS is caused by a virus that attacks the immune system and leaves its victims defenseless against illnesses. The virus is transmitted by sexual contact, contaminated needles or, less commonly, through transfused blood or its components.

At one time, it appeared that AIDS was limited to two high-risk groups—homosexual or bisexual men and intravenous drug users. Now, however, AIDS is on the increase in heterosexual populations, and some experts believe that by 1991, the incidence is likely to increase ninefold in that population. A prolific sexual history is partly to blame. "A person with multiple partners has had more chances of coming in contact with an infected person," explains Dr. Stone. "It's not just the people you sleep with; it's the people they've slept with."

So who's *not* at risk? Those partners who have both been faithful for at least five years.

HOW TO CURB CONTAGION

All the alarm about AIDS is enough to scare just about everyone away from sex. But you don't have to sign up for the monastery. "Nobody is asking you to give up sex," assures Stephen H. Zinner, M.D., chief of the Division of Infectious Diseases at Brown University's Roger Williams Hospital in Providence, Rhode Island. "What we are saying is, don't take sex for granted. Be careful and take precautions."

That begins with understanding that the AIDS virus is primarily transmitted by contact with semen and blood and that you need to protect yourself by using condoms for all sexual activity. "If you do that," says Dr. Stone, "you are on your way to protecting yourself from other STDs, too."

If you are a woman, notes Dr. Stone, you may not display any symptoms of some STDs, even though they may be present. She says that if you suspect you could have a disease, you should ask your doctor for specific testing.

If caught in time, most STDs can be cured. Chlamydia is now diagnosed earlier, thanks to two new rapid-detection tests. And while herpes is a lifelong disease, new drugs like acyclovir now control it. "Plus," adds Dr. Zinner, "it's possible that we may have a vaccine against gonorrhea, herpes and possibly other STDs in the next few years."

In the meantime, it's up to you to curb contagion. Here's how.

Limit partners. "Simply reducing the number of sexual partners and avoiding persons known to have multiple sexual partners should reduce the likelihood of exposure to an infected person," says Dr. Stone.

Seven STDs: How to Spot and Stop Them

Infection	The Signs	Tests, Treatments and Prevention
Acquired Immune Deficiency Syndrome (AIDS)	Symptoms are nonspecific but can include fatigue, weight loss, diarrhea, purple to bluish skin lesions and night sweats	Have blood serum antibody test. Avoid sexual contact with people who've had multiple or anonymous partners. Do not share needles. There is no cure, but there are various treatments for symptoms.
Chlamydia	*Men:* Painful urination, discharge or no symptoms; may coexist with gonorrhea *Women:* Yellow discharge or no symptoms	Men should have gonorrhea test; women should have vaginal cell exam. Take prescribed antibiotic. Have partners examined. Avoid sex until cured. Use condoms to prevent further infections.
Genital Herpes	Single or multiple lesions on genitalia; may be painful and shed between outbreaks	Have virus tissue culture taken. May take acyclovir to reduce symptoms. Keep infected area clean and dry. Have partners examined. Use condoms when you have no symptoms; avoid sex when you have symptoms.
Genital Warts	Single or multiple soft, fleshy, painless growths on genitalia	Have growths identified and removed by cryotherapy (freezing) or surgery. Some doctors treat with the drug podophyllin. Have partners examined. Avoid sex or use condoms during treatment.
Gonorrhea	*Men:* Discharge from the penis, frequent urination and severe burning during urination *Women:* Vaginal discharge, painful urination or no symptoms	Have specimen tested. Have partners examined. Take prescribed antibiotic. Avoid sex until cured. Use condoms to prevent reinfection.
Syphilis	Painless lesion or chancre; possibly a skin rash or other symptoms	Have a serum test. Take prescribed antibiotic. Have partners examined. Avoid sex until cured. Use condoms to prevent reinfection.

SOURCE: Adapted from *Sexually Transmitted Disease Summary—1986* (Atlanta, Ga.: Centers for Disease Control, 1986).

Look before you make love. Put passion in park if you notice unusual lesions or rashes on or discharges from your genitals or your partner's. Avoid sex until all infected persons are evaluated and treated.

Tell before you kiss. "You can't intuit if someone has an STD," reminds David J. Fletcher, M.D., medical director of MedWork at Decatur Memorial Hospital in Illinois. "Ask questions about your partner's sexual history. Listen for clues that indicate multiple or homosexual partners or IV drug use."

Use condom sense. Studies have shown that condoms prevent giving or getting chlamydia, herpes, gonorrhea and AIDS infections. They cannot, however, protect you against herpes sores or venereal warts that are not on the penis itself or not in the cervix and vagina. Using a spermicide along with a condom may make the protection even more potent. Learn how to use them properly.

Get tested and treated. Don't trust home tests or treatments, says Dr. Zinner. See your private physician or public health clinic or call the STD hotline maintained by the American Social Health Association (1-800-227-8922) for a referral to a health-care provider who specializes in STDs.

Marcia Holman

Secrets to Self-Love

Love thyself. That phrase could be the first commandment of mental health. "Of all the judgments we pass," says noted Los Angeles psychologist Nathaniel Branden, Ph.D., "none is as important as the one we pass on ourselves.

"How we feel about ourselves crucially affects virtually every aspect of our experience, from the way we function at work, in love, in sex, to the way we operate as parents, to how high in life we are likely to rise." Self-esteem, says Dr. Branden, author of *How to Raise Your Self-Esteem*, "is the key to success or failure."

There are many people, though, who have lost the key. And they're often easy to spot.

I, I, I!

For one thing, their conversations are usually centered on one subject: themselves. "People with low self-esteem always use a lot of the I, me, my, mine words," explains Gary Emery, Ph.D., director of the Los Angeles Center for Cognitive Therapy. What's more, he says, people with low self-esteem are guilty of "overpush." That is, they often overeat, overdrink, overwork or act overbearing. "They must overdo to compensate for what's lacking inside."

Perhaps the saddest part is that people who don't love themselves often find that others don't love them either. Like Rodney Dangerfield, they get no respect. They often think of themselves as losers, an evaluation that could lead to a host of psychological problems. Anxiety, drug abuse, spouse-battering, suicide, violent crimes—all can be traced to poor self-esteem, says Dr. Branden.

On the other hand, people with high self-esteem think of themselves as winners. George Burns might be a model, suggests Dr. Emery. "He doesn't appear to take himself too seriously, he's active, and he seems to have good relationships. He's got a twinkle in his eye that says he accepts himself."

The Weaker Sex

"When a woman gets the blues, she hangs her head and cries; when a man gets the blues, he takes the train and rides." There may be some truth to the old song lyric.

"Women," explains Minnesota psychologist Dwight Moore, Ph.D., "are more likely to talk to others when they feel down and to ask for support. Men, on the other hand, may cover up inferior feelings." They may become aggressive—kick the dog, chop down a tree. They may indulge in sex, or become the "strong, silent" type. They may not take the train and ride but may head for the hills in their cars instead.

The trouble is, this behavior doesn't put men on the road to reversing low self-esteem. It may even lead to depression up ahead.

The solution? Don't wait for another man to admit to the blues before you express yourself. "You have to take a risk," says Dr. Moore. By doing so, you may experience an increase in your self-esteem.

BUILD A BETTER SELF-IMAGE

Why do some of us end up short on self-esteem? We can blame our families for failing to nurture a sense of self-love. Or society for telling us we aren't up to snuff. Or Lady Luck for passing us by. But in the end, says Dr. Branden, developing healthy self-esteem is up to us. "No one else can breathe for us, no one else can think for us, no one else can thrust self-trust and self-love upon us."

Indeed, it's possible to radically transform the way you feel about yourself even if you've suffered for years with feelings of inadequacy and have had that vague sense of "I am not enough."

And when that positive transformation happens, says Dr. Branden, the rewards are great. You're likely to be more resilient when faced with adversity, form healthy relationships, earn respect and be successful—emotionally, creatively and spiritually. You might even start to look different. Your face will become relaxed, your shoulders erect, your walk purposeful, your voice clear.

And who knows, you might even develop that special twinkle in your eye—just like George Burns.

Here are some self-love suggestions.

Correct faulty thinking. The difference between people who love themselves and those who don't, say experts, is in their thinking. That conclusion grew out of work by University of Pennsylvania professor of psychiatry Aaron Beck, M.D., who discovered that "depressed people think of themselves as 'losers'—deprived, frustrated, rejected, humiliated or punished in some way."

These people are plagued with faulty thinking. They may, for example, personalize ("Everyone at the meeting was staring at me") or jump to conclusions ("I have a swollen gland. I must have cancer") or pass by the positive ("Sure, the dinner party went all right, but I burned the soufflé").

What these negative thoughts have in common, says Dr. Emery, is that they are generally wrong. "They are not conclusions reached through reason and logic."

To reverse this faulty thinking, you need to first become aware of the incorrect thoughts and then discover what's behind them. You might try dividing a piece of paper into two columns and writing out a more balanced, realistic answer for each recurrent negative thought. If, says Dr. Emery, your thought is: "This always happens to me. It will never change," then write: "Just because it happened in one case doesn't mean it has happened or will happen in every case."

Practice self-acceptance. "You can't really change yourself until you accept yourself," reminds Dr. Branden.

Learn, for example, to accept certain feelings that you may find hard to face—insecurity, envy, rage, fear—by repeating the phrase, "I am now feeling such and such (whatever the feeling is) and I accept it fully." When you learn to accept a feeling, you feel more in control of your life. Self-confidence and self-respect rise.

Build a better body image. When you feel bad about your body (oh, those hippo hips, those thunder thighs), you feel bad about yourself. How do you relate to your body? Stand in front of a mirror and listen to how you talk to your body, suggests Thomas Cash, Ph.D., professor of psychology at Old Dominion University. Do you criticize your body? Compare it to others?

Once you are aware of your thoughts, you can do the things that reinforce the good feelings about your body—things that have nothing to do with attractiveness. Luxuriate in a bath. Dance. Experiment with clothes and cosmetics that make you feel spunky and special.

Get busy. We're not talking about writing a novel or doing other large,

noble tasks, but about the more mundane, humble kind, like taking out the trash, cleaning out a drawer. Doing anything, however small, explains Dr. Emery, serves to slow down thinking and divert it from yourself. "Getting busy can completely change your state of mind by helping you gain a sense of accomplishment and power."

Give yourself feel-good rewards. Do you think, "*If* I had the right job (relationship, house, etc.), *then* I'd be happy with myself?" Why not do something to make you feel good now? Take a dream vacation. Buy a bunch of daisies. You'll soon see that self-worth starts within; you don't need someone or something to validate your existence.

Marcia Holman

Blue Mondays and Other Self-Esteem Saboteurs

There are specific times when your self-esteem is easily undermined, no matter how confident you feel. Here are 3 problem periods and how to overcome them.

Mondays. Why the letdown come Monday morning? The major reason, says psychiatrist Ronald Pies, M.D., of the New England Medical Center, Boston, is job dissatisfaction, especially if you have little control over your work. You may also start the week low if you kept late weekend hours. To

avoid feeling worn out from a disturbed sleep schedule, stick to your normal bedtime on weekends.

Holidays. Realizing that your holiday is not perfect can hit you hard, says Dr. Pies. Spare your self-esteem by reducing your imagined expectations. Cut back on commitments. Don't have all the relatives over this year. Don't knock yourself out baking cookies. Don't try to find the perfect gift. You'll feel better about yourself if you don't gorge on the goodies.

Severe winters. People often close down when they are shut in, and their self-esteem suffers, says Arthur C. Huntley, M.D., professor of psychiatry at the Medical College of Pennsylvania. This winter, make your life more stimulating. Socialize. Take a vacation to a warm climate. Surround yourself with color. Wear a red scarf instead of a gray one. Ski, skate—but get outdoors. The sunlight will lift your mood and the activity will help you feel more in control of a dismal situation.

Romantic Renewal

"It makes me feel, relaxed, calm."

"It makes me feel stimulated, full of spit and fire."

"It makes me feel sexy."

"It's better than sex."

"It's better than I remember it ever being."

Is the "it" a new drug? No. In fact, these people are describing the effects of an old, old potion, one that is perhaps more powerful and intoxicating than any pharmaceutical.

The "it" is romance. And it's the stuff that can make us fall in love again and feel like we're taking a wonderful ride to paradise.

ALTERED STATES

"Romance can indeed do wonderful things to you," says Marcia Lasswell, professor of marriage and family therapy training at the University of Southern California. "Studies have shown that when people first fall in love, their brain chemicals are altered."

Apparently, that euphoric, "walking on air" feeling that many lovestruck victims describe is not brought about by being stung by cupid's bow but by a surge in norepinephrine, the brain chemical that makes you feel good.

Other brain chemical increases may make new lovebirds feel stimulated, energized or, as they might put it, like they could "set the world on fire."

And why do people wooed by romance often claim that the world seems brighter, more vivid? Subjects falling in love, notes Dr. Lasswell, have been observed to have dilated pupils. "So it could be that their eyes are literally letting more light in."

The problem is that after a while, as with other kinds of potions, the effects of romance wear off even though love lingers on. But, romance can be as special in a mature relationship as it is in puppy love, protests William Betcher, M.D., Ph.D., a psychiatrist at McLean Hospital, Belmont, Massachusetts. In other words, you can keep that "falling in love" feeling flowing for a lifetime.

THE PERSONAL TOUCH

What does it take to recapture romance? Surprise! You don't have to be rich or particularly poetic. You don't need to be in an exotic location to experience romance—you can see it in the city lights, feel it in a snow shower. You don't need cards or candy in order to express your romantic feelings or a holiday or special occasion to tell you when to express them.

"Romance is a personal thing," echoes Dr. Lasswell. "It comes from within. To be romantic, you need to do things that make you feel happy, alive, good. And to do things that will make the other person feel the same way."

Is there a recipe for romance? No, says Dr. Betcher. But there are common ingredients that contribute to those rich, wonderful feelings. How you mix them together is up to you.

"Romance is really a state of mind," reminds Dr. Lasswell. You need to realize that the world is ripe with opportunities to release the romantic in you.

Need inspiration to rev up your romance? Try including some of the following ideas offered by real-life Romeos and Juliets.

Give love tokens. "Gifts are a tangible expression of love," says Dr. Betcher, "and when our beloved gives us something that clearly demonstrates being in tune with our true needs or desires, we feel especially loved." Love tokens need not be lavish, either, as these recollections show:

—After a special date, my boyfriend sent me a sprig of herb with a note that read simply, "Rosemary for remembrance." It really showed me that our time together meant as much to him as it did to me.

Play the Name Game

Sticks and stones will break your bones, but names can help your love life. That's right, those pet names like Snookums and Huggy Bear can help you feel closer. So can making funny faces, talking in foreign accents and generally acting like silly kids.

It's all part of "intimate play," which is a big part of romance, says William Betcher, M.D., Ph.D., in his book *Intimate Play: Creating Romance in Everyday Life.* "We all need excitement and novelty in our love relationship. Intimate play is a way of keeping that spark alive." It says, "You and I are unique and so is our relationship."

Playfulness can also ease tension and solve problems. If a wife says, for example, "Sir Lancelot, the Queen requests you not stow your armor in the middle of the castle," she is addressing the issue of housework with humor. "Playfulness softens the blow with finesse," says Dr. Betcher.

—My husband knows how much I love the beach. So for one birthday, he gave me a little plastic sandpail and invited me to join him at "the sand castle by the sea."

Especially romantic are the spontaneous, spur-of-the moment gifts that have nothing to do with birthdays and holidays:

—Once, while walking along a rocky trail littered with smooth, odd-shaped stones, my husband gathered up all the heart-shaped ones for me. I use them as paperweights—they make me feel loved.

Share experiences. Many people say they feel royally romantic when sharing experiences—both the ordinary and extraordinary kind:

—My wife and I feel totally in tune with one another when we are surrounded by nature—like sitting on our deck overlooking the woods, listening to the bullfrogs' songs.

—Sharing the birth of our son was the peak romantic experience for us. My husband was incredibly supportive—I felt so close to him.

Often the most romantic experiences are the most daring, new and out of the ordinary, says Dr. Betcher. "The purpose of seeking such novelty is to wake ourselves up so we can shake off habits and see our partners, too, with fresh eyes."

—On one camping trip my husband and I took a midnight walk through the woods in the nude—right past tents of sleeping campers. It was all misty and shadowy. We felt like the original Adam and Eve.

—Once my wife and I had a picnic in the stockroom where we worked. It was off-limits to employees and we found it dangerously delightful.

—On one particularly beautiful spring morning my husband woke up, looked out the window and said "Let's drive to Maine for a lobster dinner." Well, Maine's 6 hours away but we did it! We ended up spending the night and driving home the next morning. We had a fabulous time.

For Them, Romance Is Forever

"It's very hard to stay intimate with another person for many years and continue to recapture the feeling of wanting to be with each other, of passionate loving," says William Betcher, M.D., Ph.D. Yet many couples have retained romance for 50 years or more.

Here are their secrets for keeping that special feeling alive as the years roll by.

Continue the courtship. "Romance may continue even when sexual intercourse, for various reasons, ceases," writes gerontologist Robert N. Butler, M.D., in *Love and Sex over Sixty.* He describes the way one couple in their eighties spends their evenings. They dress in formal attire, dine with candlelight and music and hold hands. At bedtime they fall asleep in each other's arms. "I fall in love with her every day," says the husband of his wife. "My feelings grow stronger when I realize we have only a certain amount of time left."

Do something new. "We sample new restaurants and try to travel as much as possible," says one man of his 65-year marriage. "It's always a romantic adventure for us even if it's going cross-country only to visit the kids."

Retain rituals. The changing seasons can be a good reminder to renew your romantic bond. Each fall, one couple returns to the river town where they wed to toss a "good luck" pebble into the water as a wish for continued happiness together. Renewing rituals can help recapture some of the feeling of beginning a new relationship, says Dr. Betcher.

Speak the language of love. You don't have to be Keats or even have a special way with words to communicate your heartfelt feelings:

—I'll never forget the handwritten note my husband of 13 years packed in my lunch telling me how much I meant to him. He's a man who rarely writes anything—it was worth a thousand valentine cards or a float full of roses!

—One morning, for no reason at all, I awoke and found a beautiful, sentimental greeting card on my pillow that my husband had placed there when I fell asleep. I guess I had been feeling that I was being taken for granted for a while. That card erased that notion.

Plan a great escape. Going away together creates a cozy cocoon and may allow the romantic in you to reappear:

—One Christmas eve my husband and I took a room at an old country inn overlooking a frozen canal. We escaped the frantic gift-giving, the glitzy holiday glitter. The only lights were the stars shining in the sky. It was so still and quiet—we never knew just how special celebrating a holiday could be.

—We were vacationing with a few other couples and all our kids and had spent a day sailing. Later that night, my wife and I slipped away to the bay and took a moonlit sail alone. We got so caught up in the magic of it—we didn't return to the dock until dawn.

As one romantic once put it: "It's the little things that count!"

Marcia Holman

CHILDREN'S HEALTH

Easing Childhood Ills

It's 3:00 A.M. A quavery voice calls from down the darkened hall. "M-o-m-m-m-my!" You pretend you can't hear a thing. Maybe he'll go back to sleep. Then, "Daddy! Daddy, I *need* you!" Of course. What is it this time? A virus? An earache? Maybe a sore throat? You stagger out of bed to investigate.

SEE SPOTS SPREAD

It's chickenpox. The red spots all over your child's chest are unmistakable. He's also got a fever and a headache, and the spots are so itchy they're driving him bats. You knew he'd been exposed to several cases over the past three or four weeks, but since he'd felt fine except for a runny nose, you figured he'd get away with it. But no such luck. Now what are you going to do?

Pop him in a tub of water and throw in a handful of baking soda, suggests Linda Jonides, R.N., a certified pediatric nurse-practitioner in Ann Arbor, Michigan. If that doesn't stop the itch, try Benadryl Anti-Itch Cream, an over-the-counter topical antihistamine that many parents keep on hand. (When you reach your doctor in the morning, however, he may prescribe something different.) You might also want to splotch calamine lotion over the spots.

If your child's really fussy, you might want to give him a dose of acetaminophen (Tylenol). But you'll have to decide whether brevity of illness or comfort of child is more important. Pediatricians at the Johns Hopkins University School of Medicine have discovered that acetaminophen can make chicken pox hang around for about an extra day. Also, aspirin and aspirin-containing products are verboten from infancy to about 19 years of age because of their association with a neurological disorder called Reye's syndrome.

Keep Your Cool!

"The best way to treat your child's fever is to keep cool yourself," says G. James Fruthaler, Jr., M.D., staff pediatrician at the Ochsner Clinic in New Orleans. Ice-water enemas, ice baths, alcohol rubs and other common fever "remedies" are not only unnecessary, the pediatrician says, they could be considered cruel and unusual punishment.

Why? Fever is a natural defense mechanism, he explains, not a disease in need of treatment. It indicates the immune system is on the job and, when triggered by relatively minor illnesses such as viral infections or colds (as it is between 80 and 90 percent of the time), it won't rise to a harmful level unless you keep your child deprived of water or overly warm.

What should you do if a fever is cooking your kid?

Check with your doctor to find out what's causing the temperature, advises Dr. Fruthaler. Then forget it. Don't keep checking it with fever dots, strips or thermometers. If your child's fussy and uncomfortable, give him a fever-reducer such as acetaminophen (Tylenol), sponge him down with lukewarm water, let him soak—with you close by—in a tepid bath or strip off any uncomfortable sheets, blankets or clothes.

This chart should give you a reading on temperature control.

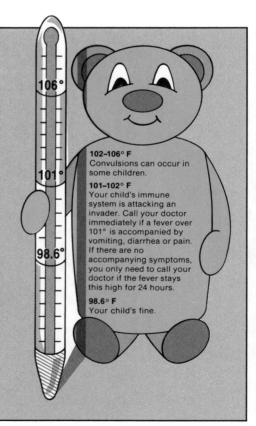

102–106° F
Convulsions can occur in some children.

101–102° F
Your child's immune system is attacking an invader. Call your doctor immediately if a fever over 101° is accompanied by vomiting, diarrhea or pain. If there are no accompanying symptoms, you only need to call your doctor if the fever stays this high for 24 hours.

98.6° F
Your child's fine.

SOOTHING CROUP

Croup, the name given to the sound made when air is breathed in through a narrowed windpipe, is another illness children seem to get frequently at night. Your child may have looked perfectly healthy all day, but he'll suddenly wake up with a barking cough. And wait till you hear him inhale: He may very well honk like a goose.

The first thing to do if you suspect croup, says Loraine Stern, M.D., associate clinical professor of pediatrics at UCLA, is to calm your child. Croup is scary and "the more upset children get," says Dr. Stern, "the worse the coughing." Fear tightens everything up.

The second thing to do is steam up the bathroom, shut the door and sit inside with your child. Sit on the floor if you have to, but keep your small person upright to ease his breathing.

You can also wrap your child in blankets and take him outside in the cool night air, says Dr. Stern. Or drive around in your car. The night air will soothe your little one's irritated windpipe and the ride will soothe his nerves. It may even help your nerves, too.

But call your pediatrician if your child begins to look gray or blue, cautions Dr. Stern. If he's not breathing well or if he won't swallow, if he sits upright with his head held forward and drools as well as coughs, take him to the emergency room. And try to be calm. "It's usually better in the morning," reassures Dr. Stern.

TOOTH DECAY IS A DISEASE

A disease? That's right! It's not one of those diseases that hits smack in the middle of the night, taking energy and the next few nights' sleep along with it. Tooth decay is more insidious than that. The only way to attack tooth decay—besides chemicals, drills and lasers—is to prevent it. How? It all begins with brushing and flossing.

"Start your kids brushing as young as possible," says pedodontist Paul F. DePaola, D.D.S., head of clinical trials and human experimentation at the prestigious Forsyth Dental Center in Boston and director of the center's Specialized Caries Research Center. Teeth should be brushed "down on the uppers" and "up on the lowers" in a circular motion. The general rule is to brush every time you eat, says Dr. DePaola, although he's willing to compromise: "One thorough brushing a day is the minimum; twice a day is preferred."

But how do you get kids to give their teeth a thorough brushing? One way is to have your child chew a "disclosing tablet" before brushing, says Dr. DePaola. The tablet, which is usually made of a harmless vegetable dye and is available at your local drugstore without a prescription, will signal any buildup of food particles and bacteria with a red splotch that even a two-year-old can't miss.

"Tell your child, 'Every place you see red is bad. You need to brush it off,'" suggests Dr. DePaola. It will probably take your child about 2 minutes to follow your instructions—about the same amount of time you can expect a child to pay attention to his teeth.

And don't forget about flouride; it's the most important cavity fighter. Fluoride has been shown to reduce tooth decay up to 65 percent. It's so important, in fact, that if you don't have fluoridated water, your child should not only brush with a fluoride toothpaste but should also take a fluoride tablet prescribed by either your dentist or pediatrician. Your dentist may also want to apply a fluoride gel directly to your child's teeth once or twice a year and perhaps "bond" the decay-prone biting surface of your child's back teeth.

Bonding means that your dentist applies a kind of plastic that seals the tooth. Most bonding, which should be done as soon after new teeth develop as possible, lasts roughly five years and usually has to be repeated. It cuts your child's decay potential drastically.

NO ESCAPING AN EARACHE

Earaches are usually caused by a strep or flu bug attacking the middle ear—sometimes as the rearguard action of a nose or throat infection, sometimes as the unfortunate side effect of propping a bottle in a baby's mouth for a long period of time.

Whatever the cause, earaches may be accompanied by fever, discharge and, in children too young to describe pain, irritability, crying and tugging or rubbing the ear that hurts. They occur in 85 percent of all children, usually under age five and usually in the fall or winter.

Children with earaches are likely to wake up screaming in the night, says Dr. Stern. When that happens, you can wrap a hot water bottle in a towel and place it against the affected ear or use a warm washcloth as a compress. Or simply pick your little one up and lean his sore ear against your chest. The warmth of your body can be just as effective—and far more comforting than a piece of cotton or a bag of rubber.

If the ear is not draining, says Dr. Stern, warm a few drops of oil— either olive or vegetable—and place it in the infected ear. "Do *not* heat the oil in a microwave," cautions Dr. Stern. "You'll fry the ear." Decongestants and antihistamines, even though they're commonly prescribed, have little or no effect, she says.

But even if your child feels fine the next morning, get him to the doctor. The earache may dissipate overnight due to your tender loving care, but the infection will probably linger until it's hit with antibiotics. And if it does, you may get an Oscar-quality performance of "Scream in the Night, Part II."

WHO SOCKED YOU?

Nosebleeds are especially common in children between the ages of four and ten. They're usually caused by a blow—from a pugilistic sibling, perhaps?—or an inquisitive finger. And sometimes an overheated, dry bedroom contributes to the problem.

In any case, bloody noses are no cause for panic. They usually can be stopped fairly simply. Doctors suggest that you have your child lean forward to avoid swallowing the blood, breathe through the mouth and pinch the nostril shut steadily for 5 minutes (no peeking).

Rarely does bleeding continue, but if it does, see your pediatrician.

SORE THROAT SOOTHERS

Even when your child's throat is as sore and irritated as a brush burn, you can usually make him more comfortable by offering cool or hot lemon drinks and turning on a cool-mist vaporizer or humidifier. Frozen fruit juice or yogurt can also help and, if you need to tempt your kid's thirst buds, adding carbonated water to pear, apple, orange or watermelon juice will frequently do the trick. If you're really hard up for a liquid strategy, however, sticking a curly or bendy straw in the glass usually tickles the most jaded pair of inflamed tonsils.

Older kids—"older" meaning they don't immediately swallow everything that goes in their mouths—can sometimes benefit from lozenges with a local anesthetic or maybe a favorite cough drop, says pediatric nurse-practitioner Jonides.

Saltwater nose drops (two to three drops of a solution of ¼ teaspoon of

How Sick Is Sick?

Your child has a fever. He's flushed. He doesn't smile even when his puppy attacks your toes. Does he have a run-of-the-mill infection, or is he seriously ill?

If *you* think it's serious, it is. But there are six key signs and sounds that can help you figure it out, says Paul McCarthy, M.D., professor of pediatrics at Yale School of Medicine. Here they are.

Observation	Normal	Moderate Impairment	Severe Impairment
Quality of cry	Strong with normal tone *or* content and not crying	Whimpering *or* sobbing	Weak *or* moaning *or* high-pitched
Reaction to parent stimulation (effect on crying when held, patted on back, jiggled on lap or carried)	Cries briefly, then stops *or* content and not crying	Cries off and on	Continual cry *or* hardly responds
State variation (going from awake to asleep or asleep to awake)	If awake, then stays awake *or* wakes up quickly	Eyes close briefly, then awakens *or* wakes up with prolonged stimulation	Will not rouse *or* falls to sleep
Color	Pink	Pale hands and feet *or* acrocyanosis (blue hands and feet)	Pale *or* blue *or* ashen (gray) *or* mottled
Hydration (moisture in skin, eyes and mouth)	Skin normal and eyes and mouth moist	Skin and eyes normal and mouth slightly dry	Skin doughy or tented, eyes sunken and eyes and mouth dry
Response to social overtures (being held, kissed, hugged, touched, talked to, comforted)	Smiles *or* (if 2 months or less) alerts	Brief smile *or* (if 2 months or less) alerts briefly	No smile, face anxious *or* dull, expressionless *or* (if 2 months or less) no alerting

salt per ½ cup of lukewarm water, four or five times a day) can at least provide comfort if the infection, which can be either bacterial or viral, is located in the upper part of your child's throat. If it's located further down—around the tonsils, for example—gargling might help.

Any sore throat that lasts longer than 24 hours, Jonides cautions, should be checked by your pediatrician.

FLUSH AWAY THE TUMMYACHE

If your child comes home from his best friend's birthday party with a stomachache, you can pretty well guess what caused it—too much cake and ice cream. You can also pretty much guess the cause if it hurts only when it's time for bed. Or school. Or any place else your child doesn't want to go.

But aside from these pains of rather obvious origin, the most common cause of recurrent stomachaches, says Jonides, is constipation, a condition that refers to the hard, dry texture of your child's stool. And the fastest way to get rid of it is to increase the fluid intake and the amount of fiber in your child's diet. Also avoid foods like cheese, peanut butter and bananas for a couple of days. Be sure to watch for additional symptoms—increased pain, fever, vomiting—that may signal another problem.

You thought enemas were the answer? No way. Fruits, vegetables and whole grain breads and cereals should be a normal part of every child's diet, but at least one study indicates that a child with recurrent abdominal pain should increase the usual amount by 10 grams a day. That's the equivalent of adding a bowl of high-fiber cereal and a slice of whole wheat bread to the diet daily. You might want to start things off by offering your child a few stewed prunes or dried figs. The impact of a single serving can be felt within 24 hours.

A SEA OF BUGS

Viruses, viruses, viruses. Sometimes it seems as though our children are swimming through a sea of micro-organisms determined to make them sneeze, cough, vomit or spend what seems like the rest of their lives on the toilet. Preschool children in day care, for example, have six to nine colds and up to four intestinal viruses a year.

Antibiotics and other medical weaponry aren't much good against most of these bugs, so how can you make your child more comfortable until his immune system overruns the enemy?

Believe it or not, some doctors suggest you spoil him. Read him stories, play games, sing songs, move the television into his room, bring him gifts, do everything you've always wanted to but were afraid would ruin his character. If he wants to stay in bed, let him. If he wants to get up, let him. If he wants to go outside on a warm day, let him. Just don't let him bounce around.

If he has a cough that doesn't produce mucus, give him a dose of an over-the-counter cough medicine containing dextromethorphan polystirex, doctors suggest. With any kind of cough, encourage your child to lie on his side or stomach at night. Also, use a cool-mist vaporizer in his room and don't smoke anywhere around him. And if he has a runny nose, don't let him leave germy tissues lying around. Make sure he puts them in the trash.

But what do you do if the bugs attack your child's gastrointestinal system? If he's an infant and he's vomiting, says Dr. Stern, skip the next feeding, wait a few hours, then start him on an over-the-counter electrolyte solution such as Pedialyte or Lytren to prevent dehydration. Let him take as much or as little as he likes.

If your child is a year old or older and is vomiting, give him 1 tablespoon of flat soda (any kind will do) or diluted apple juice. Wait 15 minutes, then try another tablespoon. If he keeps it down, great. Continue the tablespoons for a couple of hours. Do *not* give water to a child who has just vomited, cautions Dr. Stern. It can trigger a magnificent encore.

For diarrhea, Dr. Stern suggests keeping your child on clear liquids, but for no longer than 24 hours. After that, ease him back onto food with bananas, rice and applesauce.

If your child is under a year old and has diarrhea and is vomiting, or if diarrhea continues in an older child for more than a week, check with your pediatrician, says Dr. Stern. Children sometimes develop chronic nonspecific diarrhea of childhood (CNDC), which—as its name indicates—means chronic diarrhea of unknown origin. It's a condition found in normal children.

CNDC is most often triggered by a viral attack and usually stops if you increase the fat—particularly unsaturated fat like that found in margarine and peanut butter—in your child's diet until it represents 40 percent of total calories. You should also avoid wheat, milk and sugar for a few days, and don't let him drink excessively.

A study at the University of South Florida, for example, revealed that nearly 70 percent of CNDC in a group of 314 children under the age of three was caused by guzzling liquids. Apple juice, that perennial favorite of nutrition-conscious mothers, was particularly involved in aggravating the problem.

In any case, your child can resume his normal activities—school, day care, afternoon play group—as soon as he has enough energy to withstand the rigors of perpetual motion. You don't need to worry about spreading the virus to teachers or other kids. Since children with viral illnesses are contagious for five to seven days before they actually show any symptoms, you can rest assured that he's already infected everyone he knows—including you.

Ellen Michaud

Play Is Your Child's Work

What is play?

Only an adult would ask. But Michael Yogman, M.D., director of the Infant Health and Development Program at the Children's Hospital in Boston and assistant professor of pediatrics at Harvard Medical School, has an answer: "Play is children's work."

It develops creativity, learning skills, self-esteem, flexibility and vocabulary. And since the child is forced to evaluate, fantasize, consider alternatives, solve problems and make decisions during play, it also contributes to mental growth.

But play is parents' work, too, Dr. Yogman adds, because play is a medium of communication between parent and child. It's a way for you and your child to say how you feel about each other, a way for children to share things that trouble them and a way for parents to shape their children's values.

BEING A KID AGAIN

Think of what goes on during play. One parent races up and down the stairs. He's a thief escaping from jail. His son, the three-year-old police officer, races after him. "I got you, daddy!" the child gleefully screams as he grabs his dad by the arm. "You're gonna go back to *jail!* "

Obviously this young man has been taught that there are consequences to taking something that doesn't belong to him. His dad starts the play sequence by pretending to walk through a store—his living room —and whistling. He stops at an end table overflowing with books, then sneaks a look over each shoulder to see if anyone is watching. He carefully ignores the 36-inch police offi-cer peeking out from behind a chair. Instead, he grabs a book, shoves it under his sweater and turns to leave the store.

But the miniature police officer explodes out from behind his chair. "You're under *arrest!*" he yells in his best police-officer voice. The thief is then sent to jail—from which he can escape again and again to the delight of everyone concerned.

Yet for all the parental shaping that goes on during parent/child play, says Dr. Yogman, parents have got to do things that are fun for both parent and child. "You can't fool kids," he adds. If you're not having as much fun as they are, they'll know it. They'll turn off and turn away. But because they're so young it's *your* responsibility to find games and kinds of play that are mutually enjoyable. You can't just decide to teach your child some abstract idea or moral value and make up a game to go with it. You need to balance the parental shaping that may be your intent during play, says Dr. Yogman, with respect for your child. Otherwise you'll rob your kid of his creativity—one of the things he's supposed to be learning from play.

THE FOUR STAGES OF PLAY

But how do you figure out what kinds of play are both fun and educational?

Well, says Jerome L. Singer, Ph.D., a psychologist at Yale University, it may help to realize that children progress through four different kinds of play as they move from toddler to adolescent.

"The first kind of play is sensory motor play, which consists simply of feeling and touching—a baby waving his fingers in front of his eyes, enjoying the feel of sand, kicking things around and so on," says Dr. Singer. That's basically what very young children like to do.

"The second type of play is what's called make-believe or symbolic play —pretending, fantasizing, introducing elements that aren't given in the immediate situation. A child takes a stick and makes believe it's a train or an airplane or a spaceship and imitates the sound of the plane or makes believe that there are little people riding on it who talk to each other and so on." The shoplifter dad and his three-year-old police-officer son are also good examples.

Then as your child gets a little older, say around five or six, "there are games with rules such as Simon Says," says Dr. Singer. This is the third type of play. But rule games, which teach children how to cooperate, get more complex as they get older. They are supplanted around the age of seven or eight by board games, such as Clue or Stratego.

You thought board games were just for fun? They are. But educational ones like crossword-puzzle games, educational lotto games, Risk, Monopoly and Facts in Five can, psychologists say, help your child develop his ability to think logically and abstractly, identify relationships and develop and verify scientific hypotheses. They can also build self-confidence, because they give your child an opportunity to think through situations and have his thinking "rewarded" by success: he wins the game.

Eventually rule games evolve into games of mastery—the fourth kind of play—in which skills are learned that will someday be used in athletics, music and that sort of thing.

Stir Those Thoughts

How do you encourage imaginative play? Jerome L. Singer, Ph.D., a psychologist and author, with Dorothy G. Singer, of *Make Believe,** answers the question this way.

● Make an outdoor playhouse with at least 3 sides and a roof. Whether it's an elaborate log cabin or some boards secured to a tree, the playhouse will make an exciting fort, pirate's den, castle, clubhouse, store or cave from which your child can launch any number of dramatic stories and try on any number of roles. It also provides him with a private place in which to be alone to ponder the world.

● Provide a pile of sand or dirt in your backyard with pint-size shovels. Your child can build roads to Timbuktu and solve the mysteries of the ancients.

● Read your child stories. Suggest he act them out. Then suggest he make up new characters and endings. Not only will it stimulate his imagination, it'll teach him new ways to think.

● Collect a big bag of hats—baseball hats, nurses' hats, firefighters' hats, any kind of hats. Wearing a hat changes a child into another person. It helps him figure out who *he* is and develop a sensitivity to other people's feelings.

● Encourage your child to use his senses. Go outside with him to listen to the wind. Blindfold each other and walk around the house trying to identify sounds such as water running in the sink, a door or window opening or footsteps on a staircase. Have a "touching shelf" on which your child can place things he finds that have an interesting texture—feathers, scraps of velvet, even bottlecaps. Look at everyday things— hair, fabric, applesauce—under a magnifying glass. Or bake some spice cookies and encourage your child to taste the ingredients as you use them.

● Dance. And ask your kid to dance with you. Pretend you're a snowflake, a goldfish, a big stormy wind or a cloud moving through the sky. Not only does dancing improve balance and coordination, it will also help your child learn to like his own body.

These activities encourage children to explore the world around them. It also allows them to learn a deeper, richer way of perceiving experiences and teaches them a way to enhance their memories. Memories that we connect with a physical sense are always remembered in greater detail and with greater precision.

It's at that point, Dr. Yogman says, that parents may be less welcome in their child's play. "When kids are younger, they really need adults to play with them for a brief period of time to get the game going," he explains. "Some kids are really good self-starters, but many kids need that initial push from an adult."

WHEN IT'S TIME TO TAKE YOUR BOW

"After the age of six or seven, the adult can be an embarrassment," says Dr. Yogman. Parents need to be more of a catalyst than a participant. If you see your nine-year-old just sitting around, for example, you might want to suggest he get out a board game and practice strategy. Maybe with you. Maybe with a friend. Maybe alone.

But before you turn into a spectator, remember that playing with your kids also benefits *you.* It helps you get in touch with parts of yourself that are often fenced off from everyday thoughts. And play, according to at least one psychologist, is probably the single best method of stress reduction.

So the next time your kid asks you to go sledding, think twice before you say no. Think about zooming down a snow-covered hill on a red Gemini sled. Think about flying over icy bumps with your nose 6 inches off the ground. Think about the squeals and laughter as that final mogul nearly dumps you in the creek.

Then think about how much fun you'd have missed if you'd decided to be a grown-up.

Keeping up with your kids sometimes means being a kid yourself.

Ellen Michaud

Vitamins for Better Health

It's not as if a mother doesn't try. It's just that it's not always so easy when Billy locks his jaw every time you try to feed him what he should eat instead of what he wants. To make matters worse, you don't even know if (and how often!) he trades his nutritious tuna on whole wheat for a triple pack of cupcakes in the school cafeteria.

It's no wonder kids have such an easy time driving their mothers mad! How can you possibly know for sure if he's getting the proper nutrition—at least the Recommended Dietary Allowance (RDA)?

UNDERSTANDING THE RDA

Before you can best assess your child's nutritional health, you need an understanding of what the RDA is all about. Simply, the RDA is the government-established minimum limits for 13 vitamins, three minerals, nine trace elements and three electrolytes. They were designed to ensure that healthy people get an adequate intake of all the essential nutrients. But what does *minimum* mean? Does it mean your children are expected to hit 100 percent in each category every day?

"No," says Lendon Smith, M.D., a retired Oregon pediatrician and author of *Feed Your Kids Right* and *Dr. Smith's Diet Plan for Teenagers.* "Everyone who has any kids knows that they don't eat right every day. Even though we'd like them to, it's unrealistic to expect it. You should look at the overall diet. It's okay if your child doesn't get the RDA every day. But is he getting it every week?"

Another thing to remember is that getting less than 100 percent of a nutrient does not necessarily mean your child will become instantly unhealthy. Scientifically, a nutrient isn't considered on the low side until intake falls below 67 percent of the RDA, and even then, a deficiency disease isn't imminent. Knowing that alone should make you feel better if a day or two doesn't measure up.

NUTRIENTS IN SHORT SUPPLY

Not surprisingly, certain vitamins and minerals are more likely than others to be in short supply in a child's diet. One study conducted at the University of Washington tested a group of healthy children from the ages of 3½ to 9 to see how they fared on the RDA for vitamins C, B_6 and B_{12}, thiamine (B_1), riboflavin (B_2) and folate—all essential nutrients in normal childhood development. While intakes were adequate for most nutrients, some of the children showed intakes below 70 percent for folate and B_6.

Dr. Smith also feels that zinc, a trace element that aids normal growth, is often low in the average child's diet. But it's iron, more than any other nutrient, that is most commonly in short supply.

Alvin N. Eden, M.D., author of *Dr. Eden's Healthy Kids,* agrees. "I think there's a large group of children out there who are iron deficient without being anemic," says Dr. Eden, a practicing pediatrician in New York City and associate clinical professor of pediatrics at New York Hospital/Cornell University Medical Center. "For this reason I think it's important for parents to consider giving their children an iron supplement. In fact, the most important thing I tell parents is to 'think iron.' "

Of course, if children would eat liver, the best source of iron, there would never be a deficiency problem. Nor would a deficiency of zinc, selenium, chromium, vitamins A and B_{12}, riboflavin and folate ever occur. Unfortunately, when it comes to liver, most kids consider going to bed without supper the better alternative.

MEETING THE RDA

But don't despair. There are plenty of other ways to get your liver-shy kids to eat right. By including certain core foods in the diet each day, the doctors we spoke to say you'll be doing your best to help your children meet their RDA.

For breakfast, the most concentrated form of nutrition is a whole grain cereal and a fruit, either juice or whole. "Hot oatmeal with applesauce and raisins tastes great and is very nutritious," says Dr. Smith. Or for a change of taste, try serving leftovers from last night's dinner. "There's nothing wrong with a chicken leg for breakfast," he says. "It's protein."

Our experts also suggested it's best to pack a child's school lunch rather than depend on what's being served in the cafeteria. Whole wheat or other whole grain bread should always be used for sandwiches. It provides needed B vitamins. Peanut butter is just fine, but eliminate—or at least cut down on—the jelly. Instead, substitute a banana. Always include fruit in the lunchbox, too. For snacks, opt for carrot sticks or trail mix (an assortment of nuts, dried fruits and raisins).

For dinner, serve lean meat or fish, steamed vegetables and fruit for dessert. If you want to feed your kids pastry, think whole grains, and go for oatmeal cookies instead of brownies.

Allow your kids to drink only low-fat or skim milk. "Kids shouldn't drink too much milk," says Dr. Eden. "I think milk is a little overrated. Too much spoils an appetite, and it's too high in fat to be good for you. Two glasses a day is plenty."

Debora Tkac

The ABC's of Good Nutrition

Here's a handy reference list of the major vitamins and minerals, what they do and where to find them. Why not stick a copy on your refrigerator? Then tell your kids they can reach for anything on the list—but not an hour before dinner.

Nutrient	Major Functions	Good Food Sources Children Can Love	Nutrient	Major Functions	Good Food Sources Children Can Love
Vitamins A	Necessary for healthy skin, good vision and bone growth. Bolsters the body's natural immune system.	Cantaloupe, carrots, dried apricots, hard-boiled eggs, sweet potatoes, vegetable soup, watermelon	C	Helps hold cells together; can help guard against the common cold.	Baked potatoes, blackberries, blueberries, cantaloupe, cherries, orange juice, strawberries, tomato juice
Thiamine (B₁)	Helps keep nervous system functioning smoothly.	Baked beans, oatmeal, rice, rye bread, sunflower seeds, whole wheat bread	D	Works with calcium to build strong bones.	Egg yolks, milk, tuna (also plenty of sunshine)
Riboflavin (B₂)	Carries oxygen to body cells; helps build healthy blood.	Almonds, cheese (particularly Brie), lean hamburger, low-fat yogurt, milk, wild rice	E	Prevents blood clots; protects cells against oxidation; protects immune system.	Almonds, lobster, peanuts and peanut butter, pecans, sunflower seeds
Niacin	Good for memory and moods; helps lower blood fats—cholesterol and triglycerides.	Almonds, baked beans, dried dates, peanuts and peanut butter, sunflower seeds, tuna, white meat chicken, whole wheat bread	**Minerals** Calcium	Necessary for healthy bones, teeth and muscle.	Buttermilk, cheese, ice cream, low-fat yogurt, milk, whole wheat pancakes
B₆	Helps keep immune system healthy and keeps blood clots at bay.	Bananas, filbert nuts, sunflower seeds, tuna, white meat chicken	Iron	Essential for the manufacture of red blood cells.	Chicken and turkey (light and dark meat), lean hamburger, molasses, raisins, sweet potatoes
B₁₂	Necessary for healthy blood and nerves; guards against anemia.	Lamb, low-fat yogurt, milk, Swiss and cheddar cheeses, tuna, white meat chicken	Zinc	Aids normal growth; sharpens taste, smell and sight; aids wound healing.	Chicken legs, crab, hot dogs, lean hamburger, oatmeal, pork chops, shredded wheat
Folate	Aids in the normal functioning of the central nervous system.	Cantaloupe, orange juice, red beets, romaine lettuce (on sandwiches)	Magnesium	Aids calcium in forming strong teeth and bones.	Baked potatoes, bananas, beans, molasses, nuts, oatmeal, peanut butter, whole wheat spaghetti
Biotin	Helps certain enzymes utilize food.	Black raspberries, eggs, grapefruit, milk, oranges, turkey and chicken legs, whole wheat bread			

Making Your Kids Smarter

Can you make a smarter kid? You sure can.

Between 50 and 80 percent of your child's intelligence is shaped by the genetic material passed to him by you and your spouse, say the experts. That leaves a lot for you to play with. Although genetics sets the stage for your child's intellectual development, *you* control the action. You control the scripts, dialogues, costumes, characters and props. And with that kind of control, you can improve your child's intelligence.

How? "Talk," says Sheryl L. Olson, Ph.D., a psychologist at the University of Michigan. From the day your baby is born, talk to him. When you're changing a diaper, ask him how the wipe-'em feels. Ask him how fresh the clothes smell, where his puppy is, whether or not he can hear the birds singing outside his window. And every time he burbles back an answer—inadvertently or not—step up the conversation with a laugh, a smile and more chatter.

TALK TO STIMULATE BRAIN GROWTH

"Active verbal interaction is probably the most important social variable affecting a baby's cognitive competence," says Dr. Olson. Quite simply, the more verbal the parent, the more intelligent the child.

Why? Every time your child interacts in an active, positive way with his environment, his brain grows.

At birth, says Jane M. Healy, Ph.D., an educational psychologist at Cleveland State University and author of *Your Child's Mind,* the brain already contains billions of nerve cells, which are supported by a mass of connections that link them into efficient relay

systems. But the connections are only potential—they're not actually built until a nerve cell fires off a message to one of its neighbors. That's where you come in. By communicating with your child, you trigger a chemical and electronic response in the baby's brain. Every word you say, every appearance you make, every touch you apply, every finger you let your baby suck makes more connections. And each new connection increases your baby's ability to learn.

DON'T SHOUT

But as your child grows, the content of your words is almost as important as whether or not you speak, adds Dr. Olson. As her own and other studies have demonstrated, for example, telling kids what to do all the time, where to put things, what to read, where to go, where not to go—generally trying to control, direct or command a child's every move—is associated with decreasing your child's intelligence. So is shouting at your child in anger or physically punishing him.

"One of the major theories of children's cognitive development," explains Dr. Olson, "is that they need to actively explore the world in order to develop their cognitive abilities—that these cognitive abilities are actually shaped through active exploration of the environment.

"If you buy that theory, then it makes sense that moms who restrict their children's exploration very much will tend to have kids who are less intelligent than others.

"That doesn't mean a mother shouldn't control her child," Dr. Olson emphasizes. "She should." It means she should control her child in a posi-

tive way. If your child is throwing pots and pans around the kitchen floor, for example, instead of yelling "Don't do that!" say, "Would you like to put those back in the cupboard for me?" The difference between positive and restrictive discipline is as simple as that, says Dr. Olson. And it's just as effective.

Dr. Healy agrees. The fear engendered by parental shouting, physical punishment or constant restriction, she points out, can trigger a chemical reaction in the brain that disrupts the way nerve cells fire off their messages. Developing brains need lots of tender loving care, she adds. Children learn best in a positive, unpressured and emotionally secure environment.

They also learn best in an environment that gives them lots of opportunities to explore and play, says Dr. Olson. And toys that respond to them—blocks that fall over when they're swiped at, pots that make noise when they're banged—also stimulate children's learning.

But don't overstimulate your child in an effort to build a better brain. When your baby averts his eyes and maybe even his head, cautions Dr. Olson, he's telling you he's had enough. And continued overstimulation will actually interfere with his ability to learn.

Find the point at which your baby's had enough and then quit, concurs Dr. Healy. A smarter *parent* is one who learns to understand his child's language.

Marks of a Gifted Child

Is your child destined to be the next Albert Einstein? Between 2 and 3 percent of all children are intellectually "gifted," according to the experts, which generally means that they have an intelligence quotient (IQ) of 130 or more plus a specific academic aptitude — in math or languages, for example. They may also exhibit creativity, talent in the arts and an unusual amount of motivation.

Does this sound like a small person you know? Gifted children often share similar characteristics. Frequently they may be:

● Insatiable readers.
● Early talkers who develop a large vocabulary and are fascinated by words.
● Unusually curious, constantly questioning and avidly seeking information.
● Capable of intense concentration.
● Perfection seekers.
● Highly perceptive with a good sense of humor.
● Aware that they are somehow "different."

ENCOURAGE THINKING

How else can we make a smarter child? One way that's gaining momentum in schools throughout the country, says Robert Swartz, Ph.D., director of the Critical and Creative Thinking Program at the University of Massachusetts, is to help your children learn to think. "A common mistake people make is to confuse the accumulation of facts with intelligence," says Dr. Swartz. "Intelligence is the ability to use information and to use it well." Stuffing a kid's brain full of information does *not* make him more intelligent.

Besides, how can not having enough facts ever be a problem for kids who are constantly bombarded with facts, from "Sesame Street" at age 2 to "Nightline" at age 22? What may be a problem, says Dr. Swartz, is sorting through all the information and determining which is accurate and reliable and which is not. A smart kid, he points out, is going to be the one who can start to sort this out and not just accept everything that anyone tells him.

How do we get our kids to think? "The trick is to not just tell kids to think," says Dr. Swartz, "but to prompt them to do it with our questions."

If you're sitting there watching TV with your child, for example, ask your child what he thinks about the commercials. Who's the advertiser? What's he trying to sell? Who's he trying to sell it to? Do you know anybody in the neighborhood who's purchased the product? If he does, suggests Dr. Swartz, it's worth the effort to visit the neighbor and have your child ask *him* what he thinks of the product. Teaching a child to get his information from a variety of sources — not just one — is an important lesson.

In encouraging this kind of thinking, it's particularly helpful if the product involved is something to which your child can easily relate. Checking out a toy, for example, is going to be far more relevant to an eight-year-old than checking out a mop.

BE INQUISITIVE

The key is to use everyday materials and situations to instill a constructive questioning attitude in your child. You're the model, Dr. Swartz points out, and as you go through a day wondering out loud whether or not a neighborhood jungle gym is safe — "Who can we ask?" — or whether or not the new car takes you as far as the old one on a gallon of gas — "How can we check it out?" — your child will begin to ask his own questions. "Do these sneakers really make me jump higher?" "Would the salesperson know?" "Does he have a particular reason for saying that?"

BRAINSTORM

Encourage your child's questions, Dr. Swartz suggests, and help him develop the skills to find the answer. Even more, give him various problems to solve in creative ways. Brainstorming is an important part of this process.

Say the rain gutters on your house are rusted through. Point this out to your child, then ask, "What do you think will happen the next time it rains?" Then turn your brainstorming toward a solution. "What can we do about it?" "What's the one thing that nobody else has ever done?" "What's a solution that involves your hands?"

Even a child's moment of misbehavior can be an opportunity to make him smarter, says Dr. Swartz. Instead of preaching at him about the rotten thing he's done — "It's wrong. It's wrong because someone got hurt." — turn an ordinary incident into a brain-stretcher. "Can you think of any reason why what you did is wrong?" "What can you do to make it right?"

Any kid who grows up thinking his way through those kinds of questions, says Dr. Swartz, is bound to develop the essence of what we really mean by being smart — good, effective thinking.

Ellen Michaud

Understanding Childhood Allergies

Is your child allergic? Since one in every five children is allergic to something, there's a good chance that he is. And if you happen to have allergies yourself—in the form of asthma, hay fever or dermatitis—your child has a 50/50 chance of developing one, too.

How can you tell if your child has an allergy? It's not always easy.

THE TELLTALE SIGNS

Parents are often misled by symptoms that mimic a cold (sneezing and coughing), intestinal problems (colic, cramps and vomiting) or skin disorders (hives, rashes and swelling). Even wheezing or shortness of breath can be mistaken for other ailments. So be on the lookout for the following symptoms as well.

Allergic "shiners." Dark, puffy circles under the eyes are common in children with allergies and are caused by the congestion of blood in tiny blood vessels under the eyes, according to Warren Richards, M.D., head of allergy and clinical immunology at Children's Hospital of Los Angeles and clinical professor of pediatrics at the University of Southern California.

Allergic salute. "This is a gesture common to children with nasal allergy," continues Dr. Richards. "Itching prompts the child to repeatedly rub the nose, either up and down or sideways, and may cause nosebleeds. In time, this gesture can form a noticeable crease across the bridge of the nose."

Dizziness and ringing in the ears. Allergy may cause swelling and fluid retention in the arteries and smaller blood vessels feeding the ear, causing dizziness and annoying inner-ear sounds.

Mothers Give More Than Love

You are what you eat. But you are also what your mother ate while she was pregnant, doctors suspect. If your mom was binging on eggs, for example, chances are you'll be allergic to them.

"People with food allergies often crave the foods to which they're allergic," says Vincent A. Marinkovich, M.D.

"For a pregnant woman, the result is that undigested food proteins travel through the bloodstream right to the baby," says Dr. Marinkovich. The baby's immune system perceives these undigested food proteins as foreign invaders and manufactures antibodies to repel them.

But the process doesn't end there. "Once that immune system is 'turned on,' it has a good memory," he explains. "When the baby encounters that food again, the immune system remembers it as an enemy and responds as if under attack. And that means an allergic reaction."

The solution? "It's perfectly all right for mothers to eat a little bit of what they're craving," says Dr. Marinkovich. "As long as they eat some other foods at the same time. The key is to eat a well-balanced diet that can include the craved foods, but not to binge on anything."

Eczema (allergic dermatitis). Children with allergies often have hypertensive skin and are plagued by dryness, itching, redness, cracking and watery discharges. Check your child's face, neck, inside creases of both elbows, hands and knees, since those are the most common trouble spots.

Hearing difficulties. On-and-off hearing loss, popping in the ears, a feeling of fullness in the head or ear pain may be due to an allergy that causes the lower end of the eustachian tubes to swell. If hearing loss occurs at a very young age, it may interfere with speech, according to experts. Unfortunately, a school-age child with allergy-induced hearing loss may then be labeled as inattentive or not too bright.

Itchy throat. Does your child clear his throat constantly, even in his sleep? Allergy may be causing postnasal drip, which in turn causes the tickle in his throat.

SORTING OUT THE SYMPTOMS

If your child has any symptoms that may indicate an allergy, you may want to get help from an allergist. The doctor will ask you dozens of questions about what your child eats, breathes and touches and ask for the following information as well.

How long do symptoms last? If sneezing and stuffiness last a few days, then disappear, your child probably has a cold. If sniffling and congestion linger, or occur more than six times a year, allergy is probably the cause.

Are symptoms worse at certain times of the year than others? If your child's symptoms flare up in the spring and late summer or fall, then subside in winter, the child could be allergic to pollen, the powdery grains that burst from plants during the growing season. If your child feels worse during damp weather, he could be allergic to mold and mildew, which flourish during spring and fall.

Does your child suffer more during the heating season? That suggests an allergy to fumes from burning fossil fuel, especially gas.

Do you have pets? If your child's symptoms are worse when he's around animals—cats, dogs, gerbils, guinea pigs, hamsters, horses or parakeets— dander could be the trigger. And don't forget that down comforters and feather pillows fall into this category, too.

Does your child crave certain foods—or feel better if he skips a meal? Ironically, either tendency may point to a food allergy.

Did your child suffer colic as an infant? Colic often precedes food allergy later in life.

Your answers to these questions can narrow down the list of likely suspects, but to help confirm the diagnosis, your doctor may want to conduct a battery of allergy tests.

WHAT ALLERGY TESTS CAN TELL YOU

Allergy tests don't come right out and tell you exactly what your child's allergic to. They simply detect the presence or absence of specific antibodies or other immune substances that indicate the *likelihood* of an allergy.

To interpret the results, your doctor will also take your child's actual experience into consideration. "A child could have a positive reaction to dog dander [indicating allergy], for example, yet suffer no nasal problems or other allergy symptoms when around the family dog," explains Edward W.

Get Pregnant in February

Families in which allergies run rampant should time pregnancies carefully to avoid giving birth during high-risk pollen periods, concluded pediatric researchers at a university hospital in Sweden.

The reason? Allergy-prone babies born in May had *double* the chance of developing allergies as allergy-prone babies born in November.

A little planning and forethought, the researchers suggest, can avoid a childhood of sneezes and wheezes.

Hein, M.D., chief of pediatric allergy at St. Christopher's Hospital for Children in Philadelphia. "It just means that your child is *potentially* allergic to dogs." Of course, if your child experiences symptoms around the dog *and* shows a positive reaction, he's probably allergic.

The most common type of allergy test is called the scratch test. Based on a hunch about what's making your child miserable, the doctor scratches a minute amount of a suspected allergen into the surface of the skin. If a red welt (called a wheal-flare reaction) appears, your child may be allergic.

Blood tests are another possible way to identify an allergy. The MAST test, for example, is a one-step procedure that can check for allergic reactions to 35 different foods, using just a teaspoon-size sample of your child's blood.

The MAST test, says Vincent A. Marinkovich, M.D., a clinical associate professor of pediatrics at Stanford University, uses a small chamber divided into sections, each of which contains a "thread" coated with a specific allergen like cat dander, dust,

pollen, mold or a specific food. A little bit of your child's blood is added to the chamber, and doctors can then examine each thread to see if antibodies in the blood have reacted to that allergy-provoking substance. Threads that do react literally "light up" in the chamber, and the result is photographed. The picture clearly shows the cause of your allergies.

OUTGROWING ALLERGIES

But even if the tests indicate that your child is indeed allergic, says Dr. Hein, "my experience is that six out of ten allergic children tend to outgrow their symptoms. In fact, the earlier they develop an allergy, the more likely they are to outgrow it—usually around age six, or when they reach puberty."

As for asthma, adds Dr. Richards, 50 percent will feel better or be completely free of symptoms by puberty, too.

"That doesn't mean parents should sit back and do nothing, waiting for their children to outgrow the problem," Dr. Richards hastens to caution. "If a child is four years old and miserable, don't wait around. Seek treatment."

Sharon Faelten

Kids Get Stress, Too

When Jennifer Novack was seven, specialists had confirmed what the Philadelphia girl's parents feared: Scoliosis was twisting her backbone into an S-shaped curve. She would need surgery to straighten out her spine.

The operation is described by one hospital physician as about as major an orthopedic procedure as a child can have. Diane Novack remembers her daughter's operation taking more than 5 hours. Four weeks at home followed her five-week hospital stay.

But in Jennifer Novack, nurses discovered "a very up kid." There were no cries of pain and no tears. Here was a child who drew on an inner well of courage—what psychologists call the ability to cope.

Children are the silent victims of broken homes, lost jobs, crippling illnesses. How do some—Jennifer Novack, for example—handle life's stresses so well?

SOURCES OF STRESS

Certain normal stress is built into childhood, forming a sort of obstacle course mapped by nature and set with a multitude of hurdles.

"The environment places a lot of barriers to little people. High drinking fountains, high doorknobs, for example, are sources of frustration. The older a child gets, the more he ventures into a wider environment with more opportunities for stress," says Peter J. Behrens, Ph.D., psychologist and assistant professor at Pennsylvania State University.

Separation from family is a major source of stress for young children, especially anxiety that accompanies the first weeks of school or day care, adds Susan Leibmann, M.D., director of outpatient services for children,

adolescents and families at Thomas Jefferson University Hospital in Philadelphia and assistant professor at Jefferson Medical College.

"At ages four and five, their lives are their families. They are susceptible to anything that disrupts it," she says. "For school-age children, there are new demands. They have to perform cognitively. They have a new authority figure, a teacher, and they have peers to get along with."

Preadolescent years bring the stress of growth, sexual maturation and rigorous academic demands. "There is more concern with what peers have to say and a constant struggle trying to separate from the family," says Dr. Leibmann.

"Despite the stressfulness of our world, most children manage to come through it," says Norman Garmezy, Ph.D., a psychology professor at the University of Minnesota, who is conducting a 15-year study of what steels children against stress. "The majority are able to overcome the disadvantages they labor under."

CUES FOR COPING

Still, there's no instant guarantee of protection for your child from life's ups and downs. Worries, frustrations and disappointments are all part of growing up. But as a parent *you* can ease the way.

Here are some tips from child-rearing experts on how you can help your child cope.

Say "I love you." Show your child you love him, no matter what. Though this sounds obvious, it may not be so obvious when your six-year-old has dumped a quart of apple juice on the floor, the wall and himself—and you are already late for work.

A hug offered with reassurance that these things happen has curative powers that make mopping the floor and apologizing to the boss all worthwhile. Psychologists point to a loving parent as a child's most invincible armor.

Be honest. Teachers, nurses and therapists emphasize that children need straight answers in language they can understand.

"Children don't like to find out you've ever lied to them," says Lois Trouland, a registered nurse who prepares children for orthopedic surgery at the Philadelphia unit of Shriners Hospitals. "If you lie, you lose their confidence."

Master little stressors. "Parents can use everyday stressors to advantage by gradually introducing them—little bites as opposed to big chunks. In that way, children can adapt when big stressors come along," says Dr. Behrens.

Knowing, for example, that it is the nature of a five-year-old to take half the morning to find his pants, a parent might ease the tension by locating them the night before.

Keep in touch with how your child feels. The time to deal with stress is before it sets up a vicious circle of behavioral or school problems. "It means asking children directly about how they feel and what they're thinking. I recommend the 'what if' question," says Dr. Behrens. "Put the child in a hypothetical situation so he can work it through."

Parents also need to be alert to physical problems, such as poor vision, that add stress to daily activities.

Be consistent. Fred Boccella, who counsels junior high school kids in the Philadelphia school system, watches wearily when parents send conflicting cues.

"You get two parents and neither knows what the other is doing. The father says one thing, the mother the opposite. The child is getting mixed signals. He's confused. He comes to school angry and has a poor self-image. He's restless, inattentive and a poor achiever." Parents need to come to an agreement and stick with it, the counselor says.

Set goals within reach. Adults whose expectations exceed a child's timetable or abilities—insisting on early reading or entrance to an advanced scholastic program a pupil doesn't belong in, for example—are asking for trouble.

Leave time for play. Recognize that play during childhood, without direct parental supervision, is filled with learning and exploration. Play lets children try new roles. They learn at their own pace, free of adult criticism, and work out relationships with peers.

Mary Blakinger

SOS: Distress Warnings

In most settings, it takes a perceptive parent or teacher to spot what a child is unable or unwilling to express. Children signal distress with symptoms that may develop in subtle or dramatic ways.

Susan Leibmann, M.D., says there are four areas in which you can spot stressful behavior.

Emotional functioning. Trouble here can take many forms, like continual crying or whining, a sense of hopelessness, a worried outlook.

Behavior. A child might become withdrawn, aggressive or irritable. In older children, Dr. Leibmann says, symptoms could be reflected in truancy, fighting with peers or stealing.

School performance. Children overwhelmed by stress have difficulty paying attention and doing homework. Their grades drop.

Health. When stress bothers children, symptoms can be physical—headaches, insomnia, appetite changes, asthma. Parents should heed these complaints, Dr. Leibmann points out.

Does your child exhibit any of these signs? If he does, the following checklist, adapted from the Home-Rahe Social Readjustment Rating Scale, may help you figure out how your child got so overwhelmed—and just *how* overwhelmed he is.

Event	Points
1. Death of a parent	100
2. Divorce of parents	73
3. Separation of parents	65
4. Parent's jail term	63
5. Death of a close family member	63
6. Personal injury or illness	53
7. Parent's remarriage	50
8. Suspension or expulsion from school	47
9. Parents' reconciliation	45
10. Long vacation (Christmas/summer)	45
11. Parent or sibling sickness	44
12. Mother's pregnancy	40
13. Anxiety over sex	39
14. Birth or adoption of new baby	39
15. New school, classroom or teacher	39
16. Money problems at home	38
17. Death (or moving away) of close friend	37
18. Change in studies	36
19. Quarreling more with parents (or parents quarreling more)	35

Event	Points
20. Change in school responsibilities	29
21. Sibling going away to school	29
22. Family arguments with grandparents	29
23. Winning school or community awards	28
24. Mother going to work or stopping work	26
25. School beginning or ending	26
26. Change in family's living standard	25
27. Change in personal habits (bedtime, homework)	24
28. Trouble with parents (hostility, lack of communication)	23
29. Change in school hours, schedule or courses	20
30. Family's moving	20
31. New sports, hobbies, family recreation activities	19
32. Change in church activities (more involvement or less)	19
33. Change in social activities (new friends, loss of old ones, peer pressures)	18

Event	Points
34. Change in sleeping habits (staying up later, giving up nap)	16
35. Change in number of family get-togethers	15
36. Change in eating habits (going on or off diet, new way of family cooking)	15
37. Breaking home, school or community rules	11

Scoring: The points column opposite each life event gives it a numerically weighted value from 11 to 100. Add up all points and refer to the score range below.

Score Range	Interpretation
300+	Major stress
250–299	Serious stress
200–249	Moderate stress
150–199	Mild stress
11–149	Very little stress

Quelling the Cries

You've checked his diaper. You've offered him a breast. You've tried a bottle. You've even looked for a tiny hand trapped in a sleeve or a diaper pin that didn't stay closed. And he isn't feverish or vomiting. But your baby just cries and cries. He's inconsolable.

Now what do you do?

The first thing, experienced parents say, is to realize that babies cry when they're tired or hungry or wet or afraid or bored or lonely or in pain. And sometimes, particularly in the evening after dinner, they seem to cry without any reason at all. For hours.

But the next time your little person expresses dissatisfaction with the world, remember that for centuries, babies have been soothed by some combination of sound and motion. So instead of feeling like an incompetent boob who can't do anything—which is what *all* parents feel like when faced with a crying baby—try one of the following tips from other parents down in the trenches and on the front lines.

● Snuggle your baby against your chest, breathe slowly and deeply and imagine yourself deep in a tranquil forest. Hopefully baby will join you.
● Slip your baby into a front-pouch baby carrier and go about your normal activities.
● Put your baby on top of the running dryer and do your laundry. Do not, under any circumstances, leave your baby unattended.
● Hold your baby at crotch and chest, tummy down, and zoom him through the air like Superman. Keep his head a bit higher than his bottom.
● Rock your baby in a rocking chair and sing songs like "Swing Low, Sweet Chariot" and "Amazing Grace." ("We Shall Overcome" is particularly comforting—at least to the parent.) Or rock your baby in time to a rollicking sea chant like "What Shall We Do with a Drunken Sailor."
● Turn on the radio and boogie your baby across the room.
● Massage your baby with warm lotion.
● Lay your baby tummy down across your knees, then rhythmically sway him back and forth.
● Swaddle your infant with a receiving blanket.
● Put your baby in his carriage, then jiggle it up and down, push it back and forth, sway it from side to side. If you feel like running it around in circles, try that, too.

They Call It Colic

When your baby screams and draws his legs up tightly against his abdomen as though all the fiends in hell are dancing through his intestines, you can bet what you're seeing is colic.

What may help, one pediatrician says, is eliminating cow's milk from your diet for a week or two if you're breastfeeding, or from your baby's diet if you're bottle-feeding. Switch your baby to a soy-based formula such as Isomil or Soyalac instead. You might also give your baby more sucking time during feedings.

If neither of these tactics relieves your baby's obvious agony, ask your pediatrician about a prescription medication such as Donnatal or Levsin. There's no known sure cure for colic, but these 2 medications may be able to relieve its symptoms.

Baby's Screams Can Be Deafening

How loud can a baby cry? Louder than a jackhammer just 3 feet away; louder than a subway train. Even louder than a live rock concert.

In fact, a baby has the capacity for such volume that it can temporarily harm your hearing. Experts agree that noise levels in excess of 85 decibels for 8 hours or more a day can eventually harm hearing. Exposure to 115 decibels for even 15 minutes a day can do the same. Where does a baby's noise level lie, and what can you compare it to? The chart below will give you a clue.

Noise	Decibel Level
Live rock music	90 – 130
Screaming child	90 – 115
Subway train	80 – 105
Automobile horn	110
Chain saw	100
Jackhammer	100
Motorcycle	100
Alarm clock	80
Ordinary human speech	60

- Take a warm bath with your baby.
- Put your baby in an infant seat or stroller and keep him nearby while you work.
- Offer a pacifier. (The ones shaped like nipples allow less air to pass into your baby's digestive tract.)
- Put your baby in a wind-up swing.
- Put your baby in his cradle or carriage and move it next to a grandfather clock. Make sure you do not wind the weight that controls the chime.
- Hold your baby and shift your weight from foot to foot.
- Lay your baby on his back and gently put a hand on his tummy. Or hold his leg. It will make him feel more secure, doctors say.
- Tape 30 minutes of your washing machine or dishwasher. Play it back to your infant when he cries. The rhythmic swishing soothes.
- Drape your baby tummy down over a warm hot water bottle on your lap.
- Lay your baby tummy up on a bed and bounce him by quickly pushing down on the bed on either side of him.
- Tell your baby your life story in a quiet, conversational voice. The sound of your unexcited voice tells him all is well.
- Take your baby for a ride in the car. When he falls asleep, drive home, unstrap your baby's car seat and carry it into the house. Then plunk it in a crib and go take a nap yourself.
- Get a Rock-A-Bye Bear, the 11-inch teddy bear invented by an obstetrician that reproduces the sounds your baby heard *in utero*.
- Make animal noises. Say, "And here comes moo cow... Mo-o-o-o-o. And here comes duckie . . . quack-quack-quack-quack-quack-quack-quack. And here comes . . ."
- Turn on a fan or hair dryer, or leave the radio tuned to a station that's off the air. "White noise" sometimes soothes a baby.
- Spread out a blanket in the sunshine and plunk him down in the middle. If it's cold outside, spread the blanket in front of a sunny window. Think of how blissful you feel lying on a warm, sunny beach and you'll understand why it works.
- Wind up a musical stuffed animal and put it where your baby can see it.
- Blow a wet kiss in your baby's soft little belly.
- Gently blow on his toes.
- Always go to your crying baby. It's impossible to spoil an infant, say pediatricians.

GRIN AND BEAR IT

Some days, however, nothing's going to quell your baby's crying. So for those times when you'd sell your soul for 5 minutes of peace and quiet, try one of these mother-tested tips.

- Put on a pair of earphones that are intended to muffle the noise. You'll never hear a thing.
- Call a babysitter. Then go out to dinner with your best friend.
- Put your baby in his carriage, then go wash the dishes. Run the water hard so you can't hear a thing.
- Hand your screaming bundle of joy to any other warm body you can find.
- Take a deep breath and breathe out all that pent-up tension. Your baby knows you try.

Ellen Michaud

Disturbing the Peace

Your in-laws have taken you, your spouse and your new baby to a fancy restaurant for dinner. Everything was fine—at first. You sat down, put the baby in a sling, draped a napkin across your lap and picked up the oversized menu.

Now everyone is staring. Because no matter how many times you jiggle your car keys or offer a bottle, your child simply curls up his fists and screams.

It happens to everybody who thinks that their infant will find the tinkling of glassware a lullaby. He won't. More likely he'll think of it as reveille.

"You have to remember how short a baby's attention span is," says Charles Schaefer, Ph.D., a child psychologist and director of the Crying Baby Clinic at Fairleigh Dickinson University. "You can't expect him to sit still. Even at the age of a year, a baby's attention span is only 5 to 10 minutes.

"That's probably why fast-food restaurants have come into being," the psychologist adds with a chuckle. "You have to serve parents with babies fast" —before the kids have a chance to start screaming. "Even preschoolers can only be expected to sit for half an hour or so."

But what if you've no choice but to bring your baby along? In that case, says Dr. Schaefer, remember 2 things.

Bring along a bag of tricks. Bag a variety of small toys and—for slightly older kids—drawing materials. Then let your child pick out 1 toy at a time and mouth it, wave it or pass it back and forth.

Set limits on what your fellow diners have to put up with. If your child has reached his tolerance level for sitting still, get up, take him to a neutral corner—the parking lot, cloakroom, reception area—and wait until he stops crying. *You* can return when *he* returns to socially acceptable behavior.

Lessons in Potty Training

Remember the old adage, "You can lead a horse to water but you can't make him drink?" Well, in parenting, it's "You can lead a child to the potty but you can't make him pee."

And it's true. You may be in charge of everything else in your child's life, but he's in charge of his body. He's the one who decides when, where, what and how much.

Yet isn't there a way *you* can help him decide at least the where and when? There is.

READY, GET SET . . .

Read him *No More Diapers,* an engaging book for toddlers by Joae Graham Brooks, M.D., and the Boston Children's Medical Center staff. Then somewhere around his second birthday, when he's dry for several hours at a time, when he's walking, when he can follow simple instructions, you can tell him your expectations, says Eleanor Weisberger, assistant professor of child therapy at Case Western Reserve University School of Medicine and author of *When Your Child Needs You.* You can buy a potty-chair, a dozen pairs of training pants and a sponge. The sponge is for mopping up mistakes.

Then you can start to talk with him about the way his body functions, Weisberger says. Clearly label his body's by-products—urine, pee-pee, poop, B.M., tinkle, whatever—so that he connects the word with the deed. Then leave the potty-chair where he can easily reach it, Weisberger advises, and tell him what it's for. Encourage him to sit on it while he's wearing his diapers.

If a red face or grunt alerts you to imminent action, suggest he take off his diaper. Then see what happens. Just don't be overzealous, Weisberger cautions, particularly during this introductory period. But if he *does* do something in the potty, make sure he knows you think he's the best thing since sliced bread.

. . . GO!

Toilet training may take three to six months, Weisberger estimates, and parents should accept that at the outset. Part of the reason it takes so long is that when children are biologically ready to begin potty training, they're also exploring what me, myself and I is all about on a psychological level. "No! Don't want to do it. *You* do it!" is an amazingly accurate test case of who's who.

But a few months after your child's gotten comfortable with the potty-chair, pick a time when you know you're going to be available and you can let other things in your life take care of themselves. Then move the potty-chair to the bathroom. If there isn't a bathroom on the first floor, Weisberger suggests, stow the potty where your child can get to it quickly and easily. Then get out the pile of training pants you bought, stack them nearby and show the setup to your kid.

Point to the potty and tell your child that it's time for him to go to the bathroom the way the big kids do,

Weisberger suggests. Emphasize the big kid stuff and look confident.

ACCIDENTS WILL HAPPEN

But accidents are bound to happen. In fact, your child will probably continue to urinate and defecate in his training pants for the first few weeks. "Act indifferent," Weisberger advises. "Deal with your child as if he's a smart, sentient person. Potty training is not like training a dog." You don't whack him on the nose with a newspaper—or anywhere else—when he doesn't get it right.

When he does have an accident, Weisberger suggests, say, "Next time, tell me *before* you have to go." You may have to repeat your request a dozen times before he gets the idea—the concepts "before" and "after" are pretty complicated for small people—but eventually you'll get through. You can help him figure it out, however, if you say "We have to urinate in the potty *before* we can go to the pool" or "*before* we can go to the playground" or "*before*" any other anticipated treat. Eventually he'll make the connection.

When he finally does tell you he has to go to the bathroom, show him to the potty, help him with his clothes and leave him to it, Weisberger says. Don't hang around and comment or offer a magazine. You did your job. Now let him do his.

If he's still having accidents several months later, however, show him step-by-step how to rinse out his pants and mop up the rug or floor with a sponge. That's his job, too, Weisberger says firmly.

TIPS FROM A PEDIATRICIAN

But Loraine Stern, M.D., associate clinical professor of pediatrics at UCLA, prefers a more laid-back approach to accidents. "Children don't mind playing in poop," she says candidly. So teaching a kid to mop up after himself really has no value.

"Most of the time accidents occur because the kids are playing and they don't want to be bothered with going to the bathroom. We just have to accept that," the pediatrician says. "Do as little as you can get away with," in terms of correction.

Instead, be a good role model, suggests Dr. Stern. "When you have to go to the bathroom, say 'Mommy has to go potty.' Go, sit down, say, 'Mommy's going potty.' " Spell it all out. Use a doll that drinks and wets if that makes the process clearer. By drawing your child's attention to the specific steps involved in toileting, says Dr. Stern, you're doing all the training that's necessary.

Ellen Michaud

The Boot Camp Bathroom

Can you toilet train children in less than a day? "Yes!" say Nathan H. Azrin, Ph.D., and Richard M. Foxx, Ph.D., in their book *Toilet Training in Less Than a Day*. If a child is 20 months old, can remain dry for several hours at a time, knows when he's about to urinate, can follow simple instructions and walk easily from room to room without assistance, he can probably be trained by the method these 2 learning specialists originally developed to train profoundly retarded adults. Or, at least, that's what they say.

Others, however, feel differently. "Everybody wants instant," says Eleanor Weisberger, an assistant professor of child therapy. "Instant diet. Instant potatoes. With children, slower is better. Lenient with expectation is better."

Loraine Stern, M.D., agrees. "You'd have to be a psychologist to do it," she says, referring to the less-than-a-day method. "You can use their techniques, but not in one day. Some children will say, 'Mommy—potty!' and they've trained themselves. But there are others who do it slowly and gradually."

What is this controversial method? Essentially, parent, child, potty-chair, candy, tasty liquids and a doll that drinks and wets stay shut up together without distraction until either the kid gets trained or the parent gives up. You fill the doll up with water so it wets. You fill your child up with his favorite liquids so he gets the urge to wet.

"Offer the drinks every few minutes," the doctors advise. Then, force the youngster to sit on the potty until he urinates. It supposedly takes 4 hours or less for a child of "normal intelligence" to get the idea, claim Dr. Azrin and Dr. Foxx.

Carefree Babysitting

The babysitter was nervous. He rattled away about his schoolwork, his church and his sister—a dependable teenager who had been their regular sitter until she'd started a part-time job the previous weekend.

They wondered why he was nervous—then remembered he was only 13. And this was his first paying job. Still, as this young couple said good night to their four-year-old, something nagged at them. They had known the boy, at least to say hello to, for several years. They also knew his mother. His sister. They shrugged the feeling away and left.

Four hours later they returned to find a police car parked in their driveway. The sitter, surrounded by his family, claimed there had been a robbery. There hadn't. As a sensitive police investigation determined the following day, the sitter was a neglected child who was crying out for attention any way he could get it. And for the next year, the four-year-old was terrified of babysitters every time Mommy and Daddy left.

Such incidents, fortunately, are few and far between for most parents. Still, they open up a very important concern. How can you tell if a sitter's any good? How do you know if he or she is a stable, reliable person who can take care of your child, especially in an emergency? How do you spot the troubled ones?

GETTING TO KNOW YOU

The only way, says Bryna Siegel, Ph.D., a psychologist at Stanford University, is to get to know any prospective sitter. Anytime you're considering someone for in-home child care, you should invite her (or him) over for a cup of coffee or a soft drink and a chat. Establish a good rapport, says Dr. Siegel, who is also the author of *The Working Parents' Guide to Child Care,* and ask her how she got into babysitting. What kinds of things does she do to help a child adjust to his parents' leaving? How does she handle misbehavior?

Then watch how she interacts with your child, says Dr. Siegel. Does she pick him up? Does she talk to him? Touch him? Does the way she talks about children jibe with the way she acts toward *your* child?

And how does your child, assuming he's more than a few months old, seem to feel about the sitter? You should respect your child's right not to like someone, says Dr. Siegel. He shouldn't have to put up with a babysitter he doesn't like or feel comfortable with. Nor should you.

Many times, however, your prospective sitter is a teenager, and chit-chat is not going to reveal much more than what school she goes to, what subjects she likes, what sports she plays and whether or not she's free on Saturday nights.

So instead of inviting a teenager over for a chat, suggests Dr. Siegel, invite her over to sit for a few afternoons while you're in the house. Then see if the sitter knows how to handle children. Does she know how to play with a small child? Is she into buckets and balls and blocks? Or does she plop herself and your kid in front of the TV to watch MTV?

QUALITY CARE

Another area of consideration should be the babysitter's age. At what age should a teenager be considered responsible for the care of a younger child? Twelve or 13 is okay if she lives next door or across the street, says Dr. Siegel, and if you know her parents

are available for any problems. Otherwise, no child under 3 should be left with a sitter who's younger than 14.

And remember, a babysitter's family is part of her credentials. In her experience, says Dr. Siegel, quality babysitting is closely related to how interested the sitter's parents are in what she's doing.

How do you know if they're involved? A phone call to your prospective sitter's mom may give you a clue, says Dr. Siegel, and you can ask the sitter whether or not she has to clear babysitting assignments with her parents. If she does, there's a good chance that her parents care enough about *their* child to make sure she knows how to take care of *yours.*

Ellen Michaud

This Says You Care

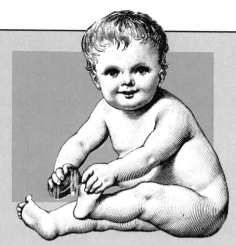

Here's a guide to share with the babysitters in your life, whether it's your own child caring for younger brothers or sisters or the friendly 14-year-old entrepreneur next door. With this detailed list of tips—compiled from interviews with Patricia Keener, M.D., a neonatologist at the Community Hospital of Indianapolis, and other safety experts—your sitter can learn what he or she needs to know to keep your children safe while you're out of the house.

Photocopy this page and give it to your babysitter after filling in all the pertinent information.

Here's what to do if there's a problem.

● If our child has trouble breathing, and especially if he or she stops breathing, call for an ambulance, then call our neighbor. The numbers are listed below. Then call us. The same rules apply for poisoning or broken bones.

● If our child gets a deep cut or bumps his head or won't obey you, call our neighbor at the number listed below.

● If our child develops a fever, begins throwing up or won't stop crying, call us.

Special Instructions

In case of fire, here are the escape plans the children have rehearsed.

MAIN ESCAPE ROUTE: _____

ALTERNATE ROUTE: _____

_____

A Few Things You Should Know

MEALS AND SNACKS: _____

_____

BATHROOM HABITS: _____

_____

BEDTIME: _____

_____

TV RULES: _____

_____

WHAT TO DO IF OUR CHILD MISBEHAVES: _____

_____

Phone Numbers You'll Need in Case of a Problem or an Emergency

POLICE: _____

FIRE: _____

AMBULANCE: _____

NEIGHBOR: _____

POISON CONTROL CENTER: _____

WHERE WE ARE: _____

Reminders

● Never leave the children alone. When it comes to getting into serious trouble, children are more inventive than a script writer for Saturday morning cartoons.

● Don't be afraid to ask for help. No one will think you're stupid if you have to call us or ask a neighbor for help or advice in handling a problem.

● Lock the doors after we leave. Never open the door to strangers. Never tell visitors you're alone. If someone or something strikes you as suspicious, call the police at the number listed above.

● If someone calls and asks for us, don't let them know you're in the house alone. Say, "They can't come to the phone right now," take a message and say, "They'll call right back." Hang up immediately on obscene calls.

● If there is a fire, get yourself and the children out of the house quickly and safely. Don't go back into the house! Call the fire department from the safety of a neighbor's house.

● In an emergency, you may also need to tell the police, ambulance or fire department our address and phone number. Here they are:

ADDRESS: _____

_____

PHONE: _____

Sibling Rivalry: Creative Combat

Jimmy toddles into the nursery, looks over his shoulder to make sure he's alone, then pinches his six-month-old sister. Hard.

Kimberly is steamed. Her sister got a new winter coat *and* a pair of leather boots, while she got only a coat. Kimberly rushes at her sister, screaming "I hate you! I hate you!"

Whether it's between babies, preteens or so-called mature adults, rivalry between siblings is more often the rule than the exception. What causes people who are basically sweet, intelligent and kind to turn on the very people they should love the most? It all goes back to the whole question of who Mom and Dad loves best. Every child wants to be number one.

"Children are very self-centered," says Lawrence Balter, Ph.D., professor of educational psychology at New York University. "They resent any interruption in their relationship with their parents. When another child comes along, they've lost their exclusivity."

But if parents are the basic cause of sibling rivalry, they can also be the cure. "Parents can make it better or worse," Dr. Balter says.

It helps to acknowledge and talk about a child's negative feelings about a brother or sister. Dr. Balter suggests, "You can say to the child, 'I know it bothers you that the baby is crying so much. And I know that it's hard that I have to spend so much time with her.'"

Parents should also keep in mind that children may be at different developmental stages that make it impossible for them to be perfect playmates.

DON'T COMPARE

What more can you do to avoid sibling rivalry or reduce existing conflicts? Never criticize one child while praising another ("Why can't you be more like your brother? He's so neat."). If you do, you may start a never-ending competition for your favor. Building

up a child at the expense of another is just as destructive.

"A parent will say, 'This is a fantastic report card,' and as an aside will say, 'I wish your brother's was a little better,'" says social worker Carole Calladine, a therapist at St. Joseph Hospital in Lorain, Ohio, and the author, with her husband, Andrew, of *Raising Brothers and Sisters without Raising the Roof.* She recommends building a positive self-image for each child that isn't based on comparisons.

Here are her other suggestions for avoiding comparisons.

Give praise in private. When it's report card time, or your child has had a noteworthy achievement, praise him in private. You'll avoid setting up rivalries or sparking jealousy, but you will still be helping to build your child's self-esteem.

Don't get caught in the fairness trap. Parents don't have to treat kids equally, from spending exactly 10 minutes playing with each to giving them the same number of Christmas

Easing the New-Baby Blues

The day that Mom brings a new baby home from the hospital is often the day that sibling rivalry begins. There's a lot that parents can do to ease the strain, advises Morris Green, M.D., professor and chairman of the Department of Pediatrics at the Indiana University School of Medicine.

If you can manage to space children 2 to 3 years apart, it can help, Dr. Green says. It's easier for parents to handle children at different developmental stages. Here are some of his other hints for helping children adjust to a new sibling.

● Tell your child about the expected addition in advance and let him get used to the idea.
● Any other changes for the older child—starting nursery school or giving up the crib—should occur 2 or 3 months before the baby's arrival.
● Prepare children in advance for

Mom's hospital stay and have them visit her there. If that's not possible, Mom should phone them or send them a photo of Mom and baby.
● Mom should take a card along to the hospital and send it home, telling the older child how much she misses him.
● Enlist the older child's help in caring for the baby.
● Set aside time each day to spend with the older child.

You Can Bury the Hatchet

Sibling rivalry may seem childish, but don't tell that to adults who are still feeling its effects. Competition with a brother or sister or the hurts inflicted by a parent's comparisons can persist for a lifetime.

But there are ways to establish new ties with your siblings—no matter what your age. Here are some of them.

● Unfreeze resentments and misunderstandings by talking openly about your feelings with brothers and sisters.

● Parents can continue to fuel competition among adult children, but you don't have to respond. When a parent says, "You should hear the way your sister talks to me," refuse to participate in the conversation. You can counter by saying, "Mom, the time we spend talking is special. Let's not spend it talking about her."

● If your parents persist in casting you and your siblings in your childhood roles when you're in their home, meet your brothers and sisters on neutral territory. It can help you establish new ways of relating.

● Be willing to recognize that your siblings may feel that they suffered because of you, too.

● Mark the beginning of your new sibling relationship with a ritual: Toast yourselves with champagne or share a hug.

---

presents. "If you're always trying to be fair and duplicate things with kids, you're creating scorekeepers," Calladine warns. "And the scorekeeping will go on and on until the parents die. Try to individualize the attention, and let them know they're special."

To avoid demands for equal treatment, Calladine suggests teaching children the difference between needs and wants. "We all need different things at different times," she explains. "Obviously a baby *needs* a great deal of time. An older kid may not need the same attention, but he *wants* to know he's special."

Describe what you feel or see. When behavior displeases you, resist comparisons. Don't say, "Why can't you be like your brother and do your homework without being told?" Instead, describe the negative behavior or the feelings that it's causing: "It's 8 o'clock and I see you haven't started your homework" or "I'm concerned that you haven't started your homework."

Do the same thing when complimenting youngsters. Don't say: "You picked up your toys! Your baby sister could never do that." Instead, say, "You put away all the toys. That is a big help to me."

NEITHER JUDGE NOR REFEREE

For the parent who is trying to avoid picking favorites, sibling fights —verbal or physical—pose major challenges. If you become the judge who decides who's right and who's wrong—"Johnny had the truck first, so he gets it"—youngsters feel you're choosing sides.

What can you do if the fights are threatening your sanity and their safety? "Conflicts in themselves are not a problem," says Calladine. "It's very helpful to teach kids how to problem-solve. Take a mediator's rather than a referee's role." Intervene only when someone might get hurt.

Here are some ways to deal with sibling fights.

Call a time-out. If things are heating up and your kids are trying to reenact the latest Hulk Hogan wrestling match, send them to their rooms to cool off. Set a specific time period for the break, such as 10 minutes.

Encourage them to solve their own conflicts. Children, regardless of their age, should be encouraged to resolve their own squabbles. Dr. Balter says that parents should suggest alternatives if children are too young to work out solutions on their own. "If you hear them arguing about who can play with the wagon, suggest they take turns, or say they both could sit in the wagon at the same time." The important thing is to let them choose. Soon they'll catch on to how it's done.

Draw up a contract. Children can work out a written contract to cover an ongoing source of arguments. For example, if kids always disagree about who does which chores, a formal contract could end the fights.

Teach them to use words. Words, not fists, should be used to resolve differences. And those words should not include name-calling. When a small child is teased, for example, teach him to say, "I don't like it when you tease me" instead of kicking. And try to keep them from saying, "You're a slimy worm."

Vicki Jarmulowksi

Kid Talk

You talk to your child every day. You can even use his buzzwords. You're so tuned in, as a matter of fact, that whether the words originated on the soccer field, the playground or the graffiti-scrawled walls of the boys' bathroom, you can speak the language. "Radical!" is not a comment on your politics but your kid's accolade to your innovative thinking.

But does that mean the two of you communicate? Does it mean you can, like, *understand*? That's an important question. A survey of 1,800 7th, 9th and 11th graders found, for example, that teens who use drugs, skip classes and booze it up are less likely to have parents who can understand—whatever language they use. Teens who *do* communicate well with their parents, the survey reveals, attend school, cope well with adolescent stress, feel good about themselves and their futures and avoid alcohol and drugs.

But just what is good communication?

It starts with listening, says Thomas Gordon, Ph.D., a California psychologist and father who developed a nationwide program to teach good parenting skills. But Parent Effectiveness Training (P.E.T.), as Dr. Gordon's program is called, doesn't just teach parents how to open their ears. It also teaches them how to open their minds.

BE A LISTENER

There are four different ways parents can effectively listen to their children, whether their kids are teens or toddlers, says Dr. Gordon. They can listen passively, for example, which means that they simply sit back and allow their child to ramble on about whatever's bothering him. This method encourages the child to share whatever's on his mind. It says, "I want to hear what you're feeling. I accept your feelings. I trust you to decide what you want to share with me. You're in charge here—it's your problem."

Sometimes that's all that's needed for a child to open up and share what he's thinking or unload something that's got him down. But sometimes your kid may wonder whether or not you're really paying attention, says Dr. Gordon. So another way of listening is to let your child ramble on, but make empathetic responses here and there. "Uh-huh." "I see." "Oh." Frequently these are just enough to let your child know you're tuned in and encourage him to continue.

Occasionally children need a little more prodding just to get started. In that case, suggests Dr. Gordon, *you* initiate the conversation. *You* open the door: "Would you like to talk about it?" "I'm interested in what you're thinking about that." "Sounds like you have some feelings about that." "Do you want to say more about that?" Notice that all these door-openers make no judgments. They're what psychologists call "open-ended." Where they lead is up to your kid.

The most effective way of listening, however, is "active listening." Think of yourself as a mirror for your child's words and you've got the gen-

Are You a Nag?

"Is your homework done yet?" "Did you clean up your room?" "When are you going to take a bath?"

Sound familiar? If it does, chances are you're a nag, someone who may be *trying* to get their child moving in a particular direction but who has unfortunately chosen one of the most annoying, ineffectual ways to do it.

Why do parents nag? "Nagging usually starts as a short-term strategy for getting your kids to do something," says Kathleen McCluskey-Fawcett, Ph.D., a mother of 4 who chairs the Department of Psychology at the University of Kansas.

It usually begins around the age of 6 or 7 as parents are beginning to feel that their children are old enough to handle the responsibility of doing some things on their own—getting ready for school, feeding the dog, making their own bed. And it's usually caused by a parental directive that either isn't clear—"Get ready to go!" rather than "Put your shoes on!"—or one that lacks consequences.

What kind of consequences? The consequences of disobedience. "You need to say to your child, 'Okay, I'm going to say this twice. If I have to say it a third time, this is what's going to happen,'" says Dr. McCluskey-Fawcett. And then follow it up with an appropriate action. "My 12-year-old was supposed to do the dishes. She didn't. So she lost her allowance—and she still had to do the dishes."

eral idea, because what you do is mirror back or repeat your child's comments—without adding any of your own. If your child says, "I'm too dumb to learn arithmetic. I'll never be able to do that stuff," an active listener will say, "You feel you're not smart enough, so you doubt you'll ever get it."

The active listener will *not* say, "You've always been a good student. Don't worry about it." That kind of cajoling statement throws up a roadblock. It says, "You're wrong. I don't accept that. I don't accept how you feel," and, by extension, "I don't accept you." Is your kid supposed to argue that he's stupid?

LEARN TO TALK

A lot of things we say to our kids unintentionally set up barriers. And most of them center around what Dr. Gordon calls "you" messages. "*You* go to your room." "*You* stop making so much noise." "*You* always want to bother me when I'm tired." All these statements stop communication dead, says Dr. Gordon. They push your child away. They create hostility, dissension and confrontation.

That's why you should kill the "you" messages and start sending "I" messages instead, says Dr. Gordon. "I can't sleep while you're making so much noise. That makes me feel grouchy." "I can't get dinner ready while you're playing on the kitchen floor. I'm afraid I won't be finished before our guests come." "I can't sleep until I know you're home safe and sound. I worry when you're late."

Notice the particular form of the message. It clearly says *I*, the parent, not *you*, the child, have a problem. It says what the problem is, how you feel about it and why. There's no apportionment of blame. That's what makes it so effective, particularly during confrontations or disagreements.

Break the Communication Gap

You and your child communicate just fine. He tells you *almost* everything —all about his friends, school, the problems he has with the tough guy down the street. But it's the "almost" that has you bothered. When it comes to one or a few particular subjects his mouth snaps shut like a clam.

How do you break this communication gap? A few well-chosen books might be the answer—preferably ones that are relevant to the particular difficulty in your child's life.

If your 8-year-old is having a problem with sibling rivalry, for example, you might pick up a copy of Judith Viorst's *I'll Fix Anthony* or Judy Blume's *Superfudge*. Then read the book and discuss it. Here are some of the questions learning specialists use to structure the discussion.

● What was the story about?
● Can you describe some of the characters?
● What was the dilemma of the main character?
● How did this dilemma happen?
● What were the choices in the story?
● How was the dilemma solved?
● How would you have solved the problem?
● Do you think that the right decision was made?
● How could this dilemma be avoided in the future?
● How do you feel when you have to make a hard decision?

This type of discussion may not solve your child's problem, but at least it will get him to talk to you about it—the two of you are *communicating*. And that in itself will go a long way toward solving the problem.

If you're about to blast your kid because he hasn't cleaned his junk out of your car, for example, state the problem in "I" message form: "I can't put my golf bag in the trunk when it's full of football gear." Tell him how you feel about it: "I'm afraid I won't be able to play golf." Then ask for some solutions: "Gee, Mom, I'll throw my stuff in the garage." There's not a kid born who doesn't want to do what he, himself, has suggested, says Dr. Gordon.

LEARN TO USE A COMPUTER

Learning how to communicate with your child may get easier in the not-too-distant future. At least it will if researchers at the University of Wisconsin have anything to say about it. That's because they've developed and are testing a series of computer programs designed to encourage family communication. Results so far have been extremely successful.

"Instead of merely answering questions and retrieving information," report the researchers in the journal *Marriage and Family Review*, "the computer acts as a facilitator by encouraging family members to share opinions, feelings and points of view."

The program "How to be Heard," for example, contains a series of computer games that focus on how family members talk to one another. One game asks for two family members to help demonstrate what happens when one person does all the talking during a game and the other can't ask a single question—not even to clarify the rules. Then the game is repeated and both family members are allowed to speak. Eventually, all family members discuss the game and compare the different outcomes produced by people who communicated and people who didn't.

Who *wins* the game? The entire family, of course.

Ellen Michaud

Playground Safety

The playground supervisor looked at her watch and sucked in her breath. "Ten seconds," she predicted. "They'll be here in 10 seconds."

As if on cue, the double steel doors leading from the cafeteria exploded open and 198 elementary school children who had been penned up all morning charged out onto the playground. The boys were in the lead. An even dozen headed out across the blacktopped basketball court to play soccer in an adjoining field. A group of girls scrambled after them to make sure that no soccer player put his dirty sneakers on their carefully chalked hopscotch squares.

Most of the older children clustered around the blacktop in tight knots, talking and occasionally grabbing the scarf or hat or muffler of someone of the opposite sex that they absolutely—*absolutely*—hated. Some of the younger children simply ran in circles—dipping and swaying so that their red, blue and yellow jackets looked like kites caught in an early March wind. The rest of the kids swarmed over, under, around and on the swings and monkey bars.

The kids looked like what they are: a mixed bag of big kids, little kids, happy kids, sad kids, smart kids, dumb kids, fast kids, slow kids, fat kids, thin kids, all kinds of kids, any kind of kids, just kids. But as the smallest of them wiggled his way to the top of the steel climber, it was evident that there was one kind of kid that they weren't—safe kids.

They weren't safe because, despite a computer-generated maintenance schedule that made sure their playground equipment was kept in tip-top condition, some of the equipment was inherently unsafe. And the hard-packed dirt underneath was a killer.

TAKING THE FALL

Hard to believe? Not when you know the statistics. More than 210,000 children were treated for injuries on United States playgrounds in 1985. And as an earlier study by the Consumer Product Safety Commission (CPSC) reveals, 72 percent of the children injured on playgrounds were hurt in falls. Falls in which a child's body hit a hard surface or hit the same piece of equipment he was climbing, or falls in which a child's body fell from one piece of equipment and hit another. Four out of every five children were ten years of age or younger.

What kind of equipment are our children getting hurt on? Climbers—monkey bars and chinning bars, for example—are responsible for 42 percent of all playground injuries, estimates the CPSC, which makes sense because climbers are used more than any other piece of equipment. Swings account for 23 percent of the injuries and are the second most used piece of equipment. Slides come in third in popularity and are responsible for 16 percent of all injuries. Merry-go-rounds and seesaws are used significantly less than other equipment, but they still account for 11 percent of all injuries.

How are our children getting hurt? They're slipping and losing their grip or their balance on monkey bars as they jump on, jump off, perform stunts or swing from rung to rung. They're leaping from swings and falling, or standing too close and getting struck. They're falling from the sides of slides, the platforms of slides

Playlot Nirvana

What do children really want in a playground? In the late 1970s, the Swedish Council for Children's Play sent 4 psychologists to 27 playgrounds to find out.

When children are offered choices, reports Eva Noren-Bjorn, one of the psychologists, they play on blacktop courts, multistructured combination equipment, sand pits (even the big kids!), multilevel playhouses with ladders, playhouses with climbing towers and slides, building boxes with giant blocks inside, hillslides, plastic play sculptures and boats—real boats, the kind with railings and masts that can stay "beached" forever on the playground while children search for buried treasure.

and the ladders of slides as a result of rough-housing, walking up and down the slide, losing their grip or their balance and just plain slipping. Occasionally they hit protruding bolts, strike the slide rim and edge, or just slip on the ladder and strike the steps.

STOP BATTERY PARKS

It may sound as though our kids are getting battered at their local school or neighborhood playground. And at some places they are. But how can we prevent it? Short of sending our kids out in body armor or forbidding—fat chance!—their sneakered feet from leaving the ground, how can we keep our children safe?

Take this book to your local playground and answer the following questions. Your answers will tell you all you need to know about creating the safe playground environment your children deserve.

How does *your* playground measure up? Is it safe? Or is it time to talk to local officials? If it is, invite other parents to come along. Then head for the officials' next public meeting and pass out copies of your answers to these questions. Go to your city or town council's meeting if it's a municipal playground or, if it's a school playground, your school board's. Hopefully, they will agree with you and implement the recommended safety measures.

Is there asphalt, concrete or any other hard surface under any playground equipment? If there is, says the CPSC, move the equipment. Or install a more resilient surface, such as bark, wood chips, shredded tires, outdoor rubber mats or synthetic turf. While these materials may not reduce the number of falls, they may very well reduce the severity of injuries—an important point since nearly half of all injuries from falls involve a child's head. A softer surface can mean the difference between a minor bruise and brain damage.

Are buildings, paths, walkways, gates, fences and other play areas such as sandboxes at least 8 feet away from the "use zone" of each piece of playground equipment? Your child needs enough room to exit slides, jump from swings and spin off merry-go-rounds without worrying about running into other objects or people. If equipment is crowded together, says the CPSC, consider moving some pieces out of the more densely populated areas. Smoothly flowing traffic will eliminate collisions between your child and his buddies.

Are there any trees, shrubs, walls, fences or other visual barriers that can hamper supervision of the area? Get rid of them. How will you—or a teacher if it's a school playground—know when the local clown is standing on his head on top of the climber if he can't be seen?

Is all metal equipment painted or galvanized to prevent rust? Are all wood surfaces treated with a nontoxic substance to prevent wood rot? If not, insist that it be done. And it's also a good idea, says the CPSC, to install or paint slip-resistant surfaces on the climbing and gripping components of all playground equipment.

Is there any opening—a swinging exercise ring, for example—that is too small to allow your child to easily withdraw his head? Obviously, anything that can trap a child in any way should be removed. If there's no other way for a child to support his weight than his head or neck, for example, he may die from strangulation.

Do you see any sharp points, corners or edges? Any protrusions or projections? Any angle that might pinch or crush an unwary finger? Cover the exposed ends of bolts or tubing, get rid of pinch and crush possibilities, and slap brightly colored tape or paint on any protrusion to make it more visible.

Are any concrete footings exposed? Cover them with earth or padding to prevent tripping or to protect your child in case of a fall, says the CPSC.

Do swings bump into one another? If so, consider removing one or two swings from a swingset, suggests the CPSC. And what are the swing seats made of? Seats should be made of lightweight materials such as plastic, canvas or rubber with smoothly finished or rounded edges. Add tire swings if you have the opportunity. Their safety record appears to be better than that of conventional swings.

Do the slides have protective barriers at the top? Barriers prevent falls while your child is changing from a climbing to a sliding position, as do platforms that are at least 10 inches in length with a width the same size as the entrance to the sliding surface. Corrugated or grooved steps and rungs that are evenly spaced—with spaces between 7 and 11 inches—can also prevent falls.

Play it safe. Inspect your child's playground for hazards beforehand so you can send your youngster to this home away from home with peace of mind and the knowledge that your community has its children's welfare at heart.

Ellen Michaud

Care and the Latchkey Child

Latchkey children—they're out of sight but never out of mind. But what are they *really* up to while Mom and Dad are at work?

Well, there's eight-year-old Mike, who cruises the streets of his neighborhood every day between 3:30 P.M. and 5:30 P.M. He rides his bike back and forth until he meets up with a half-dozen of his neighborhood buddies, usually in an alley that runs behind their houses. Nobody's parents are home, so the boys like to stay together.

What do they do? They shoot baskets, or jump their bikes over a retaining wall. Sometimes they even get into a little mischief, like chucking rocks at an empty tractor-trailer parked in a lot in the neighborhood.

Then there's nine-year-old Billy. Billy's day with his friends ends when he waves good-bye to them at the bus stop. He walks the short distance home, lets his two cocker spaniels out of the garage and bounces into the house to feed them—and himself—a snack.

Promptly at 4:00 P.M. he calls his mom. He reassures her that the door is locked, he's inside, the dogs are fed, and he's about to start his homework. And after listening to her say how much she loves him and how proud of him she is, he settles down on the couch, a dog snuggled on either side, and begins to read his history assignment.

PLANNING IS THE KEY

The difference between Mike's after-school life and Billy's is planning. When Billy's mother went back to work, she couldn't find anyone to watch him. Billy was always an obedient boy and seemed mature for his age, so she decided he could handle it on his own. So she sat down with Billy, worked out a schedule—home at 3:30 P.M., feed dogs at 3:45 P.M., call Mom at 4:00 P.M.—and a set of house rules designed to keep him safe.

Mike's mom, on the other hand, more or less took his ability to take care of himself for granted. There were no schedules, no rules. And since Mike's mom couldn't receive any phone calls at work except in an emergency, there was no way to keep in touch. Mike was simply left to fend for himself.

GROUND RULES FOR SELF-CARE

Of course, every parent would rather have a Billy than a Mike. How do you feel secure that your child is secure? How can you keep him safe and sound? Here are some tips from family therapist Helen L. Swan, a consultant to the National Committee for the Prevention of Child Abuse.

Make sure they're ready. Few children are ready to be left alone before the ages of nine or ten, says Swan. And in most areas of the country,

---

Ready or Not?

Can your child handle being left alone after school? Can you handle leaving him? To find out, take this quiz, developed by Lynette Long, Ph.D., and Thomas Long, Ed.D., authors of *The Handbook for Latchkey Children and Their Parents.* Answer each question yes or no.

1. Do you consider your child old enough to assume self-care responsibilities? ⎯⎯⎯⎯

2. Do you believe your child is mature enough to care for himself or herself? ⎯⎯⎯⎯

3. Has your child indicated that he or she would be willing to try self-care? ⎯⎯⎯⎯

4. Is your child able to solve problems? ⎯⎯⎯⎯

5. Is your child able to communicate with adults? ⎯⎯⎯⎯

6. Is your child able to complete daily tasks? ⎯⎯⎯⎯

7. Is your child generally unafraid to be alone? ⎯⎯⎯⎯

8. Is your child unafraid to enter your house alone? ⎯⎯⎯⎯

9. Can your child unlock and lock the doors to your home unassisted? ⎯⎯⎯⎯

10. Is there an adult living or working nearby that your child knows and can rely on in case of emergency? ⎯⎯⎯⎯

11. Do you have adequate household security? ⎯⎯⎯⎯

12. Do you consider your neighborhood safe? ⎯⎯⎯⎯

If you answered no to any of the above questions, your child may not be ready for self-care, say the Longs. You should delay or abandon your plans for self-care until *all* questions elicit a positive response.

a five-year-old left alone without adult supervision is legally a case of neglect.

But age, she says, should by no means be the only criterion. You also have to ask yourself if your neighborhood is safe. Even a 14-year-old shouldn't be considered safe in an area that's been hit with crime, has a high rate of delinquency or has been subject to a rash of burglaries.

Also, you need to ask yourself if your child is prepared and if your child really *wants* to stay home alone. Not just because you'd like to give him his druthers, Swan explains, but because the desire to take care of himself is indicative of his level of maturity.

A key question here is also how *long* you intend to leave your child. "Are we talking 1 hour or 5 hours?" asks Swan. "Kids who are home alone at night for 5 or 6 hours seem to be the most disturbed." Usually 3 hours is the most kids can handle.

Practice handling dangerous situations. Have your child pretend there's a fire in each room of your house, suggests Swan, who is co-author of *Alone after School,* a self-care guide that is chock-full of such practical exercises. Ask him to tell you how the fire started, how he found it and what he's going to do about it. Before you leave him alone for the first time, make sure he knows what to do in any given situation.

Test your child. Leave your child alone for a couple of hours, suggests Swan. Tell him not to leave the house and to call you at a neighbor's if there's a problem. This will give you a chance to see how well he follows directions. Did he stay put, or did he wander over to a friend's? Continue testing by leaving him for increasingly longer times with increasingly more instructions. Then talk to him about his experiences. How did he feel about being home alone?

Make rules that are appropriate for your child's level of maturity. The younger the child, the more simple the rules. A nine-year-old's "door" rule, for example, might be a flat,

---

Child Safety Checklist

Is your child safe when he's at home and you're at work? The National Parent-Teacher Association suggests that you make sure your child knows the following things.

✓ Never to go into your house or apartment if the door is ajar or a window broken.

✓ To lock the door when he comes home and to keep the doors and windows locked.

✓ To check in with you by telephone or report to a neighbor at a regularly scheduled time.

✓ To avoid walking or playing alone on the way home from school.

✓ His full name, address and telephone number—including area code.

✓ *Your* full name, the exact name of the place where you work and its telephone number.

✓ How to use both push-button and dial phones to reach the operator or report an emergency.

✓ How to carry a key so it's secure but out of sight.

✓ How to answer the telephone without letting callers know that he's home alone.

✓ How to get out of the house safely and quickly in case of fire.

"Don't answer the door." But an adolescent's might be a more complex: "Answer the door, but don't let strangers into the house. Tell them your parents can't come to the door."

Teach parenting skills. Younger children are frequently left in the care of older kids, Swan says, and the result is that the older kids feel tied down and the younger kids are afraid of being beaten up. Why? "Older brothers and sisters are just not prepared to parent," the therapist explains. "They need to be taught how to keep their little brother quiet without punching him out."

Consider a pet. A pet, particularly for only children, keeps lonely feelings at bay, says Swan, who has used the strategy herself. "My younger daughter, when she was nine, wouldn't go into the house without first going into the backyard and getting the dogs. I'd come home and she'd be reading on the couch with a dog on either side of her."

Respect your child's fear. Any child who's left alone is going to be afraid at one time or another. The

two most important things you can do to reduce that fear, says Swan, is to call your children while they're alone. If necessary, ask your employer to install a pay phone if he doesn't like you using a company phone. Also, make sure you come home on time. That extra 15 minutes it takes to pick up a loaf of bread can seem an eternity to your child.

Encourage your child to talk honestly about staying home alone. Sometimes just letting him talk about his fears or the way he feels about your work—and letting him know that you accept those feelings—can make everything right in his world. Or sometimes you can respond to a problem with small changes—dance lessons on Wednesday night, for example—that will make being alone the rest of the week more palatable.

Use your guilt. "You shouldn't feel guilty if your child is ready, able and willing to be in self-care," says Swan. "If you *do* feel guilty, that's your cue to reevaluate the situation."

Ellen Michaud

Taming Your Teenager

"Randy, you stink!" said the 16-year-old's mother bluntly. She had been unable to convince her son that the raunchy smell of basketball sneakers, adolescent glands and sweaty underwear needed attention. But her blunt comment stung him into action.

"All right," replied Randy in that derisive tone that rebellious teens reserve to slice up their parents. "I'll take a *shower.* I wouldn't want to *offend* you with my bodily *odor.*"

Angrily he threw a fresh pair of pants over his shoulder and headed for the bathroom. But not without a parting shot, "You know what?" he added viciously, "You look really *old,* Mom!"

Ouch! Is that what adolescence is all about? Mouth-to-mouth combat? A series of running battles between you and your child over cars, curfews, booze, friends and personal hygiene?

With more than 30 million young people between the ages of 12 and 20 running loose in this country, we wouldn't have the *time* for other worries if it were.

FRIENDLY PERSUASION

Fortunately, it's not. Douglas H. Powell, Ed.D., psychologist and coordinator of the Behavior Therapy Program at Harvard University Health Service, notes that it was once believed that adolescence was a time of conflict, regression and turmoil. More recent research suggests, however, that most adolescents enjoy good relationships with family and friends, cope effectively with stress and think well of themselves.

"Most kids turn out perfectly well," says Dr. Powell. They grow to maturity through quiet evolution rather than dramatic revolution. Yes, everyone goes through an identity crisis here and there, but studies indicate that the teen years are tumultuous for only one in three children. And only one teen in ten regularly experiences the fears, depressions, learning problems and crises that throw families into constant whirlpools of tension, anger, defiance and pain.

But how can you keep your family on an even keel if it's *your* kid who is rocking (and probably rolling) the boat? How can you keep the peace?

Don't overreact. "The most important thing is to be aware of the kinds of things that make you overreact," says Dr. Powell, then don't allow yourself to do it. A messy room doesn't mean your son won't be able to earn a living when he finishes school, and a string bikini doesn't mean your daughter will flunk out of school and live on the streets.

"Don't do anything that will worsen the situation," adds Dr. Powell. "Don't label behavior. Don't say, 'She's lazy!' or 'He's a poor student!' especially during a disagreement. Labels obscure more than they reveal.

"And be honest about your feelings," he adds. "Kids are like any oppressed minority group. They know what you're thinking." If your son asks to stay out until 2:00 A.M. with a group of guys you suspect may be vandalizing the neighborhood and you don't trust him not to join in, tell him straight out. Don't muddy up your relationship with deceit. Let him know

The Tipoff to Trouble

"Teenagers are always going to talk back and things like that," says Joe Sanders, Jr., M.D., of Augusta, Georgia, president of the Society for Adolescent Medicine. "In fact, I get worried about them if they're not a little bit spunky." But teens who are headed for trouble usually send up the following red flags.

A significant drop in grades. Not from an A to a B, but from A's and B's to barely passing.

Spending an inordinate amount of time alone. All kids need time alone, but the teen who isolates himself from his peers is probably having problems.

Hanging out with the wrong kids. You won't like all your child's friends. But if he seems to be running with drop-outs or druggies, he's headed for trouble.

Defying authority. Most kids will ditch school, get caught, get punished and swear never to ditch school again, says Dr. Sanders. But if you have a kid who keeps on doing it time after time, something's wrong. Most of us learn from our mistakes. Why doesn't he?

If your teen exhibits any of these problems, check with your pediatrician, youth minister or school guidance counselor or psychologist, says Dr. Sanders. Your child needs professional help.

he has some work to do before he's proved worthy of your trust.

"But don't feel the need to hyper-control," cautions Dr. Powell. "Adolescence is a time to allow increased decision-making, to gradually let go. You never let go completely—that's a piece of baloney that's been sold to the American public. But you never force your kid to do what you want. You tell him what you think. You make your personal witness—sometimes at the top of your voice—but you don't force him to do what you want unless personal safety is involved."

Know who you are. It also helps keep the family waters calm if you recognize that you are you and your kid is not you. That's right. Even if you contributed half of his genetic material, your kid is still not *you*. There's a great deal of evidence that children are born with a particular temperament, a core personality that will remain unchanged throughout adolescence, says Dr. Powell. Respect it. If you're slow and methodical and your kid is fast and intuitive, don't insist he slow down and solve a particular problem your way. His way will work just as well. For him.

REEFER MADNESS

One of the biggest obstacles to family harmony during the teen years, however, is drugs. A kid on drugs is tuned into a different world. Reason has no meaning. Talk has no form. Love has no warmth.

So how do you keep drugs away from your teen? You can't. You keep *him* away from drugs. And the best way to do that, says Alfred McAlister, Ph.D., an associate professor and associate director of the Center for Health Promotion Research and Development at the University of Texas Health Science Center, is to inoculate your teen against drugs.

No, there's no vaccine against street drugs. But just as doctors use a weakened form of the polio virus to inoculate your child against that disease, so you can use a little role-playing—a little play-acting—to inoculate him against peer pressure. Because it's peer pressure that actually causes the problem.

How? You and your teen pretend he's hanging out with a friend. You're the friend. The peer. The one who applies the pressure. You offer him a pill or a toke and he refuses. You call him a nerd, a chicken, whatever insulting name is currently on the street, and he refuses. You ridicule him. He's a baby, right?

Wrong. Your kid looks you straight in the eyes, grins from ear to ear and comes back with a snappy refusal. "I quit last year." "My girl likes my eyes the way they are." "I heard they were cutting that with dog turds."

"Your kid needs to retain his sense of self-respect, his cool," says Dr. McAlister. So you help him develop a humorous comeback. Then help him rehearse his delivery. It's the kids who are dealing who'll look like schmucks. Your kid can walk away.

BEING THERE

How else can you keep the family peace? Here are some tips from Dr. McAlister.

Love your child. Your child needs to know from birth that you love him unequivocally. Even if he reminds you of Charles Manson.

Get your kid talking. Watch for loaded—issue-oriented—TV programs and when the station breaks for a commercial, hit the mute before your kid has time to run for a sandwich. Say, "What do you think of that?" Then let him talk. And don't make judgmental statements.

Establish realistic standards. "To provide challenge and encouragement, parents should always expect just a little more than a child can do," says Dr. McAlister. "But don't set standards too high." And for every criticism you make, find something else to praise.

Stepparents should step out. Stepparents should leave rule-making and discipline to the natural parent for at least the first three years of any relationship. Sugar daddies and fairy godmothers get hugs. Stepparents get clubs.

Acknowledge your own vulnerability. Admit that you've made mistakes in your life, says Dr. McAlister. Share everyday kinds of experiences in which you don't come off like the white knight. Weren't you really more like the court jester? "I got an F in geometry"—those kinds of things. Nothing heavy-duty like "I smoked pot."

Ellen Michaud

chapter twelve

YOUR HEALTHY PET

Creature Comfort: A Pet Can Boost Your Health

Freud, Adler and Jung—the founders of modern psychology. Now there's a new trio—Fido, Morris and a tank of fish.

Psychologists are finding that pets can provide a wide variety of emotional benefits to their patients, so much so that the animals are referred to as "co-therapists." Before you reject the notion that an animal could help you feel better, consider this true story.

A psychotic blow-up is just another event at the Oakwood Forensic Center in Lima, Ohio, a hospital for the criminally insane. The patient hurls chairs across the room, rips out the phones and hurts several patients and employees before being subdued. But instead of joining his act, the other murderers, rapists and robbers surround the bird cage and aquarium, like musk-oxen fending off wolves, to protect their communal pets.

These dangerous, depressed, often suicidal patients are needed, accepted and loved by their pets, says David Lee, the psychiatric social worker who runs the pet therapy program. "The pets don't make judgments," says Lee. "They don't care if you're an ax murderer." He found that patients with pets need less medication and present fewer behavior problems than those without pets.

If a bird or fish or dog or cat can help alleviate such extreme human anguish, can they have a positive effect on those with more down-to-earth, everyday woes?

Yes, claims Tom Ferguson, M.D., "Their affection does not depend on our reaching a sales quota, meeting a deadline, or keeping the house spotless. They do not worship youth or beauty, and they care nothing for financial or social success."

"Pets stay kids forever,"adds Alan Beck, Sc.D., director of the Center for Interactions of Animals and Society, University of Pennsylvania School of Veterinary Medicine. They offer unconditional love and need to be cared for. These childlike traits can help ill, depressed, lonely humans respond in calming, loving, nurturing ways that benefit human physical and emotional health. Dr. Beck says there are some similarities between a psychologist and a golden retriever, "but at the end of the session a golden retriever will lick your face."

CAN A PET HELP YOU?

Researchers are finding that pets can indeed act as medicines. They warn, however, that a pet is by no means a panacea, and it is not the right medicine for everyone. In the first place, says Dr. Beck, you have to *like* pets for them to benefit you. His point is borne out by Leo Bustad, D.V.M., Ph.D., president of the Delta Society, an organization that encourages pet visitations in hospitals, who reported "a mistake in placement" that nearly resulted in a massacre. It seems the activity director of a nursing home selected gerbils as pets for the residents. Some residents, however, perceived the cute little rodents as rats, "something to be exterminated," says Dr. Bustad, and "beat on the cage and tried to let them out to stomp on them."

And just because an animal produces a warm fuzzy feeling in you, says Dr. Beck, that doesn't necessarily mean it can help you any more than ice cream, movies, children or video games, which can also make you feel good inside. "For the most part, pets are positive," he says. "But there are very few things that are *all* good. Nothing has that kind of intimacy, that closeness to people, without the potential for the negative. It may very well be that the real universal emotional nourishment is contact with living things. And for some people, that doesn't mean pets."

MY DOCTOR, MY PET

But for some people it does mean pets. Here are examples of healthful achievements—emotional *and* physical—in the new science of pet therapy.

Lowering blood pressure. In one study, researchers found that the blood pressure of subjects temporarily fell below its resting level when they talked to or petted a dog (interestingly, the dog's blood pressure also dropped). The pet doesn't have to be a dog. Watching fish swim about aimlessly in a tank, says Dr. Beck, "can always be counted on to lower your blood pressure."

Raising the chances of surviving a heart attack. University of Pennsylvania researchers found that of 92 heart attack patients, 94 percent of those who owned pets were still living at least one year following their heart attacks, while only 72 percent of those without pets survived that long.

Watching fish at the dentist's. "We found that contemplating fish for 15 to 20 minutes before dental surgery was at least as effective as being hypnotized," says Dr. Beck. "It looks like fish-tank contemplation is a very real phenomenon."

Taking Fifi to the marriage counselor. Indiana University researchers found that when the family dog was present in counseling sessions, emotions tempered and body language cleaned up. Another researcher says that during family arguments "one woman used to say, 'Stop fighting, you're upsetting the dog.'"

Talking to Fluffy and letting your family eavesdrop. "When family members want to say something to each other that they can't say directly, they might say it to the pet and let the other person overhear it," says the University of Maryland's Ann Cain, Ph.D. "That also lets the listener off the hook, because he doesn't have to respond directly."

Improving your image. One researcher showed pictures of an older woman with and without a dog to psychology students. Without a dog, she was perceived as industrious by 33 percent. With the dog, her industriousness score rose to 43 percent.

"This phenomenon has been exploited by politicians during elections," says Dr. Beck, explaining why politicians love to be seen kissing babies.

Boosting your health and morale. Studies suggest that people with pets have higher morale and generally overall better health than those without.

Breaking the ice. Researchers have found that people talk to each other more when an animal is present. Total strangers love to gab with each other about their pets.

Curing the couch potato. Ohio State University psychiatrist Samuel Corson, M.D., had one patient who lost 30 pounds in a month, just by walking his dog.

Civilizing your little monster. Pets are good for children, too. Lee Salk, Ph.D., clinical professor of pediatrics at New York Hospital/Cornell University Medical Center, New York City, says kids learn to be gentle by watching parents cuddle a purring cat. They learn responsibility by caring for the family dog. They learn about illness and death. "Pets even provide children with knowledge about love," says Dr. Salk. "The warmth and affection displayed by two cats or two playful dogs can go a long way in teaching a child about touching and caring."

William LeGro

A New Breed of Hospital Visitor

The boy lies unmoving in his hospital bed, his eyes open. Pillows prop him up. He doesn't move, he stares, looking at nothing. He cannot speak. Nurses swish briskly into his room, fuss over him. They wonder, "Does he even think? Is his brain beyond repair?" They don't know; he is a wall, his world is behind it. They know that if he doesn't soon reclaim his life, he will die.

Chelsea pads into the room; the nurses watch. Hope is not dead. She leaps onto the bed beside him. Wriggling onto her back, she snuggles up to him full-length, whiskered muzzle prying its way between his arm and side. Her jaws part in a pink-gummed grin, her tongue lolls, her teeth gleam. She pants, and squirms, her paws flail the air, her golden tail brushes the sheets. Like a river her love rushes to him, nudging response. Insistent, Chelsea will not be denied.

Something is happening here.

Magic is afoot, spirit is alive. The boy sees, light fills his face, he grins back at Chelsea, wiggles his elbows, pressing the limits of his wasted limbs; atrophied hands strain to touch her. He looks up in wonder, sees for the first time the white-clad women who for two years have been pouring unrequited love into him, sees their tear-filled eyes. And the lady with the leash. He hears them ask, "Do you want to get up and see the other animals?" He nods his head and smiles.

Chelsea is a golden retriever, one of several hospital and nursing home visiting pets of the Friendship Foundation in the San Francisco Bay area. Trained volunteers handle the entire project. Social worker Forest Rosengren, the lady with the leash, is director of the Friendship Foundation.

"Once you can get a child out of bed and motivated, that's a real event," Rosengren says of the brain-damaged boy and of other children suffering

from disfiguring burns, wasting diseases and crippling accidents that seem to suck from them the will to live. The pets don't even notice the savage toll; their love has no strings.

Veterinarians screen each prospective pet therapist closely and continually for health and temperament. When a wheelchair runs over Chelsea's tail, says Rosengren, "she'll just sort of clear her throat and keep smiling."

Other hospitals, like Columbia in Milwaukee, allow patients' own pets to visit. Always, there is strict immunization and infection control; here the animals are crated for their trip through the corridors. The hospitals report no mishaps, no bites, no potty problems.

Pet visitation programs are spreading. Write Delta Society, P.O. Box 1080, Renton, WA 98057-1080 for help in getting a program started in your local hospital.

Picking a Healthy Pet

When buying a new dog or cat, think small—not small in terms of size but small in terms of breeder. National chains of pet stores, for instance, usually get their purebred puppies and kittens from large commercial breeders, says Bonnie Dalzell, greyhound and borzoi breeder and University of Pennsylvania veterinary anatomist, meaning you don't know, and can't find out, anything about the animal's parents—genetic weaknesses, temperament, health—the conditions in which it was bred, born and raised, or its personality.

Although pet stores vary, says Dalzell, you most likely will be better off getting familiar with a neighborhood independent pet store. It will enable you to become familiar with the owner or manager, who can give you the information you need.

Purchasing a nonpedigreed cat may not be as big a problem, says Melinda Van Vechten, D.V.M., of the University of Pennsylvania, because cats are easy to come by. But buying a pedigreed cat carries the same caveat as buying a dog, meaning don't buy one from a commercial facility.

Municipal dog pounds are also chancy, Dalzell says, and vary widely in their policies. There again you have little or no opportunity to discover the animal's breeding and medical history.

YOUR BEST BETS

Now that you've been warned, here's what the experts say are the best places to pick up a pet.

Try a breeder. For the same cost as at a pet store, a reputable breeder may provide you with a purebred pet complete with heritage and background. Make sure you arrange for medical care, refund or exchange in case the pet has problems.

Before you buy a pet from a breeder, be sure to investigate their reputation. You can do this simply by asking previous customers. Also inspect the surroundings: Is the area clean? Is there plenty of light? Do the animals look healthy and happy? Does the breeder seem to love the animals? If you're interested in a show-quality dog, find out if the breeder is showing the animals regularly and winning.

Give me shelter. You may find that an animal shelter run by your state Humane Society or the Society for the Prevention of Cruelty to Animals is just right. Local shelters vary widely in their policies, however. Some take strays, others take only "give-aways." These pets, given up by people, may have behavior problems (which is probably why they were given away).

All in the family. Families with recent litters of puppies or kittens are almost always safer sources of paperless pets than pet stores or pounds, Dr. Van Vechten says. And the animals usually have the added benefit of not having been exposed to the array of diseases found at pet stores, shelters, pounds and kennels.

GROUND RULES

No matter where you get your puppy or kitten, there are rules and precautions you should follow for the

---

Test Your Compatibility

"Having a pet is a great responsibility," Melinda Van Vechten, D.V.M., says. "You should pick one according to your needs and your personality." Adds dog breeder Bonnie Dalzell, "If you've never had a dog before, you have to realize it's like adopting about one-fourth of a child. It makes an impact on your lifestyle. It needs care."

If you're a single person living alone, you may want to consider a cat. They also need care but are not such highly social animals as dogs; they need you, but not in the same way. A dog may not be right for the single person: "If you want to leave work, go to happy hour, then out to dinner, and get home at 11:00 P.M.," Dalzell says, "then don't expect to have an apartment left."

Whatever the pet, you have to brush it. Give it a soft bed to sleep on if it's a short-coated breed of dog. An active dog needs either space to play or your time to go out on walks. An aggressive dog needs obedience training. Indoor cats need scratching posts and litter boxes. Don't forget that pets need to be fed—pet food is the single biggest seller in the supermarket. Then there's medical care. And they all need your time and affection. Before you decide on a pet, ask yourself: Do I have the time? Do I have the space? Do I care enough? Do I have the money?

sake of the pet, your pocketbook and your peace of mind.

Get a guarantee. Wherever you buy your pet, make your purchase dependent on a veterinarian's certification of good health. This is probably the most important thing you can do when buying a pet.

Ask about the parents. Purebred animals often have genetic weaknesses. And some mixed-breed dogs are prone to some of the same genetic problems as purebreds, Dalzell notes. Ask about possible problems.

Make sure it's old enough. A puppy or kitten should be eight to nine weeks old before you take it home, Dalzell says. Puppies need that time to socialize with their littermates. "They need to learn that if they bite other dogs, they get bitten back." The same goes for cats.

Check for vaccinations. By eight weeks, a puppy should have had a distemper combination and a parvovirus shot. By the same age a kitten should have had vaccinations for feline infectious enteritis (also called feline distemper or panleukopenia), rhinotracheitis, calicivirus and pneumonitis. Ask for certification of immunization.

READING YOUR PET

Here are some basic tips that can help you pick a healthy pet. Keep in mind that you're not an expert; follow your inspection with a veterinary checkup of the chosen animal.

What does the body say? Overall, the animal should feel firm, strong and energetic, Dalzell says. It should not be listless or droopy, and it should be able to walk in a straight line without stumbling. Check its coordination.

The tummy talks. Hookworms and roundworms, common in puppies and kittens, may cause diarrhea, malnutrition, anemia and even death. A skinny body with a fat tummy, a "starving coat" (fur that stands up straight), lethargy and discharge from the eyes are signs of worms.

Don't Be Pound Foolish

Buying a mutt is not a bad idea, but if you want a purebred dog or cat, think hard before you buy, advises dog breeder and veterinary anatomist Bonnie Dalzell. "You're buying a hothouse plant," Dalzell says, "a piece of biosculpture" and "an adventure in biomedical education."

The problem? "People tend to select for the grotesque, for exaggeration," Dalzell says. That's how you get dachshunds so long they get disk problems and so low to the ground they get splinters on their chests going over wooden doorsills.

The congenital problems of show dogs tend to "slop over" into nonshow purebreds and crossbreds, she says, and so you find German shepherd/Labrador retriever mixes with hip dysplasia. If you want a purebred, Dalzell suggests you find a mismarked dog of a multicolored breed or a spotted dog that is supposed to be a solid color. And try to make sure the animal's great-great-great grandparents are still alive and healthy at 15 years of age; that bodes well for your animal.

Another tip from Dalzell: "Buy a dog from a breeder, and choose one that is able to do what it's supposed to do, instead of just looking good in the show ring; you've got a better chance of getting a healthy dog."

The problem of genetic weaknesses is not so prevalent in cats, says Melinda Van Vechten, D.V.M., but certain breeds, especially the Persian, Himalayan and Siamese, are often afflicted.

Nose around. You can't really judge health from the feel of a puppy's or kitten's nose, the experts say. But sneezing, coughing, wheezing or a runny nose and eyes can indicate a respiratory virus infection, or in puppies, canine distemper.

Give 'em the eye. The eyes should be clear, bright and free of pus or watery discharge. Don't get an animal with reddened or swollen eyes, Dr. Van Vechten advises. Test for peripheral vision by getting behind the animal while its attention is focused to the front, and dropping a tissue to the floor.

Smell the ears. They should smell waxy, not foul. The ears should be clean and free of debris that could indicate ear mites. Other symptoms of ear problems are tenderness or head-shaking or tilting. To test hearing, have someone remain in front of the animal while you get behind it and lightly clap your hands. (Note: a white, blue-eyed kitten is often deaf, and deafness is common in dalmatians.)

Open wide. The teeth should be bright and clean. The incisors—the little ones between the fangs—should meet edge to edge in most dog breeds. The breath should smell clean.

Check the skin and fur. With your hand, brush the fur backward from tail to head. The skin should look healthy. Check for patches of flaking, reddened or irritated skin, and for signs of fleas—the critters themselves or their excreta, little black flecks. The fur should be shiny in most breeds (woolly breeds, such as poodles, are the exception); a kitten that doesn't groom itself is probably sick.

William LeGro

Nutrition for a Healthier Life

SCENE: You arrive home. As you go into the kitchen to fix yourself some dinner, Fluffy appears.

YOU: Hi, Fluffy, I'm home! Did you have a nice day?

FLUFFY: Meow!

YOU: You must be hungry. *Get down off the stove!*

FLUFFY: Meoweowow!

YOU: Would you like some of my home-cooked cat food?

FLUFFY: Meourgghh!

YOU: Oh, it's not *that* bad. Don't you like okra? How about this supermarket cat chow?

FLUFFY: Meow!

YOU: What do you mean, it's mostly cornmeal? Have you been reading the labels again? Can't fool Fluffy.

Stop walking between my feet! Well, there's this moist chow that comes in a plastic bag. I've just got to tear it open and . . .

FLUFFY: Meow!

YOU: Okay, Okay! So it's mostly cornmeal, too. Oh, all right, I suppose it has to be this little can of beef chunks—*gourmet* beef chunks. *Expensive* gourmet beef chunks.

FLUFFY: Meoweow!

YOU: *Well, I've warned you not to get your tail in the refrigerator!* Yes, yes, I'm opening it as fast as I can!

FLUFFY: Purrrrr.

FIFI AND FLUFFY WANT MEAT!

Look at those fangs! Dogs and cats are meant to be carnivores, and meat, loaded with protein and fat, really is the best food you can give them. They have short intestines adapted to digesting flesh, and they may not handle vegetables well (although you can make omnivores or vegetarians of some dogs).

Cats have no need whatsoever for carbohydrates, nor do your average lie-around-all-day-and-sleep-and-scratch dogs.

"The higher the level of protein and fat, the higher the nutritional value of the food," says Susan Donoghue, V.M.D., veterinary nutritionist at the University of Pennsylvania School of Veterinary Medicine. She also says, "all pet foods are not created equal." So, there are a few things you, as a caring pet pal, should consider when developing your pet's diet.

Read the label. As in human food labeling, pet food ingredients must be listed in descending order of quantity. "Foods with labels listing meat first are better than those with grain listed first," says Dr. Donoghue. The new premium dry foods are as good as so-called canned meat "suppers." But there are good ingredients and bad ingredients in each type, she says, so you should evaluate them by looking at the label.

Dry food has its advantages. In fact, the dry pet food you buy in the supermarket is manufactured for your convenience as much as Fifi's and Fluffy's health. It's the nibble-at-will, no-can-opening, no-greasy-spoon, no-smelly-bowl, no-budget-busting pet food. It has lower levels of fat than canned meat because the fat seeps through the paper bags (you don't want that greasy bag on your car upholstery or in your kitchen cabinet). Fifi and Fluffy get to eat more for your money, thus getting pleasantly full tummies, while less protein, fat and digestibility keep their figures from becoming unbecomingly porcine.

Dry food labeled "complete and balanced for all stages of your pet's life" is good enough for most pets, says Dr. Donoghue. She warns, however, that you should not let your pet eat canned meat or the premium dry foods "free choice"; they taste too good and your animals may overeat.

Dogs are protein-wise. They can thrive on a wide range of protein levels, says Dr. Donoghue. The minimum may be 15 percent a day, and the average recommended amount is between 22 and 25 percent. Dr. Donoghue prefers 30 percent for some dogs. A show or working dog, a sick dog, a nursing mother or a growing puppy may need double the minimum.

Cats need cat food. Cats are strict carnivores, says Dr. Donoghue

Generic Dog Food Disease

Just when you thought you'd heard it all, along comes another disease—and it's the direct result of feeding your dog generic dog food.

Generic dog food uses corn as the primary source of calories, explains Susan Donoghue, V.M.D. Corn is low in protein and calcium, so manufacturers add calcium and protein-rich soybean meal. This makes the food too high in calcium, she says. The calcium binds with a soybean ingredient called phytate and prevents absorption of zinc. This leads to a zinc-deficiency dermatitis around the lips and eyes of dogs who live on generic dog food.

and, besides needing between 30 to 40 percent protein, "have some very peculiar nutritional requirements," especially an amino acid called taurine. This is one reason you shouldn't feed dog food to cats; they're unable to make sufficient taurine out of the amino acids in dog food. A taurine deficiency can cause degeneration of the retina in the eye, leading to blindness.

There is very little difference in brands or types of cat foods because cats have very strict requirements. The cat may not agree, Dr. Donoghue adds: "Cats are very individualistic; it's hard to predict what they'll like."

Feed 'em fat. It's essential to healthy skin and coat, aids digestibility of other nutrients and makes food taste good. Unlike humans, dogs and cats don't get artery-choking cholesterol problems, says Dr. Donoghue. Nutritionists recommend between 20 percent and 50 percent as an optimal level, though your pet can live on much less, as is commonly found in nonpremium dry chow.

If you think your pet can benefit from extra fat in his diet, be sure to add it gradually to avoid digestive difficulties and diarrhea, warns Dr. Donoghue. She recommends adding to dry food a whole cooked egg, which contains equal amounts of fat and protein. You could also add just oil, using 1 teaspoon of corn oil per ½ pound of dry food. Canned meat doesn't need extra fat—it already has enough.

Home cooking can be hazardous. Many people make their dog's food from scratch. The catch, says Dr. Donoghue, is that "for every ten dogs I see on home-cooked diets, nine of them have unbalanced diets. The big problem is not enough calcium, especially for puppies. It can create all sorts of problems for their bones. And, of course, there may not be enough taurine for cats."

Vitamin and mineral supplements can create imbalances of other nutri-

---

Is Fifi Too Fat?

To test your dog for fat, says the Alpo Pet Center's *Canine Nutrition and Feeding Management*, stand behind him and place both thumbs side by side on the spine with fingers spread over the ribs. With thumbs pressing on the vertebrae and fingers on the ribs, slide your hands gently backward and forward.

Ideally, you should feel a moderately thin layer of fat. If you can see protruding bones, the dog is too thin. A layer of fat that cushions the edges of the ribs, allowing only a smooth wavy feel to the chest, suggests that the dog is too fat.

As for cats, you should be able to feel but not see the ribs as individual bones.

---

ents. Clams or clam juice is taurine-rich but also very salty. Another hazard is too much liver, which can lead to vitamin A toxicity. "If you're going to make pet food at home," says Dr. Donoghue, "be prepared to learn some nutrition and how to balance diets and calculate amounts of nutrients."

They don't need supplements. For your average house pet, quality dry and canned foods have adequate amounts of vitamins and minerals, Dr. Donoghue says.

They don't need "special" diets. Your typical pet will do nicely on typical pet food. "There are a lot of marketing gimmicks in the pet food industry that aren't necessarily in the best interest of the dog," says Dr. Donoghue. It's not always a good idea, for example, to reduce protein in the diet of a healthy old dog.

Check with your vet before putting your pudgy dog on a reducing diet, and then just feed it less, suggests Dr. Donoghue. You don't need to buy an expensive "reducing diet" food. Also, she says, there's no evidence that the so-called low-ash cat foods help to prevent cats from getting urinary disease.

They don't need fiber. There is no recommended daily requirement. It's sometimes added to reducing diets. The danger is that the animal will fill up on a high-fiber diet and stop eating before its nutritional needs are met, says Dr. Donoghue.

Milk is good for pets. Moisten dry food with 1 part whole milk (or ½ part evaporated milk) to 4 parts dry food, recommends Dr. Donoghue. Like egg, it adds protein, fat and taste. Milk won't cause diarrhea if it remains part of the diet from weaning or if it's reintroduced gradually later in life over a period of five or six days.

Water your pet. "It is the most important thing in nutrition, especially for cats," says Dr. Donoghue. Fresh water should be available at all times.

William LeGro

Common Pet Diseases

Poor Fifi. The poor pup doesn't feel good today. She's hiding under the bed, quiet and annoyed with anyone who approaches. You've forgiven her for digging up the flower bed. You've told her the mailman settled out of court. Even Fluffy the cat has made peace with Fifi after having spent the night in the tree, with Fifi lying in wait below.

You wonder if Mr. Klausewitz's garbage wasn't all that good for Fifi's tummy, or if the garbage can lid he hurled at her made contact. Fifi didn't eat her gourmet dog chow last night. And she threw up this morning (why on the new sofa?) and is having a little diarrhea (okay, a *lot* of diarrhea). She won't come out and play with her favorite squeaky toy. She just lies under the bed, whining and moaning, and seems most disagreeable.

What's the matter with Fifi? It could be any of a long list of ailments. The many diseases, illnesses and injuries your dog or cat can suffer, mild or serious, share many of the same symptoms. How do you know when Fifi needs to see a doctor?

THE TOP 15 THREATS

The following information is intended only as a general guide to the ailments most often seen by veterinarians, says Kenneth Bovée, D.V.M., chief of medicine at the University of Pennsylvania School of Veterinary Medicine. Don't try to make a diagnosis yourself, but do try to notice symptoms so you can describe them to the doctor. Keep in mind that the symptoms don't always mean your pet has a given ailment.

Parvovirus. This is a highly contagious viral disease that is dangerous primarily to puppies. Bloody diarrhea is the most important and easily recognized symptom; others include loss of appetite, vomiting, fever and listlessness. Parvovirus can kill an adult dog in two to four days; 8- to 12-week-old puppies can die in a few hours, so early diagnosis is important. A preventive vaccine is 80 to 90 percent effective.

Heartworm. This condition is just what it sounds like: a worm up to a foot long (and hair-thick) that floats in blood in one of the heart's chambers. Mainly affecting dogs, it's transmitted by mosquitoes. Symptoms include coughing, shortness of breath, listlessness and poor appetite. Heart or lung failure occurs over months or years. Prevention is available in a daily or monthly pill.

Heart disease. There are many causes for heart disease other than heartworm, but the symptoms are the same. A veterinarian can diagnose heart disease with a thorough physical examination, including X-rays and electrocardiograms. If it's detected early enough, the prognosis is often good.

Distemper in dogs. This disease is different for dogs and cats, but both are highly preventable with vaccines. Symptoms of canine distemper include coughing (a puppy can die of pneumonia in the first or second week of distemper), diarrhea, listlessness and fever. Prognosis depends upon severity and early diagnosis and treatment.

Distemper in cats. This is actually feline infectious enteritis or panleukopenia and is caused by a different virus than canine distemper. Distemper hits kittens the same way that parvovirus attacks the digestive system of a puppy, and it can kill in 12 hours. Symptoms include weakness, vomiting, diarrhea (sometimes bloody) and high fever. It's a highly contagious disease. Early diagnosis and treatment are essential.

Rabies. Its symptoms are well known: personality changes, sensitivity to light, drooling or foaming at the mouth, loss of appetite and aversion to water. It moves so fast in cats that paralysis may be the only symptom you notice. Rabies is spread by the bite of an infected, often wild, animal. The extreme danger is transmission to humans. Rabies is always fatal to the animal. Prevention by a highly effective vaccine is the only way to go, and it's required by law. A rabies epidemic has been ravaging the eastern United States since 1979.

Kennel cough. This condition, also called infectious tracheobronchitis, is the most common respiratory illness in dogs, similar to the common cold in humans but more severe and potentially fatal. It is caused by a series of airborne viruses, and dogs often pick it up at boarding kennels. Stress may be a contributing factor, along with close proximity to other dogs. The main symptom is a dry, hacking cough, which usually disappears by itself within two weeks. The best prevention is a standard vaccination with parainfluenza vaccine, which is often combined with canine and parvovirus vaccines.

Respiratory infections. These are probably the most frequently seen infectious ailments in cats. All of the many varieties are very contagious and range from mild to severe. Signs are sneezing, fever, eye and nasal discharges, poor appetite, listlessness and drooling. In severe cases, the eyes may be crusted shut and nasal passages clogged from discharges. These symptoms mean the cat should be seen by a doctor. Vaccines can prevent the diseases.

Intestinal parasites. Young animals are most often affected by parasites. They are generally born with roundworms and pick up tapeworms from fleas. The roundworm-infested puppy or kitten may be very thin, have a pot belly, diarrhea and a cough. Tapeworm is the most common internal parasite of adult cats. A veterinarian must diagnose the type of worm and prescribe the proper medication.

Mange. This condition is caused by microscopic parasites called mites. The mites are common, but it's unknown why some animals get mange while others don't. There are two main types of mange, and dogs get both of them much more frequently than cats. One type is scabies, which can be transmitted to humans. (In fact, most people with scabies get it from their cats or dogs.) Symptoms of demodectic mange are obvious; lots of scratching and severely crusted skin. This type of mange actually produces severe skin changes and gives your cat or dog a moth-eaten appearance, especially around the eyes, ears and nose. Treatment involves antiparasitic dips.

Kidney disease. The causes of kidney disease, which is silent until well advanced, are varied, as is the prognosis. The most common symptoms are poor appetite, gradual weight loss, excessive thirst and, later, vomiting. Early recognition is important; this very serious disease can lead to kidney failure and death. If your pet has any of these symptoms, a yearly urinalysis and blood test are advisable.

Put a Stop to Fleas and Ticks

Fleas and ticks may be a nuisance to you, but for your pets these hopping and crawling little vampires are a real problem that crucifixes and garlic won't solve. Besides sucking Fifi's precious blood, they transmit worms and cause skin irritations and highly irritating allergies. Severe infestations of fleas can cause anemia and even kill; each flea feasts on a drop of blood daily. Dinner at Fifi's. Think about it.

Use dips to kill fleas and ticks. Use a chemical dip especially formulated for cats or dogs; they are *not* interchangeable, says Kenneth Bovée, D.V.M. Wear rubber gloves and follow the directions *to the letter.*

Pick those ticks. Ticks embed themselves in the skin, especially on the head and neck, on and in the ears and between the toes. The best way to remove ticks is to dip the animal first, paralyzing the ticks, then pick them off, says Dr. Bovée. Wear rubber gloves to avoid contact with blood (certain ticks can spread Rocky Mountain spotted fever), grasp them as close to the skin as possible and pull out with a slight twist, strongly and slowly.

One of the more endearing qualities of ticks is that you can pull their heads right off their bodies, causing a minor inflammation on Fifi's skin, which can be treated with hydrogen peroxide. Don't use tweezers on ticks because they can pop the tick and spray blood on you (Bleagghh!). And don't use the old hot match trick; it can burn Fifi's skin.

After you've removed the ticks, bathe your pet.

Treat fleas ecologically. If the buggers keep reinfesting Fifi, it's because your home, yard and doghouse are probably infested with adults, eggs and larvae. You might have to attack repeatedly to wipe out the flowering of flea culture. Flea bombs used in the home usually work. But follow bombing instructions to the letter. For severe infestations, you may have to call an exterminator.

Plan an eviction. Your pet's bed is bound to be a bed for his fleas as well. In fact it's probably their hotel. So make sure the surface of his bed can easily be washed. This is a highly effective method of control, vets say, and nothing special needs to be done other than to use soap or detergent and hot water. If your pet uses a pillow that is difficult to wash, just pitch the unwashed pillow in the dryer and make sure it gets good and hot.

Flea collars work. But only to prevent an invasion of the bloodsucking hordes. They can't wipe out an occupying army, nor can medallions or tags. And so-called natural pyrethrins are insecticides that are less effective than those used in dips and flea collars.

Also, says Dr. Bovée, there's no evidence that sulfur or brewer's yeast added to the diet works either.

Become the flea-and-tick police. Once you've eradicated the insidious enemy (forget winning their hearts and minds), you can prevent a reinvasion with judicious employment of the wide arsenal of the Strategic Anticritter Attack Force: regular use of flea collars or sprays, and washing and spraying of the indoor environment. And professional extermination if your home seems to be a target area.

Be on Poison Patrol

These days poison abounds in our environment, and dogs and cats get into it as easily as children can.

Most of the time you won't see your pet eating poison, but if you truly suspect your pet's been poisoned by any substance, even by something not mentioned here, *call a veterinarian*—no matter what time of day or night, Harold Trammel, Pharm.D., director of the Illinois Animal Poison Information Center, advises. "If the animal is sick," he says, "very little can be done at home." Your vet will have access to an animal poison control center. If a vet is unreachable, call a human poison control center.

Here is a brief rundown of some of the types of poison that your pets are likely to find.

Rodenticides. In fall and winter months, humans put out rat poison to welcome the little critters in from the cold. Warfarin is one common ingredient: It prevents production of blood-clotting proteins, thus leading to death from internal and external bleeding. Another common ingredient is strychnine; the telltale symptoms are seizures brought on by simple stimulation. Make sure to place the poisons out of reach.

Insecticides. Bug-killers are the number two cause of pet poisoning, according to Dr. Trammel. Keep your pets off your lawn for 24 to 48 hours after you've laid down the welcome mat for dandelions, crabgrass and their compadres. And, Dr. Trammel notes, one major source of insecticide poisoning is flea control: "We dip the animal, then spray the carpet, spray the doghouse, powder the cat bed, spray the animal, then put a flea collar on him." When you consider the mistakes in measuring you're liable to make—not even counting those who use dog dip on their cats—it's a wonder Fifi and Fluffy survive at all. And don't forget, cats and dogs groom themselves, increasing their exposure.

Herbicides and fertilizers are lesser but still dangerous poison sources. Gardeners with pets should not use snail bait. If your pet gets sick from grass or plants, it might not be a bad idea to get yourself tested. You could be using the wrong dilution.

Human medication. "One extra-strength Tylenol will kill a cat," says Val Beasley, D.V.M., associate director of the Poison Information Center of the University of Illinois. The ingredient to beware of is acetaminophen. It takes a little more ibuprofen (Nuprin, Advil) to do the job. Aspirin can send a cat into a coma within 6 to 12 hours and kill it, even though a safe dose can be prescribed by a veterinarian. "Well-intentioned humans have no business giving human medication to animals unless it's prescribed by their vets," says Dr. Trammel. Watch out, too, he warns, for pet medication: "Dogs will scarf down whatever they can get their mouths on."

Animal medication. Overdoses are all too common, as owners persist in believing if 1 pill is good, 2 are great, or what's good for a dog is good for a cat, or if it works for the dog, it'll work for the puppy. Wrong, wrong, wrong! If your pet has OD'd, call your vet.

Antifreeze. Given the chance, your pet will readily drink antifreeze. It's a dangerous poison. If your pet gets anywhere near exposed antifreeze, take him to a vet *immediately*. If you can't get to a vet within an hour, induce vomiting with 1 teaspoon of 3 percent hydrogen peroxide per 5 pounds of body weight. Do this even if you're not sure any antifreeze was swallowed.

Symptoms are: vomiting, possible mental confusion, heavy panting and collapse. The best prevention: have a garage change your antifreeze, says Dr. Beasley (have you ever *not* spilled the stuff doing it yourself?).

Garbage intoxication. Seriously, this is what it's called, and dogs are particularly susceptible. One way to prevent it is to train your dog to stay away from garbage. Another is to never treat your pet like a walking garbage disposal by giving him table scraps. *Never* give sweets for a treat—1 pound of chocolate will toss a 10-pound dog for a loop with severe stomach problems. Stick to pet food!

Gastrointestinal disease. Diseases or disorders of the gastrointestinal tract have a great many causes, but usually two major symptoms: vomiting and diarrhea. There are at least 50 kinds of gastrointestinal disease; if the symptoms persist or seem drastic, take your pet to a vet. But don't be unduly alarmed if your dog vomits, says Dr. Bovée. "Dogs can vomit at the drop of a hat, four or five times in a matter of hours, then turn around and eat a big meal, or what they just vomited." (You can see why cats think dogs have no class.)

Cancer. Although cancer is as ubiquitous in cats and dogs as it is in humans, by far the major dog-and-cat cancer is malignant lymphoma in its various forms. A virus causes the incurable feline leukemia viral disease complex (FeLV) and is the primary cause of cancer in cats. Cancer symptoms have a vast range depending on tumor sites; the most common symptom is chronic weight loss. Prognosis varies widely. Euthanasia is often advised for cats with FeLV to prevent the spread of the disease. An FeLV vaccine is available, but its effectiveness is unclear.

Diabetes. Dogs are particularly affected by this disease. As in humans, symptoms include excessive thirst and urination, weight loss, loss of appetite and weakness. It can occur at any age. Treatment with diet alone almost never works; insulin is usually necessary. The prognosis depends on the owner's willingness to give injections every day.

Feline urologic syndrome. This is the most common group of disorders in cats. Although it affects only 1 percent of all cats, it keeps recurring. The cause is unknown. The effectiveness of so-called low-ash or low-magnesium diets sometimes used to treat it is unproven, says Dr. Bovée.

William LeGro

Symptoms That Spell EMERGENCY!

These symptoms or conditions, indicative of a variety of illnesses or injuries, may mean your pet is in serious or life-threatening danger and needs to see a veterinarian immediately, if not sooner.

Confusion, inability to stand, shivering, paleness of the gums and mouth. These are signs of shock, a collapse of the cardiovascular system. Shock is the number one symptom that dogs and cats suffer as a result of injury and blood loss, says Kenneth Bovée, D.V.M. He advises that you take your pet's rectal temperature as you would your child's. Ask your vet if you're not sure. A subnormal temperature, down to 97°F or 98°F (normal is 101.5°F, plus or minus 1°F), signifies shock. Keep the animal warm and quiet.

Continuous rapid, frantic, noisy breathing. This is a sign of heatstroke, commonly caused by being locked in a hot car or room. In severe cases the mouth can be blue or bright red, and foaming. "Taking the temperature is absolutely critical," says Dr. Bovée. "If it's higher than 103°F, call your veterinarian and ask him what to do before you take the animal in." You can spray the animal all over with cool water. Heatstroke can cause cardiovascular collapse and shock and can kill quickly.

Abdominal swelling. This is gastric bloat, distension of the abdomen caused by gas, and follows attempts to vomit. "This is always an emergency situation," says Dr. Bovée. "You want to get the dog to the vet within 2 to 3 hours, or shock will result. You'll know it when you see it." The dog acts as if it has acute abdominal pain, paces around and is unable to find a comfortable position to lie down. The pressure of bloat makes breathing difficult and can lead to shock.

Significant bleeding. To be an emergency, bleeding must be truly profuse, says Dr. Bovée. It may be seen from a wound or from any body orifice: nose, mouth or rectum. It may appear as spontaneous purple or red blotches or bruises on the skin or gums or it can be from internal hemorrhage, although this is difficult to detect. Blood can show up in vomit, urine or stool. The result can be shock.

There is no home first aid for bruising or internal hemorrhaging. Ice packs or cold compresses may temporarily control nasal bleeding. For wounds, *do not use tourniquets*, which can cut off circulation. Instead, apply pressure in places not easily bandaged.

Diarrhea. Three features that spell emergency: if diarrhea is frequent —every 30 to 60 minutes—voluminous and accompanied by an inability to eat or drink, says Dr. Bovée, the animal may go into shock in a matter of hours if untreated.

Frequent, difficult urination with bloody urine; little or no urine; severe abdominal tenderness and depression. This is a sign of acute urinary obstruction and can occur in dogs and cats. Take the animal to the vet within 24 hours of the onset of these symptoms. If untreated, this ailment can lead to death in 60 hours. Other urinary disorders aren't as serious as urinary obstruction.

Dentistry:
New Breadth in Pet Care

Fifi just wiggled up and slurped a big, sloppy, wet kiss on your nose. You nearly keeled over from an explosive overdose of doggie breath. Your nose may never fully recover. Put the stuff in a can, add a propellant, and you'd have a substance lethal enough to control Fifi's flea population and kill your neighbor's lawn! But you don't really mind because you love Fifi and Fifi's very affectionate.

And diseased.

After all, how could anything that smells so rank be healthy? In the vast majority of cases, doggie breath—or kitty breath—is the first sign of periodontal disease, says Jean Hawkins, D.V.M., president of the American Veterinary Dental Society and editor of the *Journal of Veterinary Dentistry*. (Bad breath can also be related to diet or illness.)

The disease has two stages: The first, gingivitis, is marked by inflamed gums that bleed when pressure is applied. It is totally reversible. The second stage is periodontitis. It destroys the soft tissue and bones that teeth fit into, causing chronic abscesses, infections and, if left untreated, bone and tooth loss. Periodontitis is irreversible but controllable with proper dental care, including regular checkups and cleaning.

FANGLESS FRIENDS

Periodontal disease afflicts 95 percent of cats and dogs two years old and older, Dr. Hawkins says, and is their primary cause of tooth loss. Every gruesomely graphic photo your dentist has shown you of advanced periodontal disease in humans can easily be matched by a veterinary dentist eager to illustrate what can happen to Fifi's and Fluffy's fangs.

Fifi and Fluffy should be able to keep their teeth until they die, notes Dr. Hawkins, who is also a fellow of American Veterinary Dentistry. Researchers find it hard to induce cavities in experimental dogs fed lots of sweets and even inoculated with cavity-causing bacteria. "I guess the bacteria just don't like the mouths of dogs and cats," she says. Well, who does?

Take these steps to improve the state of your dog's and cat's mouths, and bad breath will become a not-so-mere smell of the past. And your much-abused nose will thank you.

Get your pet regular dental exams and cleanings. Before it's too late, start your pets on a comprehensive dental care program. First, get them a thorough examination and cleaning from a veterinarian knowledgeable in this fairly new field (only

Cute? Yes. But it's no joke. Your pets have the same chance as you of developing serious dental problems if they don't follow the same sensible advice. They should have their teeth brushed daily.

A Pooch You Can Smooch

Don't expect your dog to toss back her head and gargle for you, but there is mouthwash made especially to combat plaque in pets. Jean Hawkins, D.V.M., says there are prescription and over-the-counter preparations available.

She cautions you to read the labels to be sure you don't use a mouthwash containing the preservative sodium benzoate for your cat; cats can't tolerate it. Use a baby syringe and squirt it over the teeth and gums, or put the mouthwash on swabs or gauze sponges and wipe it on.

a small—but increasing—percentage of veterinarians are taught animal dental care in school). The first exam should be when the pet's baby teeth are fully in, at five to six weeks of age, says Dr. Hawkins. This is when possible bite problems can be diagnosed.

The next exam should be at six to eight months, and following that, examinations should be scheduled every year. The six-month exam is to make sure the baby teeth are shed and the permanent teeth are in the right position. A mouth crammed full of teeth is much more susceptible to plaque and periodontal disease and abnormal tooth wear.

"Animals with periodontal disease may have to have their teeth cleaned as often as once a month to start," says Dr. Hawkins, "and then every three months for a couple of times, and then every six months to control the disease."

Start your home care program when they're young. Get Fifi and

Fluffy used to having their fuzzy muzzles handled and their mouths pried open at as young as three months old, says Dr. Hawkins. At this stage, just wipe the teeth with a swab, a gauze pad or a washcloth wrapped around your finger, being sure to reach the gum line. Later, begin brushing. By six months, when all their permanent teeth are in, your pets should be accustomed to daily invasions of their mouths.

Get them their own toothbrushes. Start brushing their teeth *every day* to keep the plaque from solidifying into calculus, a substance with the consistency of concrete, that won't come off with a brush. Use adult-size brushes for large dogs, child-size for smaller dogs and cats. Always use soft-bristled brushes.

Use pet toothpaste. Dogs can tolerate human toothpaste, but cats are very sensitive to the preservative sodium benzoate found in most human toothpastes. For both dogs and cats, Dr. Hawkins recommends C.E.T. Enzymatic malt-flavored toothpaste that controls plaque, available from veterinarians. Don't use the traditional baking soda-and-salt mixture, warns Dr. Hawkins: "It's *too high* in sodium."

Make it a convenient habit for you. Keep the brush handy on a table next to your favorite living room chair or sofa and brush Fifi's and Fluffy's teeth during the evening prime-time TV shows, or any time that can fit easily into your daily routine. After their meals is best.

Praise your pet. Put your dog (if he's small enough) or cat on your lap, speak soothing words, offer lots of praise. "Happy cats and dogs are easier to handle than animals that are ignored," says Dr. Hawkins.

Cats may not cooperate. You may have noticed Fluffy has some very sharp edges and an uncooperative nature (dogs, being more eager to please, are more likely to accept dental hygiene). "My own personal cat won't let me in her mouth," says Dr.

Hawkins. "She turns into an octopus, with claws on the ends of each of her eight legs. She tucks her head down—her neck muscles are stronger than my hand muscles. She starts crawfishing backward and sideways, and she's gone."

Still, if you start her early enough in life, she will probably accept tooth brushing, or at least tooth wiping. But first, you may want to immobilize Fluffy in a pillowcase or thick towel.

This is how you do it. Concentrate on cleaning the outside of the upper cheek teeth, the fangs and the incisors (between the fangs), which will help control about 75 percent of the disease. Don't worry about brushing up and down or around and round or back and forth. Just get close to the gum line. The point is to "do a good job as quickly as you can without getting bitten," says Dr. Hawkins. The tongue will help keep the inside lower cheek teeth clean.

Alternatives aren't as good. Brushing is undoubtedly the best way to clean your pet's teeth, says Dr. Hawkins. Various other methods involve feeding your pet more food and sometimes dog biscuits, but none are substitutes for brushing.

Dry food may scrape some plaque off, but won't break off calculus, says Dr. Hawkins. Usually the animal just crunches a little and swallows.

A raw, hard carrot may do a little better and knuckle bones can help, especially on the upper cheek teeth. But you have to supervise this closely. Says Dr. Hawkins: Bones can spoil. They can get stuck on a tooth, and teeth can become impacted. The knuckle bone needs to be fresh, raw, beef only, with no fat or muscle tissue attached. If Fifi is a bone-gobbler, she can get constipated from too many bones.

Dog biscuits will help somewhat "if the dog does what he's supposed to do," she says, which is chew slowly and thoroughly. But usually a larger dog

Get Braced for This One!

Your dog's name's Fifi, but you can call her Ol' Snaggletooth. Her baby teeth didn't drop out when they were supposed to, so now one of Fifi's fangs is jutting out like a spear, and another is gouging a hole in the roof of her mouth. Fifi needs a veterinary orthodontist. That's right. Braces.

Enter Charles Williams, D.V.M., president-elect of the Academy of Veterinary Dentistry and a veterinary orthodontist. Baby teeth not dropping out is the single biggest cause of orthodontic problems, says Dr. Williams, but puppies can develop bite disorders in their brand-new adult teeth from puppy games like tug-of-war. Depending on the problem, he uses braces fairly similar to those that children receive or custom-designed bite plates.

"The dogs don't relish it," Dr. Williams says, "but in general they handle it pretty well." The treatment may last from 2 weeks to a year, but the average is 3 to 4 months. The owner has to clean the teeth religiously—some use a Water-Pik—and keep the dog away from bones and chew toys.

will just bite the bones into swallowable pieces and gulp them down. Dog biscuits add calories and salt.

Rawhide chews can be dangerous. There are some reports of intestinal impaction caused by rawhide bones, and Dr. Hawkins recommends against them. "My dog will just devour a rawhide bone instantaneously," she says, although for other dogs they may help, especially small dogs, which tend to treasure and gnaw on them.

William LeGro

Get Dogged about Exercise

You tried bicycling with your dog, but Fifi's legs were too short to reach the pedals. You took her out to jog alongside the car, but Fifi got a ticket for running a red light. You and Fifi went to an aerobics class, but Fifi was kicked out for having four left feet.

Fifi's behind is spreading like soft cream cheese. Her waist, which once resembled the isthmus of Panama, now looks more like the bulge of Brazil.

Meanwhile, Fluffy's a feline version of the Goodyear blimp. But you should talk. When you and your pets line up for a look in the mirror, the only apparent differences between human and pet are your two legs and lack of fur.

THE HIGH COST OF PAMPERED PETS

Prevention magazine columnist Amy Marder, V.M.D., says up to 40 percent of American dogs and 10 percent of American cats are obese. Corpulent canines and tubby tabbies are suspectible to the same health problems as hippopotamic humans: lameness, diabetes, heart and lung diseases and intestinal disorders.

A lack of exercise is implicated in pooch and kitty delinquency, too. In fact, Warren Eckstein, a behavior therapist for more than 30,000 pets and coauthor of *Pet Aerobics,* says that "nearly every behavior problem I have encountered in 14 years of work with animals is directly attributable to lack of exercise. Chasing a Frisbee eliminates the need to chase a tail or chew a paw." Or a sofa.

So though all may be fat and frustration, all is not lost. You can deliver your dog and cat from lard, languor and delinquency while help-

ing your own state of health. Here's a step-by-step guide.

FIRST THINGS FIRST

There are precautions you and your pet should take before diving into an exercise program.

Get a checkup. Even though your vet may look at you strangely, do ask for the equivalent of a human stress test, says Eckstein. University of Pennsylvania veterinary anatomist Bonnie Dalzell, who breeds greyhounds and borzois, says a veterinarian should check your pet for any physical defects or weaknesses that preclude certain types of exercise.

Get your pet vaccinated. Your puppy or kitten should complete its vaccination series before being exposed to diseases that can be picked up on sidewalks and in parks and playgrounds.

Don't start too young. "Small breeds of dogs are pretty mature at six months, but large breeds may not be mature until two years," Dalzell says. "The rule of thumb is: no repetitive forced exercise until your pet is skeletally mature. The kinds of exercise regimens that are good for the

Pooped Pup? Go Easy

Hard exercise can mean injuries to dogs, says dog breeder and veterinary anatomist Bonnie Dalzell. High-speed running can cause poorly healing toe injuries, and dogs have broken their necks falling over backward while leaping for a Frisbee. They're also subject to torn ligaments and muscles and sore joints.

"If the dog has periodic bouts of lameness," Dalzell says, "tires easily, isn't overweight and has no heart problems, the problem is most likely in the joints." You can help prevent joint problems by feeding your pet properly from puppyhood.

Dalzell says to avoid the super-high protein, super-high vitamin and mineral supplements that promote maximum growth. "It makes it much more likely the dog will develop joint problems later on," she says. The best prevention for injuries, though, is common sense and awareness of your pet's body and capabilities.

Exercise—it's the secret to a long and healthy life for your pet.

cardiovascular system are not good for a puppy's skeletal system. There's a real fine line between producing an athletic animal and a disaster. It's better to be on the conservative side. A quarter-mile walk is more than enough for a two-month-old puppy. The typical pattern of play for a puppy or kitten—15 minutes of play and a half hour of sleep—builds a nice, sturdy, athletic animal."

Read their body language. "Be sensitive to signs of distress—panting, inability to continue, limping, obvious stress," Dalzell says. "Dogs are so cooperative, they want to please their masters, and they may go till they drop."

Fifi should learn the basics. For their own safety, your pets need basic training in obedience before it's safe to take them out in public. They should be leash-trained. To do some of the aerobic and strength exercises that follow, your dog should know the basics—heel, sit and come.

Your cat can benefit, too. Eckstein claims considerable success at training cats to do just about everything a dog can do. "Cats are so smart," he says, "that they've convinced the public they can't be trained. But actually they're very adaptable."

IT'S EXERCISE TIME!

As in obedience training, reward your pet with praise when it does something right; be patient when it does something wrong or gets confused. Be aware when your pet seems to have had enough of one exercise, and move on to another. Work into the exercises gradually, increasing the length of the session, repetitions or weights week by week as your pet gets stronger and more fit. Here are some of the exercises Eckstein recommends in *Pet Aerobics.*

Walking, jogging and running. The perfect aerobic exercises. Determine your program according to the size, age and breed of your dog or cat. Walk, don't run, cats and short-legged

---

The Cold-Water Cool-Down

If your pet (most likely a dog) seems overheated, dog breeder and veterinary anatomist Bonnie Dalzell says, don't let him drink as much water as he wants. Drinking too much can cause gastric bloat, a condition which, if left untreated, is fatal. (For specific symptoms, see the box, "Symptoms That Spell Emergency," on page 351.)

"Air circulation is what's important," she says. "The rule of thumb is to give him a ½ cup of water or let him lick ice cubes, then walk the dog until he stops panting. Follow this with 2 cups of water, let him cool down further, then give him a bowl of water. After he's drunk all he wants, don't exercise him for 1 to 2 hours to give him a chance to absorb the water."

Another way to help cool down a dog is to hose him down with running water, Dalzell says; a bucket of water poured over him doesn't work in conditions of high humidity because it doesn't carry any of the body heat away with it.

---

dogs. For an out-of-shape pet, four repetitions are plenty to start with.

Sit-ups. It goes like this: "Sit. Up. Sit. Up." Fifi sits, then stands, then sits, then stands. You get the idea.

Jumping jacks. Tell your pet to sit, then say "Jump!" as you snap your fingers over its head, but not so far that the pet jumps up and falls backward. Eckstein says this is often sufficient, but if it doesn't work, hold his favorite toy over his head.

Push-ups. This is a repetition of sit and down commands: "Sit. Down (or lie down). Sit. Down."

Running push-up. Tell your pet to sit and stay while you position yourself across the room. Then tell him to come. When he gets halfway to you, tell him to lie down. Then repeat the "come" command. Eckstein says after a while your pet will anticipate the "down" command and simply run into it, "which, of course, is the whole point."

Ball-playing. Besides throwing a ball and having the pet fetch, you can throw or kick the ball, then chase your dog when he picks it up. Or you can play "monkey in the middle"—just let your pet get the ball often. Smaller balls like Nerf balls or any high-bouncing rubber balls are perfect for cats and smaller dogs. Cats are sprinting animals, Dalzell says, and ball-chasing is the best aerobic exercise for them.

Frisbee. Again, you have to teach your dog to fetch and to not eat the Frisbee. Dalzell offers this caution: The dog can hurt himself seriously if he leaps straight up to catch a Frisbee and falls over backward coming down, or comes down too hard on his hind legs. "Throw the Frisbee so the dog gallops and leaps like a horse to catch it. Keep it low and horizontal, not high and vertical."

Pumping iron. This is simple, too. Tie your dog or cat by its leash and special chest harness to something draggable—a vinyl sand-filled free weight plate or, for large dogs, even a spare tire. Then command your pet to come, pulling the weight. Be sure the harness is padded and fits properly. Cats and small dogs should start with ⅛- to ½-pound weights; larger dogs can start with 2 to 5 pounds. Start with two 5-minute sessions split by a rest period. To find a special pulling harness, contact a local dogsled club or ask your vet. Remember that the harness you buy at a pet store isn't the same thing.

William LeGro

Pets and Your Allergies

Milo Beeblebork sneezed, and because of that, civilization as we know it came to an end.

When Milo sneezed, he was shaving; he cut himself, and stuck toilet paper on his neck to stop the bleeding. He neglected to remove the toilet paper before he went to work, so Milo made a very bad first impression on a major client. Milo lost the account and his job, and subsequently everything else —house, Volvo, espresso machine— and became mired in poverty.

Milo's son, Isaac, grew up with a conscious desire to become powerful and a subconscious one to avenge his father's failure. Isaac Beeblebork became president and subconsciously maneuvered the nation into a confrontation with Teepeedia, the world's biggest toilet paper producer, which responded with an embargo the likes of which America's bottoms had never seen. Tension understandably rose, and when President Beeblebork got word that the infidels had mobilized their forces, he pushed the big red preemptive strike button.

A closer study of history, however, reveals that it was actually Fluffy Beeblebork, Milo's cat, who indirectly caused the end of civilization as we know it. Milo sneezed because he was allergic to cats.

All kidding aside, allergies can precipitate dreadful consequences. So here we present tips from the experts on how to handle pet allergies and thus possibly prevent your own personal Armageddon.

LIVING WITH PETS AND ALLERGIES

Allergies to pets are a major problem. One researcher estimates that as much as 20 percent of the general population is at risk of developing an allergy to pets. One allergist questioned a group of allergic pet owners to find out why they felt such attachment toward the animals that caused their runny noses, itching eyes and wheezing. The answer was predictable and understandable: Their pets also provided companionship and someone to love.

But their emotional benefits, say allergists, have to be weighed against their physical costs.

Minor-league allergy symptoms are one thing, "but an asthmatic sleeping with a cat on the pillow is literally risking his life," says John Ohman, M.D., a clinical associate professor of medicine at Tufts University and chairman of the American Academy of Allergy and Immunology's Committee on Allergy to Animals.

Dr. Ohman believes, however, that healthy coexistence of allergic owners and animals is possible—if the owners involved are prepared to go to a little extra trouble.

Deinsulate your house. Pets in well-insulated houses are definitely a problem, says Dr. Ohman. Mark Swanson, from the Allergic Diseases Research Lab of the Mayo Clinic in Rochester, Minnesota, agrees. Swanson found that a two-cat super-insulated home—one with every crack closed tight and windows triple-glazed in the name of energy efficiency—had nearly *40 times* more cat allergen by weight than an ordinary two-cat home.

The results so astounded the researchers that they tried to see if they could lower the levels. They put a high-efficiency particulate air (HEPA) filter on the furnace, but even after eight months of filtering, there was still over five times as much cat stuff in the air as in a "normal" house without any kind of air-cleaning device. Clearly, in this case, the cause of the problem was as much the fault of house design as of pussycat presence.

Get your pet out of the bedroom. But bedrooms are a problem, even in "normal" houses. Immediately after making a bed that a cat has slept on, the reading will jump up to an almost impossibly high level. "Keeping the pet out of the bedroom reduces exposure a thousandfold," explains Dr. Ohman.

Get your pet out of the house. "Keeping the pet outside the house as much as possible is also a tremendous help," says Dr. Ohman.

Groom your pet outside. While that pet is outdoors is also the time to do the things you shouldn't be doing inside. "It's okay to pet and brush your animal," explains Dr. Ohman, "but do yourself a big favor and limit that activity to outside the house. The most allergenic component of your pet's fur is so small it's invisible to the naked eye. But its small size also makes it all the more easily inhalable."

THE ALLERGIC LEGACY

Moving your pet outdoors is not a total solution, warns Dr. Ohman. "These allergens are remarkably stable and stay in the environment a very long time," he explains. "You can even boil cat antigen for hours and have very little effect on its potential to cause an allergic reaction."

The cat and dog may now be outside, but they've left a lot behind for you to remember them by. "It takes months or years for cat allergens to clear from rugs and chairs," says Dr. Ohman. But vacuuming is not the answer. "Cat allergen is extremely small and just comes back out into the air with most vacuum cleaners. And it remains suspended in the air for a long time, partly because its molecules are so tiny.

"The best procedure is actually to change the bedding and carpeting. If that's too much, at least get a fresh start in the bedroom. In most cases, there has to be a certain level of allergen in the environment to cause a reaction, so reducing the level often reduces symptoms and their severity."

A SHOT IN THE ARM

If your allergic symptoms persist and exposure simply cannot be reduced, says Dr. Ohman, "immunotherapy [allergy shots] does offer hope, although it's much more effective if the therapy begins before exposure to the animal."

Some studies—three by Swedish researchers and two by Dr. Ohman and his colleagues—have shown a significant beneficial effect of immunotherapy. And Dr. Ohman believes that the materials being used for these desensitizing injections are getting better all the time.

In Dr. Ohman's studies, patients treated with purified cat pelt extract "had significant reduction in bronchial sensitivity," and, in some cases, reduced pulmonary symptoms as well. In the Swedish studies, patients could tolerate 11 times more cat allergen after a year of treatment.

For years, studies of dog immunotherapy hadn't been promising. But researchers from Finland and Denmark, who used immunotherapy to help a group of children, found the results so impressive that dogs can now be added to the small but growing list of allergy triggers that such injections can help calm.

NO BREED IS SAFE

European researchers curious about whether one breed of cat or dog causes fewer allergic reactions than another found no distinction among breeds. People with allergies simply tend to be allergic to dogs as well as cats in general. The study estimates that 20 to 40 percent of people with allergies may react to dogs and cats, while 40 to 60 percent will develop hypersensitivity to hamsters and guinea pigs after long exposure.

So if you want furry pets, try to follow the measures in this chapter. A nice tank of tropical fish may be another answer, but be sure to keep the water and plumbing clean if you're sensitive to mold.

William LeGro with Mike McGrath

Overreaction Is the Worst Reaction

When it comes to controlling pet allergies, we're talking about the possibility of a painful separation from a loyal, faithful friend. That's why it's vitally important to first be sure that your pet really is the cause of your allergy symptoms. And new research from Canada indicates that the prime method used to determine such guilt or innocence may often be misleading.

A blood test or skinprick may be used to tell if you're allergic. If the test is positive, you're faced with either getting rid of the pet, taking extraordinary measures such as kicking the animal out of the house and refurnishing, or getting allergy shots.

But researchers at the University of British Columbia say that such test results could be wrong. In their study, they found only one-half to two-thirds of 168 children who tested positive to dogs or cats were actually allergic to them.

The researchers got their results this way: Before the testing, a thorough medical history done on each child revealed that 31 of the 168 were allergic to dogs and 51 had problems around cats. But when both skin and blood tests were run, the results showed many more positive reactions to dogs and cats than there were actual allergies.

If parents had followed the test results alone, it would have meant a 33 to 50 percent chance of putting out the pooch when he wasn't really the problem. Such "false-positive" test results, explain the researchers, indicate only that the children have been exposed to animals, not that they're allergic to them.

Basic Training for Obedient Dogs

The point of obedience training is to make your dog a responsible member of your human family. This means he should obey each member of the family equally well. Training a dog can sometimes become a test of wills. You must always win. You may want to consult some of the excellent dog-training books or even a professional trainer, but here are the basics to having a civilized dog.

THE FAR SIDE

"No way. I'll put *my* magazine down when you put yours down."

THE FOUNDATIONS OF A GOOD RELATIONSHIP

Before you can teach your dog anything, there are some basic lessons experts recommend you learn yourself.

Patience and consistency are prerequisites. "The first few times you give a command, your dog has no idea what you want," says Barbara Chapman, B.V.Sc., resident in internal medicine of small animals at the Veterinary Medical Teaching Hospital of the University of California. "As long as you're consistent in what the command means, the dog has to catch on. There's no harm in treating him as human, but don't expect him to have human mental capabilities."

Praise is a cardinal virtue. When your dog needs correction—and he will—do it immediately, and always follow it with praise to let him know you're still friends. And of course, always praise him when he does something right. An enthusiastic "good boy" is enough; don't overdo it. You don't want to get him excited.

Repetition is a requirement. Repeat all the commands, the body motions, the corrections and the praise until he learns each lesson without the leash snaps and corrections. Then teach each command without the leash.

Violence is against the rules. The American Kennel Club (AKC) says the only time you should strike your dog is when he actually threatens to bite. Otherwise, don't hit him with your hand or anything else. Hitting can become meaningless if done too often and can make your dog afraid of you. It can also lead to other problems.

Mutual confidence is a must. The AKC says confidence is the cornerstone of training. You and your dog must have confidence in each other—you that he can learn and he in your fairness and consistency. Always use a firm, confident, no-nonsense voice. Punishment is counterproductive.

Correct, don't punish. A dog is never punished. A dog is only corrected. If he doesn't sit when you tell him to, for instance, immediately guide him to a sitting position with your hands.

Get a collar and leash. The best setup is a so-called choke chain collar and leather or webbing leash. *Caution:* Be sure to put the collar on as shown in the illustration below, with the loose ring at the right of the

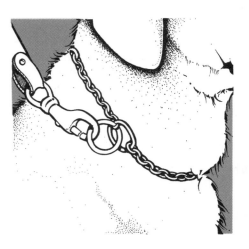

dog's neck, or you can truly end up choking your dog. The leash should be 6 feet long and ½ to 1 inch wide. Hold it so you have about 2 feet in reserve. Don't keep the leash tight—the dog will begin to tug on it in response.

Learn the art of the leash snap. The dog should always walk on your left. Holding the leash in your right hand, as shown here, snap it with your left hand. Just give the leash a quick snap (not a tug, not a pull and not hard enough to hurt) to tighten the collar, then release it. Never maintain continuous pressure. Before you put your dog on the leash, practice the leash snap by attaching it to an

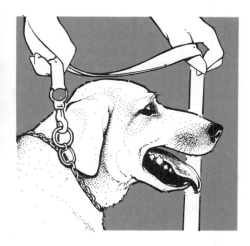

immovable object about the same height as your dog, snapping and instantly releasing.

Sign language works like words. With every exercise we mention, you can give your dog a consistent hand signal he can either see or hear. For instance, snap your fingers when you say "Sit!", hold your palm in front of his face when you command him to stay or hold your palm down when you want him to lie down. He'll learn to obey the hand signals without the verbal commands.

Make it just like school. You can start teaching basic commands when your puppy is 12 weeks old, but wait until he is six or eight months old and has completed his vaccinations before enrolling him in obedience classes. Establish regular training sessions of 15 to 30 minutes once or twice a day. After each session, take a little time to play with him to ensure good relations.

With these basic rules in mind, you and your dog are now ready to begin basic training. Remember: Basic training here does not mean boot camp.

HEEL!

Probably the most important on-leash command you can teach your dog is to heel—it ensures your control and enables you to go on to other exercises.

Start walking with your dog on your left side, giving the command, "Byron, heel!" as you take the first step. Simultaneously snap the leash lightly. Make him walk with his head level with your left leg. As you walk, practice turning right, left, forward and back, each time giving the command to heel as you snap the leash to get him into position. Follow each command with praise. If he starts to get ahead of or behind you, snap the leash to get him back in place.

SIT!

Teach your dog to sit first when you stop walking with him. When you stop, give the command "Sit!" while you press his rear into a sitting position with your left hand. Repeat. Your right hand is using the leash to hold his head up. Use your hands to make him remain sitting for a moment, then say "Heel!" and start walking. Repeat. Eventually, he will sit as soon as you stop walking.

STAY!

Tell your dog to sit while on a leash, and immediately order him to "Stay!" while keeping your hands on him if needed to reinforce it while repeating the command. Make him stay no more than 10 to 20 seconds the first few times. Slowly increase the time while reducing the number of commands until he'll stay on one command for at least 3 minutes.

DOWN!

Have your dog sit at your left side, then kneel beside him. Reach over his back with your left arm and hold his left front leg close to your body with your left hand. With your right hand, hold his right front leg. Tell him "Down!" as you gently lift his front feet off the ground and ease his body down until he's lying down. When he's down, release him slowly, keeping your left arm over his back while repeating "Down!" and "Stay!" The timing for "Down!" should be like that for "Stay!"

COME!

After your dog has learned these basic commands, surprise him one day with "Come!" While he's heeling, suddenly take a step backward and tell him, "Byron, come!" as you snap the leash to turn him around clockwise toward you. When he's turned around, keep walking backward, urging him to come toward you with gentle snaps of the leash, repeating the "come" command and praising him. When he's in full stride toward you, stop, and when he reaches you, tell him to sit.

DON'T JUMP UP!

Dogs just want to be close to human faces, and they get in the bad habit of jumping up to do this. A common way to prevent a dog from jumping is to raise your knee up as he jumps. This throws him off balance and connects his jumping immediately with his loss of balance. Dog behavior specialist William E. Campbell recommends that when the dog approaches, tell him to sit and put your hand over his head so he will look up. When he sits, crouch down and pet him, but not too enthusiastically, and praise him. After a few days of experience with you and other people, he'll get the idea. If the dog also jumps on you while *you're* sitting, anticipate his jumping and stand up before he jumps, then repeat the method above.

William LeGro

Lessons in Body Language

You made the mistake long ago of letting your dog sleep on your bed with you. But now Fifi has decided the bed's not big enough for both of you. When you approach the bed, she stares you down; when you lift the covers, she growls; if you make a move to get in, she snaps at you. You have to sleep in the guest room.

Fluffy, on the other hand, is playing Queen of the Cat Box. She won't let your new kitten near it; she stands guard and hisses when the kitten approaches.

Fifi and Fluffy are talking to you the only way they know—with their bodies. In both of these cases, they're saying, "This place is *mine.*" For other circumstances, pets have other "words," and it helps if you know what they're trying to say.

LEARNING DOGSPEAK

Dog behaviorists recognize two basic types of dogspeak: dominance and submission. Your dog should always be submissive to you and your family, even if it is dominant with other dogs, or you could end up sleeping in the guest room—or worse, the dog could become aggressive to members of your family. If your dog isn't submissive, he needs training to be so.

A dog usually won't be 100 percent dominant or submissive but will have degrees of each, depending on what other dogs or people are around, and especially where it is at the moment. But Myrna Milani, D.V.M., author of *The Body Language and Emotions of Dogs,* says, generally, your dog is dominant if he places his chin on another dog's shoulders, puts his front paws on the other's back, growls if the other dog whines or tries to move, circles and sniffs the other, looks directly at the other, holds his ears and tail erect when meeting another dog or deliberately marks the area of confrontation with urine.

Submissive body language includes tail lowered or tucked under the body, ears flattened against the head, eyes averted, rolling over and exposing the abdomen, nervous licking or swallowing, cringing or trembling or seemingly involuntary dribbling of urine.

Just because a dog is dominant doesn't mean he's brave, Dr. Milani says, and just because a dog is submissive doesn't mean he's cowardly. And as trainer William E. Campbell notes in his book *Better Behavior in Dogs and Cats,* dogs have a wide range of other expressions it's important for you to be able to read, because often the dog is talking to *you.* Some expressions, like smiling, tail-wagging, prancing and growling, are obvious.

But how do you know if a dog might attack you? If it approaches you from the front, with direct eye contact, tail and ears up and hackles raised, an attack is highly possible. An absolutely still stance with these signs is also a sign of impending attack. But direct eye contact without other aggressive signs just means the dog wants you to pay attention to him.

Dogs can read your body language, too, right down to the scowl or smile on your face. Campbell describes how dogs interpret certain human moves.

- If you crouch, especially sideways, toward a dog, it will usually approach in a friendly manner.

- When owners stand or walk side by side with strangers or outsiders, most dogs see this as a friendly relationship.
- Face-to-face meetings between owners and outsiders may trigger aggression in dogs. When an outsider stands within the family group, the dog may see this as an invasion of its pack.
- Standing absolutely still facing an aggressive dog may trigger attack. It's better to stand sideways to the dog, lean slightly away and turn smoothly with him if he starts to circle. Avoid direct eye-to-eye contact, which dogs interpret as challenging and threatening.

LEARNING CATSPEAK

"Cats aren't little dogs," says Dr. Milani, who is also author of *The Body Language and Emotions of Cats.* "Cats are the only domestic species that respond to humans the way the infant animal responds to its mother." That's why two of the most common body language signs of a cat are purring and kneading, behavior that is identical to that of nursing kittens. The cat's exquisite body-language vocabulary is based on fundamental aspects of the cat's nature: It's an asocial, predatory, highly sexual animal.

Yes, face it, cat-lovers: Fluffy is a sexpot, and many of the "words" in her body language lexicon are sexually charged. "I think this is what the allure of cats is," Dr. Milani says, "but nobody wants to say it." Well, you read it here first.

Have you ever been stroking your cat when suddenly she turns around and bites you? It could be that your stroking is imitating normal feline mating behavior. Not intentionally, of course, but Fluffy doesn't know that. It just feels good. Right after orgasm, Dr. Milani says, a female cat will "whip around and nail the male," and then roll on the floor.

Here are some other "words" in Fluffy's vocabulary.

● While being petted, Fluffy's down on her front legs and her rear end is up in the air, balanced on the toes of her back legs. It's usually a female sexual display.

● Rubbing you with her head means "You're mine," you're her territory.

● Rubbing her head on prominent objects like corners of tables, sofas and door frames (and refrigerators, the storehouses of cat food and ice cream) is both territorial and a scent-marking device left over from predomestic days to enable her to make her way through the woods at night.

● Sweet little Fluffy cusses like a sailor. Arched back, fur on end, tail straight up and ears flat mean, "Come one step closer and you're @#!$#&• mincemeat!"

● Fluffy also talks with her eyes. If she's going to attack, her pupils constrict to slits because "she wants to get a bead on you," Dr. Milani says. "The pupils are constricted, the ears are forward, the weight is balanced on the back legs. This cat is ready for action."

● If she's in a defensive mode instead of offensive, her pupils are dilated. "She wants to be left alone and wants you to give her an out," Dr. Milani says, "but she will attack if you don't leave her alone." Defensive body language includes ears flattened and the body scrunched down to the floor "to appear as little as possible," Dr. Milani says.

● If Fluffy grabs your hand with her front paws, it's likely she'll roll over

and bring up her rear paws to start shredding. And a bite is next. Dr. Milani advises you to freeze and relax to escape the full attack.

● Arching her back and lifting her tail up straight (without the fur standing up) is "a friendly sign," Dr. Milani says. "The cat is saying, 'Here I am, I'm making myself as big as possible so you can't miss the fact I'm standing in front of the refrigerator and want you to feed me and reach down and pet me.' "

● Purring can mean a lot of things. Contentment when nursing or eating or being petted is most common, of course. But cats also purr when they're concentrating on things, Dr. Milani says, kind of like a person who whistles or hums softly to himself.

William LeGro

The Tail of a Dog Fight

The traditional advice is to throw water on fighting dogs, but, says trainer William E. Campbell, "sometimes it's a stimulus to even harder fighting." Besides, can you always depend on finding a hose or bucket of water on a street? Campbell, who says he's never been bitten breaking up dog fights, gives this advice.

● In long-tailed breeds, grab the aggressor—not the victim—by the tail and lift its hind legs off the ground. This causes the dog to lose traction needed to keep up the attack. He may try to turn around and bite you, but if you've got him off the ground, he won't

be able to reach you. Without traction the dog usually panics and quits fighting.

● In short-tailed breeds, grab the aggressor by the rear feet with both hands, hold them together, and lift and rotate the rear legs sideways. Again the dog loses traction and panics. But, Campbell warns, "you have to have the physical ability to lift the dog."

● Don't try to pull one dog off using its collar. "If you get in there around the head, the dog thinks you're joining in the fight on its side, and it will fight even harder," Campbell says. And you can get bitten.

● Keep your cool. "Keep absolutely

silent," Campbell says. "Otherwise, each dog can interpret that you're cheering it on."

● If you own both dogs, Campbell says, your best move may be to just walk away. If they're fighting in your presence, it's likely a "jealousy" reaction. If you leave, they'll stop because the person they're fighting over isn't even there.

● If you use a water hose on the dogs, play the stream over their feet and legs. "It's more upsetting to them the way their nervous systems are set up than having it hit their heads," Campbell says.

Good Grooming

Good grooming—and that means from baths to pedicures—is the hallmark of a loved and cared for pet. And that goes for your favorite feline, too.

The hair on your pillow isn't yours. Your hair hasn't been short and calico-colored since that accident at Mr. Billy's Beauty Salon. You have to stop talking to spit out the fur your tongue seems to have sprouted. The Barcalounger deposits a layer of hair on Aunt Fanny's clothes, an example of hygiene she never fails to call to your attention. Between the lint trap in the dryer and the vacuum cleaner bag there's sufficient fur to make a handsome stole without endangering rare species.

In fact, you're pawing your face free of real and imagined tickling hair at the moment Fluffy makes her regal "A Star Is Born" entrance. She jumps on the bed, leaving a furry imprint as she inches closer to snuggle. Realization dawns like a new day: My furry friend needs a good grooming. So does my house.

FLY AWAY FUR!

Both dogs and cats need their coats groomed daily, say experts in the field. Cats groom themselves constantly; their sandpaper tongues pull hair into their stomachs, where fur balls can form and can cause digestive problems. Dogs seem to get dirty just lying around the house. Regular grooming with a comb or brush is one of the best ways to keep your pet clean, its coat healthy and your decor able to pass a drill-sergeant inspection.

Here are some grooming tips that could save your pet's self-respect and your time and money.

Get the proper tools. Combs are better than brushes, says Will Thompson, treasurer of the Cat Fanciers Association and an all-breed show judge. They let you untangle snarls without pulling the hair out. The best comb is stainless steel, with rounded (not pointed), narrowly spaced teeth at one end and widely spaced teeth at the other.

If you use a brush, use one with natural bristles, which doesn't break hair as easily as nylon or rubber brushes. Brushes produce a healthy massaging action when you brush down to the skin.

Scissors, used to cut out mats that can't be combed out, must be very sharp but with rounded ends to avoid stabbing your pet.

Start them young. Most dogs and cats can be taught to love having their coats groomed if you begin when they're two to four months old, the experts say. Talk soothingly, be patient but firm, and lavish your friend with praise.

Beauty or Beast: It's Time for a Bath

Your dog, Fifi, smells like something the cat dragged in—and your cat's fragrance compares unfavorably with Chanel No. 5. And Fifi agrees with authorities who say dogs need baths as seldom as possible—frequent baths remove essential oils that keep your pet's skin and coat healthy. Others say bathing at least once every 2 or 3 weeks is optimum.

Robert Schwartzman, V.M.D., senior dermatologist at the University of Pennsylvania's School of Veterinary Medicine, says there are no scientific data to back up either position. Dr. Schwartzman's position is simple: "If the dog gets dirty, I would say the dog needs a bath." The general rule is the same for cats.

Use a mild human shampoo, says Dr. Schwartzman. "It's possible certain animals are sensitive to certain shampoos," he says. "If you notice any skin irritation (redness and itching) following the shampoo, don't use it again. A thorough rinsing is very important."

Be sure to use large pieces of cotton to block the ears and remember to remove them after the bath. There's no real advantage to using eye ointments, he adds. "Just be more careful around the eyes, and use a sponge if necessary. Most dogs will close their eyes anyway."

If you do bathe your pet frequently, Dr. Schwartzman says, you can follow the shampoo with a light bath-oil rinse.

Comb them every day. While short-haired animals may not absolutely *need* it every day, it's still a good idea, but long-haired dogs and cats are a different story. "Running a wide-toothed comb through the coat once a day will remove tangles and assure you that your pet's coat is not going to fill with mats," Thompson says. "It only takes 15 seconds. Then every two or three days, use the narrow-toothed comb to take out dead hair."

Comb a cat with the lay of the coat. It's a common misconception, says Thompson, that long-haired cats should be combed *against* the lay of the coat. "Totally wrong," he says. "You do not back-comb a cat. You'll rip the coat out, and I mean that literally." To make your cat's coat fluff out, you instead lift and turn the comb clockwise with a twist of your wrist as you draw the comb backward. "Lift and turn, lift and turn," says Thompson.

With short-haired cats there's no lifting and turning, but always comb with the lay of the coat. Thompson says one very easy way to groom a cat daily is simply to wet your hands and smooth them down the coat; the loose hair will cling to your hands.

Long-haired dogs should be groomed against the lay of the coat. They generally have more and longer hair than a cat, says Jeff Reynolds, executive director of the National Dog Groomers' Association of America. Combing or brushing against the lay makes it easier to locate and remove mats, gives the coat a fuller appearance, and prepares the coat for using a flea and tick dip.

De-mat the coat. If you groom your pet every day its coat probably won't mat. Still, some dogs and cats will mat despite your best efforts, especially under and on the backs of the legs. First, grip the mat with your fingers without pulling on the skin and begin to separate the hairs, working down toward the skin. Then tease the rest of the mat out with two teeth of a wide-toothed comb, always being sure to hold the mat away from your pet so you don't poke the skin with the teeth of the comb.

Some mats may have to be cut out. Slide the comb beneath the mat to protect the skin from the scissors, and cut away. Thompson advises cornstarch powder to help remove mats on cats. Because dogs don't groom themselves as much as cats, it's safer to use commercial mat-remover liquids and sprays on them. For badly matted cats, a veterinarian may have to tranquilize the cat and cut them out, but this is a rare procedure. A professional groomer will usually use clippers to remove bad mats on a dog.

Skunked! Getting the Stink Out

Fifi the dog had a tête-á-derriere with a skunk and came out on the losing end. If you don't happen to appreciate parfum de skunk, never fear: You can deodorize both your dog or cat by immersing the animal in tomato juice.

If Fifi is, oh, say, a St. Bernard, make that *a lot* of tomato juice. Like, empty the supermarket shelves. Soak her in full-strength juice for several minutes and sponge it over her face, avoiding eyes, ears and nose, say the experts. Follow with a mild shampoo and then a white vinegar rinse using 1 tablespoon of vinegar per gallon of water.

A PAW-AND-CLAW MANICURE

A dog's nails need to be kept trimmed to prevent the foot from splaying out and causing walking problems, says Michael S. Garvey, D.V.M., chairman of the Department of Medicine at the Animal Medical Center in New York City. Often the dog will wear its nails down sufficiently just walking on a sidewalk. Otherwise, humans have to cut the nails.

Cats normally sharpen their own claws, often on your furniture. Train your cat early in life to use a heavy-duty, well-weighted scratching post. Thompson advocates trimming cats' claws because he believes the environment these days is too dangerous for cats to go outdoors and do their own manicures on trees.

You need a steady hand. You also need a confident attitude that communicates confidence to the dog or cat, because they usually don't even like having their feet handled, let alone nails cut. Be gentle and firm, speak softly and use praise effusively.

Use nail trimmers. They're available at pet stores or through your groomer; scissors aren't strong enough or sharp enough.

Cut carefully. Too little is better than too much, as Fifi and Fluffy will vigorously remind you should you cut to the "quick," the pink blood vein that can be seen in white nails. Be sure to cut *outside* the quick; for dark nails on dogs, cut only the hooklike projection. It's important to smooth the ends with a nail file. Use a cotton ball or gauze or dip your wet finger in flour and apply to the nail to stop the bleeding if you cut too far.

Control your cat. You know how cats are: inherently uncooperative, sharp-edged and very fussy about their paws. It's best to have a helper to hold Fluffy down while you clip, carefully pulling up on the scruff of the neck if Fluffy threatens to get out of control, says Thompson.

You should do back claws as well as front. He says: "Have you ever had a cat leap off your lap, leaving gouges in your thighs?" It's easy to see the quick in a cat's translucent claws. "Don't even go near the quick," says Thompson; just nip off the sharp ends.

William LeGro

How to Be Happy Together

Your puppy, Fifi, piddled and pooped all over the house and tore up the sofa while you were gone yesterday. Then, all tired out, she fell asleep. When you came home 6 hours later, she wiggled and leaped and licked joyfully to greet you. But you could only see the damage and, understandably angry, you scolded her severely. She immediately hung her head in shame, tucked her tail between her legs in guilt, squatted and piddled on the carpet.

Today when you came in the door, there was no joyful greeting. Instead, she slunk guiltily over to you with her head down and her tail between her legs. She'd trashed the house again. You say you know she did it to spite you for leaving her alone, and this time you spanked her.

It is four months later. Your home stinks, your sofa is beyond repair and Fifi is a cringing, quivering mess of a mutt, afraid of your every move. She is unhappy and you are unhappy, too.

THE LANGUAGE OF PUPPY LOVE

What went wrong here? The problem is that you and Fifi aren't speaking the same language. Fifi talks Dog, you talk People, and you're both missing the messages, says Myrna Milani, D.V.M., author of *The Body Language and Emotions of Dogs*. You could be having similar problems with your cat because Fluffy speaks Cat. If you want to be in control, it's up to you to learn Dog and Cat—and not hope Fifi and Fluffy will learn your

THE FAR SIDE

Simultaneously all three went for the ball, and the coconut-like sound of their heads hitting secretly delighted the bird.

version of People. Only when you can understand what they're telling you will you be able to respond knowledgeably and responsibly.

According to Dr. Milani, there are two keys to changing unwanted behavior in dogs and cats: A good trainer or self-help books and your own emotional attitudes. If what you perceive to be your pet's emotions—spite, jealousy, fear, sorrow—are interfering with your relationship, you must change, and you'll find your pet will change with you. Fifi and Fluffy are not a lost cause.

The behaviorist theory of animal psychology says dogs and cats react unemotionally to environmental triggers. The owner theory (for want of a better term) holds that cats and dogs think, reason, love, hate, get jealous, feel guilty and do things out of spite.

Dr. Milani believes the reality is a fusion of both views. You, in effect, can create and change the reality to suit your needs. It's your choice, Dr. Milani says, to decide if your dog or cat can think and feel. It's also your choice to simply disregard the thoughts and emotions that erode your relationship with your pet, to "get rid of the feelings that don't work for you." You just keep the positive feelings and react neutrally to the negative.

This means when Fifi acts joyous when you come home, you can feel she loves you and wants to be with you. But when she tears up the house when you're gone, you can reject the feeling that it's spite and realize she just needs training.

LEARNING DOG-THINK

First, you have to understand how a dog thinks. A dog is a social animal, a member of a pack. To Fifi, her human family is the pack, and she must know her place in it. She finds this out through her own and your body language. Her proper place in a human pack is the lowest rank, simply because humans are smarter and are responsible for her welfare and her behavior. To her, almost all humans are leaders of the pack. Those who let their dogs become the leader are asking for trouble.

Another very important thing to remember about a dog's behavior is that it has absolutely no memory of unconnected events: A dog's memory retention span is less than a minute at best; hence the old and true saying, "You have to catch them in the act."

To Fifi, there was a *direct* connection only between her body language—a joyful greeting—and *your* body language—a stern scolding. Fifi had no idea you were upset because of the mess she made hours before. The second time, Dr. Milani says, she greeted you submissively, thinking you hadn't been pleased with a joyful greeting. But instead of accepting her obeisance, you spanked her. No wonder she's a basket case!

So how can you react to Fifi's behavior problems without traumatizing her or yourself? "Don't waste time blaming yourself or seeing guilt—or spite, or stupidity or hate—in your pet," Dr. Milani says. "Concentrate your efforts on solving the problem." In Fifi's case, that means training her not to trash the house.

THAT DARN CAT!

The same general rule—disregarding negative emotions while treasuring positive ones—works for cats as well as it does for dogs, Dr. Milani says. But of course, there are differences.

"Cats are not little dogs," she says. For one thing, they're not pack animals. "The cat is the most different from us of all domestic animals. It's solitary, it's sexual, it's predatory. But everything we adore in the cat is simultaneously what we condemn in it."

We like Fluffy because she's independent. But we don't want her to be aloof when we want to cuddle. We love her when she's chasing a ball of yarn across the living room but hate her when she brings home a bird she's used the identical predatory trait to kill. Or when she sharpens those deadly claws on the couch.

Relating healthily to a cat takes the same maturity of human emo-tions as it does to relate to a dog. A cat probably has no longer memory for unnconnected events than a dog. A cat does not think in terms of spite, or hate or jealousy any more than does a dog—that is, not at all. Cats are very good at cussing you out, at questioning your privilege to even have a cat, when you don't do what they want *when* they want, Dr. Milani says.

Coming home to find the trash raided, the door frame gouged, the settee sprayed and a dead robin on the kitchen floor doesn't exactly endear Fluffy to you. But cats don't respond to discipline at all.

"The only thing that works with cats is to set up a situation where the cat chooses to do what you want it to." That and "the fear of God" technique. This is the way you train cats not to rip up the house. Cats being cats, there's not much you can do to repress their sexuality beyond neutering or spaying. And nothing stops their predatory instincts. All you can do there is to bell the cat.

THE CHOICE IS YOURS

Many people treat their pets like people. Others treat them like just another part of nature, there to serve and be dominated by man. One extreme anthropomorphizes them—assigns them human characteristics that they don't have. Especially human faults. The other extreme denies them their individuality, especially as domesticated animals. Both views do a disservice to human and animal, Dr. Milani says.

Fifi is a dog. Fluffy is a cat. They are not human beings, nor are they wildlife. Assuming these animals think and feel as we do, or assuming they have no role at all in our emotional lives, may assuage our own feelings of loneliness or inadequacy or frustration or powerlessness, Dr. Milani says. But it's our acting out of those negative feelings that can really hurt both human and pet.

Choosing to accept only the positive feelings is kind of like the theory of the unproven state called heaven, Dr. Milani says. You can't be sure heaven exists, but just in case it does, you try to be on your best behavior, and you've got nothing to lose even if there is no heaven. If your pet does indeed lack the capacity to think and feel, well then, you still succeed in making yourself feel better.

But if science someday proves your pet actually possesses the capacity to think and feel, then you've learned how to forge a connection of infinite love, a solid yet flexible bond to a form of life neither human nor wild. And in the process you will have enriched your life tremendously.

William LeGro

Join the Flock of Bird-Lovers

Without birds, none of us would be free. After all, the Declaration of Independence was signed with a *quill* pen, wasn't it?

To hear the birds squawk about it, we owe them a lot more. "People relate to us with a tremendous fascination and admiration," cackles the San Diego Chicken, the well-known mascot and cheerleader for the city's professional baseball team. "Perhaps they admire us more than any other animal because of our unique ability to fly. Humans have been trying to imitate us since the beginning of time. Man has always wanted to fly, and when he built a machine to fly in, he copied the form from a *bird*. Airplanes don't look like dogs, do they?"

Ted Giannoulas is the man with a bird's-eye view of how people relate to birds. He's played the role of the famous San Diego Chicken for 14 years and spends more than 200 days a year "flying" around the country for various events.

He knows birds inside out, so to speak, and he has some advice for people who are purchasing their first bird. "Buy a bird with a sense of humor. And most important, buy a bird who can fly slightly higher than a cat."

Avian veterinarians have some other pointers on choosing a bird.

THIS BIRD'S FOR YOU

When it comes to finding the right bird for you, Gary Gallerstein, D.V.M., author of *The Bird Owner's Home Health and Care Book*, advises you to pick a bird that will fit into your nest. Spend the time necessary to make the right decision. Read, shop around, talk to people in the know, attend bird club meetings and ask questions. Some of the larger, more beautiful birds are not good choices for the first-time bird buyer. A reputable breeder or bird pet shop can give good advice on choosing the right species for you.

Some veterinarians say a parakeet would be a good first choice. They're relatively inexpensive, some of them will talk, they can be hand-tamed and they make a very nice pet. Canaries are great, too. They will sing, and they are simple to take care of.

For the more experienced bird owner, cockatiels are very nice intermediate birds. They can be hand-tamed, a few of them whistle and talk, they have a life span longer than that of a parakeet, and they are very cheerful pets. They're in between the parakeet and the parrot.

As you get more feathers in your cap, you may want to go with more exotic types of birds, such as an Amazon, a small South American green parrot. Larger parrotlike birds, such as the macaws and cockatoos, are good talkers and make good pets for the advanced bird owner.

FOWL-WEATHER FRIENDS

Just because you live in an area where it snows doesn't mean that you have to buy a penguin instead of a parrot. Beryl Moss, vice-president of the Bird Association of California, says most pet birds don't need to winter in Miami. "Most birds climatize very well. Some very tiny finches have a problem with extreme cold, but a parakeet could break the ice on its water dish before drinking and still not have a problem. The heat doesn't bother them much either, unless it's very high temperatures combined with high humidity."

This doesn't mean you should just fly right out and buy the first bird you see. Robert Altman, D.V.M., a veterinarian with a special interest in birds, says you should turn into a bird watcher. "Observe the bird, perhaps on more than one or two occasions. It should be active, and not just sitting there puffed up. See how active it is compared with other birds in the cage. And the bird's feathers should be shiny and sleek."

When picking a place to buy a bird, Dr. Altman believes in being cagey. Check around. "You should buy it from a reliable source. A good pet shop should be the same as a good breeder. Are they knowledgeable? Is the place clean and bright? Look for a place that has a good reputation, a place where other people have had good experiences. Ask around."

Spotting Smuggled Birds

Smuggling exotic birds into this country is a big business. The human health risks involved, says Gary Gallerstein, D.V.M., make this problem especially costly.

Legally imported birds have stainless steel leg bands. Domestically raised birds may or may not have a band. The only way to protect yourself is to know your supplier. Ask a lot of questions. Remember, if the price is too good to be true, it may be a smuggled bird. All new birds should be examined by an avian veterinarian immediately after purchase.

How to Clip Those Wings

If you don't want your bird to fly the coop the first time your door opens, you might want to clip its wings.

Actually, you need clip only 1 wing to prevent flying. That will put the bird off-balance, which, of course, is the whole idea. The bird will flutter along the ground, but its flight ceiling will be limited to a few inches.

To start, have someone else hold the bird gently in a towel with the bird's belly facing up. Then all you need is a wing and scissors.

Spread the bird's wing out and clip the primary feathers, the long ones, to point B, as shown in the illustration. You can cut the feathers anywhere between point A and C to accomplish the job. Don't worry about hurting your bird. Feathers are like fingernails—the feathers are sensitive only where they grow inside the bird's skin.

This procedure will keep your adult bird from flying for about a year; then it should be done again. For younger birds, you'll have to clip monthly.

If this procedure ruffles *your* feathers, you can have an avian veterinarian do the job.

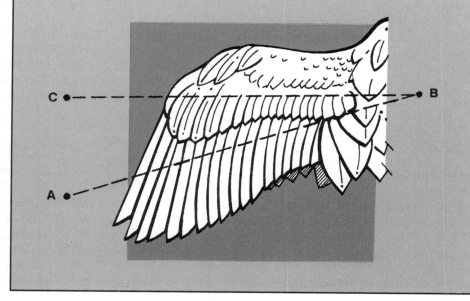

lettuce, spinach, bananas, apples. The more varied their diets, the less chance there is of them having dietary deficiencies. If you're going to give them a vitamin supplement, sprinkle it on their soft food, not in their water, because most birds do not drink much water."

GETTING A BEAKFUL

If you want your toucan to talk or want to hear prose from your parakeet, you're going to have to perch yourself in front of the cage for a while.

Billy Rodgers owned and operated a traveling bird show for 18 years. His birds did tricks. And talked. Here's how he got them to give a beakful to the audience.

"You have to use repetition. You use the same words over and over again. Don't overtire them; let them enjoy what they're doing. At the end of the session, reward them. Give them something they really like, such as a cracker with peanut butter on it. Each day hold the treat back a little longer until they finally say the word."

Don Barone

EAT LIKE A HUMAN

When it comes to feeding your bird, you can wing it, Moss says. "Most people think that all you have to do is give them seed and gravel and that's it. Actually, most pet birds will eat almost everything that a human being will eat."

Moss went on to say that her birds love her Italian cooking, and that when her family has spaghetti and meatballs, the birds get a dish of it, too.

She has other recommendations. "Most of the larger birds love chicken," she says. "They love to chew on the chicken bones, and it's good for them; they need the protein. They also love fruit and vegetables, except for avocados, which can poison them. They love carrots, broccoli, corn,

Life in a Fish Bowl

Bubble.

Bubble.

Bubble.

Da dummm.

You catch a glimpse of a fin swimming by.

Da dummm.

The surface of the water starts churning.

Dum *dum* dum *dum* dum *dummmmmmmm* . . .

The feeding frenzy begins. All your pretty, "tame" tropical fish race madly for those red and green flakes you just put in your aquarium.

Then, as suddenly as it began, the fish relax, and the flakes drift gently to the bottom of the tank, coming to rest on the tiny blue stones. You watch as a small red and blue fish swims in and out of a pink castle. A stream of bubbles rises from the ceramic helmet of the deep-sea diver, causing waves in the corner of your tank. It's safe to go back to the water. In fact, some psychologists recommend it.

THE AGE OF AQUARIUMS

"I will often advise people to get their own aquariums," says Ginger Hamilton, Ph.D., a psychologist who deals with people and their pets. "Fish are very relaxing to watch. It's almost like you go into a trance when you watch them. You tend to tune yourself out of your external environment and tune yourself more into your internal environment through the soothing repetitive movement of the fish. It's sort of like tank therapy."

It's a therapy, in fact, that many people have taken a liking to. Accord-

ing to people in the industry, fish are a *very* popular hobby.

You've heard the story of the one that got away? Well, in Florida, it seems, millions get away. David Boozer, executive director of the Florida Tropical Fish Farmers Association, says the state of Florida produces 95 percent of the domestically raised tropical fish in the country, with annual retail sales of $120 million. At about a dollar per fish, that's a lot of fish.

"We ship 15,000 to 20,000 boxes of ornamental fish a week," he says. "That represents about four million fish. Recent statistics show that collecting fish is the second largest hobby in the world, second only to photography."

FISH: URBAN ANIMALS

The reasons why fish are so popular as pets are obvious. They're relatively inexpensive to keep, they're inexpensive to feed, they don't chew furniture or leave fur on your pillow. They're also welcome just about anywhere.

"No Pets Allowed!!!" Oh, you can have a dog or cat, but it can also mean an extra $1,000 security deposit on your apartment. Deanimalizing fee, you know.

If you're yearning for a pet but live in confined or restricted quarters, fish may be the answer.

Fish live in aquariums, but they also live perfectly in apartments. "America is becoming more urbanized," says Boozer. "People are living more and more in condominiums and apartments, lots of places that have

restrictions on pets. You can pretty much get away with having an aquarium no matter where you live."

FISHING FOR ROOMMATES

Deciding on getting a fish is the easy part. Deciding on what kind of fish to get, however, is another matter. With hundreds if not thousands of species around, how do you choose which fish is best for you? In fact, how do you even find the best place to buy your fish?

One of the best-known tropical fish experts in the world, Herbert Axelrod, M.D., Ph.D., author of *Dr. Axelrod's Atlas of Freshwater Aquarium Fishes,* recommends that you trust your nose.

"If a fish store smells like fish, it has dead or dying fish around, so you shouldn't buy fish there. I also would absolutely stay away from five-and-dime-type stores because the people there don't really know anything about fish. The best place to buy fish is from a store that specializes in tropical fish, preferably one that *only* sells tropical fish."

One hint: Don't buy the ones that are floating belly-up. Dr. Axelrod says that it's pretty hard for a novice to tell if a fish is healthy or not but that there are some fish that are pretty safe bets for the beginner to buy.

"For the beginner, buy any of the popular live-bearing fish, especially guppies. If somebody wants something more colorful, I would suggest white cloud mountain fish. All of these fish are fairly hardy, and can live at room temperatures."

FISHING FOR ADVICE?

Before you buy your fish, says Dr. Axelrod, you need to have a home for it. You should buy an aquarium first.

When it comes to buying and setting up an aquarium, Brian Montague, curator of the National Aquarium in Washington, D.C., has some tank tips.

● Read all you can about fish and setting up an aquarium before making a purchase.

● Decide what size aquarium your space can accommodate and you're willing to care for. Most experts recommend a 10- or 20-gallon aquarium for beginners.

● Make sure that the fish you buy will not outgrow the aquarium. Ask how big the fish will get. One fish, for example—a snakehead—starts out at about 1½ inches but ends up over 3 *feet* long. Not a good choice for a 3-gallon desk aquarium.

● Start out with a freshwater setup. It's easier for beginners than a saltwater tank.

● As a general rule of thumb, figure 1 gallon of water per inch of fish.

Thus, a 10-gallon tank could support a 10-inch fish.

● The more surface area a filter has, the better filter it will be. It's not how big the filter container is but the amount of material that acts as a filter that's important. Filters work better under the gravel, but are harder to clean when they need cleaning. Although box filters don't have much surface area and need frequent cleaning, they are much easier to clean. You won't have to break the whole tank down to do it.

● Live plants look better than plastic plants to us—and to the fish. They tend to eat them. If you have live plants you will need a plant growth bulb installed in the aquarium light housing. Montague says that if you have large fish that eat the plants and you don't want to keep replacing them, use plastic plants. They aren't as appetizing.

● For decorations in the tank, don't use anything metal because you don't want rust in the tank. Use plastics, ceramics, natural rock or driftwood. If you use your own rocks or driftwood, make sure they are thoroughly cleaned

and disinfected before you put them in the tank. Most beginners should purchase rocks or wood; they have usually been cleaned and disinfected. Look for a label or ask a salesperson if you're not sure.

CLEANING THE AQUARIUM

Mike Shaw knows about cleaning fish aquariums. He's the curator of fishes at Sea World in San Diego, California. They have aquariums there ranging in size from 50 gallons to the 430,000-gallon shark aquarium, which you clean *very carefully.* He has a staff of 12 full-time aquarists cleaning his aquariums. He offers these tips for cleaning yours.

● There's a lot of work involved in keeping an aquarium looking nice, but you have to maintain it on a regular basis—about two or three times a week.

● Clean the glass of the tank often with a pad or brush so that algae don't have a chance to become established. When cleaning near the bottom, be careful not to drag up sand or gravel that can scratch the glass.

● Never empty the aquarium completely when changing the water. Change 10 to 25 percent of the water at a time. "Fish are used to a certain kind of water, even if it's bad water," Shaw says.

Don Barone

"Telefishion"—The New Way to Relax

If you've always thought that what you see on television is a bit fishy, the new aquarium video cassette tape will confirm your belief.

This new-wave video, which is available through video catalogs, consists of nothing more than fish swimming in an aquarium, complete with bubble sounds, and it may be just the right thing for those who don't want to dive right in and get their hands wet with taking care of fish.

For 30 minutes or so, you'll have an electronic 19-inch aquarium playing in your living room, and while it's not exactly the same as owning a real fish aquarium, Ginger Hamilton, Ph.D., believes it may have some of the same benefits. "It should help a person relax just as watching a real fish aquarium would."

You've always been able to buy a species of fish named Beta. Now it seems you can get them in VHS, too.

Illustration Credits

Janet Bohn: p. 206
Jack Crane: p. 73
Lisa Farkas: pp. 116–19
Leslie Flis: pp. 8, 58, 93, 128, 161, 167, 185, 203, 210, 232, 265, 310, 324
Frank Fretz: pp. 11, 223
Jean Gardner: pp. 81, 136, 182, 195
Kathleen M. Geosits: pp. 27, 132–33, 141, 177, 178, 187, 197, 204, 208, 225, 298, 315, 318, 319, 335
Stewart Jackson: pp. 14, 15, 22, 33, 42, 50, 61, 149, 154, 190, 191, 201, 238, 245, 248, 273, 358 (right), 359, 367
Acey Lee: pp. 5, 268
Wally Neibart: pp. 28, 56, 57, 240, 352, 354, 362

Index

Page references in *italic* indicate boxes, charts and tables. References in **boldface** indicate illustrations.

Rodale Press, Inc., publishes PREVENTION®, the better health magazine.
For information on how to order your subscription,
write to PREVENTION®, Emmaus, PA 18098.